CROSSWORD
LISTS

CROSSWORD LISTS

Edited by

Anne Stibbs

BLOOMSBURY

First published 1989

Copyright © Bloomsbury Publishing Limited

Bloomsbury Publishing Limited, 2 Soho Square, London W1V 5DE

A CIP record for this title is available from the British Library.

ISBN 07475 03451

Compiled and typeset by
Market House Books, Ltd., Aylesbury
Printed and bound by
Richard Clay Ltd., Bungay, Suffolk

INTRODUCTION

This book is a companion to the *Bloomsbury Crossword Solver,* which lists words in alphabetical order according to their number of letters. Here we have listed words under categories—people, places, birds, animals, fish, breeds of dog, Greek gods, names of drinks, and so on, in the hope that the user can quickly find the required answer to a clue. We have chosen the contents for their usefulness. There are, for example, over 2300 known named varieties of *Salmonella,* but they are not listed here. We have tried to concentrate on the words that actually appear in crosswords. We have also tried to present the information in the most helpful way. Usually, this means listing the words in length order—3-letter, 4-letter, 5-letter words, etc., and then in alphabetical order within each section. In some cases we have used simple alphabetical or logical order and some information is presented in tabular form.

We have also included additional information in many of the lists; for example, the birth and death dates of people or the colours of gemstones. This is partly to help the reader to find the correct word, but we also hope that owners of the book will find it a useful reference source in its own right.

While most of the lists are collections of things, there are also lists of types of words—for example, palindromes, back words, homophones (words that sound like others), abbreviations and acronyms, and common two-word phrases. The book also contains well-known foreign words and phrases and American-British variants. To help the reader find his way about, there is a Contents page that lists all the tables and lists in the order in which they appear in the book. In addition, there is an index in the back of the book. This gives the tables and lists in alphabetical order, but also includes cross references. For instance, a reader interested in 'jewels' will be directed to the list of *gemstones*, 'girl' might indicate a girl's first name, listed under *first names*, and so on. The index also contains hints on solving cryptic clues. There are many conventions used by setters of crosswords—'love' often indicates the letter O, 'cardinal' might be a compass point, N, S, E, or W, twisted could suggest an anagram, etc. A selection of these has been included in the index.

In using the book, the reader should also be aware of the inflection of words. The most common, for the purpose of crosswords, is the use of plurals, and it is usually apparent from the wording of the clue whether the answer is a singular or plural. When nouns have regular plurals, only the singular forms have been included. Another point is that verbs are invariably shown with

—ize endings. The alternative *—ise* ending may have been used in the puzzle. The same principle applies to nouns ending with *—ization*.

The editor would like to thank all the people who have been involved in the production of this book. Their names are listed under **ACKNOWLEDG-MENTS.**

Finally we would like to say that some crossword purists regard the use of a book like this as 'cheating.' We, however, prefer to think of it as 'research.' We hope that this book will be helpful to people who like crossword puzzles, and in particular to those who research their solutions.

Anne Stibbs
Aylesbury 1989

ACKNOWLEDGMENTS

Beth Bonham
Eve Daintith
John Daintith
Joan Gallagher
Robert Kerr
David Pickering
Kathy Rooney
Jessica Scholes
Gwen Shaw
Kate Smith
Brenda Tomkins
Edmund Wright

CONTENTS

GEOGRAPHY

COUNTRIES OF THE WORLD

AFGHANISTAN
  Capital: Kabul
  Currency: afghani (pul)
  Legislature: Central Committee
  Admin. Div.: Province

ALBANIA
  Capital: Tirana
  Currency: lek (qindar)
  Legislature: People's Assembly (Kuvënd Popullor)
  Admin. Div.: People's Council

ALGERIA
  Capital: Algiers
  Currency: dinar (centime)
  Legislature: National Assembly

ARGENTINA
  Capital: Buenos Aires
  Currency: austral (centavo)
  Legislature: National Congress: Senate; H of Deputies
  Admin. Div.: Province

AUSTRALIA
  Capital: Canberra
  Currency: dollar (cent)
  Legislature: Federal Parliament: Senate; H of Representatives
  Admin. Div.: State

AUSTRIA
  Capital: Vienna
  Currency: schilling (groschen)
  Legislature: National Assembly: Nationalrat (National Council); Bundesrat (Federal Council)
  Admin. Div.: Federal State

BANGLADESH
  Capital: Dhaka
  Currency: taka (poisha)
  Legislature: Parliament

BELGIUM
  Capital: Brussels
  Currency: franc (centime)
  Legislature: Senate; Chamber of Representatives
  Admin. Div.: Province

BOLIVIA
  Capital: La Paz
  Currency: boliviano (centavo)
  Legislature: Congress: Senate; Chamber of Deputies
  Admin. Div.: Department

BOTSWANA
  Capital: Gaborone
  Currency: pula (thebe)
  Legislature: National Assembly

BRAZIL
  Capital: Brasilia
  Currency: cruzado (centavo)
  Legislature: National Congress: Senate; Chamber of Deputies
  Admin. Div.: State

BULGARIA
  Capital: Sofia
  Currency: lev (stotinka)
  Legislature: National Assembly
  Admin. Div.: People's Council

BURMA
  Capital: Rangoon
  Currency: kyat (pya)
  Legislature: People's Assembly

CAMBODIA
  Capital: Phnom Penh
  Currency: riel (sen)
  Legislature: National Assembly

CANADA
  Capital: Ottawa
  Currency: dollar (cent)
  Legislature: Parliament: Upper House; H of Commons
  Admin. Div.: Province

CHILE
  Capital: Santiago
  Currency: peso (centavo)
  Admin. Div.: Region

CHINA
  Capital: Peking
  Currency: yuan (fen)
  Legislature: National People's Congress
  Admin. Div.: Province

COLOMBIA
  Capital: Bogotá
  Currency: peso (centavo)
  Legislature: Congress: Senate; H of Representatives
  Admin. Div.: Départmento

COSTA RICA
  Capital: San José
  Currency: colón (céntimo)
  Legislature: Legislative Assembly

CUBA
  Capital: Havana
  Currency: peso (centavo)

Legislature: National Assembly of People's
  Power
Admin. Div.: Province
CYPRUS
  Capital: Nicosia
  Currency: pound (cent)
  Legislature: H of Representatives
CZECHOSLOVAKIA
  Capital: Prague
  Currency: koruna (heller)
  Legislature: Federal Assembly: H of the
    People; H of the Nations
DENMARK
  Capital: Copenhagen
  Currency: krone (öre)
  Legislature: Folketing (Diet)
  Admin. Div.: Municipality
DOMINICAN REPUBLIC
  Capital: Santo Domingo
  Currency: peso (centavo)
  Legislature: Congress
  Admin. Div.: Province
ECUADOR
  Capital: Quito
  Currency: sucre (centavo)
  Legislature: National Congress
  Admin. Div.: Province
EGYPT
  Capital: Cairo
  Currency: pound (piastre)
  Legislature: People's Assembly
  Admin. Div.: Governorate
EL SALVADOR
  Capital: San Salvador
  Currency: colón (centavo)
  Legislature: Assembly
ETHIOPIA
  Capital: Addis Ababa
  Currency: birr (cent)
  Legislature: Shengo (National Assembly)
FINLAND
  Capital: Helsinki
  Currency: markka (penni)
  Legislature: Parliament: Eduskunta-
    Riksdagen (Chamber)
  Admin. Div.: Province
FRANCE
  Capital: Paris
  Currency: franc (centime)
  Legislature: Parliament: National Assembly;
    Senate
  Admin. Div.: Département
THE GAMBIA
  Capital: Banjul
  Currency: dalasi (butut)
  Legislature: House of Representatives
  Admin. Div.: District
GERMANY, DEMOCRATIC REPUBLIC OF
  (East Germany)
  Capital: East Berlin
  Currency: Mark (Pfennig)

Legislature: People's Chamber
  (Volkskammer)
Admin. Div.: County
GERMANY, FEDERAL REPUBLIC OF (West
  Germany)
  Capital: Bonn
  Currency: Deutsche Mark (Pfennig)
  Legislature: Bundestag (Federal Diet);
    Bundersrat (Federal Council)
  Admin. Div.: County
GHANA
  Capital: Accra
  Currency: cedi (pesewa)
  Legislature: Provisional National Defence
    Council
  Admin. Div.: Region
GREECE
  Capital: Athens
  Currency: drachma (lepton)
  Legislature: Parliament
  Admin. Div.: Nomoi (Prefecture)
GUATEMALA
  Capital: Guatemala City
  Currency: quetzal (centavo)
  Legislature: Legislative Assembly
HAITI
  Capital: Port-au-Prince
  Currency: gourde (centime)
  Legislature: National Assembly
  Admin. Div.: Département
HONDURAS
  Capital: Tegucigalpa
  Currency: lempira (centavo)
  Legislature: Congress of Deputies
  Admin. Div.: Department
HONG KONG
  Capital: Victoria
  Currency: dollar (cent)
  Legislature: Executive Council; Legislative
    Council
  Admin. Div.: District
HUNGARY
  Capital: Budapest
  Currency: forint (filler)
  Legislature: Parliament (Országgyülés)
  Admin. Div.: County
ICELAND
  Capital: Reykjavik
  Currency: króna (eyrir)
  Legislature: Parliament (Althingi): Upper
    House; Lower House
  Admin. Div.: Commune
INDIA
  Capital: New Delhi
  Currency: rupee (paisa)
  Legislature: Parliament: Council of States
    (Rajya Sabha); H of the People (Lok
    Sabha)
  Admin. Div.: State
INDONESIA
  Capital: Jakarta

Currency: rupiah (sen)
Legislature: People's Consultative Assembly
Admin. Div.: Province

IRAN
Capital: Tehran
Currency: rial (dinar)
Legislature: Islamic Consultative Assembly
  (Majlis)
Admin. Div.: Province (Ostán)

IRAQ
Capital: Baghdad
Currency: dinar (fils)
Legislature: National Assembly
Admin. Div.: Governorate

IRELAND, REPUBLIC OF
Capital: Dublin
Currency: pound (pence)
Legislature: Parliament (Oireachtas): H of
  Representatives (Dáil); Senate (Seanad)
Admin. Div.: County

ISRAEL
Capital: Jerusalem
Currency: shekel (agora)
Legislature: Knesset
Admin. Div.: Municipality

ITALY
Capital: Rome
Currency: lira (centesimo)
Legislature: Parliament: Chamber of
  Deputies; Senate
Admin. Div.: Region

JAMAICA
Capital: Kingston
Currency: dollar (cent)
Legislature: H of Representatives; Senate
Admin. Div.: Parish

JAPAN
Capital: Tokyo
Currency: yen
Legislature: Diet: H of Representatives
  (Shugi-in); H of Councillors (Sangi-in)
Admin. Div.: Prefecture

JORDAN
Capital: Amman
Currency: dinar (fils)
Legislature: Parliament
Admin. Div.: District (Muhafaza)

KENYA
Capital: Nairobi
Currency: shilling (cent)
Legislature: National Assembly
Admin. Div.: Province

**KOREA, DEMOCRATIC PEOPLE'S REPUBLIC
OF (North Korea)**
Capital: P'yöngyang
Currency: won (chon)
Legislature: Supreme People's Assembly
Admin. Div.: Province

KOREA, REPUBLIC OF (South Korea)
Capital: Seoul
Currency: won (jeon)

Legislature: National Assembly
Admin. Div.: Province

KUWAIT
Capital: Kuwait
Currency: dinar (fils)
Legislature: National Assembly
Admin. Div.: Governorate

LAOS
Capital: Vientiane
Currency: kip (at)
Legislature: People's Supreme Council
Admin. Div.: Province

LEBANON
Capital: Beirut
Currency: pound (piastre)
Legislature: Parliament
Admin. Div.: Governorate

LIBERIA
Capital: Monrovia
Currency: dollar (cent)
Legislature: National Assembly: Senate; H of
  Representatives
Admin. Div.: County

LIBYA
Capital: Tripoli
Currency: dinar (dirham)
Legislature: General People's Congress

LUXEMBOURG
Capital: Luxembourg
Currency: franc
Legislature: Council of State

MADAGASCAR
Capital: Antananaivo
Currency: franc malgache
Legislature: National People's Assembly
Admin. Div.: Province

MALAWI
Capital: Lilongwe
Currency: kwacha (tambala)
Legislature: Parliament

MALAYSIA
Capital: Kuala Lumpur
Currency: dollar (cent)
Legislature: Parliament: H of
  Representatives (Dewan Ra'ayat); Senate
  (Dewan Negara)
Admin. Div.: State

MALTA
Capital: Valletta
Capital: lira (cent)
Legislature: Parliament: H of
  Representatives

MAURITIUS
Capital: Port Louis
Currency: rupee (cent)
Legislature: Legislative Assembly

MEXICO
Capital: Mexico City
Currency: peso (centavo)
Legislature: General Congress: Chamber of
  Deputies; Senate

Admin. Div.: State
MONGOLIA
Capital: Ulan Bator
Currency: tugrik (mongo)
Legislature: Great People's Khural
Admin. Div.: Province
MOROCCO
Capital: Rabat
Currency: dirham (centime)
Legislature: Parliament
Admin. Div.: Province
NEPAL
Capital: Kathmandu
Currency: rupee (paisa)
Legislature: Panchayat
Admin. Div.: Zone
NETHERLANDS
Capital: Amsterdam
Currency: florin (cent)
Legislature: Parliament (Staten-Generaal):
First Chamber; Second Chamber
Admin. Div.: Province
NEW ZEALAND
Capital: Wellington
Currency: dollar (cent)
Legislature: Parliament: H of
Representatives
Admin. Div.: Region
NICARAGUA
Capital: Managua
Currency: córdoba (centavo)
Legislature: National Assembly
Admin. Div.: Region
NIGERIA
Capital: Abuja
Currency: naira (kobo)
Admin. Div.: State
NORWAY
Capital: Oslo
Currency: krone (öre)
Legislature: Storting: Lagting; Odelsting
Admin. Div.: Fylker
PAKISTAN
Capital: Islamabad
Currency: rupee (paisa)
Legislature: Parliament: National Assembly;
Senate
Admin. Div.: Province
PANAMA
Capital: Panama City
Currency: balboa (cent)
Legislature: Legislative Assembly
Admin. Div.: Province
PARAGUAY
Capital: Asunción
Currency: guarani (céntimo)
Legislature: Parliament: Senate; Chamber of
Deputies
Admin. Div.: Department
PERU
Capital: Lima

Currency: inti (centimo)
Legislature: Congress: Senate; Chamber of
Deputies
Admin. Div.: Department
PHILIPPINES
Capital: Manila
Currency: peso (centavo)
Legislature: Congress: Upper House; H of
Representatives
Admin. Div.: Region
POLAND
Capital: Warsaw
Currency: zloty (grosz)
Legislature: Sejm
Admin. Div.: Voivodship
PORTUGAL
Capital: Lisbon
Currency: escudo (centavo)
Legislature: Assembly of the Republic
Admin. Div.: District
ROMANIA
Capital: Bucharest
Currency: leu (ban)
Legislature: Grand National Assembly
Admin. Div.: County
SAUDI ARABIA
Capital: Riyadh
Currency: riyal (halalas)
Legislature: Assembly
Admin. Div.: Region
SEYCHELLES
Capital: Victoria
Currency: rupee (cent)
Legislature: People's Assembly
SIERRA LEONE
Capital: Freetown
Currency: leone (cent)
Legislature: Parliament
Admin. Div.: Province
SINGAPORE
Capital: Singapore City
Currency: dollar (cent)
Legislature: Parliament
SOUTH AFRICA
Capital: Pretoria
Currency: rand (cent)
Legislature: Parliament: H of
Representatives, H of Delegates, H of
Assembly
Admin. Div.: Province
SPAIN
Capital: Madrid
Currency: peseta (céntimo)
Legislature: Cortes: Congress of Deputies;
Senate
Admin. Div.: Autonomous Community
SRI LANKA
Capital: Colombo
Currency: rupee (cent)
Legislature: Parliament
Admin. Div.: District

SUDAN
  Capital: Khartoum
  Currency: pound (piastre)
  Legislature: National Assembly
  Admin. Div.: Region
SWEDEN
  Capital: Stockholm
  Currency: krona (öre)
  Legislature: Riksdag
  Admin. Div.: Län
SWITZERLAND
  Capital: Bern
  Currency: franc (centime)
  Legislature: Parliament: Standerat;
    Nationalrat
  Admin. Div.: Canton
SYRIA
  Capital: Damascus
  Currency: pound (piastre)
  Legislature: People's Council
  Admin. Div.: Mohafaza
TAIWAN
  Capital: Taipei
  Currency: dollar (cent)
  Legislature: National Assembly
  Admin. Div.: County
TANZANIA
  Capital: Dodoma
  Currency: shilling (cent)
  Legislature: National Assembly
  Admin. Div.: Region
THAILAND
  Capital: Bangkok
  Currency: baht (stangs)
  Legislature: National Assembly: Senate; H of
    Representatives
  Admin. Div.: Province (Changwad)
TUNISIA
  Capital: Tunis
  Currency: dinar (millieme)
  Legislature: National Assembly
  Admin. Div.: Gouvernorat
TURKEY
  Capital: Ankara
  Currency: lira (kurus)
  Legislature: Grand National Assembly
  Admin. Div.: Il
UGANDA
  Capital: Kampala
  Currency: shilling (cent)
  Legislature: National Resistance Council
  Admin. Div.: Province
UNITED KINGDOM
  Capital: London

  Currency: pound (pence)
  Legislature: Parliament: H of Lords; H of
    Commons
  Admin. Div.: County
UNITED STATES OF AMERICA
  Capital: Washington, DC
  Currency: dollar (cent)
  Legislature: Congress: Senate; H of
    Representatives
  Admin. Div.: State
URUGUAY
  Capital: Montevideo
  Currency: peso (centésimo)
  Legislature: Chamber; Senate
  Admin. Div.: Department
USSR (SOVIET UNION)
  Capital: Moscow
  Currency: rouble (copeck)
  Legislature: Supreme Soviet of the USSR:
    Council of the Union; Council of
    Nationalities
VENEZUELA
  Capital: Caracas
  Currency: bolivar
  Legislature: Congress: Senate; Chamber of
    Deputies
  Admin. Div.: State
VIETNAM
  Capital: Hanoi
  Currency: dong (xu)
  Legislature: National Assembly
  Admin. Div.: Province
YUGOSLAVIA
  Capital: Belgrade
  Currency: dinar (para)
  Legislature: Federal Assembly: Federal
    Chamber; Chamber of Republics and
    Autonomous Provinces
ZAÏRE
  Capital: Kinshasa
  Currency: zaïre (likuta)
  Legislature: National Legislative Council
  Admin. Div.: Region
ZAMBIA
  Capital: Lusaka
  Currency: kwacha (ngwee)
  Legislature: National Assembly
  Admin. Div.: Province
ZIMBABWE
  Capital: Harare
  Currency: dollar (cent)
  Legislature: Parliament: Senate; H of
    Assembly
  Admin. Div.: Province

ENGLISH COUNTIES

COUNTY (Administrative Centre)

4
AVON (Bristol)
KENT (Maidstone)
5
DEVON (Exeter)
ESSEX (Chelmsford)
SALOP (name for
Shropshire between
1974 and 1980)
WIGHT, ISLE OF
(Newport, IOW)
6
DORSET (Dorchester)
DURHAM (Durham)
SURREY (Kingston
Upon Thames)
SUSSEX, EAST
(Lewes)
SUSSEX, WEST
(Chichester)
7
CUMBRIA (Carlisle)
NORFOLK (Norwich)
*RUTLAND (Oakham)
SUFFOLK (Ipswich)
8
CHESHIRE (Chester)
CORNWALL (Truro)
SOMERSET (Taunton)

9
BERKSHIRE
(Reading)
CLEVELAND
(Middlesborough)
HAMPSHIRE
(Winchester)
WILTSHIRE
(Trowbridge)
†W. MIDLANDS
(Birmingham)
10
*CUMBERLAND
(Carlisle)
DERBYSHIRE
(Matlock)
HUMBERSIDE
(Beverley)
LANCASHIRE
(Preston)
†MERSEYSIDE
(Liverpool)
N. YORKSHIRE
(Northallerton)
SHROPSHIRE
(Shrewsbury)
†S. YORKSHIRE
(Barnsley)
†W. YORKSHIRE
(Wakefield)

11
OXFORDSHIRE
(Oxford)
†TYNE AND WEAR
(Newcastle-Upon-
Tyne)
*WESTMORLAND
(Kendal)
12
BEDFORDSHIRE
(Bedford)
LINCOLNSHIRE
(Lincoln)
WARWICKSHIRE
(Warwick)
13
*HEREFORDSHIRE
(Hereford)
HERTFORDSHIRE
(Hertford)
STAFFORDSHIRE
(Stafford)
14
CAMBRIDGESHIRE
(Cambridge)
LEICESTERSHIRE
(Leicester)
NORTHUMBERLAND
(Morpeth)

15
BUCKINGHAMSHIRE
(Aylesbury)
GLOUCESTERSHIRE
(Gloucester)
*HUNTINGDONSHIRE
(Huntingdon)
NOTTINGHAMSHIRE
(Nottingham)
16
NORTHAMPTON-
SHIRE
(Northampton)
17
†GREATER
MANCHESTER
(Manchester)
20
HEREFORD AND
WORCESTER
(Worcester)

*indicates a former
county
† metropolitan county

WELSH COUNTIES

COUNTY (Administrative Centre)

5
CLWYD (Mold)
DYFED (Carmarthen)
GWENT (Cwmbran)
POWYS (Llandrindod
Wells)
7
GWYNEDD
(Caernarfon)
8
*ANGLESEY
(Llangefni)
9
*GLAMORGAN
(Cardiff)

9 —continued
*MERIONETH
(Dolgellan)
10
*FLINTSHIRE (Mold)
S. GLAMORGAN
(Cardiff)
W. GLAMORGAN
(Swansea)
11
*BRECONSHIRE
(Brecon)
*RADNORSHIRE
(Llandrindod Wells)

12
*DENBIGHSHIRE
(Ruthin)
MID GLAMORGAN
(Cardiff)
13
*CARDIGANSHIRE
(Aberystwyth)
*MONMOUTHSHIRE
(Newport)
*PEMBROKESHIRE
(Haverfordwest)

15
*CAERNARFON-
SHIRE (Caernarfon)
*CARMARTHEN-
SHIRE
(Carmarthen)
*MONTGOMERY-
SHIRE (Welshpool)

*indicates a former
county

SCOTTISH REGIONS AND COUNTIES

REGION OR COUNTY (Administrative Centre)

3
*AYR (Ayr)
4
*BUTE (Rothesay)
FIFE (Fife)
*FIFE (Cupar)
5
*ANGUS (Forfar)
*BANFF (Banff)
*MORAY (Elgin)
*NAIRN (Nairn)
*PERTH (Perth)
6
*ARGYLL
  (Lochgilphead)
*LANARK (Hamilton)
ORKNEY (Kirkwall)
*ORKNEY (Kirkwall)
7
*BERWICK (Duns)
BORDERS (Newton
  St. Boswells)
CENTRAL (Stirling)

7 —continued
*KINROSS (Kinross)
LOTHIAN (Edinburgh)
*PEEBLES (Peebles)
*RENFREW (Paisley)
*SELKIRK (Selkirk)
TAYSIDE (Dundee)
*WIGTOWN
  (Stranraer)
*ZETLAND (Lerwick)
8
*ABERDEEN
  (Aberdeen)
*DUMFRIES
  (Dumfries)
GRAMPIAN
  (Aberdeen)
HIGHLAND
  (Inverness)
*ROXBURGH
  (Newtown St.
  Boswells)
SHETLAND (Lerwick)

8 —continued
*STIRLING (Stirling)
9
*CAITHNESS (Wick)
*DUMBARTON
  (Dumbarton)
*INVERNESS
  (Inverness)
10
*KINCARDINE
  (Stonehaven)
*MIDLOTHIAN
  (Edinburgh)
*SUTHERLAND
  (Golspie)
11
*CLACKMANNAN
  (Alloa)
*EAST LOTHIAN
  (Haddington)
STRATHCLYDE
  (Glasgow)

11 —continued
*WEST LOTHIAN
  (Linlithgow)
12
WESTERN ISLES
  (Lewis)
13
*KIRKCUDBRIGHT
  (Kirkcudbright)
15
*ROSS AND
  CROMARTY
  (Dingwall)
19
DUMFRIES AND
  GALLOWAY
  (Dumfries)

  *indicates former
  Scottish county

COUNTIES OF NORTHERN IRELAND

COUNTY (County Town)

4
DOWN (Downpatrick)
6
ANTRIM (Belfast)

6 —continued
ARMAGH (Armagh)
TYRONE (Omagh)

9
FERMANAGH
  (Enniskillen)

11
LONDONDERRY
  (Londonderry)

REPUBLIC OF IRELAND PROVINCES

CONNACHT   LEINSTER   MUNSTER   ULSTER

REPUBLIC OF IRELAND COUNTIES

4	6	7 —continued	8 —continued
CORK	CARLOW	LEITRIM	LONGFORD
MAYO	DUBLIN	WEXFORD	MONAGHAN
5	GALWAY	WICKLOW	**9**
CAVAN	OFFALY	**8**	ROSCOMMON
CLARE	**7**	KILKENNY	TIPPERARY
KERRY	DONEGAL	LAOIGHIS	WATERFORD
LOUTH	KILDARE	LIMERICK	WESTMEATH
MEATH			
SLIGO			

AMERICAN STATES

STATE	ABBREVIA-TION	NICKNAME	CAPITAL
ALABAMA	ALA	CAMELLIA	MONTGOMERY
ALASKA	ALAS		JUNEAU
ARIZONA	ARIZ	OCOTILLO	PHOENIX
ARKANSAS	ARK		LITTLE ROCK
CALIFORNIA	CAL	GOLDEN	SACRAMENTO
COLORADO	COLO	CENTENNIAL	DENVER
CONNECTICUT	CONN	NUTMEG	HARTFORD
DELAWARE	DEL	DIAMOND	DOVER
FLORIDA	FLA	SUNSHINE	TALLAHASSEE
GEORGIA	GA	PEACH	ATLANTA
HAWAII	HA	ALOHA	HONOLULU
IDAHO	IDA	GEM	BOISE
ILLINOIS	ILL	PRAIRIE	SPRINGFIELD
INDIANA	IND	HOOSIER	INDIANAPOLIS
IOWA	IA	HAWKEYE	DES MOINES
KANSAS	KAN	SUNFLOWER	TOPEKA
KENTUCKY	KY	BLUEGRASS	FRANKFORT
LOUISIANA	LA	PELICAN	BATON ROUGE
MAINE	ME	PINETREE	AUGUSTA
MARYLAND	MD	OLDLINE	ANNAPOLIS
MASSACHUSETTS	MASS	BAY	BOSTON
MICHIGAN	MICH	WOLVERINE	LANSING
MINNESOTA	MINN	NORTHSTAR	ST. PAUL
MISSISSIPPI	MISS	MAGNOLIA	JACKSON
MISSOURI	MO	SHOWME	JEFFERSON CITY
MONTANA	MONT	TREASURE	HELENA
NEBRASKA	NEBR	CORNHUSKER	LINCOLN
NEVADA	NEV	SILVER	CARSON CITY
NEW HAMPSHIRE	NH	GRANITE	CONCORD
NEW JERSEY	NJ	GARDEN	TRENTON
NEW MEXICO	N MEX	LAND OF ENCHANTMENT	SANTA FÉ
NEW YORK	NY	EMPIRE	ALBANY
NORTH CAROLINA	NC	TARHEEL	RALEIGH
NORTH DAKOTA	N DAK	SIOUX	BISMARCK
OHIO	OH	BUCKEYE	COLUMBUS

OKLAHOMA	OKLA	SOONER	OKLAHOMA CITY
OREGON	OREG	BEAVER	SALEM
PENNSYLVANIA	PA	KEYSTONE	HARRISBURG
RHODE ISLAND	RI	OCEAN	PROVIDENCE
SOUTH CAROLINA	SC	PALMETTO	COLUMBIA
SOUTH DAKOTA	S DAK	COYOTE	PIERRE
TENNESSEE	TENN	VOLUNTEER	NASHVILLE
TEXAS	TEX	LONESTAR	AUSTIN
UTAH	UT	MORMAN	SALT LAKE CITY
VERMONT	VT	GREEN MOUNTAIN	MONTPELIER
VIRGINIA	VA	OLD DOMINION	RICHMOND
WASHINGTON	WASH	EVERGREEN	OLYMPIA
WEST VIRGINIA	W VA	MOUNTAIN	CHARLESTON
WISCONSIN	WIS	BADGER	MADISON
WYOMING	WYO	EQUALITY	CHEYENNE

AUSTRALIAN STATES AND TERRITORIES

AUSTRALIAN CAPITAL TERRITORY	NEW SOUTH WALES NORTHERN TERRITORY	QUEENSLAND SOUTH AUSTRALIA TASMANIA	VICTORIA WESTERN AUSTRALIA

TOWNS AND CITIES

AFGHANISTAN

5
HERAT
KABUL

8
KANDAHAR

ALGERIA

4
ORAN

7
ALGIERS

ANGOLA

6
LOBITO
LUANDA

ARGENTINA

7
CORDOBA
LA PLATA
ROSARIO

11
BAHIA BLANCA
BUENOS AIRES

AUSTRALIA

5
PERTH

6
DARWIN
HOBART
SYDNEY

8
ADELAIDE
BRISBANE
CANBERRA

9
MELBOURNE
NEWCASTLE

12
ALICE SPRINGS

AUSTRIA

6
VIENNA

8
SALZBURG

9
INNSBRUCK

BANGLADESH

5
DHAKA

10
CHITTAGONG

BELGIUM

5
GHENT
LIÈGE
NAMUR
YPRES

6
BRUGES
DINANT
OSTEND

7
ANTWERP
MALINES

8
BRUSSELS

BRAZIL

5
BELEM

6
RECIFE

8
BRASILIA
SAO PAULO

11
PORTO ALEGRE

12
RIO DE JANEIRO

13
BELO HORIZONTE

BULGARIA

5
SOFIA
VARNA

BURMA

3
AVA

7
RANGOON

8
MANDALAY

CANADA

6
OTTAWA
QUEBEC
REGINA

7
CALGARY
HALIFAX
ST JOHN'S
TORONTO
8
EDMONTON
HAMILTON
KINGSTON
MONTREAL
VICTORIA
WINNIPEG
9
VANCOUVER
SASKATOON
10
THUNDER BAY
11
FREDERICTON
12
NIAGARA FALLS
13
CHARLOTTETOWN

CHILE

8
SANTIAGO
10
VALPARAISO

CHINA

4
LUTA
SIAN
5
WUHAN
6
ANSHAN
CANTON
DAIREN
FUSHUN
HARBIN
MUKDEN
PEKING
TSINAN
7
BEIJING
KUNMING
LANCHOW
NANKING
TAIYUAN
8
SHANGHAI
SHENYANG
TIENTSIN
9
CHANGCHUN
CHUNGKING

10
PORT ARTHUR

COLOMBIA

4
CALI
6
BOGOTÁ
9
CARTAGENA
12
BARRANQUILLA

CZECHOSLOVAKIA

4
BRNO
6
PRAGUE
10
BRATISLAVA

EGYPT

4
GIZA
SUEZ
5
ASWAN
CAIRO
LUXOR
TANTA
6
THEBES
7
MANSURA
MEMPHIS
ZAGAZIG
8
ISMAILIA
PORT SAID
10
ALEXANDRIA

ENGLAND

3
ELY
EYE
RYE
WEM
4
BATH
BRAY
BUDE
BURY
CLUN
DEAL
DISS
ETON
HOLT

4 —continued
HOVE
HULL
HYDE
INCE
LEEK
LOOE
LYDD
ROSS
RYDE
SHAP
WARE
WARK
YARM
YORK
5
ACTON
ALTON
BACUP
BLYTH
BOURN
CALNE
CHARD
CHEAM
COLNE
COWES
CREWE
DERBY
DOVER
EGHAM
EPSOM
FILEY
FOWEY
FROME
GOOLE
HAWES
HEDON
HURST
HYTHE
LEEDS
LEIGH
LEWES
LOUTH
LUTON
MARCH
OLNEY
OTLEY
POOLE
REETH
RIPON
RISCA
RUGBY
SARUM
SELBY
STOKE
STONE
TEBAY
THAME
TRING
TRURO
WELLS

5 —continued
WIGAN
6
ALFORD
ALSTON
ASHTON
BARNET
BARROW
BARTON
BATLEY
BATTLE
BAWTRY
BEDALE
BELPER
BODMIN
BOGNOR
BOLTON
BOOTLE
BOSTON
BRUTON
BUNGAY
BURTON
BUXTON
CASTOR
COBHAM
CROMER
DARWEN
DUDLEY
DURHAM
EALING
ECCLES
EPPING
EXETER
GORING
HANLEY
HARLOW
HARROW
HAVANT
HENLEY
HEXHAM
HOWDEN
ILFORD
ILKLEY
ILSLEY
JARROW
KENDAL
LEYTON
LONDON
LUDLOW
LYNTON
LYTHAM
MALDON
MALTON
MARLOW
MASHAM
MORLEY
NASEBY
NELSON
NESTON
NEWARK
NEWENT

6 —continued	7 —continued	7 —continued	7 —continued
NEWLYN	BILSTON	LEYBURN	WAREHAM
NEWTON	BOURTON	LINCOLN	WARWICK
NORHAM	BOWFELL	MALVERN	WATCHET
OAKHAM	BRANDON	MARGATE	WATFORD
OLDHAM	BRISTOL	MATLOCK	WEOBLEY
ORMSBY	BRIXHAM	MOLESEY	WICKWAR
OSSETT	BROMLEY	MORETON	WINDSOR
OUNDLE	BURNHAM	MORPETH	WINSLOW
OXFORD	BURNLEY	MOSSLEY	WINSTER
PENRYN	BURSLEM	NEWBURY	WISBECK
PEWSEY	CAISTOR	NEWPORT	WORKSOP
PINNER	CATFORD	NORWICH	8
PUDSEY	CAWSTON	OLDBURY	ABINGDON
PUTNEY	CHARING	OVERTON	ALFRETON
RAMSEY	CHATHAM	PADSTOW	ALNMOUTH
REDCAR	CHEADLE	PENRITH	AMESBURY
RIPLEY	CHEDDAR	POULTON	AMPTHILL
ROMNEY	CHESHAM	PRESCOT	AXBRIDGE
ROMSEY	CHESTER	PRESTON	AYCLIFFE
RUGELY	CHORLEY	RAINHAM	BAKEWELL
SEAHAM	CLACTON	READING	BARNSLEY
SEATON	CLIFTON	REDHILL	BERKELEY
SELSEY	CRAWLEY	REDRUTH	BEVERLEY
SETTLE	CROYDON	REIGATE	BICESTER
SNAITH	DARSLEY	RETFORD	BIDEFORD
ST IVES	DATCHET	ROMFORD	BOLSOVER
STROOD	DAWLISH	ROSSALL	BRACKLEY
STROUD	DEVIZES	ROYSTON	BRADFORD
SUTTON	DORKING	RUNCORN	BRAMPTON
THIRSK	DOUGLAS	SALFORD	BRIDPORT
THORNE	DUNSTER	SALTASH	BRIGHTON
TOTNES	ELSTREE	SANDOWN	BROMYARD
WALTON	ENFIELD	SAXELBY	BROSELEY
WATTON	EVERTON	SEAFORD	CAMBORNE
WESTON	EVESHAM	SHIFNAL	CARLISLE
WHITBY	EXMOUTH	SHIPLEY	CATERHAM
WIDNES	FAREHAM	SHIPTON	CHERTSEY
WIGTON	FARNHAM	SILLOTH	CLEVEDON
WILTON	FELTHAM	SKIPTON	CLOVELLY
WITHAM	GLOSSOP	SPILSBY	COVENTRY
WITNEY	GOSPORT	STAINES	CREDITON
WOOLER	GRIMSBY	STILTON	DAVENTRY
YEOVIL	HALIFAX	ST NEOTS	DEBENHAM
7	HAMPTON	SUDBURY	DEDWORTH
ALNWICK	HARWICH	SUNBURY	DEPTFORD
ANDOVER	HAWORTH	SWANAGE	DEWSBURY
APPLEBY	HELSTON	SWINDON	EGREMONT
ARUNDEL	HEYWOOD	SWINTON	EVERSLEY
ASHFORD	HITCHIN	TAUNTON	FAKENHAM
AYLSHAM	HONITON	TELFORD	FALMOUTH
BAMPTON	HORNSEA	TENBURY	FOULNESS
BANBURY	HORNSEY	TETBURY	GRANTHAM
BARKING	HORSHAM	THAXTED	GRANTOWN
BECCLES	IPSWICH	TILBURY	HADLEIGH
BEDFORD	IXWORTH	TORQUAY	HAILSHAM
BELFORD	KESWICK	TWYFORD	HALSTEAD
BERWICK	KINGTON	VENTNOR	HASTINGS
BEWDLEY	LANCING	WALSALL	HATFIELD
BEXHILL	LANGTON	WALTHAM	HELMSLEY
BiCKLEY	LEDBURY	WANTAGE	HEREFORD

8 —continued	8 —continued	9 —continued	9 —continued
HERNE BAY	TUNSTALL	GREENWICH	TOWCESTER
HERTFORD	UCKFIELD	GRINSTEAD	TYNEMOUTH
HINCKLEY	UXBRIDGE	GUILDFORD	ULVERSTON
HOLBEACH	WALLASEY	HARROGATE	UPMINSTER
HUNMANBY	WALLSEND	HASLEMERE	UPPINGHAM
ILKESTON	WANSTEAD	HAVERHILL	UTTOXETER
KEIGHLEY	WESTBURY	HAWKHURST	WAINFLEET
KINGSTON	WETHERAL	HOLMFIRTH	WAKEFIELD
LAVENHAM	WETHERBY	ILCHESTER	WARKWORTH
LECHLADE	WEYMOUTH	IMMINGHAM	WEYBRIDGE
LISKEARD	WOODFORD	KETTERING	WHERNSIDE
LONGTOWN	WOOLWICH	KING'S LYNN	WHITHAVEN
LYNMOUTH	WORTHING	KINGSWEAR	WIMBLEDON
MARYPORT	YARMOUTH	LAMBOURNE	WINCANTON
MIDHURST	**9**	LANCASTER	WOKINGHAM
MINEHEAD	ALDEBURGH	LEICESTER	WOODSTOCK
NANTWICH	ALDERSHOT	LICHFIELD	WORCESTER
NEWHAVEN	ALLENDALE	LIVERPOOL	WYMONDHAM
NUNEATON	ALRESFORD	LONGRIDGE	**10**
ORMSKIRK	AMBLESIDE	LOWESTOFT	ACCRINGTON
OSWESTRY	ASHBOURNE	LYME REGIS	ALDBOROUGH
PENZANCE	ASHBURTON	LYMINGTON	ALTRINCHAM
PERSHORE	AVONMOUTH	MAIDSTONE	BARNSTAPLE
PETERLEE	AYLESBURY	MANSFIELD	BEDLINGTON
PETWORTH	BLACKBURN	MIDDLETON	BELLINGHAM
PEVENSEY	BLACKPOOL	NEWCASTLE	BILLERICAY
PLAISTOW	BLANDFORD	NEWMARKET	BIRKENHEAD
PLYMOUTH	BLISWORTH	NEW ROMNEY	BIRMINGHAM
RAMSGATE	BRACKNELL	NORTHWICH	BRIDGNORTH
REDDITCH	BRAINTREE	OTTERBURN	BRIDGWATER
RICHMOND	BRENTFORD	PEMBRIDGE	BROMSGROVE
RINGWOOD	BRENTWOOD	PENISTONE	BROXBOURNE
ROCHDALE	BRIGHOUSE	PENKRIDGE	BUCKINGHAM
ROTHBURY	BROUGHTON	PENYGHENT	CANTERBURY
SALTBURN	CAMBRIDGE	PICKERING	CARSHALTON
SANDGATE	CARNFORTH	ROCHESTER	CHELMSFORD
SANDWICH	CASTLETON	ROTHERHAM	CHELTENHAM
SEDBERGH	CHESILTON	SALISBURY	CHICHESTER
SHANKLIN	CHINGFORD	SALTFLEET	CHIPPENHAM
SHELFORD	CLITHEROE	SEVENOAKS	CHULMLEIGH
SHIPSTON	CONGLETON	SHEERNESS	COGGESHALL
SIDMOUTH	CRANBORNE	SHEFFIELD	COLCHESTER
SKEGNESS	CRANBROOK	SHERBORNE	CULLOMPTON
SLEAFORD	CREWKERNE	SMETHWICK	DARLINGTON
SOUTHEND	CRICKLADE	SOUTHGATE	DORCHESTER
SPALDING	CUCKFIELD	SOUTHPORT	DUKINFIELD
STAFFORD	DARTMOUTH	SOUTHWELL	EASTBOURNE
ST ALBANS	DEVONPORT	SOUTHWOLD	ECCLESHALL
STAMFORD	DONCASTER	STARCROSS	FARNINGHAM
STANHOPE	DONINGTON	ST AUSTELL	FOLKESTONE
STANWELL	DROITWICH	STEVENAGE	FRESHWATER
ST HELENS	DRONFIELD	STOCKPORT	GILLINGHAM
STOCKTON	DUNGENESS	STOKESLEY	GLOUCESTER
STRATTON	DUNSTABLE	STOURPORT	HALESWORTH
SURBITON	ELLESMERE	STRATFORD	HARTLEPOOL
SWAFFHAM	FAVERSHAM	TARPORLEY	HASLINGDON
TAMWORTH	FLEETWOOD	TAVISTOCK	HEATHFIELD
THETFORD	GATESHEAD	TENTERDEN	HORNCASTLE
THORNABY	GODALMING	TODMORDEN	HORNCHURCH
TIVERTON	GRAVESEND	TONBRIDGE	HUNGERFORD

10 —continued

HUNSTANTON
HUNTINGDON
ILFRACOMBE
KENILWORTH
KINGSCLERE
KIRKOSWALD
LAUNCESTON
LEAMINGTON
LEOMINSTER
LITTLEPORT
MAIDENHEAD
MALMESBURY
MANCHESTER
MEXBOROUGH
MICHELDEAN
MIDDLEWICH
MILDENHALL
NAILSWORTH
NOTTINGHAM
OKEHAMPTON
ORFORDNESS
PANGBOURNE
PATRINGTON
PEACEHAVEN
PONTEFRACT
PORTISHEAD
PORTSMOUTH
POTTER'S BAR
RAVENGLASS
ROCKINGHAM
SAXMUNDHAM
SHEPPERTON
SHERINGHAM
SHREWSBURY
STALBRIDGE
ST LEONARDS
STOWMARKET
SUNDERLAND
TEDDINGTON
TEIGNMOUTH
TEWKESBURY
THAMESMEAD
TORRINGTON
TROWBRIDGE
TWICKENHAM
WALSINGHAM
WARMINSTER
WARRINGTON
WASHINGTON
WEDNESBURY
WELLINGTON
WESTWARD HO
WHITCHURCH
WHITSTABLE
WHITTLESEY
WILLENHALL
WINCHELSEA
WINCHESTER
WINDERMERE
WINDLESHAM

10 —continued

WIRKSWORTH
WITHERNSEA
WOODBRIDGE
WORKINGTON

11

BASINGSTOKE
BEARMINSTER
BOGNOR REGIS
BOURNEMOUTH
BRIDLINGTON
BUNTINGFORD
CLEETHORPES
COCKERMOUTH
EAST RETFORD
GLASTONBURY
GREAT MARLOW
GUISBOROUGH
HALTWHISTLE
HAMPTON WICK
HATHERLEIGH
HIGH WYCOMBE
INGATESTONE
LEYTONSTONE
LITTLESTONE
LUDGERSHALL
LUTTERWORTH
MABLETHORPE
MANNINGTREE
MARKET RASEN
MARLBOROUGH
MUCH WENLOCK
NEW BRIGHTON
NEWTON ABBOT
NORTHAMPTON
PETERSFIELD
POCKLINGTON
RAWTENSTALL
SCARBOROUGH
SHAFTESBURY
SOUTHAMPTON
SOUTH MOLTON
STALYBRIDGE
ST MARGARET'S
STOURBRIDGE
TATTERSHALL
WALLINGFORD
WALTHAMSTOW
WESTMINSTER
WHITECHURCH
WOODHALL SPA

12

ATTLEBOROUGH
BEXHILL-ON-SEA
CASTLE RISING
CHESTERFIELD
CHRISTCHURCH
GAINSBOROUGH
GREAT GRIMSBY
GREAT MALVERN

12 —continued

HUDDERSFIELD
INGLEBOROUGH
LONG STRATTON
LOUGHBOROUGH
MACCLESFIELD
MILTON KEYNES
MORECAMBE BAY
NORTH BERWICK
NORTH SHIELDS
NORTH WALSHAM
PETERBOROUGH
SHOEBURYNESS
SHOTTESBROOK
SOUTH SHIELDS
STOKE-ON-TRENT

13

BARNARD CASTLE
BERKHAMPSTEAD
BISHOP'S CASTLE
BOROUGHBRIDGE
BRIGHTLINGSEA
BURTON-ON-TRENT
BURY ST EDMUNDS
CHIPPING ONGAR
FINCHAMPSTEAD
GODMANCHESTER
GREAT YARMOUTH
HIGHAM FERRERS
KIDDERMINSTER
KIRKBY STEPHEN
KNARESBOROUGH
LITTLEHAMPTON
LYTHAM ST ANNES
MARKET DEEPING
MARKET DRAYTON
MELCOMBE REGIS
MELTON MOWBRAY
MIDDLESBROUGH
NORTHALLERTON
SAFFRON WALDEN
SHEPTON MALLET
WOLVERHAMPTON
WOOTTON BASSET

14

BERWICK-ON-TWEED
BISHOP AUCKLAND
BISHOPS WALTHAM
CHIPPING BARNET
CHIPPING NORTON
HEMEL HEMPSTEAD
KIRKBY LONSDALE
MARKET BOSWORTH
MORTIMER'S CROSS
STOCKTON-ON-TEES
STONY STRATFORD
SUTTON COURTNEY
TUNBRIDGE WELLS
WELLINGBOROUGH
WEST HARTLEPOOL

15+

ASHTON-UNDER-
  LYNE
BARROW-IN-
  FURNESS
BISHOP'S
  STORTFORD
BURNHAM-ON-
  CROUCH
CASTLE DONINGTON
LEIGHTON BUZZARD
NEWCASTLE-ON-
  TYNE
ST LEONARDS-ON-
  SEA
STRATFORD-ON-
  AVON
SUTTON COLDFIELD
WELWYN GARDEN
  CITY
WESTON-SUPER-
  MARE

FRANCE

3

AIX
PAU

4

ALBI
CAEN
LYON
METZ
NICE

5

ARLES
ARRAS
BREST
DIJON
EVIAN
LILLE
LYONS
MACON
NANCY
NIMES
PARIS
REIMS
ROUEN
TOURS
TULLE

6

AMIENS
BAYEUX
CALAIS
CANNES
DIEPPE
LE MANS
NANTES
RHEIMS
ST MALO

6 —continued
TOULON
VERDUN

7
AJACCIO
ALENÇON
AVIGNON
BAYONNE
DUNKIRK
LE HAVRE
LIMOGES
LOURDES
ORLÉANS

8
BESANÇON
BIARRITZ
BORDEAUX
BOULOGNE
CHARTRES
GRENOBLE
SOISSONS
ST TROPEZ
TOULOUSE

9
ABBEVILLE
CHERBOURG
DUNKERQUE
MARSEILLE
MONTAUBAN
PERPIGNAN
ST ETIENNE

10
MARSEILLES
MONTELIMAR
STRASBOURG
VERSAILLES

11
ARMENTIÈRES
MONTPELLIER

15
CLERMONT-
  FERRAND

**GERMAN
DEMOCRATIC
REPUBLIC**

4
GERA
SUHL

5
HALLE

6
BERLIN
ERFURT

7
COTTBUS
DRESDEN
LEIPZIG
POTSDAM

7 —continued
ROSTOCK
SPANDAU

8
SCHWERIN

9
FRANKFURT
MAGDEBURG

11
BRANDENBURG

13
KARL-MARX-STADT

GREECE

6
ATHENS
SPARTA
THEBES

7
CORINTH
MYCENAE
PIRAEUS

8
SALONIKA

HUNGARY

4
PÉCS

8
BUDAPEST

INDIA

4
AGRA

5
AJMER
ALWAR
DELHI
KOTAH
PATNA
POONA
SIMLA

6
BARODA
BHOPAL
BOMBAY
HOWRAH
IMPHAL
INDORE
JAIPUR
JHANSI
KANPUR
KOHIMA
MADRAS
MEERUT
MYSORE
NAGPUR
RAMPUR

7
BENARES
GWALIOR
JODHPUR
LUCKNOW

8
AGARTALA
AMRITSAR
CALCUTTA
CAWNPORE
JAMALPUR
SHILLONG
SRINAGAR
VARANASI

9
AHMEDABAD
ALLAHABAD
BANGALORE
HYDERABAD

10
CHANDIGARH
DARJEELING
JAMSHEDPUR
TRIVANDRUM

11
BHUBANESWAR

INDONESIA

7
BANDUNG
JAKARTA

8
SURABAJA

9
PALEMBANG

IRAN

6
ABADAN
SHIRAZ
TABRIZ
TEHRAN

7
ISFAHAN
MASHHAD

IRAQ

5
BASRA
MOSUL

7
BAGHDAD
KARBALA

IRELAND

4
BRAY
COBH
CORK

5
BALLA
BOYLE
CLARE
KELLS
SLIGO

6
ARKLOW
BANTRY
CARLOW
CASHEL
DUBLIN
GALWAY
TRALEE

7
ATHLONE
BLARNEY
CLONMEL
DUNDALK
KILDARE
SHANNON
WEXFORD
WICKLOW
YOUGHAL

8
CLONTARF
DROGHEDA
KILKENNY
LIMERICK
LISTOWEL
MAYNOUTH
RATHDRUM

9
CONNEMARA
KILLARNEY
ROSCOMMON
TIPPERARY
WATERFORD

10
SHILLELAGH

11
BALLYMURPHY

ISRAEL

4
GAZA

5
HAIFA
JAFFA

7
TEL AVIV

9
BEERSHEBA
JERUSALEM

ITALY

4
BARI
PISA

4 —continued
ROME

5
GENOA
MILAN
OSTIA
PADUA
PARMA
SIENA
TRENT
TURIN

6
NAPLES
REGGIO
VENICE
VERONA

7
BOLOGNA
MESSINA
PALERMO
POMPEII
RAVENNA
SALERNO
SAN REMO
TRIESTE
VATICAN

8
FLORENCE
SYRACUSE

9
AGRIGENTO

JAPAN

4
KOBE

5
KYOTO
OSAKA
TOKYO

6
NAGOYA

7
FUKUOKA
SAPPORO

8
NAGASAKI
YOKOHAMA

9
HIROSHIMA

10
KITAKYUSHU

KENYA

4
LAMU

7
MOMBASA
NAIROBI

KOREA

5
SEOUL

9
PANMUNJON

LEBANON

4
TYRE

5
SIDON

6
BEIRUT

7
TRIPOLI

LIBYA

4
HOMS

6
TOBRUK

MALI

6
BAMAKO

8
TIMBUKTU

MEXICO

6
JUAREZ
PUEBLA

8
ACAPULCO
VERACRUZ

9
MONTERREY

11
GUADALAJARA

MOROCCO

3
FEZ

5
RÀBAT

6
AGADIR
MEKNES

7
TANGIER

8
TANGIERS

9
MARRAKECH
MARRAKESH

10
CASABLANCA

NETHERLANDS

5
HAGUE

6
ARNHEM
LEIDEN
LEYDEN

7
UTRECHT

8
THE HAGUE

9
AMSTERDAM
DORDRECHT
EINDHOVEN
ROTTERDAM

NEW ZEALAND

6
NAPIER
NELSON

7
DUNEDIN

8
AUCKLAND

10
WELLINGTON

12
CHRISTCHURCH

NIGERIA

4
KANO

5
ABUJA
ENUGU
LAGOS

6
IBADAN

NORTHERN IRELAND

4
MUFF

5
DOAGH
GLYNN
KEADY
LARNE
LOUTH
NEWRY
OMAGH
TOOME

6
ANTRIM
AUGHER

6 —continued
BELCOO
BERAGH
CALLAN
CARNEY
COMBER
LURGAN
RAPHOE
SHRULE

7
BELFAST
BELLEEK
CALEDON
CARRICK
CLOGHER
DERVOCK
DUNDRUM
DUNMORE
FINTONA
GILFORD
GLENARM
LIFFORD
LISBURN

8
AHOGHILL
BALLYBAY
DUNGIVEN
HILLTOWN
PORTRUSH
STRABANE
TRILLICK

9
BALLINTRA
BALLYMENA
BALLYMORE
BANBRIDGE
BELTURBET
BUSHMILLS
COLERAINE
COOKSTOWN
DUNGANNON
GLASLOUGH
KILLYBEGS
KIRCUBBIN
MONEYMORE
NEWCASTLE
PORTADOWN
RASHARKIN
ROSTREVOR
TOVERMORE

10
BALLYBOFIR
BALLYCLARE
BALLYHAISE
BALLYMONEY
BALLYRONEY
CASTLEDERG
CASTLEFINN
CUSHENHALL
DONAGHADEL

10 —continued
GLENGARIFF
KILCONNELL
MARKETHILL
PORTAFERRY
SAINTFIELD
STRANGFORD
STRANORLAR
TANDERAGEE

11
BALLYCASTLE
BALLYGAWLEY
CARRICKMORE
CROSSMAGLEN
DOWNPATRICK
DRAPERSTOWN
ENNISKILLEN
LETTERKENNY
LONDONDERRY
MAGHERAFELT
PORTGLENONE
RANDALSTOWN
RATHFRYLAND

12
CASTLEBLANEY
CASTLE DAWSON
CASTLEWELLAN
FIVE MILE TOWN
HILLSBOROUGH
INISHTRAHULL
SLIEVE DONARD
STEWARTSTOWN

13
BROOKEBOROUGH
CARRICKFERGUS
DERRYGONNELLY

14
NEWTOWN
  STEWART

NORWAY

4
OSLO

6
BERGEN

9
TRONDHEIM

PAKISTAN

6
LAHORE
QUETTA

7
KARACHI

8
PESHAWAR

9
HYDERABAD

10
RAWALPINDI

PERU

4
LIMA

5
CUZCO

POLAND

4
LODZ

5
POSEN

6
DANZIG
GDANSK
KRAKOW
LUBLIN
WARSAW

7
BRESLAU

8
PRZEMYSL

PORTUGAL

6
LISBON
OPORTO

SAUDI ARABIA

5
MECCA

6
JEDDAH
MEDINA
RIYADH

SCOTLAND

3
AYR
UIG

4
ALVA
BARR
DUNS
ELIE
KIRN
LUSS
NIGG
OBAN
REAY
RONA
STOW
WICK

5
ALLOA
ANNAN

5 —continued
APPIN
AVOCH
AYTON
BANFF
BEITH
BRORA
BUNAW
BUSBY
CERES
CLOVA
CLUNE
CRAIL
CUPAR
DENNY
DOWNE
ELGIN
ELLON
ERROL
FYVIE
GOVAN
INSCH
ISLAY
KEISS
KEITH
KELSO
LAIRG
LARGO
LEITH
NAIRN
PERTH
SALEN
TROON

6
ABOYNE
ALFORD
BARVAS
BEAULY
BERVIE
BIGGAR
BO'NESS
BUCKIE
CARRON
CAWDOR
COMRIE
CRIEFF
CULLEN
CULTER
DOLLAR
DRYMEN
DUNBAR
DUNDEE
DUNLOP
DUNNET
DUNOON
DYSART
EDZELL
FINDON
FORFAR
FORRES
GIRVAN

6 —continued
GLAMIS
HAWICK
HUNTLY
IRVINE
KILLIN
KILMUN
LANARK
LAUDER
LESLIE
LINTON
LOCHEE
MEIGLE
MOFFAT
PLADDA
RESTON
RHYNIE
ROSYTH
ROTHES
SHOTTS
THURSO
TONGUE
WISHAW
YARROW

7
AIRDRIE
BALFRON
BALLOCH
BANAVIE
BOWMORE
BRAEMAR
BRECHIN
BRODICK
CANOBIE
CANTYRE
CARBOST
CARGILL
CARLUKE
CRATHIE
CULROSS
CUMNOCK
DENHOLM
DOUGLAS
DUNKELD
DUNNING
EVANTON
FAIRLIE
FALKIRK
GALSTON
GIFFORD
GLASGOW
GLENCOE
GOLSPIE
GOUROCK
GRANTON
GUTHRIE
HALKIRK
KENMORE
KESSOCK
KILMORY
KILSYTH

7 —continued	8 —continued	9 —continued	10 —continued
KINROSS	DUNBEATH	CALLANDER	JOHNSHAVEN
KINTORE	DUNBLANE	CARSTAIRS	KILCREGGAN
LAMLASH	DUNSCORE	DUMBARTON	KILLENAULE
LARBERT	EARLSTON	EDINBURGH	KILMAINHAM
LYBSTER	EYEMOUTH	FERINTOSH	KILMALCOLM
MACDUFF	FINDHORN	FOCHABERS	KILMARNOCK
MAYBOLE	FORTROSE	INCHKEITH	KILWINNING
MELDRUM	GLENLUCE	INVERARAY	KINCARDINE
MELROSE	GREENLAW	INVERNESS	KINGSBARNS
MELVICH	GREENOCK	JOHNSTONE	KIRKMAIDEN
METHVEN	HAMILTON	KILDRUMMY	KIRKOSWALD
MILMUIR	INVERARY	KINGUSSIE	KIRRIEMUIR
MONIKIE	INVERURY	KIRKCALDY	LENNOXTOWN
MUTHILL	JEANTOWN	LEADHILLS	LESMAHAGOW
NEWPORT	JEDBURGH	LOCHGELLY	LINLITHGOW
PAISLEY	KILBRIDE	LOCHINVAR	LIVINGSTON
PEEBLES	KILNIVER	LOCHNAGAR	MILNATHORT
POLMONT	KILRENNY	LOCKERBIE	MOTHERWELL
POOLEWE	KINGHORN	LOGIERAIT	PITTENWEEM
PORTREE	KIRKWALL	MAUCHLINE	PORTOBELLO
PORTSOY	LANGHOLM	MILNGAVIE	RUTHERGLEN
RENFREW	LATHERON	PETERHEAD	STONEHAVEN
SADDELL	LEUCHARS	PITLOCHRY	STONEHOUSE
SARCLET	LOANHEAD	PORT ELLEN	STONEYKIRK
SCOURIE	MARKINCH	PRESTWICK	STRATHAVEN
SELKIRK	MARYKIRK	RICCARTON	STRATHEARN
STANLEY	MONIAIVE	RONALDSAY	STRATHMORE
STRATHY	MONTROSE	ROTHIEMAY	TWEEDMOUTH
TARBERT	MONYMUSK	SALTCOATS	WEST CALDER
TARLAND	MUIRKIRK	SHIELDAIG	WILSONTOWN
TAYPORT	NEILSTON	SLAMANNAN	
TRANENT	NEWBURGH	ST ANDREWS	**11**
TUNDRUM	NEWMILNS	STEWARTON	ABERCHIRDER
TURRIFF	PENICUIK	ST FILLANS	BALQUHIDDER
ULLSTER	PITSLIGO	STRANRAER	BANNOCKBURN
YETHOLM	POOLTIEL	STRATHDON	BLAIRGOWRIE
8	QUIRAING	STRONTIAN	CAMPBELTOWN
ABERDEEN	ROTHESAY	THORNHILL	CHARLESTOWN
ABERLADY	ST FERGUS	TOBERMORY	CUMBERNAULD
ABINGTON	STIRLING	TOMINTOUL	DRUMMELZIER
ARBROATH	STRICHEN		DUNFERMLINE
ARMADALE	TALISKER	**10**	ECCLEFECHAN
ARROCHAR	TARANSAY	ABBOTSFORD	FETTERCAIRN
AULDEARN	TRAQUAIR	ACHNASHEEN	FORT WILLIAM
BALLATER	ULLAPOOL	ANSTRUTHER	FRASERBURGH
BANCHORY	WHITHORN	APPLECROSS	HELENSBURGH
BARRHILL	WOODSIDE	ARDRISHAIG	INVERGORDON
BEATTOCK	**9**	AUCHINLECK	KIRKMICHAEL
BLANTYRE	ABERFELDY	BALLANTRAE	LOSSIEMOUTH
BURGHEAD	ABERFOYLE	BLACKADDER	LOSTWITHIEL
CANISBAY	ARDROSSAN	CARNOUSTIE	MAXWELLTOWN
CARNWATH	BERRIDALE	CARSPHAIRN	MUSSELBURGH
CREETOWN	BETTYHILL	CASTLETOWN	PORT GLASGOW
CROMARTY	BLACKLARG	COATBRIDGE	PORT PATRICK
DALKEITH	BRACADALE	COLDINGHAM	PRESTONPANS
DALMALLY	BRAERIACH	COLDSTREAM	PULTNEYTOWN
DINGWALL	BROADFORD	DALBEATTIE	STRATHBLANE
DIRLETON	BROUGHTON	DRUMLITHIE	
DUFFTOWN	BUCKHAVEN	EAST LINTON	**12**
DUMFRIES	CAIRNTOUL	GALASHIELS	AUCHTERARDER
		GLENROTHES	BALLACHULISH

12 —continued
EAST KILBRIDE
FORT AUGUSTUS
GARELOCHHEAD
INNERLEITHEN
LAWRENCEKIRK
PORTMAHOMACK
STRATHPEFFER
TILLICOULTRY

13
AUCHTERMUCHTY
CASTLE DOUGLAS
COCKBURNSPATH
DALMELLINGTON
INVERKEITHING
INVERKEITHNIE
KIRKCUDBRIGHT
KIRKINTILLOCH
NEWTON STEWART
ROTHIEMURCHUS

SOUTH AFRICA

6
DURBAN
SOWETO

8
CAPE TOWN
MAFEKING
PRETORIA

9
KIMBERLEY
LADYSMITH

10
SIMONSTOWN

11
GRAHAMSTOWN
SHARPEVILLE

12
BLOEMFONTEIN
JOHANNESBURG

13
PORT ELIZABETH

SPAIN

4
VIGO

5
CADIZ

6
BILBAO
MADRID
MALAGA

7
BADAJOZ
CORDOBA
GRANADA
SEVILLE

8
ALICANTE
PAMPLONA
VALENCIA
ZARAGOZA

9
BARCELONA
CARTAGENA
LAS PALMAS
SANTANDER
SARAGOSSA

12
SAN SEBASTIAN

SRI LANKA

5
GALLE
KANDY

7
COLOMBO

11
TRINCOMALEE

SUDAN

6
BERBER

7
DONGOLA

8
KHARTOUM
OMDURMAN

SWEDEN

5
MALMÖ

7
UPPSALA

8
GÖTEBORG

9
STOCKHOLM

10
GOTHENBURG

11
HELSINGBORG

SWITZERLAND

4
BÂLE
BERN

5
BASEL
BASLE

6
GENEVA
ZURICH

7
LUCERNE

8
LAUSANNE

SYRIA

4
HOMS

6
ALEPPO

7
PALMYRA

8
DAMASCUS

TANZANIA

6
DODOMA

8
ZANZIBAR

TURKEY

5
IZMIR

6
ANKARA
SMYRNA

7
ERZERUM

8
ISTANBUL

9
BYZANTIUM

14
CONSTANTINOPLE

USA

4
GARY
LIMA
RENO
TROY
WACO
YORK

5
AKRON
BOISE
BRONX
BUTTE
FLINT
MIAMI
OMAHA
OZARK
SALEM
SELMA
TULSA
UTICA

6
ALBANY
AUSTIN
BANGOR
BILOXI
BOSTON
CAMDEN
CANTON
DALLAS
DAYTON
DENVER
DULUTH
EL PASO
EUGENE
FRESNO
LOWELL
MOBILE
NASSAU
NEWARK
OXNARD
PEORIA
ST PAUL
TACOMA
TOLEDO
TOPEKA
TUCSON
URBANA

7
ABILENE
ANAHEIM
ATLANTA
BOULDER
BUFFALO
CHICAGO
CONCORD
DETROIT
HAMPTON
HOBOKEN
HOUSTON
JACKSON
KEY WEST
LINCOLN
MADISON
MEMPHIS
MODESTO
NEW YORK
NORFOLK
OAKLAND
ORLANDO
PHOENIX
RALEIGH
READING
ROANOKE
SAGINAW
SAN JOSÉ
SEATTLE
SPOKANE
ST LOUIS
WICHITA
YONKERS

8
BERKELEY
BROOKLYN
COLUMBUS
DEARBORN
GREEN BAY
HANNIBAL
HARTFORD
HONOLULU
LAKELAND
LAS VEGAS
NEW HAVEN
OAK RIDGE
PALO ALTO
PASADENA
PORTLAND
RICHMOND
SAN DIEGO
SANTA ANA
SAVANNAH
STAMFORD
STOCKTON
SYRACUSE
WHEELING

9
ANCHORAGE
ANNAPOLIS
ARLINGTON
BALTIMORE
BETHLEHEM
CAMBRIDGE
CHAMPAIGN
CHARLOTTE
CLEVELAND
DES MOINES
FAIRBANKS
FORT WAYNE
FORT WORTH
GALVESTON
HOLLYWOOD
JOHNSTOWN
KALAMAZOO
LANCASTER
LEXINGTON
LONG BEACH
MANHATTAN
MILWAUKEE
NASHVILLE
NEW LONDON
NORTHEAST
PRINCETON
RIVERSIDE
ROCHESTER
WATERBURY
WORCESTER
YPSILANTI

10
ATOMIC CITY
BATON ROUGE
BIRMINGHAM

10 —continued
CHARLESTON
CINCINATTI
EVANSVILLE
GREENSBORO
GREENVILLE
HARRISBURG
HUNTSVILLE
JERSEY CITY
KANSAS CITY
LITTLE ROCK
LONG BRANCH
LOS ANGELES
LOUISVILLE
MIAMI BEACH
MONTGOMERY
NEW BEDFORD
NEW ORLEANS
PITTSBURGH
PROVIDENCE
SACRAMENTO
SAINT LOUIS
SAN ANTONIO
WASHINGTON
YOUNGSTOWN

11
ALBUQUERQUE
CEDAR RAPIDS
CHATTANOOGA
GRAND RAPIDS
MINNEAPOLIS
NEWPORT NEWS
PALM SPRINGS
SCHENECTADY
SPRINGFIELD

12
ATLANTIC CITY
BEVERLY HILLS
FAYETTEVILLE
INDEPENDENCE
INDIANAPOLIS
JACKSONVILLE
NEW BRUNSWICK
NIAGARA FALLS
OKLAHOMA CITY
PHILADELPHIA
POUGHKEEPSIE
SALT LAKE CITY
SAN FRANCISCO
SANTA BARBARA

13
CORPUS CHRISTI
ST PETERSBURGH

14
FORT LAUDERDALE

15
COLORADO
   SPRINGS

USSR

3
UFA

4
BAKU
KIEV
LVOV
OMSK
RIGA

5
BREST
GORKY
KAZAN
MEMEL
MINSK
PINSK
PSKOV
VILNA
YALTA

6
KAUNAS
MOSCOW
ODESSA
TIFLIS

7
ALMA-ATA
DONETSK
IRKUTSK
ISFAHAN
KALININ
KHARKOV
LEMBERG
TALLINN
TBILISI
VILNIUS
YAKUTSK
YEREVAN

8
NOVGOROD
SMOLENSK
TASHKENT

9
ASTRAKHAN
CHERKESSK
KARAGANDA
KRIVOI ROG
KUIBYSHEV
LENINGRAD
SAMARKAND
VOLGOGRAD

10
KÖNIGSBERG
SEVASTOPOL
STALINGRAD
SVERDLOVSK

11
KALININGRAD

11 —continued
NOVOSIBIRSK
VLADIVOSTOK

14
DNEPROPETROVSK

VENEZUELA

7
CARACAS

9
MARACAIBO

WALES

3
USK

4
BALA
HOLT
MOLD
PYLE
RHYL

5
CHIRK
FLINT
NEATH
NEVIN
TENBY
TOWYN

6
AMLWCH
BANGOR
BRECON
BUILTH
CONWAY
MARGAM
RUABON
RUTHIN

7
CARBURY
CARDIFF
CWMBRAN
DENBIGH
MAESTEG
NEWPORT
NEWTOWN
ST ASAPH
SWANSEA
WREXHAM

8
ABERAVON
ABERDARE
ABERGELE
BARMOUTH
BRIDGEND
CAERLEON
CARDIGAN
CHEPSTOW
DOLGELLY

8 —continued
EBBW VALE
HAWARDEN
HOLYHEAD
HOLYWELL
KIDWELLY
KNIGHTON
LAMPETER
LLANELLY
LLANRWST
MONMOUTH
PEMBROKE
RHAYADER
SKERRIES
SKIFNESS
TALGARTH
TREDEGAR
TREGARON

9
ABERAERON
ABERDOVEY
ABERFFRAW
BEAUMARIS
CARNARVON
CRICCIETH
FESTINIOG
FISHGUARD
LLANBERIS
LLANDUDNO
NEW RADNOR
PONTYPOOL
PORTHCAWL
PORTMADOC
PWHLLHELI
WELSHPOOL

10
CADER IDRIS
CAERNARFON
CAERNARVON
CARMARTHEN
CRICKHOWEL
FFESTINIOG
LLANDOVERY
LLANFYLLIN
LLANGADOCK
LLANGOLLEN
LLANIDLOES
MONTGOMERY
PLINLIMMON
PONTYPRIDD
PORTH NIGEL
PORT TALBOT
PRESTEIGNE

11
ABERGAVENNY
ABERYSTWYTH
MACHYNLLETH
OYSTERMOUTH

12
LLANDILOFAWR
LLANTRISSANT

13
HAVERFORDWEST
MERTHYR TYDFIL

WEST GERMANY

4
BONN
KIEL
KÖLN

5
ESSEN
MAINZ
TRIER
WORMS

6
AACHEN
BERLIN
BOCHUM
BREMEN
CASSEL
KASSEL
LÜBECK
MUNICH
TRÈVES

7
COBLENZ
COLOGNE
HAMBURG
HANOVER
HOMBURG
KOBLENZ
MÜNCHEN

8
AUGSBURG
DORTMUND
HANNOVER
MANNHEIM
NÜRNBERG

9
BRUNSWICK
DARMSTADT
FRANKFURT
NUREMBERG
STUTTGART

9 —continued
WIESBADEN
WUPPERTAL

10
BADEN BADEN
BAD HOMBURG
DÜSSELDORF
HEIDELBERG

11
SAARBRÜCKEN

13
AIX-LA-CHAPELLE

YUGOSLAVIA

5
SPLIT

6
SKOPJE
ZAGREB

8
BELGRADE
SARAJEVO

9
LJUBLJANA

ZAÏRE

8
KINSHASA

10
LUBUMBASHI

PORTS

ALGERIA

4
ORAN
6
SKIKDA
7
ALGIERS
9
PORT ARZEW

ANGOLA

6
LOBITO
LUANDA

ARGENTINA

7
LA PLATA
11
BUENOS AIRES

AUSTRALIA

6
SYDNEY
7
DAMPIER
GEELONG
8
ADELAIDE
BRISBANE

9
MELBOURNE
NEWCASTLE
10
FREEMANTLE
11
PORT JACKSON
12
PORT ADELAIDE

BELGIUM

6
OSTEND
7
ANTWERP
9
ZEEBRUGGE

BENIN

7
COTONOU
9
PORTO NOVO

BRAZIL

4
PARA
5
BELEM
6
RECIFE
SANTOS
7
TOBARAO

10
PERNAMBUCO
12
RIO DE JANEIRO

BULGARIA

5
VARNA

BURMA

5
AKYAB
6
SITTWE
7
RANGOON
8
MOULMEIN

CAMEROON

6
DOUALA

CANADA

7
HALIFAX
KITIMAT
8
MONTREAL
9
CHURCHILL
ESQUIMALT
OWEN SOUND
VANCOUVER
11
THREE RIVERS

CHANNEL ISLANDS

8
ST HELIER
11
SAINT HELIER
ST PETER PORT

CHILE

5
ARICA
8
COQUIMBO
10
VALPARAISO

CHINA

4
AMOY
6
CHEFOO

6 —continued
HANKOW
SWATOW
WEIHAI
7
FOOCHOW
YINGKOW
8
SHANGHAI
TIENTSIN
10
PORT ARTHUR

COLUMBIA

9
CARTAGENA
12
BARRANQUILLA
BUENAVENTURA

CORSICA

6
BASTIA
7
AJACCIO

CUBA

6
HAVANA
14
SANTIAGO DE CUBA

CYPRUS

7
LARNACA
8
LIMASSOL

DENMARK

6
ODENSE
7
AALBORG
HORSENS
8
ELSINORE
9
HELSINGÖR
10
COPENHAGEN
13
FREDERIKSHAVN

ECUADOR

9
GUAYAQUIL

EGYPT

4
SUEZ
8
DAMIETTA
PORT SAID
10
ALEXANDRIA

ENGLAND

4
HULL
5
DOVER
6
LONDON
7
CHATHAM
GRIMSBY
HARWICH
TILBURY
8
FALMOUTH
NEWHAVEN
PENZANCE
PLYMOUTH
PORTLAND
SANDWICH
WEYMOUTH
9
AVONMOUTH
DEVONPORT
GRAVESEND
KING'S LYNN
LIVERPOOL
NEWCASTLE
SHEERNESS
10
BARNSTAPLE
COLCHESTER
FELIXSTOWE
FOLKESTONE
HARTLEPOOL
PORTSMOUTH
SUNDERLAND
TEIGNMOUTH
WHITSTABLE
11
CINQUE PORTS
SOUTHAMPTON
12
NORTH SHIELDS
PORT SUNLIGHT
13
MIDDLESBROUGH

FINLAND

8
HELSINKI

FRANCE

5
BREST
6
CALAIS
CANNES
DIEPPE
TOULON
7
DUNKIRK
LE HAVRE
8
BORDEAUX
BOULOGNE
HONFLEUR
9
CHERBOURG
FOS-SUR-MER
MARSEILLE
10
LA ROCHELLE
MARSEILLES

FRENCH GUIANA

7
CAYENNE

**GERMAN
DEMOCRATIC
REPUBLIC**

6
WISMAR
7
ROSTOCK

GHANA

4
TEMA
8
TAKORADI

GREECE

5
CANEA
CORFU
6
PATRAS
RHODES
7
PIRAEUS

8
NAVARINO

10
HERMOPOLIS

11
HERMOUPOLIS

HAWAII

8
HONOLULU

11
PEARL HARBOR

HUNGARY

8
BUDAPEST

INDIA

6
BOMBAY
COCHIN
HALDIA
KANDLA
MADRAS

8
CALCUTTA
COCANADA
KAKINADA

11
MASULIPATAM
PONDICHERRY

12
MASULIPATNAM

INDONESIA

6
PADANG

7
JAKARTA

8
MACASSAR
MAKASSAR
PARADEEP

IRAN

6
ABADAN

7
BUSHIRE

IRAQ

5
BASRA

IRELAND

4
COBH

4 —continued
CORK

7
DONEGAL
DUNDALK
YOUGHAL

8
DUNLEARY

12
DUN LAOGHAIRE

ISRAEL

4
ACRE
AKKO
ELAT

5
EILAT
HAIFA

6
ASHDOD

ITALY

4
BARI

5
GAETA
GENOA
OSTIA
TRANI

6
ANCONA
NAPLES
VENICE

7
LEGHORN
MARSALA
MESSINA
PALERMO
SALERNO
TRAPANI
TRIESTE

8
BRINDISI

IVORY COAST

7
ABIDJAN

JAMAICA

8
KINGSTON

9
PORT ROYAL

10
MONTEGO BAY

JAPAN

4
KOBE

5
KOCHI
OSAKA

8
HAKODATE
NAGASAKI
YOKOHAMA

9
HIROSHIMA
KAGOSHIMA

11
SHIMONOSEKI

KENYA

7
MOMBASA

KUWAIT

12
MINA AL-AHMADI

LEBANON

6
BEIRUT

LIBYA

7
TRIPOLI

8
BENGHAZI

MADAGASCAR

8
TAMATAVE

MALAYSIA

6
PENANG

9
PORT KLANG

10
GEORGE TOWN

12
KOTAKINABALU

MAURITANIA

10
NOUAKCHOTT

MAURITIUS

9
PORT LOUIS

MEXICO

7
GUAYMAS

8
VERA CRUZ

MOROCCO

4
SAFI

5
CEUTA
RABAT

6
AGADIR
TETUÁN

7
MELILLA
MOGADOR
TANGIER

9
ESSAOUIRA

10
CASABLANCA

14
MINA HASSAN TANI

MOZAMBIQUE

5
BEIRA

6
MAPUTO

NETHERLANDS

5
DELFT

8
FLUSHING

9
AMSTERDAM
EUROPOORT
ROTTERDAM

10
VLISSINGEN

NEW ZEALAND

6
NELSON

8
AUCKLAND
GISBORNE

9
LYTTELTON

NIGERIA

5
LAGOS

12
PORT HARCOURT

NORTHERN IRELAND

7
BELFAST

NORWAY

4
OSLO

6
BERGEN
LARVIK
NARVIK
TROMSO

9
STAVANGER
TRONDHEIM

10
CHRISTIANA
HAMMERFEST

13
CHRISTIANSUND

PAKISTAN

6
CHALNA

7
KARACHI

PANAMA

5
COLON

6
BALBOA

9
CRISTOBAL

PAPUA NEW GUINEA

11
PORT MORESBY

**PEOPLE'S
DEMOCRATIC
REPUBLIC OF
YEMEN**

4
ADEN

PERU

3
ILO

6
CALLAO

8
MATARINI

10
SAN JUAN BAY

PHILIPPINES

4
CEBU

6
MANILA

POLAND

6
DANZIG
GDANSK
GDYNIA

7
STETTIN

8
SZCZECIN

9
KOLOBRZEG

PORTUGAL

6
LISBON
OPORTO

PUERTO RICO

7
SAN JUAN

ROMANIA

10
CONSTANTSA

SAUDI ARABIA

6
JEDDAH

SCOTLAND

4
TAIN
WICK

5
LEITH
SCAPA

6
DUNBAR
DUNDEE

8
GREENOCK

9
ARDROSSAN
SCAPA FLOW
STORNAWAY

11
GRANGEMOUTH
PORT GLASGOW

SENEGAL

5
DAKAR

SIERRA LEONE

8
FREETOWN

SOUTH AFRICA

6
DURBAN

8
CAPE TOWN

9
MOSSEL BAY
PORT NATAL

10
EAST LONDON
SIMONSTOWN

11
RICHARD'S BAY

13
PORT ELIZABETH

SOUTH KOREA

5
PUSAN

SPAIN

5
PALMA
PALOS

6
BILBAO
FERROL
MALAGA

7
CORUNNA
FUNCHAL

8
ALICANTE
ARRECIFE
LA CORUÑA

9
ALGECIRAS
BARCELONA
CARTAGENA
LAS PALMAS
PORT MAHON

SRI LANKA

5
GALLE

7
COLOMBO

SUDAN

6
SUAKIN

9
PORT SUDAN

SWEDEN

5
LULEA
MALMÖ
WISBY
YSTAD

6
KÄLMAR

8
GÖTEBORG
HALMSTAD
NYKÖPING

9
STOCKHOLM

10
GOTHENBURG

11
HELSINGBORG

TAIWAN

6
TAINAN

7
KEELUNG

9
KAOHSIUNG

TANZANIA

6
MTWARA

11
DAR ES SALAAM

**TRINIDAD AND
TOBAGO**

11
PORT-OF-SPAIN

TURKEY

5
IZMIR

6
SMYRNA

8
ISTANBUL

14
CONSTANTINOPLE

URUGUAY

10
MONTEVIDEO

USA

4
ERIE
7
DETROIT
HOUSTON
NEW YORK
NORFOLK
SEATTLE
8
NEW HAVEN
9
BALTIMORE
GALVESTON
NANTUCKET
PENSACOLA
.10
BRIDGEPORT
CHARLESTON
JERSEY CITY
LOS ANGELES
NEW BEDFORD
NEW ORLEANS
PERTH AMBOY
PORTSMOUTH
11
ROCK HARBOUR
12
SAN FRANCISCO

USSR

4
BAKU
OKHA
RIGA
5
KERCH
REVAL
YALTA
6
IZMAIL
ODESSA
7
OKHOTSK
TALLINN
8
NAKHODKA
PECHENGA
TAGANROG
TIKSI BAY
9
ARCHANGEL
LENINGRAD
11
VLADIVOSTOK
13
PETROPAVLOVSK

VENEZUELA

8
LA GUIARA
12
PUERTO HIERRO

13
PUERTO CABELLO

WALES

7
CARDIFF
SWANSEA
8
HOLYHEAD
LLANELLI
PEMBROKE
9
PORTMADOC
12
MILFORD HAVEN

WEST GERMANY

4
KIEL
5
EMDEN
6
BREMEN
7
HAMBURG
8
CUXHAVEN
9
FLENSBURG
10
TRAVEMÜNDE
11
BREMERHAVEN

13
WILHELMSHAVEN

YEMEN ARAB REPUBLIC

5
MOCHA
6
AHMEDI
7
HODEIDA

YUGOSLAVIA

3
BAR
4
PULA
5
KOTOR
6
RIJEKA
7
CATTARO
9
DUBROVNIK

ZAÏRE

6
MATADI
9
MBUJI-MAYI

ISLANDS

4
BALI
CEBU
CUBA
EDGE
GUAM
JAVA
OAHU
SARK
5
BANKS
CERAM
CORFU
CRETE
DEVON
HAITI
LEYTE
LUZON

5 —continued
MALTA
PANAY
SAMAR
TIMOR
6
BAFFIN
BORNEO
CYPRUS
FLORES
HAINAN
HAWAII
HONSHU
JERSEY
KODIAK
KYUSHU
MADURA
NEGROS

6 —continued
PENANG
RHODES
SICILY
TAHITI
TAIWAN
7
BAHRAIN
BARENTS
BERMUDA
CELEBES
CORSICA
CURACAO
GOTLAND
GRENADA
ICELAND
IRELAND
JAMAICA

7 —continued
MADEIRA
MAJORCA
MINDORO
OKINAWA
PALAWAN
SHIKOKU
ST LUCIA
SUMATRA
WRANGEL
8
ALDERNEY
BARBADOS
DOMINICA
GUERNSEY
HOKKAIDO
HONG KONG
MALAGASY

8 —continued
MELVILLE
MINDANAO
SAKHALIN
SARDINIA
SOMERSET
SRI LANKA
SULAWESI
TASMANIA
TENERIFE
TRINIDAD
UNALASKA
VICTORIA
VITI LEVU
ZANZIBAR

9
ANTICOSTI
AUSTRALIA

9 —continued
ELLESMERE
GREENLAND
HALMAHERA
ISLE OF MAN
MANHATTAN
MAURITIUS
NANTUCKET
NEW GUINEA
SINGAPORE
ST VINCENT
VANCOUVER

10
CAPE BRETON
GUADELOUPE
HISPANIOLA
LONG ISLAND
MADAGASCAR

10 —continued
MARTINIQUE
NEW BRITAIN
NEW IRELAND
NEW ZEALAND
PUERTO RICO

11
AXEL HEIBERG
GUADALCANAL
ISLE OF PINES
ISLE OF WIGHT
SOUTHAMPTON

12
BOUGAINVILLE
GREAT BRITAIN
NEW CALEDONIA
NEWFOUNDLAND
NOVAYA ZEMLYA

13
NORTH EAST LAND
PRINCE OF WALES
PRINCE PATRICK
SANTA CATALINA

14
TIERRA DEL FUEGO

15
MARTHA'S
 VINEYARD
WEST SPITSBERGEN

18
PRINCE EDWARD
 ISLAND

OCEANS AND SEAS

3 & 4
ARAL (SEA)
AZOV (SEA OF)
DEAD (SEA)
JAVA (SEA)
KARA (SEA)
RED (SEA)
ROSS (SEA)
SAVA (SEA)

5
BANDA (SEA)
BLACK (SEA)
CHINA (SEA)
CORAL (SEA)
IRISH (SEA)
JAPAN (SEA OF)
NORTH (SEA)
TIMOR (SEA)
WHITE (SEA)

6
AEGEAN (SEA)
ARCTIC (OCEAN)
BALTIC (SEA)
BERING (SEA)
CELTIC (SEA)
INDIAN (OCEAN)
INLAND (SEA)
IONIAN (SEA)
LAPTEV (SEA)
NANHAI (SEA)
TASMAN (SEA)
YELLOW (SEA)

7
ANDAMAN (SEA)
ARABIAN (SEA)
ARAFURA (SEA)

7 —continued
BARENTS (SEA)
BEHRING (SEA)
CASPIAN (SEA)
DONG HAI (SEA)
GALILEE (SEA OF)
MARMARA (SEA OF)
OKHOTSK (SEA OF)
PACIFIC (OCEAN)
WEDDELL (SEA)

8
ADRIATIC (SEA)
AMUNDSEN (SEA)
ATLANTIC (OCEAN)
BEAUFORT (SEA)
HUANG HAI (SEA)
LIGURIAN (SEA)

8 —continued
SARGASSO (SEA)
TIBERIAS (SEA OF)

9
ANTARCTIC (OCEAN)
CARIBBEAN (SEA)
EAST CHINA (SEA)
GREENLAND (SEA)

10+
BELLINGSHAUSEN
 (SEA)
MEDITERRANEAN
 (SEA)
PHILIPPINE (SEA)
SETO-NAIKAI (SEA)
SOUTH CHINA (SEA)

LAKES AND LOCHS

LAKE (Country)

3
AWE (Scotland)
VAN (Turkey)

4
BALA (Wales)
CHAD (West Africa)
COMO (Italy)
ERIE (Canada, USA)
EYRE (Australia)

4 —continued
KIVU (Zaïre, Rwanda)
NEMI (Italy)
NESS (Scotland)
TANA (Ethiopia)

5
FOYLE (Ireland)
GARDA (Italy)
GREAT (Australia)

5 —continued
GREAT (USA,
 Canada)
HURON (USA,
 Canada)
KIOGA (Uganda)
KYOGA (Uganda)
LÉMAN (Switzerland,
 France)

5 —continued
LEVEN (Scotland)
LOCHY (Scotland)
MAREE (Scotland)
NEAGH (Northern
 Ireland)
NYASA (Malawi,
 Tanzania,
 Mozambique)

5 —continued
ONEGA (Soviet
  Union)
TAUPO (New
  Zealand)
URMIA (Iran)

6
ALBERT (Uganda,
  Zaïre)
BAIKAL (Soviet
  Union)
EDWARD (Uganda,
  Zaïre)
GENEVA (Switzerland,
  France)
KARIBA (Zambia,
  Zimbabwe)
LADOGA (Soviet
  Union)
LOMOND (Scotland)
LOP NOR (China)
MALAWI (Malawi,
  Tanzania,
  Mozambique)
MOBUTU (Uganda,
  Zaïre)
NASSER (Egypt)
NATRON (Tanzania)
PEIPUS (Soviet
  Union)
POYANG (China)

6 —continued
RUDOLF (Kenya,
  Ethiopia)
SAIMAA (Finland)
VÄNERN (Sweden)

7
BALATON (Hungary)
DERWENT (England)
KATRINE (Scotland)
KOKO NOR (China)
LUCERNE
  (Switzerland)
NU JIANG (China,
  Burma)
ONTARIO (Canada,
  USA)
QINGHAI (China)
ST CLAIR (USA,
  Canada)
TORRENS (Australia)
TURKANA (Kenya,
  Ethiopia)

8
BALKHASH (Soviet
  Union)
CHIEMSEE (West
  Germany)
CONISTON (England)
DONGTING (China)
GRASMERE
  (England)

8 —continued
ISSYK KUL (Soviet
  Union)
MAGGIORE (Italy,
  Switzerland)
MAZURIAN (Poland)
MENINDEE (Australia)
MICHIGAN (USA)
NEUSIEDL (Austria,
  Hungary)
SUPERIOR (USA,
  Canada)
TITICACA (Peru,
  Bolivia)
TONLE SAP
  (Kampuchea)
TUNG-T'ING (China)
VICTORIA (Uganda,
  Tanzania, Kenya)
WINNIPEG (Canada)

9
ATHABASCA
  (Canada)
BANGWEULU
  (Zambia)
CHAMPLAIN (USA)
CONSTANCE (West
  Germany)
ENNERDALE
  (England)

9 —continued
GREAT BEAR
  (Canada)
GREAT SALT (USA)
MARACAIBO
  (Venezuela)
THIRLMERE
  (England)
TRASIMENO (Italy)
ULLSWATER
  (England)
WAST WATER
  (England)

10+
BUTTERMERE
  (England)
GREAT SLAVE
  (Canada)
IJSSELMEER
  (Netherlands)
KARA-BOGAZ-GOL
  (Soviet Union)
OKEECHOBEE (USA)
TANGANYIKA (Zaïre,
  Burundi, Tanzania,
  Zambia)
VIERWALDSTÄTTER-
  SEE (Switzerland)
WINDERMERE
  (England)

RIVERS

RIVER (Country)

2 & 3
AIN (France)
ALN (England)
BUG (USSR, Poland,
  E. Germany)
CAM (England)
DEE (Scotland, Wales,
  England)
DON (USSR,
  Scotland, England,
  France, Australia)
EMS (W. Germany,
  Netherlands)
ESK (Australia)
EXE (England)
FAL (England)
FLY (New Guinea)
HAN (China)
KWA (Zaïre)
LEA (England)
LEE (Ireland)

2 & 3 —continued
LOT (France)
OB (USSR)
PO (Italy)
RED (USA)
RUR (W. Germany)
RYE (England)
TAY (Scotland)
URE (England)
USA (USSR)
USK (Wales, England)
WEY (England)
WYE (Wales, England)
YEO (England)

4
ADDA (Italy)
ADUR (England)
AIRE (England,
  France)
ALMA (USSR)

4 —continued
AMUR (Mongolia,
  USSR, China)
ARNO (Italy)
ARUN (Nepal)
AUBE (France)
AVON (England)
BEAS (India)
BURE (England)
CHER (France)
COLN (England)
DART (England)
DOON (Scotland)
DOVE (England)
EBRO (Spain)
EDEN (England,
  Scotland)
ELBE (W. Germany, E.
  Germany,
  Czechoslovakia)
EMBA (USSR)

4 —continued
ISIS (England)
JUBA (E. Africa)
KAMA (USSR)
KURA (Turkey, USSR)
LAHN (W. Germany)
LECH (W. Germany,
  Austria)
LENA (USSR)
LUNE (England)
LÜNE (W. Germany)
MAAS (Netherlands)
MAIN (W. Germany,
  Northern Ireland)
MIÑO (Spain)
MOLE (England)
NILE (Sudan, Egypt)
ODER (W. Germany,
  E. Germany,
  Czechoslovakia,
  Poland)

4 —continued
OHIO (USA)
OISE (France)
OUSE (England)
OXUS (USSR)
PEEL (Australia, USA)
RAVI (India, Pakistan)
REDE (England)
RUHR (W. Germany)
SAAR (W. Germany,
France)
SIDA (USSR)
SPEY (Scotland)
TAFF (Wales)
TAJO (Spain)
TARN (France)
TAWE (Wales)
TAWI (India)
TEES (England)
TEJO (Brazil)
TEST (England)
TYNE (Scotland,
England)
URAL (USSR)
VAAL (South Africa)
WEAR (England)
YARE (England)

5
ADIGE (Italy)
AISNE (France)
ALLAN (Scotland,
Syria)
ALLER (Spain, W.
Germany)
ANNAN (Scotland)
BENUE (Nigeria)
BRENT (England)
CAMEL (England)
CHARI (Cameroon,
Chad)
CLYDE (Scotland,
Canada)
COLNE (England)
CONGO (Zaïre)
DNEPR (USSR)
DOUBS (France,
Switzerland)
DOURO (Spain,
Portugal)
DOVEY (Wales)
DRAVA (Italy, Austria,
Yugoslavia,
Hungary)
DUERO (Spain)
DVINA (USSR)
FORTH (Scotland)
FROME (Australia)
INDUS (India,
Pakistan, China)
JAMES (USA,
Australia)

5 —continued
JUMNA (India)
JURUÁ (Brazil)
KAFUE (Zambia)
KASAI (Angola, Zaïre)
KUBAN (USSR)
LIPPE (W. Germany)
LOIRE (France)
MARNE (France)
MAROS (Indonesia)
MEUSE (France,
Belgium)
MINHO (Spain,
Portugal)
MURES (Romania,
Hungary)
NEGRO (Spain, Brazil,
Argentina, Bolivia,
Paraguay, Uruguay,
Venezuela)
NEMAN (USSR)
NIGER (Nigeria, Mali,
Guinea)
OTTER (England)
PEACE (Canada,
USA)
PEARL (USA, China)
PECOS (USA)
PIAVE (Italy)
PURUS (Brazil)
RANCE (France)
RHINE (Switzerland,
W. Germany,
Netherlands)
SAALE (E. Germany,
W. Germany)
SAÔNE (France)
SEINE (France)
SLAVE (Canada)
SNAKE (USA)
SOMME (France)
STOUR (England)
SWALE (England)
TAGUS (Portugal,
Spain)
TAMAR (England)
TIBER (Italy)
TRENT (England)
TWEED (England,
Scotland)
VOLGA (USSR, USA)
VOLTA (Ghana)
WESER (W. Germany)
XINGU (Brazil)
ZAÏRE (Zaïre)

6
ALLIER (France)
AMAZON (Peru,
Brazil)
ANGARA (USSR)
BÍO-BÍO (Chile)

6 —continued
CHENAB (Pakistan)
CLUTHA (New
Zealand)
COOPER (Australia)
COQUET (England)
CROUCH (England)
DANUBE (W.
Germany, Austria,
Romania, Hungary,
Czechoslovakia,
Bulgaria)
DNESTR (USSR)
ESCAUT (Belgium,
France)
FRASER (Canada)
GAMBIA (The
Gambia, Senegal)
GANGES (India)
GLOMMA (Norway)
HUDSON (USA)
HUNTER (Australia)
IRTYSH (USSR)
ITCHEN (England)
JAPURÁ (Brazil)
JORDAN (Israel,
Jordan)
KOLYMA (USSR)
LIFFEY (Eire)
LODDON (Australia,
England)
MAMORÉ (Brazil,
Bolivia)
MEDINA (USA)
MEDWAY (England)
MEKONG (Laos,
China)
MERSEY (England)
MONNOW (England,
Wales)
MURRAY (Australia,
Canada)
NECKAR (W.
Germany)
NEISSE (Poland,
Germany)
OGOOUÉ (Gabon)
ORANGE (South
Africa)
ORWELL (England)
PARANÁ (Brazil)
PLATTE (USA)
RIBBLE (England)
ST JOHN (Liberia,
USA)
SALADO (Argentina,
Cuba, Mexico)
SEVERN (England)
SUTLEJ (Pakistan,
India, China)
THAMES (England)

6 —continued
TICINO (Italy,
Switzerland)
TIGRIS (Iraq, Turkey)
TUGELA (South
Africa)
USSURI (China,
USSR)
VIENNE (France)
VLTAVA
(Czechoslovakia)
WABASH (USA)
WEAVER (England)
YELLOW (China,
USA, Papua New
Guinea)

7
BERMEJO (Argentina)
CAUVERY (India)
DAMODAR (India)
DARLING (Australia)
DERWENT (England)
DURANCE (France)
GARONNE (France)
GIRONDE (France)
HELMAND
(Afghanistan)
HOOGHLY (India)
HUANG HO (China)
LACHLAN (Australia)
LIMPOPO (South
Africa, Zimbabwe,
Mozambique)
LUALABA (Zaïre)
MADEIRA (Brazil)
MARAÑÓN (Brazil,
Peru)
MARITSA (Bulgaria)
MOSELLE (W.
Germany)
ORONTES (Syria)
PECHORA (USSR)
POTOMAC (USA)
SALWEEN (Burma,
China)
SCHELDT (Belgium)
SENEGAL (Senegal)
SHANNON (Eire)
SONGHUA (Vietnam,
China)
SUNGARI (China)
SUWANNEE (USA)
URUGUAY (Uruguay,
Brazil)
VISTULA (Poland)
WAIKATO (New
Zealand)
XI JIANG (China)
YANGTZE (China)
YENISEI (USSR)

7 —continued
ZAMBEZI (Zambia,
Angola, Zimbabwe,
Mozambique)

8
AMU DARYA (USSR)
ARAGUAIA (Brazil)
ARKANSAS (USA)
CANADIAN (USA)
CHARENTE (France)
COLORADO (USA)
COLUMBIA (USA)
DEMERARA (Guyana)
DORDOGNE (France)
GODAVARI (India)
MANAWATU (New
Zealand)
MENDERES (Turkey)
MISSOURI (USA)
PARAGUAY
(Paraguay)

8 —continued
PUTUMAYO
(Ecuador)
RÍO BRAVO (Mexico)
SAGUENAY (Canada)
SYR DARYA (USSR)
TORRIDGE (England)
TUNGUSKA (USSR)
VOLTURNO (Italy)
WANSBECK
(England)
WINDRUSH (England)

9
ATHABASCA
(Canada)
CHURCHILL (Canada)
ESSEQUIBO (Guyana)
EUPHRATES (Iraq)
GREAT OUSE
(England)
HSI CHIANG (China)
IRRAWADDY (Burma)

9 —continued
MACKENZIE
(Australia)
MAGDALENA
(Colombia)
RIO GRANDE
(Jamaica)
TENNESSEE (USA)

10
CHANG JIANG
(China)
CHAO PHRAYA
(Thailand)
COPPERMINE
(Canada)
HAWKESBURY
(Australia)
SHENANDOAH (USA)
ST LAWRENCE (USA)

11
ASSINIBOINE
(Canada)

11 —continued
BRAHMAPUTRA
(Tibet, India)
MISSISSIPPI (USA)
SHATT AL-ARAB
(Iran, Iraq)
SUSQUEHANNA
(USA)
YELLOWSTONE
(USA)

12
GUADALQUIVIR
(Spain)
MURRUMBIDGEE
(Australia)
RÍO DE LA PLATA
(Argentina,
Uruguay)
SASKATCHEWAN
(Canada)

MOUNTAINS AND HILLS

MOUNTAIN (Country)

3
ASO (MT) (Japan)
IDA (MT) (Turkey)

4
ALPS (France,
Switzerland, Italy,
Austria)
BLUE (MTS)
(Australia)
COOK (MT) (New
Zealand)
ETNA (MT) (Sicily)
HARZ (MTS) (East
Germany, West
Germany)
JAYA (MT)
(Indonesia)
JURA (MTS) (France,
Switzerland)
OSSA (MT) (Australia)
RIGI (Switzerland)
URAL (MTS) (Soviet
Union)

5
ALTAI (MTS) (Soviet
Union, China,
Mongolia)
ANDES (South
America)
ATHOS (MT) (Greece)

5 —continued
ATLAS (MTS)
(Morocco, Algeria)
BLACK (MTS) (Wales)
COAST (MTS)
(Canada)
EIGER (Switzerland)
ELGON (MT)
(Uganda, Kenya)
GHATS (India)
KAMET (MT) (India)
KENYA (MT) (Kenya)
LENIN (PEAK) (Soviet
Union)
LOGAN (MT)
(Canada)
PELÉE (MT)
(Martinique)
ROCKY (MTS) (USA,
Canada)
SAYAN (MTS) (Soviet
Union)
SNOWY (MTS)
(Australia)
TATRA (MTS)
(Poland,
Czechoslovakia)
WEALD (THE)
(England)

6
ARARAT (MT)
(Turkey)
BALKAN (MTS)
(Bulgaria)
CARMEL (MT) (Israel)
EGMONT (MT) (New
Zealand)
ELBERT (MT) (USA)
ELBRUS (MT) (Soviet
Union)
ELBURZ (MTS)
(Soviet Union)
EREBUS (MT) (Ross
Island)
HERMON (MT) (Syria,
Lebanon)
HOGGAR (MTS)
(Algeria)
KUNLUN (MTS)
(China)
LADAKH (RANGE)
(India)
MATOPO (HILLS)
(Zimbabwe)
MENDIP (HILLS)
(England)
MOURNE (MTS)
(Northern Ireland)

6 —continued
OLIVES (MT OF)
(Israel)
PAMIRS (Soviet
Union, China,
Afghanistan)
PINDUS (MTS)
(Greece, Albania)
TAURUS (MTS)
(Turkey)
VOSGES (France)
ZAGROS (MTS) (Iran)

7
AHAGGAR (MTS)
(Algeria)
BERNINA
(Switzerland)
BROCKEN (East
Germany)
CHEVIOT (HILLS)
(United Kingdom)
CHIANTI (Italy)
EVEREST (MT)
(Nepal, Tibet)
OLYMPUS (MT)
(Greece)
PALOMAR (MT) (USA)
RAINIER (MT) (USA)

7 —continued

RORAIMA (MT)
(Brazil, Guyana,
Venezuela)
RUAPEHU (MT) (New
Zealand)
SKIDDAW (England)
SNOWDON (Wales)
ST ELIAS (MTS)
(Alaska, Yukon)
TIBESTI (MTS) (Chad,
Libya)

8

ARDENNES
(Luxembourg,
Belgium, France)
BEN NEVIS (Scotland)
CAMBRIAN (MTS)
(Wales)
CAUCASUS (MTS)
(Soviet Union)
CÉVENNES (France)
CHILTERN (HILLS)
(England)
COTOPAXI (Ecuador)
COTSWOLD (HILLS)
(England)
FLINDERS (RANGE)
(Australia)
FUJIYAMA (Japan)
HYMETTUS (MT)
(Greece)
JUNGFRAU
(Switzerland)
KAIKOURA (RANGES)
(New Zealand)
MUSGRAVE
(RANGES)
(Australia)
PENNINES (England)
PYRENEES (France,
Spain)
STANOVOI (RANGE)
(Soviet Union)
TIAN SHAN (Soviet
Union, China,
Mongolia)
VESUVIUS (Italy)

9

ACONCAGUA (MT)
(Argentina)

9 —continued

ALLEGHENY (MTS)
(USA)
ANNAPURNA (MT)
(Nepal)
APENNINES (Italy)
CAIRNGORM (MTS)
(Scotland)
DOLOMITES (Italy)
DUNSINANE
(Scotland)
GRAMPIANS
(Scotland)
HAMERSLEY
(RANGE) (Australia)
HELVELLYN
(England)
HIMALAYAS (S Asia)
HINDU KUSH (Central
Asia)
HUASCARÁN (Peru)
KARAKORAM
(RANGE) (China,
Pakistan, India)
KOSCIUSKO (MT)
(Australia)
MONT BLANC
(France, Italy)
NANDA DEVI (MT)
(India)
PACARAIMA (MTS)
(Brazil, Venezuela,
Guyana)
PARNASSUS (MT)
(Greece)
RUWENZORI (MTS)
(Uganda-Zaïre)
TIRICH MIR (MT)
(Pakistan)
ZUGSPITZE (West
Germany)

10

ADIRONDACK (MTS)
(USA)
CADER IDRIS (Wales)
CANTABRIAN (MTS)
(Spain)
CARPATHIAN (MTS)
(Czechoslovakia,
Poland, Romania,
Soviet Union)

10 —continued

CHIMBORAZO (MT)
(India)
DHAULAGIRI (MT)
(Nepal)
ERZGEBIRGE
(Czechoslovakia,
East Germany)
KEBNEKAISE
(Sweden)
LAMMERMUIR
(HILLS) (Scotland)
MACDONNELL
(RANGES)
(Australia)
MAJUBA HILL (South
Africa)
MATTERHORN
(Switzerland, Italy)
MIDDLEBACK
(RANGE) (Australia)
MONTSERRAT
(Spain)
MOUNT LOFTY
(RANGES)
(Australia)

11

ANTI-LEBANON
(MTS) (Lebanon,
Syria)
APPALACHIAN (MTS)
(USA)
DRAKENSBERG
(MTS) (South
Africa)
JOTUNHEIMEN
(Norway)
KILIMANJARO (MT)
(Tanzania)
MONADHLIATH (MTS)
(Scotland)
NANGA PARBAT (MT)
(Pakistan)
SCAFELL PIKE
(England)
SIERRA MADRE
(Mexico)

12

CITLALTÉPETL
(Mexico)

12 —continued

GODWIN AUSTEN
(MT) (Pakistan)
GOLAN HEIGHTS
(Syria)
GRAN PARADISO
(Italy)
INGLEBOROUGH
(England)
KANCHENJUNGA
(MT) (Nepal)
PEAK DISTRICT
(England)
POPOCATÉPETL
(MT) (Mexico)
SIDING SPRING (MT)
(Australia)
SIERRA MORENA
(Spain)
SIERRA NEVADA
(Spain, USA)
WARRUMBUNGLE
(RANGE) (Australia)

13

CARRANTUOHILL
(Ireland)
COMMUNISM PEAK
(Soviet Union)
GROSSGLOCKNER
(Austria)
KANGCHENJUNGA
(MT) (Nepal)
KOMMUNIZMA PIK
(Soviet Union)
OJOS DEL SALADO
(Argentina, Chile)
SIERRA MAESTRA
(Cuba)

14+

BERNESE
OBERLAND
(Switzerland)
FICHTELGEBIRGE
(West Germany)
FINSTERAARHORN
(Switzerland)
MACGILLICUDDY'S
REEKS (Ireland)
SHIRÉ HIGHLANDS
(Malawi)

VOLCANOES

VOLCANO (Country)

3
ASO (Japan)
AWU (Indonesia)

4
ETNA (Sicily)
FOGO (Cape Verde
  Islands)
GEDE (Indonesia)
KABA (Indonesia)
LAKI (Iceland)
NILA (Indonesia)
POAS (Costa Rica)
SIAU (Indonesia)
TAAL (Philippines)

5
AGUNG (Indonesia)
ASAMA (Japan)
ASKJA (Iceland)
DEMPO (Indonesia)
FUEGO (Guatemala)
HEKLA (Iceland)
KATLA (Iceland)
MANAM (Bismarck
  Archipelago)
MAYON (Philippines)
NOYOE (Iceland)
OKMOK (USA)
PALOE (Indonesia)
PELÉE (W. Indies)
SPURR (USA)

6
ALCEDO (Galapagos
  Islands)
AMBRIM (Vanuatu
  Republic)
BIG BEN (Heard
  Island)
BULENG (Indonesia)
COLIMA (Mexico)
DUKONO (Indonesia)
IZALCO (El Salvador)
KATMAI (USA)
LASCAR (Chile)
LASSEN (USA)
LLAIMA (Chile)
LOPEVI (Vanuatu
  Republic)

6 —continued
MARAPI (Indonesia)
MARTIN (USA)
MEAKAN (Japan)
MERAPI (Indonesia)
MIHARA (Japan)
O'SHIMA (Japan)
OSORNO (Chile)
PACAYA (Guatemala)
PAVLOF (USA)
PURACÉ (Colombia)
SANGAY (Ecuador)
SEMERU (Indonesia)
SLAMAT (Indonesia)
TACANA (Guatemala)
UNAUNA (Indonesia)

7
ATITLAN (Guatemala)
BÁRCENA (Mexico)
BULUSAN
  (Philippines)
DIDICAS (Philippines)
EL MISTI (Peru)
GALERAS (Colombia)
JORULLO (Mexico)
KILAUEA (USA)
OMETEPE
  (Nicaragua)
PUYEHUE (Chile)
RUAPEHU (New
  Zealand)
SABRINA (Azores)
SOPUTAN (Indonesia)
SURTSEY (Iceland)
TERNATE (Indonesia)
TJAREME (Indonesia)
TOKACHI (Japan)
TORBERT (USA)
TRIDENT (USA)
VULCANO (Italy)

8
BOGOSLOF (USA)
CAMEROON
  (Cameroon)
COTOPAXI (Ecuador)

8 —continued
DEMAVEND (Iran)
FONUALEI (Tonga
  Islands)
FUJIYAMA (Japan)
HUALALAI (USA)
KERINTJI (Indonesia)
KRAKATAU
  (Indonesia)
KRAKATOA
  (Indonesia)
MAUNA LOA (USA)
NIUAFO'OU (Tonga
  Islands)
RINDJANI (Indonesia)
SANGEANG
  (Indonesia)
TARAWERA (New
  Zealand)
VESUVIUS (Italy)
YAKEDAKE (Japan)

9
AMBUROMBU
  (Indonesia)
BANDAI-SAN (Japan)
CLEVELAND (USA)
COSEGUINA
  (Nicaragua)
COTACACHI
  (Ecuador)
GAMKONORA
  (Indonesia)
GRIMSVÖTN (Iceland)
KORYAKSKY (USSR)
MOMOTOMBO
  (Nicaragua)
MYOZIN-SYO (Japan)
NGAURUHOE (New
  Zealand)
PARICUTIN (Mexico)
RININAHUE (Chile)
SANTORINI (Greece)
STROMBOLI (Italy)
TONGARIRO (New
  Zealand)

10
ACATENANGO
  (Guatemala)
CAPELINHOS
  (Azores)
CERRO NEGRO
  (Nicaragua)
GUALLATIRI (Chile)
HIBOK HIBOK
  (Philippines)
ICHINSKAYA (USSR)
LONG ISLAND
  (Bismarck
  Archipelago)
MIYAKEJIMA (Japan)
NYAMIAGIRA (Zaïre)
NYIRAGONGO (Zaïre)
SANTA MARIA
  (Guatemala)
SHISHALDIN (USA)
TUNGURAHUA
  (Ecuador)
VILLARRICA (Chile)

11
GREAT SITKIN (USA)
KILIMANJARO
  (Tanzania)
LA SOUFRIÈRE (W.
  Indies)
TUPUNGATITO
  (Chile)
WHITE ISLAND (New
  Zealand)

12
HUAINAPUTINA
  (Peru)
POPOCATAPETL
  (Mexico)
SARYCHEV PEAK
  (USSR)

13
KLYUCHEVSKAYA
  (USSR)

DESERTS

4
GILA
GOBI
THAR
5
NAMIB
NEFUD
NEGEV
OLMOS
ORDOS
SINAI
STURT
6
ARUNTA
GIBSON
MOJAVE

6 —continued
NUBIAN
SAHARA
SYRIAN
UST'-URT
7
ALASHAN
ARABIAN
ATACAMA
KARA KUM
MORROPE
PAINTED
SECHURA
SIMPSON
8
COLORADO

8 —continued
KALAHARI
KYZYL KUM
MUYUNKUM
VIZCAINO
9
BLACK ROCK
DASHT-I-LUT
DZUNGARIA
10
AUSTRALIAN
BET-PAK-DALA
GREAT SANDY
PATAGONIAN
RUB'AL KHALI

11
DASHT-I-KAVIR
DASHT-I-MARGO
DEATH VALLEY
13
GREAT SALT LAKE
GREAT VICTORIA
14
BOLSON DE MAPIMI
16
TURFAN
  DEPRESSION

ANIMALS AND PLANTS

ANIMALS

2 & 3
AI
APE
ASS
BAT
CAT
DOG
ELK
FOX
GNU
KOB
PIG
RAT
YAK

4
ANOA
BEAR
CAVY
CONY
DEER
GAUR
GOAT
HARE
IBEX
KUDU
LION
LYNX
MINK
MOLE
MULE
ORYX
PACA
PIKA
PUMA
SAKI
SEAL
SIKA
TAHR
TITI
VOLE
WOLF
ZEBU

5
ADDAX
BISON
BONGO
CAMEL
CHIRU
CIVET
COATI

5 —continued
COYPU
DHOLE
DINGO
DRILL
ELAND
FOSSA
GAYAL
GENET
GORAL
HINNY
HORSE
HUTIA
HYENA
HYRAX
INDRI
KIANG
KOALA
LEMUR
LIGER
LLAMA
LORIS
MOOSE
MOUSE
NYALA
OKAPI
ORIBI
OTTER
OUNCE
PANDA
POTTO
RATEL
SABLE
SAIGA
SEROW
SHEEP
SHREW
SKUNK
SLOTH
STOAT
TAPIR
TIGER
TIGON
WHALE
ZEBRA

6
AGOUTI
ALPACA
AOUDAD
ARGALI

6 —continued
AUROCH
AYE-AYE
BABOON
BADGER
BEAVER
BOBCAT
CATTLE
CHITAL
COLUGO
COUGAR
COYOTE
CUSCUS
DESMAN
DIK-DIK
DONKEY
DUGONG
DUIKER
ERMINE
FENNEC
FERRET
FISHER
GALAGO
GELADA
GERBIL
GIBBON
GOPHER
GRISON
GUENON
HYAENA
IMPALA
JACKAL
JAGUAR
JERBOA
LANGUR
MAMMAL
MARGAY
MARMOT
MARTEN
MONKEY
MUSK OX
NILGAI
NUMBAT
NUTRIA
OCELOT
OLINGO
ONAGER
POSSUM
RABBIT
RED FOX
RODENT

6 —continued
SEA COW
SERVAL
SIFAKA
TENREC
VERVET
VICUNA
WALRUS
WAPITI
WEASEL
WISENT
WOMBAT

7
ACOUCHI
ANT BEAR
BANTENG
BIGHORN
BLESBOK
BLUE FOX
BUFFALO
CANE RAT
CARACAL
CARIBOU
CHAMOIS
CHEETAH
COLOBUS
DASYURE
DOLPHIN
ECHIDNA
FELIDAE
GAZELLE
GEMSBOK
GERENUK
GIRAFFE
GLUTTON
GORILLA
GRAMPUS
GUANACO
GYMNURE
HAMSTER
LEMMING
LEOPARD
LINSANG
MACAQUE
MAMMOTH
MANATEE
MARKHOR
MEERKAT
MOLE RAT

7 —continued
MOON RAT
MOUFLON
MUSKRAT
NARWHAL
NOCTULE
OPOSSUM
PACK RAT
PANTHER
PECCARY
POLECAT
PRIMATE
RACCOON
RED DEER
ROE DEER
RORQUAL
SEALION
SIAMANG
SOUSLIK
SUN BEAR
TAMARIN
TAMAROU
TARSIER
WALLABY
WARTHOG
WILDCAT
ZORILLA

8
AARDVARK
AARDWOLF
ANTEATER
ANTELOPE
AXIS DEER
BABIRUSA
BONTEBOK
BUSHBABY
BUSHBUCK
CACHALOT
CAPYBARA
CHIPMUNK
DORMOUSE
ELEPHANT
ENTELLUS
FRUIT BAT
HEDGEHOG
IRISH ELK
KANGAROO
KINKAJOU
MANDRILL
MANGABEY
MARMOSET
MONGOOSE
MUSK DEER
MUSQUASH
PANGOLIN
PLATYPUS

8 —continued
PORPOISE
REEDBUCK
REINDEER
RUMINANT
SEA OTTER
SEI WHALE
SQUIRREL
STEINBOK
TALAPOIN
TAMANDUA
VISCACHA
WALLAROO
WATER RAT
WILD BOAR

9
ARCTIC FOX
ARMADILLO
BANDICOOT
BINTURONG
BLACK BEAR
BLACKBUCK
BLUE WHALE
BROWN BEAR
DEER MOUSE
DESERT RAT
DROMEDARY
FLYING FOX
GOLDEN CAT
GROUNDHOG
GUINEA PIG
HAMADRYAS
MARSUPIAL
MONOTREME
MOUSE DEER
ORANG-UTAN
PACHYDERM
PALM CIVET
PAMPAS CAT
PHALANGER
POLAR BEAR
PORCUPINE
PRONGHORN
PROSIMIAN
SILVER FOX
SITATUNGA
SLOTH BEAR
SOLENODON
SPRINGBOK
THYLACINE
TREE SHREW
WATERBUCK
WATER VOLE
WOLVERINE
WOODCHUCK

10
ANGWANTIBO

10 —continued
BARBARY APE
BOTTLENOSE
CACOMISTLE
CHEVROTAIN
CHIMPANZEE
CHINCHILLA
CHIROPTERA
FALLOW DEER
FIELDMOUSE
GOLDEN MOLE
HARTEBEEST
HONEY MOUSE
HOODED SEAL
JAGUARUNDI
KODIAK BEAR
MONA MONKEY
OTTER SHREW
PALLAS'S CAT
PILOT WHALE
PINE MARTEN
POUCHED RAT
PRAIRIE DOG
RACCOON DOG
RHINOCEROS
RIGHT WHALE
SPERM WHALE
SPRINGHAAS
TIMBER WOLF
VAMPIRE BAT
WATER SHREW
WHITE WHALE
WILDEBEEST

11
BARBASTELLE
BARKING DEER
DOUROUCOULI
FLYING LEMUR
GRASS MONKEY
GRIZZLY BEAR
HARBOUR SEAL
HONEY BADGER
KANGAROO RAT
KILLER WHALE
LEOPARD SEAL
PATAS MONKEY
PIPISTRELLE
PRAIRIE WOLF
RAT KANGAROO
RED SQUIRREL
SEROTINE BAT
SNOW LEOPARD

12
ELEPHANT SEAL
HARVEST MOUSE
HIPPOPOTAMUS

12 —continued
HORSESHOE BAT
HOWLER MONKEY
JUMPING MOUSE
KLIPSPRINGER
MOUNTAIN LION
POCKET GOPHER
RHESUS MONKEY
ROAN ANTELOPE
SNOWSHOE HARE
SPIDER MONKEY
TREE KANGAROO
WATER BUFFALO
WOOLLY MONKEY

13
ANTHROPOID APE
CRABEATER SEAL
DORCAS GAZELLE
HUMPBACK WHALE
MARSUPIAL MOLE
ROYAL ANTELOPE
SABLE ANTELOPE
TASMANIAN WOLF

14
CAPUCHIN MONKEY
CLOUDED LEOPARD
FLYING SQUIRREL
GROUND SQUIRREL
MOUNTAIN BEAVER
NEW WORLD
  MONKEY
OLD WORLD
  MONKEY
PÈRE DAVID'S DEER
SPECTACLED BEAR
SQUIRREL MONKEY
TASMANIAN DEVIL

15+
CHINESE WATER
  DEER
DUCK-BILLED
  PLATYPUS
FLYING PHALANGER
PROBOSCIS
  MONKEY
PYGMY
  HIPPOPOTAMUS
SCALY-TAILED
  SQUIRREL
WHITE RHINOCEROS
WOOLLY
  RHINOCEROS
WOOLLY SPIDER
  MONKEY

ANIMALS AND THEIR GENDER

ANIMAL	MALE	FEMALE
ANTELOPE	BUCK	DOE
ASS	JACKASS	JENNYASS
BADGER	BOAR	SOW
BEAR	BOAR	SOW
BOBCAT	TOM	LIONESS
BUFFALO	BULL	COW
CAMEL	BULL	COW
CARIBOU	STAG	DOE
CAT	TOM	QUEEN
CATTLE	BULL	COW
CHICKEN	COCK	HEN
COUGAR	TOM	LIONESS
COYOTE	DOG	BITCH
DEER	STAG	DOE
DOG	DOG	BITCH
DONKEY	JACKASS	JENNYASS
DUCK	DRAKE	DUCK
ELAND	BULL	COW
ELEPHANT	BULL	COW
FERRET	JACK	JILL
FISH	COCK	HEN
FOX	FOX	VIXEN
GIRAFFE	BULL	COW
GOAT	BILLYGOAT	NANNYGOAT
GOOSE	GANDER	GOOSE
HARE	BUCK	DOE
HARTEBEAST	BULL	COW
HORSE	STALLION	MARE
IMPALA	RAM	EWE
JACKRABBIT	BUCK	DOE
KANGAROO	BUCK	DOE
LEOPARD	LEOPARD	LEOPARDESS
LION	LION	LIONESS
MOOSE	BULL	COW
OX	BULLOCK	COW
PEACOCK	PEACOCK	PEAHEN
PHEASANT	COCK	HEN
PIG	BOAR	SOW
RHINOCEROS	BULL	COW
ROEDEER	ROEBUCK	DOEDEER
SEAL	BULL	COW
SHEEP	RAM	EWE
SWAN	COB	PEN
TIGER	TIGER	TIGRESS
WALRUS	BULL	COW
WEASEL	BOAR	COW
WHALE	BULL	COW
WOLF	DOG	BITCH
ZEBRA	STALLION	MARE

ANIMALS AND THEIR YOUNG

ANIMAL	YOUNG	ANIMAL	YOUNG
ANTELOPE	KID	HARE	LEVERET
BADGER	CUB	HARTEBEAST	CALF
BEAR	CUB	HAWK	CHICK
BEAVER	KITTEN	HORSE	FOAL
BOBCAT	KITTEN	JACKRABBIT	KITTEN
BUFFALO	CALF	KANGAROO	JOEY
CAMEL	CALF	LEOPARD	CUB
CARIBOU	FAWN	LION	CUB
CAT	KITTEN	MONKEY	INFANT
CATTLE	CALF	OX	STOT
CHICKEN	CHICK	PHEASANT	CHICK
COUGAR	KITTEN	PIG	PIGLET
COYOTE	PUPPY	RHINOCEROS	CALF
DEER	FAWN	ROEDEER	KID
DOG	PUPPY	SEAL	CALF
DUCK	DUCKLING	SHEEP	LAMB
ELAND	CALF	SKUNK	KITTEN
ELEPHANT	CALF	SWAN	CYGNET
ELK	CALF	TIGER	CUB
FISH	FRY	TOAD	TADPOLE
FROG	TADPOLE	WALRUS	CUB
FOX	CUB	WEASEL	KIT
GIRAFFE	CALF	WHALE	CALF
GOAT	KID	WOLF	CUB
GOOSE	GOSLING	ZEBRA	FOAL

COLLECTIVE TERMS

ANIMAL	COLLECTIVE TERM	ANIMAL	COLLECTIVE TERM
ANTELOPE	HERD	DOG	PACK
APE	SHREWDNESS	DONKEY	DROVE
ASS	DROVE	DUCK	PADDLING
BADGER	CETE	ELAND	HERD
BEAR	SLEUTH	ELEPHANT	HERD
BEAVER	COLONY	ELK	GANG
BLOODHOUND	SUTE	FERRET	BUSINESS
BOAR	SOUNDER	FISH	SCHOOL
BUFFALO	HERD	FOX	TROOP
CAMEL	TRAIN	GELDING	BRACE
CARIBOU	HERD	GIRAFFE	HERD
CAT	CLUSTER	GOAT	FLOCK
CATTLE	HERD	GOOSE	GAGGLE
CHAMOIS	HERD	HARE	HUSKE
CHICKEN	FLOCK	HARTEBEAST	HERD
CHOUGH	CHATTERING	HAWK	CAST
COLT	RAG	HORSE	HERD
COOT	FLEET	IMPALA	COUPLE
COYOTE	PACK	JACKRABBIT	HUSK
DEER	HERD	KANGAROO	TROOP

ANIMAL	COLLECTIVE TERM	ANIMAL	COLLECTIVE TERM
KINE	DROVE	ROEDEER	BEVY
LEOPARD	LEAP	ROOK	BUILDING
LION	PRIDE	SEAL	POD
MOLE	LABOUR	SHEEP	FLOCK
MONKEY	TROOP	SNAKE	KNOT
MOOSE	HERD	TOAD	NEST
MOUSE	NEST	WALRUS	POD
OX	TEAM	WEASEL	PACK
PEACOCK	PRIDE	WHALE	SCHOOL
PHEASANT	BROOD	WOLF	PACK
PIG	TRIP	ZEBRA	HERD
RHINOCEROS	CRASH		

BREEDS OF CATS

3
REX

4
MANX

5
CREAM
SMOKE
TABBY

6
BIRMAN
HAVANA

7
BURMESE
PERSIAN
RED SELF
SIAMESE

7—continued
SPOTTED
TURKISH

8
DEVON REY
RED TABBY

9
BLUE CREAM

10
ABYSSINIAN
BROWN TABBY
CHINCHILLA
CORNISH REY

11
BLUE BURMESE
BRITISH BLUE

11—continued
COLOURPOINT
RUSSIAN BLUE
SILVER TABBY

12
BROWN BURMESE

13
CHESTNUT BROWN
RED ABYSSINIAN
TORTOISESHELL

14
LONG HAIRED BLUE
TORTIE AND WHITE

15
RED-POINT SIAMESE

18
BLUE-POINTED
  SIAMESE
SEAL-POINTED
  SIAMESE
TORTIE-POINT
  SIAMESE

19
LILAC-POINTED
  SIAMESE
TABBY-POINTED
  SIAMESE

20+
CHOCOLATE-
  POINTED SIAMESE

BREEDS OF DOGS

3
PUG

4
PULI

5
BOXER
CORGI
HUSKY
SPITZ

6
BEAGLE
BORZOI
BRIARD
COLLIE
KELPIE
POODLE
SALUKI

6—continued
SETTER

7
BASENJI
BULLDOG
GRIFFON
HARRIER
LOWCHEN
MALTESE
MASTIFF
POINTER
SAMOYED
SHELTIE
SHIH TZU
SPANIEL
TERRIER
WHIPPET

8 AIREDALE
ALSATIAN
CHOW CHOW
ELKHOUND
FOXHOUND
KEESHOND
PAPILLON
SHEEPDOG

9
CHIHUAHUA
DACHSHUND
DALMATIAN
DEERHOUND
GREAT DANE
GREYHOUND
LHASA APSO
PEKINGESE

9—continued
RETRIEVER
SCHNAUZER
STAGHOUND
ST BERNARD

10
BLOODHOUND
FOX TERRIER
OTTERHOUND
POMERANIAN
ROTTWEILER
SCHIPPERKE
WEIMARANER
WEIMERANER
WELSH CORGI

11
AFGHAN HOUND

11—continued
BASSET HOUND
BULL MASTIFF
BULL TERRIER
IBIZAN HOUND
IRISH SETTER
SKYE TERRIER

12
CAIRN TERRIER
FINNISH SPITZ
IRISH TERRIER
JAPANESE CHIN
NEWFOUNDLAND
PHARAOH HOUND
SILKY TERRIER
WELSH TERRIER

13
AFFENPINSCHER
BORDER TERRIER
BOSTON TERRIER

13—continued
COCKER SPANIEL
ENGLISH SETTER
HUNGARIAN PULI

14
GERMAN SHEPHERD
IRISH WOLFHOUND

15
AIREDALE TERRIER
ALASKAN
   MALAMUTE
GOLDEN RETRIEVER
HUNGARIAN VIZSLA
LAKELAND TERRIER
SCOTTISH TERRIER
SEALYHAM TERRIER
SPRINGER SPANIEL

16
KERRY BLUE
   TERRIER

16—continued
PYRENEAN
   MOUNTAIN
SHETLAND
   SHEEPDOG
YORKSHIRE
   TERRIER

17
BEDLINGTON
   TERRIER
DOBERMANN
   PINSCHER
LABRADOR
   RETRIEVER

18
JACK RUSSELL
   TERRIER
KING CHARLES
   SPANIEL

18—continued
LARGE
   MUNSTERLANDER
OLD ENGLISH
   SHEEPDOG
RHODESIAN
   RIDGEBACK

20
DANDIE DINMONT
   TERRIER
STAFFORDSHIRE
   BULL TERRIER
WEST HIGHLAND
   WHITE TERRIER
WIREHAIRED
   POINTING
   GRIFFON

BREEDS OF HORSES AND PONIES

3
COB
DON

4
ARAB
BARB
FELL
POLO
RUSS

5
DALES
FJORD
HUCUL
KONIK
LOKAI
ORLOV
PINTO
SHIRE
TERSK
TIMOR
WELSH

6
ALBINO

6—continued
BASUTO
EXMOOR
MERENS
MORGAN
TARPAN
VIATKA

7
CASPIAN
COMTOIS
CRIOLLO
FURIOSA
HACKNEY
JUTLAND
LLANERO
MUSTANG
NORIKER
QUARTER
SORRAIA

8
BUDEONNY
CAMARGUE

8—continued
DARTMOOR
GALICEÑO
HIGHLAND
HOLSTEIN
KABARDIN
KARABAIR
KARABAKH
LUSITANO
PALOMINO
SHETLAND

9
AKHAL-TEKE
ALTER-REAL
APPALOOSA
CONNEMARA
FALABELLA
HAFLINGER
KNABSTRUP
NEW FOREST
OLDENBURG
PERCHERON

9—continued
SCHLESWIG

10
ANDALUSIAN
AVELIGNESE
CLYDESDALE
GELDERLAND
HANOVERIAN
IRISH DRAFT
LIPIZZANER

11
NOVOKIRGHIZ

12
CLEVELAND BAY
SUFFOLK PUNCH
THOROUGHBRED

13
WELSH MOUNTAIN

16
TENNESSEE
   WALKING

BREEDS OF CATTLE

3
GIR

5
DEVON
KERRY
LUING

6
DEXTER
JERSEY
SUSSEX

7
BEEFALO
BRANGUS

8
AYRSHIRE
FRIESIAN
GALLOWAY
GUERNSEY
HEREFORD
HIGHLAND
LIMOUSIN

9
CHAROLAIS
SHORTHORN
SIMMENTAL

10
BROWN SWISS

10—continued
LINCOLN RED
MURRAY GREY
WELSH BLACK

11
JAMAICA HOPE

11—continued
MARCHIGIANA

13
ABERDEEN ANGUS
DROUGHTMASTER
TEXAS LONGHORN

BREEDS OF SHEEP

4
LONK
MULE
SOAY

5
CARDY
CHIOS
JACOB
LLEYN
MORFE
TEXEL

6
AWASSI
MASHAM
MERINO

6—continued
ROMNEY

7
CHEVIOT
GOTLAND
KARAKUL
LACAUNE
SUFFOLK

8
HERDWICK
LONGMYND
POLWARTH
PORTLAND
SHETLAND

9
HEBRIDEAN
LONGWOOLS
OLDENBERG
ROUGH FELL
SWALEDALE
TEESWATER

10
CORRIEDALE
DORSET HORN
EXMOOR HORN
POLL DORSET

11
MANX LOGHTAN

11—continued
WENSLEYDALE

13
WELSH MOUNTAIN
WILTSHIRE HORN

15
FRIES MELKSCHAAP

17
SCOTTISH
   BLACKFACE

18
WHITEFACED
   WOODLAND

BREEDS OF PIGS

5
DUROC
WELSH

8
PIETRAIN
TAMWORTH

9
BERKSHIRE
HAMPSHIRE

10
LARGE WHITE

15
SWEDISH LANDRACE

17
BRITISH
   SADDLEBACK

17—continued
GLOUCESTER OLD
   SPOT

BREEDS OF POULTRY

4
BUFF (goose)

5
MARAN (chicken)
PEARL (guinea fowl)
PEKIN (duck)
ROMAN (goose)
ROUEN (duck)
WHITE (guinea fowl)

6
ANCONA (chicken)
CAYUGA (duck)

6—continued
EMBDEN (goose)
SILKIE (chicken)

7
AFRICAN (goose)
CHINESE (goose)
CRESTED (duck)
DORKING (chicken)
LEGHORN (chicken)
MUSCOVY (duck)
PILGRIM (goose)

8
LAVENDER (guinea
   fowl)
TOULOUSE (goose)

9
AYLESBURY (duck)
WELSUMMER
   (chicken)

10
BARNVELDER
   (chicken)

10—continued
BELTSVILLE (turkey)
BOURBON RED
   (turkey)
INDIAN GAME
   (chicken)
ROSS RANGER
   (chicken)
SEBASTOPOL
   (goose)

11	12—continued	13—continued	14—continued
CUCKOO MARAN (chicken)	NARRAGANSETT (turkey)	KHAKI CAMPBELL (duck)	RHODE ISLAND RED (chicken)
LIGHT SUSSEX (chicken)	PLYMOUTH ROCK (chicken)	MAMMOTH BRONZE (turkey)	WELSH HARLEQUIN (duck)
12	WHITE HOLLAND (turkey)	WHITE AUSTRIAN (turkey)	WHITE WYANDOTTE (chicken)
BLACK NORFOLK (turkey)	**13**	**14**	**15**
INDIAN RUNNER (duck)	BUFF ORPINGTON (duck)	BLACK EAST INDIE (duck)	CAMBRIDGE BRONZE (turkey)

BIRDS

3	5 —continued	6 —continued	7 —continued
AUK	EIDER	MARTIN	GRACKLE
EMU	FINCH	MERLIN	HARRIER
JAY	GOOSE	MOTMOT	HAWK OWL
MOA	GREBE	ORIOLE	HOATZIN
OWL	HERON	OSPREY	JACAMAR
TIT	HOBBY	PARROT	JACKDAW
TUI	MACAW	PEEWIT	KESTREL
4	MYNAH	PETREL	LAPWING
CHAT	NODDY	PIGEON	MALLARD
COLY	OUZEL	PLOVER	MANAKIN
COOT	PIPIT	PUFFIN	MARABOU
CROW	PRION	QUELEA	MINIVET
DODO	QUAIL	RATITE	MOORHEN
DOVE	RAVEN	ROLLER	OILBIRD
DUCK	ROBIN	SHRIKE	ORTOLAN
GULL	SCAUP	SISKIN	OSTRICH
HAWK	SERIN	TAKAHE	PEACOCK
HUIA	SNIPE	THRUSH	PEAFOWL
IBIS	STILT	TOUCAN	PELICAN
KAGU	STORK	TROGON	PENGUIN
KITE	**6**	TURACO	PINTAIL
KIWI	AVOCET	TURKEY	POCHARD
KNOT	BARBET	WHIDAH	QUETZAL
LARK	BULBUL	WHYDAH	REDPOLL
LORY	CANARY	WIGEON	REDWING
RAIL	CHOUGH	**7**	ROSELLA
RHEA	CONDOR	ANTBIRD	SEAGULL
ROOK	CUCKOO	BABBLER	SERIEMA
RUFF	CURLEW	BARN OWL	SKIMMER
SHAG	DARTER	BITTERN	SKYLARK
SKUA	DIPPER	BLUETIT	SPARROW
SMEW	DRONGO	BUNTING	SUNBIRD
SWAN	DUNLIN	BUSTARD	SWALLOW
TEAL	FALCON	BUZZARD	TANAGER
TERN	FULMAR	COAL TIT	TINAMOU
WREN	GANNET	COURSER	TOURACO
5	GODWIT	DUNNOCK	VULTURE
BOOBY	HOOPOE	EMU WREN	WAGTAIL
CRAKE	JABIRU	FANTAIL	WARBLER
CRANE	JACANA	FINFOOT	WAXBILL
DIVER	KAKAPO	FISH OWL	WAXWING
EAGLE	LINNET	GADWALL	WRYBILL
EGRET	MAGPIE	GOSHAWK	WRYNECK

8

ACCENTOR
AVADAVAT
BATELEUR
BEE-EATER
BLACKCAP
BLUEBIRD
BOATBILL
BOBOLINK
CARACARA
CARDINAL
COCKATOO
CURASSOW
DABCHICK
DOTTEREL
EAGLE OWL
FISH HAWK
FLAMINGO
GAMEBIRD
GARGANEY
GREAT TIT
GROSBEAK
HAWFINCH
HORNBILL
LOVEBIRD
LYREBIRD
MANNIKIN
MEGAPODE
MUTE SWAN
NIGHTJAR
NUTHATCH
OVENBIRD
OXPECKER
PARAKEET
PHEASANT
PYGMY OWL
REDSHANK
REDSTART
REEDLING
RIFLEMAN
ROCK DOVE
SCOPS OWL
SCREAMER
SEA EAGLE
SHELDUCK
SHOEBILL
SNOWY OWL
SONGBIRD
STARLING
SWIFTLET
TAWNY OWL
TITMOUSE
TRAGOPAN
WHEATEAR
WHIMBREL
WHINCHAT
WHIPBIRD
WHITE-EYE
WILDFOWL
WOODCHAT
WOODCOCK

9

ALBATROSS
BALD EAGLE
BLACKBIRD
BLACK SWAN
BOWERBIRD
BRAMBLING
BROADBILL
BULLFINCH
CASSOWARY
CHAFFINCH
COCKATIEL
CORMORANT
CORNCRAKE
CROSSBILL
CURRAWONG
FIELDFARE
FIRECREST
FRANCOLIN
FRIARBIRD
FROGMOUTH
GALLINULE
GOLDCREST
GOLDENEYE
GOLDFINCH
GUILLEMOT
GYRFALCON
HILL MYNAH
KITTIWAKE
LITTLE OWL
MERGANSER
MOUSEBIRD
PARTRIDGE
PHALAROPE
PTARMIGAN
RAZORBILL
RED GROUSE
RIFLEBIRD
RING OUZEL
SANDPIPER
SCRUB BIRD
SNAKEBIRD
SNOW GOOSE
SPOONBILL
STONECHAT
THICKHEAD
THORNBILL
TRUMPETER
TURNSTONE

10

ARCTIC TERN
BEARDED TIT
BRENT GOOSE
BUDGERIGAR
CHIFFCHAFF
CRESTED TIT
DEMOISELLE
DIVING DUCK
FLYCATCHER
GRASSFINCH
GREENFINCH

10 —continued

GREENSHANK
GUINEA FOWL
HAMMERHEAD
HARPY EAGLE
HONEYEATER
HONEY GUIDE
HOODED CROW
JUNGLE FOWL
KINGFISHER
KOOKABURRA
MALLEE FOWL
MUTTONBIRD
NIGHT HERON
NUTCRACKER
PRATINCOLE
SACRED IBIS
SADDLEBACK
SAGE GROUSE
SANDERLING
SANDGROUSE
SCREECH OWL
SHEARWATER
SHEATHBILL
SONG THRUSH
SUN BITTERN
TAILORBIRD
TROPIC BIRD
TURTLE DOVE
WEAVERBIRD
WOODPECKER
WOOD PIGEON
ZEBRA FINCH

11

BLACK GROUSE
BRUSH TURKEY
BUTCHERBIRD
BUTTON QUAIL
CANADA GOOSE
CARRION CROW
DIAMONDBIRD
FRIGATE BIRD
GNATCATCHER
GOLDEN EAGLE
HERRING GULL
HUMMINGBIRD
LAMMERGEIER
LAUGHING OWL
MOCKINGBIRD
MUSCOVY DUCK
NIGHTINGALE
REED WARBLER
SNOW BUNTING
SPARROWHAWK
STONE CURLEW
STORM PETREL
TREECREEPER
WALLCREEPER
WEAVERFINCH
WHITETHROAT
WOODCREEPER

11 —continued

WREN BABBLER

12

BURROWING OWL
CAPERCAILLIE
CUCKOO-SHRIKE
DABBLING DUCK
FAIRY PENGUIN
FLOWERPECKER
GREYLAG GOOSE
HEDGE SPARROW
HONEYCREEPER
HOUSE SPARROW
LANNER FALCON
MANDARIN DUCK
MARSH HARRIER
MISTLE THRUSH
MOURNING DOVE
PERCHING DUCK
SHOVELER DUCK
STANDARDWING
UMBRELLA BIRD
WHIPPOORWILL
YELLOWHAMMER

13

ADJUTANT STORK
AMERICAN EAGLE
BARNACLE GOOSE
CROCODILE BIRD
ELEPHANT BIRDS
FAIRY BLUEBIRD
HARLEQUIN DUCK
HAWAIIAN GOOSE
LONG-TAILED TIT
OYSTERCATCHER
PASSERINE BIRD
SECRETARY BIRD
WHISTLING DUCK
WHOOPING CRANE

14

BEARDED VULTURE
BIRD OF PARADISE
DARWIN'S FINCHES
EMPEROR PENGUIN
GOLDEN PHEASANT
GRIFFON VULTURE
OWLET FROGMOUTH
PLAINS-WANDERER

15+

BALTIMORE ORIOLE
GREAT CRESTED
  GREBE
IVORY-BILLED
  WOODPECKER
LAUGHING JACKASS
PASSENGER PIGEON
PEREGRINE FALCON
PHILIPPINE EAGLE
TYRANT
  FLYCATCHER

FISH

3
COD
DAB
EEL
GAR
IDE
RAY

4
BASS
CARP
CHAR
CHUB
DACE
DORY
FISH
GOBY
HAKE
LING
OPAH
ORFE
PIKE
RUDD
SHAD
SOLE
TOPE
TUNA

5
BLEAK
BREAM
BRILL
DANIO
GRUNT
GUPPY
LOACH
MOLLY
PERCH
PORGY
ROACH
SAURY
SHARK
SKATE
SMELT
SPRAT
TENCH
TETRA
TROUT
TUNNY

6
BARBEL
BELUGA
BLENNY
BONITO
BOWFIN
BURBOT

6 —continued
GUNNEL
KIPPER
MARLIN
MINNOW
MULLET
PLAICE
PUFFER
REMORA
SAITHE
SALMON
TARPON
TURBOT
WEEVER
WRASSE

7
ALEWIFE
ANCHOVY
BATFISH
CATFISH
CICHLID
CROAKER
DOGFISH
EELPOUT
GARFISH
GARPIKE
GOURAMI
GROUPER
GUDGEON
GURNARD
HADDOCK
HAGFISH
HALIBUT
HERRING
HOGFISH
ICEFISH
LAMPREY
MUDFISH
OARFISH
PIRANHA
POLLACK
POMPANO
RATFISH
SARDINE
SAWFISH
SCULPIN
SEA BASS
SNAPPER
SUNFISH
TELEOST
TORPEDO
WHITING

8
ALBACORE

8 —continued
BLUEFISH
BRISLING
BROTULID
BULLHEAD
CAVE FISH
CHARACIN
CHIMAERA
DEVIL RAY
DRAGONET
DRUMFISH
FILEFISH
FLATFISH
FLATHEAD
FLOUNDER
FROGFISH
GOLDFISH
GRAYLING
JOHN DORY
LUNGFISH
MACKEREL
MANTA RAY
MONKFISH
MOONFISH
MORAY EEL
PILCHARD
PIPEFISH
SAILFISH
SEA BREAM
SEA HORSE
SEA PERCH
SEA ROBIN
SKIPJACK
STINGRAY
STURGEON
SWAMP EEL
TOADFISH
WOLF FISH

9
ANGELFISH
BARRACUDA
BLUE SHARK
CLINGFISH
CONGER EEL
GLASSFISH
GLOBEFISH
GOOSEFISH
GRENADIER
KILLIFISH
LATIMERIA
LEMON SOLE
MURRAY COD
PEARLFISH
PIKEPERCH

9 —continued
PILOT FISH
PLACODERM
PORBEAGLE
RED MULLET
RED SALMON
STARGAZER
STONE BASS
STONEFISH
SWORDFISH
SWORDTAIL
THREADFIN
TIGERFISH
TOP MINNOW
TRUNKFISH
WHITEBAIT
WHITEFISH
WRECKFISH
ZEBRA FISH

10
ANGLERFISH
ARCHER FISH
BOMBAY DUCK
COELACANTH
CORNETFISH
CYCLOSTOME
DAMSELFISH
DRAGONFISH
FLYING FISH
GHOST SHARK
GUITAR FISH
LUMPSUCKER
MIDSHIPMAN
MUDSKIPPER
NEEDLEFISH
NURSE SHARK
PADDLEFISH
PARROT FISH
PINK SALMON
PLACODERMI
RIBBONFISH
SHIELD FERN
SILVERSIDE
TIGER SHARK
WHALE SHARK
WHITE SHARK

11
ELECTRIC EEL
ELECTRIC RAY
GOBLIN SHARK
HATCHETFISH
LANTERN FISH
MOORISH IDOL
STICKLEBACK

11 —continued
SURGEONFISH
TRIGGERFISH
12+
BASKING SHARK
CLIMBING PERCH

12+ —continued
FIGHTING FISH
FOUR-EYED FISH
GREENLAND SHARK
HAMMERHEAD
 SHARK

12+ —continued
LABYRINTH FISH
MACKEREL SHARK
MILLER'S THUMB
MOUTHBROODER
PORCUPINE FISH

12+ —continued
REQUIEM SHARK
SCORPION FISH
SOCKEYE SALMON
THRESHER SHARK
YELLOWFIN TUNA

SEASHELLS

3
SUN
4
HARP
5
TULIP
6
NUTMEG
7
JUNONIA
SUNDIAL
8
DYE MUREX
LION'S PAW
NOBLE PEN
PHEASANT
TURK'S CUP
9
ANGEL WING
BAT VOLUTE
BURSA FROG
GIANT CLAM
PINK CONCH
ROTA MUREX
SPINY VASE
TELESCOPE
TENT OLIVE
WEDGE CLAM
10
BLUE MUSSEL
COAT-OF-MAIL
CROWN CONCH
DELPHINULA
DRUPE SNAIL
EYED COWRIE
PAPERY RAPA
QUAHOG CLAM
SCALED WORM
WINGED FROG
11
BEAR PAW CLAM
CAMEO HELMET
CLIONE SNAIL
FRONS OYSTER
GREEN TURBAN
HEART COCKLE
MUSIC VOLUTE

11—continued
ONYX SLIPPER
OSTRICH FOOT
PAPER BUBBLE
PEARL OYSTER
SACRED CHANK
TEXTILE CONE
TIGER COWRIE
12
AMORIA VOLUTE
ATLANTIC CONE
FLORIDA MITER
GAUDY ASAPHIS
GOLDEN COWRIE
GOLDEN TELLIN
LIMA FILE CLAM
MONEY COWRIES
PACIFIC AUGER
PARTRIDGE TUN
PELICAN'S FOOT
SCOTCH BONNET
SPIKED LIMPET
SPINDLE TIBIA
13
ANGULAR VOLUTE
BABLYON TURRID
BLEEDING TOOTH
CARDINAL MITER
COMMERCIAL TOP
COSTATE COCKLE
FIGHTING CONCH
GEOGRAPHY CONE
JACKKNIFE CLAM
JAPANESE CONES
PAPER NAUTILUS
PRICKLY HELMET
RIDGED ABALONE
SPIRAL BABYLON
SUNRISE TELLIN
TURKEY WING ARK
VENUS COMB CLAM
14
CHANNELED WHELK
DISTAFF SPINDLE
ELEGANT FIMBRIA
EPISCOPAL MITER
IMPERIAL VOLUTE

14—continued
INDONESIAN CLAM
LEUCODON COWRIE
LEWIS' MOON SNAIL
LIGHTNING WHELK
PANAMANIAN CONE
PHILIPPINE CONE
POLYNESIAN CONE
TAPESTRY TURBAN
TRITON'S TRUMPET
VENUS COMB
 MUREX

15
BITTERSWEET CLAM
BULL-MOUTH
 HELMET
JAPANESE CARRIER
NEW ENGLAND
 WHELK
PANAMANIAN
 AUGER
PILGRIM'S SCALLOP
SUNBURST CARRIER
TURRITELLA SNAIL
WATERING POT
 CLAM
WEST INDIAN CHANK
WEST AFRICAN
 CONE

16
ASIAN MOON
 SCALLOP
ATLANTIC SURF
 CLAM
DONKEY EAR
 ABALONE
EDIBLE BAY
 SCALLOP
FRILLED
 DOGWINKLE
GLORY-OF-INDIA
 CONE
ORANGE-MOUTH
 OLIVE
PAGODA
 PERIWINKLE

16—continued
PERPLICATE
 VOLUTE
PINK-MOUTHED
 MUREX
ROOSTERTAIL
 CONCH
WEDDING CAKE
 VENUS
17
AUSTRALIAN
 TRUMPET
CHAMBERED
 NAUTILUS
FLORIDA HORSE
 CONCH
PACIFIC WING
 OYSTER
SANTA CRUZ
 LATIAXIS
VIOLET SPIDER
 CONCH
18
ATLANTIC DEER
 COWRIE
GIANT KNOBBED
 CERITH
GLORY-OF-THE-
 SEAS CONE
GREAT KEYHOLE
 LIMPET
PACIFIC GRINNING
 TUN
PRECIOUS
 WENTLETRAP
WHITE-SPOTTED
 MARGIN
19
TANKERVILLE'S
 ANCILLA
20+
ARTHRITIC SPIDER
 CONCH
ATLANTIC THORNY
 OYSTER
COLOURFUL
 ATLANTIC MOON

20+ —continued
ELEPHANT'S SNOUT
   VOLUTE

20+ —continued
IMBRICATE CUP-
   AND-SAUCER

20+ —continued
MIRACULOUS
   THATCHERIA

REPTILES AND AMPHIBIANS

3
ASP
BOA
OLM
4
FROG
NEWT
TOAD
5
ADDER
AGAMA
COBRA
GECKO
KRAIT
MAMBA
SIREN
SKINK
SNAKE
TOKAY
VIPER
6
CAYMAN
GAVIAL
IGUANA
LIZARD
MOLOCH
MUGGER
PYTHON
TAIPAN
TURTLE
ZALTYS

7
AXOLOTL
GHARIAL
REPTILE
TUATARA
8
ANACONDA
BASILISK
BULLFROG
CONGO EEL
MATAMATA
MOCCASIN
MUDPUPPY
PIT VIPER
RINGHALS
SEA SNAKE
SLOWWORM
TERRAPIN
TORTOISE
TREE FROG
9
ALLIGATOR
BLINDWORM
BOOMSLANG
BOX TURTLE
CAECILIAN
CHAMELEON
CROCODILE
HAIRY FROG
PUFF ADDER
TREE SNAKE

9 —continued
VINE SNAKE
WART SNAKE
WHIP SNAKE
10
BLACK SNAKE
BUSHMASTER
CHUCKWALLA
CLAWED FROG
COPPERHEAD
CORAL SNAKE
FER-DE-LANCE
GLASS SNAKE
GRASS SNAKE
HELLBENDER
HORNED TOAD
NATTERJACK
POND TURTLE
SALAMANDER
SAND LIZARD
SIDEWINDER
WATER SNAKE
WORM LIZARD
11
AMPHISBAENA
CONSTRICTOR
COTTONMOUTH
DIAMONDBACK
FLYING SNAKE
GABOON VIPER
GILA MONSTER

11 —continued
GOLIATH FROG
GREEN TURTLE
HORNED VIPER
MIDWIFE TOAD
RATTLESNAKE
SMOOTH SNAKE
12
FLYING LIZARD
HORNED LIZARD
KOMODO DRAGON
13
BEARDED LIZARD
FRILLED LIZARD
GIANT TORTOISE
MANGROVE SNAKE
MONITOR LIZARD
RUSSELL'S VIPER
SPADEFOOT TOAD
WATER MOCCASIN
14+
FIRE SALAMANDER
HAWKSBILL TURTLE
LEATHERBACK
   TURTLE
SNAKE-NECKED
   TURTLE
SOFT-SHELLED
   TURTLE

INSECTS

3
ANT
BEE
BUG
FLY
4
FLEA
GNAT
WASP
5
APHID
DRONE
LOUSE

5 —continued
MIDGE
6
BEDBUG
BEETLE
BOT FLY
CAPSID
CHAFER
CHIGOE
CICADA
EARWIG
GAD FLY
HORNET

6 —continued
IO MOTH
LOCUST
LOOPER
MAGGOT
MANTIS
MAYFLY
SAWFLY
THRIPS
WEEVIL
7
ANTLION
ARMY ANT

7 —continued
BLOWFLY
CRICKET
CUTWORM
DIPTERA
FIRE ANT
FIREFLY
KATYDID
MONARCH (butterfly)
PEACOCK (butterfly)
PROTURA
RINGLET
SANDFLY

7 —continued
SATYRID (butterfly)
SKIPPER (butterfly)
STYLOPS
TERMITE
WAX MOTH

8
ALDERFLY
ARMY WORM
BLACKFLY
BOOKWORM
CINNABAR
CRANEFLY
FIREBRAT
FRUIT FLY
GALL WASP
GLOWWORM
GOAT MOTH
GREENFLY
HAWK MOTH
HONEY ANT
HONEYBEE
HORNTAIL
HORSE FLY
HOUSEFLY
HOVERFLY
LACEWING
LADYBIRD
LUNA MOTH
MASON BEE
MEALWORM
MEALYBUG
MILKWEED (butterfly)
MOSQUITO
PHASMIDA
PLANT BUG
PUSS MOTH
SHEEP KED
SILKWORM
SNAKEFLY
STINK BUG
STONEFLY
WATER BUG
WHITE FLY
WIREWORM
WOODWASP
WOODWORM

9
AMAZON ANT
ANOPHELES
BLOODWORM

9 —continued
BOOKLOUSE
BRIMSTONE
BUMBLEBEE
CADDIS FLY
CHINCH BUG
COCKROACH
CORN BORER
DAMSELFLY
DOBSONFLY
DOR BEETLE
DRAGONFLY
DRIVER ANT
GALL MIDGE
GROUND BUG
GYPSY MOTH
ICHNEUMON
LAC INSECT
NYMPHALID
 (butterfly)
OIL BEETLE
OWLET MOTH
ROBBER FLY
SCREWWORM
SHIELD BUG
SWIFT MOTH
TIGER MOTH
TSETSE FLY
WARBLE FLY
WHIRLIGIG

10
BARK BEETLE
BLUEBOTTLE
BOLL WEEVIL
CACTUS MOTH
COCKCHAFER
COLEOPTERA
DIGGER WASP
DROSOPHILA
DUNG BEETLE
FRITILLARY
FROGHOPPER
HAIRSTREAK
JUNE BEETLE
LEAF BEETLE
LEAF HOPPER
LEAF INSECT
PAPILIONID (butterfly)
PHYLLOXERA
POND SKATER

10 —continued
POTTER WASP
RED ADMIRAL
 (butterfly)
ROVE BEETLE
SILVERFISH
SPANISH FLY
SPIDER WASP
SPITTLEBUG
SPRINGTAIL
STAG BEETLE
TINEID MOTH
TREEHOPPER
WEBSPINNER
WOOLLY BEAR

11
ASSASSIN BUG
BACKSWIMMER
BAGWORM MOTH
BLACK BEETLE
BRISTLETAIL
BUFFALO GNAT
BUSH CRICKET
CANTHARIDIN
CATERPILLAR
CLICK BEETLE
CLOTHES MOTH
CODLING MOTH
EMPEROR MOTH
GRASSHOPPER
MOLE CRICKET
NOCTUID MOTH
PAINTED LADY
 (butterfly)
PLANT HOPPER
PYRALID MOTH
SCALE INSECT
SCORPION FLY
STICK INSECT
SWALLOWTAIL
 (butterfly)
TIGER BEETLE
TUSSOCK MOTH
WATER BEETLE

12
CABBAGE WHITE
 (butterfly)
CACTOBLASTIS
CARPENTER BEE

12 —continued
CARPET BEETLE
CECROPIA MOTH
DIVING BEETLE
GROUND BEETLE
HERCULES MOTH
PEPPERED MOTH
SCARAB BEETLE
SEXTON BEETLE
WATER BOATMAN
WATER STRIDER

13
BLISTER BEETLE
BURYING BEETLE
CLEARWING MOTH
COTTON STAINER
DADDY LONGLEGS
ELM BARK BEETLE
GEOMETRID MOTH
GIANT WATER BUG
GOLIATH BEETLE
LEAFCUTTER ANT
LEAFCUTTER BEE
SATURNIID MOTH
SOLDIER BEETLE
TORTOISESHELL
 (butterfly)
UNDERWING MOTH
WATER SCORPION

14+
AMBROSIA BEETLE
BOMBARDIER
 BEETLE
CABBAGE ROOT FLY
CAMBERWELL
 BEAUTY (butterfly)
COLORADO BEETLE
CUCKOO-SPIT
 INSECT
DARKLING BEETLE
DEATH'S-HEAD
 MOTH
DEATHWATCH
 BEETLE
DEVIL'S COACH
 HORSE
HERCULES BEETLE
SLAVE-MAKING ANT
TORTOISE BEETLE

PLANTS AND FLOWERS

3
ABE
HOP
IVY
RYE
4
DOCK
FERN
FLAG (*Iris*)
FLAX
HEMP
IRIS (flag, sweet flag, gladdon)
JUTE
LILY
PINK (carnation)
RAPE
REED
RICE
ROSE
RUSH
TARE
UPAS
WOAD
5
AGAVE
ASTER (Michaelmas daisy)
AVENS
BRIAR
CANNA
CYCAD
DAISY
HENNA
JALAP
KUDZU
LOTUS
LUPIN
OXLIP (*Primula*)
PANSY (*Viola*)
PEONY
PHLOX
POPPY
SEDGE
SENNA
SISAL
TULIP
VIOLA (pansy, violet)
6
ALLIUM
ALSIKE (clover)
BALSAM
BLUETS
BRYONY

6 —continued
CACTUS
CLOVER (trefoil)
COLEUS
COTTON
COWPEA
CROCUS
DAHLIA
DARNEL
FESCUE
HYSSOP
MADDER
MEDICK
MILLET
NETTLE (*Urtica*)
ORCHID
PETREA
PEYOTE (cactus)
RATTAN
SALVIA
SPURGE
SQUILL (*Scilla*)
SUNDEW
TEASEL
THRIFT
TWITCH (couch grass)
VIOLET (*Viola*)
YARROW
ZINNIA
7
ACONITE (monkshood)
ALFALFA
ALKANET
ANEMONE
ASTILBE
BEGONIA
BISTORT (snakeroot)
BRACKEN (fern)
BUGLOSS
BULRUSH (reed mace)
BURDOCK
CAMPION
CATMINT
CLARKIA
COWSLIP (*Primula*)
DAY LILY
DOGBANE
DOG ROSE
FIGWORT
FREESIA
FROG-BIT

7 —continued
GENTIAN
GLADDON (*Iris*)
GUARANA
HEMLOCK
HENBANE
HONESTY (*Lunaria*)
JONQUIL (*Narcissus*)
KINGCUP (marsh marigold)
LOBELIA
MILFOIL (yarrow)
MULLEIN (Aaron's rod)
OPUNTIA (prickly pear)
PAPYRUS
PETUNIA
PIGWEED
PRIMULA (cowslip, primrose)
RAGWORT
ROSELLE
SAGUARO
SANICLE
SPURREY
THISTLE
TIMOTHY
TOBACCO
TREFOIL (clover)
VERBENA (vervain)
VERVAIN (*Verbena*)
8
ACANTHUS
AGRIMONY
ARUM LILY (cuckoopint, lords-and-ladies)
ASPHODEL
AURICULA
BEDSTRAW
BERGENIA
BINDWEED (*Convolvulus*)
BLUEBELL
CATBRIER
CAT'S TAIL (reedmace)
CHARLOCK
CLEAVERS (goosegrass)
CLEMATIS (old man's beard, traveller's joy)

8 —continued
CROWFOOT
CYLCAMEN
DAFFODIL
DIANTHUS
EELGRASS
EUCHARIS (amazon lily)
FLEABANE
FLEAWORT
FOXGLOVE (*Digitalis*)
FUMITORY
GERANIUM (*Pelargonium*)
GLOXINIA
GOUTWEED (ground elder)
HAREBELL
HAWKWEED
HENEQUEN
HIBISCUS (rose of China, rose of Sharon)
HORNWORT
HYACINTH
ICE PLANT
KNAPWEED
LADY FERN
LARKSPUR
LUNGWORT
MARIGOLD
MILKWEED
MILKWORT
MOSS PINK (*Phlox*)
PLANTAIN
PLUMBAGO
POLYPODY
PRIMROSE (*Primula*)
REEDMACE (bulrush, cat's-tail)
ROCK ROSE
SAINFOIN
SALTWORT
SAMPHIRE
SCABIOUS
SEED FERN
SELF HEAL
SHAMROCK (clover, medick, wood sorrel)
SNOWDROP

8 —continued
SOAPWORT
SWEET PEA
TOAD LILY (fritillary)
TUBEROSE
VALERIAN
VERONICA
(speedwell)
WAXPLANT
WOODBINE (virginia
creeper)
WOODRUSH
WORMWOOD

9
AARON'S ROD
(mullein)
AMARYLLIS
(belladonna lily)
ANTHURIUM
AQUILEGIA
(columbine)
ARROWROOT
BLUEGRASS
BROOMRAPE
BRYOPHYTE
BUCKWHEAT
BUTTERCUP
CAMPANULA
(Canterbury bell)
CANDYTUFT
CARNATION (pink)
CELANDINE
CHICKWEED
CINERARIA
COCKLEBUR
COCKSFOOT
(orchard grass)
COLTSFOOT
COLUMBINE
(Aquilegia)
CORDGRASS
CORN POPPY
CORYDALIS
CYMBIDIUM (orchid)
DANDELION
DEVIL'S FIG (prickly
poppy)
DOG VIOLET
EDELWEISS
EGLANTINE (sweet
briar)
EYEBRIGHT
GERMANDER
GLADIOLUS
GLASSWORT
GOLDENROD
(Solidago)
GOOSEFOOT
(pigweed)
GRASS TREE
GROUND IVY

9 —continued
GROUNDSEL
HELLEBORE
(christmas rose)
HERB PARIS
HOLLYHOCK
HORSETAIL
HOUSELEEK
IMPATIENS (touch-
me-not, busy Lizzie)
JABORANDI
MARE'S TAIL
MONEYWORT
(creeping jenny)
MONKSHOOD
(aconite)
MOSCHATEL
(townhall clock)
NARCISSUS (jonquil)
PATCHOULI
PIMPERNEL
PYRETHRUM
QUILLWORT
ROYAL FERN
SAFFLOWER
SAXIFRAGE (London
pride)
SNAKEROOT (bistort)
SPEEDWELL
(Veronica)
SPIKENARD
STONECROP
SUNFLOWER
SWEET FLAG (Iris)
TORMENTIL
WATER LILY
WITCHWEED
WOUNDWORT

10
AGAPANTHUS
AMARANTHUS (love-
lies-bleeding)
AMAZON LILY
ASPIDISTRA
BELLADONNA
(deadly nightshade)
BUSY LIZZIE
BUTTERWORT
CHARMOMILE
CINQUEFOIL
CITRONELLA
CLIFFBREAK (fern)
CORNCOCKLE
CORNFLOWER
COUCH GRASS
(twitch, quack
grass)
COW PARSLEY
CRANESBILL
CUCKOOPINT (arum
lily)

10 —continued
DAMASK ROSE
DRAGONROOT
DYER'S BROOM
FRITILLARY (snake's
head, leopard lily,
toad lily)
GAILLARDIA (blanket
flowers)
GOATSBEARD
GOOSEGRASS
(cleavers)
GRANADILLA
(passionflower)
GREENBRIER
(catbrier)
HELIOTROPE
HERB ROBERT
JIMSONWEED (thorn
apple)
LADY'S SMOCK
MARGUERITE (oxeye
daisy)
MIGNONETTE
MONTBRETIA
MOONFLOWER
(morning glory)
NASTURTIUM
OPIUM POPPY
OXEYE DAISY
(marguerite)
PENNYROYAL
PERIWINKLE
POLYANTHUS
(Primula)
QUACK GRASS
(couch grass)
SHIELD FERN
SNAKE'S HEAD
SNAPDRAGON
(Antirrhinum)
SOW THISTLE
SPIDERWORT
SPLEENWORT
STITCHWORT
SWEET BRIAR
(eglantine)
THORN APPLE
(jimsonweed)
TOUCH-ME-NOT
WALLFLOWER
WATERCRESS
WELSH POPPY
WILLOWHERB
WOOD SORREL

11
ANTIRRHINUM
(snapdragon)
BISHOP'S WEED
(ground elder)

11 —continued
BITTERSWEET
(woody nightshade)
BLADDERWORT
CALCEOLARIA
CANARY GRASS
CONVOLVULUS
(bindweed)
FIG MARIGOLD
FORGET-ME-NOT
GILLYFLOWER
(gilliflower, pink,
carnation)
GLOBE FLOWER
GROUND ELDER
(goutweed, bishop's
weed)
HELLEBORINE
(orchid)
HONEYSUCKLE
IPECACUANHA
KANGAROO PAW
LADY'S SLIPPER
LEOPARD LILY
(fritillary, blackberry
lily)
LONDON PRIDE
(saxifrage)
LOVE-IN-A-MIST
MARRAM GRASS
MARSH MALLOW
MEADOWSWEET
PAMPAS GRASS
PONTENTILLA
(cinquefoil)
PRICKLY PEAR
(cactus)
RAGGED ROBIN
RED-HOT POKER
ROSE OF CHINA
(Hibiscus)
RUBBER PLANT
SEA LAVENDER
SHRIMP PLANT
SPIDER PLANT
ST JOHN'S WORT
(Hibiscus)
STRAWFLOWER
WELWITSCHIA
WINTERGREEN

12
AUTUMN CROCUS
(meadow saffron)
CENTURY PLANT
COMPASS PLANT
(turpentine plant)
GLOBE THISTLE
MONKEYFLOWER

12 —continued
MORNING GLORY
  (moonflower)
OLD MAN CACTUS
OLD MAN'S BEARD
  (*Clematis*)
ORCHARD GRASS
  (cocksfoot)
PITCHER PLANT
PRICKLY POPPY
  (devil's fig)
QUAKING GRASS
ROSE OF SHARON
  (*Hibiscus*)
SOLOMON'S SEAL
SWEET WILLIAM
VENUS FLYTRAP

13
AFRICAN VIOLET
BIRD'S NEST FERN
BLEEDING HEART
CALYPSO ORCHID
CARRION FLOWER
CHRISTMAS ROSE
  (hellebore)
CHRYSANTHEMUM

13 —continued
CREEPING JENNY
  (moneywort)
ELEPHANT GRASS
GARLIC MUSTARD
  (jack-by-the-hedge)
GRAPE HYACINTH
MARSH MARIGOLD
  (kingcup)
MEADOW SAFFRON
  (autumn crocus)
PASSIONFLOWER
  (granadilla)
RANUNCULACEAE
ROSE OF JERICHO
SLIPPER ORCHID
TOWNHALL CLOCK
  (moschatel)
TRAVELLER'S JOY
  (*Clematis*)
WINTER ACONITE

14
BELLADONNA LILY
  (*Amaryllis*)
BLACKBERRY LILY
  (leopard lily)

14 —continued
BLANKET FLOWERS
CANTERBURY BELL
  (*Campanula*)
CASTOR-OIL PLANT
HEDGEHOG CACTUS
JACK-BY-THE-
  HEDGE (garlic
  mustard)
LORDS-AND-LADIES
  (arum lily)
MAIDENHAIR FERN
TRUMPET CREEPER

15+
BIRD-OF-PARADISE
  FLOWER
BIRD'S NEST
  ORCHID
BLACK NIGHTSHADE
DEADLY
  NIGHTSHADE
  (belladonna)
DOG'S TOOTH
  VIOLET

15+ —continued
ENCHANTER'S
  NIGHTSHADE
GRASS OF
  PARNASSUS
LILY-OF-THE-VALLEY
LOVE-LIES-
  BLEEDING
  (*Amaranthus*)
MICHAELMAS DAISY
  (*Aster*)
ORGAN-PIPE
  CACTUS
SNOW-ON-THE-
  MOUNTAIN
SQUIRTING
  CUCUMBER
STAR OF
  BETHLEHEM
TURPENTINE PLANT
  (compass plant)
WOODY
  NIGHTSHADE
  (bittersweet)

TREES AND SHRUBS

3
ASH
BOX
ELM
FIG
FIR
MAY (hawthorn)
OAK
TEA
YEW

4
ANIL
COCA
DATE (palm)
KAVA
KOLA (cola)
NIPA (palm)
PALM
PINE
TEAK

5
ALDER
ASPEN
BALSA
BEECH (*Fagus*)
BIRCH
BROOM
CACAO

5 —continued
CAPER
CEDAR
EBONY
ELDER
ERICA (heath,
  heather)
FURZE (gorse)
GORSE (furze)
HAZEL
HEATH (*Erica*)
HOLLY
KARRI
LARCH
LILAC
MAPLE
OSIER (willow)
PECAN (hickory)
ROWAN (mountain
  ash)
SAVIN (juniper)
YUCCA

6
ACACIA
AZALEA
BAMBOO
BANYAN
BAOBAB

6 —continued
BONSAI
BO TREE
CASSIA
DAPHNE
DATURA
DEODAR (cedar)
DERRIS
DURIAN
GINKGO (maidenhair
  tree)
GOMUTI (sugar palm)
JARRAH
JINBUL (coolabar)
JUJUBE
LAUREL
LOCUST (carob tree,
  St John's bread)
MIMOSA
MOOLAR (coolabar)
MYRTLE
NUTMEG
ORACHE
POPLAR
PRIVET
PROTEA
REDBUD (judas tree)

6 —continued
RED GUM
  (*Eucalyptus*)
SALLOW (willow)
SALVIA
SAPPAN
SPRUCE
WILLOW

7
AMBOYNA
ARBUTUS
BEBEERU
  (greenheart)
BLUE GUM
  (*Eucalyptus*)
CAMELIA
CORK OAK
CYPRESS
DOGWOOD
DURMAST (oak)
FUCHSIA
GUM TREE
  (*Eucalyptus*)
HEATHER (*Erica*, ling)
HEMLOCK
HICKORY (pecan)
HOLM OAK (holly
  oak)

7 —continued
JASMINE
JUNIPER
MUGWORT
(wormwood)
OIL PALM
PALMYRA
REDWOOD
ROSEBAY (oleander)
SEQUOIA (redwood,
wellingtonia, big
tree)
SOURSOP
SPIRAEA
SYRINGA (lilac, mock
orange)

8
BARBERRY (*Berberis*)
BASSWOOD
BAYBERRY
BERBERIS (barberry)
BERGAMOT
BLACKBOX
(coolabar)
BOX ELDER (maple)
CALABASH
CINCHONA
COOLABAR (jinbul,
moolar, blackbox,
dwarf box)
CORKWOOD (balsa)
DWARF BOX
(coolabar)
EUONYMUS (spindle
tree)
GARDENIA
GUAIACUM
HAWTHORN (may)
HORNBEAM
IRONWOOD
JAPONICA
LABURNUM (golden
chain, golden rain)
LAVENDER
MAGNOLIA (umbrella
tree)
OLEANDER (rosebay)
QUANDONG
RAMBUTAN
ROSEWOOD
SAGO PALM

8 —continued
SALTBUSH
SILKY OAK
SWEET GUM
SWEETSOP
SYCAMORE (maple)
TAMARISK
TOLU TREE
VIBURNUM (snowball
tree)
WISTERIA
WOODBINE (virginia
creeper)
WORMWOOD
(mugwort)

9
ARAUCARIA
(monkey puzzle
tree)
BEARBERRY
BUCKTHORN
CAROB TREE (locust)
CORAL TREE
EUPHORBIA (crown
of thorns,
poinsettia, snow-on-
the-mountain)
FIRETHORN
(pyracantha)
FLAME TREE
(flamboyant)
FORSYTHIA (golden
bell)
JACARANDA
JUDAS TREE
(redbud)
KALANCHOE
KAURI PINE
MANGROVES
MISTLETOE
PLANE TREE
POINCIANA
POISON IVY
SASSAFRAS
SATINWOOD
SCREW PINE
STINKWOOD
STONE PINE
SWEETWOOD
(greenheart)
TULIP TREE

9 —continued
WHITEBEAM

10
ARBOR VITAE
BIRD CHERRY
BRAZILWOOD
COFFEE TREE
COTTONWOOD
DOUGLAS FIR
DRAGON TREE
EUCALYPTUS (blue
gum, red gum)
FRANGIPANI (pagoda
tree, temple flower)
GOLDEN BELL
(forsythia)
GOLDEN RAIN
(laburnum)
GREENHEART
(sweetwood,
bebeeru)
JOSHUA TREE
MANGOSTEEN
MOCK ORANGE
PAGODA TREE
(frangipani)
POINSETTIA
PYRACANTHA
RAFFIA PALM
RUBBER TREE
WITCH HAZEL
YELLOWWOOD

11
BOTTLEBRUSH
CABBAGE PALM
CAMPHOR TREE
CHAULMOOGRA
COTONEASTER
CYPRESS PINE
DAWN REDWOOD
GOLDEN CHAIN
(laburnum)
GUELDER ROSE
HONEY LOCUST
JUMPING BEAN
MOUNTAIN ASH
(rowan)
PENCIL CEDAR
(juniper)
PHYLLANTHUS

11 —continued
SERVICE TREE
SLIPPERY ELM
SPINDLE TREE
STEPHANOTIS
TALIPOT PALM

12
CHERRY LAUREL
CREOSOTE BUSH
CUCUMBER TREE
CUSTARD APPLE
(soursop, sweetsop)
INCENSE CEDAR
MONKEY PUZZLE
SNOWBALL TREE
ST JOHN'S BREAD
(locust)
SWAMP CYPRESS
TEMPLE FLOWER
(frangipani)
TREE OF HEAVEN
UMBRELLA TREE
(*Magnolia*)

13
BOUGAINVILLEA
BUTCHER'S BROOM
CROWN OF THORNS
HORSE CHESTNUT
JAPANESE CEDAR
JAPANESE MAPLE
PAPER MULBERRY
PEACOCK FLOWER
(flamboyant)
WAYFARING TREE

14+
FLAMBOYANT TREE
(flame tree, peacock
flower)
FLOWERING
CURRANT
JERUSALEM
CHERRY
MAIDENHAIR TREE
(ginkgo)
STRAWBERRY TREE
TRAVELLER'S TREE
TURPENTINE TREE
VIRGINIA CREEPER
(woodbine)

FRUIT, VEGETABLES, AND PULSES

3
FIG
PEA

3 —continued
YAM

4
BEET
EDDO (taro)

4 —continued
KALE
KIWI

4 —continued
LEEK
LIME (linden)
OKRA (lady's fingers, gumbo)
PEAR
PLUM
SLOE
TARO (eddo, dasheen, elephant's ear)

5
APPLE
CAROB
CHARD (swiss chard)
CRESS
GRAPE
GUAVA
GUMBO (okra)
LEMON
MANGO
MELON (musk, honeydew, canteloupe, water)
OLIVE
ONION (spring onion, scallion)
PEACH
SWEDE

6
ALMOND
BANANA
CARROT
CASHEW
CELERY
CHERRY
CITRON
COB NUT
DAMSON
ENDIVE
LENTIL
LICHEE
LINDEN (lime)
LITCHI
LOQUAT
LYCHEE (litchi, lichee)
MANIOC (cassava)

6 —continued
MARROW
MEDLAR
ORANGE
PAWPAW
PEANUT (groundnut)
POTATO
PRUNUS (plum, almond, apricot, cherry)
QUINCE
RADISH
SQUASH
TOMATO
TURNIP
WALNUT

7
APRICOT
AVOCADO
BRAMBLE (blackberry)
BULLACE (plum)
CABBAGE
CASSAVA (manioc)
CHICORY
CURRANT
DASHEEN (taro)
FILBERT
GENIPAP
GHERKIN
KUMQUAT
LETTUCE
PARSNIP
PUMPKIN
RHUBARB
SALSIFY
SATSUMA (tangerine)
SHALLOT
SPINACH

8
BEETROOT
BILBERRY (blaeberry, huckleberry, whortleberry)
BRASSICA (broccoli, cabbage)
BROCCOLI

8 —continued
CAPSICUM (sweet pepper, chilli, paprika)
CELERIAC (knob celery)
CHESTNUT
CHICK PEA
CUCUMBER
DEWBERRY
EARTHNUT (groundnut)
EGGPLANT (aubergine)
KOHLRABI (cabbage)
MANDARIN (tangerine)
MULBERRY
MUNG BEAN (green gram)
MUSHROOM
OLEASTER (russian olive, trebizond date)
SCALLION
SOYA BEAN
TAMARIND
ZUCCHINI (courgette)

9
ARTICHOKE
ASPARAGUS
AUBERGINE (eggplant)
BLAEBERRY (bilberry)
BROAD BEAN
COCODEMER
COURGETTE (marrow, zucchini)
CRAB APPLE
CRANBERRY
CROWBERRY
GREENGAGE
GROUNDNUT (peanut, earthnut)
MANGETOUT
NECTARINE
PERSIMMON

9 —continued
PINEAPPLE
PISTACHIO
RASPBERRY
SAPODILLA
STAR APPLE
SWEET CORN
TANGERINE

10
BLACKBERRY (bramble)
CLEMENTINE
ELDERBERRY
FRENCH BEAN (kidney bean)
GOOSEBERRY
GRAPEFRUIT (*Citrus Paradisi*)
KIDNEY BEAN
LOGANBERRY
REDCURRANT
RUNNER BEAN
SNAKE GOURD
STRAWBERRY

11
CAULIFLOWER
COCONUT PALM
HORSE-RADISH
HUCKLEBERRY (bilberry)
POMEGRANATE
SWEET POTATO

12+
BLACKCURRANT
BRUSSELS SPROUT
ELEPHANT'S EAR (taro)
JERUSALEM ARTICHOKE
LADY'S FINGERS (okra)
MANGEL-WURZEL (beet)
WATER CHESTNUT
WHORTLEBERRY (bilberry)

FUNGI

4
CÈPE
5
MOREL
YEAST

6
AGARIC
INK CAP
7
AMANITA
BLEWITS

7—continued
BOLETUS
CANDIDA
TRUFFLE
8
DEATH CAP

8—continued
MUSHROOM
PUFFBALL
9
CUP FUNGUS
EARTHSTAR

9—continued
FLY AGARIC
PSILOCYBE
RUST FUNGI
STINKHORN
TOADSTOOL

10
BREAD MOULD
CHAMPIGNON
11
ASCOMYCETES
ASPERGILLUS
CHANTERELLE

11—continued
HONEY FUNGUS
PENICILLIUM
SLIME MOULDS
13
BRACKET FUNGUS

14
BASIDIOMYCETES
15
PARASOL
   MUSHROOM

FERNS

4
TREE
5
ROYAL
7
BRACKEN

7—continued
OSMUNDA
8
LADY FERN
POLYPODY
STAGHORN

9
BIRD'S NEST
10
CLIFFBRAKE
DRYOPTERIS

10—continued
MAIDENHAIR
SPLEENWORT
11
HART'S TONGUE

PEOPLE

ARTISTS, SCULPTORS, AND ARCHITECTS

3

ARP, Jean (1887–1966; French sculptor and poet)

DOU, Gerrit (1613–75; Dutch painter)

FRY, Roger (1866–1934; British painter and art critic)

LOW, Sir David (1871–1963; New Zealand-born cartoonist)

4

ADAM, Robert (1728–92; British architect and interior designer)

CAPP, Al (Alfred Caplin, 1909–79; US cartoonist)

CUYP, Aelbert Jacobsz (1620–91; Dutch landscape painter)

DADD, Richard (1817–86; British painter)

DALI, Salvador (1904–89; Spanish surrealist painter)

DIOR, Christian (1905–57; French fashion designer)

DORÉ, Gustave (1832–83; French illustrator, painter, and sculptor)

DUFY, Raoul (1877–1953; French painter)

ERTÉ (Romain de Tirtoff, 1892–   ; French fashion illustrator and designer, born in Russia)

ETTY, William (1787–1849; British painter)

GABO, Naum (Naum Neemia Pevsner, 1890–1977; Russian sculptor)

GOES, Hugo van der (c. 1440–82; Flemish painter)

GOYA, Francesco de (1746–1828; Spanish painter)

GRIS, Juan (José Victoriano González, 1887–1927; Spanish-born cubist painter)

GROS, Antoine Jean, Baron (1771–1835; French painter)

HALS, Frans (c. 1581–1666; Dutch painter)

HILL, David Octavius (1802–70; Scottish painter and photographer)

HUNT, William Holman (1827–1910; British painter)

JOHN, Augustus (1878–1961; British painter)

KAHN, Louis Isadore (1901–74; US architect)

KENT, William (1685–1748; English architect, landscape gardener, and interior designer)

KLEE, Paul (1879–1940; Swiss painter and etcher)

LAMB, Henry (1885–1960; Australian-born British painter)

4—continued

LELY, Sir Peter (Pieter van der Faes, 1618–80; English portrait painter of Dutch descent)

LOOS, Adolph (1870–1933; Austrian architect)

MAES, Nicolas (or N Maas, 1634–93; Dutch painter)

MARC, Franz (1880–1916; German expressionist painter)

MIRÓ, Joan (1893–1983; Spanish painter)

NASH, John (1752–1835; British architect)

NASH, Paul (1889–1946; British painter)

NEER, Aert van der (c. 1603–77; Dutch landscape painter)

OPIE, John (1761–1807; British portrait and history painter)

RENI, Guido (1575–1642; Italian painter)

ROSA, Salvator (1615–73; Italian painter and etcher)

SHAW, Norman (1831–1912; British architect)

WARD, Sir Leslie (1851–1922; British caricaturist)

WEST, Benjamin (1738–1820; British painter of American birth)

WOOD, Christopher (1901–30; English painter)

WOOD, Grant (1892–1942; US painter)

WOOD, John, of Bath (1704–54; English architect)

WREN, Sir Christopher (1632–1723; English architect and scientist)

ZORN, Anders (1860–1920; Swedish artist)

5

AALTO, Alvar (1898–1976; Finnish architect)

ATGET, Eugène (1856–1927; French photographer)

BACON, Francis (1909–   ; British painter, born in Dublin)

BACON, John (1740–99; British neoclassical sculptor)

BAKST, Léon (Lev Samoilovich Rosenberg, 1866–1924; Russian artist)

BALLA, Giacomo (1871–1958; Italian futurist painter)

BARRY, Sir Charles (1795–1860; British architect)

BLAKE, Peter (1932–   ; British painter)

BOSCH, Hieronymus (Jerome van Aeken, c. 1450–c. 1516; Dutch painter)

BOUTS, Dierick (c. 1400–75; Netherlandish painter)

5—continued

BROWN, Capability (Lancelot B, 1716–83; British landscape gardener)

BROWN, Ford Madox (1821–93; British painter, born in Calais)

BURRA, Edward (1905–76; British painter)

CAMPI, Giulio (1502–72; Italian Renaissance architect)

COROT, Jean Baptiste Camille (1796–1875; French landscape painter)

CRANE, Walter (1845–1915; British illustrator, painter, and designer of textiles and wallpaper)

CROME, John (1768–1821; British landscape painter and etcher)

DAGLY, Gerhard (c. 1653–?1714; Belgian artist)

DANBY, Francis (1793–1861; Irish painter)

DANCE, George (c. 1700–68; British architect)

DAVID, Gerard (c. 1460–1523; Netherlandish painter)

DAVID, Jacques Louis (1748–1825; French neoclassical painter)

DEGAS, Edgar (1834–1917; French painter and sculptor)

DENIS, Maurice (1870–1943; French painter, designer, and art theorist)

DÜRER, Albrecht (1471–1528; German painter)

ENSOR, James Sydney, Baron (1860–1949; Belgian painter)

ERNST, Max (1891–1976; German artist)

FOLEY, John Henry (1818–74; British sculptor)

GADDI, Taddeo (c. 1300–?1366; Florentine painter)

GIBBS, James (1682–1754; British architect)

GILES, Carl Ronald (1916–   ; British cartoonist)

GORKY, Arshile (Vosdanig Adoian, 1905–48; US painter, born in Armenia)

GOYEN, Jan Josephszoon van (1596–1656; Dutch landscape painter and etcher)

GRANT, Duncan James Corrowr (1885–1978; British painter and designer)

GROSZ, George (1893–1959; German painter and draughtsman)

HOMER, Winslow (1836–1910; US painter)

HOOCH, Pieter de (1629–c. 1684; Dutch painter)

HORTA, Victor (1861–1947; Belgian architect)

JOHNS, Jasper (1930–   ; US artist)

JONES, Inigo (1573–1652; English classical architect)

KEENE, Charles Samuel (1823–91; British artist and illustrator)

KLIMT, Gustav (1862–1918; Viennese Art Nouveau artist)

KLINT, Kaare (1888–1954; Danish furniture designer)

5—continued

LEACH, Bernard (1887–1979; British potter, born in Hong Kong)

LEECH, John (1817–64; British caricaturist)

LÉGER, Fernand (1881–1955; French painter)

LE VAU, Louis (1612–70; French baroque architect)

LIPPI, Fra Filippo (c. 1406–69; Florentine painter)

LOTTO, Lorenzo (c. 1480–1556; Venetian painter)

LOWRY, L S (1887–1976; British painter)

MACKE, August (1887–1914; German painter)

MANET, Edouard (1832–83; French painter)

MENGS, Anton Raphael (1728–79; German painter)

METSU, Gabriel (1629–67; Dutch painter)

MONET, Claude (1840–1926; French impressionist painter)

MOORE, Henry (1898–1986; British sculptor)

MOSES, Grandma (Anna Mary Robertson M, 1860–1961; US primitive painter)

MUNCH, Edvard (1863–1944; Norwegian painter and printmaker)

MYRON (5th century BC; Athenian sculptor)

NADAR (Gaspard Felix Tournachon, 1820–1910; French photographer and caricaturist)

NERVI, Pier Luigi (1891–1979; Italian architect)

NOLAN, Sir Sidney (1917–   ; Australian painter)

NOLDE, Emil (E Hansen, 1867–1956; German expressionist painter and printmaker)

OUDRY, Jean-Baptiste (1686–1755; French rococo painter and tapestry designer)

PHYFE, Duncan (or Fife, 1768–1854; US cabinetmaker and furniture designer, born in Scotland)

PIPER, John (1903–   ; British painter and writer)

PUGIN, Augustus Welby Northmore (1812–52; British architect and theorist)

QUANT, Mary (1934–   ; British fashion designer)

REDON, Odilon (1840–1916; French symbolist painter and lithographer)

RICCI, Sebastiano (1659–1734; Venetian painter)

RILEY, Bridget Louise (1931–   ; British painter)

RODIN, Auguste (1840–1917; French sculptor)

SCOTT, Sir George Gilbert (1811–78; British architect)

SHAHN, Ben (1898–1969; Lithuanian-born US artist)

SOANE, Sir John (1753–1837; British architect)

STEEN, Jan (c. 1626–79; Dutch painter)

STOSS, Veit (c. 1445–1533; German gothic sculptor and woodcarver)

5—continued

TOBEY, Mark (1890–1976; US painter)

VICKY (Victor Weisz, 1913–66; British cartoonist, born in Berlin)

WATTS, George Frederick (1817–1904; British artist)

WYATT, James (1747–1813; British architect)

6

ALBERS, Josef (1888–1976; German abstract painter)

ARCHER, Thomas (1668–1743; English baroque architect)

BEATON, Sir Cecil (1904–80; British photographer)

BEHZAD (c. 1455–c. 1536; Persian painter)

BENTON, Thomas Hart (1889–1975; US painter)

BEWICK, Thomas (1753–1828; British wood engraver)

BOUDIN, Eugène (1824–98; French painter)

BOULLE, André Charles (or Buhl, 1642–1732; French cabinetmaker)

BRANDT, Bill (1905– ; British photographer)

BRAQUE, Georges (1882–1963; French painter)

BRATBY, John (1928– ; British painter and writer)

BREUER, Marcel Lajos (1902–81; US architect, born in Hungary)

BUFFET, Bernard (1928– ; French painter)

BUTLER, Reg Cotterell (1913–81; British sculptor)

CALDER, Alexander (1898– ; US sculptor)

CALLOT, Jacques (c. 1592–1635; French graphic artist)

CANOVA, Antonio (1757–1822; Italian sculptor)

CARDIN, Pierre (1922– ; French fashion designer)

CASSON, Sir Hugh (1910– ; British architect)

CHANEL, Coco (Gabrielle C, 1883–1971; French fashion designer)

CLOUET, Jean (c. 1485–1540; French portrait painter)

COOPER, Samuel (1609–72; British miniaturist)

COSWAY, Richard (1742–1821; British portrait miniaturist)

COTMAN, John Sell (1782–1842; British landscape watercolourist and etcher)

DERAIN, André (1880–1954; French postimpressionist painter)

DE WINT, Peter (1784–1849; British landscape painter)

EAKINS, Thomas (1844–1916; US painter)

FLORIS, Cornelis (1514–75; Flemish artist)

FLORIS, Frans (c. 1516–70; Flemish artist)

FULLER, Richard Buckminster (1895–1983; US inventor and architect)

6—continued

FUSELI, Henry (Johann Heinrich Füssli, 1741–1825; British painter of Swiss birth)

GÉRARD, François, Baron (1770–1837; French painter)

GIOTTO (Giotto di Bondone, c. 1266–1337; Italian painter and architect)

GIRTIN, Thomas (1775–1802; British landscape painter)

GOUJON, Jean (c. 1510–68; French Renaissance sculptor)

GREUZE, Jean-Baptiste (1725–1805; French painter)

GUARDI, Francesco (1712–93; Venetian painter)

HOLLAR, Wenceslaus (1607–77; Bohemian etcher)

HOUDON, Jean Antoine (1741–1828; French sculptor)

INGRES, Jean-Auguste-Dominique (1780–1867; French painter)

ISABEY, Jean Baptiste (1767–1855; French portrait painter and miniaturist)

JOCHHO (d. 1057; Japanese sculptor)

KNIGHT, Dame Laura (1877–1970; British painter)

LASDUN, Sir Denys (1914– ; British architect)

LA TOUR, Georges de (1593–1652; French painter)

LA TOUR, Maurice-Quentin de (1704–88; French portrait pastellist)

LE BRUN, Charles (1619–90; French history and portrait painter and designer)

LE NAIN, Antoine (c. 1588–1648; French painter)

LE NAIN, Louis (c. 1593–1648; French painter)

LE NAIN, Mathieu (c. 1607–77; French painter)

LESCOT, Pierre (c. 1510–78; French architect)

LONGHI, Pietro (Pietro Falca, 1702–85; Venetian painter)

LURCAT, Jean (1892–1966; French painter)

MARINI, Marino (1901–80; Italian sculptor and painter)

MARTIN, John (1789–1854; British painter)

MASSYS, Quentin (or Matsys, Messys, Metsys, c. 1466–1530; Flemish painter)

MILLET, Jean François (1814–75; French painter)

MOREAU, Gustave (1826–98; French symbolist painter)

MORONI, Giovanni Battista (c. 1525–78; Italian painter)

MORRIS, William (1834–96; British designer and artist)

OLIVER, Isaac (?1556–1617; English portrait miniaturist, born in France)

6—continued

OROZCO, José (1883–1949; Mexican mural painter)

OSTADE, Adrian van (1610–85; Dutch painter and etcher)

PALMER, Samuel (1805–81; British landscape painter and etcher)

PAXTON, Sir Joseph (1801–65; British architect)

PISANO, Andrea (Andrea de Pontedera, c. 1290–1348; Italian sculptor)

PISANO, Nicola (c. 1220–c. 1278; Italian sculptor)

RENOIR, Pierre Auguste (1841–1919; French impressionist painter)

RIBERA, José de (or Jusepe R, 1591–1652; Spanish-born painter and etcher)

RIVERA, Diego (1886–1957; Mexican mural painter)

ROMNEY, George (1734–1802; British portrait painter)

ROTHKO, Mark (Marcus Rothkovitch, 1903–70; Russian-born US painter)

RUBENS, Peter Paul (1577–1640; Flemish painter)

SCARFE, Gerald (1936– ; British cartoonist)

SEARLE, Ronald William Fordham (1920– ; British cartoonist)

SESSHU (Sesshu Toyo, 1420–1506; Japanese landscape painter)

SEURAT, Georges (1859–91; French painter)

SIGNAC, Paul (1863–1935; French painter and art theorist)

SISLEY, Alfred (1839–99; Impressionist painter)

SLUTER, Claus (c. 1345–1406; Dutch sculptor)

SPENCE, Sir Basil (1907– ; British architect)

STUBBS, George (1724–1806; British animal painter)

TANGUY, Yves (1900–55; French surrealist painter)

TISSOT, James Joseph Jacques (1836–1902; French painter and etcher)

TITIAN (Tiziano Vecellio, c. 1488–1576; Venetian painter)

TURNER, Joseph Mallord William (1775–1851; British landscape and marine painter)

VASARI, Giorgio (1511–74; Italian painter, architect, and writer)

VOYSEY, Charles Francis Annesley (1857–1941; British architect and designer)

WARHOL, Andy (Andrew Warhola, 1926–87; US pop artist)

WEYDEN, Rogier van der (c. 1400–64; Flemish painter)

WILKIE, Sir David (1785–1841; Scottish painter)

WILSON, Richard (1714–82; British landscape painter)

6—continued

WRIGHT, Frank Lloyd (1869–1959; US architect)

XIA GUI (or Hsia Knei, c. 1180–c. 1230, Chinese landscape painter)

ZEUXIS (late 5th century BC; Greek painter)

7

ALBERTI, Leon Battista (1404–72; Italian Renaissance architect)

ALLSTON, Washington (1779–1843; US Romantic painter)

ANTENOR (late 6th century BC; Athenian sculptor)

APELLES (4th century BC; Greek painter)

ASTBURY, John (1688–1743; English potter)

BARLACH, Ernst (1870–1938; German expressionist sculptor and playwright)

BASSANO, Jacopo (Jacopo or Giacomo da Ponte, c. 1517–92; Italian painter)

BEHRENS, Peter (1868–1940; German architect)

BELLINI, Jacopo (c. 1400–c. 1470; Venetian painter)

BERNINI, Gian Lorenzo (1598–1680; Italian sculptor and architect)

BONNARD, Pierre (1867–1947; French painter)

BORGLUM, Gutzon (1867–1941; US sculptor)

BOUCHER, François (1703–70; French rococo painter)

BROUWER, Adriaen (c. 1605–38; Flemish painter)

CAMERON, Julia Margaret (1815–79; British photographer, born in Calcutta)

CASSATT, Mary (1844–1926; US painter)

CELLINI, Benvenuto (1500–71; Florentine goldsmith and sculptor)

CENNINI, Cennino (c. 1370–c. 1440; Florentine painter)

CÉZANNE, Paul (1839–1906; French postimpressionist painter)

CHAGALL, Marc (1887–1985; Russian-born painter and printmaker)

CHARDIN, Jean-Baptiste-Siméon (1699–1779; French painter)

CHIRICO, Giorgio de (1888–1978; Italian painter, born in Greece)

CIMABUE, Giovanni (Cenni de Peppi, c. 1240–c. 1302; Florentine painter)

CLODION (Claude Michel, 1738–1814; French rococo sculptor)

COURBET, Gustave (1819–77; French painter)

DAUMIER, Honoré (1808–79; French caricaturist, painter, and sculptor)

DELORME, Philibert (?1510–70; French Renaissance architect)

DELVAUX, Paul (1897– ; Belgian painter)

DUCHAMP, Marcel (1887–1968; French artist)

7—continued

EL GRECO (Domeníkos Theotokópoulos, 1541–1614; Painter of Greek parentage, born in Crete)

EPSTEIN, Sir Jacob (1880–1959; British sculptor of US birth)

EXEKIAS (6th century BC; Athenian potter and vase painter)

FABERGÉ, Peter Carl (1846–1920; Russian goldsmith and jeweller)

FLAXMAN, John Henry (1755–1826; British sculptor and book illustrator)

FONTANA, Domenico (1543–1607; Italian architect)

FOUQUET, Jean (c. 1420–81; French painter and manuscript illuminator)

GAUGUIN, Paul (1848–1903; French postimpressionist painter)

GIBBONS, Grinling (1648–1721; English wood carver and sculptor)

GILLRAY, James (1756–1815; British caricaturist)

GOZZOLI, Benozzo (Benozzo di Lese, 1420–97; Florentine painter)

GROPIUS, Walter (1883–1969; German architect)

GUARINI, Guarino (1624–83; Italian baroque architect)

HASSALL, John (1868–1948; British artist)

HERRERA, Juan de (1530–97; Spanish architect)

HOBBEMA, Meindert (1638–1709; Dutch landscape painter)

HOCKNEY, David (1937– ; British painter, draughtsman, and printmaker)

HOGARTH, William (1697–1764; British painter and engraver)

HOKUSAI (Katsushika H, 1760–1849; Japanese painter and book illustrator)

HOLLAND, Henry (1745–1806; British architect)

HOPPNER, John (1758–1810; British portrait painter)

ICTINUS (5th century BC; Greek architect)

JOHNSON, Cornelius (Janssen van Ceulen, 1593–1661; English portrait painter)

KNELLER, Sir Godfrey (1646–1723; English portrait painter of German birth)

LALIQUE, René (1860–1945; French Art Nouveau jeweller and glassmaker)

LAMERIE, Paul de (1688–1751; English silversmith)

L'ENFANT, Pierre-Charles (1754–1825; US architect and town planner of French birth)

LE NÔTRE, André (1613–1700; French landscape gardener)

LIMBURG, Pol de (active c. 1400–c. 1416; French manuscript illuminator)

LIMOSIN, Léonard (or Limousin, c. 1505–c. 1577; French artist)

7—continued

LOCHNER, Stefan (c. 1400–51; German painter)

LUTYENS, Sir Edwin Landseer (1869–1944; British architect)

MACLISE, Daniel (1806–70; Irish portrait and history painter)

MADERNA, Carlo (1556–1629; Roman architect)

MAILLOL, Aristide (1861–1944; French sculptor)

MANSART, François (or Mansard, 1596–1666; French classical architect)

MARTINI, Simone (c. 1284–1344; Italian painter)

MATISSE, Henri (1869–1954; French painter and sculptor)

MEMLING, Hans (or Memlinc, c. 1430–1494; German painter)

MILLAIS, Sir John Everett (1829–96; British painter)

MORANDI, Giorgio (1890–1964; Italian still-life painter and etcher)

MORISOT, Berthe (1841–95; French painter)

MORLAND, George (1763–1804; British painter)

MURILLO, Bartolomé Esteban (1617–82; Spanish painter)

NEUMANN, Balthasar (1687–1753; German architect)

O'KEEFFE, Georgia (1887–1986; US painter)

ORCAGNA, Andrea (Andrea di Cione, c. 1308–c. 1368; Florentine artist)

PALISSY, Bernard (1510–89; French potter)

PASMORE, Victor (1908– ; British artist)

PATINIR, Joachim (or Patenier, c. 1485–1524; Flemish painter)

PEVSNER, Antoine (1886–1962; Russian sculptor and painter)

PHIDIAS (c. 490–c. 417 BC; Athenian sculptor)

PICABIA, Francis (1879–1953; French painter and writer)

PICASSO, Pablo (1881–1973; Spanish artist)

POLLOCK, Jackson (1912–56; US painter)

POUSSIN, Nicolas (1594–1665; French painter)

PRUD'HON, Pierre Paul (1758–1823; French painter and draughtsman)

RACKHAM, Arthur (1867–1939; British watercolourist and book illustrator)

RAEBURN, Sir Henry (1756–1823; Scottish portrait painter)

RAPHAEL (Raffaello Sanzio, 1483–1520; Italian Renaissance painter and architect)

REDOUTÉ, Pierre Joseph (1759–1841; French flower painter)

ROBERTS, Tom (1856–1931; Australian painter, born in Britain)

ROUAULT, Georges (1871–1958; French artist)

7—continued

RUBLYOV, Andrey (or A Rublev, c. 1370–1430; Russian icon painter)

SARGENT, John Singer (1856–1925; US portrait painter, born in Florence)

SCHIELE, Egon (1890–1918; Austrian expressionist painter)

SEGHERS, Hercules Pieterzoon (c. 1589–c. 1638; Dutch landscape painter and etcher)

SHEPARD, Ernest Howard (1879–1976; British artist)

SICKERT, Walter Richard (1860–1942; British impressionist painter and etcher, born in Munich)

SNOWDON, Antony Armstrong-Jones, Earl of (1930–   ; British photographer)

SNYDERS, Frans (1579–1657; Flemish animal painter)

SOUTINE, Chaim (1893–1943; Lithuanian-born painter, who emigrated to Paris)

SPENCER, Sir Stanley (1891–1959; British painter)

TENNIEL, Sir John (1820–1914; British cartoonist and book illustrator)

TIBALDI, Pellegrino (1527–96; Italian architect and painter)

TIEPOLO, Giovanni Battista (1696–1770; Venetian rococo painter)

UCCELLO, Paolo (P di Dono, 1397–1475; Florentine painter and craftsman)

UTRILLO, Maurice (1883–1955; French painter)

VAN DYCK, Sir Anthony (or Vandyke, 1599–1641; Flemish baroque painter)

VAN EYCK, Jan (c. 1390–1441; Flemish painter)

VAN GOGH, Vincent (1853–90; Dutch postimpressionist painter)

VERMEER, Jan (1632–75; Dutch painter)

VIGNOLA, Giacomo da (1507–73; Roman mannerist architect)

WATTEAU, Antoine (1684–1721; French rococo painter)

ZADKINE, Ossip (1890–1967; French sculptor of Russian birth)

ZOFFANY, Johann (c. 1733–1810; German-born English painter)

ZUCCARO, Federico (1543–1609; Italian painter)

ZUCCARO, Taddeo (1529–66; Italian painter)

8

AALTONEN, Wäinö (1894–1966; Finnish sculptor)

AMMANATI, Bartolommeo (1511–92; Florentine mannerist architect and sculptor)

ANGELICO, Fra (Guido di Pietro, c. 1400–55; Italian painter)

ANNIGONI, Pietro (1910–   ; Italian painter)

ANTELAMI, Benedetto (active 1177–1233; Italian sculptor)

8—continued

BECKMANN, Max (1884–1950; German expressionist painter)

BOCCIONI, Umberto (1882–1916; Italian futurist painter and sculptor)

BRAMANTE, Donato (1444–1514; Italian Renaissance architect)

BRANCUSI, Constantin (1876–1957; Romanian sculptor)

BRONZINO, Il (Agnolo di Cosimo, 1503–72; Florentine mannerist painter)

CARRACCI, Annibale (1560–1609; Italian painter)

CASTAGNO, Andrea del (Andrea di Bartolo de Simone, c. 1421–57; Italian painter)

CHAMBERS, Sir William (1723–96; British architect and interior designer)

CRESSENT, Charles (1685–1768; French cabinetmaker)

CRIVELLI, Carlo (c. 1430–95; Venetian painter)

DAUBIGNY, Charles-François (1817–78; French landscape painter)

DELAUNAY, Robert (1885–1941; French painter)

DRYSDALE, Sir Russell (1912–81; Australian painter, born in England)

DUBUFFET, Jean (1901–85; French painter and sculptor)

FILARETE (Antonio Averlino, c. 1400–c. 1469; Italian Renaissance architect)

FRAMPTON, Sir George James (1860–1928; British sculptor)

GHIBERTI, Lorenzo (c. 1378–1455; Florentine Renaissance sculptor)

GIORDANO, Luca (1632–1705; Neapolitan painter, nicknamed LUCA FA PRESTO)

GOSSAERT, Jan (c. 1478–c. 1532; Flemish painter)

GUERCINO (Giovanni Francesco Barbieri, 1591–1666; Italian painter)

HEPWORTH, Dame Barbara (1903–75; British sculptor)

HILLIARD, Nicholas (1547–1619; English portrait miniaturist)

JACOBSEN, Arne (1902–71; Danish architect and designer of furniture and wallpaper)

JONGKIND, Johan Barthold (1819–91; Dutch landscape painter and etcher)

JORDAENS, Jakob (1593–1678; Flemish painter)

KIRCHNER, Ernst Ludwig (1880–1938; German expressionist painter and printmaker)

LANDSEER, Sir Edwin Henry (1802–73; British artist)

LAWRENCE, Sir Thomas (1769–1830; British painter)

LIPCHITZ, Jacques (1891–1973; Lithuanian cubist sculptor)

8—continued

LOMBARDO, Pietro (c. 1438–1515; Italian sculptor and architect)

LYSIPPUS (4th century BC; Court sculptor of Alexander the Great)

MAGRITTE, René (1898–1967; Belgian surrealist painter)

MALEVICH, Kazimir (1878–1935; Russian painter and art theorist)

MANTEGNA, Andrea (c. 1431–1506; Italian Renaissance painter and engraver)

MASACCIO (Tommaso di Giovanni di Simone Guidi, 1401–28; Florentine painter)

MASOLINO (Tommaso di Cristoforo Fini, 1383–?1447; Italian painter)

MEEGEREN, Hans van (1889–1947; Dutch painter)

MONDRIAN, Piet (Pieter Cornelis Mondriaan, 1872–1944; Dutch painter)

MULREADY, William (1786–1863; British painter)

MUNNINGS, Sir Alfred (1878–1959; British painter)

NIEMEYER, Oscar (1907–   ; Brazilian architect)

PALLADIO, Andrea (1508–80; Italian architect)

PIRANESI, Giambattista (1720–78; Italian etcher)

PISSARRO, Camille (1830–1903; French impressionist painter, born in the West Indies)

PONTORMO, Jacopo da (J Carrucci, 1494–1557; Italian mannerist painter)

REYNOLDS, Sir Joshua (1723–92; British portrait painter)

ROBINSON, William Heath (1872–1944; British cartoonist and book illustrator)

ROUSSEAU, Henri (1844–1910; French painter)

ROUSSEAU, Théodore (1812–67; French Romantic painter)

RUISDAEL, Jacob van (?1628–82; Dutch landscape painter)

SAARINEN, Eero (1910–61; US architect, born in Finland)

SASSETTA (Stefano di Giovanni, c. 1392–c. 1450; Italian painter)

SEVERINI, Gino (1883–1966; Italian painter)

SHERATON, Thomas (1751–1806; British furniture designer)

SOUFFLOT, Jacques Germain (1713–80; French architect)

SULLIVAN, Louis Henry (1856–1924; US architect)

TERBORCH, Gerard (1617–81; Dutch painter)

VANBRUGH, Sir John (1664–1726; English architect)

VASARELY, Victor (1908–   ; Hungarian-born painter)

8—continued

VERONESE, Paolo (P Caliari, 1528–88; Italian painter)

VLAMINCK, Maurice de (1876-1958; French painter)

VUILLARD, Édouard (1868–1940; French artist)

WEDGWOOD, Josiah (1730–95; British potter, industrialist, and writer)

WHISTLER, James McNeill (1834–1903; US painter)

WHISTLER, Rex (1905–44; British artist)

WOOLLETT, William (1735–85; British engraver)

ZURBARÁN, Francisco de (1598–1664; Spanish painter)

9

ALTDORFER, Albrecht (c. 1480–1538; German artist)

BARTHOLDI, Frédéric August (1834–1904; French sculptor)

BEARDSLEY, Aubrey Vincent (1872–98; British illustrator)

BONINGTON, Richard Parkes (1801–28; British painter)

BORROMINI, Francesco (1599–1667; Italian baroque architect)

BOURDELLE, Émile (1861–1929; French sculptor)

CANALETTO (Antonio Canal, 1697–1768; Venetian painter)

CARPACCIO, Vittore (c. 1460–c. 1525; Venetian painter)

CAVALLINI, Pietro (c. 1250–c. 1330; Italian painter)

COCKERELL, Charles Robert (1788–1863; British architect)

CONSTABLE, John (1776–1837; British landscape painter)

CORNELIUS, Peter von (1783–1867; German painter)

CORREGGIO (Antonio Allegri, c. 1494–1534; Italian Renaissance painter)

COURRÈGES, André (1923–   ; French fashion designer)

DE KOONING, Willem (1904–   ; US painter of Dutch birth)

DELACROIX, Eugène (1798–1863; French Romantic painter)

DELAROCHE, Paul (1797–1859; French history and portrait painter)

DONATELLO (Donato de Nicolo di Betti Bardi, c. 1386–1466; Florentine sculptor)

FABRITIUS, Carel (1622–54; Dutch painter)

FEININGER, Lyonel (1871–1956; US painter and illustrator)

FRAGONARD, Jean Honoré (1732–1806; French rococo painter)

FRIEDRICH, Caspar David (1774–1840; German Romantic landscape painter)

9—continued

GÉRICAULT, Théodore (1791–1824; French painter)

GIORGIONE (c. 1477–1510; Italian painter)

GREENAWAY, Kate (1846–1901; British artist and book illustrator)

GREENOUGH, Horatio (1805–52; US neoclassical sculptor)

GRÜNE'.VALD, Matthias (Mathis Gothardt, d. 1528; German painter)

HAWKSMOOR, Nicholas (1661–1736; English baroque architect)

HIROSHIGE (Ando Tokitaro, 1797–1858; Japanese colour-print artist)

HONTHORST, Gerrit von (1590–1656; Dutch painter)

JAWLENSKY, Alexey von (1864–1941; Russian expressionist painter)

KANDINSKY, Wassily (1866–1944; Russian expressionist painter and art theorist)

KAUFFMANN, Angelica (1741–1807; Swiss painter)

KOKOSCHKA, Oskar (1886–1980; Austrian expressionist painter and writer)

LISSITZKY, El (Eliezer L, 1890–1941; Russian painter and architect)

MESTROVIĆ, Ivan (1883–1962; US sculptor, born in Yugoslavia)

MUYBRIDGE, Eadweard (Edward James Muggeridge, 1830–1904; US photographer, born in Britain)

NICHOLSON, Ben (1894–1982; British artist)

NOLLEKENS, Joseph (1737–1823; British neoclassical sculptor)

OLDENBURG, Claes; (1929–   ; US sculptor, born in Sweden)

PISANELLO (Antonio Pisano, c. 1395–c. 1455; Italian international gothic painter, draughtsman, and medallist)

ROUBILLAC, Louis François (or L F Roubiliac, 1695–1762; French sculptor)

SIQUEIROS, David Alfaro (1896–1974; Mexican painter)

STIEGLITZ, Alfred (1864–1946; US photographer)

THORNHILL, Sir James (1675–1734; English baroque decorative painter)

VELÁZQUEZ, Diego Rodriguez de Silva (1599–1660; Spanish painter)

VITRUVIUS (Marcus Vitruvius Pollio, 1st century BC; Roman architect)

WOUWERMAN, Philips (1619–68; Dutch painter)

10

ALMA-TADEMA, Sir Lawrence (1836–1912; Dutch painter)

ALTICHIERO (c. 1330–c. 1390; Italian painter)

ARCHIPENKO, Alexander (1887–1964; Russian-born sculptor and painter)

ARCIMBOLDO, Giuseppe (1527–93; Mannerist painter)

10—continued

BERRUGUETE, Alonso (c. 1480–1561; Castillian painter)

BERRUGUETE, Pedro (c. 1450–c. 1504; Castillian painter)

BOTTICELLI, Sandro (Alessandro di Mariano Filipepi, c. 1445–1510; Florentine Renaissance painter)

BURLINGTON, Richard Boyle, 3rd Earl of (1694–1753; English architect)

BURNE-JONES, Sir Edward Coley (1833–98; Pre-Raphaelite painter)

CARAVAGGIO (Michelangelo Merisi, 1573–1610; Italian painter)

CHAMPAIGNE, Philippe de (1602–74; French portrait painter)

CRUIKSHANK, George (1792–1872; British caricaturist, painter, and illustrator)

EUPHRONIOS (late 6th–early 5th centuries BC; Athenian potter and vase painter)

GIACOMETTI, Alberto (1901–66; Swiss sculptor and painter)

LORENZETTI, Ambrogio (c. 1290–?1348; Italian painter)

MACKINTOSH, Charles Rennie (1868–1928; Scottish architect and designer)

MEISSONIER, Jean-Louis-Ernest (1815–91; French painter)

MODIGLIANI, Amedeo (1884–1920; Italian painter and sculptor)

MOHOLY-NAGY, László (1895–1946; Hungarian artist)

MOTHERWELL, Robert (1915–   ; US abstract painter)

POLLAIUOLO, Antonio (c. 1432–98; Florentine Renaissance artist)

POLYCLITUS (5th century BC; Greek sculptor)

PRAXITELES (mid-4th century BC; Athenian sculptor)

RICHARDSON, Henry Hobson (1838–86; US architect)

ROWLANDSON, Thomas (1756–1827; British caricaturist)

SCHWITTERS, Kurt (1887–1958; German artist and poet)

SENEFELDER, Aloys (1771–1834; German playwright and engraver)

SIGNORELLI, Luca (c. 1441–1523; Italian Renaissance painter)

SUTHERLAND, Graham Vivian (1903–80; British artist)

TANGE KENZO (1913–   ; Japanese architect)

TINTORETTO (Jacopo Robusti, 1518–94; Venetian painter)

VAN DE VELDE, Henry (1863–1957; Belgian Art Nouveau architect, interior designer, and painter)

VERROCCHIO, Andrea del (Andrea del Cione, c. 1435–88; Italian sculptor, painter, and goldsmith)

10—continued

WATERHOUSE, Alfred (1830–1905; British architect)

ZUCCARELLI, Francesco (1702–88; Italian painter)

11

ABERCROMBIE, Sir Patrick (1879–1957; British architect)

BARTOLOMMEO, Fra (Baccio della Porta, c. 1472–1517; Florentine Renaissance painter)

BUTTERFIELD, William (1814–1900; British architect)

CALLICRATES (5th century BC; Athenian architect)

CALLIMACHUS (late 5th century BC; Greek sculptor)

CHIPPENDALE, Thomas (1718–79; British cabinetmaker)

CHODOWIECKI, Daniel Nikolaus (1726–1801; German painter and engraver)

DELLA ROBBIA, Luca (1400–82; Florentine Renaissance sculptor)

DOMENICHINO (Domenico Zampieri, 1581–1641; Italian painter)

GHIRLANDAIO, Domenico (Domenico di Tommaso Bigordi, 1449–94; Florentine painter)

GIAMBOLOGNA (Giovanni da Bologna *or* Jean de Boulogne, 1529–1608; Italian mannerist sculptor)

GISLEBERTUS (early 12th century; French romanesque sculptor)

HEPPLEWHITE, George (d. 1786; British furniture designer and cabinetmaker)

LE CORBUSIER (Charles-Édouard Jeanneret, 1887–1965; French architect, born in Switzerland)

TERBRUGGHEN, Hendrik (1588–1629; Dutch painter)

THORVALDSEN, Bertel (*or* B Thorwaldsen, 1768–1844; Danish sculptor)

12

BRUNELLESCHI, Filippo (1377–1446; Italian architect)

FANTIN-LATOUR, Henri (1836–1904; French painter)

GAINSBOROUGH, Thomas (1727–88; British portrait and landscape painter)

GAUDÍ Y CORNET, Antonio (1852–1926; Spanish architect)

GIULIO ROMANO (Giulio Pippi, c. 1499–1546; Italian mannerist painter and architect)

LICHTENSTEIN, Roy (1923– ; US painter)

LUCA FA PRESTO (Nickname of Luca Giordano)

PALMA VECCHIO, Jacopo (J Negretti, c. 1480–1528; Italian painter)

PARMIGIANINO (Girolamo Francesco Maria Mazzola, 1503–40; Italian painter)

12—continued

PINTURICCHIO (Bernardino di Betto, c. 1454–1513; Italian Renaissance painter)

RAUSCHENBERG, Robert (1925– ; US artist)

SAINT-LAURENT, Yves (1936– ; French fashion designer)

SCHIAPARELLI, Elsa (1896–1973; Italian-born fashion designer)

VIOLLET-LE-DUC, Eugène Emmanuel (1814–79; French architect and author)

WINTERHALTER, Franz Xavier (1806–73; German painter and lithographer)

13

LORENZO MONACO (Piero di Giovanni, c. 1370–1425; Italian painter)

PIERO DI COSIMO (P di Lorenzo, 1462–1521; Florentine Renaissance painter)

WILLIAMS-ELLIS, Sir Clough (1883–1978; Welsh architect)

14

ANDREA DEL SARTO (Andrea d'Agnolo, 1486–1530; Italian painter)

BÉRAIN THE ELDER, Jean (1637–1711; French designer, engraver, and painter)

CARTIER-BRESSON, Henri (1908– ; French photographer)

CLAUDE LORRAINE (Claude Gellée, 1600–82; French landscape painter)

COUSIN THE ELDER, Jean (1490–1560; French artist and craftsman)

GAUDIER-BRZESKA, Henri (1891–1915; French sculptor)

LUCAS VAN LEYDEN (Lucas Hugensz *or* Jacobsz, c. 1494–1533; Dutch artist)

MIES VAN DER ROHE, Ludwig (1886–1969; German architect)

15

CRANACH THE ELDER, Lucas (Lucas Müller, 1472–1553; German artist)

HARDOUIN-MANSART, Jules (1646–1708; French baroque architect)

KITAGAWA UTAMARO (1753–1806; Japanese artist)

LEONARDO DA VINCI (1452–1519; Italian artistic and scientific genius of the Renaissance)

TOULOUSE-LAUTREC, Henri de (1864–1901; French artist)

16

BRUEGHEL THE ELDER, Pieter (*or* Bruegel, 1525–69; Flemish painter)

FISCHER VON ERLACH, Johann Bernhard (1656–1723; Austrian architect)

PUVIS DE CHAVANNES, Pierre (1824–98; French painter)

REMBRANDT VAN RIJN (1606–69; Dutch painter and etcher)

16—continued

UTAGAWA KUNIYOSHI (Igusa Magosaburo, 1797–1861; Japanese painter and printmaker)

17

DOMENICO VENEZIANO (active c. 1438–1461; Italian painter)

GENTILE DA FABRIANO (Niccolo di Giovanni di Massio, c. 1370–1427; Florentine painter)

HERRERA THE YOUNGER, Francisco de (1622–85; Spanish baroque painter and architect)

HOLBEIN THE YOUNGER, Hans (c. 1497–1543; German painter)

TENIERS THE YOUNGER, David (1610–90; Flemish painter)

18

ANTONELLO DA MESSINA (c. 1430–c. 1479; Italian painter)

18—continued

JACOPO DELLA QUERCIA (c. 1374–1438; Italian Renaissance sculptor)

LEIGHTON OF STRETTON, Frederic, Baron (1830–96; British painter and sculptor)

19

DUCCIO DI BUONINSEGNA (c. 1255–c. 1318; Italian painter)

PIERO DELLA FRANCESCA (c. 1420–92; Italian Renaissance painter)

20

DESIDERIO DA SETTIGNANO (c. 1430–64; Italian Renaissance sculptor)

MICHELANGELO BUONARROTI (1475–1564; Italian sculptor, painter, and architect)

MICHELOZZO DI BARTOLOMMEO (1396–1472; Florentine Renaissance sculptor and architect)

WRITERS, PLAYWRIGHTS, AND POETS

3

FRY, Christopher (C Harris, 1907–   ; British dramatist)

GAY, John (1685–1732; British poet and dramatist)

KYD, Thomas (1558–94; English dramatist)

PAZ, Octavio (1914–   ; Mexican poet)

SUE, Eugène (Joseph Marie S, 1804–57; French novelist)

4

AGEE, James (1909–55; US poet and novelist)

AMIS, Kingsley (1922–   ; British novelist and poet)

ASCH, Sholem (1880–1957; Jewish novelist)

BANA (7th century AD; Sanskrit writer)

BAUM, L Frank (1856–1919; US novelist)

BENN, Gottfried (1886–1956; German poet)

BLOK, Aleksandr Aleksandrovich (1880–1921; Russian symbolist poet)

BÖLL, Heinrich (1917–85; German novelist)

BOLT, Robert Oxton (1924–   ; British dramatist)

BUCK, Pearl S (1892–1973; US novelist)

CARY, Joyce (1888–1957; British novelist)

CRUZ, Sor Juana Inéz de la (1651–95; Mexican poet)

DAHL, Roald (1916–   ; British author)

DEUS, João de (1830–96; Portuguese poet)

DU FU (or Tu Fu; 712–70 AD; Chinese poet)

FORD, Ford Madox (Ford Hermann Hueffer, 1873–1939; British novelist)

FORD, John (1586–c. 1640; English dramatist)

4—continued

FOXE, John (1516–87; English religious writer)

GALT, John (1779–1839; Scottish novelist)

GIDE, André (1869–1951; French novelist and critic)

GRAY, Thomas (1716–71; British poet)

GUNN, Thomson W (1929–   ; British poet)

HART, Moss (1904–61; US dramatist)

HOGG, James (1770–1835; Scottish poet and writer)

HOOD, Thomas (1799–1845; British poet)

HOPE, Anthony (Sir Anthony Hope Hawkins; 1863–1933; British novelist)

HUGO, Victor (1802–85; French poet, dramatist, and novelist)

HUNT, Leigh (1784–1859; British poet and journalist)

KIVI, Alexis (A Stenvall, 1834–72; Finnish poet, dramatist, and novelist)

LAMB, Charles (1775–1834; British essayist and critic)

LEAR, Edward (1812–88; British artist and poet)

LIVY (Titus Livius, 59 BC–17 AD; Roman writer)

LOTI, Pierre (Julien Viaud; 1850–1923; French novelist)

LYLY, John (c. 1554–1606; English dramatist and writer)

MANN, Thomas (1875–1955; German novelist)

MUIR, Edwin (1887–1959; Scottish poet)

NASH, Ogden (1902–71; US humorous writer)

4—continued

NEXØ, Martin Andersen (1869–1954; Danish novelist)

OVID (Publius Ovidius Naso 43 BC–17 AD; Roman poet)

OWEN, Wilfred (1893–1918; British poet)

POPE, Alexander (1688–1744; British poet)

READ, Sir Herbert (1893–1968; British poet)

RHYS, Jean (1894–1979; British novelist)

ROTH, Philip (1933–   ; US novelist)

ROWE, Nicholas (1674–1718; British dramatist)

RUIZ, Juan (c. 1283–c. 1350; Spanish poet)

SADE, Donatien Alphonse François, Marquis de (1740–1814; French novelist)

SA'DI (Mosleh al-Din S, c. 1215–92; Persian poet)

SAKI (H H Munro, 1870–1916; British humorous short-story writer)

SAND, George (Aurore Dupin, Baronne Dudevant, 1804–76; French novelist)

SHAW, George Bernard (1856–1950; Irish dramatist)

SNOW, C P, Baron (1905–80; British novelist)

TATE, Allen (1899–   ; US poet and critic)

TATE, Nahum (1652–1715; British poet)

URFÉ, Honoré d' (1568–1625; French novelist)

VEGA, Lope Félix de (1562–1635; Spanish poet and dramatist)

WAIN, John (1925–   ; British novelist and poet)

WARD, Artemus (Charles Farrar Browne, 1834–67; US humorous writer)

WARD, Mrs Humphry (1851–1920; British novelist)

WEBB, Mary (1881–1927; British novelist)

WEST, Dame Rebecca (Cicely Isabel Fairfield, 1892–1983; British novelist and journalist)

WEST, Nathanael (Nathan Weinstein, 1903–40; US novelist)

WOOD, Mrs Henry (1814–87; British novelist)

WREN, P C (1885–1941; British novelist)

WYSS, Johann Rudolph (1782–1830; Swiss writer)

ZOLA, Émile (1840–1902; French novelist)

5

ADAMS, Henry (1838–1918; US historian)

ADAMS, Richard (1920–   ; British novelist)

AGNON, Shmuel Yosef (Samuel Josef Czaczkes, 1888–1970; Jewish novelist)

ALBEE, Edward (1928–   ; US dramatist)

ARANY, János (1817–82; Hungarian poet)

AUDEN, W H (1907–73; British poet)

BABEL, Isaac Emmanuilovich (1894–1941; Russian short-story writer)

BARTH, John (1930–   ; US novelist)

BATES, H E (1905–74; British writer)

BEHAN, Brendan (1923–64; Irish playwright)

BELLO, Andrés (1781–1865; Venezuelan scholar and poet)

5—continued

BELYI, Andrei (Boris Nikolaevich Bugaev, 1880–1934; Russian symbolist poet and critic)

BEMBO, Pietro (1470–1547; Italian scholar)

BENDA, Julien (1867–1956; French novelist and philosopher)

BENÉT, Stephen Vincent (1898–1943; US poet and novelist)

BETTI, Ugo (1892–1953; Italian dramatist)

BOWEN, Elizabeth (1899–1973; British novelist, born in Dublin)

BRANT, Sebastian (?1458–1521; German poet)

BROCH, Hermann (1886–1951; Austrian novelist)

BUNIN, Ivan Alekseevich (1879–1953; Russian poet and novelist)

BURNS, Robert (1759–96; Scottish poet)

BUTOR, Michel (1926–   ; French experimental novelist and critic)

BYRON, George Gordon, Lord (1788–1824; British poet)

CAMUS, Albert (1913–60; French novelist)

CAREW, Thomas (c. 1595–1640; British poet)

CLARE, John (1793–1864; British poet)

COLUM, Padraic (Patrick Colm; 1881–1972; Irish poet)

CRAIK, Dinah Maria Mulock (1826–87; British novelist)

CRANE, Hart (1899–1932; US poet)

CRANE, Stephen (1871–1900; US novelist)

DARÍO, Rubén (Félix García Sarmiento; 1867–1916; Nicaraguan poet)

DEFOE, Daniel (1660–1731; British novelist)

DONNE, John (1572–1631; English poet)

DOYLE, Sir Arthur Conan (1859–1930; British author)

DUMAS, Alexandre (1802–70; French novelist and dramatist)

DURAS, Marguerite (1914–   ; French novelist)

ELIOT, George (Mary Ann Evans, 1819–80; British novelist)

ELIOT, T S (1888–1965; Anglo-American poet, critic, and dramatist)

ELYOT, Sir Thomas (c. 1490–1546; English scholar)

EWALD, Johannes (1743–81; Danish poet and playwright)

FROST, Robert Lee (1874–1963; US poet)

GENET, Jean (1910–86; French novelist and dramatist)

GOGOL, Nikolai Vasilievich (1809–52; Russian novelist and dramatist)

GORKI, Maksim (Aleksei Maksimovich Peshkov; 1868–1936; Russian novelist)

GOSSE, Sir Edmund (1849–1928; British critic)

GOWER, John (c. 1330–1408; English poet)

GRASS, Günter (1927–   ; German novelist and poet)

5—continued

GREEN, Henry (Henry Vincent Yorke; 1905–73; British novelist)

HAFIZ, Shams al-Din Muhammad (?1326–90; Persian lyric poet)

HALLE, Adam de la (c. 1240–90; French poet and musician)

HARDY, Thomas (1840–1928; British novelist and poet)

HARTE, Brett (1836–1902; US short-story writer)

HAŠEK, Jaroslav (1883–1923; Czech novelist)

HEINE, Heinrich (1797–1856; German Jewish poet and writer)

HENRY, O (William Sidney Porter, 1862–1910; US short-story writer)

HESSE, Hermann (1877–1962; German novelist and poet)

HOMER (8th century BC; Greek epic poet)

HOOFT, Pieter Corneliszoon (1581–1647; Dutch poet)

IBSEN, Henrik (1828–1906; Norwegian playwright and poet)

JAMES, Henry (1843–1916; US novelist and critic)

JARRY, Alfred (1873–1907; French dramatist)

JONES, David (1895–1974; Anglo-Welsh writer)

JONES, LeRoi (1934– ; US dramatist and poet)

JOYCE, James (1882–1941; Irish novelist and poet)

KAFKA, Franz (1883–1924; Czech writer)

KEATS, John (1795–1821; British poet)

KEMAL, Namik (1840–88; Turkish poet, novelist, and dramatist)

KESEY, Ken (1935– ; US novelist)

LEWIS, C S (1898–1963; British writer)

LEWIS, Matthew Gregory (1775–1818; British novelist)

LEWIS, Sinclair (1885–1951; US novelist)

LEWIS, Wyndham (1882–1957; British novelist)

LODGE, Thomas (1558–1625; English poet, dramatist, and writer)

LOWRY, Malcolm (1909–57; British novelist)

LUCAN (Marcus Annaeus Lucanus, 39–65 AD; Roman poet)

MAROT, Clément (1496–1544; French poet)

MARSH, Dame Ngaio (1899–1981; New Zealand detective-story writer)

MARTÍ, José Julián (1853–95; Cuban poet)

MASON, A E W (1865–1948; British novelist)

MILNE, A A (1882–1956; British novelist and dramatist)

MOORE, Marianne (1887–1972; US poet)

MOORE, Thomas (1779–1852; Irish poet)

MURRY, John Middleton (1889–1957; British literary critic)

MUSIL, Robert (1880–1942; Austrian novelist)

5—continued

MYERS, F W H (1843–1901; British essayist and poet)

NASHE, Thomas (1567–c. 1601; British dramatist)

NOYES, Alfred (1880–1958; British poet)

ODETS, Clifford (1906–63; US dramatist)

O'HARA, John (1905–70; US novelist)

OPITZ, Martin (1597–1639; German poet)

ORCZY, Baroness Emmusca (1865–1947; British novelist)

OTWAY, Thomas (1652–85; British dramatist)

OUIDA (Marie Louise de la Ramée, 1839–1908; British novelist)

PAN GU (or P'an Ku; 32–92 AD; Chinese historian)

PATON, Alan (1903– ; South African novelist)

PEAKE, Mervyn (1911–68; British novelist)

PEELE, George (1556–96; English dramatist)

PÉGUY, Charles (1873–1914; French poet and essayist)

PERSE, Saint-John (Alexis Saint-Léger, 1887–1975; French poet)

PLATH, Sylvia (1932–63; US poet and writer)

POUND, Ezra (1885–1972; US poet and critic)

POWYS, John Cowper (1872–1963; British novelist)

PRIOR, Matthew (1664–1721; British poet)

PULCI, Luigi (1432–84; Italian poet)

RAINE, Kathleen (1908– ; British poet)

READE, Charles (1814–84; British novelist)

RILKE, Rainer Maria (1875–1926; Austrian poet)

ROLFE, Frederick William (1860–1913; British novelist)

SACHS, Hans (1494–1576; German poet and folk dramatist)

SACHS, Nelly (1891–1970; German Jewish poet and dramatist)

SAGAN, Françoise (Françoise Quoirez, 1935– ; French writer)

SCOTT, Sir Walter (1771–1832; Scottish novelist)

SETON, Ernest Thompson (1860–1946; US writer)

SHUTE, Nevil (Nevil Shute Norway, 1899–1960; British novelist)

SIMMS, William Gilmore (1806–70; US novelist)

SMART, Christopher (1722–71; British poet)

SMITH, Stevie (Florence Margaret S, 1902–71; British poet)

SPARK, Muriel (1918– ; British novelist)

STAËL, Anne Louise Germaine Necker, Madame de (1766–1817; French writer)

STEIN, Gertrude (1874–1946; US writer)

STORM, Theodor Woldsen (1817–1888; German writer)

STOWE, Harriet Beecher (1811–96; US novelist)

5—continued

SVEVO, Italo (Ettore Schmitz, 1861–1928; Italian novelist)

SWIFT, Jonathan (1667–1745; Anglo-Irish poet and satirist)

SYNGE, John Millington (1871–1909; Anglo-Irish dramatist)

TASSO, Torquato (1544–95; Italian poet)

TIECK, Ludwig (1773–1853; German writer)

TWAIN, Mark (Samuel Langhorne Clemens, 1835–1910; US novelist)

UDALL, Nicholas (1505–56; English dramatist)

VARRO, Marcus Terentius (116–27 BC; Roman scholar and poet)

VERNE, Jules (1828–1905; French writer)

VIDAL, Gore (1925– ; US novelist and essayist)

VIGNY, Alfred de (1797–1863; French poet, novelist, and dramatist)

WALEY, Arthur (1889–1966; British translator and poet)

WAUGH, Evelyn (1903–66; British novelist)

WEISS, Peter (1916–82; German dramatist and novelist)

WELLS, H G (1866–1946; British novelist)

WHITE, Patrick (1912– ; Australian novelist)

WHITE, T H (1906–64; British novelist)

WILDE, Oscar (O. Fingal O'Flahertie Wills W, 1854–1900; British dramatist and poet)

WOLFE, Charles (1791–1823; Irish poet)

WOLFE, Thomas (1900–38; US novelist)

WOOLF, Virginia (1882–1941; British novelist)

WYATT, Sir Thomas (1503–42; English poet)

YEATS, William Butler (1865–1939; Irish poet and dramatist)

YONGE, Charlotte (1823–1901; British novelist)

ZWEIG, Arnold (1887–1968; East German-Jewish novelist)

ZWEIG, Stefan (1881–1942; Austrian Jewish writer)

6

ACCIUS, Lucius (170–c. 85 BC; Roman tragic dramatist)

ADAMOV, Arthur (1908–70; French dramatist)

ALCOTT, Louisa May (1832–88; US novelist)

ALDISS, Brian W (1925– ; British novelist)

ALEMÁN, Mateo (1547–?1614; Spanish writer)

ALGREN, Nelson (1909–81; US novelist)

AMBLER, Eric (1909– ; British novelist)

ANDRIĆ, Ivo (1892–1975; Serbian writer)

ARAGON, Louis (1897–1982; French poet, novelist, and journalist)

ASCHAM, Roger (1515–68; English scholar and writer)

ASIMOV, Isaac (1920– ; US science fiction writer, born in Russia)

AUBREY, John (1626–97; English antiquary)

AUSTEN, Jane (1775–1817; British novelist)

AZORÍN (José Martinéz Ruíz, 1874–1967; Spanish novelist, essayist, and critic)

6—continued

AZUELA, Mariano (1873–1952; Mexican novelist)

BALZAC, Honoré de (1799–1850; French novelist)

BARHAM, Richard Harris (1788–1845; British humorous writer)

BARKER, George (1913– ; British poet)

BARNES, William (1801–86; British poet)

BAROJA, Pío (1872–1956; Spanish novelist)

BARRÈS, Maurice (1862–1923; French writer)

BARRIE, Sir James (1860–1937; British dramatist and novelist)

BELLAY, Joachim de (1522–60; French poet)

BELLOC, Hilaire (1870–1953; British poet and essayist)

BELLOW, Saul (1915– ; Canadian-born US novelist)

BESANT, Sir Walter (1836–1901; British novelist)

BIALIK, Chaim Nachman (1873–1934; Jewish poet and translator)

BIERCE, Ambrose Gwinnett (1842–?1914; US writer)

BINYON, Laurence (1869–1943; British poet)

BLYTON, Enid (1897–1968; British writer of children's books)

BORGES, Jorge Luis (1899–1986; Argentinian writer)

BORROW, George Henry (1803–81; British writer)

BRECHT, Bertolt (1898–1956; German dramatist and poet)

BRETON, André (1896–1966; French poet)

BRIDIE, James (Osborne Henry Mavor; 1888–1951; British dramatist)

BRONTË, Anne (1820–49; British novelist)

BRONTË, Charlotte (1816–55; British novelist)

BRONTË, Emily (1818–48; British novelist)

BROOKE, Rupert (1887–1915; British poet)

BROWNE, Sir Thomas (1605–82; English writer)

BRYANT, William Cullen (1794–1878; US poet, journalist, and critic)

BUCHAN, John, 1st Baron Tweedsmuir (1875–1940; British novelist)

BUNYAN, John (1628–88; English writer)

BÜRGER, Gottfried (1747–94; German poet)

BURNEY, Fanny (Mrs Frances Burney D'Arblay; 1752–1840; British novelist)

BUTLER, Samuel (1612–80; British satirical poet)

BUTLER, Samuel (1835–1902; British novelist)

CAMÕES, Luís de (c. 1524–80; Portuguese poet)

CAPOTE, Truman (1924–84; US novelist)

CARSON, Rachel Louise (1907–64; US science writer)

CAVAFY, Constantine (C Kavafis, 1863–1933; Greek poet)

6—continued

CÉLINE, Louis Ferdinand (L F Destouches, 1884–1961; French novelist)

CIBBER, Colley (1671–1757; British dramatist)

CLARKE, Marcus (1846–81; Australian novelist, born in London)

COLMAN, George (1732–94; British dramatist)

CONRAD, Joseph (Teodor Josef Konrad Watęcz Korzeniowski, 1857–1924; Polish-born British novelist)

COOPER, James Fenimore (1789–1851; US novelist)

COWLEY, Abraham (1618–67; English poet)

COWPER, William (1731–1800; British poet)

CRABBE, George (1754–1832; British poet)

CRONIN, A J (1896–1981; British novelist)

DANIEL, Samuel (?1562–1619; English poet, dramatist, and critic)

DAUDET, Alphonse (1840–97; French novelist)

DAVIES, W H (1871–1940; British poet)

DEKKER, Thomas (c. 1572–1632; British dramatist and pamphleteer)

DOWSON, Ernest (1867–1900; British poet)

DRYDEN, John (1631–1700; British poet)

DUNBAR, William (c. 1460–c. 1530; Scots poet)

ÉLUARD, Paul (Eugène Grindel, 1895–1952; French poet)

EMPSON, Sir William (1906–84; British poet and critic)

ENNIUS, Quintus (238–169 BC; Roman poet)

EVELYN, John (1620–1706; English diarist)

FOUQUÉ, Friedrich Heinrich Karl, Baron de la Motte (1777–1843; German novelist and dramatist)

FOWLES, John (1926– ; British novelist)

FRANCE, Anatole (Jacques Anatole François Thibault, 1844–1924; French novelist)

FRISCH, Max (1911– ; Swiss dramatist and novelist)

FUGARD, Athol (1932– ; South African dramatist)

FULLER, Roy (1912– ; British poet and novelist)

FULLER, Thomas (1608–61; British historian)

GEORGE, Stefan (1868–1933; German poet)

GIBBON, Edward (1737–94; British historian)

GIBRAN, Khalil (1883–1931; Lebanese mystic and poet)

GOETHE, Johann Wolfgang von (1749–1832; German poet)

GRAVES, Robert (1895–1985; British poet, critic, and novelist)

GREENE, Graham (1904– ; British novelist)

GREENE, Robert (c. 1558–92; English dramatist)

HAMSUN, Knut (1859–1952; Norwegian novelist)

HARRIS, Joel Chandler (1848–1908; US novelist and short-story writer)

6—continued

HEBBEL, Friedrich (1813–63; German dramatist)

HELLER, Joseph (1923– ; US novelist)

HESIOD (8th century BC; Greek poet)

HILTON, James (1900–54; British novelist)

HOLMES, Oliver Wendell (1809–94; US essayist and poet)

HORACE (Quintus Horatius Flaccus; 65–8 BC; Roman poet)

HUDSON, W H (1841–1922; British naturalist and writer)

HUGHES, Richard (1900–76; British novelist)

HUGHES, Ted (1930– ; British poet)

HUGHES, Thomas (1822–96; British writer)

IRVING, Washington (1783–1859; US short-story writer)

ISAACS, Jorge (1837–95; Colombian novelist)

JENSEN, Johannes (1873–1950; Danish novelist and poet)

JONSON, Ben (1572–1637; English dramatist and poet)

KAISER, Georg (1878–1945; German dramatist)

KELLER, Gottfried (1819–90; German-Swiss poet and novelist)

KLEIST, Heinrich von (1777–1811; German dramatist)

LACLOS, Pierre Choderlos de (1741–1803; French novelist)

LANDOR, Walter Savage (1775–1864; British poet and prose writer)

LANIER, Sidney (1842–81; US poet)

LARKIN, Philip (1922–85; British poet)

LAWLER, Ray (1921– ; Australian dramatist)

LE FANU, Sheridan (1814–73; Irish novelist)

LEONOV, Leonid (1899– ; Soviet novelist and playwright)

LESAGE, Alain-René (1668–1747; French novelist)

LONDON, Jack (1876–1916; US novelist)

LOWELL, Amy (1874–1925; US poet)

LOWELL, James Russell (1819–91; US poet)

LOWELL, Robert (1917–77; US poet)

LU HSÜN (or Chou Shu-jen; 1881–1936; Chinese writer)

MACHEN, Arthur (1863–1947; Welsh novelist)

MAILER, Norman (1923– ; US novelist and journalist)

MALORY, Sir Thomas (?1400–71; English writer)

MERCER, David (1928–80; British dramatist)

MILLAY, Edna St Vincent (1892–1950; US poet)

MILLER, Arthur (1915– ; US dramatist)

MILLER, Henry (1891–1980; US novelist)

MILTON, John (1608–74; English poet)

MOLNÁR, Ferenc (1878–1952; Hungarian dramatist)

MORGAN, Charles (1894–1958; British novelist and dramatist)

6—continued

MÖRIKE, Eduard Friedrich (1804–75; German poet and novelist)

MUNTHE, Axel (1857–1949; Swedish author)

MUSSET, Alfred de (1810–57; French poet and dramatist)

NERUDA, Pablo (Neftalí Ricardo Reyes; 1904–73; Chilean poet)

NERVAL, Gérard de (Gérard Labrunie; 1808–55; French poet)

NESBIT, Edith (1858–1924; British children's writer)

O'BRIEN, Flann (Brian O'Nolan; 1911–66; Irish novelist and journalist)

O'CASEY, Sean (1880–1964; Irish dramatist)

O'NEILL, Eugene (1888–1953; US dramatist)

ORWELL, George (Eric Blair; 1903–50; British novelist, born in India)

PARKER, Dorothy Rothschild (1893–1967; US humorous writer)

PAVESE, Cesare (1908–50; Italian novelist and poet)

PETÖFI, Sándor (1823–49; Hungarian poet)

PINDAR (518–438 BC; Greek poet)

PINERO, Sir Arthur Wing (1855–1934; British dramatist)

PINTER, Harold (1930–   ; British dramatist)

PIOZZI, Hester Lynch (1741–1821; British writer)

PLOMER, William (1903–73; South African poet and novelist)

PORTER, Katherine Anne (1890–1980; US short-story writer and novelist)

PORTER, Peter (1929–   ; British poet)

POTTER, Beatrix (1866–1943; British children's writer)

POTTER, Stephen (1900–70; British writer)

POWELL, Anthony (1905–   ; British novelist)

PROUST, Marcel (1871–1922; French novelist)

RACINE, Jean (1639–99; French dramatist)

RAMSAY, Allan (?1685–1758; Scottish poet)

RANSOM, John Crowe (1888–1974; US poet)

RUNYON, Damon (1884–1946; US humorous writer)

SAPPER (H C McNeile, 1888–1937; British novelist)

SAPPHO (c. 612–c. 580 BC; Greek poet)

SARDOU, Victorien (1831–1908; French dramatist)

SARTRE, Jean-Paul (1905–80; French philosopher, novelist, dramatist, and critic)

SAVAGE, Richard (c. 1696–1743; British poet)

SAYERS, Dorothy L (1893–1957; British writer)

SIDNEY, Sir Philip (1554–86; English poet)

SILONE, Ignazio (Secondo Tranquilli, 1900–78; Italian novelist)

SINGER, Isaac Bashevis (1904–   ; US novelist and short-story writer)

SMILES, Samuel (1812–1904; British writer)

6—continued

STEELE, Sir Richard (1672–1729; British essayist and dramatist)

STERNE, Laurence (1713–68; British novelist)

STOKER, Bram (Abraham S, 1847–1912; Irish novelist)

STOREY, David (1933–   ; British novelist and dramatist)

SURREY, Henry Howard, Earl of (1517–47; English poet)

SYMONS, Arthur (1865–1945; British poet and critic)

TAGORE, Rabindranath (1861–1941; Indian poet)

THOMAS, Dylan (1914–53; Welsh poet)

THOMAS, Edward (1878–1917; British poet)

TOLLER, Ernst (1893–1939; German playwright and poet)

TRAVEN, B (Berick Traven Torsvan, 1890–1969; US novelist)

UHLAND, Ludwig (1787–1862; German poet)

UNDSET, Sigrid (1882–1949; Norwegian novelist)

UPDIKE, John (1932–   ; US novelist and short-story writer)

VALÉRY, Paul (1871–1945; French poet, essayist, and critic)

VILLON, François (1431–?1463; French poet)

VIRGIL (Publius Vergilius Maro, 70–19 BC; Roman poet)

VONDEL, Joost van den (1587–1679; Dutch dramatist and poet)

WALLER, Edmund (1606–87; British poet)

WALTON, Izaak (1593–1683; English writer)

WARTON, Joseph (1722–1800; British poet and critic)

WERFEL, Franz (1890–1945; Austrian Jewish poet, dramatist, and novelist)

WESKER, Arnold (1932–   ; British dramatist)

WILDER, Thornton (1897–1975; US novelist and dramatist)

WILSON, Colin (1931–   ; British critic and novelist)

WILSON, Edmund (1895–1972; US critic and essayist)

WILSON, Sir Angus (1913–   ; British novelist)

WOTTON, Sir Henry (1568–1639; English poet)

WRIGHT, Judith (1915–   ; Australian poet)

WRIGHT, Richard (1908–60; US novelist and critic)

7

ADDISON, Joseph (1672–1719; British essayist and poet)

AELFRIC (c. 955–c. 1020; Anglo-Saxon prose writer)

ALARCÓN, Pedro Antonio de (1833–91; Spanish novelist)

ALBERTI, Raphael (1902–   ; Spanish poet)

ALCAEUS (6th century BC; Greek lyric poet)

7—continued

ALDANOV, Mark (M Aleksandrovich Landau, 1886–1957; Russian novelist)

ALDRICH, Thomas Bailey (1836–1907; US short-story writer and poet)

ALEGRÍA, Ciro (1909–61; Peruvian novelist)

ALFIERI, Vittorio, Count (1749–1803; Italian poet and dramatist)

ANEIRIN (6th century AD; Welsh poet)

ARETINO, Pietro (1492–1556; Italian satirist)

ARIOSTO, Ludovico (1474–1533; Italian poet)

ARRABAL, Fernando (1932– ; Spanish playwright and novelist)

BALCHIN, Nigel (1908–70; British novelist)

BALDWIN, James Arthur (1924–87; US novelist, essayist, and dramatist)

BARBOUR, John (1316–95; Scottish poet)

BECKETT, Samuel (1906– ; Irish novelist, dramatist, and poet)

BEDDOES, Thomas Lovell (1803–49; British poet)

BENNETT, Arnold (1837–1931; British novelist)

BENTLEY, Edmund Clerihew (1875–1956; British writer)

BERGMAN, Hjalmar (1883–1931; Swedish novelist and dramatist)

BLUNDEN, Edmund Charles (1896–1974; British poet and critic)

BOIARDO, Matteo Maria, Conte di Scandiano (1441–94; Italian poet)

BOILEAU(-Despréaux), Nicolas (1636–1711; French poet and critic)

BOSWELL, James (1740–95; Scottish writer)

BO ZHU YI (or Po Chü-i; 772–846; Chinese poet)

BRADLEY, Andrew Cecil (1851–1935; British literary critic)

BRIDGES, Robert Seymour (1844–1930; British poet)

BÜCHNER, Georg (1813–37; German dramatist)

BURGESS, Anthony (John Burgess Wilson; 1917– ; British novelist and critic)

BURNETT, Frances Eliza Hodgson (1849–1924; British novelist)

CAEDMON (d. c. 680 AD; English poet)

CAO CHAN (or Zao Zhan; ?1715–63; Chinese novelist)

CAROSSA, Hans (1878–1956; German novelist)

CARROLL, Lewis (Charles Lutwidge Dodgson; 1832–98; British writer)

CHAPMAN, George (c. 1560–1634; British poet and dramatist)

CHAUCER, Geoffrey (c. 1342–1400; English poet)

CHEKHOV, Anton Pavlovich (1860–1904; Russian dramatist and short-story writer)

CHÉNIER, André de (1762–94; French poet, born in Istanbul)

7—continued

CHU YUAN (c. 343 BC–c. 289 BC; Chinese poet)

CLAUDEL, Paul (1868–1955; French dramatist and poet)

CLELAND, John (1709–89; English novelist)

COCTEAU, Jean (1889–1963; French poet and artist)

COLETTE (Sidonie-Gabrielle C, 1873–1954; French novelist)

COLLINS, William (1721–59; British poet)

COLLINS, William Wilkie (1824–89; British novelist)

CORELLI, Marie (1854–1924; British novelist)

CRASHAW, Richard (c. 1613–49; British poet)

CREELEY, Robert (1926– ; US poet)

DA PONTE, Lorenzo (1749–1838; Italian author)

DELEDDA, Grazia (1871–1936; Italian novelist)

DICKENS, Charles (1812–70; British novelist)

DINESEN, Isak (Karen Blixen, Baroness Blixen-Finecke, 1885–1962; Danish author)

DOUGLAS, Gavin (?1474–1522; Scottish poet)

DOUGLAS, Norman (1868–1952; British novelist)

DRABBLE, Margaret (1939– ; British novelist)

DRAYTON, Michael (1563–1631; English poet)

DREISER, Theodore (1871–1945; US novelist)

DUHAMEL, Georges (1884–1966; French novelist)

DUNSANY, Edward John Moreton Drax Plunkett, 18th Baron (1878–1957; Irish author)

DURRELL, Lawrence George (1912– ; British novelist and poet, born in India)

EMERSON, Ralph Waldo (1803–82; US essayist and poet)

ERCILLA, Alonso de (1533–94; Spanish poet)

EUPOLIS (late 5th century BC; Greek dramatist)

FERRIER, Susan Edmonstone (1782–1854; Scottish novelist)

FEYDEAU, Georges (1862–1921; French playwright)

FIRBANK, Ronald (1886–1926; British novelist)

FLECKER, James Elroy (1884–1915; British poet)

FLEMING, Ian (1908–64; British author)

FLEMING, Paul (1609–40; German poet)

FONTANE, Theodor (1819–98; German novelist)

FORSTER, E M (1879–1970; British novelist)

FOSCOLO, Ugo (1778–1827; Italian poet)

FRENEAU, Philip (1752–1832; US poet)

FRÖDING, Gustaf (1860–1911; Swedish lyric poet)

GASKELL, Elizabeth Cleghorn (1810–65; British novelist)

7—continued

GAUTIER, Théophile (1811–72; French poet)

GILBERT, Sir William Schwenk (1836–1911; British comic dramatist)

GISSING, George Robert (1857–1903; British novelist)

GOLDING, William (1911–   ; British novelist)

GOLDONI, Carlo (1707–93; Italian comic playwright)

GRAHAME, Kenneth (1859–1932; British children's writer)

GUARINI, Giovanni Battista (1538–1612; Italian poet)

HAGGARD, Sir H Rider (1856–1925; British novelist)

HAMMETT, Dashiell (1894–1961; US novelist)

HARTLEY, L P (1895–1972; British novelist)

HELLMAN, Lillian (1905–84; US dramatist)

HERBERT, George (1593–1633; English poet)

HERRICK, Robert (1591–1674; English poet)

HEYWOOD, Thomas (c. 1574–1641; English dramatist)

HOLBERG, Ludvig, Baron (1684–1754; Danish playwright and poet)

HOPKINS, Gerard Manley (1844–89; British poet)

HOUSMAN, A E (1859–1936; British poet and scholar)

IBN EZRA, Abraham Ben Meir (1093–1167; Hebrew poet and scholar)

IONESCO, Eugène (1912–   ; French dramatist)

JEFFERS, Robinson (1887–1962; US poet)

JIMÉNEZ, Juan Ramón (1881–1958; Spanish poet)

JUVENAL (Decimus Junius Juvenalis, c. 60– c. 130 AD; Roman satirist)

KÄSTNER, Erich (1899–1974; German novelist and poet)

KAUFMAN, George S (1889–1961; US dramatist)

KENDALL, Henry (1841–82; Australian poet)

KEROUAC, Jack (1922–69; US novelist)

KIPLING, Rudyard (1865–1936; British writer and poet)

KLINGER, Friedrich Maximilian von (1752–1831; German dramatist)

LABICHE, Eugène (1815–88; French dramatist)

LARDNER, Ring (1885–1933; US short-story writer)

LAXNESS, Halldór (1902–   ; Icelandic novelist and essayist)

LAYAMON (early 13th century; English poet)

LEACOCK, Stephen (1869–1944; English-born Canadian humorist)

LE CARRÉ, John (David Cornwell, 1931–   ; British novelist)

LESSING, Doris (1919–   ; British novelist)

LESSING, Gotthold Ephraim (1729–81; German dramatist and writer)

7—continued

LINDSAY, Vachel (1879–1931; US poet)

LYDGATE, John (c. 1370–c. 1450; English poet)

MACHAUT, Guillaume de (c. 1300–77; French poet)

MALAMUD, Bernard (1914–86; US novelist)

MALRAUX, André (1901–76; French novelist and essayist)

MANZONI, Alessandro (1785–1873; Italian poet and novelist)

MARLOWE, Christopher (1564–93; English dramatist and poet)

MARRYAT, Captain Frederick (1792–1848; British novelist)

MARSTON, John (1576–1634; English dramatist)

MARTIAL (Marcus Valerius Martialis, c. 40– c. 104 AD; Roman poet)

MARVELL, Andrew (1621–78; English poet)

MASTERS, Edgar Lee (1868–1950; US poet)

MAUGHAM, W Somerset (1874–1965; British novelist and dramatist)

MAURIAC, François (1885–1970; French novelist)

MAUROIS, André (Émile Herzog; 1885–1967; French biographer, novelist, and critic)

MÉRIMÉE, Prosper (1803–70; French novelist)

MISHIMA, Yukio (Kimitake Hiraoka; 1925–70; Japanese novelist and playwright)

MISTRAL, Frédéric (1830–1914; French poet)

MISTRAL, Gabriela (Lucila Godoy Alcayaga, 1889–1957; Chilean poet)

MOLIÈRE (Jean-Baptiste Poquelin, 1622–73; French dramatist)

MONTAGU, Lady Mary Wortley (1689–1762; English writer)

MONTALE, Eugenio (1896–1981; Italian poet)

MORAVIA, Alberto (Alberto Pincherle, 1907–   ; Italian novelist)

MURDOCH, Dame Iris (1919–   ; British novelist)

NABOKOV, Vladimir (1899–1977; US novelist)

NAEVIUS, Gnaeus (c. 270–c. 200 BC; Roman poet)

NAIPAUL, V S (1932–   ; West Indian novelist)

NOVALIS (Friedrich Leopold, Freiherr von Hardenberg; 1772–1801; German poet and writer)

O'CONNOR, Frank (Michael O'Donovan; 1903–66; Irish short-story writer)

OSBORNE, John (1929–   ; British dramatist)

PATMORE, Coventry (1823–96; British poet)

PEACOCK, Thomas Love (1785–1866; British satirical novelist)

PLAUTUS, Titus Maccius (c. 254–184 BC; Roman dramatist)

PRÉVERT, Jacques (1900–77; French poet)

PUSHKIN, Aleksandr (1799–1837; Russian poet, novelist, and dramatist)

PYNCHON, Thomas (1937–   ; US novelist)

7—continued

QUENEAU, Raymond (1903–79; French novelist and poet)

RANSOME, Arthur Mitchell (1884–1967; British journalist and children's writer)

REGNIER, Henri François Joseph de (1864–1936; French poet)

RICHLER, Mordecai (1931– ; Canadian novelist)

RIMBAUD, Arthur (1854–91; French poet)

ROLLAND, Romain (1866–1944; French novelist, dramatist, and essayist)

ROMAINS, Jules (Louis Farigoule; 1885–1972; French poet, novelist, and dramatist)

RONSARD, Pierre de (1524–85; French poet)

ROSTAND, Edmond (1868–1918; French dramatist)

ROUSSEL, Raymond (1877–1933; French writer and dramatist)

SAROYAN, William (1908–81; US dramatist and fiction writer)

SASSOON, Siegfried (1886–1967; British poet and writer)

SCARRON, Paul (1610–60; French poet, dramatist, and satirist)

SEFERIS, George (Georgios Seferiadis, 1900–71; Greek poet)

SHAFFER, Peter (1926– ; British dramatist)

SHELLEY, Percy Bysshe (1792–1822; British poet)

SIMENON, Georges (1903– ; Belgian novelist)

SIMONOV, Konstantin (1915–79; Soviet novelist, playwright, poet, and journalist)

SITWELL, Edith (1887–1964; British poet and writer)

SKELTON, John (c. 1460–1529; English poet)

SOUTHEY, Robert (1774–1843; British poet and writer)

SOYINKA, Wole (1934– ; Nigerian dramatist and poet)

SPENDER, Stephen (1909– ; British poet and critic)

SPENSER, Edmund (c. 1552–99; English poet)

STEVENS, Wallace (1879–1955; US poet)

SURTEES, Robert Smith (1803–64; British novelist)

TERENCE (Publius Terentius Afer, c. 185–c. 159 BC; Roman dramatist)

THESPIS (6th century BC; Greek poet)

THOMSON, James (1700–48; British poet)

THURBER, James (1894–1961; US humorous writer and cartoonist)

TOLKIEN, J R R (1892–1973; British scholar and writer)

TOLSTOY, Leo, Count (1828–1910; Russian writer)

TRAVERS, Ben (1886–1980; British dramatist)

TUTUOLA, Amos (1920– ; Nigerian writer)

VAUGHAN, Henry (c. 1622–95; English poet)

7—continued

VICENTE, Gil (c. 1465–1536; Portuguese dramatist)

WALLACE, Edgar (1875–1932; British novelist)

WALPOLE, Sir Hugh (1884–1941; British novelist)

WEBSTER, John (c. 1580–c. 1625; English dramatist)

WHARTON, Edith (1862–1937; US novelist)

WHITMAN, Walt (1819–92; US poet)

WIELAND, Christoph Martin (1733–1813; German novelist and poet)

YESENIN, Sergei Aleksandrovich (1895–1925; Russian poet)

8

ABU NUWAS (c. 762–c. 813 AD; Arab poet)

ANACREON (6th century BC; Greek lyric poet)

ANCHIETA, José de (1534–97; Portuguese poet)

ANDERSEN, Hans Christian (1805–75; Danish author)

ANDERSON, Sherwood (1876–1941; US author)

APULEIUS, Lucius (2nd century AD; Roman writer and rhetorician)

ASTURIAS, Miguel Ángel (1899–1974; Guatemalan novelist and poet)

BANDEIRA, Manuel Carneiró de Sousa (1886–1968; Brazilian poet)

BANVILLE, Théodore Faullain de (1823–89; French poet)

BARBUSSE, Henri (1873–1935; French novelist)

BEAUMONT, Francis (1584–1616; British dramatist)

BEAUVOIR, Simone de (1908–86; French novelist and essayist)

BECKFORD, William (?1760–1844; British writer)

BEERBOHM, Sir Max (1872–1956; British caricaturist and writer)

BELINSKY, Vissarion (1811–48; Russian literary critic)

BENCHLEY, Robert Charles (1889–1945; US humorist)

BERANGER, Pierre Jean de (1780–1857; French poet and songwriter)

BERNANOS, Georges (1888–1948; French novelist)

BETJEMAN, Sir John (1906–84; British poet)

BJØRNSON, Bjørnstjerne (1832–1910; Norwegian novelist, poet, and playwright)

BRADBURY, Ray (1920– ; US science-fiction writer)

BRENTANO, Clemens (1778–1842; German writer)

BROWNING, Robert (1812–89; British poet)

CAMPBELL, Roy (1901–57; South African poet)

8—continued

CAMPBELL, Thomas (1777–1844; British poet)

CARDUCCI, Giosuè (1835–1907; Italian poet and critic)

CASTILHO, Antonio Feliciano de (1800–75; Portuguese poet)

CATULLUS, Valerius (*c.* 84–*c.* 54 BC; Roman poet)

CHANDLER, Raymond (1888–1959; US novelist)

CHARTIER, Alain (*c.* 1385–*c.* 1440; French poet and prose writer)

CHRISTIE, Dame Agatha (1891–1976; British author of detective fiction and playwright)

CLAUDIAN (*c.* 370–404 AD; Roman poet)

CONGREVE, William (1670–1729; British dramatist)

CONSTANT, Benjamin (1767–1830; French novelist)

CROMPTON, Richmal (Richmal Crompton Lamburn, 1890–1969; British children's author)

CUMMINGS, e e (1894–1962; US poet)

CYNEWULF (early 9th century AD; Anglo-Saxon religious poet)

DAVENANT, Sir William (1606–68; English dramatist and poet)

DAY LEWIS, C (1904–72; British poet and critic)

DE LA MARE, Walter (1873–1956; British poet, novelist, and anthologist)

DONLEAVY, J P (1926–   ; Irish-American novelist)

ETHEREGE, Sir George (*c.* 1635–*c.* 1692; English dramatist)

FARQUHAR, George (1678–1707; Irish dramatist)

FAULKNER, William (1897–1962; US novelist)

FIELDING, Henry (1707–54; British novelist and dramatist)

FIRDAUSI (Abul Qasim Mansur; *c.* 935–*c.* 1020; Persian poet)

FLAUBERT, Gustave (1821–80; French novelist)

FLETCHER, John (1579–1625; English dramatist)

FORESTER, C S (1899–1966; British novelist)

GINSBERG, Allen (1926–   ; US poet)

GONCOURT, Edmond de (1822–96; French writer)

HENRYSON, Robert (15th century; Scottish poet)

HOCHHUTH, Rolf (1933–   ; Swiss dramatist)

HUYSMANS, Joris Karl (1848–1907; French novelist)

JEAN PAUL (Johann Paul Friedrich Richter, 1763–1825; German novelist)

KALIDASA (5th century AD; Indian poet)

KINGSLEY, Charles (1819–79; British writer)

KOESTLER, Arthur (1905–83; British writer)

8—continued

KOTZEBUE, August von (1761–1819; German dramatist and novelist)

LAFORGUE, Jules (1860–87; French poet)

LAGERLÖF, Selma Ottiliana Lovisa (1858–1940; Swedish novelist)

LANGLAND, William (*c.* 1330–*c.* 1400; English poet)

LAS CASES, Emmanuel, Comte de (1776–1842; French writer)

LAWRENCE, D H (1885–1930; British novelist, poet, and painter)

LEOPARDI, Giacomo (1798–1837; Italian poet)

LOCKHART, John Gibson (1794–1854; Scottish biographer and journalist)

LONGINUS (1st century AD; Greek rhetorician)

LOVELACE, Richard (1618–57; English Cavalier poet)

MACAULAY, Dame Rose (1881–1958; British novelist)

MACLEISH, Archibald (1892–1982; US poet)

MACNEICE, Louis (1907–63; Irish-born British poet)

MALHERBE, François de (1555–1628; French poet and critic)

MALLARMÉ, Stéphane (1842–98; French poet)

MARIVAUX, Pierre Carlet de Chamblain de (1688–1763; French dramatist)

MARQUAND, J P (1893–1960; US novelist)

MCCARTHY, Mary (1912–   ; US novelist)

MELVILLE, Herman (1819–91; US novelist)

MENANDER (*c.* 341–*c.* 290 BC; Greek dramatist)

MEREDITH, George (1828–1909; British poet and novelist)

MICHELET, Jules (1798–1874; French historian)

MITCHELL, Margaret (1909–49; US novelist)

NEKRASOV, Nikolai Alekseevich (1821–78; Russian poet)

NICOLSON, Sir Harold (1886–1968; British literary critic)

PALGRAVE, Francis Turner (1824–97; British poet and anthologist)

PERELMAN, S J (1904–79; US humorous writer)

PERRAULT, Charles (1628–1703; French poet and fairytale writer)

PETRARCH (Francesco Petrarca, 1304–74; Italian poet)

PHAEDRUS (1st century AD; Roman writer)

PHILEMON (*c.* 368–*c.* 264 BC; Greek dramatist)

PLUTARCH (*c.* 46–*c.* 120 AD; Greek biographer and essayist)

RABELAIS, François (1483–1553; French satirist)

RADIGUET, Raymond (1903–23; French novelist)

8—continued

RATTIGAN, Sir Terence (1911–77; British dramatist)

REMARQUE, Erich Maria (1898–1970; German novelist)

RICHARDS, Frank (Charles Hamilton, 1876–1961; British children's writer)

RUNEBERG, Johan Ludvig (1804–77; Finnish poet)

SALINGER, J D (1919–   ; US novelist)

SANDBURG, Carl (1878–1967; US poet)

SARRAUTE, Nathalie (1902–   ; French novelist, born in Russia)

SCALIGER, Julius Caesar (1484–1558; Italian humanist scholar)

SCHILLER, Friedrich (1759–1805; German dramatist, poet, and writer)

SHADWELL, Thomas (c. 1642–92; British dramatist)

SHERIDAN, Richard Brinsley (1751–1816; Anglo-Irish dramatist)

SILLITOE, Alan (1928–   ; British novelist)

SINCLAIR, Upton (1878–1968; US novelist)

SMOLLETT, Tobias (1721–71; British novelist)

SPILLANE, Mickey (Frank Morrison S, 1918–   ; US detective-story writer)

STENDHAL (Henri Beyle, 1783–1842; French novelist)

STOPPARD, Tom (1937–   ; British dramatist)

SUCKLING, Sir John (1609–42; English poet and dramatist)

SU DONG PO (or Su Tung-p'o, 1036–1101; Chinese poet)

TALIESIN (6th century AD; Welsh poet)

TENNYSON, Alfred, Lord (1809–92; British poet)

THOMPSON, Francis (1859–1907; British poet and critic)

TIBULLUS, Albius (c. 55–c. 19 BC; Roman poet)

TOURNEUR, Cyril (c. 1575–1626; English dramatist)

TRAHERNE, Thomas (c. 1637–74; English poet)

TRILLING, Lionel (1905–75; US literary critic)

TROLLOPE, Anthony (1815–82; British novelist)

TULSIDAS (c. 1532–1623; Indian poet)

TURGENEV, Ivan (1818–83; Russian novelist)

VERLAINE, Paul (1844–96; French poet)

VOLTAIRE (François-Marie Arouet, 1694–1778; French writer)

VONNEGUT, Kurt (1922–   ; US novelist)

WEDEKIND, Frank (1864–1918; German dramatist)

WHITTIER, John Greenleaf (1807–92; US poet)

WILLIAMS, Tennessee (1911–83; US dramatist)

WILLIAMS, William Carlos (1883–1963; US poet)

8—continued

ZAMYATIN, Yevgenii Ivanovich (1884–1937; Russian novelist)

9

AESCHYLUS (c. 525–456 BC; Greek tragic dramatist)

AINSWORTH, W Harrison (1805–82; British historical novelist)

AKHMATOVA, Anna (Anna Andreevna Gorenko, 1889–1966; Russian poet)

ALDINGTON, Richard (1892–1962; British poet, novelist, and biographer)

ALLINGHAM, Margery (1904–66; British detective-story writer)

ARBUTHNOT, John (1667–1735; Scottish writer)

AYCKBOURN, Alan (1939–   ; British dramatist)

BLACKMORE, R D (1825–1900; British historical novelist)

BLACKWOOD, Algernon Henry (1869–1951; British novelist and short-story writer)

BOCCACCIO, Giovanni (1313–75; Italian writer and poet)

BURROUGHS, Edgar Rice (1875–1950; US novelist)

BURROUGHS, William (1914–   ; US novelist)

CERVANTES, Miguel de (1547–1616; Spanish novelist)

CHARTERIS, Leslie (L Charles Bowyer Yin, 1907–   ; British novelist)

CHURCHILL, Charles (1731–64; British poet)

COLERIDGE, Samuel Taylor (1772–1834; British poet)

CORNEILLE, Pierre (1606–84; French dramatist)

D'ANNUNZIO, Gabriele (1863–1938; Italian poet, novelist, and dramatist)

DE LA ROCHE, Mazo (1885–1961; Canadian novelist)

DE QUINCEY, Thomas (1785–1859; British essayist and critic)

DICKINSON, Emily (1830–86; US poet)

DOOLITTLE, Hilda (1886–1961; US poet)

DOS PASSOS, John (1896–1970; US novelist)

DU MAURIER, George (1834–96; British caricaturist and novelist)

ECKERMANN, Johann Peter (1792–1854; German writer)

EDGEWORTH, Maria (1767–1849; Anglo-Irish writer)

EHRENBERG, Iliya Grigorievich (1891–1967; Soviet author)

EURIPIDES (c. 480–406 BC; Greek dramatist)

FROISSART, Jean (1337–c. 1400; French chronicler and poet)

GIRAUDOUX, Jean (1882–1944; French dramatist and novelist)

GOLDSMITH, Oliver (1730–74; Anglo-Irish writer)

9—continued

GONCHAROV, Ivan Aleksandrovich (1812–91; Russian novelist)

GOTTSCHED, Johann Christoph (1700–66; German critic)

GREENWOOD, Walter (1903–   ; British novelist)

HAUPTMANN, Gerhart (1862–1946; German dramatist)

HAWTHORNE, Nathaniel (1804–64; US novelist and short-story writer)

HEMINGWAY, Ernest (1899–1961; US novelist)

HIGHSMITH, Patricia (1921–   ; US author of crime fiction)

HÖLDERLIN, Friedrich (1770–1843; German poet)

ISHERWOOD, Christopher (1904–86; British novelist)

JEFFERIES, Richard (1848–87; British novelist and naturalist)

KLOPSTOCK, Friedrich Gottlieb (1724–1803; German poet)

LA BRUYÈRE, Jean de (1645–96; French satirist)

LA FAYETTE, Mme de (Marie Madeleine, Comtesse de L F, 1634–93; French novelist)

LAMARTINE, Alphonse de (1790–1869; French poet)

LAMPEDUSA, Giuseppe Tomasi di (1896–1957; Italian novelist)

LERMONTOV, Mikhail (1814–41; Russian poet and novelist)

LINKLATER, Eric (1889–1974; Scottish novelist)

LLEWELLYN, Richard (R D V L Lloyd, 1907–83; Welsh novelist)

LOMONOSOV, Mikhail Vasilievich (1711–65; Russian poet)

LOVECRAFT, H P (1890–1937; US novelist and short-story writer)

LUCRETIUS (Titus Lucretius Carus, c. 95–c. 55 BC; Roman philosopher and poet)

MACKENZIE, Sir Compton (1883–1972; British novelist)

MALAPARTE, Curzio (Kurt Erich Suckert; 1898–1957; Italian novelist and dramatist)

MANSFIELD, Katherine (Kathleen Mansfield Beauchamp, 1888–1923; New Zealand short-story writer)

MARINETTI, Filippo Tommaso (1876–1944; Italian poet and novelist)

MARTINEAU, Harriet (1802–76; British writer)

MASEFIELD, John (1878–1967; British poet)

MASSINGER, Philip (1583–1640; English dramatist)

MCCULLERS, Carson (1917–67; US novelist and playwright)

MIDDLETON, Thomas (1580–1627; English dramatist)

9—continued

MONSARRAT, Nicholas (John Turney, 1910–79; British novelist)

MONTAIGNE, Michel de (1533–92; French essayist)

MUTANABBI, Abu At-Tayyib Ahmad Ibn Husayn al- (915–65 AD; Arab poet)

O'FLAHERTY, Liam (1897–1984; Irish novelist)

PARKINSON, Northcote (1909–   ; British author)

PASTERNAK, Boris (1890–1960; Russian poet and novelist)

POLIZIANO (or Politian; 1454–94; Italian poet and scholar)

PRITCHETT, V S (1900–   ; British short-story writer and critic)

RADCLIFFE, Ann (1764–1823; British novelist)

ROCHESTER, John Wilmot, 2nd Earl of (1647–80; British poet)

SACKVILLE, Thomas, 1st Earl of Dorset (1536–1608; British poet and dramatist)

SCHREINER, Olive (1855–1920; South African novelist)

SHENSTONE, William (1714–63; British poet)

SHOLOKHOV, Mikhail (1905–   ; Soviet novelist)

SOPHOCLES (c. 496–406 BC; Greek dramatist)

STEINBECK, John (1902–68; US novelist)

STEVENSON, Robert Louis (1850–94; British novelist)

STURLUSON, Snorri (1178–1241; Icelandic poet)

SWINBURNE, Algernon Charles (1837–1909; British poet)

THACKERAY, William Makepeace (1811–63; British novelist)

TSVETAEVA, Marina (1892–1941; Russian poet)

UNGARETTI, Giuseppe (1888–1970; Italian poet)

VERHAEREN, Émile (1844–96; Belgian poet)

VITTORINI, Elio (1908–66; Italian novelist)

WERGELAND, Henrik Arnold (1808–45; Norwegian poet)

WODEHOUSE, Sir P G (1881–1975; US humorous writer)

WYCHERLEY, William (1640–1716; English dramatist)

10

BAUDELAIRE, Charles (1821–67; French poet)

BILDERDIJK, Willem (1756–1831; Dutch poet and dramatist)

CAVALCANTI, Guido (c. 1255–1300; Italian poet)

CHATTERJEE, Bankim Chandra (1838–94; Indian novelist)

CHATTERTON, Thomas (1752–70; British poet)

10—continued

CHESTERTON, G K (1874–1936; British essayist, novelist, and poet)

CONSCIENCE, Hendrik (1812–83; Flemish novelist)

DAZAI OSAMU (Tsushima Shuji; 1909–48; Japanese novelist)

DIO CASSIUS (*c.* 150–235 AD; Roman historian)

DRINKWATER, John (1882–1937; British poet and dramatist)

DÜRRENMATT, Friedrich (1921–   ; Swiss dramatist and novelist)

FITZGERALD, Edward (1809–83; British poet)

FITZGERALD, F Scott (1896–1940; US novelist)

GALSWORTHY, John (1867–1933; British novelist and dramatist)

JEAN DE MEUN (*c.* 1240–*c.* 1305; French poet)

KHLEBNIKOV, Velimir (Victor K, 1885–1922; Russian poet)

LA FONTAINE, Jean de (1621–95; French poet)

LAGERKVIST, Pär (1891–1974; Swedish novelist, poet, and dramatist)

LONGFELLOW, Henry Wadsworth (1807–82; US poet)

MACDIARMID, Hugh (Christopher Murray Grieve, 1892–1978; Scottish poet)

MANDELSTAM, Osip (1891–?1938; Russian poet)

MAUPASSANT, Guy de (1850–93; French short-story writer and novelist)

MCGONAGALL, William (1830–1902; Scottish poet)

MICKIEWICZ, Adam (1798–1855; Polish poet)

OSTROVSKII, Aleksandr Nikolaevich (1823–86; Russian dramatist)

PIRANDELLO, Luigi (1867–1936; Italian dramatist and novelist)

PROPERTIUS, Sextus (*c.* 50–*c.* 16 BC; Roman poet)

RICHARDSON, Henry Handel (Ethel Florence R, 1870–1946; Australian novelist)

RICHARDSON, Samuel (1689–1761; British novelist)

RUTHERFORD, Mark (William Hale White, 1831–1913; British novelist)

SCHNITZLER, Arthur (1862–1931; Austrian Jewish dramatist and novelist)

STRINDBERG, August (1849–1912; Swedish dramatist and writer)

TANNHÄUSER (*c.* 1200–*c.* 1270; German poet)

THEOCRITUS (*c.* 310–250 BC; Greek poet)

VAN DER POST, Sir Laurens (1906–   ; South African novelist)

10—continued

WILLIAMSON, Henry (1895–1977; British novelist)

WORDSWORTH, William (1770–1850; British poet)

XENOPHANES (6th century BC; Greek poet)

11

ANZENGRUBER, Ludwig (1839–89; Austrian dramatist and novelist)

APOLLINAIRE, Guillaume (Wilhelm de Kostrowitzky, 1880–1918; French poet)

ARCHILOCHUS (*c.* 680–*c.* 640 BC; Greek poet)

BACCHYLIDES (*c.* 516–*c.* 450 BC; Greek lyric poet)

BLESSINGTON, Marguerite, Countess of (1789–1849; Irish author)

CALLIMACHUS (*c.* 305–*c.* 240 BC; Greek poet)

CASTIGLIONE, Baldassare (1478–1529; Italian writer)

DOSTOIEVSKI, Fedor Mikhailovich (1821–81; Russian novelist)

EICHENDORFF, Josef, Freiherr von (1788–1857; German writer)

GARCÍA LORCA, Federico (1898–1936; Spanish poet and dramatist)

GRILLPARZER, Franz (1791–1872; Austrian dramatist)

KAZANTZAKIS, Nikos (1885–1957; Greek novelist and poet)

LAUTRÉAMONT, Comte de (Isidore Ducasse, 1846–70; French writer)

MAETERLINCK, Maurice (1862–1949; Belgian poet and dramatist)

MATSUO BASHO (Matsuo Munefusa, 1644–94; Japanese poet)

MAYAKOVSKII, Vladimir (1893–1930; Russian poet)

MONTHERLANT, Henry de (1896–1972; French novelist and dramatist)

'OMAR KHAYYAM (?1048–?1122; Persian poet)

PÉREZ GALDÓS, Benito (1843–1920; Spanish novelist)

SHAKESPEARE, William (1564–1616; English dramatist)

SIENKIEWICZ, Henryk (1846–1916; Polish novelist)

STIERNHIELM, Georg Olofson (1598–1672; Swedish poet)

YEVTUSHENKO, Yevgenii (1933–   ; Soviet poet)

12

ARISTOPHANES (*c.* 450–*c.* 385 BC; Greek comic dramatist)

BEAUMARCHAIS, Pierre-Augustin Caron de (1732–99; French dramatist)

BLASCO IBÁÑEZ, Vicente (1867–1928; Spanish novelist)

12—continued

FERLINGHETTI, Lawrence (1919–   ; US poet)

FEUCHTWANGER, Lion (1884–1958; German novelist and dramatist)

HOFMANNSTHAL, Hugo von (1874–1929; Austrian poet and dramatist)

LÓPEZ DE AYALA, Pero (c. 1332–c. 1407; Spanish poet and chronicler)

MARTIN DU GARD, Roger (1881–1958; French novelist)

MATTHEW PARIS (c. 1200–59; English chronicler)

ROBBE-GRILLET, Alain (1922–   ; French novelist)

SAINT-EXUPÉRY, Antoine de (1900–44; French novelist)

SOLZHENITSYN, Aleksandr (1918–   ; Russian novelist)

VOZNESENSKII, Andrei (1933–   ; Soviet poet)

13

BERTRAN DE BORN (?1140–?1215; French troubadour poet)

CASTELO BRANCO, Camilo (1825–95; Portuguese novelist)

CHATEAUBRIAND, Vicomte de (1768–1848; French writer)

CSOKONAI VITÉZ, Mihaly (1773–1805; Hungarian poet)

HARISHCHANDRA (1850–85; Hindi poet, dramatist, and essayist, also known as Bharatendu)

MARIE DE FRANCE (12th century AD; French poet)

TIRSO DE MOLINA (Gabriel Téllez, c. 1584–1648; Spanish dramatist)

ZEAMI MOTOKIYO (1363–c. 1443; Japanese playwright)

14

BRILLAT-SAVARIN, Anthelme (1755–1826; French writer)

COMPTON-BURNETT, Dame Ivy (1892–1969; British novelist)

DAFYDD AP GWILYM (c. 1320–c. 1380; Welsh poet)

DANTE ALIGHIERI (1265–1321; Italian poet)

DROSTE-HÜLSHOFF, Annette von (1797–1848; German poet and novelist)

GÓNGORA Y ARGOTE, Luis de (1561–1627; Spanish poet)

GRIMMELSHAUSEN, Hans Jacob Christoph von (c. 1625–76; German novelist)

JACOPONE DA TODI (c. 1236–1306; Italian religious poet)

LECONTE DE LISLE, Charles Marie René (1818–94; French poet)

OEHLENSCHLÄGER, Adam (1779–1850; Danish poet and playwright)

PRÉVOST D'EXILES, Antoine François, Abbé (1697–1763; French novelist)

14—continued

SULLY-PRUDHOMME, René François Armand (1839–1907; French poet)

WOLLSTONECRAFT, Mary (1759–97; British writer)

ZORRILLA Y MORAL, José (1817–93; Spanish poet and dramatist)

15

ALARCÓN Y MENDOZA, Juan Ruiz de (1581–1639; Spanish dramatist)

DIODORUS SICULUS (1st century BC; Greek historian)

PLINY THE YOUNGER (Gaius Plinius Caecilius Secundus, c. 61–c. 113 AD; Roman writer)

16

CHRÉTIEN DE TROYES (12th century AD; French poet)

CYRANO DE BERGERAC, Savinien (1619–55; French writer and dramatist)

KAWABATA YASUNARI (1899–1972; Japanese novelist)

PETRONIUS ARBITER (1st century AD; Roman satirist)

17

CALDERÓN DE LA BARCA, Pedro (1600–81; Spanish dramatist)

GUILLAUME DE LORRIS (13th century; French poet and author)

TANIZAKI JUN-ICHIRO (1886–1965; Japanese novelist)

18

APOLLONIUS OF RHODES (3rd century BC; Greek epic poet)

KAKINOMOTO HITOMARO (c. 680–710; Japanese poet)

THOMAS OF ERCELDOUNE (13th century; English poet and prophet)

19

BENOIT DE SAINTE-MAURE (12th century AD; French poet)

CHIKAMATSU MONZAEMON (Sugimori Nobumori; 1653–1724; Japanese dramatist)

VILLIERS DE L'ISLE-ADAM, Philippe Auguste, Comte de (1838–89; French poet, novelist, and dramatist)

20+

BERNARDIN DE SAINT-PIERRE, Jacques Henri (1737–1814; French naturalist and writer)

DIONYSIUS OF HALICARNASSUS (1st century BC; Greek historian)

DRUMMOND OF HAWTHORNDEN, William (1585–1649; Scots poet)

ECHEGARAY Y EIZAGUIRRE, José (1832–1916; Spanish dramatist)

GOTTFRIED VON STRASSBURG (13th century; German poet)

20+—continued
WALTHER VON DER VOGELWEIDE (*c.* 1170–
c. 1230; German poet)

20+—continued
WOLFRAM VON ESCHENBACH (*c.* 1170–
c. 1220; German poet)

MUSICIANS AND COMPOSERS

3
BAX, Sir Arnold Edward Trevor (1883–1953;
British composer)

4
ADAM, Adolphe-Charles (1803–56; French
composer)
ARNE, Thomas Augustine (1710–78; British
composer)
BACH, Johann Sebastian (1685–1750;
German composer and keyboard player)
BERG, Alban (1885–1935; Austrian composer)
BING, Sir Rudolf (1902– ; British opera
administrator)
BLOW, John (1649–1708; English composer)
BÖHM, Karl (1894–1981; Austrian conductor)
BULL, John (*c.* 1562–1628; English composer
and organist)
BUSH, Alan Dudley (1900– ; British
composer)
BUTT, Dame Clara (1873–1936; British
contralto singer)
BYRD, William (?1543–1623; English
composer)
CAGE, John (1912– ; US composer)
HESS, Dame Myra (1890–1965; British pianist)
IVES, Charles (1874–1954; US composer)
LALO, Édouard (1823–92; French composer)
LILL, John (1944– ; British pianist)
LIND, Jenny (1820–87; Swedish soprano)
NONO, Luigi (1924– ; Italian composer)
ORFF, Carl (1895–1982; German composer
and conductor)
WOLF, Hugo (1860–1903; Austrian composer)
WOOD, Sir Henry (1869–1944; British
conductor)

5
ALKAN, Charles Henri Valentin (C H V
Morhange, 1813–88; French pianist and
composer)
ARRAU, Claudio (1903– ; Chilean pianist)
AUBER, Daniel François Esprit (1782–1871;
French composer)
AURIC, Georges (1899– ; French composer)
BAKER, Dame Janet (1933– ; British mezzo-
soprano)
BERIO, Luciano (1925– ; Italian composer)
BIZET, Georges (Alexandre César Léopold B,
1838–75; French composer)
BLISS, Sir Arthur Edward Drummond (1891–
1975; British composer)

5—continued
BLOCH, Ernest (1880–1959; Swiss-born
composer)
BOEHM, Theobald (1794–1881; German
flautist)
BOULT, Sir Adrian (1889–1983; British
conductor)
BOYCE, William (*c.* 1710–79; British
composer)
BREAM, Julian Alexander (1933– ; British
guitarist and lutenist)
BRIAN, Havergal (1876–1972; British
composer)
BRUCH, Max (1838–1920; German composer)
BÜLOW, Hans Guido, Freiherr von (1830–94;
German pianist and conductor)
DAVIS, Sir Colin (1927– ; British conductor)
D'INDY, Vincent (1851–1931; French
composer)
DUFAY, Guillaume (*c.* 1400–74; Burgundian
composer)
DUKAS, Paul (1865–1935; French composer)
DUPRÉ, Marcel (1886–1971; French organist
and composer)
ELGAR, Sir Edward (1857–1934; British
composer)
EVANS, Sir Geraint (1922– ; Welsh baritone)
FALLA, Manuel de (1876–1946; Spanish
composer)
FAURÉ, Gabriel (1845–1924; French
composer and organist)
FIELD, John (1782–1837; Irish pianist and
composer)
FRIML, Rudolph (1879–1972; Czech-born
composer and pianist)
GIGLI, Beniamino (1890–1957; Italian tenor)
GLUCK, Christoph Willibald (1714–87;
German composer)
GOBBI, Tito (1915–84; Italian baritone)
GRIEG, Edvard Hagerup (1843–1907;
Norwegian composer)
GROVE, Sir George (1820–1900; British
musicologist)
HALLÉ, Sir Charles (Karl Hallé, 1819–1895;
German conductor and pianist)
HAYDN, Franz Joseph (1732–1809; Austrian
composer)
HENZE, Hans Werner (1926– ; German
composer)
HOLST, Gustav (1874–1934; British composer
and teacher)

5—continued

IBERT, Jacques (1890–1962; French composer)

LEHÁR, Franz (Ferencz L, 1870–1948; Hungarian composer)

LISZT, Franz (Ferencz L, 1811–86; Hungarian pianist and composer)

LOCKE, Matthew (c. 1622–77; English composer)

LULLY, Jean Baptiste (Giovanni Battista Lulli, 1632–87; French composer)

MELBA, Dame Nellie (Helen Porter Armstrong, 1861–1931; Australian soprano)

MOORE, Gerald (1899–1987; British pianist)

MUNCH, Charles (1892–1968; French conductor)

OGDON, John (1937– ; British pianist)

PARRY, Sir Hubert (1848–1918; British composer)

PATTI, Adelina (Adela Juana Maria, 1843–1919; Italian-born operatic soprano)

PEARS, Sir Peter (1910–86; British tenor)

RAVEL, Maurice (1875–1937; French composer)

REGER, Max (1873–1916; German composer, organist, and teacher)

SATIE, Erik (1866–1925; French composer)

SHARP, Cecil (1859–1924; British musician)

SOLTI, Sir Georg (1912– ; Hungarian-born British conductor)

SOUSA, John Philip (1854–1933; US composer and bandmaster)

SPOHR, Louis (Ludwig S, 1784–1859; German violinist and composer)

STERN, Isaac (1920– ; Russian-born US violinist)

SZELL, George (1897–1970; Hungarian conductor)

TEYTE, Dame Maggie (1888–1976; British soprano)

VERDI, Giuseppe (1813–1901; Italian composer)

WEBER, Carl Maria von (1786–1826; German composer)

WEILL, Kurt (1900–50; German composer)

WIDOR, Charles Marie (1844–1937; French organist and composer)

6

ARNOLD, Malcolm (1921– ; British composer)

BARBER, Samuel (1910–81; US composer)

BARTÓK, Béla (1881–1945; Hungarian composer)

BISHOP, Sir Henry Rowley (1786–1855; British composer and conductor)

BOULEZ, Pierre (1925– ; French composer and conductor)

BRAHMS, Johannes (1833–97; German composer)

BRIDGE, Frank (1879–1941; British composer)

6—continued

BURNEY, Charles (1726–1814; British musicologist, organist, and composer)

BUSONI, Ferruccio (1866–1924; Italian virtuoso pianist and composer)

CALLAS, Maria (Maria Anna Kalageropoulos, 1923–77; US-born soprano)

CARTER, Elliott (1908– ; US composer)

CARUSO, Enrico (1873–1921; Italian tenor)

CASALS, Pablo (Pau C, 1876–1973; Spanish cellist, conductor, and composer)

CHOPIN, Frédéric (François, 1810–49; Polish composer)

CLARKE, Jeremiah (?1673–1707; English composer and organist)

CORTOT, Alfred (1877–1962; French pianist and conductor)

COWELL, Henry (1897–1965; US composer)

CURWEN, John (1816–80; British teacher who perfected the Tonic Sol-fa system)

CURZON, Sir Clifford (1907–82; British pianist)

DAVIES, Sir Peter Maxwell (1934– ; British composer)

DELIUS, Frederick (1862–1934; British composer)

DIBDIN, Charles (1745–1814; British composer, actor, and singer)

DUPARC, Henri (Marie Eugène Henri Foucques D, 1848–1933; French composer)

DVOŘÁK, Antonín (1841–1904; Czech composer)

ENESCO, Georges (G Enescu, 1881–1955; Romanian violinist and composer)

FLOTOW, Friedrich von (1812–83; German composer)

FRANCK, César Auguste (1822–90; Belgian composer, organist, and teacher)

GALWAY, James (1939– ; Irish flautist)

GLINKA, Mikhail Ivanovich (1804–57; Russian composer)

GOUNOD, Charles François (1818–93; French composer)

GRÉTRY, André Ernest Modeste (1741–1813; Belgian composer)

GROVES, Sir Charles (1915– ; British conductor)

HALÉVY, Jacques François (Fromental Elias Levy, 1799–1862; French composer)

HANDEL, George Frederick (1685–1759; German composer)

HARRIS, Roy (1898–1979; US composer)

HOTTER, Hans (1909– ; German baritone)

HUMMEL, Johann Nepomuk (1778–1837; Hungarian pianist and composer)

JOCHUM, Eugen (1902– ; German conductor)

KODÁLY, Zoltan (1882–1967; Hungarian composer)

KRENEK, Ernst (1900– ; Austrian composer)

6—continued

LASSUS, Roland de (c. 1532–94; Flemish composer)

LIGETI, György (1923–   ; Hungarian composer)

MAAZEL, Lorin (1930–   ; US conductor)

MAHLER, Gustav (1860–1911; Austrian composer and conductor)

MORLEY, Thomas (1557–1603; English composer, music printer, and organist)

MOZART, Wolfgang Amadeus (1756–91; Austrian composer)

PREVIN, André (Andreas Ludwig Priwin, 1929–   ; German-born conductor, pianist, and composer)

RAMEAU, Jean Philippe (1683–1764; French composer)

RUBBRA, Edmund (1901–86; British composer)

SCHÜTZ, Heinrich (1585–1672; German composer)

TALLIS, Thomas (c. 1505–85; English composer)

VARÈSE, Edgard (1883–1965; French composer)

WAGNER, Richard (1813–83; German composer)

WALTER, Bruno (B W Schlesinger, 1876–1962; German conductor)

WALTON, Sir William (1902–83; British composer)

WEBERN, Anton von (1883–1945; Austrian composer)

7

ALBÉNIZ, Isaac Manuel Francisco (1860–1909; Spanish composer and pianist)

ALLEGRI, Gregorio (1582–1652; Italian composer)

ANTHEIL, George (1900–59; US composer)

BABBITT, Milton (1916–   ; US composer)

BEECHAM, Sir Thomas (1879–1961; British conductor)

BELLINI, Vincenzo (1801–35; Italian opera composer)

BENNETT, Richard Rodney (1936–   ; British composer)

BENNETT, Sir William Sterndale (1816–75; British pianist)

BERLIOZ, Hector (1803–69; French composer and conductor)

BORODIN, Aleksandr Porfirevich (1833–87; Russian composer)

BRENDEL, Alfred (1931–   ; Austrian pianist)

BRITTEN, Benjamin, Baron (1913–76; British composer and pianist)

CABALLÉ, Montserrat (1933–   ; Spanish soprano)

CACCINI, Giulio (c. 1545–c. 1618; Italian singer and composer)

CAMPION, Thomas (or Campian, 1567–1620; English composer)

7—continued

CAVALLI, Francesco (1602–76; Italian composer)

COPLAND, Aaron (1900–   ; US composer)

CORELLI, Arcangelo (1653–1713; Italian violinist and composer)

DEBUSSY, Claude (1862–1918; French composer)

DELIBES, Leo (1836–91; French composer)

DOMINGO, Placido (1941–   ; Spanish tenor)

DOWLAND, John (1563–1626; English composer and lutenist)

FARNABY, Giles (c. 1565–1640; English composer)

FERRIER, Kathleen (1912–53; British contralto)

GALUPPI, Baldassare (1706–85; Venetian composer)

GIBBONS, Orlando (1583–1625; English composer, organist, and virginalist)

GIULINI, Carlo Maria (1914–   ; Italian conductor)

HAMMOND, Dame Joan (1912–   ; British soprano)

HOFMANN, Joseph Casimir (1876–1957; Polish-born pianist)

IRELAND, John Nicholson (1879–1962; British composer)

JANÁČEK, Leoš (1854–1928; Czech composer)

JOACHIM, Joseph (1831–1907; Hungarian violinist and composer)

KARAJAN, Herbert von (1908–   ; Austrian conductor)

KUBELIK, Rafael (1914–   ; Czech conductor)

LAMBERT, Constant (1905–51; British composer and conductor)

LEHMANN, Lilli (1848–1929; German soprano)

LEHMANN, Lotte (1885–1976; German soprano)

MALCOLM, George John (1917–   ; British harpsichordist)

MARTINŮ, Bohuslav (1890–1959; Czech composer)

MENOTTI, Gian Carlo (1911–   ; Italian-born US composer)

MENUHIN, Sir Yehudi (1916–   ; British violinist)

MILHAUD, Darius (1892–1974; French composer)

MONTEUX, Pierre (1875–1964; French conductor)

NICOLAI, Otto Ehrenfried (1810–49; German conductor and composer)

NIELSEN, Carl (1865–1931; Danish composer and conductor)

NIKISCH, Arthur (1855–1922; Hungarian conductor)

NILSSON, Birgit Marta (1918–   ; Swedish soprano)

7—continued

OKEGHEM, Jean d' (*c.* 1425–*c.* 1495; Flemish composer)

ORMANDY, Eugene (E Blau, 1899–1985; Hungarian-born US conductor)

PÉROTIN (Latin name: Perotinus Magnus, *c.* 1155–*c.* 1202; French composer)

POULENC, Francis (1899–1963; French composer)

PUCCINI, Giacomo (1858–1924; Italian opera composer)

PURCELL, Henry (1659–95; English composer and organist)

RICHTER, Hans (1843–1916; Hungarian conductor)

RICHTER, Sviatoslav (1914–   ; Soviet pianist)

RODRIGO, Joaquín (1902–   ; Spanish composer)

ROSSINI, Gioacchino Antonio (1792–1868; Italian composer)

ROUSSEL, Albert (1869–1937; French composer)

RUGGLES, Carl (1876–1971; US composer)

SALIERI, Antonio (1750–1825; Italian composer and conductor)

SARGENT, Sir Malcolm (1895–1967; British conductor)

SCHUMAN, William (1910–   ; US composer)

SMETANA, Bedřich (1824–84; Bohemian composer)

SOLOMON (S Cutner, 1902–   ; British pianist)

STAINER, Sir John (1840–1901; British composer and organist)

STAMITZ, Johann (Jan Stamic, 1717–57; Bohemian composer)

STRAUSS, Richard (1864–1949; German composer and conductor)

THIBAUD, Jacques (1880–1953; French violinist)

THOMSON, Virgil (1896–   ; US composer and conductor)

TIPPETT, Sir Michael (1905–   ; British composer)

VIVALDI, Antonio (1678–1741; Italian composer and violinist)

WARLOCK, Peter (Philip Heseltine, 1894–1930; British composer and music scholar)

WEELKES, Thomas (*c.* 1575–1623; English composer and organist)

WELLESZ, Egon (1885–1974; Austrian composer)

XENAKIS, Yannis (1922–   ; Greek composer)

8

ALBINONI, Tomaso (1671–1750; Italian composer)

ANSERMET, Ernest (1883–1969; Swiss conductor)

BERKELEY, Sir Lennox Randal Francis (1903–   ; British composer)

8—continued

BRUCKNER, Anton (1824–96; Austrian composer and organist)

CHABRIER, Emmanuel (1841–94; French composer)

CHAUSSON, Ernest (1855–99; French composer)

CIMAROSA, Domenico (1749–1801; Italian composer)

CLEMENTI, Muzio (1752–1832; Italian pianist and composer)

COUPERIN, François (1668–1733; French composer)

DOHNÁNYI, Ernö (Ernst von D, 1877–1960; Hungarian composer and pianist)

FLAGSTAD, Kirsten Malfrid (1895–1962; Norwegian soprano)

GERSHWIN, George (Jacob Gershvin, 1898–1937; US composer)

GESUALDO, Carlo, Prince of Venosa (*c.* 1560–1631; Italian composer)

GLAZUNOV, Aleksandr Konstantinovich (1865–1936; Russian composer)

GOOSSENS, Sir Eugene (1893–1962; British conductor and composer)

GRAINGER, Percy Aldridge (1882–1961; Australian composer and pianist)

GRANADOS, Enrique (1867–1916; Spanish composer and pianist)

HONEGGER, Arthur (1892–1955; French composer)

HOROWITZ, Vladimir (1904–   ; Russian pianist)

KREISLER, Fritz (1875–1962; Austrian violinist)

MACONCHY, Elizabeth (1907–   ; British composer)

MARENZIO, Luca (1553–99; Italian composer)

MASCAGNI, Pietro (1863–1945; Italian composer)

MASSENET, Jules (1842–1912; French composer)

MELCHIOR, Lauritz (1890–1973; Danish tenor)

MESSAGER, André (1853–1929; French composer and conductor)

MESSIAEN, Olivier (1908–   ; French composer, organist, and teacher)

MILSTEIN, Nathan (1904–   ; US violinist)

MUSGRAVE, Thea (1928–   ; Scottish composer)

OISTRAKH, David (1908–75; Russian violinist)

PAGANINI, Niccolò (1782–1840; Italian violinist)

PHILIDOR, André Danican (d. 1730; French musician)

RESPIGHI, Ottorino (1879–1936; Italian composer)

SCHNABEL, Artur (1882–1951; Austrian pianist)

8—continued

SCHUBERT, Franz (1797–1828; Austrian composer)

SCHUMANN, Elisabeth (1885–1952; German-born soprano)

SCHUMANN, Robert (1810–56; German composer)

SCRIABIN, Alexander (1872–1915; Russian composer and pianist)

SESSIONS, Roger (1896–1985; US composer)

SIBELIUS, Jean (Johan Julius Christian S, 1865–1957; Finnish composer)

STANFORD, Sir Charles (1852–1924; Irish composer)

SULLIVAN, Sir Arthur (1842–1900; British composer)

TAVERNER, John (c. 1495–1545; English composer)

TE KANAWA, Dame Kiri (1944– ; New Zealand soprano)

TELEMANN, Georg Philipp (1681–1767; German composer)

VICTORIA, Tomás Luis de (c. 1548–1611; Spanish composer)

WILLIAMS, John (1941– ; Australian guitarist)

ZABALETA, Nicanor (1907– ; Spanish harpist)

9

ADDINSELL, Richard (1904–77; British composer)

ASHKENAZY, Vladimir (1937– ; Russian pianist and conductor)

BALAKIREV, Mili Alekseevich (1837–1910; Russian composer)

BARENBOIM, Daniel (1942– ; Israeli pianist and composer)

BEETHOVEN, Ludwig van (1770–1827; German composer)

BERNSTEIN, Leonard (1918– ; US conductor, composer, and pianist)

BOULANGER, Nadia (1887–1979; French composer, teacher, and conductor)

BUXTEHUDE, Dietrich (1637–1707; Danish organist and composer)

CHALIAPIN, Feodor Ivanovich (1873–1938; Russian bass)

CHERUBINI, Maria Luigi (1760–1842; Italian composer)

CHRISTOFF, Boris (1919– ; Bulgarian singer)

DOLMETSCH, Arnold (1858–1940; British musician and instrument maker)

DONIZETTI, Gaetano (1797–1848; Italian composer)

DUNSTABLE, John (d. 1453; English composer)

HINDEMITH, Paul (1895–1963; German composer and viola player)

HODDINOTT, Alun (1929– ; Welsh composer)

9—continued

KLEMPERER, Otto (1885–1973; German conductor)

LANDOWSKA, Wanda (1877–1959; Polish-born harpsichordist)

MACKERRAS, Sir Charles (1925– ; US-born Australian conductor)

MALIPIERO, Gian Francesco (1882–1973; Italian composer and teacher)

MEYERBEER, Giacomo (Jacob Liebmann Beer, 1791–1864; German composer and pianist)

OFFENBACH, Jacques (J Eberst, 1819–80; French composer)

PAVAROTTI, Luciano (1935– ; Italian tenor)

PERGOLESI, Giovanni (1710–36; Italian composer)

SCARLATTI, Domenico (1685–1757; Italian composer, harpsichordist, and organist)

STOKOWSKI, Leopold (1882–1977; British-born conductor)

TORTELIER, Paul (1914– ; French cellist)

TOSCANINI, Arturo (1867–1957; Italian conductor)

10

BARBIROLLI, Sir John (1899–1970; British conductor)

BIRTWISTLE, Harrison (1934– ; British composer)

BOCCHERINI, Luigi (1743–1805; Italian violoncellist and composer)

GALLI-CURCI, Amelita (1882–1963; Italian soprano)

LOS ANGELES, Victoria de (1923– ; Spanish soprano)

MENGELBERG, William (1871–1951; Dutch conductor)

MONTEVERDI, Claudio (1567–1643; Italian composer)

MUSSORGSKI, Modest Petrovich (1839–81; Russian composer)

PADEREWSKI, Ignacy (1860–1941; Polish pianist and composer)

PALESTRINA, Giovanni Pierluigi da (?1525–94; Italian composer)

PENDERECKI, Krzysztof (1933– ; Polish composer)

PRAETORIUS, Michael (M Schultheiss, 1571–1621; German composer)

RAWSTHORNE, Alan (1905–71; British composer)

RUBINSTEIN, Anton (1829–94; Russian pianist and composer)

RUBINSTEIN, Artur (1888–1982; Polish-born pianist)

SAINT-SAËNS, Camille (1835–1921; French composer, conductor, pianist, and organist)

SCHOENBERG, Arnold (1874–1951; Austrian-born composer)

SKALKOTTAS, Nikos (1904–49; Greek composer)

10—continued

STRADIVARI, Antonio (?1644–1737; Italian violin maker)

STRAVINSKY, Igor (1882–1971; Russian-born composer)

SUTHERLAND, Dame Joan (1926– ; Australian soprano)

TETRAZZINI, Luisa (1871–1940; Italian soprano)

VILLA-LOBOS, Heitor (1887–1959; Brazilian composer)

11

CHARPENTIER, Gustave (1860–1956; French composer)

FURTWÄNGLER, Wilhelm (1886–1954; German conductor)

HUMPERDINCK, Engelbert (1854–1921; German composer)

LEONCAVALLO, Ruggiero (1858–1919; Italian composer)

LESCHETIZKY, Theodor (1830–1915; Polish pianist and piano teacher)

LUTOSLAWSKI, Witold (1913– ; Polish composer)

MENDELSSOHN, Felix (Jacob Ludwig Felix Mendelssohn-Bartholdy, 1809–47; German composer)

RACHMANINOV, Sergei (1873–1943; Russian composer, pianist, and conductor)

SCHWARZKOPF, Elisabeth (1915– ; German soprano)

STOCKHAUSEN, Karlheinz (1928– ; German composer)

SZYMANOWSKI, Karol (1882–1937; Polish composer)

11—continued

TCHAIKOVSKY, Peter Ilich (1840–93; Russian composer)

WOLF-FERRARI, Ermanno (1876–1948; Italian composer)

12

DALLAPICCOLA, Luigi (1904–1975; Italian composer and pianist)

GUIDO D'AREZZO (c. 990–c. 1050; Italian monk and musical theorist)

KHACHATURIAN, Aram Ilich (1903–78; Soviet composer)

KOUSSEVITSKY, Sergei (1874–1951; Russian composer)

13

ROUGET DE L'ISLE, Claude Joseph (1760–1836; French composer)

14

FISCHER-DIESKAU, Dietrich (1925– ; German baritone)

JAQUES-DALCROZE, Émile (1865–1950; Swiss composer)

JOSQUIN DES PREZ (c. 1450–1521; Flemish composer)

RIMSKY-KORSAKOV, Nikolai (1844–1908; Russian composer)

15

COLERIDGE-TAYLOR, Samuel (1875–1912; British composer)

VAUGHAN WILLIAMS, Ralph (1872–1958; British composer)

17

STRAUSS THE YOUNGER, Johann (1825–99; Austrian violinist, conductor, and composer)

POPULAR MUSICIANS

2
U2

3
ABC
ANT, Adam
DAY, Doris
ENO, Brian
JAM, The
LEE, Brenda
MUD
O.M.D. (Orchestral Manoeuvres in the Dark)
ONO, Yoko
RAY, Johnny
REA, Chris
UFO
VEE, Bobby
WAR

3—continued
WHO, The
YES

4
10CC
ABBA
AC/DC
ANKA, Paul
BAEZ, Joan
BAND, The
BART, Lionel
BECK, Jeff
BLUE, Barry
BROS
BUSH, Kate
BYRD, Charlie
CARS, The
CASH, Johnny
CHER

4—continued
CHIC
COLE, Nat 'King'
COMO, Perry
CURE, The
DION
DURY, Ian
EDDY, Duane
FAME, Georgie
FORD, Tennessee Ernie
FREE
FURY, Billy
GAYE, Marvin
GETZ, Stan
IDOL, Billy
JOEL, Billy
JOHN, Elton
KALE, J J

4—continued
KERN, Jerome
KIDD, Johnny
KING, B B
KING, Carole
KING, Jonathon
KISS
KITT, Eartha
LOWE, Nick
LULU
LYNN, Vera
MANN, Barry
MAZE
MONK, Thelonius
MOST, Mickie
MOVE, The
NICE, The
PAUL, Billy
PIAF, Edith

4—continued
REED, Lou
RICH, Charlie
ROSS, Diana
RUSH
SADE
SHAW, Artie
SHAW, Sandie
STYX
T REX
UB40
WHAM!
WOLF, Howlin'
WOOD, Roy
WRAY, Link

5
ADLER, Larry
ADLER, Lou
ASWAD
BAKER, Peter 'Ginger'
BASIE, Count
BERRY, Chuck
BLACK, Cilla
BOLAN, Marc
BONDS, Gary US
BOONE, Pat
BOWIE, David
BREAD
BROWN, James
BYRDS, The
CHINN, Nicky
CLARK, Dave
CLARK, Petula
CLASH, The
CLIFF, Jimmy
COHEN, Leonard
COOKE, Sam
CREAM, The
CROCE, Jim
DARIN, Bobby
DAVIS, Miles
DAVIS, Sammy, Jnr
DAVIS, Spencer,
  Group
DELLS, The
DOORS, The
DYLAN, Bob
ESSEX, David
FACES, The
FERRY, Bryan
FLACK, Roberta
FREED, Alan
GREEN, Al
HALEY, Bill
HANDY, William
  Christopher
HAYES, Isaac
HEART
HINES, Earl
HOLLY, Buddy
JAMES, Bob

5—continued
JAMES, Tommy, &
  The Shondells
JARRE, Jean-Michel
JONES, Quincy
JONES, Tom
KINKS, The
KLEIN, Allen
LAINE, Frankie
LEWIS, Huey, & The
  News
LEWIS, Jerry Lee
LYMON, Frankie, &
  The Teenagers
MCCOY, Van
MOORE, Gary
MOYET, Alison
NUMAN, Gary
O'JAYS, The
PERRY, Richard
PRICE, Alan
PROBY, P J
QUEEN
REDDY, Helen
SAXON
SAYER, Leo
SCOTT, Ronnie
SEGER, Bob
SIMON, Carly
SLADE
SMITH, Bessie
STARR, Ringo
STING
SWEET, The
TATUM, Art
WHITE, Barry
WYMAN, Bill
YAZOO
YOUNG, Neil
YOUNG, Paul
ZAPPA, Frank
ZZ TOP

6
ALPERT, Herb
ARGENT
ATKINS, Chet
ATWELL, Winifred
AVALON, Frankie
BALDRY, Long John
BASSEY, Shirley
BECHET, Sidney
BENSON, George
BERLIN, Irving
BOLDEN, Buddy
BONEY M
BOSTON
BROWNE, Jackson
BURDON, Eric
CHAPIN, Harry
COCKER, Joe
COODER, Ry

6—continued
COOPER, Alice
COUGAR, John
CREOLE, Kid, & The
  Coconuts
CROSBY, Bing
DAMNED, The
DEKKER, Desmond
DENVER, John
DOMINO, Fats
DR HOOK
EAGLES, The
EASTON, Sheena
EQUALS, The
FABIAN
FAMILY
FISHER, Eddie
GELDOF, Bob
HARRIS, Emmylou
HOOKER, John Lee
HUNTER, Ian
JAGGER, Mick
JOLSON, Al
JOPLIN, Janis
KNIGHT, Gladys, &
  The Pips
KOOPER, Al
KORNER, Alexis
KRAMER, Billy J
LAUPER, Cyndi
LEIBER, Jerry
LENNON, John
LERNER, Alan Jay
MARLEY, Bob, & The
  Wailers
MARTIN, George
MARTIN, John
MATHIS, Johnny
MAYALL, John
MCLEAN, Don
MIDLER, Bette
MILLER, Glenn
MILLER, Steve
MINGUS, Charlie
MONTEZ, Chris
MORTON, Jelly Roll
NELSON, Ricky
NELSON, Willie
NEWMAN, Randy
NUGENT, Ted
OSMOND, Donny
PALMER, Robert
PARKER, Charlie
PARKER, Colonel
  Tom
PARTON, Dolly
PAXTON, Tom
PITNEY, Gene
POLICE, The
PORTER, Cole
PRINCE

6—continued
REEVES, Jim
REVERE, Paul, & The
  Raiders
RICHIE, Lionel
RIVERS, Johnny
ROGERS, Kenny
SEDAKA, Neil
SEEGER, Pete
SIMONE, Nina
SLEDGE, Percy
SUMMER, Donna
TAUPIN, Bernie
TAYLOR, James
THOMAS, B J
TROGGS, The
TURNER, Ike & Tina
TWITTY, Conway
VALENS, Ritchie
VINTON, Bobby
WALLER, Fats
WATERS, Muddy
WEBBER, Andrew
  Lloyd
WILSON, Jackie
WINTER, Edgar
WINTER, Johny
WOMACK, Bobby
WONDER, Stevie

7
AMERICA
ANIMALS, The
BALLARD, Hank
BEATLES
BEE GEES, The
BENNETT, Tony
BLONDIE
BON JOVI
BRUBECK, Dave
CALVERT, Eddie
CASSIDY, David
CHAPMAN, Mike
CHARLES, Ray
CHECKER, Chubby
CLAPTON, Eric
CLOONEY, Rosemary
COCHRAN, Eddie
COLLINS, Judy
COLLINS, Phil
DE BURGH, Chris
DIAMOND, Neil
DIDDLEY, Bo
DONEGAN, Lonnie
DONOVAN
EDMUNDS, Dave
EPSTEIN, Brian
FRANCIS, Connie
GABRIEL, Peter
GENESIS
GLITTER, Gary
GOODMAN, Benny

7—continued
GUTHRIE, Woody
HAMPTON, Lionel
HANCOCK, Herbie
HENDRIX, Jimi
HOLIDAY, Billie
HOLLIES, The
JACKSON, Mahalia
JACKSON, Michael
JACKSON, Millie
JARREAU, Al
LOFGREN, Nils
MADNESS
MADONNA
MANILOW, Barry
MARTINO, Al
MICHAEL, George
MONKEES, The
NILSSON
ORBISON, Roy
OSMONDS, The
PERKINS, Carl
PRESLEY, Elvis
PRESTON, Billy
RAINBOW
REDDING, Otis
RICHARD, Cliff
RICHARD, Keith
RODGERS, Richard
  Charles
RUSSELL, Leon
SANTANA
SCRAGGS, Boz
SEEKERS, The
SHADOWS, The
SHANKAR, Ravi
SHANNON, Del
SINATRA, Frank
SPECTOR, Phil
SQUEEZE
STEVENS, Cat
STEWART, Rod
TRAFFIC
TURTLES, The
VAUGHAN, Sarah
VINCENT, Gene
WAKEMAN, Rick
WARWICK, Dionne
WHITMAN, Slim
WIZZARD
WYNETTE, Tammy
ZOMBIES, The

8
ANDERSEN, Eric
AZNAVOUR, Charles
CAMPBELL, Glen
CHI-LITES, The
COASTERS, The
COLTRANE, John
CRYSTALS, The
DRIFTERS, The

8—continued
FOUR ACES, The
FOUR TOPS, The
FRAMPTON, Peter
FRANKLIN, Aretha
HAMLISCH, Marvin
HARRISON, George
HAWKWIND
HEATWAVE
INK SPOTS
JENNINGS, Waylon
MARSALIS, Wynton
MAYFIELD, Curtis
MEAT LOAF
MINNELLI, Liza
MIRACLES, The
MITCHELL, Joni
MORRISON, Van
OLDFIELD, Mike
OSBOURNE, Ozzy
PETERSON, Oscar
  Emmanuel
PICKETTS, Wilson
PLATTERS, The
RAFFERTY, Gerry
ROBINSON, Smokey
RONETTES, The
RONSTADT, Linda
SONDHEIM, Stephen
SPECIALS, The
STIGWOOD, Robert
STROLLER, Mike
SUPREMES, The
ULTRAVOX
VANDROSS, Luther

9
AIR SUPPLY
ARMSTRONG, Louis
BACHARACH, Burt
BADFINGER
BEACH BOYS, The
BEEFHEART, Captain
BELAFONTE, Harry
BUCKS FIZZ
CHIPMUNKS, The
CRUSADERS, The
ELLINGTON, Duke
FAITHFULL, Marianne
FOGELBERG, Dan
FOREIGNER
GILLESPIE, Dizzy
GOLDSBORO, Booby
GRAPPELLI,
  Stephane
LEADBELLY
LITTLE EVA
LYTTELTON,
  Humphrey
MARMALADE
MCCARTNEY, Paul
MEN AT WORK

9—continued
MOTORHEAD
O'SULLIVAN, Gilbert
PINK FLOYD
REINHARDT, Django
ROSE ROYCE
ROXY MUSIC
SCORPIONS
SEARCHERS, The
SHIRELLES, The
SIMPLY RED
STATUS QUO
STEELY DAN
STREISAND, Barbra
THIN LIZZY
TOWNSHEND, Pete
URIAH HEEP
YARDBIRDS, The

10
AMEN CORNER
BAD COMPANY
BANANARAMA
CARMICHAEL, Hoagy
CARPENTERS, The
COMMODORES, The
DEEP PURPLE
DR FEELGOOD
DURAN DURAN
EURYTHMICS, The
FITZGERALD, Ella
FUNKADELIC
IRON MAIDEN
JETHRO TULL
LITTLE FEAT
LONG RYDERS, The
MOODY BLUES
MUNGO JERRY
NEWTON-JOHN,
  Olivia
PRETENDERS, The
SCOTT-HERON, Gil
SEX PISTOLS, The
SMALL FACES, The
STRANGLERS, The
STYLISTICS, The
WASHINGTON, Dinah
WHITESNAKE
ZAGER & EVANS

11
ARMATRADING, Joan
BEIDERBECKE, Bix
CULTURE CLUB
DIRE STRAITS
FOUNDATIONS
FOUR SEASONS, The
HUMAN LEAGUE
IMPRESSIONS, The
JACKSON FIVE
JOY DIVISION
KING CRIMSON

11—continued
LED ZEPPELIN
LINDISFARNE
MANFRED MANN
MARVELETTES, The
OHIO PLAYERS
PET SHOP BOYS
PROCUL HARUM
SIMPLE MINDS
SPRINGFIELD, Dusty
SPRINGFIELD, Rick
SPRINGSTEEN, Bruce
TEMPTATIONS, The
THEODORAKIS, Mikis
WISHBONE ASH

12
BLACK SABBATH
BOOMTOWN RATS
COCKNEY REBEL
FLEETWOOD MAC
GRATEFUL DEAD
HALL AND OATES
HOT CHOCOLATE
HOUSEMARTINS, The
SONNY AND CHER
STYLE COUNCIL
TALKING HEADS
YOUNG RASCALS,
  The

13
HAMMERSTEIN II,
  Oscar
ISLEY BROTHERS
KRISTOFFERSON,
  Kris
LITTLE RICHARD
LOVIN' SPOONFUL
MAMAS AND PAPAS
MOTT THE HOOPLE
REO SPEEDWAGON
ROLLING STONES,
  The
SPANDAU BALLET
STAPLE SINGERS
TEARS FOR FEARS
THREE DOG NIGHT

14
ALLMAN BROTHERS
BAY CITY ROLLERS
BLUE OYSTER CULT
DOOBIE BROTHERS
FIFTH DIMENSION
HERMAN'S HERMITS
JON AND VANGELIS
KOOL AND THE
  GANG
SEALS AND CROFTS

15
DETROIT SPINNERS
EVERLEY BROTHERS

16
AVERAGE WHITE BAND
BOOKER T AND THE MG'S
EARTH WIND AND FIRE
PETER, PAUL AND MARY

17
GRAND FUNK RAILROAD
JEFFERSON AIRPLANE
RIGHTEOUS BROTHERS

17—continued
SIMON AND GARFUNKEL
SWINGING BLUE JEANS

18
BLOOD SWEAT AND TEARS
BUFFALO SPRINGFIELD
FAIRPORT CONVENTION
PUBLIC IMAGE LIMITED

19
BARCLAY JAMES HARVEST

20+
BACHMAN-TURNER OVERDRIVE
CREEDENCE CLEARWATER REVIVAL
CROSBY, STILLS, NASH AND YOUNG
DEXYS MIDNIGHT RUNNERS
ELECTRIC LIGHT ORCHESTRA

20+—continued
EMERSON, LAKE AND PALMER
FREDDIE AND THE DREAMERS
GERRY AND THE PACEMAKERS
K C AND THE SUNSHINE BAND
SIOUXSIE AND THE BANSHEES
SLY AND THE FAMILY STONE

STAGE AND SCREEN PERSONALITIES

3
BOW, Clara (US film actress)
COX, Robert (English comic actor)
FOY, Eddie (US actor)
HAY, Will (British comedian)
LEE, Gypsy Rose (US entertainer)
RAY, Satyajit (Indian film director)
RIX, Sir Brian (British actor)
SIM, Alastair (Scottish actor)

4
ARNE, Susanna Maria (British actress)
BIRD, Theophilus (English actor)
BOND, Edward (British dramatist)
CANE, Andrew (English actor)
COBB, Lee J (US actor)
COOK, Peter (British comedy actor)
DALY, Augustin (US theatre manager)
DEAN, James (US film actor)
DUFF, Mrs (US actress)
DUSE, Eleonora (Italian actress)
FORD, John (US film director)
GISH, Lillian (US actress)
GOLD, Jimmy (British comedian)
GRAY, Dulcie (British actress)
GRAY, 'Monsewer' Eddie (British comedian)
HALL, Sir Peter (British theatre director)
HOPE, Bob (US comedian, born in Britain)
KEAN, Edmund (British actor)
KNOX, Teddy (British comedian)
LAHR, Bert (US actor)
LANG, Fritz (German film director)
LEAN, Sir David (British film director)
LUNT, Alfred (US actor)
OWEN, Alun Davies (British dramatist)
PAGE, Geraldine (US actress)
PIAF, Edith (French cabaret and music-hall performer)

4—continued
RANK, J Arthur (British industrialist and film executive)
REED, Sir Carol (British film director)
REID, Beryl (British actress)
RIGG, Diana (British actress)
SHER, Anthony (British actor)
TATE, Harry (British music-hall comedian)
TREE, Sir Herbert Beerbohm (British actor and theatre manager)
WEST, Mae (US actress)

5
ALLEN, Chesney (British comedian)
ALLEN, Woody (US film actor and director)
ARMIN, Robert (British actor)
ASTON, Anthony (Irish actor)
BADEL, Alan (British actor)
BARON, André (French actor)
BARON, Michel (French actor)
BARRY, Elizabeth (English actress)
BARRY, Spranger (Irish actor)
BATES, Alan (British actor)
BETTY, William Henry West (British boy actor)
BLOOM, Claire (British actress)
BOOTH, Barton (British actor)
BOOTH, Edwin Thomas (US actor)
BOOTH, Junius Brutus (US actor)
BOYER, Charles (French film actor)
BRICE, Fanny (US actress)
BROOK, Peter (British theatre director)
BROWN, Pamela (British actor)
BRYAN, Dora (British actress)
CAPRA, Frank (US film director, born in Italy)
CAREY, Joyce (British actress)
CARNÉ, Marcel (French film director)
CLAIR, René (French film director)
CLIVE, Kitty (British actress)
CONTI, Italia (British actress)

5—continued

DAVIS, Bette (US film actress)
DENCH, Dame Judi (British actress)
EDWIN, John (British actor)
EKHOF, Konrad (German actor and director)
EVANS, Dame Edith (British actress)
FLYNN, Errol (Australian actor, born in Tasmania)
FONDA, Henry (US film actor and director)
GABIN, Jean (French film actor)
GABLE, Clark (US film actor)
GARBO, Greta (Swedish actress)
GOZZI, Carlo (Italian dramatist)
GRANT, Cary (US film actor, born in England)
GWYNN, Nell (English actress)
HAIGH, Kenneth (British actor)
HANDL, Dame Irene (British actress)
HAWKS, Howard (US film director)
HICKS, Sir Seymour (British actor-manager)
IRONS, Jeremy (British actor)
KAZAN, Elia (US stage and film director and novelist)
KELLY, Grace (US film actress)
KORDA, Sir Alexander (British film producer and director)
LA RUE, Danny (British female impersonator)
LEIGH, Vivien (British actress)
LENYA, Lotte (German actress and singer)
LIFAR, Serge (Russian ballet dancer and choreographer)
LLOYD, Harold (US film comedian)
LLOYD, Marie (British music-hall entertainer)
LOREN, Sophia (Italian film actress)
LOSEY, Joseph (US film director)
MAYER, Louis B (US film producer, born in Russia)
MILES, Bernard (British theatre director and actor)
MILLS, Sir John (British actor)
MOORE, Dudley (British actor and songwriter)
NERVO, Jimmy (British comedian)
NIVEN, David (British film actor)
PAIGE, Elaine (British actress and singer)
PASCO, Richard (British actor)
PETIT, Roland (French ballet dancer and choreographer)
POLUS (Greek tragic actor)
POPOV, Alexei Dmitrevich (Soviet director)
POPOV, Oleg Konstantinovich (Russian clown)
POWER, Tyrone (US actor)
PRYCE, Jonathan (British actor)
ROBEY, Sir George Edward (British music-hall comedian)
SMITH, Maggie Natalie (British actress)
TERRY, Dame Ellen Alice (British actress)
TOPOL, Chaim (Israeli actor)
TRACY, Spencer (US film actor)
TUTIN, Dorothy (British actress)
WAJDA, Andrzej (Polish film director)
WAYNE, John (US film actor)

6

ADRIAN, Max (British actor)
AINLEY, Henry (British actor)
AITKEN, Maria (British actress)
ALIZON (French actor)
ALLEYN, Edward (English actor)
ARNAUD, Yvonne Germaine (French actress)
ARTAUD, Antonin (French actor, poet, producer, and theoretician of the theatre)
ASHTON, Sir Frederick (British ballet dancer and choreographer, born in Ecuador)
ATKINS, Eileen (British actress)
BALCON, Sir Michael (British film producer)
BARDOT, Brigitte (French film actress)
BARNUM, Phineas Taylor (US showman)
BAYLIS, Lilian (British theatre manager)
BÉJART, Joseph (French actor)
BÉJART, Maurice (French ballet dancer and choreographer)
BENSON, Sir Frank (British actor-manager)
BLASIS, Carlo (Italian dance teacher)
BOCAGE (French actor)
BOGART, Humphrey (US film actor)
BRANDO, Marlon (US actor)
BRIERS, Richard (British actor)
BROOKE, Gustavus Vaughan (British actor)
BROUGH, Lionel (British actor)
BROWNE, Robert (English actor)
BRYANT, Michael (British actor)
BUÑUEL, Luis (Spanish film director)
BURTON, Richard Walter (British actor, born in Wales)
CAGNEY, James (US actor)
CALLOW, Simon (British actor)
CANTOR, Eddie (US singer and actor)
CASSON, Sir Lewis (British actor and director)
CIBBER, Colley (British actor-manager)
COLMAN, Ronald (British actor)
CONWAY, William Augustus (British actor)
COOPER, Dame Gladys (British actress)
COOPER, Gary (US film actor)
COWARD, Sir Noël (British dramatist, composer, and actor)
COWELL, Joe Leathley (British actor)
CRANKO, John (British choreographer, born in South Africa)
CROSBY, Bing (US popular singer and film actor)
CURTIS, Tony (US film actor)
DE SICA, Vittorio (Italian film director)
DEVINE, George Alexander Cassady (British theatre manager, director, and actor)
DIGGES, Dudley (British actor)
DISNEY, Walt (US film producer and animator)
DRAPER, Ruth (US actress)
DREYER, Carl Theodor (Danish film director)
DUNCAN, Isadora (US dancer)
FIELDS, Gracie (British popular entertainer)
FIELDS, W C (US actor)
FINLAY, Frank (British actor)
FINNEY, Albert (British actor)

6—continued
FLEURY (French actor)
FOKINE, Michel (Russian ballet dancer and choreographer)
FORMAN, Miloš (Czech film director)
FORMBY, George (British music hall singer)
GODARD, Jean-Luc (French film director)
GORING, Marius (British actor)
GRAHAM, Martha (US ballet dancer and choreographer)
GUITRY, Sacha (French actor and dramatist)
HARLOW, Jean (US film actress)
HERZOG, Werner (German film director)
HILLER, Dame Wendy (British actress)
HOWARD, Leslie (British actor of Hungarian descent)
IRVING, Sir Henry (British actor and manager)
JACOBI, Derek (British actor)
JOLSON, Al (US actor and singer)
JORDAN, Dorothy (British actress)
JOUVET, Louis (French actor and theatre director)
KEATON, Buster (US comedian of silent films)
KEMBLE, John Philip (British actor and manager)
KENDAL, Felicity (British actress)
KOONEN, Alisa Georgievna (Soviet actress)
LANDEN, Dinsdale (British actor)
LAUDER, Sir Harry (Scottish singer and music-hall comedian)
LEMMON, Jack (US actor)
LESSER, Anton (British actor)
LILLIE, Beatrice Gladys (British actress, born in Canada)
LIPMAN, Maureen (British actress)
MARTIN, Mary (US actress)
MASSEY, Daniel (British actor)
MASSEY, Raymond Hart (Canadian actor)
MCEWAN, Geraldine (British actress)
MCKERN, Leo (Australian actor)
MERMAN, Ethel (US actress)
MONROE, Marilyn (US film actress)
MORLEY, Robert (British actor)
O'TOOLE, Peter (British actor)
PETIPA, Marius (French dancer and choreographer)
PORTER, Eric (British actor)
QUAYLE, Sir Anthony (British actor)
RACHEL (French actress)
RÉJANE (French actress)
ROBSON, Dame Flora (British actress)
ROGERS, Ginger (US actress and singer)
ROWLEY, Thomas (English dramatist and actor)
SHUTER, Ned (British actor)
SINDEN, Donald (British actor)
STEELE, Tommy (British singer and actor)
STREEP, Meryl (US actress)
SUZMAN, Janet (British actress)
TAYLOR, Elizabeth (US film actress, born in England)

6—continued
TEARLE, Godfrey Seymour (British actor)
TEMPLE, Shirley (US film actress)
TILLEY, Vesta (British music-hall entertainer)
WARREN, William (US actor, born in Britain)
WELLES, Orson (US film actor and director)
WILDER, Billy (US film director, born in Austria)
WOLFIT, Sir Donald (British actor and manager)

7
ACHURCH, Janet (British actress)
ACKLAND, Joss (British actor)
AESOPUS, Claudius (Roman tragic actor)
ALLGOOD, Sara (Irish actress)
ANTOINE, André (French actor, director, and theatre manager)
BEAUVAL (French actor)
BELLAMY, George Anne (British actress)
BENNETT, Hywel (British actor, born in Wales)
BENNETT, Jill (British actress)
BERGMAN, Ingmar (Swedish film and stage director)
BERGMAN, Ingrid (Swedish actress)
BERGNER, Elisabeth (Austrian actress)
BLAKELY, Colin (British actor)
BOGARDE, Dirk (British film actor of Dutch descent)
BRANAGH, Kenneth (British actor)
BRESSON, Robert (French film director)
BURBAGE, Richard (English actor)
CALVERT, Louis (British actor)
CASARÉS, Maria (French actress)
CELESTE, Céline (French actress)
CHABROL, Claude (French film director)
CHAPLIN, Charlie (US film actor, born in Britain)
COLBERT, Claudette (US film actress, born in France)
COLLIER, Constance (British actress)
COMPTON, Fay (British actress)
CONDELL, Henry (English actor)
CORALLI, Jean (Italian ballet dancer and choreographer)
CORNELL, Katharine (US actress)
DEBURAU, Jean-Gaspard (French pantomimist, born in Bohemia)
DÉJAZET, Pauline-Virginie (French actress)
DELYSIA, Alice (French actress and singer)
DE MILLE, Cecil B (US film producer and director)
DENISON, Michael (British actor)
DOGGETT, Thomas (British actor)
DOTRICE, Roy (British actor)
DOUGLAS, Kirk (US film actor)
DURANTE, Jimmy (US actor and singer, known as 'Schnozzle')
ELLIOTT, Denholm (British actor)
FELLINI, Federico (Italian film director)
FONTEYN, Dame Margot (British ballet dancer)

7—continued

GARLAND, Judy (US singer and film actress)
GARRICK, David (English actor)
GIELGUD, Sir John (British actor)
GINGOLD, Hermione (British actress)
GOLDWYN, Samuel (US film producer)
GREGORY, Lady Augusta (Irish theatre patron and dramatist)
GUTHRIE, Tyrone (British theatre director)
HANCOCK, Sheila (British actress)
HANCOCK, Tony (British comedian)
HAWTREY, Sir Charles (British actor-manager)
HEPBURN, Audrey (British actress)
HEPBURN, Katharine (US actress)
HOFFMAN, Dustin (US film actor)
HORDERN, Sir Michael (British actor)
HOUDINI, Harry (US magician)
IFFLAND, August Wilhelm (German actor)
JACKSON, Glenda (British actress)
JOHNSON, Dame Celia (British actress)
KARLOFF, Boris (British character actor)
KUBRICK, Stanley (US film writer, director, and producer)
LACKAYE, Wilton (US actor)
LANGTRY, Lillie (British actress, known as the 'Jersey Lily')
LAROQUE (French actor)
LÉOTARD, Jules (French acrobat and music-hall performer)
MARCEAU, Marcel (French mime)
MARKOVA, Dame Alicia (British ballet dancer)
MASSINE, Léonide (Russian ballet dancer and choreographer)
MCKENNA, Siobhán (Irish actress)
MCQUEEN, Steve (US film actor)
MICHELL, Keith (Australian actor)
NUREYEV, Rudolf (Russian ballet dancer)
OLIVIER, Laurence Kerr, Lord (British actor)
OXBERRY, William (British actor)
PAVLOVA, Anna (Russian ballet dancer)
PAXINOU, Katina (Greek actress)
PLUMMER, Christopher (Canadian actor)
PORTMAN, Eric (British actor)
QUILLEY, Denis (British actor)
RAMBERT, Dame Marie (British ballet dancer and choreographer)
REDFORD, Robert (US film actor)
RISTORI, Adelaide (Italian actress)
ROBARDS, Jason (US actor)
ROBBINS, Jerome (US ballet dancer and choreographer)
ROBESON, Paul Bustil (US Black actor)
RUSSELL, Ken (British film director)
SALVINI, Tommaso (Italian actor)
SELLERS, Peter (British comic actor)
SIDDONS, Sarah (English actress)
STEWART, James (US film actor)
STRITCH, Elaine (US actress)
TEMPEST, Dame Marie (British actress)
ULANOVA, Galina (Russian ballet dancer)

7—continued

USTINOV, Peter Alexander (British actor, director, and dramatist)
VESTRIS, Madame (British actress)
WITHERS, Googie (British actress)

8

ABINGTON, Frances (British actress)
ALDRIDGE, Ira Frederick (US actor)
ANDERSON, Dame Judith (Australian actress)
ANDREINI, Francesco (Italian actor-manager and playwright)
ANDREINI, Giovanni Battista (Italian actor)
ANDREINI, Isabella (Italian actress)
ASHCROFT, Dame Peggy (British actress)
BADDELEY, Hermione (British actress)
BANCROFT, Anne (US actress)
BANKHEAD, Tallulah (US actress)
BARRAULT, Jean-Louis (French actor and director)
BERKELEY, Busby (US dance director)
BORISOVA, Yulia Konstantinovna (Soviet actress)
BRASSEUR, Pierre (French actor)
BUCHANAN, Jack (Scottish actor-manager)
CALDWELL, Zoë (Australian actress)
CAMPBELL, Mrs Patrick (British actress)
CHANNING, Carol (US actress and singer)
CLEMENTS, Sir John (British actor-manager)
CRAWFORD, Joan (US film actress)
CRAWFORD, Michael (British actor)
DANCOURT, Florent (French actor and playwright)
DE LA TOUR, Frances (British actress)
DE VALOIS, Dame Ninette (British ballet dancer and choreographer, born in Ireland)
DEVRIENT, Ludwig (German actor)
DIETRICH, Marlene (German film actress and singer)
DUFRESNE (French actor)
ESTCOURT, Richard (English actor)
FLAHERTY, Robert (US film director)
FLANAGAN, Bud (British comedian)
FLORENCE, William Jermyn (US actor)
FLORIDOR (French actor)
GRENFELL, Joyce (British actress)
GRIERSON, John (British film director)
GRIMALDI, Joseph (British clown)
GUINNESS, Sir Alec (British actor)
HARRISON, Rex (British actor)
HELPMANN, Sir Robert Murray (Australian ballet dancer, choreographer, and actor)
KUROSAWA, Akira (Japanese film director)
KYNASTON, Ned (English actor)
LANSBURY, Angela (US actress)
LAUGHTON, Charles (British actor)
LAWRENCE, Gertrude (British actress)
LEIGHTON, Margaret (British actress)
MACREADY, William Charles (British actor and theatre manager)
MATTHEWS, Jessie (British actress)
MCKELLEN, Ian (British actor)

8—continued

MERCOURI, Melina (Greek actress and politician)
NAUGHTON, Charlie (British comedian)
NAZIMOVA, Alla (Russian actress)
NIJINSKY, Vaslav (Russian ballet dancer)
PICKFORD, Mary (Canadian-born US film actress)
POLANSKI, Roman (Polish film director, born in Paris)
REDGRAVE, Corin (British actor)
REDGRAVE, Lynn (British actress)
REDGRAVE, Sir Michael (British actor)
REDGRAVE, Vanessa (British actress)
ROBINSON, Edward G (US film actor, born in Romania)
SCOFIELD, Paul (British actor)
SELZNICK, David O (US film producer)
STROHEIM, Erich von (US film director and actor)
THOMPSON, Emma (British actress)
VISCONTI, Luchino (Italian film director)
WHITELAW, Billie (British actress)
WILLIAMS, Kenneth (British comic actor)
WILLIAMS, Michael (British actor)
ZIEGFELD, Florenz (US theatrical producer)

9

ANTONIONI, Michelangelo (Italian film maker)
BARKWORTH, Peter (British actor)
BARRYMORE, Ethel (US actress)
BARRYMORE, John (US actor)
BARRYMORE, Lionel (US actor)
BARRYMORE, Maurice (British actor)
BELLECOUR (French actor)
BELLEROSE (French actor-manager)
BERIOSOVA, Svetlana (Russian ballet dancer)
BERNHARDT, Sarah (French actress)
BETTERTON, Thomas (English actor)
CHEVALIER, Maurice (French singer and actor)
COURTENAY, Tom (British actor)
DIAGHILEV, Sergei (Russian ballet impresario)
DU MAURIER, Sir Gerald (British actor-manager)
FAIRBANKS, Douglas (US film actor)
FAVERSHAM, William (US actor)
FERNANDEL (French comedian)
FEUILLÈRE, Edwige (French actress)
GRAMATICA, Irma (Italian actress)
GROSSMITH, George (British actor)
GRÜNDGENS, Gustav (German actor)
LAPOTAIRE, Jane (British actress)
MACMILLAN, Sir Kenneth (British ballet dancer and choreographer)
MONCRIEFF, Gladys (Australian actress)
NICHOLSON, Jack (US film actor)
PECKINPAH, Sam (US film director)
PLEASENCE, Donald (British actor)
PLOWRIGHT, Joan Anne (British actress)
PREMINGER, Otto (US film director, born in Austria)

9—continued

REINHARDT, Max (Austrian theatre director)
STERNBERG, Josef von (US film director, born in Austria)
STREISAND, Barbra (US singer and actress)
THORNDIKE, Dame Sybil (British actress)
VALENTINO, Rudolf (US film actor, born in Italy)

10

BALANCHINE, George (US ballet dancer and choreographer, born in Russia)
BASSERMANN, Albert (German actor)
BELLEROCHE (French actor)
BERTOLUCCI, Bernardo (Italian film director)
BOUCICAULT, 'Dot' (British actor-manager)
BOUCICAULT, Nina (British actress)
CARTWRIGHT, William (English actor)
CUNNINGHAM, Merce (US dancer and choreographer)
D'OYLY CARTE, Richard (British theatre impresario and manager)
EISENSTEIN, Sergei (Russian film director)
FASSBINDER, Rainer Werner (German film director)
LITTLE TICH (British music-hall comedian)
LITTLEWOOD, Joan (British theatre director)
MONTFLEURY (French actor)
RICHARDSON, Ian (British actor)
RICHARDSON, Sir Ralph (British actor)
ROSSELLINI, Roberto (Italian film director)
RUTHERFORD, Dame Margaret (British actress)
WOFFINGTON, Peg (Irish actress)
ZEFFIRELLI, G Franco (Italian director and stage designer)

11

BEAUCHÂTEAU (French actor)
BIANCOLELLI, Giuseppe Domenico (French actor)
BRACEGIRDLE, Anne (English actress)
BRAITHWAITE, Dame Lilian (British actress)
COURTNEIDGE, Dame Cicely (British actress)
DAUVILLIERS (French actor)
MACLIAMMÓIR, Micheál (Irish actor and dramatist)
MASTROIANNI, Marcello (Italian actor)
MISTINGUETT (French singer and comedienne)
SCHLESINGER, John (British film and theatre director)

12

BRUSCAMBILLE (French actor)
MARX BROTHERS (US family of comic film actors)
STANISLAVSKY, Konstantin (Russian actor and theatre director)

13

ROSCIUS GALLUS, Quintus (Roman comic actor)

14
MIZOGUCHI KENJI (Japanese film director)
15
FFRANGCON-DAVIES, Gwen (British actress)
FORBES-ROBERTSON, Sir Johnston (British actor-manager)

15—continued
GRANVILLE-BARKER, Harley (British theatre director)
KOBAYASHI MASAKI (Japanese film director)

SCIENTISTS AND INVENTORS

3
DAM, Carl Peter Henrik (1895–1976; Danish biochemist)
KAY, John (1704–c. 1764; British inventor)
LEE, Tsung-Dao (1926– ; US physicist)
OHM, Georg Simon (1787–1854; German physicist)
RAY, John (1627–1705; English naturalist)
4
ABEL, Niels Henrik (1802–29; Norwegian mathematician)
ABEL, Sir Frederick Augustus (1827–1902; British chemist)
ADER, Clément (1841–1926; French engineer and inventor)
AIRY, Sir George Biddell (1801–92; British astronomer)
BAER, Karl Ernest von (1792–1876; Russian embryologist)
BELL, Alexander Graham (1847–1922; Scottish scientist and inventor)
BENZ, Karl (1844–1929; German engineer)
BIRÓ, Laszlo (1900–85; Hungarian inventor)
BOHR, Niels Henrik David (1885–1962; Danish physicist)
BORN, Max (1882–1970; British physicist)
BOSE, Sir Jagadis Chandra (1858–1937; Indian plant physiologist and physicist)
COHN, Ferdinand Julius (1839–1884; German botanist)
COKE, Thomas William, of Holkham, Earl of Leicester (1752–1842; British agriculturalist)
CORT, Henry (1740–1800; British inventor)
DAVY, Sir Humphry (1778–1829; British chemist and inventor)
EADS, John Buchanan (1820–87; US civil engineer)
FUST, Johann (1400–66; German printer)
GOLD, Thomas (1920– ; Austrian-born astronomer)
GRAY, Asa (1810–88; US botanist)
HAHN, Otto (1879–1968; German chemist and physicist)
HESS, Victor Francis (1883–1964; US physicist)
HOWE, Elias (1819–67; US inventor)
KOCH, Robert (1843–1910; German bacteriologist)

4—continued
LAND, Edwin Herbert (1909– ; US inventor)
LAUE, Max Theodor Felix Von (1879–1960; German physicist)
LOEB, Jacques (1859–1924; US zoologist)
MACH, Ernst (1838–1916; Austrian physicist)
MAYO (family of US medical researchers)
OTIS, Elisha Graves (1811–61; US inventor)
OTTO, Nikolaus August (1832–91; German engineer)
RABI, Isidor Isaac (1898– ; US physicist)
RYLE, Sir Martin (1918–84; British astronomer)
SWAN, Sir Joseph Wilson (1828–1914; British physicist)
TODD, Alexander Robertus, Baron (1907– ; British biochemist)
TULL, Jethro (1674–1741; English agriculturalist and inventor of the seed drill)
UREY, Harold Clayton (1893–1981; US physicist)
WATT, James (1736–1819; British engineer)
YANG, Chen Ning (1922– ; US physicist)
5
ADAMS, John Couch (1819–92; English astronomer)
AIKEN, Howard Hathaway (1900–73; US mathematician)
AMICI, Giovanni Battista (1786–1863; Italian astronomer, microscopist, and optical instrument maker)
ASTON, Francis William (1877–1945; British chemist)
AVERY, Oswald Theodore (1877–1955; Canadian bacteriologist)
BACON, Roger (c. 1214–c. 1292; English scientist)
BAILY, Francis (1774–1844; British amateur astronomer)
BAIRD, John Logie (1888–1946; British electrical engineer)
BAKER, Sir Benjamin (1840–1907; British civil engineer)
BANKS, Sir Joseph (1743–1820; British botanist and explorer)
BATES, Henry Walter (1825–92; British naturalist and explorer)

5—continued

BEEBE, Charles William (1877–1962; US explorer and naturalist)

BETHE, Hans Albrecht (1906– ; US physicist)

BLACK, Joseph (1728–99; Scottish physician and chemist)

BLOCH, Felix (1905– ; US physicist)

BONDI, Sir Hermann (1919– ; British cosmologist and mathematician)

BOOLE, George (1815–64; British mathematician)

BOSCH, Carl (1874–1940; German chemist)

BOTHE, Walther Wilhelm Georg Franz (1891–1957; German experimental physicist)

BOVET, Daniel (1907– ; Swiss pharmacologist)

BOWEN, Norman Levi (1887–1956; Canadian experimental petrologist)

BOWER, Frederick Orpen (1855–1948; British botanist)

BOYLE, Robert (1627–91; British physicist and chemist)

BRAGG, Sir William Henry (1862–1942; British physicist)

BRAHE, Tycho (1546–1601; Danish astronomer)

BROWN, Robert (1773–1858; Scottish botanist)

BÜRGE, Joost (1552–1632; Swiss mathematician)

CHAIN, Sir Ernst Boris (1906–79; British biochemist)

CREED, Frederick (1871–1957; Canadian inventor)

CRICK, Francis Harry Compton (1916– ; British biophysicist)

CURIE, Marie (1867–1934; Polish chemist)

CURIE, Pierre (1859–1906; French physicist)

DEBYE, Peter Joseph Wilhelm (1884–1966; Dutch physicist and chemist)

DIELS, Otto Paul Hermann (1876–1954; German chemist)

DIRAC, Paul Adrien Maurice (1902–84; British physicist)

ELTON, Charles (1900– ; British zoologist)

EULER, Leonhard (1707–83; Swiss mathematician)

EVANS, Oliver (1755–1819; American engineer)

FABRE, Jean Henri (1823–1915; French entomologist)

FABRY, Charles (1867–1945; French physicist)

FERMI, Enrico (1901–54; US physicist)

FREGE, Gottlob (1848–1925; German mathematician and logician)

GABOR, Dennis (1900–79; British electrical engineer)

GALLE, Johann Gottfried (1812–1910; German astronomer)

5—continued

GAUSS, Karl Friedrich (1777–1855; German mathematician)

GEBER (14th century; Spanish alchemist)

GIBBS, Josiah Willard (1839–1903; US physicist)

GÖDEL, Kurt (1906–78; US mathematician)

HABER, Fritz (1868–1934; German chemist and inventor)

HARDY, Godfrey Harold (1877–1947; British mathematician)

HENRY, Joseph (1797–1878; US physicist)

HERTZ, Heinrich Rudolf (1857–94; German physicist)

HOOKE, Robert (1635–1703; British physicist)

HOYLE, Sir Fred (1915– ; British astronomer)

JEANS, Sir James Hopwood (1877–1946; British mathematician and astronomer)

JOULE, James Prescott (1818–89; British physicist)

KOLBE, Hermann (1818–84; German chemist)

KREBS, Sir Hans Adolf (1900–81; British biochemist)

LAWES, Sir John Bennet (1814–1900; British agriculturalist)

LIBBY, Willard Frank (1908–80; US chemist)

LODGE, Sir Oliver Joseph (1851–1940; British physicist)

LYELL, Sir Charles (1797–1875; British geologist)

MAXIM, Sir Hiram Stevens (1840–1916; British inventor)

MAYER, Julius Robert Von (1814–78; German physicist)

MONGE, Gaspard (1746–1818; French mathematician)

MONOD, Jacques-Lucien (1910–76; French biochemist)

MORSE, Samuel Finley Breese (1791–1872; US inventor)

NOBEL, Alfred Bernhard (1833–96; Swedish chemist)

NOBLE, Sir Andrew (1831–1915; British physicist)

PAULI, Wolfgang (1900–58; US physicist)

POPOV, Aleksandr Stepanovich (1859–1905; Russian physicist)

PROUT, William (1785–1850; British chemist and physiologist)

RAMAN, Sir Chandrasekhara Venkata (1888–1970; Indian physicist)

REBER, Grote (1911– ; US astronomer)

RHINE, Joseph Banks (1895–1980; US psychologist)

ROSSE, William Parsons, 3rd Earl Of (1800–67; Irish astronomer)

SEGRÈ, Emilio (1905– ; US physicist)

SMITH, Sir Keith Macpherson (1890–1955; Australian aviator)

5—continued

SODDY, Frederick (1877–1956; British chemist)

STAHL, Georg Ernst (1660–1734; German physician and chemist)

TATUM, Edward Lawrie (1909–75; US geneticist)

TESLA, Nikola (1856–1943; US electrical engineer)

VOLTA, Alessandro Giuseppe Antonio Anastasio, Count (1745–1827; Italian physicist)

WEBER, Ernst Heinrich (1795–1878; German physiologist)

WHITE, Gilbert (1720–93; English naturalist)

YOUNG, Thomas (1773–1829; British physician and physicist)

6

ACHARD, Franz Karl (1753–1821; German chemist)

ADRIAN, Edgar Douglas, 1st Baron (1889–1977; British physiologist)

AGNESI, Maria Gaetana (1718–99; Italian mathematician and philosopher)

ALFVÉN, Hannes Olof Gösta (1908– ; Swedish astrophysicist)

AMPÈRE, André Marie (1775–1836; French physicist)

APPERT, Nicolas (1750–1841; French inventor)

ARCHER, Frederick Scott (1813–57; British inventor and sculptor)

BAEYER, Adolf Von (1835–1917; German chemist)

BEADLE, George Wells (1903– ; US geneticist)

BODONI, Giambattista (1740–1813; Italian printer)

BOLYAI, János (1802–60; Hungarian mathematician)

BONNET, Charles (1720–93; Swiss naturalist)

BORDET, Jules Jean Baptiste Vincent (1870–1961; Belgian bacteriologist)

BOVERI, Theodor Heinrich (1862–1915; German cell biologist)

BRAMAH, Joseph (1748–1814; British engineer and inventor)

BRIGGS, Henry (1561–1630; English mathematician)

BRUNEL, Isambard Kingdom (1806–59; British engineer)

BUFFON, Georges Louis Leclerc, Comte de (1707–88; French naturalist)

BUNSEN, Robert Wilhelm (1811–99; German chemist)

CALVIN, Melvin (1911– ; US biochemist)

CANTOR, Georg (1845–1918; Russian mathematician)

CARNOT, Sadi (1796–1832; French scientist and soldier)

CARREL, Alexis (1873–1944; French surgeon)

6—continued

CARVER, George Washington (1864–1943; US agriculturalist)

CAUCHY, Augustin Louis, Baron (1789–1857; French mathematician)

CAXTON, William (c. 1422–91; first English printer)

CAYLEY, Arthur (1821–95; British mathematician)

CAYLEY, Sir George (1773–1857; British engineer and pioneer designer of flying machines)

CUVIER, Georges, Baron (1769–1832; French zoologist)

DALTON, John (1766–1844; British chemist)

DARWIN, Charles Robert (1809–1882; British naturalist)

DE BARY, Heinrich Anton (1831–88; German botanist)

DE DUVE, Christian (1917– ; Belgian biochemist)

DREYER, Johan Ludvig Emil (1852–1926; Danish astronomer)

DU MONT, Allen Balcom (1901–65; US engineer)

DUNLOP, John Boyd (1840–1921; Scottish inventor)

ECKERT, John Presper (1919– ; US electronics engineer)

EDISON, Thomas Alva (1847–1931; US inventor)

ENDERS, John Franklin (1897– ; US microbiologist)

ENGLER, Gustav Heinrich Adolf (1844–1930; German botanist)

EUCLID (c. 300 BC; Greek mathematician)

FERMAT, Pierre de (1601–65; French mathematician)

FINSEN, Niels Ryberg (1860–1904; Danish physician)

FOKKER, Anthony Hermann Gerard (1890–1939; Dutch aircraft manufacturer)

FRANCK, James (1882–1964; US physicist)

FRISCH, Karl Von (1886–1982; Austrian zoologist)

FRISCH, Otto Robert (1904–79; Austrian-born physicist)

FULTON, Robert (1765–1815; American inventor)

GALOIS, Évariste (1811–32; French mathematician)

GALTON, Sir Francis (1822–1911; British scientist)

GEIGER, Hans (1882–1945; German physicist)

GESNER, Conrad (1516–65; Swiss physician)

GRAHAM, Thomas (1805–69; British physicist)

HALLEY, Edmund (1656–1742; British astronomer)

HEVESY, George Charles Von (1885–1966; Hungarian-born chemist)

6—continued

HOOKER, Sir William Jackson (1785–1865; British botanist)

HUBBLE, Edwin Powell (1889–1953; US astronomer)

HUTTON, James (1726–97; Scottish physician)

HUXLEY, Thomas Henry (1825–95; British biologist)

JANSKY, Karl Guthe (1905–50; US radio engineer)

JENSON, Nicolas (c. 1420–80; French printer)

JOLIOT, Frédéric (1900–59; French physicist)

KELVIN, William Thomson, 1st Baron (1824–1907; Scottish physicist)

KEPLER, Johannes (1571–1630; German astronomer)

KINSEY, Alfred (1894–1956; US zoologist and sociologist)

LANDAU, Lev Davidovich (1908–68; Soviet physicist)

LARTET, Édouard Armand Isidore Hippolyte (1801–71; French archaeologist)

LIEBIG, Justus, Baron Von (1803–73; German chemist)

LORENZ, Konrad (1903– ; Austrian zoologist)

LOVELL, Sir Bernard (1913– ; British astronomer)

LOWELL, Percival (1855–1916; US astronomer)

MARKOV, Andrei Andreevich (1856–1922; Russian mathematician)

MARTIN, Archer John Porter (1910– ; British biochemist)

MARTIN, Pierre-Émile (1824–1915; French engineer)

MCADAM, John Loudon (1756–1836; British inventor)

MENDEL, Gregor Johann (1822–84; Austrian botanist)

MORGAN, Thomas Hunt (1866–1945; US geneticist)

MORLEY, Edward Williams (1838–1923; US chemist)

MORRIS, Desmond John (1928– ; British zoologist)

MULLER, Hermann Joseph (1890–1967; US geneticist)

MÜLLER, Paul Hermann (1899–1965; Swiss chemist)

NAPIER, John (1550–1617; Scottish mathematician)

NERNST, Walther Hermann (1864–1941; German physical chemist)

NEWTON, Sir Isaac (1642–1727; British physicist and mathematician)

OLBERS, Heinrich Wilhelm Matthäus (1758–1840; German astronomer)

PASCAL, Blaise (1623–62; French mathematician and physicist)

6—continued

PENNEY, William George, Baron (1909– ; British mathematician)

PERKIN, Sir William Henry (1838–1907; British chemist)

PERRIN, Jean-Baptiste (1870–1942; French physicist)

PLANCK, Max Karl Ernst Ludwig (1858–1947; German physicist)

POWELL, Cecil Frank (1903–69; British physicist)

PROUST, Joseph-Louis (1754–1826; French chemist)

RAMSAY, Sir William (1852–1916; Scottish chemist)

RENNIE, John (1761–1821; British civil engineer)

SANGER, Frederick (1918– ; British biochemist)

SAVERY, Thomas (c. 1650–1715; English engineer)

SHOLES, Christopher Latham (1819–90; US inventor)

SINGER, Isaac Merrit (1811–75; US inventor)

SLOANE, Sir Hans (1660–1753; British physician and naturalist)

STOKES, Sir George Gabriel (1819–1903; British physicist and mathematician)

STRUVE, Otto (1897–1963; US astronomer)

SUTTON, Walter Stanborough (1877–1916; US geneticist)

TALBOT, William Henry Fox (1800–77; British botanist and physicist)

TAYLOR, Brook (1685–1737; English mathematician)

TAYLOR, Frederick Winslow (1856–1915; US engineer)

TELLER, Edward (1908– ; US physicist)

TOWNES, Charles Hard (1915– ; US physicist)

VAUBAN, Sébastian Le Prestre de (1633–1707; French military engineer)

WALLIS, Sir Barnes (1887–1979; British aeronautical engineer)

WALTON, Ernest Thomas Sinton (1903– ; Irish physicist)

WATSON, James Dewey (1928– ; US geneticist)

WIENER, Norbert (1894–1964; US mathematician)

WIGNER, Eugene Paul (1902– ; US physicist)

WILSON, Charles Thomson Rees (1869–1959; British physicist)

WILSON, Edmund Beecher (1856–1939; US biologist)

WÖHLER, Friedrich (1800–82; German chemist)

WRIGHT, Orville (1871–1948; US aviator)

YUKAWA, Hideki (1907–81; Japanese physicist)

6—continued

ZEEMAN, Pieter (1865–1943; Dutch physicist)

7

AGASSIZ, Jean Louis Rodolphe (1807–73; Swiss natural historian)

ALVAREZ, Luis Walter (1911–   ; US physicist)

AUDUBON, John James (1785–1851; US naturalist)

BABBAGE, Charles (1792–1871; British mathematician and inventor)

BARDEEN, John (1908–   ; US physicist)

BARNARD, Edward Emerson (1857–1923; US astronomer)

BATESON, William (1861–1926; British biologist)

BATTANI, Al- (c. 858–929; Islamic astronomer)

BERGIUS, Friedrich (1884–1949; German chemist)

BORLAUG, Norman (1914–   ; US plant breeder)

BRAILLE, Louis (1809–52; French inventor of system of writing and printing for the blind)

BROUWER, Luitzen Egbertus Jan (1881–1966; Dutch mathematician)

BURBANK, Luther (1849–1926; US plant breeder)

CANDELA, Felix (1910–   ; Mexican engineer)

CARDANO, Girolamo (1501–76; Italian mathematician)

COMPTON, Arthur Holly (1892–1962; US physicist)

CORRENS, Carl Erich (1864–1933; German botanist and geneticist)

COULOMB, Charles Augustin de (1736–1806; French physicist)

CROOKES, Sir William (1832–1919; British physicist)

CURTISS, Glenn (1878–1930; US aviator and aeronautical engineer)

DAIMLER, Gottlieb (1834–1900; German inventor)

DANIELL, John Frederic (1790–1845; British chemist)

DE LA RUE, Warren (1815–89; British astronomer)

DE VRIES, Hugo Marie (1848–1935; Dutch botanist)

DOPPLER, Christian Johann (1803–53; Austrian physicist)

DRIESCH, Hans Adolf Eduard (1867–1941; German zoologist)

EICHLER, August Wilhelm (1839–87; German botanist)

FARADAY, Michael (1791–1867; British chemist and physicist)

FEYNMAN, Richard Phillips (1918–   ; US physicist)

FISCHER, Emil Hermann (1852–1919; German chemist)

7—continued

FLEMING, Sir John Ambrose (1849–1945; British electrical engineer)

FOURIER, Jean Baptiste Joseph, Baron (1768–1830; French mathematician and physicist)

FRESNEL, Augustin Jean (1788–1827; French physicist)

GAGARIN, Yuri Alekseevich (1934–68; Soviet cosmonaut)

GALVANI, Luigi (1737–98; Italian physician)

GILBERT, William (1544–1603; English physicist)

GODDARD, Robert Hutchings (1882–1945; US physicist)

GREGORY, James (1638–75; Scottish mathematician and astronomer)

HAECKEL, Ernst Heinrich (1834–1919; German zoologist)

HAWORTH, Sir Walter Norman (1883–1950; British biochemist)

HELMONT, Jan Baptist van (1580–1644; Belgian alchemist and physician)

HERMITE, Charles (1822–1901; French mathematician)

HILBERT, David (1862–1943; German mathematician)

HODGKIN, Alan Lloyd (1914–   ; British physiologist)

HODGKIN, Dorothy Mary Crowfoot (1910–   ; British biochemist)

HOPKINS, Sir Frederick Gowland (1861–1947; British biochemist)

HUGGINS, Sir William (1824–1910; British astronomer)

HUYGENS, Christiaan (1629–95; Dutch astronomer and physicist)

JUSSIEU (French family of botanists)

KAPITZA, Peter Leonidovich (1894–1984; Soviet physicist)

KENDALL, Edward Calvin (1886–1972; US biochemist)

KENDREW, Sir John Cowdery (1917–   ; British biochemist)

KHORANA, Har Gobind (1922–   ; US biochemist)

KIDINNU (4th century BC; Babylonian mathematician and astronomer)

KOZIREV, Nikolai Aleksandrovich (1908–   ; Soviet astronomer)

LALANDE, Joseph-Jérôme le Français de (1732–1807; French astronomer)

LAMARCK, Jean-Baptiste de Monet, Chevalier de (1744–1829; French naturalist)

LAMBERT, Johann Heinrich (1728–77; German mathematician and astronomer)

LANGLEY, Samuel Pierpont (1834–1906; US astronomer)

LAPLACE, Pierre Simon, Marquis de (1749–1827; French mathematician and astronomer)

7—continued

LESSEPS, Ferdinand de (1805–94; French diplomat)

LOCKYER, Sir Joseph Norman (1836–1920; British astronomer)

LORENTZ, Hendrick Antoon (1853–1928; Dutch physicist)

LUMIÈRE, Auguste (1862–1954; French photographer and inventor)

LYSENKO, Trofim Denisovich (1898–1976; Soviet biologist)

MARCONI, Guglielmo (1874–1937; Italian electrical engineer)

MAXWELL, James Clerk (1831–79; Scottish physicist)

MEITNER, Lise (1878–1968; Austrian physicist)

MESSIER, Charles (1730–1817; French astronomer)

MOSELEY, Henry Gwyn Jeffries (1887–1915; British physicist)

NEUMANN, John Von (1903–57; US mathematician)

OERSTED, Hans Christian (1777–1851; Danish physicist)

ONSAGER, Lars (1903–76; US chemist)

OSTWALD, Wilhelm (1853–1932; German chemist)

PARSONS, Sir Charles Algernon (1854–1931; British engineer)

PASTEUR, Louis (1822–95; French chemist and microbiologist)

PAULING, Linus Carl (1901– ; US chemist)

PICCARD (family of Swiss scientists)

POISSON, Siméon Dénis (1781–1840; French mathematician)

PRANDTL, Ludwig (1875–1953; German physicist)

PTOLEMY (or Claudius Ptolemaeus, 2nd century AD; Egyptian mathematician, astronomer, and geographer)

PURCELL, Edward Mills (1912– ; US physicist)

RÉAUMUR, René-Antoine Ferchault de (1683–1757; French physicist)

RIEMANN, Georg Friedrich Bernhard (1826–66; German mathematician)

RUMFORD, Benjamin Thompson, Count (1753–1814; American-born scientist)

SANDAGE, Allan Rex (1926– ; US astronomer)

SCHEELE, Carl Wilhelm (1742–86; Swedish chemist)

SCHWANN, Theodor (1810–82; German physiologist)

SEABORG, Glenn Theodore (1912– ; US physicist)

SHEPARD, Jr, Allan Bartlett (1923– ; US astronaut)

SIEMENS, Ernst Werner von (1816–92; German electrical engineer)

7—continued

SIMPSON, George Gaylord (1902– ; US palaeontologist)

SZILARD, Leo (1898–1964; US physicist)

TELFORD, Thomas (1757–1834; British civil engineer)

THENARD, Louis-Jacques (1777–1857; French chemist)

THOMSON, Sir Joseph John (1856–1940; British physicist)

TUPOLEV, Andrei Niklaievich (1888–1972; Soviet designer)

TYNDALL, John (1820–93; Irish physicist)

VAVILOV, Nikolai Ivanovich (1887–1943; Soviet plant geneticist)

WAKSMAN, Selman Abraham (1888–1973; US microbiologist)

WALLACE, Alfred Russel (1823–1913; British naturalist)

WEGENER, Alfred Lothar (1880–1930; German geologist)

WHITNEY, Eli (1765–1825; American inventor)

WHITTLE, Sir Frank (1907– ; British aeronautical engineer)

WILKINS, Maurice Hugh Frederick (1916– ; New Zealand physicist)

ZIEGLER, Karl (1898–1973; German chemist)

8

AGRICOLA, Georgius (1494–1555; German physician and mineralogist)

ANDERSON, Carl David (1905– ; US physicist)

ÅNGSTRÖM, Anders Jonas (1814–74; Swedish physicist and astronomer)

AVOGADRO, Amedeo, Conte di Quaregna e Ceretto (1776–1856; Italian physicist)

BAKEWELL, Robert (1725–95; British agriculturalist)

BESSEMER, Sir Henry (1813–98; British engineer and inventor)

BIRKHOFF, George David (1864–1944; US mathematician)

BJERKNES, Vilhelm Friman Koren (1862–1951; Norwegian meteorologist and physicist)

BLACKETT, Patrick Maynard Stuart, Baron (1897–1974; British physicist)

BRATTAIN, Walter Houser (1902– ; US physicist)

BREWSTER, Sir David (1781–1868; Scottish physicist)

BRIDGMAN, Percy Williams (1882–1961; US physicist)

BRINDLEY, James (1716–72; British canal builder)

BUSHNELL, David (1742–1824; US inventor; built the first submarine)

CALMETTE, Albert Léon Charles (1863–1933; French bacteriologist)

CHADWICK, Sir James (1891–1974; British physicist)

8—continued

CLAUSIUS, Rudolf Julius Emanuel (1822–88; German physicist)

CROMPTON, Samuel (1753–1827; British inventor)

CULPEPER, Nicholas (1616–54; English physician)

DAGUERRE, Louis-Jacques-Mandé (1789–1851; French inventor)

DEDEKIND, Richard (1831–1916; German mathematician)

DE FOREST, Lee (1873–1961; US electrical engineer)

DE MORGAN, Augustus (1806–71; British mathematician and logician)

EINSTEIN, Albert (1879–1955; German physicist)

ERICSSON, John (1803–89; US naval engineer and inventor)

FOUCAULT, Jean Bernard Léon (1819–68; French physicist)

GASSENDI, Pierre (1592–1655; French physicist)

GELL-MANN, Murray (1929– ; US physicist)

GUERICKE, Otto Von (1602–86; German physicist)

HAMILTON, Sir William Rowan (1805–65; Irish mathematician)

HERSCHEL, Sir William (1738–1822; British astronomer)

ILYUSHIN, Sergei Vladimirovich (1894–1977; Soviet aircraft designer)

IPATIEFF, Vladimir Nikolaievich (1867–1952; US physicist)

JACQUARD, Joseph-Marie (1752–1834; French inventor)

KENNELLY, Arthur Edwin (1861–1939; US electrical engineer)

KLAPROTH, Martin Heinrich (1743–1817; German chemist)

KOROLIOV, Sergei Pavlovich (1906–66; Soviet aeronautical engineer)

LAGRANGE, Joseph Louis, Comte de (1736–1813; French mathematician and astronomer)

LANGMUIR, Irving (1881–1957; US chemist)

LAWRENCE, Ernest Orlando (1901–58; US physicist)

LEGENDRE, Adrien Marie (1752–1833; French mathematician)

LEMAÎTRE, Georges Édouard, Abbé (1894–1966; Belgian priest and astronomer)

LEUCKART, Karl Georg Friedrich Rudolph (1822–98; German zoologist)

LINNAEUS, Carolus (Carl Linné; 1707–78; Swedish botanist)

LIPSCOMB, William Nunn (1919– ; US chemist)

LONSDALE, Dame Kathleen (1903–71; Irish physicist)

8—continued

MAUDSLAY, Henry (1771–1831; British engineer)

MCMILLAN, Edwin Mattison (1907– ; US physicist)

MERCATOR, Gerardus (1512–94; Flemish geographer)

MEYERHOF, Otto Fritz (1884–1951; US biochemist)

MILLIKAN, Robert Andrews (1868–1953; US physicist)

MITCHELL, Reginald Joseph (1895–1937; British aeronautical engineer)

MULLIKEN, Robert Sanderson (1896–1986; US chemist and physicist)

NEWCOMEN, Thomas (1663–1729; English blacksmith and inventor of steam engine)

OLIPHANT, Sir Mark Laurence Elwin (1901– ; Australian physicist)

POINCARÉ, Jules Henri (1854–1912; French mathematician)

RAYLEIGH, John William Strutt, 3rd Baron (1842–1919; British physicist)

RHETICUS (1514–76; German mathematician)

ROBINSON, Sir Robert (1886–1975; British chemist)

ROEBLING, John Augustus (1806–69; US engineer)

ROENTGEN, Wilhelm Konrad (1845–1923; German physicist)

SABATIER, Paul (1854–1941; French chemist)

SAKHAROV, Andrei Dimitrievich (1921– ; Soviet physicist)

SHOCKLEY, William Bradfield (1910– ; US physicist)

SHRAPNEL, Henry (1761–1842; British army officer, who invented the shrapnel shell)

SIKORSKY, Igor Ivan (1889–1972; US aeronautical engineer)

STIRLING, James (1692–1770; Scottish mathematician)

VAN ALLEN, James Alfred (1914– ; US physicist)

VAN'T HOFF, Jacobus Henricus (1852–1911; Dutch chemist)

WEISMANN, August Friedrich Leopold (1834–1914; German biologist)

WOODWARD, Robert Burns (1917– ; US chemist)

ZERNICKE, Frits (1888–1966; Dutch physicist)

ZWORYKIN, Vladimir Kosma (1889–1982; US physicist)

9

ABU AL-WAFA (940–98 AD; Persian mathematician and astronomer)

ARKWRIGHT, Sir Richard (1732–92; British inventor)

ARMSTRONG, Edwin Howard (1890–1954; US electrical engineer)

ARMSTRONG, William George, Baron (1810–1900; British engineer)

9—continued

ARRHENIUS, Svante August (1859–1927; Swedish physicist and chemist)

BECQUEREL, Henri (1852–1908; French physicist)

BERNOULLI (family of Swiss mathematicians and physicists)

BERTHELOT, Marcelin (1827–1907; French chemist)

BERZELIUS, Jöns Jakob, Baron (1779–1848; Swedish chemist)

BOLTZMANN, Ludwig Eduard (1844–1906; Austrian physicist)

BRONOWSKI, Jacob (1908–74; British mathematician)

CAVENDISH, Henry (1731–1810; British physicist)

CHEBISHEV, Pafnuti Lvovich (1821–94; Russian mathematician)

CHERENKOV, Pavel Alekseievich (1904– ; Soviet physicist)

COCKCROFT, Sir John Douglas (1897–1967; British physicist)

CORNFORTH, Sir John Warcup (1917– ; Australian chemist)

D'ALEMBERT, Jean Le Rond (1717–83; French mathematician)

DAUBENTON, Louis Jean Marie (1716–1800; French naturalist)

DAVENPORT, Charles Benedict (1866–1944; US zoologist)

EDDINGTON, Sir Arthur Stanley (1882–1944; British theoretical astronomer)

ENDLICHER, Stephan Ladislaus (1804–49; Hungarian botanist)

FIBONACCI, Leonardo (c. 1170–c. 1230; Italian mathematician)

FLAMSTEED, John (1646–1719; English astronomer)

GAY-LUSSAC, Joseph Louis (1778–1850; French chemist and physicist)

GUTENBERG, Johann (c. 1400–c. 1468; German printer)

HEAVISIDE, Oliver (1850–1925; British physicist)

HELMHOLTZ, Hermann Ludwig Ferdinand Von (1821–94; German physicist and physiologist)

HOPKINSON, John (1849–98; British physicist and electrical engineer)

JOHANNSEN, Wilhelm Ludvig (1857–1927; Danish geneticist)

JOSEPHSON, Brian David (1940– ; British physicist)

KIRCHHOFF, Gustav Robert (1824–87; German physicist)

KURCHATOV, Igor Vasilievich (1903–60; Soviet physicist)

LANKESTER, Sir Edwin Ray (1847–1929; British zoologist)

9—continued

LAVOISIER, Antoine Laurent (1743–94; French chemist)

LEDERBERG, Joshua (1925– ; US geneticist)

LEVERRIER, Urbain Jean Joseph (1811–77; French astronomer)

LIOUVILLE, Joseph (1809–82; French mathematician)

MACINTOSH, Charles (1766–1843; Scottish chemist)

MACMILLAN, Kirkpatrick (d. 1878; Scottish inventor)

MICHELSON, Albert Abraham (1852–1931; US physicist)

NICHOLSON, William (1753–1815; British chemist)

NIRENBERG, Marshall Warren (1927– ; US biochemist)

PELLETIER, Pierre Joseph (1788–1842; French chemist)

PRIESTLEY, Joseph (1733–1804; British chemist)

REMINGTON, Eliphalet (1793–1863; US inventor)

SCHLEIDEN, Matthias Jakob (1804–81; German botanist)

STEINMETZ, Charles Proteus (1865–1923; US electrical engineer)

TINBERGEN, Nikolaas (1907– ; Dutch zoologist and pioneer ethologist)

ZSIGMONDY, Richard Adolph (1865–1929; Austrian chemist)

ZUCKERMAN, Solly, Baron (1904–84; British anatomist)

10

ARCHIMEDES (c. 287–c. 212 BC; Greek mathematician and inventor)

ARROWSMITH, Aaron (1750–1823; British cartographer)

BARKHAUSEN, Heinrich (1881–1956; German physicist)

BERTHOLLET, Claude Louis, Comte (1748–1822; French chemist and physician)

BLENKINSOP, John (1783–1831; British engineer)

CANNIZZARO, Stanislao (1826–1910; Italian chemist)

CARTWRIGHT, Edmund (1743–1823; British inventor)

COPERNICUS, Nicolaus (1473–1543; Polish astronomer)

DOBZHANSKY, Theodosius (1900–75; US geneticist)

FITZGERALD, George Francis (1851–1901; Irish physicist)

FOURNEYRON, Benoît (1802–67; French engineer)

FRAUNHOFER, Joseph Von (1787–1826; German physicist)

10—continued

HARGREAVES, James (d. 1778; English inventor)

HEISENBERG, Werner Karl (1901–76; German physicist)

HIPPARCHUS (c. 190–c. 120 BC; Greek astronomer)

HOFMEISTER, Wilhelm Friedrich Benedict (1824–77; German botanist)

INGENHOUSZ, Jan (1730–99; Dutch physician and plant physiologist)

KOLMOGOROV, Andrei Nikolaevich (1903– ; Soviet mathematician)

LILIENTHAL, Otto (1848–96; German aeronautical engineer)

LIPPERSHEY, Hans (d. c. 1619; Dutch lens grinder)

MAUPERTUIS, Pierre Louis Moreau de (1698–1759; French mathematician)

MENDELEYEV, Dimitrii Ivanovich (1834–1907; Russian chemist)

METCHNIKOV, Ilya Ilich (1845–1916; Russian zoologist)

RUTHERFORD, Ernest, 1st Baron (1871–1937; English physicist)

SOMMERFELD, Arnold Johannes Wilhelm (1868–1951; German physicist)

STAUDINGER, Hermann (1881–1965; German chemist)

STEPHENSON, George (1781–1848; British engineer)

SWAMMERDAM, Jan (1637–80; Dutch naturalist and microscopist)

TORRICELLI, Evangelista (1608–47; Italian physicist)

TOURNEFORT, Joseph Pitton de (1656–1708; French botanist)

TREVITHICK, Richard (1771–1833; British engineer)

WATSON-WATT, Sir Robert Alexander (1892–1973; Scottish physicist)

WHEATSTONE, Sir Charles (1802–75; British physicist)

11

AL-KHWARIZMI, Muhammed Ibn Musa (c. 780–c. 850 AD; Arabic mathematician)

BASKERVILLE, John (1706–75; British printer)

BHOSKHARA II (1114–c. 1185; Indian mathematician)

CHAMBERLAIN, Owen (1920– ; US physicist)

GOLDSCHMIDT, Richard Benedict (1878–1958; US geneticist)

HINSHELWOOD, Sir Cyril Norman (1897–1967; British chemist)

JOLIOT-CURIE, Irène (1896–1956; French physicist)

LE CHÂTELIER, Henri-Louis (1850–1936; French chemist)

11—continued

LEEUWENHOEK, Antonie van (1632–1723; Dutch scientist)

LOBACHEVSKI, Nikolai Ivanovich (1793–1856; Russian mathematician)

MONTGOLFIER, Jacques-Étienne (1745–99; French balloonist and inventor)

NOSTRADAMUS (1503–66; French physician and astrologer)

OPPENHEIMER, J Robert (1904–67; US physicist)

SCHRÖDINGER, Erwin (1887–1961; Austrian physicist)

SHERRINGTON, Sir Charles Scott (1857–1952; British physiologist)

SPALLANZANI, Lazzaro (1729–99; Italian physiologist)

TSIOLKOVSKI, Konstantin Eduardovich (1857–1935; Russian aeronautical engineer)

VAN DER WAALS, Johannes Diderik (1637–1923; Dutch physicist)

12

AMBARTSUMIAN, Viktor Amazaspovich (1908– ; Soviet astrophysicist)

SZENT-GYÖRGYI, Albert (1893–1986; US biochemist)

13

ARAGO FRANÇOIS (1786–1853; French astronomer and physicist)

CHANDRASEKHAR, Subrahmanyan (1910– ; US astronomer)

REGIOMONTANUS (1436-76; German astronomer and mathematician)

14

GALILEO GALILEI (1564–1642; Italian mathematician, physicist, and astronomer)

15

EUDOXUS OF CNIDUS (c. 408–c. 355 BC; Greek astronomer and mathematician)

16

HERO OF ALEXANDRIA (mid-1st century AD; Greek engineer and mathematician)

17

APOLLONIUS OF PERGA (c. 261–c. 190 BC; Greek mathematician)

18

ARISTARCHUS OF SAMOS (c. 310–230 BC; Greek astronomer)

LECOQ DE BOISBAUDRAN, Paul-Émile (1838–1912; French chemist)

PAPPUS OF ALEXANDRIA (3rd century BC; Greek mathematician)

19

DIOSCORIDES PEDANIUS (c. 40–c. 90 AD; Greek physician)

KEKULÉ VON STRADONITZ, Friedrich August (1829–96; German chemist)

20+
BOYD-ORR OF BRECHIN MEARNS, John, 1st
Baron (1880–1971; Scottish scientist)
DIOPHANTUS OF ALEXANDRIA (mid-3rd
century AD; Greek mathematician)
ERATOSTHENES OF CYRENE (c. 276–c. 194
BC; Greek astronomer)

20+—continued
GEOFFROY SAINT-HILAIRE, Étienne (1772–
1844; French naturalist)
SOSIGENES OF ALEXANDRIA (1st century BC;
Greek astronomer)

EXPLORERS, PIONEERS, AND ADVENTURERS

4
BYRD, Richard E (1888–1957; US explorer)
CANO, Juan Sebastián del (c. 1460–1526;
Spanish navigator)
COOK, Captain James (1728–79; British
navigator)
DIAS, Bartolomeu (c. 1450–c. 1500;
Portuguese navigator)
EYRE, Edward John (1815–1901; British
explorer)
GAMA, Vasco da (c. 1469–1524; Portuguese
navigator)
HUME, Hamilton (1797–1873; Australian
explorer)
HUNT, John, Baron (1910–   ; British
mountaineer)
KIDD, William (c. 1645–1701; Scottish sailor)
PARK, Mungo (1771–c. 1806; Scottish
explorer)
POLO, Marco (c. 1254–1324; Venetian
traveller)
ROSS, Sir James Clark (1800–62; British
explorer)
SOTO, Hernando de (?1496–1542; Spanish
explorer)

5
BAKER, Sir Samuel White (1821–93; British
explorer)
BARTH, Heinrich (1821–65; German explorer
and geographer)
BOONE, Daniel (1734–1820; American
pioneer)
BRUCE, James (1730–94; British explorer)
BURKE, Robert O'Hara (1820–61; Irish
explorer)
CABOT, John (Giovanni Caboto,
c. 1450–c. 1499; Italian explorer)
DAVIS, John (or J Davys, c. 1550–1605)
English navigator)
FUCHS, Sir Vivian (1908–   ; British explorer)
LAIRD, Macgregor (1808–61; Scottish
explorer)
OATES, Lawrence Edward Grace (1880–1912;
British explorer)
OÑATE, Juan de (d. 1630; Spanish
conquistador)

5—continued
PARRY, Sir William Edward (1790–1855;
British navigator)
PEARY, Robert Edwin (1856–1920; US
explorer)
SCOTT, Robert Falcon (1868–1912; British
explorer)
SPEKE, John Hanning (1827–64; British
explorer)
STURT, Charles (1795–1869; British explorer)
TEACH, Edward (d. 1718; British pirate)

6
ALCOCK, Sir John (1892–1919; British
aviator)
BAFFIN, William (c. 1584–1622; English
navigator)
BALBOA, Vasco Núñez de (c. 1475–1517;
Spanish explorer)
BERING, Vitus Jonassen (1681–1741; Danish
navigator)
BRAZZA, Pierre Paul François Camille
Savorgnan de (1852–1905; French explorer)
BROOKE, Sir James (1803–68; British
explorer)
BURTON, Sir Richard (1821–90; British
explorer)
CABRAL, Pedro Álvares (?1467–1520;
Portuguese navigator)
CARSON, Kit (Christopher C, 1809–68; US
frontiersman)
CORTÉS, Hernán (1485–1547; Spanish
conquistador)
HUDSON, Henry (d. 1611; English navigator)
MORGAN, Sir Henry (c. 1635–88; Welsh
buccaneer)
NANSEN, Fridtjof (1861–1930; Norwegian
explorer)
NOBILE, Umberto (1885–1978; Italian aviator)
STUART, John McDouall (1815–66; Scottish
explorer)
TASMAN, Abel Janszoon (c. 1603–c. 1659;
Dutch navigator)

7
BARENTS, Willem (c. 1550–97; Dutch
navigator)
BLÉRIOT, Louis (1872–1936; French aviator)

7—continued

CARPINI, Giovanni da Pian del (*c.* 1180–*c.* 1252; Italian traveller)

CARTIER, Jacques (1491–1557; French navigator)

CÓRDOBA, Francisco Fernández de (d. 1518; Spanish explorer)

COVILHÃ, Pêro da (*c.* 1460–*c.* 1526; Portuguese explorer)

DAMPIER, William (*c.* 1652–1715; English explorer)

EARHART, Amelia (1898–1937; US aviator)

FRÉMONT, John C (1813–90; US explorer)

GILBERT, Sir Humphrey (*c.* 1539–83; English navigator)

HAWKINS, Sir John (1532–95; English navigator)

HILLARY, Sir Edmund (1919–   ; New Zealand mountaineer and explorer)

HINKLER, Herbert John Lewis (1892–1933; Australian aviator)

LA SALLE, Robert Cavelier, Sieur de (1643–87; French explorer)

MCCLURE, Sir Robert John Le Mesurier (1807–73; Irish explorer)

PIZARRO, Francisco (*c.* 1475–1541; Spanish conquistador)

PYTHEAS (4th century BC; Greek navigator)

RALEIGH, Sir Walter (1554–1618; British explorer)

SELKIRK, Alexander (1676–1721; Scottish sailor)

STANLEY, Sir Henry Morton (1841–1904; British explorer)

WILKINS, Sir George Hubert (1888–1958; British explorer)

WRANGEL, Ferdinand Petrovich, Baron von (1794–1870; Russian explorer)

8

AMUNDSEN, Roald (1872–1928; Norwegian explorer)

COLUMBUS, Christopher (1451–1506; Italian navigator)

COUSTEAU, Jacques Yves (1910–   ; French underwater explorer)

FLINDERS, Matthew (1774–1814; British navigator and hydrographer)

FRANKLIN, Sir John (1786–1847; British explorer)

MAGELLAN, Ferdinand (*c.* 1480–1521; Portuguese explorer)

MARCHAND, Jean Baptiste (1863–1934; French explorer)

VESPUCCI, Amerigo (1454–1512; Italian navigator)

9

BLANCHARD, Jean Pierre François (1753–1809; French balloonist)

CHAMPLAIN, Samuel de (1567–1635; French explorer)

FROBISHER, Sir Martin (*c.* 1535–94; English navigator)

HEYERDAHL, Thor (1914–   ; Norwegian ethnologist)

IBERVILLE, Pierre Le Moyne, Sieur d' (1661–1706; French-Canadian explorer)

LEICHARDT, Ludwig (1813–48; German explorer)

LINDBERGH, Charles A (1902–74; US aviator)

MARQUETTE, Jacques (1637–75; French explorer)

PAUSANIAS (2nd century AD; Greek traveller)

RASMUSSEN, Knud Johan Victor (1879–1933; Danish explorer)

VANCOUVER, George (*c.* 1758–98; British navigator)

VELÁSQUEZ, Diego (?1465–1522; Spanish explorer)

10

BARBAROSSA (Khayr ad-Din, d. 1546; Turkish pirate)

ERIC THE RED (late 10th century; Norwegian explorer)

SHACKLETON, Sir Ernest Henry (1874–1922; British explorer)

11

IBN BATTUTAH (1304–?1368; Arab traveller)

LA CONDAMINE, Charles Marie de (1701–74; French geographer)

LIVINGSTONE, David (1813–73; Scottish missionary and explorer)

PONCE DE LEON, Juan (1460–1521; Spanish explorer)

12

BOUGAINVILLE, Louis Antoine de (1729–1811; French navigator)

LEIF ERIKSSON (11th century; Icelandic explorer)

NORDENSKJÖLD, Nils Adolf Erik, Baron (1832–1901; Swedish navigator)

14

BELLINGSHAUSEN, Fabian Gottlieb, Baron von (1778–1852; Russian explorer)

DUMONT D'URVILLE, Jules Sébastien César (1790–1842; French navigator)

17

HENRY THE NAVIGATOR (1394–1460; Portuguese navigator and patron of explorers)

WORLD LEADERS

3

FOX, Charles James (1749–1806; British Whig politician)

LIE, Trygve (Halvdan) (1896–1968; Norwegian Labour politician)

4

BENN, Anthony Neil Wedgwood (1925– ; British Labour politician)

BLUM, Léon (1872–1950; French socialist)

BOSE, Subhas Chandra (c. 1897–c. 1945; Indian nationalist leader)

COOK, Sir Joseph (1860–1947; Australian statesman)

DÍAZ, Porfirio (1830–1915; Mexican soldier)

FOOT, Michael (Mackintosh) (1913– ; British Labour politician)

HILL, Sir Rowland (1795–1879; British postal expert)

HOLT, Harold Edward (1908–67; Australian statesman)

HOWE, Sir Richard Edward Geoffrey (1926– ; British Conservative politician)

HULL, Cordell (1871–1955; US Democratic politician)

KING, Jr, Martin Luther (1929–68; US Black civil-rights leader)

KING, William Lyon Mackenzie (1874–1950; Canadian statesman)

KIRK, Norman Eric (1923–74; New Zealand statesman)

MEIR, Golda (1898–1978; Israeli stateswoman)

NAGY, Imre (1896–1958; Hungarian statesman)

OWEN, Dr David (1938– ; British Social Democrat politician)

RHEE, Syngman (1875–1965; Korean statesman)

RUSK, David Dean (1909– ; US statesman)

TOJO (Hideki) (1884–1948; Japanese general)

TONE, Theobald Wolfe (1763–98; Irish nationalist)

TUTU, Desmond (1931– ; South African clergyman)

WARD, Sir Joseph George (1856–1930; New Zealand statesman)

5

AGNEW, Spiro Theodore (1918– ; US Republican politician)

ASTOR, Nancy Witcher, Viscountess (1879–1964; British politician)

BANDA, Hastings Kamuzu (1905– ; Malawi statesman)

5—continued

BEGIN, Menachem (1913– ; Israeli statesman)

BERIA, Lavrenti Pavlovich (1899–1953; Soviet politician)

BEVAN, Aneurin (1897–1960; British Labour politician)

BEVIN, Ernest (1881–1951; British politician)

BOTHA, Louis (1862–1919; South African statesman)

BOTHA, Pieter Willem (1916– ; South African statesman)

CLARK, Charles Joseph (1939– ; Canadian statesman)

DAYAN, Moshe (1915–81; Israeli general)

DEBRÉ, Michel (1912– ; French statesman)

DESAI, Shri Morarji Ranchhodji (1896– ; Indian statesman)

DE WET, Christian Rudolf (1854–1922; Afrikaner politician and soldier)

EBERT, Friedrich (1871–1925; German statesman)

EMMET, Robert (1778–1803; Irish nationalist)

FLOOD, Henry (1732–91; Irish politician)

LAVAL, Pierre (1883–1945; French statesman)

LENIN, Vladimir Ilich (V I Ulyanov, 1870–1924; Russian revolutionary)

LODGE, Henry Cabot (1850–1924; US Republican politician)

LYNCH, Jack (1917– ; Irish statesman)

LYONS, Joseph Aloysius (1879–1939; Australian statesman)

MANIN, Daniele (1804–57; Italian patriot)

MBOYA, Tom (1930–69; Kenyan politician)

MENON, Krishna (Vengalil Krishnan Krishna Menon, 1896–1974; Indian diplomat)

NEHRU, Jawaharlal (1889–1964; Indian statesman)

NKOMO, Joshua (1917– ; Zimbabwean politician)

OBOTE, Apollo Milton (1925– ; Ugandan statesman)

PERÓN, Juan Domingo (1895–1974; Argentine statesman)

SADAT, Anwar (1918–81; Egyptian statesman)

SMITH, Ian Douglas (1919– ; Rhodesian prime minister)

SMUTS, Jan Christiaan (1870–1950; South African statesman and general)

SPAAK, Paul Henri (1899–1972; Belgian statesman)

STEEL, David Martin Scott (1938– ; British politician)

VANCE, Cyrus (1917– ; US statesman)

5—continued

VILLA, Pancho (Francesco V, 1878–1923;
Mexican revolutionary)

6

ARAFAT, Yassir (1929–   ; Palestinian leader)

BARTON, Sir Edmund (1849–1920; Australian
statesman)

BHUTTO, Benazir (1953–   ; Pakistani
politician)

BHUTTO, Zulfikar Ali (1928–79; Pakistani
statesman)

BORDEN, Sir Robert Laird (1854–1937;
Canadian statesman)

BRANDT, Willy (1913–   ; West German
statesman)

BRIGHT, John (1811–89; British radical
politician)

BUTLER, Richard Austen, Baron (1902–82;
British Conservative politician)

CHIRAC, Jacques (1932–   ; French
statesman)

COATES, Joseph Gordon (1878–1943; New
Zealand statesman)

COBDEN, Richard (1804–65; British politician
and economist)

CRIPPS, Sir Richard Stafford (1889–1952;
British Labour politician)

CURTIN, John Joseph (1885–1945; Australian
statesman)

CURZON, George Nathaniel, 1st Marquess
(1859–1925; British politician)

DAVITT, Michael (1846–1906; Irish nationalist)

DEAKIN, Alfred (1856–1919; Australian
statesman)

DJILAS, Milovan (1911–   ; Yugoslav
politician)

DUBČEK, Alexander (1921–   ; Czechoslovak
statesman)

DULLES, John Foster (1888–1959; US
Republican politician and diplomat)

ERHARD, Ludwig (1897–1977; German
statesman)

FADDEN, Sir Arthur William (1895–1973;
Australian statesman)

FISHER, Andrew (1862–1928; Australian
statesman)

FLEURY, André Hercule de, Cardinal (1653–
1743; French statesman)

FORBES, George William (1869–1947; New
Zealand statesman)

FRANCO, Francisco (1892–1975; Spanish
general and statesman)

FRASER, John Malcolm (1930–   ; Australian
statesman)

FRASER, Peter (1884–1950; New Zealand
statesman)

GANDHI, Indira (1917–84; Indian
stateswoman)

GANDHI, Mohandas Karamchand (1869–1948;
Indian nationalist leader)

6—continued

GÖRING, Hermann Wilhelm (1893–1946;
German Nazi politician)

GORTON, John Grey (1911–   ; Australian
statesman)

GRIVAS, Georgios (1898–1974; Greek
general)

HEALEY, Denis Winston (1917–   ; British
Labour politician)

HUGHES, William Morris (1864–1952;
Australian statesman)

JUÁREZ, Benito Pablo (1806–72; Mexican
statesman)

KAUNDA, Kenneth David (1924–   ; Zambian
statesman)

KRUGER, Stephanus Johannes Paulus (1825–
1904; Afrikaner statesman)

MARCOS, Ferdinand Edralin (1917–   ;
Philippine statesman)

MASSEY, William Ferguson (1856–1925; New
Zealand statesman)

MOBUTU, Sese Seko (Joseph Désiré M,
1930–   ; Zaïrese statesman)

MOSLEY, Sir Oswald Ernald (1896–1980;
British fascist)

NASSER, Gamal Abdel (1918–70; Egyptian
statesman)

O'BRIEN, Conor Cruise (1917–   ; Irish
diplomat)

O'NEILL, Terence, Baron (1914–   ; Northern
Irish statesman)

PÉTAIN, Henri Philippe (1856–1951; French
general and statesman)

POWELL, John Enoch (1912–   ; British
politician)

QUAYLE, Dan (1947–   ; US politician)

REVERE, Paul (1735–1818; American
revolutionary

RHODES, Cecil John (1853–1902; South
African financier and statesman)

SAVAGE, Michael Joseph (1872–1940; New
Zealand statesman)

SEDDON, Richard John (1845–1906; New
Zealand statesman)

STALIN, Joseph (1879–1953; Soviet
statesman)

SUÁREZ, Adolfo, Duke of (1932–   ; Spanish
statesman)

THORPE, John Jeremy (1929–   ; British
Liberal politician)

WATSON, John Christian (1867–1941;
Australian statesman)

WILKES, John (1725–97; British journalist and
politician)

ZAPATA, Emiliano (?1877–1919; Mexican
revolutionary)

7

ACHESON, Dean Gooderham (1893–1971; US
lawyer and statesman)

ASHDOWN, Paddy (1941–   ; Social and
Liberal Democrat politician)

7—continued

ATATÜRK, Kemal (Mustafa Kemal, 1881–1938; Turkish statesman)

BATISTA (y Zaldívar), Fulgencio (1901–73; Cuban statesman)

BENNETT, Richard Bedford, Viscount (1870–1947; Canadian statesman)

BOLÍVAR, Simón (1783–1830; South American statesman)

BORMANN, Martin (1900–45; German Nazi leader)

CLINTON, de Witt (1769–1828; US statesman)

COLLINS, Michael (1890–1922; Irish nationalist)

GADDAFI, Moammar Al- (or Qaddafi, 1942– ; Libyan colonel and statesman)

GRATTAN, Henry (1746–1820; Irish politician)

GRIMOND, Joseph (1913– ; British politician)

GROMYKO, Andrei (1909– ; Soviet statesman)

HIMMLER, Heinrich (1900–45; German Nazi politician)

HOLLAND, Sir Sidney George (1893–1961; New Zealand statesman)

HUSSEIN (ibn Talal) (1935– ; King of Jordan

JENKINS, Roy Harris (1920– ; British politician and historian)

KINNOCK, Neil (1942– ; Labour politician)

KOSYGIN, Aleksei Nikolaevich (1904–80; Soviet statesman)

LUMUMBA, Patrice Hemery (1925–61; Congolese statesman)

MACLEOD, Iain Norman (1913–70; British Conservative politician)

MANDELA, Nelson (Rolihlahla) (1918– ; South African lawyer and politician)

MAZZINI, Giuseppe (1805–72; Italian patriot)

MCMAHON, William (1908– ; Australian statesman)

MENZIES, Sir Robert Gordon (1894–1978; Australian statesman)

MINTOFF, Dominic (1916– ; Maltese statesman)

MOLOTOV, Vyacheslav Mikhailovich (1890–1986; Soviet statesman)

NYERERE, Julius Kambarage (1922– ; Tanzanian statesman)

PAISLEY, Ian (1926– ; Northern Irish politician)

PARNELL, Charles Stewart (1846–91; Irish politician)

PEARSON, Lester Bowles (1897–1972; Canadian statesman)

RAFFLES, Sir Thomas Stamford (1781–1826; British colonial administrator)

SALAZAR, António de Oliveira (1889–1970; Portuguese dictator)

SCHMIDT, Helmut (1918– ; West German statesman)

7—continued

SCULLIN, James Henry (1876–1953; Australian statesman)

SHASTRI, Shri Lal Bahadur (1904–66; Indian statesman)

SUHARTO (1921– ; Indonesian statesman and general)

TROTSKY, Leon (1879–1940; Russian revolutionary)

TRUDEAU, Pierre Elliott (1919– ; Canadian statesman)

VORSTER, Balthazar Johannes (1915–83; South African statesman)

WHITLAM, Edward Gough (1916– ; Australian statesman)

8

ADENAUER, Konrad (1876–1967; German statesman)

AMIN DADA, Idi (c. 1925– ; Ugandan politician and president)

AYUB KHAN, Mohammad (1907–74; Pakistani statesman)

BEN BELLA, Ahmed (1916– ; Algerian statesman)

BISMARCK, Otto Eduard Leopold, Prince Von (1815–98; Prussian statesman)

BREZHNEV, Leonid Ilich (1906–82; Soviet statesman)

BUKHARIN, Nikolai Ivanovich (1888–1938; Soviet politician)

BULGANIN, Nikolai Aleksandrovich (1895–1975; Soviet statesman)

COSGRAVE, William Thomas (1880–1965; Irish statesman)

CROSSMAN, Richard Howard Stafford (1907–74; British Labour politician)

DALADIER, Édouard (1884–1970; French statesman)

DE GAULLE, Charles André Joseph Marie (1890–1970; French general and statesman)

DE VALERA, Eamon (1882–1975; Irish statesman)

DOLLFUSS, Engelbert (1892–1934; Austrian statesman)

DUVALIER, François (1907–71; Haitian politician)

EICHMANN, Adolf (1906–62; German Nazi politician)

FRANKLIN, Benjamin (1706–90; US diplomat)

GOEBBELS, Paul Joseph (1897–1945; German Nazi politician)

GRIFFITH, Arthur (1872–1922; Irish journalist and nationalist)

HARRIMAN, William Averell (1891–1986; US diplomat)

HASTINGS, Warren (1732–1818; British colonial administrator)

HIROHITO (1901–89; Emperor of Japan)

HOLYOAKE, Sir Keith Jacka (1904–83; New Zealand statesman)

8—continued

HONECKER, Erich (1912– ; East German statesman)

HUMPHREY, Hubert Horatio (1911–1978; US Democratic politician)

IBARRURI, Dolores (1895– ; Spanish politician)

KENYATTA, Jomo (c. 1891–1978; Kenyan statesman)

KHOMEINI, Ayatollah Ruholla (1900– ; Iranian Shiite Muslim leader)

MALENKOV, Georgi Maksimilianovich (1902–88; Soviet statesman)

MCCARTHY, Joseph Raymond (1908–57; US Republican senator)

MORRISON, Herbert Stanley, Baron (1888–1965; British Labour politician)

MUZOREWA, Bishop Abel Tendekayi (1925– ; Zimbabwean statesman)

O'CONNELL, Daniel (1775–1847; Irish politician)

O'HIGGINS, Bernardo (?1778–1842; Chilean national hero)

PINOCHET, Augusto (1915– ; Chilean general)

PODGORNY, Nikolai (1903– ; Soviet statesman)

POINCARÉ, Raymond (1860–1934; French statesman)

POMPIDOU, Georges Jean Raymond (1911–74; French statesman)

QUISLING, Vidkun Abraham Lauritz Jonsson (1887–1945; Norwegian army officer and Nazi collaborator)

RASPUTIN, Grigori Yefimovich (c. 1872–1916; Russian mystic)

SIHANOUK, Norodim, Prince (1923– ; King of Cambodia)

SIKORSKI, Władysław (1881–1943; Polish general and statesman)

ULBRICHT, Walter (1893–1973; East German statesman)

VERWOERD, Hendrik Frensch (1901–66; South African statesman)

WALDHEIM, Kurt (1918– ; Austrian diplomat and statesman)

WEIZMANN, Chaim Azriel (1874–1952; Israeli statesman)

WELENSKY, Sir Roy (1907– ; Rhodesian statesman)

WILLIAMS, Shirley Vivien Teresa Brittain (1930– ; British politician)

9

AGA KHAN IV (1936– ; Imam (of the Ismaili sect of Muslims)

BEN-GURION, David (1886–1973; Israeli statesman)

CASTRO RUZ, Fidel (1926– ; Cuban statesman)

CHOU EN-LAI (or Zhou En Lai, 1898–1976; Chinese communist statesman)

9—continued

CHURCHILL, Lord Randolph Henry Spencer (1849–95; British Conservative politician)

GAITSKELL, Hugh (1906–63; British politician)

GARIBALDI, Giuseppe (1807–82; Italian soldier)

GORBACHOV, Mikhail Sergeevich (1931– ; Soviet statesman)

HENDERSON, Arthur (1863–1935; British Labour politician)

HO CHI MINH (Nguyen That Thanh, 1890–1969; Vietnamese statesman)

KISSINGER, Henry Alfred (1923– ; US diplomat and political scientist)

LA GUARDIA, Fiorello Henry (1882–1947; US politician)

LUXEMBURG, Rosa (1871–1919; German revolutionary)

MACDONALD, James Ramsay (1866–1937; British statesman)

MACDONALD, Sir John Alexander (1815–91; Canadian statesman)

MUSSOLINI, Benito Amilcare Andrea (1883–1945; Italian fascist dictator)

PANKHURST, Emmeline (1858–1928; British suffragette)

STEVENSON, Adlai Ewing (1900–65; US Democratic politician)

10

BERNADOTTE, Jean Baptiste Jules (c. 1763–1844; French marshal)

CARRINGTON, Peter Alexander Rupert, 6th Baron (1919– ; British Conservative politician)

CLEMENCEAU, Georges (1841–1929; French statesman)

KHRUSHCHEV, Nikita Sergeevich (1894–1971; Soviet statesman)

LEE KUAN YEW (1923– ; Singaporean statesman)

MAO TSE-TUNG (or Mao Ze Dong, 1893–1976; Chinese communist statesman)

MITTERRAND, François Maurice (1916– ; French socialist politician)

RIBBENTROP, Joachim von (1893–1946; German Nazi politician)

VOROSHILOV, Kliment Yefremovich (1881–1969; Soviet marshal and statesman)

11

ABDUL RAHMAN, Tunku (1903–73; Malaysian statesman)

CASTLEREAGH, Robert Stewart, Viscount (1769–1822; British statesman)

DIEFENBAKER, John George (1895–1979; Canadian statesman)

HORE-BELISHA, Isaac Leslie, 1st Baron (1893–1957; British politician)

11—continued
MAKARIOS III, Mikhail Khristodolou Mouskos (1913–77; Cypriot churchman and statesman)
MOUNTBATTEN (of Burma), Louis, 1st Earl (1900–79; British admiral and colonial administrator)
SELWYN LLOYD, John, Baron (1904–78; British Conservative politician)
WILBERFORCE, William (1759–1833; British philanthropist)

12
BANDARANAIKE, Solomon (1899–1959; Sri Lankan statesman)
FREI MONTALVA, Eduardo (1911–82; Chilean statesman)
HAMMARSKJÖLD, Dag (1905–61; Swedish international civil servant)
MENDÈS-FRANCE, Pierre (1907–82; French statesman)
PAPADOPOULOS, George (1919–   ; Greek colonel)

13
CHIANG KAI-SHEK (or Jiang Jie Shi, 1887–1975; Nationalist Chinese soldier and statesman)

14
ALLENDE GOSSENS, Salvador (1908–73; Chilean statesman)
CLIVE OF PLASSEY, Robert, Baron (1725–74; British soldier and colonial administrator)

15
GISCARD D'ESTAING, Valéry (1926–   ; French statesman)

20+
AYATOLLAH RUHOLLA KHOMEINI. See KHOMEINI, Ayatollah Ruholla.
HAILSHAM OF ST MARYLEBONE, Baron (Quintin Mcgarel Hogg, 1907–   )

MILITARY LEADERS

3
LEE, Robert E (1807–70; US Confederate commander)
NEY, Michel, Prince of Moscow (1769–1815; French marshal)

4
ALBA, Fernando Alvarez de Toledo, Duke of (1507–83; Spanish general)
BART, Jean (1650–1702; French admiral)
BYNG, George, Viscount Torrington (1663–1733; English admiral)
DIAZ, Porfirio (1830–1915; Mexican soldier)
FOCH, Ferdinand (1851–1929; French marshal)
HAIG, Douglas, 1st Earl (1861–1928; British field marshal)
HOOD, Samuel, 1st Viscount (1724–1816; British admiral)
HOWE, Richard, Earl (1726–99; British admiral)
JODL, Alfred (1890–1946; German general)
RAIS, Gilles de (or G de Retz, 1404–40; French marshal)
RÖHM, Ernst (1887–1934; German soldier)
ROON, Albrecht, Graf von (1803–79; Prussian general)
SAXE, Maurice, Comte de (1696–1750; Marshal of France)
SLIM, William Joseph, 1st Viscount (1891–1970; British field marshal)
TOGO (Heihachiro) (1847–1934; Japanese admiral)

5
ANDRÉ, John (1751–80; British soldier)
ANSON, George Anson, Baron (1697–1762; British admiral)
BLAKE, Robert (1599–1657; English admiral)
BLIGH, William (1754–1817; British admiral)
CIMON (d. c. 450 BC; Athenian general and politician)
DEWEY, George (1837–1917; US admiral)
DRAKE, Sir Francis (1540–96; English navigator and admiral)
EL CID (Rodrigo Diáz de Vivar, c. 1040–99; Spanish warrior)
GATES, Horatio (?1728–1806; American general)
HAWKE, Edward, 1st Baron (1705–81; British admiral)
JONES, John Paul (1747–92; American naval commander)
LALLY, Thomas, Comte de (1702–66; French general)
LEVEN, Alexander Leslie, 1st Earl of (1580–1661; Scottish general)
MOORE, Sir John (1761–1809; British general)
MURAT, Joachim (1767–1815; French marshal)
PERRY, Matthew C (1794–1858; US naval officer)
PRIDE, Thomas (d. 1658; English parliamentary soldier)

5—continued

SULLA, Lucius Cornelius (*c.* 138−78 BC; Roman dictator)

TILLY, Johan Tserclaes, Graf von (1559−1632; Bavarian general)

TROMP, Maarten (1598−1653; Dutch admiral)

WOLFE, James (1727−59; British soldier)

6

AETIUS, Flavius (d. 454 AD; Roman general)

ARNOLD, Benedict (1741−1801; American general)

BAYARD, Pierre Terrail, Seigneur de (*c.* 1473−1524; French soldier)

BEATTY, David, 1st Earl (1871−1936; British admiral)

BENBOW, John (1653−1702; English naval officer)

CRONJE, Piet Arnoldus (*c.* 1840−1911; South African general)

CUSTER, George Armstrong (1839−76; US cavalry general)

DARLAN, Jean (Louis Xavier) François (1881−1942; French admiral)

DÖNITZ, Karl (1891−1981; German admiral)

DUNDEE, John Graham of Claverhouse, 1st Viscount (*c.* 1649−89; Scottish soldier)

DUNOIS, Jean d'Orléans, Comte de (1403−68; French general)

FISHER, John Arbuthnot, 1st Baron (1841−1920; British admiral)

FRENCH, John, 1st Earl of Ypres (1852−1925; British field marshal)

FULLER, J F C (1878−1966; British soldier)

GINKEL, Godert de, 1st Earl of Athlone (1644−1703; Dutch general)

GORDON, Charles George (1833−85; British general)

GRANBY, John Manners, Marquess of (1721−70; British soldier)

GREENE, Nathaneal (1742−86; American general)

HALSEY, William F (1882−1959; US admiral)

JOFFRE, Joseph Jacques Césaire (1852−1931; French marshal)

KEITEL, Wilhelm (1882−1946; German field marshal)

KLÉBER, Jean Baptiste (1753−1800; French general)

KONIEV, Ivan Stepanovich (1897−1973; Soviet marshal)

MARIUS, Gaius (*c.* 157−86 BC; Roman general)

MOLTKE, Helmuth, Graf von (1800−91; Prussian field marshal)

MOREAU, Jean Victor (1763−1813; French general)

NAPIER (of Magdala), Robert Cornelis, 1st Baron (1810−90; British field marshal)

NAPIER, Sir Charles James (1782−1853; British general)

NARSES (*c.* 480−574 AD; Byzantine general)

6—continued

NELSON, Horatio, Viscount (1758−1805; British admiral)

NIMITZ, Chester W (1885−1966; US admiral)

OUTRAM, Sir James (1803−63; British soldier)

PATTON, George S (1885−1945; US general)

PAULUS, Friedrich (1890−1957; German field marshal)

PÉTAIN, (Henri) Philippe (1856−1951; French general and statesman)

RAEDER, Erich (1876−1960; German admiral)

RAGLAN, Fitzroy James Henry Somerset, 1st Baron (1788−1855; British field marshal)

RODNEY, George Brydges, 1st Baron (1719−92; British admiral)

ROMMEL, Erwin (1891−1944; German general)

RUPERT, Prince (1619−82; Cavalry officer)

RUYTER, Michiel Adriaanszoon de (1607−76; Dutch admiral)

TEDDER, Arthur William, 1st Baron (1890−1967; British air marshal)

VERNON, Edward (1684−1757; British admiral)

WAVELL, Archibald Percival, 1st Earl (1883−1950; British field marshal)

WILSON, Henry Maitland, 1st Baron (1881−1964; British field marshal)

WILSON, Sir Henry Hughes (1864−1922; British field marshal)

ZHUKOV, Georgi Konstantinovich (1896−1974; Soviet marshal)

7

AGRIPPA, Marcus Vipsanius (?63−12 BC; Roman general)

ALLENBY, Edmund Henry Hynman, 1st Viscount (1861−1936; British field marshal)

ARTIGAS, José Gervasio (1764−1850; national hero of Uruguay)

ATHLONE, Alexander Cambridge, 1st Earl of (1874−1957; British soldier)

BAZAINE, Achille François (1811−88; French marshal)

BERWICK, James Fitzjames, Duke of (1670−1734; Marshal of France)

BLÜCHER, Gebhard Leberecht von, Prince of Wahlstatt (1742−1819; Prussian general)

BRADLEY, Omar Nelson (1893−1981; US general)

DECATUR, Stephen (1779−1820; US naval officer)

DENIKIN, Anton Ivanovich (1872−1947; Russian general)

DOWDING, Hugh Caswall Tremenheere, 1st Baron (1882−1970; British air chief marshal)

FAIRFAX, Thomas, 3rd Baron (1612−71; English general)

JACKSON, Andrew (1767−1845; US statesman and general)

JACKSON, Stonewall (Thomas Jonathan J, 1824−63; US Confederate general)

7—continued

KOLCHAK, Alexander Vasilievich (1874–1920; Russian admiral)

LAMBERT, John (1619–83; English parliamentary general)

LYAUTEY, Louis Hubert Gonzalve (1854–1934; French marshal)

MASSÉNA, André (?1756–1817; French marshal)

METAXAS, Ioannis (1871–1941; Greek general)

MORTIER, Édouard Adolphe Casimir Joseph, Duc de Trévise (1768–1835; French marshal)

PHILLIP, Arthur (1738–1814; British admiral)

REGULUS, Marcus Attilus (d. c. 251 BC; Roman general)

ROBERTS, Frederick Sleigh, 1st Earl (1832–1914; British field marshal)

SHERMAN, William Tecumseh (1820–91; US Federal general)

SHOVELL, Sir Cloudesley (1650–1707; English admiral)

SUVOROV, Aleksandr Vasilievich, Count (1729–1800; Russian field marshal)

TANCRED (c. 1078–1112; Norman Crusader)

TIRPITZ, Alfred von (1849–1930; German admiral)

TURENNE, Henri de la Tour d'Auvergne, Vicomte de (1611–75; French marshal)

VENDÔME, Louis Joseph, Duc de (1654–1712; French marshal)

VILLARS, Claude Louis Hector, Duc de (1653–1734; French marshal)

WALLACE, Lew (1827–1905; US soldier)

WINGATE, Orde Charles (1903–44; British soldier)

WRANGEL, Peter Nikolaievich, Baron (1878–1928; Russian general)

8

AGRICOLA, Gnaeus Julius (40–93 AD; Roman governor)

ANGLESEY, Henry William Paget, 1st Marquess of (1768–1854; British field marshal)

AUGEREAU, Pierre François Charles, Duc de Castiglione (1757–1816; French marshal)

BADOGLIO, Pietro (1871–1956; Italian general)

BERTRAND, Henri Gratien, Comte (1773–1844; French marshal)

BOURMONT, Louis Auguste Victor de Ghaisnes, Comte de (1773–1846; French marshal)

BURGOYNE, John (1722–92; British general)

CAMPBELL, Colin, Baron Clyde (1792–1863; British field marshal)

CARDIGAN, James Thomas Brudenell, 7th Earl of (1797–1868; British cavalry officer)

CARRANZA, Venustiano (1859–1920; Mexican statesman and soldier)

8—continued

COCHRANE, Thomas, 10th Earl of Dundonald (1775–1860; British admiral)

CROMWELL, Oliver (1599–1658; English soldier and statesman)

GUESCLIN, Bertrand du (c. 1320–80; French commander)

HANNIBAL (247–c. 183 BC; Carthaginian general)

IRONSIDE, William Edmund, 1st Baron (1880–1959; British field marshal)

JELLICOE, John Rushworth, 1st Earl (1859–1935; British admiral)

KORNILOV, Lavrentia Georgievich (1870–1918; Russian general)

LUCULLUS, Lucius Licinius (d. c. 57 BC; Roman general)

LYSANDER (d. 395 BC; Spartan general)

MARSHALL, George C (1880–1959; US general)

MONTCALM, Louis Joseph de Montcalm-Grozon, Marquis de (1712–59; French general)

O'HIGGINS, Bernardo (?1778–1842; Chilean national hero)

PERSHING, John J (1860–1948; US general)

SANDWICH, John Montagu, 4th Earl of (1718–92; first lord of the admiralty)

SHERIDAN, Philip H (1831–88; US Federal general)

STILICHO, Flavius (d. 408 AD; Roman general)

STILWELL, Joseph W (1883–1946; US general)

WOLSELEY, Garnet Joseph, 1st Viscount (1833–1913; British field marshal)

9

ANGOULÊME, Charles de Valois, Duc d' (1573–1650; French soldier)

ANTIPATER (397–319 BC; Macedonian general)

ANTONESCU, Ion (1882–1946; Romanian general)

ARISTIDES (the Just) (c. 520–c. 468 BC; Athenian statesman)

BONAPARTE, Napoleon (1769–1821; French emperor)

DUMOURIEZ, Charles François Du Périer (1739–1823; French general)

GNEISENAU, August, Graf Neithardt von (1760–1831; Prussian field marshal)

GRENVILLE, Sir Richard (?1541–91; British sailor)

HASDRUBAL (d. 207 BC; Carthaginian general)

KITCHENER (of Khartoum), Horatio Herbert, 1st Earl (1850–1916; British field marshal)

LAFAYETTE, Marie Joseph Gilbert Motier, Marquis de (1757–1834; French general and politician)

MACARTHUR, Douglas (1880–1964; US general)

9—continued

MARCELLUS, Marcus Claudius (d. 208 BC; Roman general)

MCCLELLAN, George B (1826–85; Federal general)

MILTIADES (c. 550–489 BC; Athenian general)

NEWCASTLE, William Cavendish, Duke of (1592–1676; English soldier)

OLDCASTLE, Sir John (c. 1378–1417; English soldier)

PRETORIUS, Andries (1799–1853; Afrikaner leader)

RUNDSTEDT, Gerd von (1875–1953; German field marshal)

SANTA ANNA, Antonio López de (1794–1876; Mexican soldier)

TRENCHARD, Hugh Montague, 1st Viscount (1873–1956; The first British air marshal)

10

ABERCROMBY, Sir Ralph (1734–1801; British general)

ALANBROOKE, Alan Francis Brooke, 1st Viscount (1883–1963; British field marshal)

ALCIBIADES (c. 450–404 BC; Athenian general and politician)

ANTIGONUS I (c. 382–301 BC; Macedonian general)

AUCHINLECK, Sir Claude (1884–1981; British field marshal)

BELISARIUS (c. 505–65 AD; Byzantine general)

BERNADOTTE, Jean Baptiste Jules (1763–1844)

CORNWALLIS, Charles, 1st Marquess (1738–1805; British general)

CUMBERLAND, William Augustus, Duke of (1721–65; British general)

ENVER PASHA (1881–1922; Turkish soldier)

FLAMININUS, Titus Quinctius (c. 230–c. 174 BC; Roman general)

HINDENBURG, Paul von Beneckendorff und von (1847–1934; German general)

KESSELRING, Albert (1885–1960; German general)

KUBLAI KHAN (1215–94; Mongol conqueror of China)

MANNERHEIM, Carl Gustaf Emil, Baron von (1867–1951; Finnish general)

MONTGOMERY (of Alamein), Bernard Law, 1st Viscount (1887–1976; British field marshal)

OGLETHORPE, James Edward (1696–1785; English general)

RICHTHOFEN, Manfred, Freiherr von (1892–1918; German air ace)

SCHLIEFFEN, Alfred, Graf von (1833–1913; German general)

TIMOSHENKO, Semyon Konstantinovich (1895–1970; Soviet marshal)

VILLENEUVE, Pierre (1763–1806; French admiral)

10—continued

WELLINGTON, Arthur Wellesley, Duke of (1769–1852; British general)

11

ALBUQUERQUE, Alfonso de (1453–1515; Portuguese governor in India)

BADEN-POWELL, Robert Stephenson Smyth, 1st Baron (1857–1941; British general)

BEAUHARNAIS, Alexandre, Vicomte de (1760–94; French general)

BRAUCHITSCH, Walther von (1881–1948; German general)

COLLINGWOOD, Cuthbert, 1st Baron (1750–1810; British admiral)

EPAMINONDAS (c. 418–362 BC; Theban general)

LIDDELL HART, Sir Basil Henry (1895–1970; British soldier)

MARLBOROUGH, John Churchill, 1st Duke of (1650–1722; British general)

MÜNCHHAUSEN, Karl Friedrich, Freiherr von (1720–97; German soldier)

PONIATOWSKI, Józef (1763–1813; Marshal of France)

WALLENSTEIN, Albrecht Wenzel von (1583–1634; Bohemian-born general)

12

IBRAHIM PASHA (1789–1848; Ottoman general)

13

EUGÈNE OF SAVOY, Prince (1663–1736; Austrian general)

FABIUS MAXIMUS, Quintus (d. 203 BC; Roman general)

HAMILCAR BARCA (d. c. 229 BC; Carthaginian general)

14

BARCLAY DE TOLLY, Mikhail Bogdanovich, Prince (1761–1818; Russian field marshal)

CLIVE OF PLASSEY, Robert, Baron (1725–74; British soldier and colonial administrator)

15

CASSIUS LONGINUS, Gaius (d. 42 BC; Roman general)

SCIPIO AFRICANUS (236–183 BC; Roman general)

16

ALEXANDER OF TUNIS, Harold, 1st Earl (1891–1969; British field marshal)

17

HOWARD OF EFFINGHAM, Charles, 2nd Baron (1536–1624; English Lord High Admiral)

20+

BERNHARD OF SAXE-WEIMAR, Duke (1604–39; German general)

SCIPIO AEMILIANUS AFRICANUS (c. 185–129 BC; Roman general)

PRIME MINISTERS OF GREAT BRITAIN (FROM 1721)

NAME (TERM)

ROBERT WALPOLE (1721–42)
SPENCER COMPTON, EARL OF WILMINGTON (1742–43)
HENRY PELHAM (1743–54)
THOMAS PELHAM-HOLLES, DUKE OF NEWCASTLE (1754–56)
WILLIAM CAVENDISH, DUKE OF DEVONSHIRE (1756–57)
THOMAS PELHAM-HOLLES, DUKE OF NEWCASTLE (1757–62)
JOHN STUART, EARL OF BUTE (1762–63)
GEORGE GRENVILLE (1763–65)
CHARLES WATSON-WENTWORTH, MARQUIS OF ROCKINGHAM (1765–66)
WILLIAM PITT, EARL OF CHATHAM (1766–68)
AUGUSTUS HENRY FITZROY, DUKE OF GRAFTON (1768–70)
FREDERICK NORTH (1770–82)
CHARLES WATSON-WENTWORTH, MARQUIS OF ROCKINGHAM (1782)
WILLIAM PETTY, EARL OF SHELBURNE (1782–83)
WILLIAM HENRY CAVENDISH BENTINCK, DUKE OF PORTLAND (1783)
WILLIAM PITT (SON OF EARL OF CHATHAM) (1783–1801)
HENRY ADDINGTON (1801–04)
WILLIAM PITT (1804–06)
WILLIAM WYNDHAM GRENVILLE, BARON GRENVILLE (1806–07)
WILLIAM BENTINCK, DUKE OF PORTLAND (1807–09)
SPENCER PERCEVAL (1809–12)
ROBERT BANKS JENKINSON, EARL OF LIVERPOOL (1812–27)
GEORGE CANNING (1827)
FREDERICK JOHN ROBINSON, VISCOUNT GODERICH (1827–28)
ARTHUR WELLESLEY, DUKE OF WELLINGTON (1828–30)
CHARLES GREY, EARL GREY (1830–34)
WILLIAM LAMB, VISCOUNT MELBOURNE (1834)
ROBERT PEEL (1834–35)
WILLIAM LAMB, VISCOUNT MELBOURNE (1835–41)
ROBERT PEEL (1841–46)
JOHN RUSSELL (1846–52)
EDWARD GEORGE GEOFFREY SMITH STANLEY, EARL OF DERBY (1852)

GEORGE HAMILTON GORDON, EARL OF ABERDEEN (1852–55)
HENRY JOHN TEMPLE, VISCOUNT PALMERSTON (1855–58)
EDWARD STANLEY, EARL OF DERBY (1858–59)
HENRY TEMPLE, VISCOUNT PALMERSTON (1859–65)
JOHN RUSSELL, EARL RUSSELL (1865–66)
EDWARD STANLEY, EARL OF DERBY (1866–68)
BENJAMIN DISRAELI (1868)
WILLIAM EWART GLADSTONE (1868–74)
BENJAMIN DISRAELI, EARL (1876) OF BEACONSFIELD (1874–80)
WILLIAM EWART GLADSTONE (1880–85)
ROBERT A. T. GASCOYNE-CECIL, MARQUIS OF SALISBURY (1885–86)
WILLIAM EWART GLADSTONE (1886)
ROBERT GASCOYNE-CECIL, MARQUIS OF SALISBURY (1886–92)
WILLIAM EWART GLADSTONE (1892–94)
ARCHIBALD PHILIP PRIMROSE, EARL OF ROSEBERY (1894–95)
ROBERT GASCOYNE-CECIL, MARQUIS OF SALISBURY (1895–1902)
ARTHUR JAMES BALFOUR (1902–05)
HENRY CAMPBELL-BANNERMAN (1905–08)
HERBERT HENRY ASQUITH (1908–16)
DAVID LLOYD GEORGE (1916–22)
ANDREW BONAR LAW (1922–23)
STANLEY BALDWIN (1923–24)
JAMES RAMSAY MACDONALD (1924)
STANLEY BALDWIN (1924–29)
JAMES RAMSAY MACDONALD (1929–35)
STANLEY BALDWIN (1935–37)
NEVILLE CHAMBERLAIN (1937–40)
WINSTON CHURCHILL (1940–45)
CLEMENT RICHARD ATTLEE (1945–51)
WINSTON CHURCHILL (1951–55)
ANTHONY EDEN (1955–57)
HAROLD MACMILLAN (1957–63)
ALEC DOUGLAS-HOME (1963–64)
HAROLD WILSON (1964–70)
EDWARD HEATH (1970–74)
HAROLD WILSON (1974–76)
JAMES CALLAGHAN (1976–79)
MARGARET THATCHER (1979–   )

THE PRESIDENTS OF THE UNITED STATES OF AMERICA

NAME (TERM)

GEORGE WASHINGTON (1789–97)
JOHN ADAMS (1797–1801)
THOMAS JEFFERSON (1801–09)
JAMES MADISON (1809–17)
JAMES MONROE (1817–25)
JOHN QUINCY ADAMS (1825–29)
ANDREW JACKSON (1829–37)
MARTIN VAN BUREN (1837–41)
WILLIAM HENRY HARRISON (1841)
JOHN TYLER (1841–45)
JAMES KNOX POLK (1845–49)
ZACHARY TAYLOR (1849–50)
MILLARD FILLMORE (1850–53)
FRANKLIN PIERCE (1853–57)
JAMES BUCHANAN (1857–61)
ABRAHAM LINCOLN (1861–65)
ANDREW JOHNSON (1865–69)
ULYSSES SIMPSON GRANT (1869–77)
RUTHERFORD BIRCHARD HAYES (1877–81)
JAMES ABRAM GARFIELD (1881)
CHESTER ALAN ARTHUR (1881–85)

GROVER CLEVELAND (1885–89)
BENJAMIN HARRISON (1889–93)
GROVER CLEVELAND (1893–97)
WILLIAM MCKINLEY (1897–1901)
THEODORE ROOSEVELT (1901–09)
WILLIAM HOWARD TAFT (1909–13)
WOODROW WILSON (1913–21)
WARREN GAMALIEL HARDING (1921–23)
CALVIN COOLIDGE (1923–29)
HERBERT CLARK HOOVER (1929–33)
FRANKLIN DELANO ROOSEVELT (1933–45)
HARRY S TRUMAN (1945–53)
DWIGHT DAVID EISENHOWER (1953–61)
JOHN FITZGERALD KENNEDY (1961–63)
LYNDON BAINES JOHNSON (1963–69)
RICHARD MILHOUS NIXON (1969–74)
GERALD RUDOLPH FORD (1974–77)
JAMES EARL CARTER (1977–81)
RONALD WILSON REAGAN (1981–89)
GEORGE HERBERT WALKER BUSH
(1989–   )

RULERS OF ENGLAND

KINGS OF KENT

HENGEST (c. 455–488)
GERIC surnamed OISC (488–?512)
OCTA (?512–?)
EORMENRIC (?–560)
ETHELBERT I (560–616)
EADBALD (616–640)
EARCONBERT (640–664)
EGBERT I (664–673)
HLOTHERE* (673–685)
EADRIC* (685–686)
SUAEBHARD* (676–692)
OSWINI* (?688–?690)
WIHTRED* (690–725)
ETHELBERT II* (725–762)
EADBERT* (?725–?762)
ALRIC* (c. 750s)
EARDWULF* (747–762)
SIGERED* (?762)
EANMUND* (c. 759–765)
HEABERHT* (764–765)
EGBERT II (c. 765–780)
EALHMUND (784–786)
EADBERT (PRAEN) (796–798)
EADWALD (?798 or 807)

CUTHRED (798–807)
BALDRED (?–825)

KINGS OF DEIRA

AELLI (c. 560–590)
EDWIN (?590–592)
ETHELFRITH (592–616)
EDWIN (616–632)
OSRIC (632–633)
OSWALD (ST.) (633–641)
OSWINE (644–651)
ETHELWALD (651–654)

KINGS OF NORTHUMBRIA

ETHELFRITH (592–616)
EDWIN (616–632)
OSWALD (ST.) (633–641)
OSWIU (654–670)
EGFRITH (670–685)
ALDFRITH (685–704)
OSRED I (704–716)
COENRED (716–718)
OSRIC (718–729)
CEOLWULF (729–737)

EADBERT (737–758)
OSWULF (c. 758)
ETHELWALD MOLL (758–765)
ALCHRED (765–774)
ETHELRED I (774–778)
ELFWALD I (778–788)
OSRED II (788–790)
ETHELRED I (790–796)
OSBALD (796)
EARDWULF (796–806)
ELFWALD II (806–808)
EARDWULF (?808)
EANRED (808–840)
ETHELRED II (840–844)
REDWULF (844)
ETHELRED II (844–849)
OSBERT (849–862)
AELLE (862–867)
EGBERT I (867–873)
RICSIG (873–876)
EGBERT II (876–?878)

KINGS OF MERCIA

CEARL (c. 600)
PENDA (632–654)
WULFHERE (657–674)
ETHELRED (674–704)
COENRED (704–709)
CEOLRED (709–716)
ETHELBALD (716–?757)
BEORNRED (757)
OFFA (757–796)
EGFRITH (796)
COENWULF (796–?821)
CEOLWULF I (821–823)
BEORNWULF (823–825)
LUDECAN (825–827)
WIGLAF (827–840)
BEORHTWULF (840–852)
BURGRED (852–874)
CEOLWULF II (874–?883)

KINGS OF THE WEST SAXONS

CERDIC (519–534)
CYNRIC (534–560)
CEAWLIN (560–591)
CEOL (591–597)
CEOLWULF (597–611)
CYNEGILS (611–643)
CENWALH (643–672)
SEAXBURH (Queen) (?672–?674)
AESCWINE (674–676)
CENTWINE (676–685)
CAEDWALLA (685–688)
INI (688–726)
AETHELHEARD (726–?740)
CUTHRED (740–756)
SIGEBERHT (756–757)
CYNEWULF (757–786)
BEORHTRIC (786–802)
EGBERT (802–839)

ETHELWULF (839–855)
ETHELBALD (855–860)
ETHELBERT (860–866)
ETHELRED (866–871)
ALFRED (871–899)
EDWARD THE ELDER (899–925)
ATHELSTAN (925–939)
EDMUND (939–946)
EDRED (946–955)

RULERS OF ENGLAND

EDWY (955–959)
EDGAR (959–975)
EDWARD THE MARTYR (975–979)
ETHELRED (979–1013)
SWEGN FORKBEARD (1013–14)
ETHELRED (1014–16)
EDMUND IRONSIDE (1016)
CANUTE (1016–35)
HAROLD HAREFOOT (1035–40)
HARTACNUT (1040–42)
EDWARD THE CONFESSOR (1042–66)
HAROLD GODWINSON (1066)
EDGAR ETHELING (1066)
WILLIAM I (THE CONQUEROR) (1066–87)
WILLIAM II (RUFUS) (1087–1100)
HENRY I (1100–35)
STEPHEN (1135–54)
HENRY II (1154–89)
RICHARD I (1189–99)
JOHN (1199–1216)
HENRY III (1216–72)
EDWARD I (1272–1307)
EDWARD II (1307–27)
EDWARD III (1327–77)
RICHARD II (1377–99)
HENRY IV (1399–1413)
HENRY V (1413–22)
HENRY VI (1422–61; 1470–71)
EDWARD IV (1461–83)
EDWARD V (1483)
RICHARD III (1483–85)
HENRY VII (1485–1509)
HENRY VIII (1509–47)
EDWARD VI (1547–53)
JANE (LADY JANE GREY) (1553)
MARY (1553–58)
PHILIP* (1554–58)
ELIZABETH I (1558–1603)
JAMES I (1603–25)
CHARLES I (1625–49)
THE COMMONWEALTH (1649–60; OLIVER
    CROMWELL (LORD PROTECTOR, 1653–
    58); RICHARD CROMWELL (LORD
    PROTECTOR, 1658–59))
CHARLES II (1660–85)
JAMES II (1685–88)
WILLIAM AND MARY (1689–1694)
WILLIAM III (1694–1702)
ANNE (1702–14)
GEORGE I (1714–27)

GEORGE II (1727–60)
GEORGE III (1760–1820)
GEORGE IV (1820–30)
WILLIAM IV (1830–37)
VICTORIA (1837–1901)
EDWARD VII (1901–10)

GEORGE V (1910–36)
EDWARD VIII (DUKE OF WINDSOR) (1936)
GEORGE VI (1936–52)
ELIZABETH II (1952–   )

* Joint rulers

NOBEL PRIZE WINNERS

PHYSICS

1901	W RÖNTGEN (GER)	1938	E FERMI (ITALY)
1902	H ANTOON LORENTZ (NETH)	1939	E LAWRENCE (US)
	P ZEEMAN (NETH)	1943	O STERN (US)
1903	A BECQUEREL (FR)	1944	I RABI (US)
	P CURIE (FR)	1945	W PAULI (AUSTRIA)
	M CURIE (FR)	1946	P BRIDGMAN (US)
1904	LORD RAYLEIGH (GB)	1947	SIR E APPLETON (GB)
1905	P LENARD (GER)	1948	P BLACKETT (GB)
1906	SIR J J THOMSON (GB)	1949	H YUKAWA (JAPAN)
1907	A A MICHELSON (US)	1950	C POWELL (GB)
1908	G LIPPMANN (FR)	1951	SIR J COCKCROFT (GB)
1909	G MARCONI (ITALY)		E WALTON (IRE)
	K BRAUN (GER)	1952	F BLOCH (US)
1910	J VAN DER WAALS (NETH)		E PURCELL (US)
1911	W WIEN (GER)	1953	F ZERNIKE (NETH)
1912	N G DALÉN (SWED)	1954	M BORN (GB)
1913	H KAMERLINGH ONNES (NETH)		W BOTHE (GER)
1914	M VON LAUE (GER)	1955	W LAMB, JR (US)
1915	SIR W BRAGG (GB)		P KUSCH (US)
	SIR L BRAGG (GB)	1956	W SHOCKLEY (US)
1916	(NO AWARD)		J BARDEEN (US)
1917	C BARKLA (GB)		W BRATTAIN (US)
1918	M PLANCK (GER)	1957	TSUNG-DAO LEE (CHINA)
1919	J STARK (GER)		C N YANG (CHINA)
1920	C GUILLAUME (SWITZ)	1958	P A CHERENKOV (USSR)
1921	A EINSTEIN (SWITZ)		I M FRANK (USSR)
1922	N BOHR (DEN)		I Y TAMM (USSR)
1923	R MILLIKAN (US)	1959	E SEGRÈ (US)
1924	K SIEGBAHN (SWED)		O CHAMBERLAIN (US)
1925	J FRANCK (GER)	1960	D GLASER (US)
	G HERTZ (GER)	1961	R HOFSTADTER (US)
1926	J PERRIN (FR)		R MÖSSBAUER (GER)
1927	A H COMPTON (US)	1962	L D LANDAU (USSR)
	C WILSON (GB)	1963	J H D JENSEN (GER)
1928	SIR O RICHARDSON (GB)		M G MAYER (US)
1929	PRINCE L DE BROGLIE (FR)		E P WIGNER (US)
1930	SIR C RAMAN (INDIA)	1964	C H TOWNES (US)
1931	(NO AWARD)		N G BASOV (USSR)
1932	W HEISENBERG (GER)		A M PROKHOROV (USSR)
1933	P A M DIRAC (GB)	1965	J S SCHWINGER (US)
	E SCHRÖDINGER (AUSTRIA)		R P FEYNMAN (US)
1934	(NO AWARD)		S TOMONAGA (JAPAN)
1935	SIR J CHADWICK (GB)	1966	A KASTLER (FR)
1936	V HESS (AUSTRIA)	1967	H A BETHE (US)
	C ANDERSON (US)	1968	L W ALVAREZ (US)
1937	C DAVISSON (US)	1969	M GELL-MANN (US)
	SIR G P THOMSON (GB)	1970	H ALVÉN (SWED)

	L NÉEL (FR)	1919	(NO AWARD)
1971	D GABOR (GB)	1920	W NERNST (GER)
1972	J BARDEEN (US)	1921	F SODDY (GB)
	L N COOPER (US)	1922	F ASTON (GB)
	J R SCHRIEFFER (US)	1923	F PREGL (AUSTRIA)
1973	L ESAKI (JAPAN)	1924	(NO AWARD)
	I GIAEVER (US)	1925	R ZSIGMONDY (AUSTRIA)
	B JOSEPHSON (GB)	1926	T SVEDBERG (SWED)
1974	SIR M RYLE (GB)	1927	H WIELAND (GER)
	A HEWISH (GB)	1928	A WINDAUS (GER)
1975	J RAINWATER (US)	1929	SIR A HARDEN (GB)
	A BOHR (DEN)		H VON EULER-CHELPIN (SWED)
	B MOTTELSON (DEN)	1930	H FISCHER (GER)
1976	B RICHTER (US)	1931	K BOSCH (GER)
	S TING (US)		F BERGIUS (GER)
1977	P W ANDERSON (US)	1932	I LANGMUIR (US)
	SIR N F MOTT (GB)	1933	(NO AWARD)
	J H VAN VLECK (US)	1934	H UREY (US)
1978	P L KAPITSA (USSR)	1935	F JOLIOT-CURIE (FR)
	A A PENZIAS (US)		I JOLIOT-CURIE (FR)
	R W WILSON (US)	1936	P DEBYE (NETH)
1979	S L GLASHOW (US)	1937	SIR W HAWORTH (GB)
	A SALAM (PAK)		P KARRER (SWITZ)
	S WEINBERG (US)	1938	R KUHN (GER)
1980	J CRONIN (US)	1939	A BUTENANDT (GER)
	V FITCH (US)		L RUZICKA (SWITZ)
1981	K SIEGBAHN (SWED)	1943	G DE HEVESY (HUNG)
	N BLOEMBERGEN (US)	1944	O HAHN (GER)
	A SCHAWLOW (US)	1945	A VIRTANEN (FIN)
1982	K G WILSON (US)	1946	J SUMNER (US)
1983	S CHANDRASEKHAR (US)		J NORTHROP (US)
	W FOWLER (US)		W STANLEY (US)
1984	C RUBBIA (ITALY)	1947	SIR R ROBINSON (GB)
	S VAN DER MEER (NETH)	1948	A TISELIUS (SWED)
1985	K VON KLITZING (GER)	1949	W GIAUQUE (US)
1986	E RUSKA (GER)	1950	O DIELS (GER)
	G BINNIG (GER)		K ALDER (GER)
	H ROHRER (SWITZ)	1951	E MCMILLAN (US)
1987	A MÜLLER (SWITZ)		G SEABORG (US)
	G BEDNORZ (GER)	1952	A MARTIN (GB)

CHEMISTRY

			R SYNGE (GB)
		1953	H STAUDINGER (GER)
1901	J V HOFF (NETH)	1954	L C PAULING (US)
1902	E FISCHER (GER)	1955	V DU VIGNEAUD (US)
1903	S ARRHENIUS (SWED)	1956	N SEMYONOV (USSR)
1904	SIR W RAMSAY (GB)		SIR C HINSHELWOOD (GB)
1905	A VON BAEYER (GER)	1957	SIR A TODD (GB)
1906	H MOISSAN (FR)	1958	F SANGER (GB)
1907	E BUCHNER (GER)	1959	J HEYROVSKY (CZECH)
1908	LORD RUTHERFORD (GB)	1960	W LIBBY (US)
1909	W OSTWALD (GER)	1961	M CALVIN (US)
1910	O WALLACH (GER)	1962	J C KENDREW (GB)
1911	M CURIE (FR)		M F PERUTZ (GB)
1912	V GRIGNARD (FR)	1963	G NATTA (ITALY)
	P SABATIER (FR)		K ZIEGLER (GER)
1913	A WERNER (SWITZ)	1964	D M C HODGKIN (GB)
1914	T RICHARDS (US)	1965	R B WOODWARD (US)
1915	R WILLSTÄTTER (GER)	1966	R S MULLIKEN (US)
1916	(NO AWARD)	1967	M EIGEN (GER)
1917	(NO AWARD)		R G W NORRISH (GB)
1918	F HABER (GER)		G PORTER (GB)

1968	L ONSAGER (US)		J J R MACLEOD (GB)
1969	D H R BARTON (GB)	1924	W EINTHOVEN (NETH)
	O HASSEL (NOR)	1925	(NO AWARD)
1970	L F LELOIR (ARG)	1926	J FIBIGER (DEN)
1971	G HERZBERG (CAN)	1927	J WAGNER VON JAUREGG
1972	C B ANFINSEN (US)		(AUSTRIA)
	S MOORE (US)	1928	C NICOLLE (FR)
	W H STEIN (US)	1929	C EIJKMAN (NETH)
1973	E FISCHER (GER)		SIR F HOPKINS (GB)
	G WILKINSON (GB)	1930	K LANDSTEINER (US)
1974	P J FLORY (US)	1931	O WARBURG (GER)
1975	J W CORNFORT (AUSTR)	1932	E D ADRIAN (GB)
	V PRELOG (SWITZ)		SIR C SHERRINGTON (GB)
1976	W M LIPSCOMB (US)	1933	T H MORGAN (US)
1977	I PRIGOGINE (BELGIUM)	1934	G R MINOT (US)
1978	P MITCHELL (GB)		W P MURPHY (US)
1979	H C BROWN (US)		G H WHIPPLE (US)
	G WITTIG (GER)	1935	H SPEMANN (GER)
1980	P BERG (US)	1936	SIR H H DALE (GB)
	W GILBERT (US)		O LOEWI (GER)
	F SANGER (GB)	1937	A SZENT-GYÖRGYI (HUNG)
1981	K FUKUI (JAPAN)	1938	C HEYMANS (BELG)
	R HOFFMANN (POL)	1939	G DOMAGK (GER)
1982	A KLUG (GB)	1943	H DAM (DEN)
1983	H TAUBE (US)		E A DOISY (US)
1984	R B MERRIFIELD (US)	1944	J ERLANGER (US)
1985	H HAUPTMAN (US)		H S GASSER (US)
	J KARLE (US)	1945	SIR A FLEMING (GB)
1986	D HERSCHBACH (US)		E B CHAIN (GB)
	Y TSEH LEE (US)		LORD FLOREY (AUSTR)
	J POLANYI (CAN)	1946	H J MULLER (US)
1987	D CRAM (US)	1947	C F CORI (US)
	J LEHN (FR)		G T CORI (US)
	C PEDERSEN (US)		B HOUSSAY (ARG)
		1948	P MÜLLER (SWITZ)

PHYSIOLOGY OR MEDICINE

		1949	W R HESS (SWITZ)
1901	E VON BEHRING (GER)		A E MONIZ (PORT)
1902	SIR R ROSS (GB)	1950	P S HENCH (US)
1903	N R FINSEN (DEN)		E C KENDALL (US)
1904	I PAVLOV (RUSS)		T REICHSTEIN (SWITZ)
1905	R KOCH (GER)	1951	M THEILER (S AF)
1906	C GOLGI (ITALY)	1952	S A WAKSMAN (US)
	S RAMÓN Y CAJAL (SPAIN)	1953	F A LIPMANN (US)
1907	A LAVERAN (FR)		SIR H A KREBS (GB)
1908	P EHRLICH (GER)	1954	J F ENDERS (US)
	I MECHNIKOV (RUSS)		T H WELLER (US)
1909	E KOCHER (SWITZ)		F ROBBINS (US)
1910	A KOSSEL (GER)	1955	A H THEORELL (SWED)
1911	A GULLSTRAND (SWED)	1956	W FORSSMANN (GER)
1912	A CARREL (FR)		D RICHARDS (US)
1913	C RICHET (FR)		A F COURNAND (US)
1914	R BÁRÁNY (AUSTRIA)	1957	D BOVET (ITALY)
1915	(NO AWARD)	1958	G W BEADLE (US)
1916	(NO AWARD)		E L TATUM (US)
1917	(NO AWARD)		J LEDERBERG (US)
1919	J BORDET (BELG)	1959	S OCHOA (US)
1920	A KROGH (DEN)		A KORNBERG (US)
1921	(NO AWARD)	1960	SIR F MACFARLANE BURNET
1922	A V HILL (GB)		(AUSTR)
	O MEYERHOF (GER)		P B MEDAWAR (GB)
1923	SIR F G BANTING (CAN)	1961	G VON BÉKÉSY (US)

1962	F H C CRICK (GB)
	J D WATSON (US)
	M WILKINS (GB)
1963	SIR J C ECCLES (AUSTR)
	A L HODGKIN (GB)
	A F HUXLEY (GB)
1964	K BLOCH (US)
	F LYNEN (GER)
1965	F JACOB (FR)
	A LWOFF (FR)
	J MONOD (FR)
1966	C B HUGGINS (US)
	F P ROUS (US)
1967	H K HARTLINE (US)
	G WALD (US)
	R A GRANIT (SWED)
1968	R W HOLLEY (US)
	H G KHORANA (US)
	M W NIRENBERG (US)
1969	M DELBRÜCK (US)
	A D HERSHEY (US)
	S E LURIA (US)
1970	J AXELROD (US)
	SIR B KATZ (GB)
	U VON EULER (SWED)
1971	E W SUTHERLAND, JR (US)
1972	G M EDELMAN (US)
	R R PORTER (GB)
1973	K VON FRISCH (GER)
	K LORENZ (GER)
	N TINBERGEN (NETH)
1974	A CLAUDE (US)
	C DE DUVE (BELG)
	G E PALADE (BELG)
1975	D BALTIMORE (US)
	R DULBECCO (US)
	H M TEMIN (US)
1976	B S BLUMBERG (US)
	D G GAJDUSEK (US)
1977	R S YALOW (US)
	R GUILLEMIN (US)
	A V SCHALLY (US)
1978	W ARBER (SWITZ)
	D NATHANS (US)
	H SMITH (US)
1979	A M CORMACK (US)
	G N HOUNSFIELD (GB)
1980	G SNELL (US)
	J DAUSSET (FR)
	B BENACERRAF (US)
1981	R SPERRY (US)
	D HUBEL (US)
	T WIESEL (SWED)
1982	S K BERGSTROM (SWED)
	B I SAMUELSON (SWED)
	J R VANE (GB)
1983	B MCCLINTOCK (US)
1984	N K JERNE (DEN)
	G J F KÖHLER (GER)
	C MILSTEIN (GB)
1985	J GOLDSTEIN (US)

	M BROWN (US)
1986	S COHEN (US)
	R LEVI-MONTALCINI (ITALY)
1987	S TONEGAWA (JAPAN)

LITERATURE

1901	S PRUDHOMME (FR)
1902	T MOMMSEN (GER)
1903	B BJØRNSON (NOR)
1904	F MISTRAL (FR)
	J ECHEGARAY Y EIZAGUIRRE (SPAIN)
1905	H SIENKIEWICZ (POL)
1906	G CARDUCCI (ITALY)
1907	R KIPLING (GB)
1908	R EUCKEN (GER)
1909	S LAGERLÖF (SWED)
1910	P VON HEYSE (GER)
1911	M MAETERLINCK (BELG)
1912	G HAUPTMANN (GER)
1913	SIR R TAGORE (INDIA)
1914	(NO AWARD)
1915	R ROLLAND (FR)
1916	V VON HEIDENSTAM (SWED)
1917	K GJELLERUP (DEN)
	H PONTOPPIDAN (DEN)
1919	C SPITTELER (SWITZ)
1920	K HAMSUN (NOR)
1921	A FRANCE (FR)
1922	J BENAVENTE Y MARTINEZ (SPAIN)
1923	W B YEATS (IRE)
1924	W S REYMONT (POL)
1925	G B SHAW (IRE)
1926	G DELEDDA (ITALY)
1927	H BERGSON (FR)
1928	S UNDSET (NOR)
1929	T MANN (GER)
1930	S LEWIS (US)
1931	E A KARLFELDT (SWED)
1932	J GALSWORTHY (GB)
1933	I BUNIN (USSR)
1934	L PIRANDELLO (ITALY)
1935	(NO AWARD)
1936	E O'NEILL (US)
1937	R M DU GARD (FR)
1938	P BUCK (US)
1939	F E SILLANPÄÄ (FIN)
1943	(NO AWARD)
1944	J V JENSEN (DEN)
1945	G MISTRAL (CHILE)
1946	H HESSE (SWITZ)
1947	A GIDE (FR)
1948	T S ELIOT (GB)
1949	W FAULKNER (US)
1950	B RUSSELL (GB)
1951	P F LAGERKVIST (SWED)
1952	F MAURIAC (FR)
1953	SIR WINSTON CHURCHILL (GB)
1954	E HEMINGWAY (US)
1955	H K LAXNESS (ICE)
1956	J R JIMÉNEZ (SPAIN)

1957	A CAMUS (FR)	1916	(NO AWARD)
1958	B L PASTERNAK (DECLINED	1917	INTERNATIONAL RED CROSS
	AWARD) (USSR)		COMMITTEE (FOUNDED, 1863)
1959	S QUASIMODO (ITALY)	1919	W WILSON (US)
1960	S J PERSE (FR)	1920	L BOURGEOIS (FR)
1961	I ANDRIĆ (YUGOS)	1921	K BRANTING (SWED)
1962	J STEINBECK (US)		C L LANGE (NOR)
1963	G SEFERIS (GR)	1922	F NANSEN (NOR)
1964	J P SARTRE (DECLINED AWARD)	1923	(NO AWARD)
	(FR)	1924	(NO AWARD)
1965	M SHOLOKHOV (USSR)	1925	SIR A CHAMBERLAIN (GB)
1966	S Y AGNON (ISR)		C G DAWES (US)
	N SACHS (SWED)	1926	A BRIAND (FR)
1967	M A ASTURIAS (GUAT)		G STRESEMANN (GER)
1968	K YASUNARI (JAPAN)	1927	F BUISSON (FR)
1969	S BECKETT (IRE)		L QUIDDE (GER)
1970	A I SOLZHENITSYN (USSR)	1928	(NO AWARD)
1971	P NERUDA (CHILE)	1929	F B KELLOGG (US)
1972	H BÖLL (GER)	1930	N SÖDERBLOM (SWED)
1973	P WHITE (AUSTR)	1931	J ADDAMS (US)
1974	E JOHNSON (SWED)		N M BUTLER (US)
	H MARTINSON (SWED)	1932	(NO AWARD)
1975	E MONTALE (ITALY)	1933	SIR N ANGELL (GB)
1976	S BELLOW (US)	1934	A HENDERSON (GB)
1977	S ALEIXANDRE (SPAIN)	1935	C VON OSSIETZKY (GER)
1978	I B SINGER (US)	1936	C S LAMAS (ARG)
1979	O ALEPOUDELLIS (GREECE)	1937	VISCOUNT CECIL OF CHELWOOD
1980	C MILOSZ (US)		(GB)
1981	E CANETTI (BULG)	1938	NANSEN INTERNATIONAL OFFICE
1982	G GARCIA MARQUEZ (COLOMBIA)		FOR REFUGEES (FOUNDED, 1931)
1983	W GOLDING (GB)	1939	(NO AWARD)
1984	J SEIFERT (CZECH)	1943	(NO AWARD)
1985	C SIMON (FR)	1944	INTERNATIONAL RED CROSS
1986	W SOYINKA (NIGERIA)		COMMITTEE (FOUNDED, 1863)
1987	J BRODSKY (US)	1945	C HULL (US)
		1946	E G BALCH (US)

PEACE

			J R MOTT (US)
1901	J H DUNANT (SWITZ)	1947	AMERICAN FRIENDS' SERVICE
	F PASSY (FR)		COMMITTEE (US)
1902	E DUCOMMUN (SWITZ)		FRIENDS' SERVICE COUNCIL
	C A GOBAT (SWITZ)		(LONDON)
1903	SIR W CREMER (GB)	1948	(NO AWARD)
1904	INSTITUTE OF INTERNATIONAL	1949	LORD BOYD-ORR (GB)
	LAW (FOUNDED, 1873)	1950	R BUNCHE (US)
1905	BARONESS VON SUTTNER	1951	L JOUHAUX (FR)
	(AUSTRIA)	1952	A SCHWEITZER (ALSATIAN)
1906	T ROOSEVELT (US)	1953	G C MARSHALL (US)
1907	E TEODORO MONETA (ITALY)	1954	OFFICE OF THE UNITED NATIONS
	L RENAULT (FR)		HIGH COMMISSIONER FOR
1908	K P ARNOLDSON (SWED)		REFUGEES (FOUNDED, 1951)
1909	BARON D'ESTOURNELLES DE	1955	(NO AWARD)
	CONSTANT (FR)	1956	(NO AWARD)
	A BEERNAERT (BELG)	1957	L B PEARSON (CAN)
1910	INTERNATIONAL PEACE BUREAU	1958	D G PIRE (BELG)
	(FOUNDED, 1891)	1959	P J NOEL-BAKER (GB)
1911	T ASSER (NETH)	1960	A J LUTHULI (S AF)
	A FRIED (AUSTRIA)	1961	D HAMMARSKJÖLD (SWED)
1912	E ROOT (US)	1962	L C PAULING (US)
1913	H LAFONTAINE (BELG)	1963	INTERNATIONAL RED CROSS
1914	(NO AWARD)		COMMITTEE (FOUNDED, 1863)
1915	(NO AWARD)		

LEAGUE OF RED CROSS SOCIETIES (GENEVA)
1964 M LUTHER KING, JR (US)
1965 UNITED NATIONS CHILDREN'S FUND (FOUNDED, 1946)
1966 (NO AWARD)
1967 (NO AWARD)
1968 R CASSIN (FR)
1969 INTERNATIONAL LABOUR ORGANISATION (FOUNDED, 1919)
1970 N E BORLAUG (US)
1971 W BRANDT (GER)
1972 (NO AWARD)
1973 H KISSINGER (US)
LE DUC THO (DECLINED AWARD) (N VIET)
1974 S MACBRIDE (IRE)
E SATO (JAPAN)
1975 A S SAKHAROV (USSR)
1976 MRS B WILLIAMS (N IRE)
MISS M CORRIGAN (N IRE)
1977 AMNESTY INTERNATIONAL (FOUNDED IN UK, 1961)
1978 A SADAT (EGYPT)
M BEGIN (ISR)
1979 MOTHER TERESA (YUGOS)
1980 A P ESQUIVEL (ARG)
1981 OFFICE OF THE U N HIGH COMMISSION FOR REFUGEES (FOUNDED, 1951)
1982 A GARCIA ROBLES (MEX)
MRS A MYRDAL (SWED)
1983 L WALESA (POL)
1984 BISHOP D TUTU (S AF)
1985 INTERNATIONAL PHYSICIANS FOR THE PREVENTION OF NUCLEAR WAR (FOUNDED, 1980)
1986 E WIESEL (US)
1987 OSCAR ARIAS SÁNCHEZ (COSTA RICA)

SPORTSMEN

3

ALI, Muhammad (Cassius Marcellus Clay, 1942– ; US boxer)
COE, Sebastian (1956– ; British middle-distance runner)
LEE, Bruce (1940–73; US kungfu expert)

4

ASHE, Arthur (1943– ; US tennis player)
BORG, Bjorn (1956– ; Swedish tennis player)
CLAY, Cassius. See Ali, Muhammed
CRAM, Steve (1960– ; British middle-distance runner)
DUKE, Geoffrey E (1923– ; British racing motorcyclist)
GRAF, Steffi (1969– ; W German tennis player)
HILL, Graham (1929–75; British motor-racing driver)
HOAD, Lewis Alan (1934– ; Australian tennis player)
HUNT, James (1947– ; British motor-racing driver)
JOHN, Barry (1945– ; Welsh Rugby Union footballer)
KING, Billie Jean (born Moffitt, 1943– ; US tennis player)
MILO (late 6th century BC; Greek wrestler)
MOSS, Stirling (1929– ; British motor-racing driver)
PELÉ (1940– ; Brazilian Association footballer)
WADE, Virginia (1945– ; British tennis player)

5

BRUNO, Frank (1961– ; British heavyweight boxer)
BUDGE, Don (1916– ; US tennis player)
BUENO, Maria (1939– ; Brazilian tennis player)
BUSBY, Matt (1909– ; British Association footballer)
CLARK, Jim (1937–68; British motor-racing driver)
COURT, Margaret (born Smith, 1942– ; Australian tennis player)
CURRY, John Anthony (1949– ; British ice skater)
EVERT, Christine (1954– ; US tennis player)
GRACE, William Gilbert (1848–1915; British cricketer)
GREIG, Tony (1946– ; Rhodesian-born cricketer)
HAGEN, Walter Charles (1892–1969; US professional golfer)
HOBBS, Jack (1882–1963; British cricketer)
HOGAN, Ben (1912– ; US professional golfer)
HOYLE, Edmond (1672–1769; British authority on card games)
JEEPS, Dickie (1931– ; British Rugby Union footballer)
JONES, Bobby (1902–71; US amateur golfer)
LAUDA, Niki (1949– ; Austrian motor-racing driver)
LAVER, Rod (1938– ; Australian tennis player)
LEWIS, Carl (1961– ; US athlete)

5—continued

LLOYD, Clive (1944– ; West Indian cricketer)

LOUIS, Joe (1914–81; US boxer)

MEADE, Richard (1938– ; British three-day-event horse rider)

MEADS, Colin Earl (1935– ; New Zealand Rugby Union footballer)

MOORE, Bobby (1941– ; British Association footballer)

NURMI, Paavo Johannes (1897–1973; Finnish middle-distance and long-distance runner)

OVETT, Steve (1955– ; British middle-distance runner)

OWENS, Jesse (1913–80; US sprinter, long jumper, and hurdler)

PERRY, Fred (1909– ; British tennis and table-tennis player)

SMITH, Harvey (1938– ; British showjumper and equestrian)

SPITZ, Mark Andrew (1950– ; US swimmer)

VIREN, Lasse Artturi (1949– ; Finnish middle-distance and long-distance runner)

6

BORDER, Allan (1955– ; Australian cricketer)

BOTHAM, Ian (1955– ; British cricketer)

BROOME, David (1940– ; British show-jumper)

BROUGH, Louise (1923– ; US tennis player)

CAWLEY, Evonne (*born* Goolagong, 1951– ; Australian tennis player)

CRUYFF, Johann (1947– ; Dutch Association footballer)

D'INZEO, Colonel Piero (1923– ; Italian show jumper and equestrian)

EDBERG, Stefan (1966– ; Swedish tennis player)

FANGIO, Juan Manuel (1911– ; Argentinian motor-racing driver)

HUTTON, Len (1916– ; British cricketer)

KARPOV, Anatoly (1951– ; Soviet chess player)

KEEGAN, Kevin (1951– ; British footballer)

LASKER, Emanuel (1868–1941; German chess player)

MORPHY, Paul Charles (1837–84; US chess player)

PALMER, Arnold (1929– ; US professional golfer)

RAMSEY, Alf (1922– ; British Association footballer)

RHODES, Wilfred (1877–1973; British cricketer)

SHEENE, Barry (1950– ; British racing motorcyclist)

SMYTHE, Pat (1928– ; British showjumper and equestrian)

SOBERS, Gary (1936– ; West Indian cricketer)

TUNNEY, Gene (1897–1978; US boxer)

7

BRABHAM, Jack (1926– ; Australian motor-racing driver)

BRADMAN, Donald George (1908– ; Australian cricketer)

CARNERA, Primo (1906–67; Italian boxer)

COMPTON, Denis (1918– ; British cricketer)

CONNORS, Jimmy (1952– ; US tennis player)

COWDREY, Colin (1932– ; British cricketer)

DEMPSEY, Jack (1895– ; US boxer)

FISCHER, Bobby (1943– ; US chess player)

FRAZIER, Joe (1944– ; US boxer)

HAMMOND, Wally (1903–65; British cricketer)

LENGLEN, Suzanne (1899–1938; French tennis player)

MCBRIDE, Willie John (1939– ; Irish Rugby Union footballer)

MCENROE, John (1959– ; US tennis player)

SPASSKY, Boris (1937– ; Soviet chess player)

STEWART, Jackie (1939– ; British motor-racing driver)

SURTEES, John (1934– ; British racing motorcyclist and motor-racing driver)

TREVINO, Lee (1939– ; US golfer)

TRUEMAN, Fred (1931– ; British cricketer)

WHYMPER, Edward (1840–1911; British mountaineer)

WINKLER, Hans Günter (1926– ; West German showjumper)

ZÁTOPEK, Emil (1922– ; Czech long-distance runner)

8

AGOSTINI, Giacomo (1944– ; Italian racing motorcyclist)

ALEKHINE, Alexander (1892–1946; French chess player)

CAMPBELL, Sir Malcolm (1885–1949; British land- and water-speed racing driver)

CHARLTON, Bobby (1937– ; British Association footballer)

COMANECI, Nadia (1961– ; Romanian gymnast)

HAILWOOD, Mike (1940–81; British racing motorcyclist)

HAWTHORN, Mike (1929–58; British motor-racing driver)

JOSELITO (1895–1920; Spanish matador)

KORCHNOI, Victor (1931– ; Soviet chess player)

LINDWALL, Raymond Russell (1921– ; Australian cricketer)

MATTHEWS, Stanley (1915– ; British Association footballer)

NEWCOMBE, John (1944– ; Australian tennis player)

NICKLAUS, Jack William (1940– ; US golfer)

RICHARDS, Sir Gordon (1904–86; British jockey)

8—continued

RICHARDS, Viv (1952– ; West Indian cricketer)

ROBINSON, Sugar Ray (1920– ; US boxer)

ROSEWALL, Ken (1934– ; Australian tennis player)

SULLIVAN, John Lawrence (1858–1918; US boxer)

THOMPSON, Daley (1958– ; British decathlete)

WILLIAMS, J P R (1949– ; Welsh Rugby Union footballer)

9

BANNISTER, Roger (1929– ; British middle distance runner)

BONINGTON, Chris (1934– ; British mountaineer)

BOTVINNIK, Mikhail Moiseivich (1911– ; Soviet chess player)

D'OLIVIERA, Basil Lewis (1931– ; South African-born cricketer)

GOOLAGONG, Evonne. *See* Cawley, Evonne

LLEWELLYN, Harry (1911– ; British show-jumper and equestrian)

PETROSIAN, Tigran Vartanovich (1929–84; Soviet chess player)

SCHMELING, Max (1905– ; German boxer)

SUTCLIFFE, Herbert (1894–1978; British cricketer)

SZEWINSKA, Irena (1946– ; Polish athlete)

10

CARPENTIER, Georges (1894–1975; French boxer)

CULBERTSON, Ely (1891–1955; US bridge authority)

IMRAN KHAN (1952– ; Pakistani cricketer)

JUANTORENA, Alberto (1951– ; Cuban middle-distance runner)

WILLS MOODY, Helen (1905– ; US tennis player)

11

BALLESTEROS, Severiano (1957– ; Spanish golfer)

CONSTANTINE, Learie Nicholas, Baron (1902–71; West Indian cricketer)

FITZSIMMONS, Bob (1862–1917; New Zealand boxer)

NAVRATILOVA, Martina (1956– ; Czech-born US tennis player)

TURISHCHEVA, Ludmilla (1952– ; Soviet gymnast)

WEISSMULLER, Johnny (1904–84; US swimmer)

13

TENZING NORGAY (*c.* 1914–86; Sherpa mountaineer)

19

CAPABLANCA Y GRAUPERA, José Raúl (1888–1942; Cuban chess player)

RANJITSINHJI VIBHAJI, Kumar Shri, Maharajah Jam Sahib of Nawanagar (1872–1933; Indian cricketer)

THE ARTS

ART TERMS

2
OP

3
FEC
INC
OIL
POP

4
BODY
BUST
CAST
DADA
HERM
KORE
SIZE
SWAG
TERM
WASH

5
BRUSH
BURIN
CHALK
EASEL
FECIT
GESSO
GLAZE
MODEL
NAIVE
PIETÀ
PUTTO
SALON
SCULP
SECCO
SEPIA
STYLE
TONDO

6
ASHCAN
BISTRE
CANVAS
CUBISM
FRESCO
GOTHIC
GROUND
KIT-CAT
KITSCH
KOUROS
LIMNER
MAESTÀ

6 —continued
MEDIUM
MOBILE
MOSAIC
PASTEL
PATINA
PENCIL
PURISM
RELIEF
ROCOCO
SCHOOL
SKETCH
STUCCO
STYLUS
TUSCAN
VEDUTA
VERISM

7
ACADEMY
ARCHAIC
ATELIER
BAROQUE
BAUHAUS
BITUMEN
BODEGÓN
CABINET
CAMAÏEU
CARTOON
COLLAGE
COSMATI
DIPTYCH
DRAWING
ECORCHÉ
ETCHING
GOUACHE
IMPASTO
INCIDIT
LINOCUT
LOST WAX
MODELLO
MONTAGE
PALETTE
PIGMENT
POCHADE
REALISM
SCUMBLE
SFUMATO
SINOPIA
TEMPERA
VANITAS

7 —continued
VARNISH
WOODCUT

8
ABSTRACT
AIR-BRUSH
ALLEGORY
ANCIENTS
AQUATINT
ARMATURE
ARRICCIO
BARBIZON
BOZZETTO
CARYATID
CHARCOAL
DRÔLERIE
DRYPOINT
EMULSION
FIXATIVE
FROTTAGE
FUTURISM
GRAFFITI
HATCHING
INTAGLIO
INTONACO
MANDORLA
MAQUETTE
PASTICHE
PLEURANT
POUNCING
PREDELLA
REPOUSSÉ
SCULPSIT
STAFFAGE
TACHISME
TESSERAE
TRECENTO
TRIPTYCH
VENETIAN

9
ALLA PRIMA
ANTI-CERNE
AQUARELLE
AUTOGRAPH
BRUSHWORK
BYZANTINE
CAPRICCIO
COLOURIST
DISTEMPER
ENGRAVING

9 —continued
GRISAILLE
GROTESQUE
INTIMISME
LANDSCAPE
MAHLSTICK
MAULSTICK
MEZZOTINT
MINIATURE
POLYPTYCH
PRIMITIVE
SCULPTURE
STILL LIFE
STIPPLING
SYMBOLISM
TENEBRISM
VORTICISM

10
ARRICCIATO
ART NOUVEAU
ASSEMBLAGE
AUTOMATISM
AVANTGARDE
BIOMORPHIC
CARICATURE
CIRE-PERDUE
CRAQUELURE
FLORENTINE
METALPOINT
MONOCHROME
MORBIDEZZA
NATURALISM
PENTIMENTO
PROVENANCE
QUADRATURA
REPOUSSOIR
ROMANESQUE
SURREALISM
SYNTHETISM
TURPENTINE
XYLOGRAPHY

11
BAMBOCCANTI
BIEDERMEIER
CAROLINGIAN
CHIAROSCURO
CONTÉ CRAYON
DIVISIONISM
ECLECTICISM
ILLUSIONISM

11 —continued
IMPRIMATURA
LITHOGRAPHY
MASTERPIECE
PERSPECTIVE
PICTURESQUE
POINTILLISM
PORTRAITURE
RENAISSANCE
RETROUSSAGE

11 —continued
STYLIZATION
SUPREMATISM
TROMPE L'OEIL
WATERCOLOUR

12
ACRYLIC PAINT
ANAMORPHOSIS
CLOISONNISME

12 —continued
CONTRAPPOSTO
COUNTERPROOF
ILLUMINATION
PRECISIONISM
QUATTROCENTO
SUPERREALISM

13
ARCHITECTONIC

13 —continued
EXPRESSIONISM
FÊTE CHAMPÊTRE
IMPRESSIONISM
PAPIERS COLLÉS

14
CONSTRUCTIVISM

ARCHITECTURAL TERMS

3
BAY
CAP
DIE
EYE
KEY

4
AMBO
ANTA
APSE
ARCH
BAND
BEAD
BELL
BOSS
DADO
DAIS
DOME
FRET
FROG
FUST
NAVE
PELE
STOA

5
AISLE
AMBRY
ARRIS
ATTIC
CONGÉ
CROWN
CRYPT
DORIC
FOILS
GABLE
GLYPH
HELIX
INLAY
IONIC
LOBBY
NEWEL
ROMAN
SCAPE
SHAFT

5 —continued
SHANK
TALON
TENIA
TUDOR
VERGE

6
ABACUS
ACCESS
ALCOVE
ARCADE
ATRIUM
ATTICK
AUMBRY
BELFRY
BONNET
BROACH
CANOPY
CHEVET
COLUMN
CORONA
CRENEL
CUPOLA
DAGGER
DENTIL
DIAPER
FAÇADE
FILLET
FINIAL
FLÈCHE
FRESCO
FRIEZE
GABLET
GAZEBO
GOTHIC
GUTTAE
HEROIC
LESENE
LINTEL
LINTOL
LOGGIA
LOUVRE
MANTEL
MERLON

6 —continued
METOPE
MUTULE
NORMAN
OCULUS
PAGODA
PATERA
PLINTH
PULPIT
QUADRA
REGULA
ROCOCO
SCAPUS
SCROLL
SEDILE
SOFFIT
TROPHY
URELLA
VESTRY
VOLUTE
WREATH
XYSTUS
ZIG-ZAG

7
ANNULET
ARCH RIB
ASTYLAR
BALCONY
BAROQUE
BASTION
BOULTIN
BUTMENT
CAPITAL
CAVETTO
CHANCEL
CHEVRON
CORNICE
CROCHET
CROCKET
DISTYLE
ECHINUS
ENCARPA
ENTASIS
EUSTYLE

7 —continued
FESTOON
FLEURON
FLUTING
GADROON
GALILEE
GALLERY
LACUNAR
LANTERN
LATTICE
LEQUEAR
LUNETTE
NARTHEX
NULLING
OBELISK
ORATORY
PARVISE
PORTAIL
PORTICO
POSTERN
PTEROMA
REEDING
REGENCY
REREDOS
ROSETTE
ROTUNDA
ROUNDEL
SCALLOP
SPANISH
SYSTYLE
TESSARA
TONDINO
TRACERY
TRUMEAU

8
ABUTMENT
ACANTHUS
AEDICULA
APOPHYGE
ASTRAGAL
ATLANTES
BALUSTER
BARTIZAN
BASILICA

8 —continued

BEAK HEAD
CARYATID
CIMBORIO
CINCTURE
CRENELLE
CRESTING
CYMATIUM
DIASTYLE
DIPTERAL
DOG-TOOTH
EDGE ROLL
EXTRADOS
FORMERET
GARGOYLE
INTRADOS
KEEL ARCH
KEYSTONE
LICH GATE
LYCH GATE
MISERERE
PAVILION
PEDESTAL
PEDIMENT
PILASTER
PREDELLA
PULPITUM
ROCAILLE
SPANDREL
SPANDRIL
TORCHING
TRANSEPT
TRIGLYPH
TYMPANUM
VERANDAH

8 —continued

VIGNETTE
WAINSCOT

9

ACROPOLIS
ANTEFIXAE
ANTHEMION
APEX STONE
ARABESQUE
ARCH BRICK
ARCHIVOLT
ATTIC BASE
BIRD'S BEAK
BYZANTINE
CAMPANILE
CANEPHORA
CARTOUCHE
CAULICOLI
CLOISTERS
COLONNADE
COMPOSITE
DRIPSTONE
FOLIATION
GROTESQUE
HEXASTYLE
HYPOCAUST
HYPOSTYLE
INGLE NOOK
LABEL STOP
LACUNARIA
LINENFOLD
MEZZANINE
MOULDINGS
OCTASTYLE

9 —continued

PALLADIAN
REFECTORY
SGRAFFITO
STRAPWORK
STYLOBATE
TRABEATED
TRIFORIUM
TRILITHON
VESTIBULE
ZOOPHORUS

10

ACROTERION
AMBULATORY
ARAEOSTYLE
ARCHITRAVE
BALDACHINO
BALL FLOWER
BALUSTRADE
BATTLEMENT
CINQUEFOIL
COLONNETTE
CORINTHIAN
EGG AND DART
ENRICHMENT
HAGIOSCOPE
LADY CHAPEL
LANCET ARCH
MISERICORD
MODILLIONS
PIETRA DURA
PRESBYTERY
PYCNOSTYLE

10 —continued

QUATREFOIL
ROMANESQUE
ROOD SCREEN
ROSE WINDOW
SEXPARTITE
TETRASTYLE
TRACHELION

11

CASTELLATED
ENTABLATURE
FAN VAULTING
HARELIP ARCH
LEADED LIGHT
MANTELPIECE
MANTELSHELF
ORIEL WINDOW
RENAISSANCE
RETICULATED

12

AMPHITHEATRE
BLIND TRACERY
COCKLE STAIRS
EGG AND TONGUE
LANCET WINDOW
PORTE-COCHÈRE

13

AMPHI-PROSTYLE

14

ANGULAR CAPITAL
FLYING BUTTRESS
HYPOTRACHELION

LITERARY TERMS

3

ODE
WIT

4

EPIC
FOOT
IAMB
MYTH

5

ELEGY
FABLE
GENRE
ICTUS
IRONY
LYRIC
METRE
NOVEL
OCTET
PROSE

5 —continued

RHYME
STYLE
THEME
VERSE

6

BALLAD
BATHOS
CESURA
CLICHÉ
DACTYL
HUBRIS
LAMENT
MONODY
OCTAVE
PARODY
PATHOS
SATIRE
SCHOOL

6 —continued

SEPTET
SESTET
SIMILE
SONNET
STANZA
STRESS
SYMBOL

7

CAESURA
CONCEIT
COUPLET
DICTION
ELISION
EPIGRAM
EPISTLE
EPITAPH
EUPHONY
FABLIAU

7 —continued

HUMOURS
IMAGERY
NEMESIS
PARADOX
PROSODY
PYRRHIC
REALISM
SPONDEE
SUBPLOT
TRAGEDY
TROCHEE

8

ALLEGORY
ANAPAEST
AUGUSTAN
DIDACTIC
ELEMENTS
EXEMPLUM

8 —continued
EYE RHYME
METAPHOR
OXYMORON
PASTORAL
QUATRAIN
RHETORIC
SCANSION
SYLLABLE
TRIMETER
9
AMBIGUITY
ASSONANCE
BURLESQUE
CATHARSIS
CLASSICAL
EUPHEMISM
FREE VERSE
HALF RHYME
HEXAMETER
HYPERBOLE

9 —continued
MONOMETER
OCTAMETER
PARARHYME
10
BLANK VERSE
CARICATURE
DENOUEMENT
EPIC SIMILE
HEPTAMETER
MOCK HEROIC
NATURALISM
PENTAMETER
PICARESQUE
SPOONERISM
SUBJECTIVE
TETRAMETER
11
ANACHRONISM
COURTLY LOVE
END STOPPING

11 —continued
ENJAMBEMENT
GOTHIC NOVEL
HORATIAN ODE
MALAPROPISM
NOBLE SAVAGE
OBJECTIVITY
TRAGICOMEDY
12
ALLITERATION
ONOMATOPOEIA
13
ANTHROPOMORPH
HEROIC COUPLET
INTERNAL RHYME
14
EXISTENTIALISM
FEMININE ENDING
MILTONIC SONNET
ROMANTIC POETRY
SENTIMENTALITY

15
MASCULINE ENDING
PATHETIC FALLACY
PERSONIFICATION
16
PETRARCHAN
  SONNET
18
METAPHYSICAL
  POETRY
NEGATIVE
  CAPABILITY
OMNISCIENT
  NARRATOR
20+
STREAM OF
  CONSCIOUSNESS

MUSICAL TERMS

TERM – definition

1 & 2
F – loud
FF - very loud
MF – half loud
P – soft
PP – very soft
SF – strongly accented
3
BIS – repeat
DIM – becoming softer
PED – abbr. for pedal
PIÙ – more
PIZ – plucked
RFZ – accentuated
RIT – slowing down, holding back
SFZ – strongly accented
TEN – held
VIF – lively (Fr.)
4
CODA – final part of a movement
MOTO – motion
RALL – slowing down
SINO – up to; until
TIEF – deep; low (Ger.)
5
AD LIB – at will
ASSAI – very
BUFFO – comic
DOLCE – sweet
FORTE – loud
LARGO – very slow

5 —continued
LENTO – slowly
MESTO – sad, mournful
MEZZO – half
MOLTO – very much
MOSSO – moving, fast
PIANO – soft
QUASI – almost, as if
SEGNO – sign
SENZA – without
SOAVE – sweet; gentle
STARK – strong, loud (Ger.)
TACET – instrument is silent
TANTO – so much
TEMPO – the speed of a composition
TUTTI – all
ZOPPA – in syncopated rhythm
6
ADAGIO – slow
AL FINE – to the end
CHIUSO – stopped (of a note); closed
DA CAPO – from the beginning
DEHORS – outside; prominent
DIVISI – divided
DOPPIO – double
FACILE – easy, fluent
LEGATO – bound, tied (of notes), smoothly
MARCIA – march
NIENTE – nothing
NOBILE – noble
RETENU – held back

6 —continued
SEMPRE – always, still
SUBITO – immediately
TENUTO – held

7
AGITATO – agitated; rapid tempo
ALLEGRO – lively, brisk
AL SEGNO – as far as the sign
AMOROSO – loving, emotional
ANIMATO – spirited
ATTACCA – attack; continue without a pause
CALANDO – ebbing; lessening of tempo
CODETTA – small coda; to conclude a
  passage
CON BRIO – with vigour
DOLENTE – sorrowful
ESTINTO – extremely softly, almost without
  tone
GIOCOSO – merry; playful
MARCATO – accented
MORBIDO – soft, delicate
PESANTE – heavily, firmly
SCHNELL – fast (Ger.)
SFOGATO – effortless; in a free manner
SORDINO – mute
STRETTO – accelerating or intensifying;
  overlapping of entries of fugue

8
A BATTUTA – return to strict time
A PIACERE – as you please
BRILLANT – brilliant
COL CANTO – accompaniment to follow solo
  line
COL LEGNO – to strike strings with stick of
  the bow
CON FUOCO – fiery; vigorous
DAL SEGNO – from the sign
IN MODO DI – in the manner of
MAESTOSO – majestic
MODERATO – moderately
PORTANDO – carrying one note into the next
RITENUTO – slowing down, holding back
SOURDINE – mute (Fr.)
STACCATO – detached
VIVEMENT – lively (Fr.)

9
ADAGIETTO – quite slow
CANTABILE – in a singing fashion

9 —continued
CANTILENA – lyrical, flowing
FIORITURA – decoration of a melody
GLISSANDO – sliding scale played on
  instrument
MENO MOSSO – slower pace
MEZZA VOCE – at half power
OBBLIGATO – not to be omitted
PIUTTOSTO – somewhat
PIZZICATO – plucked
SCHNELLER – faster (Ger.)
SFORZANDO – strongly accented
SIN'AL FINE – up to the end
SLENTANDO – slowing down
SOSTENUTO – sustained
SOTTO VOCE – quiet subdued tone

10
AFFETTUOSO – tender
ALLA CACCIA – in hunting style
ALLARGANDO – broadening; more dignified
ALLEGRETTO – quite lively, brisk
DIMINUENDO – becoming softer
FORTISSIMO – very loud
MEZZOFORTE – half loud
NOBILMENTE – nobly
PERDENDOSI – dying away gradually
PIANISSIMO – very soft
PORTAMENTO – carrying one note into the
  next
RAVVIVANDO – quickening
RITARDANDO – slowing down, holding back
SCHERZANDO – joking; playing
SCHLEPPEND – dragging; deviating from
  correct speed (Ger.)
SCORREVOLE – gliding; fluent
STRINGENDO – tightening; intensification

11
ACCELERANDO – accelerating
AFFRETTANDO – hurrying
MINACCIANDO – menacing
RALLENTANDO – slowing down
RINFORZANDO – accentuated

12
ALLA CAPPELLA – in church style
LEGGERAMENTE – lightly

13
LEGGIERAMENTE – lightly

TONIC SOL-FA

DOH	ME	SOH	TE
RAY	FAH	LAH	

MUSICAL INSTRUMENTS

2
UD (lute)
YÜ (scraper)

3
BIN (vina)
KIT (fiddle)
LUR (horn)
OUD (ud)
SAZ (lute)
SHÔ (mouth organ)
TAR (drum; lute)
UTI (lute)

4
BATA (drum)
BIWA (lute)
CH'IN (zither)
DRUM
FIFE
FUYE (flute)
GONG
HARP
HORN
KENA (quena)
KHEN (mouth organ)
KOTO (zither)
LIRA (fiddle)
LUTE
LYRA (lyre)
LYRE
MU YÜ (drum)
MVET (zither)
OBOE
OUTI (lute)
P'I P'A (lute)
PIPE
ROTE (lyre)
RUAN (lute)
SONA (shawm)
TRO-U (fiddle)
URUA (clarinet)
VINA (stringed
    instrument related
    to sitar)
VIOL
WHIP (percussion)
ZOBO (mirliton)

5
AULOI (shawm)
BANJO
BELLS
BHAYA (kettledrum)
BUGLE
BUMPA (clarinet)
CELLO

5 —continued
CHANG (dulcimer)
CHIME
CLAVE
COBZA (lute)
CORNU (trumpet)
CRWTH (lyre)
DAULI (drum)
DHOLA (drum)
DOBRO (guitar)
ERH-HU (fiddle)
FIDEL (fiddle)
FIDLA (zither)
FLUTE
GAITA (bagpipe)
GAJDY (bagpipe)
GUSLE (fiddle)
HURUK (drum)
KAKKO (drum)
KANUN (qanun)
KAZOO (mirliton)
KERAR (lyre)
KO-KIU (fiddle)
MBILA (xylophone)
NGOMA (drum)
NGURU (flute)
OKEDO (drum)
ORGAN
PIANO
PI NAI (shawm)
PU-ILU (clappers)
QANUN (zither)
QUENA (flute)
RASPA (scraper)
REBAB (fiddle)
REBEC (fiddle)
SARON
    (metallophone)
SHAWM
SHENG (mouth organ)
SITAR (lute)
TABLA (drum)
TABOR (drum)
TAIKO (drum)
TIBIA (shawm)
TIPLE (shawm)
TI-TZU (flute)
TUDUM (drum)
TUMYR (drum)
TUPAN (drum)
VIOLA
YUN LO (gong)
ZURLA (shawm)
ZURNA (shawm)

6
ALBOKA (hornpipe)
ARGHUL (clarinet)
BAGANA (lyre)
BINIOU (bagpipe)
CARNYX (trumpet)
CHAKAY (zither)
CHA PEI (lute)
CORNET
CURTAL (double
    reed)
DARBUK (drum)
FANDUR (fiddle)
FIDDLE
FUJARA (flute)
GEKKIN (lute)
GENDER
    (metallophone)
GONGUE
    (percussion)
GUITAR
HU CH'IN (fiddle)
HUMMEL (zither)
KENONG (gong)
KISSAR (lyre)
KOBORO (drum)
LIRICA (fiddle)
LIRONE (fiddle)
LITUUS (trumpet)
LONTAR (clappers)
MAYURI (lute)
MOROPI (drum)
NAKERS (drums)
NAQARA (drums)
NTENGA (drum)
O-DAIKO (drum)
OMBGWE (flute)
P'AI PAN (clappers)
POMMER (shawm)
RACKET (double
    reed)
RAMKIE (lute)
RATTLE
SANTIR (dulcimer)
SHAING (horn)
SHAKER
SHANAI (shawm)
SHIELD (percussion)
SHOFAR (horn)
SOPILE (shawm)
SPINET
SPOONS (clappers)
SRALAY (shawm)
SURNAJ (shawm)

6 —continued
SWITCH (percussion)
SYRINX (panpipe)
TAM-TAM (gong)
TOM-TOM (drum)
TXISTU (flute)
VALIHA (zither)
VIELLE (fiddle)
VIOLIN
YANGUM (dulcimer)
ZITHER

7
ADENKUM (stamping
    tube)
ALPHORN (trumpet)
ANKLUNG (rattle)
ATUMPAN
    (kettledrum)
BAGPIPE
BARYTON (viol)
BASSOON
BODHRAN (drum)
BONNANG (gong)
BOW HARP
BOX LYRE
BUCCINA (trumpet)
BUISINE (trumpet)
BUMBASS
CELESTE
CHANGKO (drum)
CITTERN
CORNETT
COWBELL
CROTALS
    (percussion)
CYMBALS
DA-DAIKO (drum)
DIPLICE (clarinet)
DUGDUGI (drum)
ENZENZE (zither)
FITHELE (fiddle)
GADULKA (fiddle)
GITTERN
GLING-BU (flute)
HULA IPU
    (percussion)
INGUNGU (drum)
ISIGUBU (drum)
KACHAPI (zither)
KALUNGU (talking
    drum)
KAMANJE (fiddle)
KANTELE (zither)
KEMANAK (clappers)

7 —continued
KITHARA (lyre)
KOMUNGO (zither)
MACHETE (lute)
MANDOLA (lute)
MARACAS
    (percussion)
MASENQO (fiddle)
MIGYAUN (zither)
MOKUGYO (drum)
MURUMBU (drum)
MUSETTE (bagpipe)
MUSETTE (shawm)
OBUKANO (lyre)
OCARINA (flute)
OCTAVIN (wind)
ORPHICA (piano)
PANDORA (cittern)
PANPIPE
PIANINO
PIBCORN (hornpipe)
PICCOLO
PIFFARO (shawm)
QUINTON (viol)
RESHOTO (drum)
RINCHIK (cymbals)
SACKBUT (trombone)
SALPINX (trumpet)
SAMISEN (lute)
SANTOOR (dulcimer)
SARANGI (fiddle)
SARINDA (fiddle)
SAW-THAI (fiddle)
SAXHORN
SAXTUBA
SERPENT
SHIWAYA (flute)
SISTRUM (rattle)
SORDINE (kit)
SORDONE (double
    reed)
SPAGANE (clappers)
TAM ÂM LA (gong)
TAMBURA (lute)
TERBANG (drum)
THEORBO (lute)
TIKTIRI (clarinet)
TIMPANI
TRUMPET
TSUZUMI (drum)
UJUSINI (flute)
UKULELE
VIHUELA (guitar)
VIOLONE (viol)
WHISTLE
YUN NGAO (gong)
ZUMMARA (clarinet)

8
ALGHAITA (shawm)
ALTOHORN
AUTOHARP

8 —continued
BANDOURA (lute)
BASS DRUM
BASS HORN
BOMBARDE (shawm)
BOUZOUKI (lute)
BOWL LYRE
BUZZ DISK
CALLIOPE
    (mechanical organ)
CARILLON
CHIME BAR
CIMBALOM (dulcimer)
CIPACTLI (flute)
CLAPPERS
CLARINET
CLAVICOR (brass
    family)
CLAW BELL
COURTAUT (double
    reed)
CRECELLE (cog
    rattle)
CRUMHORN (double
    reed)
DULCIMER
DVOYNICE (flute)
GONG DRUM
HANDBELL
HAND HORN
HAWKBELL
JEW'S HARP
KAYAKEUM (zither)
KHUMBGWE (flute)
LANGLEIK (zither)
LANGSPIL (zither)
LAP ORGAN
    (melodeon)
MANDOLIN (lute)
MELODEON
MELODICA
MIRLITON (kazoo)
MRIDANGA (drum)
OLIPHANT (horn)
O-TSUZUMI (drum)
OTTAVINO (virginal)
P'AI HSIAO (panpipe)
PENORCON (cittern)
POCHETTE (kit)
PSALTERY (zither)
PUTORINO (trumpet)
RECORDER
RKAN-DUNG
    (trumpet)
RKAN-LING (horn)
RONÉAT-EK
    (xylophone)
SAN HSIEN (lute)
SIDE DRUM
SLIT DRUM
SONAJERO (rattle)

8 —continued
SRINGARA (fiddle)
SURBAHAR (lute)
TALAMBAS (drum)
TARABUKA (drum)
TAROGATO (clarinet;
    shawm)
TIMBALES (drum)
TRIANGLE
TRO-KHMER (fiddle)
TROMBONE
VIOLETTA (viol)
VIRGINAL
YANGCHIN (dulcimer)
YUEH CH'IN (lute)
ZAMPOGNA
    (bagpipe)

9
ACCORDION
ANGLE HARP
ARPANETTA (zither)
BALALAIKA (lute)
BANDURRIA (lute)
BANJOLELE
BASSONORE
    (bassoon)
BOMBARDON (tuba)
CASTANETS
CHALUMEAU
    (clarinet)
COG RATTLE
COMPONIUM
    (mechanical organ)
CORNEMUSE
    (bagpipe)
CORNOPEAN (brass
    family)
CROOK HORN
DAIBYOSHI (drum)
DARABUKKE (drum)
DJUNADJAN (zither)
DUDELSACK
    (bagpipes)
DVOJACHKA (flute)
EUPHONIUM (brass
    family)
FLAGEOLET (flute)
FLEXATONE
    (percussion)
GONG AGENG
HACKBRETT
    (dulcimer)
HARMONICA
HARMONIUM
HYDRAULIS (organ)
KELONTONG (drum)
KÖNIGHORN (brass
    family)
LAUNEDDAS
    (clarinet)
MANDOBASS (lute)

9 —continued
MANDOLONE (lute)
MORIN-CHUR (fiddle)
ORPHARION (cittern)
PICCO PIPE (flute)
PIEN CH'ING
    (lithophone)
ROMMELPOT (drum)
SAXOPHONE
TALLHARPA (lyre)
TOTOMBITO (zither)
TUBA-DUPRÉ
WOOD BLOCK
WURLITZER
XYLOPHONE
XYLORIMBA
    (xylophone)

10
BANANA DRUM
BARREL DRUM
BASSANELLO
    (double reed)
BASSET HORN
BIBLE REGAL (organ)
BICITRABIN (vina)
BIRD SCARER
BONGO DRUMS
BULL-ROARER
CHENGCHENG
    (cymbals)
CHITARRONE (lute)
CLAVICHORD
CLAVIORGAN
COLASCIONE (lute)
CONTRABASS
    (double bass)
COR ANGLAIS
DIDGERIDOO
    (trumpet)
DOUBLE BASS
FLUGELHORN
FRENCH HORN
GEIGENWERK
    (mechanical
    harpsichord)
GONG CHIMES
GRAND PIANO
HANDLE DRUM
HURDY GURDY
KETTLEDRUM
LITHOPHONE
    (percussion)
MANDOCELLO (lute)
MELLOPHONE (horn)
MOSHUPIANE (drum)
MOUTH ORGAN
OPHICLEIDE (brass
    family)
RANASRINGA (horn)
SAXOTROMBA
SHAKUHACHI (flute)

10 —continued
SOUSAPHONE
SPITZHARFE (zither)
SYMPHONIUM (mouth organ)
TAMBOURINE (drum)
TEPONAZTLI (drum)
THUMB PIANO (jew's harp)
TIN WHISTLE
TLAPIZTALI (flute)
TSURI DAIKO (drum)

11
AEOLIAN HARP
ANGEL CHIMES
BARREL ORGAN
BELL CITTERN
BIVALVE BELL
BLADDER PIPE
BOARD ZITHER
CLAPPER BELL
FIPPLE FLUTE
GAMBANG KAYA (xylophone)
GUITAR-BANJO
HAND TRUMPET
HARPSICHORD
HECKELPHONE (oboe)
NYCKELHARPA
PAIMENSARVI (horn)

11 —continued
PANHUÉHUETL (drum)
SARON DEMONG (metallophone)
SLEIGH BELLS
SPIKE FIDDLE
THEORBO-LUTE
UCHIWA DAIKO (drum)
VIOLA D'AMORE (viol)
VIOLONCELLO

12
DIPLO-KITHARA (zither)
GANSA GAMBANG (metallophone)
GANSA JONGKOK (metallophone)
GLOCKENSPIEL (metallophone)
GUITAR-VIOLIN
HI-HAT CYMBALS
KANTELEHARPE (lyre)
MANDOLINETTO (ukulele)
PEACOCK SITAR (lute)

12 —continued
RAUSCHPFEIFE (double reed)
SARRUSOPHONE (brass)
SHOULDER HARP
STOCK-AND-HORN (hornpipe)
TIPPOO'S TIGER (organ)
TUBULAR BELLS
VIOLA DA GAMBA (viol)
WHISTLE FLUTE

13
COCKTAIL DRUMS
CONTRABASSOON
DOUBLE BASSOON (contrabassoon)
HARDANGERFELE (fiddle)
HECKELCLARINA (clarinet)
SAVERNAKE HORN
SCHRILLPFEIFE (flute)
SLIDE TROMBONE
VIOLA BASTARDA (viol)

14
CLARINET D'AMORE
CLAVICYTHERIUM (harpsichord)
CYTHARA ANGLICA (harp)
JINGLING JOHNNY
TLAPANHUÉHUETL (drum)
TRICCABALLACCA (clappers)

15
CLASSICAL GUITAR
MOOG SYNTHESIZER
TURKISH CRESCENT (jingling johnny)

16
CHINESE WOOD BLOCK
CHITARRA BATTENTE (guitar)
CYLINDRICAL DRUMS
DEUTSCHE SCHALMEI (double reed)
STRUMENTO DI PORCO (zither)

THEATRICAL TERMS

2
OP
SM

3
ACT
ARC
ASM
GEL
HAM
LEG
PIT
RUN
SET

4
BLUE
BOOK
BOOM
DROP
EXIT
FLAT
GAFF
GOBO
GODS

4 —continued
GRID
IRIS
LEKO
MASK
OLIO
PIPE
PROP
RAIL
RAKE
SOCK
TABS
TAIL
WING

5
ABOVE
ACTOR
AD LIB
AGENT
APRON
ARENA
ASIDE
BELOW

5 —continued
BRACE
CLOTH
CLOUD
FLIES
FLOAT
FOYER
GAUZE
GLORY
HALLS
HEAVY
HOIST
INSET
LYRIC
MANET
ODEUM
PERCH
SCENE
SCRIM
SKENE
SLIPS
SLOTE
SOUND

5 —continued
STAGE
STALL
STILE
TRAPS
TRUCK
VISOR

6
BARREL
BATTEN
BOARDS
BORDER
BOX SET
BRIDGE
BUSKER
CELLAR
CENTRE
CIRCLE
CRITIC
DIMMER
GEGGIE
GROOVE
MAKE-UP

6 —continued
NEUMES
OLD MAN
POSTER
PUPPET
RETURN
RUNWAY
SCRUTO
SEA ROW
TEASER
TELARI
TOGGLE
WALK-ON

7
ACT DROP
ACTRESS
AULAEUM
BALCONY
BENEFIT
CALL BOY
CATWALK
CIRCUIT
CURTAIN
DIORAMA
FLIPPER
GALLERY
JORNADA
MANAGER
MATINÉE
ON STAGE
PINSPOT
RAIN BOX
ROLL-OUT
ROSTRUM
ROYALTY
SCENERY
SKY DOME
SPOT BAR
TABLEAU
TOP DROP
TRILOGY
TUMBLER
TWO-FOLD
UPSTAGE
VALANCE

8
AUDITION
BLACKOUT
BOOK FLAT
BOOK WING
CALL DOOR
CHAIRMAN
CUT-CLOTH
DESIGNER
DIRECTOR
DUMB SHOW
ELEVATOR
EPILOGUE
FAUTEUIL
FOX WEDGE

8 —continued
JUVENILE
LASHLINE
LIBRETTO
LIGHTING
OFF STAGE
OLD WOMAN
PANORAMA
PARADISO
PARALLEL
PASS DOOR
PLATFORM
PLAYBILL
PRODUCER
PROLOGUE
PROMPTER
SCENARIO
SET PIECE
SILL IRON
3IPARIUM
SKY CLOTH
STAR TRAP
VAMP TRAP
WARDROBE

9
ACOUSTICS
BACKCLOTH
BACKSTAGE
BOAT TRUCK
BOX OFFICE
CALL BOARD
CARPET CUT
CYCLORAMA
DOWNSTAGE
FAN EFFECT
FOOTLIGHT
GRAVE TRAP
GREEN ROOM
GROUNDROW
HAND-PROPS
HEMP HOUSE
LIGHT PIPE
LIMELIGHT
LOFT BLOCK
NOISES OFF
OPEN STAGE
ORCHESTRA
PENNY GAFF
PERIAKTOI
PROJECTOR
PROMENADE
PROVINCES
REFLECTOR
REHEARSAL
REPERTORY
ROD-PUPPET
ROPE HOUSE
SAND-CLOTH
SCENE DOCK
SET WATERS
SIGHT LINE

9 —continued
SKY BORDER
SLAPSTICK
SLIP STAGE
SOUBRETTE
SPOTLIGHT
STAGE CREW
STAGE DOOR
STAGE PROP
STAGE RAKE
THREE-FOLD
THROWLINE
THYRISTOR
TORMENTOR
TRAVELLER
TRICKWORK
WATER ROWS

10
ANTI-MASQUE
AUDITORIUM
AVANT-GARDE
BUILT STUFF
CORNER TRAP
CURTAIN SET
DRAG ARTIST
FLOODLIGHT
FOLLOW SPOT
GHOST GLIDE
HALL KEEPER
HOUSE LIGHT
IMPRESARIO
INNER STAGE
LYCOPODIUM
MARIONETTE
PIPE BATTEN
PROMPT SIDE
SADDLE-IRON
SCIOPTICON
SHOW PORTAL
SPECTATORY
STAGE CLOTH
STRIP LIGHT
THUNDER RUN
TREE BORDER
UNDERSTUDY

11
BACKING FLAT
BOOK CEILING
BORDER LIGHT
BRISTLE TRAP
CURTAIN CALL
DRESS CIRCLE
FALLING FLAP
FORMAL STAGE
FRESNEL SPOT
LIGHT BATTEN
LOW COMEDIAN
OFF-BROADWAY
PROFILE SPOT
RISE-AND-SINK

11 —continued
ROLL CEILING
SCENE RELIEF
SPIELTREPPE
STAGE-KEEPER
STROBE LIGHT
SWITCHBOARD
TRITAGONIST
UPPER CIRCLE
WAGGON STAGE
WIND MACHINE

12
ACTOR-MANAGER
AMPHITHEATRE
AUTHOR'S NIGHT
CAULDRON TRAP
CEILING-CLOTH
CHOREOGRAPHY
CONCERT PARTY
CORSICAN TRAP
COSTUME DRAMA
CURTAIN-MUSIC
FLYING EFFECT
FRONT OF HOUSE
LIGHT CONSOLE
LOBSTERSCOPE
MASKING PIECE
PEPPER'S GHOST
PROFILE BOARD
REVERBERATOR
RUNDHORIZONT
SCISSOR CROSS
SOUND EFFECTS
STAGE MANAGER
STAGE SETTING
STEREOPTICON
STICHOMYTHIA
STOCK COMPANY
THUNDERSHEET
TRANSPARENCY
TWOPENNY GAFF

13
DETAIL SCENERY
DEUS EX MACHINA
IMPROVISATION
LATERNA MAGICA
MAZARINE FLOOR
PLATFORM STAGE
PORTAL OPENING
SAFETY CURTAIN
STAGE LIGHTING
SUPERNUMERARY
WORD REHEARSAL

14
CONTOUR CURTAIN
COURTROOM
   DRAMA
DRAPERY SETTING
DRESS REHEARSAL
FOOTLIGHTS TRAP

14 —continued

GENERAL UTILITY
JACKKNIFE STAGE
KUPPELHORIZONT
MEZZANINE FLOOR
OFF-OFF-
 BROADWAY
PAGEANT LANTERN
PRIVATE THEATRE
PROSCENIUM ARCH
REVOLVING STAGE
STAGE DIRECTION

15

BARN DOOR
 SHUTTER
FLEXIBLE STAGING
HAND WORKED
 HOUSE
INCIDENTAL MUSIC
MULTIPLE SETTING
PROSCENIUM
 DOORS

15 —continued

QUICK-CHANGE
 ROOM
STAGE-DOOR
 KEEPER
TRAVERSE CURTAIN

16

ALIENATION EFFECT
ASPHALEIAN
 SYSTEM
COMPOSITE
 SETTING
DRAMATIS
 PERSONAE
DRAWING-ROOM
 DRAMA
PROSCENIUM
 BORDER
TOURING
 COMPANIES

17

CUP-AND-SAUCER
 DRAMA

18

BESPEAK
 PERFORMANCE
CARBON ARC
 SPOTLIGHT
DRUM-AND-SHAFT
 SYSTEM
FEMALE
 IMPERSONATOR
GRAND MASTER
 CONTROL
LINSEN-
 SCHEINWERFER
TECHNICAL
 REHEARSAL

19

COUNTERWEIGHT
 SYSTEM

19 —continued

SIMULTANEOUS
 SETTING
TRANSFORMATION
 SCENE

20

ADVERTISEMENT
 CURTAIN
ASSISTANT STAGE
 MANAGER
CARRIAGE-AND-
 FRAME SYSTEM
CHARIOT-AND-POLE
 SYSTEM
PROMENADE
 PRODUCTIONS
SILICON
 CONTROLLED
 RECTIFIER
SYNCHRONOUS
 WINCH SYSTEM

BALLET TERMS

4

BRAS
DEMI
JETÉ
PLIÉ
POSÉ
SAUT
TUTU
VOLÉ

5

ARQUÉ
BARRE
BATTU
BEATS
BRISÉ
COLLÉ
COUPÉ
DÉCOR
ÉLÈVE
FONDU
LIGNE
PASSÉ
PIQUÉ
PIVOT
PORTÉ
ROSIN
SAUTÉ
SERRÉ
TOMBÉ

6

APLOMB
À TERRE

6 —continued

ATTACK
BAISSÉ
BALLON
CAMBRÉ
CHAINÉ
CHANGÉ
CHASSÉ
CROISÉ
DÉGAGÉ
DÉTIRÉ
DEVANT
ÉCARTÉ
ÉFFACÉ
ÉLANCÉ
ENTRÉE
ÉPAULÉ
ÉTENDU
ÉTOILE
FAILLI
JARRET
MONTER
PENCHÉ
POINTE
RELEVÉ
RETIRÉ
VOYAGÉ

7

ALLONGÉ
ARRONDI
ATTAQUE
BALANCÉ

7 —continued

DANSEUR
DÉBOITÉ
ÉCHAPPÉ
EMBOITÉ
ÉTENDRE
FOUETTÉ
JARRETÉ
LEOTARD
MAILLOT
MARQUER
POISSON
RAMASSÉ
RETOMBÉ
SISSONE
SOUTENU
TAQUETÉ

8

ASSEMBLÉ
ATTITUDE
BACK BEND
BALLONNÉ
BALLOTTÉ
BATTERIE
CABRIOLE
CAGNEAUX
CORYPHÉE
DANSEUSE
DÉBOULÉS
DERRIÈRE
DÉTOURNÉ
GLISSADE

8 —continued

PISTOLET
RENVERSÉ
SERPETTE
SPOTTING
STULCHIK
TONNELET

9

ARABESQUE
BALLABILE
COU DE PIED
DÉVELOPPÉ
ÉLÉVATION
ENTRECHAT
ENVELOPPÉ
ÉQUILIBRE
HORTENSIA
JUPONNAGE
LIMBERING
MARCHEUSE
PAS DE DEUX
PIROUETTE
RACCOURCI
RÉVÉRENCE
REVOLTADE

10

BATTEMENTS
ENLÈVEMENT
ÉPAULEMENT
SOUBRESAUT
TAQUETERIE

11
CONTRETEMPS
PAS DE BASQUE
12
CHOREOGRAPHY
ENCHAÎNEMENT
GARGOUILLADE

13
CHOREOGRAPHER
CORPS DE BALLET
14
CLOSED POSITION
DIVERTISSEMENT

14 —continued
PRIMA BALLERINA
15
AUTOUR DE LA
  SALLE

17
RÉGISSEUR-
  GÉNÉRALE

NOVEL TITLES

NOVEL (Author)

3
SHE (H Rider Haggard)
4
DR NO (Ian Fleming)
EMMA (Jane Austen)
GIGI (Colette)
NANA (Émile Zola)
5
CHÉRI (Colette)
KIPPS (H G Wells)
SCOOP (Evelyn Waugh)
SYBIL (Benjamin Disraeli)
ZADIG (Voltaire)
6
AMELIA (Henry Fielding)
BEN HUR (Lew Wallace)
CHOCKY (John Wyndham)
LOLITA (Vladimir Nabokov)
PAMELA (Henry Fielding)
ROB ROY (Walter Scott)
7
CAMILLA (Fanny Burney)
CANDIDE (Voltaire)
CECILIA (Fanny Burney)
DRACULA (Bram Stoker)
EREWHON (Samuel Butler)
EVELINA (Fanny Burney)
IVANHOE (Walter Scott)
REBECCA (Daphne Du Maurier)
SHIRLEY (Charlotte Brontë)
THE FALL (Albert Camus)
ULYSSES (James Joyce)
8
ADAM BEDE (George Eliot)
CRANFORD (Mrs Gaskell)
JANE EYRE (Charlotte Brontë)
LUCKY JIM (Kingsley Amis)
SWAN SONG (John Galsworthy)
THE IDIOT (Fyodor Mikhailovich Dostoevsky)
THE MAGUS (John Fowles)
THE REBEL (Albert Camus)
TOM JONES (Henry Fielding)
VILLETTE (Charlotte Brontë)
WAVERLEY (Walter Scott)

9
AGNES GREY (Anne Brontë)
BILLY LIAR (Keith Waterhouse)
CONINGSBY (Benjamin Disraeli)
DUBLINERS (James Joyce)
GLENARVON (Lady Caroline Lamb)
HARD TIMES (Charles Dickens)
I CLAUDIUS (Robert Graves)
KIDNAPPED (R L Stevenson)
LOVE STORY (Erich Segal)
ROGUE MALE (Geoffrey Household)
THE CHIMES (Charles Dickens)
THE DEVILS (Fyodor Mikhailovich
  Dostoevsky)
THE HEROES (Charles Kingsley)
THE HOBBIT (J R R Tolkien)
THE PLAGUE (Albert Camus)
VICE VERSA (F Anstey)
10
ANIMAL FARM (George Orwell)
BLEAK HOUSE (Charles Dickens)
CANCER WARD (Alexander Solzhenitsyn)
CLAYHANGER (Arnold Bennett)
DON QUIXOTE (Cervantes)
GOLDFINGER (Ian Fleming)
IN CHANCERY (John Galsworthy)
KENILWORTH (Walter Scott)
LORNA DOONE (R D Blackmore)
PERSUASION (Jane Austen)
THE RAINBOW (D H Lawrence)
TITUS ALONE (Mervyn Peake)
TITUS GROAN (Mervyn Peake)
VANITY FAIR (William Makepeace Thackeray)
11
BLACK BEAUTY (Anna Sewell)
BURMESE DAYS (George Orwell)
CAKES AND ALE (W Somerset Maugham)
COUSIN BETTE (Honoré de Balzac)
DAISY MILLER (Henry James)
GORMENGHAST (Mervyn Peake)
LITTLE WOMEN (Louisa M Alcott)
LOST HORIZON (James Hilton)
MIDDLEMARCH (George Eliot)
MRS DALLOWAY (Virginia Woolf)
OLIVER TWIST (Charles Dickens)

11 —continued
SILAS MARNER (George Eliot)
THE BIG SLEEP (Raymond Chandler)
THE OUTSIDER (Albert Camus)
WAR AND PEACE (Leo Tolstoy)
WOMEN IN LOVE (D H Lawrence)

12
ANNA KARENINA (Leo Tolstoy)
A SEVERED HEAD (Iris Murdoch)
BARNABY RUDGE (Charles Dickens)
BRIGHTON ROCK (Graham Greene)
CASINO ROYALE (Ian Fleming)
DOMBEY AND SON (Charles Dickens)
FRANKENSTEIN (Mary Shelley)
GUY MANNERING (Walter Scott)
HEADLONG HALL (Thomas Love Peacock)
LITTLE DORRIT (Charles Dickens)
MADAME BOVARY (Gustave Flaubert)
MOLL FLANDERS (Daniel Defoe)
OF MICE AND MEN (John Steinbeck)
ROGUE JUSTICE (Geoffrey Household)
ROOM AT THE TOP (John Braine)
THE DECAMERON (Boccaccio)
THE GO-BETWEEN (L P Hartley)
THE LOST WORLD (Arthur Conan Doyle)
THE MOONSTONE (Wilkie Collins)
THE PROFESSOR (Charlotte Brontë)

13
A KIND OF LOVING (Stan Barstow)
A MODERN COMEDY (John Galsworthy)
BRAVE NEW WORLD (Aldous Huxley)
DANIEL DERONDA (George Eliot)
DOCTOR ZHIVAGO (Boris Pasternak)
FANNY AND ZOOEY (J D Salinger)
JACOB FAITHFUL (Captain Marryat)
JUST-SO STORIES (Rudyard Kipling)
LES MISÉRABLES (Victor Hugo)
LIVE AND LET DIE (Ian Fleming)
LIZA OF LAMBETH (W Somerset Maugham)
MANSFIELD PARK (Jane Austen)
NORTH AND SOUTH (Mrs Gaskell)
PINCHER MARTIN (William Golding)
SKETCHES BY BOZ (Charles Dickens)
SMILEY'S PEOPLE (John Le Carré)
SONS AND LOVERS (D H Lawrence)
TARKA THE OTTER (Henry Williamson)
THE BLUE LAGOON (H de Vere Stacpoole)
THE CHRYSALIDS (John Wyndham)
THE GOLDEN BOWL (Henry James)
THE HISTORY MAN (Malcolm Bradbury)
THE LAST TYCOON (F Scott Fitzgerald)
THÉRÈSE RAQUIN (Émile Zola)
ZULEIKA DOBSON (Max Beerbohm)

14
A MAN OF PROPERTY (John Galsworthy)
A ROOM OF ONE'S OWN (Virginia Woolf)
A ROOM WITH A VIEW (E M Forster)
A TOWN LIKE ALICE (Neville Shute)
CHANGING PLACES (David Lodge)
CIDER WITH ROSIE (Laurie Lee)

14 —continued
CROTCHET CASTLE (Thomas Love Peacock)
DEATH ON THE NILE (Agatha Christie)
DECLINE AND FALL (Evelyn Waugh)
GOODBYE, MR CHIPS (James Hilton)
JUDE THE OBSCURE (Thomas Hardy)
LORD OF THE FLIES (William Golding)
NIGHTMARE ABBEY (Thomas Love Peacock)
OUR MAN IN HAVANA (Graham Greene)
PICKWICK PAPERS (Charles Dickens)
RITES OF PASSAGE (William Golding)
ROBINSON CRUSOE (Daniel Defoe)
THE AMBASSADORS (Henry James)
THE CORAL ISLAND (R M Ballantyne)
THE FIRST CIRCLE (Alexander Solzhenitsyn)
THE FORSYTE SAGA (John Galsworthy)
THE GREAT GATSBY (F Scott Fitzgerald)
THE KRAKEN WAKES (John Wyndham)
THE LONG GOODBYE (Raymond Chandler)
THE SECRET AGENT (Joseph Conrad)
THE SILVER SPOON (John Galsworthy)
THE TIME MACHINE (H G Wells)
THE WATER-BABIES (Charles Kingsley)
THE WHITE MONKEY (John Galsworthy)
THE WOODLANDERS (Thomas Hardy)
TREASURE ISLAND (R L Stevenson)
TRISTRAM SHANDY (Laurence Sterne)
WHAT MAISIE KNEW (Henry James)

15
A CHRISTMAS CAROL (Charles Dickens)
A FAREWELL TO ARMS (Ernest Hemingway)
A PASSAGE TO INDIA (E M Forster)
COLD COMFORT FARM (Stella Gibbons)
EUSTACE AND HILDA (L P Hartley)
GONE WITH THE WIND (Margaret Mitchell)
GOODBYE TO BERLIN (Christopher
  Isherwood)
NORTHANGER ABBEY (Jane Austen)
OUR MUTUAL FRIEND (Charles Dickens)
PORTRAIT OF A LADY (Henry James)
PORTRAIT OF CLARE (Francis Brett Young)
STRAIT IS THE GATE (André Gide)
THE COUNTRY GIRLS (Edna O'Brien)
THE INVISIBLE MAN (H G Wells)
THE SECRET GARDEN (Frances Hodgson
  Burnett)
THE SILMARILLION (J R R Tolkien)
THE TRUMPET MAJOR (Thomas Hardy)
THE WHITE COMPANY (Arthur Conan Doyle)
THE WOMAN IN WHITE (Wilkie Collins)
THREE MEN IN A BOAT (Jerome K Jerome)

16
A CLOCKWORK ORANGE (Anthony Burgess)
A TALE OF TWO CITIES (Charles Dickens)
DAVID COPPERFIELD (Charles Dickens)
GULLIVER'S TRAVELS (Jonathan Swift)
MARTIN CHUZZLEWIT (Charles Dickens)
MR MIDSHIPMAN EASY (Captain Marryat)
NICHOLAS NICKLEBY (Charles Dickens)
TENDER IS THE NIGHT (F Scott Fitzgerald)

16 —continued
TEN LITTLE NIGGERS (Agatha Christie)
THE GRAPES OF WRATH (John Steinbeck)
THE PLUMED SERPENT (D H Lawrence)
THE SCARLET LETTER (Nathaniel
  Hawthorne)
WUTHERING HEIGHTS (Emily Brontë)

17
ALICE IN WONDERLAND (Lewis Carroll)
DR JEKYLL AND MR HYDE (R L Stevenson)
GREAT EXPECTATIONS (Charles Dickens)
KING SOLOMON'S MINES (H Rider Haggard)
MY BROTHER JONATHAN (Francis Brett
  Young)
POINT COUNTER POINT (Aldous Huxley)
PRIDE AND PREJUDICE (Jane Austen)
THE DEVILS OF LOUDUN (Aldous Huxley)
THE DIARY OF A NOBODY (G and W
  Grossmith)
THE LORD OF THE RINGS (J R R Tolkien)
THE MIDWICH CUCKOOS (John Wyndham)
THE MILL ON THE FLOSS (George Eliot)
THE WAR OF THE WORLDS (H G Wells)
THE WINGS OF THE DOVE (Henry James)
WIVES AND DAUGHTERS (Mrs Gaskell)

18
A HIGH WIND IN JAMAICA (Richard Hughes)
ANNA OF THE FIVE TOWNS (Arnold Bennett)
CRIME AND PUNISHMENT (Fyodor
  Dostoevsky)
NINETEEN EIGHTY-FOUR (George Orwell)
SWALLOWS AND AMAZONS (Arthur
  Ransome)
THE CATCHER IN THE RYE (J D Salinger)
THE MOON AND SIXPENCE (W Somerset
  Maugham)
THE OLD MAN AND THE SEA (Ernest
  Hemingway)
THE PRISONER OF ZENDA (Anthony Hope)
THE THIRTY-NINE STEPS (John Buchan)
THE THREE MUSKETEERS (Alexandre
  Dumas)

19
BRIDESHEAD REVISITED (Evelyn Waugh)
FOR WHOM THE BELL TOLLS (Ernest
  Hemingway)
SENSE AND SENSIBILITY (Jane Austen)
THE DAY OF THE TRIFFIDS (John Wyndham)
THE GULAG ARCHIPELAGO (Alexander
  Solzhenitsyn)
THE HISTORY OF MR POLLY (H G Wells)
THE MAN IN THE IRON MASK (Alexandre
  Dumas)
THE OLD CURIOSITY SHOP (Charles
  Dickens)
THE PILGRIM'S PROGRESS (John Bunyan)
THE RIDDLE OF THE SANDS (Erskine
  Childers)
THE SCARLET PIMPERNEL (Baroness Orczy)
THE SCREWTAPE LETTERS (C S Lewis)

19 —continued
THE VICAR OF WAKEFIELD (Oliver
  Goldsmith)
THE WIND IN THE WILLOWS (Kenneth
  Grahame)
TOM BROWN'S SCHOOLDAYS (Thomas
  Hughes)

20+
A CONNECTICUT YANKEE IN KING
  ARTHUR'S COURT (Mark Twain)
A DANCE TO THE MUSIC OF TIME (Anthony
  Powell)
AS I WALKED OUT ONE MIDSUMMER
  MORNING (Laurie Lee)
CHILDREN OF THE NEW FOREST (Captain
  Marryat)
FAR FROM THE MADDING CROWD (Thomas
  Hardy)
JOHN HALIFAX, GENTLEMAN (Mrs Craik)
KEEP THE ASPIDISTRA FLYING (George
  Orwell)
LADY CHATTERLEY'S LOVER (D H
  Lawrence)
LARK RISE TO CANDLEFORD (Flora
  Thompson)
LITTLE LORD FAUNTLEROY (Frances
  Hodgson Burnett)
MURDER ON THE ORIENT EXPRESS (Agatha
  Christie)
OUT OF THE SILENT PLANET (C S Lewis)
AROUND THE WORLD IN EIGHTY DAYS
  (Jules Verne)
TESS OF THE D'URBERVILLES (Thomas
  Hardy)
THE ADVENTURES OF HUCKLEBERRY FINN
  (Mark Twain)
THE ADVENTURES OF TOM SAWYER (Mark
  Twain)
THE BEAUTIFUL AND DAMNED (F Scott
  Fitzgerald)
THE BRIDE OF LAMMERMOOR (Walter Scott)
THE BROTHERS KARAMAZOV (Fyodor
  Mikhailovich Dostoevsky)
THE CRICKET ON THE HEARTH (Charles
  Dickens)
THE FRENCH LIEUTENANT'S WOMAN (John
  Fowles)
THE HEART OF MIDLOTHIAN (Walter Scott)
THE HISTORY OF HENRY ESMOND (William
  Makepeace Thackeray)
THE HONOURABLE SCHOOLBOY (John Le
  Carré)
THE INNOCENCE OF FATHER BROWN (G K
  Chesterton)
THE ISLAND OF DOCTOR MOREAU (H G
  Wells)
THE LAST OF THE MOHICANS (James
  Fenimore Cooper)
THE MEMOIRS OF SHERLOCK HOLMES
  (Arthur Conan Doyle)

20+ —continued

THE MYSTERIES OF UDOLPHO (Mrs Radcliffe)

THE MYSTERIOUS AFFAIR AT STYLES (Agatha Christie)

THE MYSTERY OF EDWIN DROOD (Charles Dickens)

THE PICTURE OF DORIAN GRAY (Oscar Wilde)

THE PRIME OF MISS JEAN BRODIE (Muriel Spark)

THE RED BADGE OF COURAGE (Stephen Crane)

20+ —continued

THE RETURN OF THE NATIVE (Thomas Hardy)

THE TENANT OF WILDFELL HALL (Anne Brontë)

TINKER, TAILOR, SOLDIER, SPY (John Le Carré)

TWENTY THOUSAND LEAGUES UNDER THE SEA (Jules Verne)

TWO YEARS BEFORE THE MAST (Richard Henry Dana)

UNDER THE GREENWOOD TREE (Thomas Hardy)

PLAY TITLES

TITLE (Playwright)

4

LOOT (Joe Orton)

ROSS (Terence Rattigan)

5

CASTE (T W Robertson)

FAUST (Goethe)

MEDEA (Euripides)

ROOTS (Arnold Wesker)

6

GHOSTS (Henrik Ibsen)

HAMLET (William Shakespeare)

HENRY V (William Shakespeare)

PHÈDRE (Jean Racine)

PLENTY (David Hare)

STRIFE (John Galsworthy)

7

AMADEUS (Peter Shaffer)

ATHALIE (Jean Racine)

CANDIDA (G B Shaw)

ELECTRA (Sophocles)

GALILEO (Bertolt Brecht)

HENRY IV (William Shakespeare)

HENRY VI (William Shakespeare)

JUMPERS (Tom Stoppard)

MACBETH (William Shakespeare)

OTHELLO (William Shakespeare)

THE LARK (Jean Anouilh)

THE ROOM (Harold Pinter)

VOLPONE (Ben Jonson)

8

ANTIGONE (Sophocles)

HAY FEVER (Noël Coward)

KING JOHN (William Shakespeare)

KING LEAR (William Shakespeare)

PERICLES (William Shakespeare)

PETER PAN (J M Barrie)

TARTUFFE (Molière)

THE BIRDS (Aristophanes)

8 —continued

THE FROGS (Aristophanes)

THE MISER (Molière)

9

ALL MY SONS (Arthur Miller)

BILLY LIAR (Willis Hall and Keith Waterhouse)

CAVALCADE (Noël Coward)

CYMBELINE (William Shakespeare)

DR FAUSTUS (Christopher Marlowe)

FLARE PATH (Terence Rattigan)

GOLDEN BOY (Clifford Odets)

HAPPY DAYS (Samuel Beckett)

HENRY VIII (William Shakespeare)

PYGMALION (G B Shaw)

RICHARD II (William Shakespeare)

SAINT JOAN (G B Shaw)

THE CIRCLE (W Somerset Maugham)

THE CRITIC (Sheridan)

THE DEVILS (John Whiting)

THE RIVALS (Sheridan)

10

ALL FOR LOVE (John Dryden)

ANDROMAQUE (Jean Racine)

AURENG-ZEBE (John Dryden)

CORIOLANUS (William Shakespeare)

I AM A CAMERA (John Van Druten)

OEDIPUS REX (Sophocles)

RICHARD III (William Shakespeare)

THE BACCHAE (Euripides)

THE BALCONY (Jean Genet)

THE HOSTAGE (Brendan Behan)

THE SEAGULL (Anton Chekhov)

THE TEMPEST (William Shakespeare)

UNCLE VANYA (Anton Chekhov)

11

A DOLL'S HOUSE (Henrik Ibsen)

AS YOU LIKE IT (William Shakespeare)

JOURNEY'S END (R C Sherriff)

11 —continued
LOVE FOR LOVE (William Congreve)
PANDORA'S BOX (Frank Wedekind)
ROOKERY NOOK (Ben Travers)
THE BANKRUPT (Alexander Ostrovsky)
THE CONTRAST (Royall Tyler)
THE CRUCIBLE (Arthur Miller)
THE WILD DUCK (Henrik Ibsen)

12
AFTER THE FALL (Arthur Miller)
ANNA CHRISTIE (Eugene O'Neill)
BEDROOM FARCE (Alan Ayckbourn)
BLITHE SPIRIT (Noël Coward)
BLOOD WEDDING (García Lorca)
CHARLEY'S AUNT (Brandon Thomas)
DUEL OF ANGELS (Jean Giraudoux)
JULIUS CAESAR (William Shakespeare)
MAJOR BARBARA (G B Shaw)
PRIVATE LIVES (Noël Coward)
THE ALCHEMIST (Ben Jonson)
THE ANATOMIST (James Bridie)
THE APPLE CART (G B Shaw)
THE BROKEN JUG (Heinrich von Kleist)
THE CARETAKER (Harold Pinter)
THE MOUSETRAP (Agatha Christie)
THREE SISTERS (Anton Chekhov)
TWELFTH NIGHT (William Shakespeare)

13
ARMS AND THE MAN (G B Shaw)
A TASTE OF HONEY (Shelagh Delaney)
HOBSON'S CHOICE (Harold Brighouse)
LE MISANTHROPE (Molière)
QUALITY STREET (J M Barrie)
THE ACHARNIANS (Aristophanes)
THE DUMB WAITER (Harold Pinter)
THE JEW OF MALTA (Christopher Marlowe)
THE LINDEN TREE (J B Priestley)
THE MAGISTRATE (Pinero)
THE MATCHMAKER (Thornton Wilder)
THE WHITE DEVIL (John Webster)
THE WINSLOW BOY (Terence Rattigan)
TIMON OF ATHENS (William Shakespeare)
UNDER MILK WOOD (Dylan Thomas)

14
AN IDEAL HUSBAND (Oscar Wilde)
MAN AND SUPERMAN (G B Shaw)
ROMEO AND JULIET (William Shakespeare)
SEPARATE TABLES (Terence Rattigan)
THE CORN IS GREEN (Emlyn Williams)
THE COUNTRY GIRL (Clifford Odets)
THE DEEP BLUE SEA (Terence Rattigan)
THE FIRE-RAISERS (Max Frisch)
THE GHOST SONATA (August Strindberg)
THE OLD BACHELOR (William Congreve)
THE PHILANDERER (G B Shaw)
THE TROJAN WOMEN (Euripides)
THE WINTER'S TALE (William Shakespeare)
THIS HAPPY BREED (Noël Coward)

15
BARTHOLOMEW FAIR (Ben Jonson)

15 —continued
DANGEROUS CORNER (J B Priestley)
DESIGN FOR LIVING (Noël Coward)
HEARTBREAK HOUSE (G B Shaw)
LOOK BACK IN ANGER (John Osborne)
MARRIAGE À LA MODE (John Dryden)
PRESENT LAUGHTER (Noël Coward)
THE CONSTANT WIFE (W Somerset
   Maugham)
THE ICEMAN COMETH (Eugene O'Neill)
TITUS ANDRONICUS (William Shakespeare)
TWO NOBLE KINSMEN (William Shakespeare)
VENICE PRESERVED (Thomas Otway)
WAITING FOR GODOT (Samuel Beckett)

16
A CUCKOO IN THE NEST (Ben Travers)
AN INSPECTOR CALLS (J B Priestley)
CAT ON A HOT TIN ROOF (Tennessee
   Williams)
DEATH OF A SALESMAN (Arthur Miller)
LOVE'S LABOUR'S LOST (William
   Shakespeare)
PILLARS OF SOCIETY (Henrik Ibsen)
RING ROUND THE MOON (Jean Anouilh)
THE ADDING MACHINE (Elmer Rice)
THE AMERICAN DREAM (Edward Albee)
THE BIRTHDAY PARTY (Harold Pinter)
THE CHERRY ORCHARD (Anton Chekhov)
THE COCKTAIL PARTY (T S Eliot)
THE FAMILY REUNION (T S Eliot)
THE MASTER BUILDER (Henrik Ibsen)
WHAT THE BUTLER SAW (Joe Orton)

17
A MAN FOR ALL SEASONS (Robert Bolt)
AN ITALIAN STRAW HAT (Eugène Labiche)
ARSENIC AND OLD LACE (Joseph Kesselring)
BAREFOOT IN THE PARK (Neil Simon)
JUNO AND THE PAYCOCK (Sean O'Casey)
MEASURE FOR MEASURE (William
   Shakespeare)
ROMANOFF AND JULIET (Peter Ustinov)
THE BEAUX' STRATAGEM (George Farquhar)
THE COMEDY OF ERRORS (William
   Shakespeare)
THE DEVIL'S DISCIPLE (G B Shaw)
THE DOCTOR'S DILEMMA (G B Shaw)
THE DUCHESS OF MALFI (John Webster)
THE GLASS MENAGERIE (Tennessee
   Williams)
THE GOOD-NATURED MAN (Oliver
   Goldsmith)
THE SCHOOL FOR WIVES (Molière)
THE SUPPLIANT WOMEN (Aeschylus)
'TIS PITY SHE'S A WHORE (John Ford)

18
AN ENEMY OF THE PEOPLE (Henrik Ibsen)
ANTONY AND CLEOPATRA (William
   Shakespeare)
CAESAR AND CLEOPATRA (G B Shaw)
FIVE FINGER EXERCISE (Peter Shaffer)

18 —continued

FRENCH WITHOUT TEARS (Terence Rattigan)

LADY WINDERMERE'S FAN (Oscar Wilde)

SHE STOOPS TO CONQUER (Oliver Goldsmith)

SUDDENLY LAST SUMMER (Tennessee Williams)

THE BROWNING VERSION (Terence Rattigan)

THE ROMANS IN BRITAIN (Howard Brenton)

TROILUS AND CRESSIDA (William Shakespeare)

19

ANDROCLES AND THE LION (G B Shaw)

CHIPS WITH EVERYTHING (Arnold Wesker)

MUCH ADO ABOUT NOTHING (William Shakespeare)

TAMBURLAINE THE GREAT (Christopher Marlowe)

THE MERCHANT OF VENICE (William Shakespeare)

THE SCHOOL FOR SCANDAL (Sheridan)

THE TAMING OF THE SHREW (William Shakespeare)

WHAT EVERY WOMAN KNOWS (J M Barrie)

20+

ACCIDENTAL DEATH OF AN ANARCHIST (Dario Fo)

ALL GOD'S CHILLUN GOT WINGS (Eugene O'Neill)

ALL'S WELL THAT ENDS WELL (William Shakespeare)

A MIDSUMMER NIGHT'S DREAM (William Shakespeare)

20+ —continued

A STREETCAR NAMED DESIRE (Tennessee Williams)

A WOMAN OF NO IMPORTANCE (Oscar Wilde)

CAPTAIN BRASSBOUND'S CONVERSION (G B Shaw)

ENTERTAINING MR SLOANE (Joe Orton)

INADMISSIBLE EVIDENCE (John Osborne)

MOURNING BECOMES ELECTRA (Eugene O'Neill)

MURDER IN THE CATHEDRAL (T S Eliot)

ROSENCRANTZ AND GUILDENSTERN ARE DEAD (Tom Stoppard)

THE ADMIRABLE CRICHTON (J M Barrie)

THE BARRETTS OF WIMPOLE STREET (Rudolf Besier)

THE CAUCASIAN CHALK CIRCLE (Bertolt Brecht)

THE GOVERNMENT INSPECTOR (Nikolai Gogol)

THE IMPORTANCE OF BEING EARNEST (Oscar Wilde)

THE LADY'S NOT FOR BURNING (Christopher Fry)

THE MERRY WIVES OF WINDSOR (William Shakespeare)

THE SECOND MRS TANQUERAY (Pinero)

THE TWO GENTLEMEN OF VERONA (William Shakespeare)

WHO'S AFRAID OF VIRGINIA WOOLF? (Edward Albee)

FICTIONAL CHARACTERS

CHARACTER (*Title*, Author)

3

FOX, Brer (*Uncle Remus*, J. C. Harris)

GOG (*The Tower of London*, W. H. Ainsworth)

HUR, Judah (*Ben Hur*, L. Wallace)

JIM, 'Lord' (*Lord Jim*, J. Conrad)

KIM (*Kim*, Rudyard Kipling)

LEE, General Robert E. (*Abraham Lincoln*, J. Drinkwater)

LEE, Lorelei (*Gentlemen Prefer Blondes*, Anita Loos)

OWL (*Winnie the Pooh*, A. A. Milne)

ROO (*Winnie the Pooh*, A. A. Milne)

TOM (*The Water Babies*, C. Kingsley)

TOM, 'Uncle' (*Uncle Tom's Cabin*, Harriet B. Stowe)

4

ABEL (*Middlemarch*, George Eliot)

CASS, Eppie (*Silas Marner*, George Eliot)

4 —continued

CASY, Rev. Jim (*The Grapes of Wrath*, J. Steinbeck)

CUFF, Sergeant (*The Moonstone*, W. Collins)

DEAN, Ellen (*Wuthering Heights*, Emily Brontë)

EAST (*Tom Brown's Schooldays*, T. Hughes)

EASY, John (*Mr Midshipman Easy*, Captain Marryat)

EYRE, Jane (*Jane Eyre*, Charlotte Brontë)

FAWN, Lord Frederic (*Phineas Finn*, A. Trollope)

FELL, Dr Gideon (*The Black Spectacles*, J. Dickson Carr)

FINN, Huckleberry (*Huckleberry Finn, Tom Sawyer*, M. Twain)

FINN, Phineas (*Phineas Finn*, A. Trollope)

4 —continued

GRAY, Dorian (*The Picture of Dorian Gray*, Oscar Wilde)

GRAY, Nelly (*Faithless Nelly Gray*, T. Hood)

GUNN, Ben (*Treasure Island*, R. L. Stevenson)

HOOK, Captain James (*Peter Pan*, J. M. Barrie)

HYDE, Edward (*Dr Jekyll and Mr Hyde*, R. L. Stevenson)

JUDY (*Wee Willie Winkie*, R. Kipling)

LAMB, Leonard (*Middlemarch*, George Eliot)

MOLE, Mr (*The Wind in the Willows*, K. Grahame)

NANA (*Peter Pan*, J. M. Barrie)

NASH, Richard (Beau) (*Monsieur Beaucaire*, Booth Tarkington)

PUCK (Robin Goodfellow) (*Puck of Pook's Hill*, R. Kipling)

RAMA (Tiger Tiger) (*The Jungle Book*, R. Kipling)

REED, Mrs (*Jane Eyre*, Charlotte Brontë)

RIDD, John (*Lorna Doone*, R. D. Blackmore)

SEAL, Basil (*Put Out More Flags*, E. Waugh)

SMEE (*Peter Pan*, J. M. Barrie)

TOAD, Mr (*The Wind in the Willows*, K. Grahame)

TROY, Sergeant Francis (*Far from the Madding Crowd*, T. Hardy)

VANE, Harriet (*Strong Poison*, Dorothy L. Sayers)

VANE, Lady Isabel (*East Lynne*, Mrs Henry Wood)

WOLF, 'Brer' (*Uncle Remus*, J. C. Harris)

5

ADLER, Irene (*The Adventures of Sherlock Holmes*, A. Conan Doyle)

AKELA (*The Jungle Book*, R. Kipling)

ALIBI, Tom (*Waverley*, W. Scott)

ATHOS (*The Three Musketeers*, Alexandre Dumas)

BALOO (*The Jungle Book*, R. Kipling)

BLAKE, Franklin (*The Moonstone*, W. Collins)

BONES, Captain Billy (*Treasure Island*, R. L. Stevenson)

BOOBY, Sir Thomas (*Joseph Andrews*, H. Fielding)

BRUFF (*The Moonstone*, W. Collins)

BULBO, Prince (*The Rose and the Ring*, W. M. Thackeray)

CHANT, Mercy (*Tess of the D'Urbervilles*, T. Hardy)

CLACK, Drusilla (*The Moonstone*, W. Collins)

CLARE, Angel (*Tess of the D'Urbervilles*, T. Hardy)

DARCY, Fitzwilliam (*Pride and Prejudice*, Jane Austen)

DEANS, Effie/Jeanie (*The Heart of Midlothian*, W. Scott)

DIXON, James (*Lucky Jim*, K. Amis)

DOONE, Lorna (*Lorna Doone*, R. D. Blackmore)

5 —continued

EAGER, Rev. Cuthbert (*Room with a View*, E. M. Forster)

FANNY (*Fanny's First Play*, G. B. Shaw)

FLYNN, Father James (*The Dubliners*, J. Joyce)

GESTE, Beau (*Beau Geste*, P. C. Wren)

GWYNN, Nell (*Simon Dale*, A. Hope)

HANDS, Israel (*Treasure Island*, R. L. Stevenson)

HATCH, Bennet (*The Black Arrow*, R. L. Stevenson)

JONES, Tom (*Tom Jones*, H. Fielding)

KANGA (*Winnie the Pooh*, A. A. Milne)

KIPPS, Arthur (*Kipps*, H. G. Wells)

LEIGH, Captain Sir Amyas (*Westward Ho!*, C. Kingsley)

MAGOG (*The Tower of London*, W. H. Ainsworth)

MARCH, Amy/Beth/Josephine (Jo)/Meg (*Little Women*, etc., Louisa M. Alcott)

MERCY (*Pilgrim's Progress*, J. Bunyan)

MITTY, Walter (*The Secret Life of Walter Mitty*, J. Thurber)

MOORE, Mrs (*A Passage to India*, E. M. Forster)

O'HARA, Kimball (*Kim*, Rudyard Kipling)

O'HARA, Scarlett (*Gone with the Wind*, Margaret Mitchell)

OTTER, Mr (*The Wind in the Willows*, K. Grahame)

PAGET, Jean (*A Town like Alice*, N. Shute)

POLLY, Alfred (*The History of Mr Polly*, H. G. Wells)

POOLE, Grace (*Jane Eyre*, Charlotte Brontë)

PORGY (*Porgy*, Du Bose Heywood)

PRISM, Miss Laetitia (*The Importance of Being Earnest*, Oscar Wilde)

PUNCH (*Wee Willie Winkie*, R. Kipling)

READY, Masterman (*Masterman Ready*, F. Marryat)

REMUS, Uncle (*Uncle Remus* series, J. C. Harris)

RYDER, Charles (*Brideshead Revisited*, E. Waugh)

SALLY (*Sally in Our Alley*, H. Carey)

SAMBO (*Just So Stories*, R. Kipling)

SHARP, Rebecca (Becky) (*Vanity Fair*, W. M. Thackeray)

SLOPE, Rev. Obadiah (*Barchester Towers*, A. Trollope)

SLOTH (*Pilgrim's Progress*, J. Bunyan)

SMITH, Winston (*1984*, G. Orwell)

SNOWE, Lucy (*Villette*, Charlotte Brontë)

TARKA (*Tarka the Otter*, H. Williamson)

THUMB, Tom (*The Tale of Two Bad Mice*, Beatrix Potter)

TOPSY (*Uncle Tom's Cabin*, Harriet B. Stowe)

UNCAS (*The Last of the Mohicans*, J. Fennimore Cooper)

6

AITKEN (*Prester John*, J. Buchan)
ARAMIS (*The Three Musketeers*, Alexandre Dumas)
AYESHA (*She*, H. Rider Haggard)
BENNET, Catherine/Elizabeth/Jane/Lydia/ Mary (*Pride and Prejudice*, Jane Austen)
BESSIE (*Jane Eyre*, Charlotte Brontë)
BINKIE, Lady Grizzel (*Vanity Fair*, W. M. Thackeray)
BOVARY, Emma (*Madame Bovary*, G. Flaubert)
BUTLER, Rhett (*Gone with the Wind*, Margaret Mitchell)
CACKLE (*Vanity Fair*, W. M. Thackeray)
CARDEW, Cecily (*The Importance of Being Earnest*, Oscar Wilde)
CRUSOE, Robinson (*Robinson Crusoe*, D. Defoe)
DANGLE (*The Critic*, R. B. Sheridan)
EEYORE (*Winnie the Pooh*, A. A. Milne)
ELAINE (*Idylls of the King*, Lord Tennyson)
'FRIDAY' (*Robinson Crusoe*, D. Defoe)
FRITHA (*The Snow Goose*, P. Gallico)
GARTER, Polly (*Under Milk Wood*, D. Thomas)
GATSBY, Major Jay (*The Great Gatsby*, F. Scott Fitzgerald)
GEORGE (*Three Men in a Boat*, J. K. Jerome)
GERARD, Etienne (*The Exploits of Brigadier Gerard*, A. Conan Doyle)
GILPIN, John (*John Gilpin*, W. Cowper)
GLOVER, Catherine (*The Fair Maid of Perth*, W. Scott)
GORDON, Squire (*Black Beauty*, A. Sewell)
GRIMES (*The Water Babies*, C. Kingsley)
HANNAY, Richard (*The Thirty-Nine Steps*, J. Buchan)
HARKER, Jonathan/Minna (*Dracula*, Bram Stoker)
HARMAN, Joe (*A Town like Alice*, N. Shute)
HAROLD, Childe (*Childe Harold's Pilgrimage*, Lord Byron)
HEARTS, King of/Knave of/Queen of (*Alice in Wonderland*, L. Carroll)
HOLMES, Mycroft (*The Return of Sherlock Holmes*, A. Conan Doyle)
HOLMES, Sherlock (*A Study in Scarlet, The Sign of Four, The Hound of the Baskervilles*, etc., A. Conan Doyle)
HOOPER, Fanny (*Fanny by Gaslight*, M. Sadleir)
JEEVES (*Thank you, Jeeves*, P. G. Wodehouse)
JEKYLL, Henry (*Dr Jekyll and Mr Hyde*, R. L. Stevenson)
LAURIE (*Little Women*, Louisa M. Alcott)
LAURIE, Annie (*Annie Laurie*, Douglass)
LEGREE, Simon (*Uncle Tom's Cabin*, Harriet B. Stowe)
LINTON, Edgar (*Wuthering Heights*, Emily Brontë)

6 —continued

MANGAN, Boss (*Heartbreak House*, G. B. Shaw)
MANSON, Dr Andrew (*The Citadel*, A. J. Cronin)
MARPLE, Jane (*A Pocket Full of Rye*, Agatha Christie)
MERLIN (*Idylls of the King*, Lord Tennyson)
MODRED, Sir (*Idylls of the King*, Lord Tennyson)
MOREAU, André-Louis (*Scaramouche*, R. Sabatini)
MOREAU, Dr (*The Island of Dr Moreau*, H. G. Wells)
MORGAN, Angharad/Huw (*How Green Was My Valley*, R. Llewellyn)
MORGAN, Organ (*Under Milk Wood*, D. Thomas)
MOWGLI (*The Jungle Book*, R. Kipling)
NUTKIN, Squirrel, (*The Tale of Squirrel Nutkin*, Beatrix Potter)
OMNIUM, Duke of (Family name Palliser) (*The Barsetshire series*, Angela Thirkell)
PICKLE, Peregrine (*Peregrine Pickle*, T. Smollett)
PIGLET, Henry Pootel (*Winnie the Pooh*, A. A. Milne)
POIROT, Hercule (*The Mysterious Affair at Styles*, Agatha Christie)
RABBIT (*Winnie the Pooh*, A. A. Milne)
RABBIT, 'Brer' (*Uncle Remus*, J. C. Harris)
RABBIT, The White (*Alice in Wonderland*, L. Carroll)
RIVERS, St John (*Jane Eyre*, Charlotte Brontë)
RUSTUM (*Sohrab and Rustum*, M. Arnold)
SAWYER, Tom (*The Adventures of Tom Sawyer*, M. Twain)
SHANDY, Tristram (*Tristram Shandy*, L. Sterne)
SILVER, Long John (*Treasure Island*, R. L. Stevenson)
SIMNEL, Lambert (*Perkin Warbeck*, John Ford)
SOHRAB (*Sohrab and Rustum*, M. Arnold)
TEMPLE, Miss (*Jane Eyre*, Charlotte Brontë)
THORNE, Dr Thomas (*Doctor Thorne*, A. Trollope)
THORPE, Isabella (*Northanger Abbey*, Jane Austen)
TILNEY, Henry (*Northanger Abbey*, Jane Austen)
TURNER, Jim (Captain Flint) (*Swallows and Amazons*, A. Ransome)
UMPOPA (*King Solomon's Mines*, H. Rider Haggard)
WALKER, John/Roger/Susan/Titty/Vicky (*Swallows and Amazons*, A. Ransome)
WESTON, Mrs (*Emma*, Jane Austen)
WILKES, Ashley/India (*Gone with the Wind*, Margaret Mitchell)

6 —continued

WIMSEY, Lord Peter Death Bredon (*Whose Body?*, Dorothy L. Sayers)

7

AISGILL, Alice (*Room at the Top*, J. Braine)

BAGSTER (*Middlemarch*, George Eliot)

BEESLEY (*Lucky Jim*, Kingsley Amis)

BINGLEY, Charles (*Pride and Prejudice*, Jane Austen)

BRANDON, Colonel (*Sense and Sensibility*, Jane Austen)

CANDOUR, Mrs (*The School for Scandal*, R. B. Sheridan)

CHESNEY, Jack (*Charley's Aunt,* Brandon Thomas)

COLLINS, Rev. William (*Pride and Prejudice*, Jane Austen)

CYPRESS, Mr (*Nightmare Abbey*, T. L. Peacock)

DANVERS, Mrs (*Rebecca*, Daphne du Maurier)

DESPAIR, Giant (*Pilgrim's Progress*, J. Bunyan)

DRACULA, Count (*Dracula*, Bram Stoker)

EPICENE (*Epicene*, B. Jonson)

FAIRFAX, Gwendolen (*The Importance of Being Earnest*, Oscar Wilde)

FAIRFAX, Jane (*Emma*, J. Austen)

FAIRFAX, Mrs (*Jane Eyre*, Charlotte Brontë)

FAIRLIE, Frederick (*Woman in White*, W. Collins)

FAUSTUS (*The History of Dr Faustus*, C. Marlowe)

FORSYTE, Fleur/Irene/Jolyon/Jon/Soames (*The Forsyte Saga*, J. Galsworthy)

GALAHAD (*Idylls of the King*, Lord Tennyson)

GERAINT (*Idylls of the King*, Lord Tennyson)

GRANTLY, Bishop of Barchester (*The Warden*, *Barchester Towers*, A. Trollope)

HAWKINS, Jim (*Treasure Island*, R. L. Stevenson)

HENTZAU, Rupert of (*The Prisoner of Zenda*, A. Hope)

HERRIES, Francis (*Rogue Herries*, H. Walpole)

HIGGINS, Henry (*Pygmalion*, G. B. Shaw)

IVANHOE, Wilfred, Knight of (*Ivanhoe*, W. Scott)

JENKINS, Rev. Eli (*Under Milk Wood*, D. Thomas)

KEELDAR, Shirley (*Shirley*, Charlotte Brontë)

LAMPTON, Joe (*Room at the Top*, J. Braine)

LATIMER, Darsie (*Redgauntlet*, W. Scott)

LAWLESS (*The Black Arrow*, R. L. Stevenson)

LINCOLN, Abraham (*Abraham Lincoln*, J. Drinkwater)

LUCIFER (*Faustus*, C. Marlowe)

MESSALA (*Ben Hur*, L. Wallace)

MICHAEL, Duke of Strelsau (*The Prisoner of Zenda*, A. Hope)

MINIVER, Mrs Caroline (*Mrs Miniver*, Jan Struther)

7 —continued

MORLAND, Catherine (*Northanger Abbey*, Jane Austen)

NOKOMIS (*Song of Hiawatha*, H. W. Longfellow)

PORTHOS (*The Three Musketeers*, Alexandre Dumas)

PROUDIE, Dr/Mrs (*Framley Parsonage*, A. Trollope)

RAFFLES, A. J. (*Raffles* series, E. W. Hornung)

RANDALL, Rebecca (*Rebecca of Sunnybrook Farm*, Kate D. Wiggin)

RATTLER, Martin (*Martin Rattler*, R. M. Ballantyne)

REBECCA (*Rebecca*, Daphne du Maurier)

REBECCA (*Rebecca of Sunnybrook Farm*, Kate D. Wiggin)

RED KING (*Alice Through the Looking Glass*, L. Carroll)

ROBSART, Amy (*Kenilworth*, W. Scott)

SANDERS (Sandi) (*Sanders of the River*, E. Wallace)

SHELTON, Richard (*The Black Arrow*, R. L. Stevenson)

SHIPTON, Mother (*The Luck of Roaring Camp*, Bret Harte)

SMOLLET, Captain (*Treasure Island*, R. L. Stevenson)

SORRELL, Christopher (Kit) (*Sorrell and Son*, W. Deeping)

ST CLARE, Evangeline (Little Eva) (*Uncle Tom's Cabin*, Harriet B. Stowe)

TIDDLER, Tom (*Adam's Opera*, Clemence Dane)

WARBECK, Perkin (*Perkin Warbeck*, John Ford)

WESTERN, Mrs/Sophia/Squire, (*Tom Jones*, H. Fielding)

WILLIAM (*Just William*, Richmal Crompton)

WINSLOW, Ronnie (*The Winslow Boy*, T. Rattigan)

WOOSTER, Bertie (*Thank You, Jeeves*, P. G. Wodehouse)

8

ABSOLUTE, Sir Anthony (*The Rivals*, R. B. Sheridan)

ANGELICA (*The Rose and the Ring*, W. M. Thackeray)

APOLLYON (*Pilgrim's Progress*, J. Bunyan)

ARMITAGE, Jacob (*The Children of the New Forest*, Captain Marryat)

BACKBITE, Sir Benjamin (*The School for Scandal*, R. B. Sheridan)

BAGHEERA (*The Jungle Book*, R. Kipling)

BLACK DOG (*Treasure Island*, R. L. Stevenson)

CARRAWAY, Nick (*The Great Gatsby*, F. Scott Fitzgerald)

CASAUBON, Rev. Edward, (*Middlemarch*, George Eliot)

8 —continued

CRAWFURD, David (*Prester John*, J. Buchan)

CRICHTON, Bill (*The Admirable Crichton*, J. M. Barrie)

DASHWOOD, Henry (*Sense and Sensibility*, Jane Austen)

DE BOURGH, Lady Catherine (*Pride and Prejudice*, Jane Austen)

DE WINTER, Maximilian (*Rebecca*, Daphne du Maurier)

EARNSHAW, Catherine (*Wuthering Heights*, Emily Brontë)

EVERDENE, Bathsheba (*Far from the Madding Crowd*, T. Hardy)

FFOULKES, Sir Andrew (*The Scarlet Pimpernel*, Baroness Orczy)

FLANDERS, Moll (*Moll Flanders*, D. Defoe)

FLASHMAN (*Tom Brown's Schooldays*, T. Hughes)

GLORIANA (*The Faërie Queen*, E. Spenser)

GOLLANTZ, Emmanuel (*Young Emmanuel*, N. Jacob)

GULLIVER, Lemuel (*Gulliver's Travels*, J. Swift)

GUNGA DIN (*Barrack-room Ballads*, R. Kipling)

HIAWATHA (*The Song of Hiawatha*, H. W. Longfellow)

KNIGHTLY, George (*Emma*, J. Austen)

LANCELOT, Sir (*Idylls of the King*, Lord Tennyson)

LANGUISH, Lydia (*The Rivals*, R. B. Sheridan)

LAURENCE, Theodore (*Little Women*, Louisa M. Alcott)

LESSWAYS, Hilda (*The Clayhanger Trilogy*, Arnold Bennett)

LESTRADE, of Scotland Yard (*A Study in Scarlet*, A. Conan Doyle)

LOCKWOOD (*Wuthering Heights*, Emily Brontë)

MACAVITY (*Old Possum's Book of Practical Cats*, T. S. Eliot)

MALAPROP, Mrs (*The Rivals*, R. B. Sheridan)

MARY JANE (*When We Were Very Young*, A. A. Milne)

MORIARTY, Professor James (*Memoirs of Sherlock Holmes*, A. Conan Doyle)

O'FERRALL, Trilby (*Trilby*, George du Maurier)

OLIFAUNT, Nigel (*The Fortunes of Nigel*, W. Scott)

O'TRIGGER, Sir Lucius (*The Rivals*, R. B. Sheridan)

PALLISER, Lady Glencora/Plantagenet (*Phineas Finn*, A. Trollope)

PRIMROSE, Dr Charles (*The Vicar of Wakefield*, O. Goldsmith)

QUANTOCK, Mrs Daisy (*Queen Lucia*, E. F. Benson)

RED QUEEN (*Alice Through the Looking Glass*, L. Carroll)

8 —continued

SHOTOVER, Captain (*Heartbreak House*, G. B. Shaw)

ST BUNGAY, Duke of (*Phineas Finn*, A. Trollope)

SVENGALI (*Trilby*, George du Maurier)

THATCHER, Becky (*The Adventures of Tom Sawyer*, M. Twain)

TRISTRAM (*Idylls of the King*, Lord Tennyson)

TULLIVER, Maggie/Tom (*The Mill on the Floss*, George Eliot)

VERINDER, Lady Julia (*The Moonstone*, W. Collins)

WATER RAT (Ratty) (*The Wind in the Willows*, K. Grahame)

WAVERLEY, Edward (*Waverley*, W. Scott)

WHITEOAK (family) (*The Whiteoak Chronicles*, Mazo de la Roche)

WHITE-TIP (*Tarka the Otter*, Henry Williamson)

WHITTIER, Pollyanna (*Pollyanna*, Eleanor H. Porter)

WILLIAMS, Percival William (*Wee Willie Winkie*, R. Kipling)

WORTHING, John (*The Importance of Being Earnest*, Oscar Wilde)

9

ABBEVILLE, Horace (*Cannery Row*, J. Steinbeck)

ABLEWHITE, Godfrey (*The Moonstone*, W. Collins)

ALLWORTHY, Squire (*Tom Jones*, H. Fielding)

BABBERLEY, Lord Fancourt (*Charley's Aunt*, Brandon Thomas)

BARRYMORE (*The Hound of the Baskervilles*, A. Conan Doyle)

BRACKNELL, Lady (*The Importance of Being Earnest*, Oscar Wilde)

BULSTRODE, Nicholas (*Middlemarch*, George Eliot)

CHAINMAIL (*Crotchet Castle*, T. L. Peacock)

CHRISTIAN (*Pilgrim's Progress*, J. Bunyan)

CHURCHILL, Frank (*Emma*, Jane Austen)

D'ARTAGNAN (*The Three Musketeers*, Alexandre Dumas)

DOOLITTLE, Eliza (*Pygmalion*, G. B. Shaw)

GREYSTOKE, Lord (*Tarzan series*, E. R. Burroughs)

GUINEVERE (*Idylls of the King*, Lord Tennyson)

INDIAN JOE (*The Adventures of Tom Sawyer*, M. Twain)

LEICESTER, Earl of (*Kenilworth*, W. Scott)

MACGREGOR, Robin (*Rob Roy*, W. Scott)

MARCH HARE, The (*Alice in Wonderland*, L. Carroll)

MARCHMAIN, Lady Cordelia/Lady Julia/Lord Sebastian/ Marquis of/Teresa/The Earl of Brideshead (*Brideshead Revisited*, E. Waugh)

9 —continued

MEHITABEL, the cat (*Archy and Mehitabel*, D. Marquis)

MERRILIES, Meg (*Guy Mannering*, W. Scott)

MINNEHAHA (*The Song of Hiawatha*, H. W. Longfellow)

MONCRIEFF, Algernon (*The Importance of Being Earnest*, Oscar Wilde)

PENDENNIS, Arthur (Pen) (*Pendennis*, W. M. Thackeray)

PERCIVALE (*Idylls of the King*, Lord Tennyson)

RED KNIGHT (*Alice Through the Looking Glass*, L. Carroll)

ROCHESTER, Bertha/Edward Fairfax (*Jane Eyre*, Charlotte Brontë)

SHERE KHAN (Lungri) (*The Jungle Book*, R. Kipling)

SOUTHDOWN, Earl of (*Vanity Fair*, W. M. Thackeray)

TAMERLANE (*Tamerlane*, N. Rowe)

TANQUERAY, Aubrey (*The Second Mrs Tanqueray*, A. W. Pinero)

TIGER LILY (*Peter Pan*, J. M. Barrie)

TRELAWNEY, Rose (*Trelawney of the Wells*, A. W. Pinero)

TRELAWNEY, Squire (*Treasure Island*, R. L. Stevenson)

TWITCHETT, Mrs Tabitha (*The Tale of Tom Kitten*, Beatrix Potter)

VIRGINIAN, The (*The Virginian*, O. Wister)

WAYNFLETE, Lady Cicely (*Captain Brassbound's Conversion*, G. B. Shaw)

WOODHOUSE, Emma/Isabella (*Emma*, Jane Austen)

10

ABRAMS MOSS (*Pendennis*, W. M. Thackeray)

ALLAN-A-DALE (*Ivanhoe*, W. Scott)

ARROWPOINT (*Daniel Deronda*, George Eliot)

BELLADONNA (*Vanity Fair*, W. M. Thackeray)

CHALLENGER, Professor (*The Lost World*, A. Conan Doyle)

CRIMSWORTH, William (*The Professor*, Charlotte Brontë)

EVANGELINE (*Evangeline*, H. W. Longfellow)

FAUNTLEROY, Lord Cedric Errol (*Little Lord Fauntleroy*, F. H. Burnett)

GOODFELLOW, Robin (*St Ronan's Well*, W. Scott)

HEATHCLIFF (*Wuthering Heights*, Emily Brontë)

HORNBLOWER, Horatio (The *Hornblower* series, C. S. Forester)

HUNCA MUNCA (*The Tale of Two Bad Mice*, Beatrix Potter)

HUNTER-DUNN, Joan (*A Subaltern's Love Song*, J. Betjeman)

JACKANAPES (*Jackanapes*, Juliana H. Ewing)

LETHBRIDGE, Daphne (*The Dark Tide*, Vera Brittain)

10 —continued

MAN IN BLACK (*A Citizen of the World*, O. Goldsmith)

MAULEVERER, Lord (*Cranford*, Mrs Gaskell)

MOCK TURTLE, THE (*Alice in Wonderland*, L. Carroll)

PUDDLEDUCK, Jemima (*The Tale of Jemima Puddleduck*, Beatrix Potter)

QUATERMAIN, Allan (*King Solomon's Mines*, H. Rider Haggard)

RASSENDYLL, Rudolf (*The Prisoner of Zenda*, A. Hope)

STARKADDER, Judith/Old Mrs (*Cold Comfort Farm*, Stella Gibbons)

TINKER BELL (*Peter Pan*, J. M. Barrie)

TWEEDLEDEE (*Alice Through the Looking-Glass*, L. Carroll)

TWEEDLEDUM (*Alice Through the Looking-Glass*, L. Carroll)

UNDERSHAFT, Barbara (*Major Barbara*, G. B. Shaw)

WILLOUGHBY, John (*Sense and Sensibility*, Jane Austen)

WINDERMERE, Lord Arthur/Margaret (*Lady Windermere's Fan*, Oscar Wilde)

11

ADDENBROOKE, Bennett (*Raffles*, E. W. Hornung)

DURBEYFIELD, Tess (*Tess of the D'Urbervilles*, T. Hardy)

JABBERWOCKY (*Alice Through the Looking-Glass*, L. Carroll)

MACCROTCHET (*Crotchet Castle*, T. L. Peacock)

MONTMORENCY, the dog (*Three Men in a Boat*, J. K. Jerome)

REDGAUNTLET, Sir Arthur Darsie (*Redgauntlet*, W. Scott)

TAMBURLAINE (*Tamburlaine*, C. Marlowe)

TAM O'SHANTER (*Tam O'Shanter*, R. Burns)

TIGGY-WINKLE, Mrs (*The Tale of Mrs Tiggy-Winkle*, Beatrix Potter)

TITTLEMOUSE, Mrs Thomasina (*The Tale of Mrs Tittlemouse*, Beatrix Potter)

TRUMPINGTON, Lady (*The Virginians*, W. M. Thackeray)

12

BROCKLEHURST (*Jane Eyre*, Charlotte Brontë)

CAPTAIN FLINT (*Swallows and Amazons*, A. Ransome)

FRANKENSTEIN, Victor (*Frankenstein*, M. W. Shelley)

HUMPTY-DUMPTY (*Alice Through the Looking-Glass*, L. Carroll)

PENNYFEATHER, Paul (*Decline and Fall*, E. Waugh)

13

WINNIE-THE-POOH (Edward Bear) (*Winnie-the-Pooh*, A. A. Milne)

14

MARKHAM, Gilbert (*The Tenant of Wildfell Hall*, Anne Brontë)

MEPHISTOPHELES (*Doctor Faustus*, C. Marlowe)

RIKKI-TIKKI-TAVI (*The Jungle Book*, R. Kipling)

SAMUEL WHISKERS (*The Tale of Samuel Whiskers*, Beatrix Potter)

14 —continued

WORDLY-WISEMAN (*Pilgrim's Progress*, J. Bunyan)

15

OGMORE-PRITCHARD, Mrs (*Under Milk Wood*, D. Thomas)

VALIANT-FOR-TRUTH (*Pilgrim's Progress*, J. Bunyan)

VIOLET ELIZABETH (*Just William*, Richmal Crompton)

DICKENSIAN CHARACTERS

CHARACTER (Novel)

2

JO (Bleak House)

3

AMY (Oliver Twist)

BET, Betsy (Oliver Twist)

BUD, Rosa (Edwin Drood)

CLY (A Tale of Two Cities)

GAY, Walter (Dombey and Son)

JOE (Pickwick Papers)

TOX, Miss (Dombey and Son)

4

ANNE (Dombey and Son)

BAPS (Dombey and Son)

BEGS, Mrs Ridger (David Copperfield)

BRAY, Madeline (Nicholas Nickleby)

BRAY, Walter (Nicholas Nickleby)

DICK, Mr (Oliver Twist)

DUFF (Oliver Twist)

FIPS, Mr (Martin Chuzzlewit)

FOGG (Pickwick Papers)

GAMP, Mrs Sarah (Martin Chuzzlewit)

GRIP (Barnaby Rudge)

HAWK, Sir Mulberry (Nicholas Nickleby)

HEEP, Uriah (David Copperfield)

HUGH (Barnaby Rudge)

JOWL, Mat (The Old Curiosity Shop)

JUPE, Cecilia (Hard Times)

KAGS (Oliver Twist)

KNAG, Miss (Nicholas Nickleby)

LIST, Isaac (The Old Curiosity Shop)

MANN, Mrs (Oliver Twist)

MARY (Pickwick Papers)

MELL, Charles (David Copperfield)

MIFF, Mrs (Dombey and Son)

OMER (David Copperfield)

PEAK (Barnaby Rudge)

PELL, Solomon (Pickwick Papers)

PEPS, Dr Parker (Dombey and Son)

POTT, Minverva (Pickwick Papers)

'RIAH (Our Mutual Friend)

RUGG, Anastasia (Little Dorrit)

TIGG, Montague (Martin Chuzzlewit)

4 —continued

WADE, Miss (Little Dorrit)

WEGG, Silas (Our Mutual Friend)

5

ADAMS, Jack (Dombey and Son)

ALLEN, Arabella/Benjamin (Pickwick Papers)

BATES, Charley (Oliver Twist)

BETSY (Pickwick Papers)

BRASS, Sally/Sampson (The Old Curiosity Shop)

BRICK, Jefferson (Martin Chuzzlewit)

BROWN, Alice/Mrs (Dombey and Son)

BUZUZ, Sergeant (Pickwick Papers)

CASBY, Christopher (Little Dorrit)

CHICK, John/Louisa (Dombey and Son)

CLARE, Ada (Bleak House)

CLARK (Dombey and Son)

CLIVE (Little Dorrit)

CROWL (Nicholas Nickleby)

CRUPP, Mrs (David Copperfield)

DAISY, Solomon (Barnaby Rudge)

DAVID (Nicholas Nickleby)

DAWES, Mary (Dombey and Son)

DINGO, Professor (Bleak House)

DIVER, Colonel (Martin Chuzzlewit)

DONNY, Mrs (Bleak House)

DOYCE, Daniel (Little Dorrit)

DROOD, Edwin (Edwin Drood)

DUMPS, Nicodemus (Pickwick Papers)

FAGIN (Oliver Twist)

FLITE, Miss (Bleak House)

GILES (Oliver Twist)

GILLS, Solomon (Dombey and Son)

GOWAN, Harry (Little Dorrit)

GREEN, Tom (Barnaby Rudge)

GRIDE, Arthur (Nicholas Nickleby)

GUPPY, William (Bleak House)

HEXAM, Charlie/Jesse/Lizzie (Our Mutual Friend)

JANET (David Copperfield)

JONES, Mary (Barnaby Rudge)

KROOK (Bleak House)

5 —continued

LOBBS, Maria/'Old' (Pickwick Papers)
LORRY, Jarvis (A Tale of Two Cities)
LUCAS, Solomon (Pickwick Papers)
LUPIN, Mrs (Martin Chuzzlewit)
MEALY (David Copperfield)
'MELIA (Dombey and Son)
MIGGS, Miss (Barnaby Rudge)
MILLS, Julia (David Copperfield)
MOLLY (Great Expectations)
MOULD (Martin Chuzzlewit)
NANCY (Oliver Twist)
NANDY, John Edward (Little Dorrit)
NOGGS, Newman (Nicholas Nickleby)
PERCH (Dombey and Son)
PINCH, Ruth/Tom (Martin Chuzzlewit)
PRICE, 'Tilda (Nicholas Nickleby)
PROSS, Miss/Solomon (A Tale of Two Cities)
QUALE (Bleak House)
QUILP, Daniel (The Old Curiosity Shop)
RUDGE, Barnaby/Mary (Barnaby Rudge)
SALLY, Old (Oliver Twist)
SCOTT, Tom (The Old Curiosity Shop)
SHARP (David Copperfield)
SIKES, Bill (Oliver Twist)
SLURK (Pickwick Papers)
SLYME, Chevy (Martin Chuzzlewit)
SMIKE (Nicholas Nickleby)
SNOBB, The Hon (Nicholas Nickleby)
SQUOD, Phil (Bleak House)
STAGG (Barnaby Rudge)
TOOTS, Mr P (Dombey and Son)
TRABB (Great Expectations)
TRENT, Frederick/Nellie (The Old Curiosity Shop)
TWIST, Oliver (Oliver Twist)
VENUS, Mr (Our Mutual Friend)
WATTY (Pickwick Papers)

6

BADGER, Dr Bayham/Laura/Malta/Matthew/ Quebec/Woolwich (Bleak House)
BAILEY, Benjamin (Martin Chuzzlewit)
BAILEY, Captain (David Copperfield)
BAMBER, Jack (Pickwick Papers)
BANTAM, Angelo Cyrus (Pickwick Papers)
BARKER, Phil (Oliver Twist)
BARKIS (David Copperfield)
BARLEY, Clara (Great Expectations)
BARNEY (Oliver Twist)
BEDWIN, Mrs (Oliver Twist)
BETSEY, Jane (Dombey and Son)
BITZER (Hard Times)
BOFFIN, Henrietta/Nicodemus (Our Mutual Friend)
BONNEY (Nicholas Nickleby)
BRIGGS (Dombey and Son)
BUMBLE (Oliver Twist)
BUNSBY, Captain (Dombey and Son)
CARKER, Harriet/James/John (Dombey and Son)
CARTON, Sydney (A Tale of Two Cities)

6 —continued

CHEGGS, Alick (The Old Curiosity Shop)
CLARKE (Pickwick Papers)
CODGER, Mrs (Martin Chuzzlewit)
CODLIN, Thomas (The Old Curiosity Shop)
CONWAY, General (Barnaby Rudge)
CORNEY, Mrs (Oliver Twist)
CURDLE (Nicholas Nickleby)
CUTLER, Mr/Mrs (Nicholas Nickleby)
CUTTLE, Captain Ned (Dombey and Son)
DARNAY, Charles (A Tale of Two Cities)
DARTLE, Rosa (David Copperfield)
DENNIS, Ned (Barnaby Rudge)
DIBABS, Mrs (Nicholas Nickleby)
DODSON (Pickwick Papers)
DOMBEY, Fanny/Florence/Louisa/Paul (Dombey and Son)
DORKER (Nicholas Nickleby)
DORRIT, Amy/Edward/Fanny/Frederick/ William (Little Dorrit)
DOWLER, Captain (Pickwick Papers)
FEEDER (Dombey and Son)
FEENIX (Dombey and Son)
FIZKIN, Horatio (Pickwick Papers)
FOLIAR (Nicholas Nickleby)
GEORGE (The Old Curiosity Shop)
GEORGE (Pickwick Papers)
GEORGE, Mr (Bleak House)
GORDON, Lord George (Barnaby Rudge)
GRAHAM, Mary (Martin Chuzzlewit)
GROVES, 'Honest' James (The Old Curiosity Shop)
GUNTER (Pickwick Papers)
HARMON, John (Our Mutual Friend)
HARRIS, Mrs (Martin Chuzzlewit)
HAWDON, Captain (Bleak House)
HIGDEN, Betty (Our Mutual Friend)
HOMINY, Major (Martin Chuzzlewit)
HOWLER, Rev M (Dombey and Son)
JARLEY, Mrs (The Old Curiosity Shop)
JASPER, Jack (Edwin Drood)
JINGLE, Alfred (Pickwick Papers)
KETTLE, La Fayette (Martin Chuzzlewit)
LAMMLE, Alfred (Our Mutual Friend)
LOBLEY (Edwin Drood)
LUMLEY, Dr (Nicholas Nickleby)
MAGNUS, Peter (Pickwick Papers)
MALDEN, Jack (David Copperfield)
MARLEY, Jacob (A Christmas Carol)
MARTON (The Old Curiosity Shop)
MAYLIE, Harrie/Mrs/Rose (Oliver Twist)
MERDLE, Mr (Little Dorrit)
MILVEY, Rev Frank (Our Mutual Friend)
MIVINS (Pickwick Papers)
MODDLE, Augustus (Martin Chuzzlewit)
MORFIN (Dombey and Son)
MULLET, Professor (Martin Chuzzlewit)
NIPPER, Susan (Dombey and Son)
PANCKS (Little Dorrit)
PERKER (Pickwick Papers)
PHUNKY (Pickwick Papers)

6 —continued

PIPKIN, Nathaniel (Pickwick Papers)
PIRRIP, Philip (Great Expectations)
POCKET, Herbert/Matthew/Sarah (Great Expectations)
POGRAM, Elijah (Martin Chuzzlewit)
RADDLE, Mr and Mrs (Pickwick Papers)
RIGAUD, Monsieur (Little Dorrit)
SAPSEA, Thomas (Edwin Drood)
SAWYER, Bob (Pickwick Papers)
SCALEY (Nicholas Nickleby)
SLEARY, Josephine (Hard Times)
'SLOPPY' (Our Mutual Friend)
SOWNDS (Dombey and Son)
STRONG, Dr (David Copperfield)
TACKER (Martin Chuzzlewit)
TAPLEY, Mark (Martin Chuzzlewit)
TARTAR (Edwin Drood)
TIPPIN, Lady (Our Mutual Friend)
TISHER, Mrs (Edwin Drood)
TOODLE (Dombey and Son)
TUPMAN, Tracy (Pickwick Papers)
VARDEN, Dolly/Gabriel (Barnaby Rudge)
VHOLES (Bleak House)
VUFFIN (The Old Curiosity Shop)
WALKER, Mick (David Copperfield)
WARDLE, Emily/Isabella/Mr/Rachel (Pickwick Papers)
WELLER, Sam/Tony (Pickwick Papers)
WILFER, Bella/Lavinia/Reginald (Our Mutual Friend)
WILLET, Joe/John (Barnaby Rudge)
WINKLE, Nathaniel (Pickwick Papers)
WOPSLE (Great Expectations)

7

BAILLIE, Gabriel (Pickwick Papers)
BANGHAM, Mrs (Little Dorrit)
BARBARA (The Old Curiosity Shop)
BARBARY, Miss (Bleak House)
BARDELL, Mrs Martha/Tommy (Pickwick Papers)
BAZZARD (Edwin Drood)
BELLING, Master (Nicholas Nickleby)
BLIMBER, Dr (Dombey and Son)
BLOTTON (Pickwick Papers)
BOBSTER, Cecilia/Mr (Nicholas Nickleby)
BOLDWIG, Captain (Pickwick Papers)
BROGLEY (Dombey and Son)
BROOKER (Nicholas Nickleby)
BROWDIE, John (Nicholas Nickleby)
BULLAMY (Martin Chuzzlewit)
CHARLEY (David Copperfield)
CHESTER, Edward/Sir John (Barnaby Rudge)
CHILLIP, Dr (David Copperfield)
CHIVERY, John (Little Dorrit)
CHOLLOP, Hannibal (Martin Chuzzlewit)
CHUFFEY (Martin Chuzzlewit)
CLEAVER, Fanny (Our Mutual Friend)
CLENNAM, Arthur (Little Dorrit)
CLUBBER, Sir Thomas (Pickwick Papers)
CRACKIT, Toby (Oliver Twist)

7 —continued

CRAWLEY, Young Mr (Pickwick Papers)
CREAKLE (David Copperfield)
CREWLER, Mrs/Rev Horace/Sophy (David Copperfield)
CRIMPLE, David (Martin Chuzzlewit)
CROOKEY (Pickwick Papers)
DAWKINS, Jack (Oliver Twist)
DEDLOCK, Sir Leicester/Volumnia (Bleak House)
DEFARGE, Madame (A Tale of Two Cities)
DOLLOBY (David Copperfield)
DRUMMLE, Bentley (Great Expectations)
DUBBLEY (Pickwick Papers)
DURDLES (Edwin Drood)
EDMUNDS, John (Pickwick Papers)
ESTELLA (Great Expectations)
FLEMING, Agnes (Oliver Twist)
GABELLE, Theophile (A Tale of Two Cities)
GARGERY, Biddy/Joe/Pip (Great Expectations)
GARLAND, Abel/Mrs/Mr (The Old Curiosity Shop)
GASPARD (A Tale of Two Cities)
GAZINGI, Miss (Nicholas Nickleby)
GENERAL, Mrs (Little Dorrit)
GILBERT, Mark (Barnaby Rudge)
GRANGER, Edith (Dombey and Son)
GRIDLEY (Bleak House)
GRIMWIG (Oliver Twist)
GRUDDEN, Mrs (Nicholas Nickleby)
HAGGAGE, Dr (Little Dorrit)
HEYLING, George (Pickwick Papers)
JAGGERS (Great Expectations)
JELLYBY, Caddy/Mrs/Peepy (Bleak House)
JINKINS (Martin Chuzzlewit)
JOBLING, Dr John (Martin Chuzzlewit)
JOBLING, Tony (Bleak House)
JOHNSON, Mr (Nicholas Nickleby)
JORKINS (David Copperfield)
KEDGICK, Captain (Martin Chuzzlewit)
KENWIGS, Morleena (Nicholas Nickleby)
LARKINS, Mr (David Copperfield)
LEEFORD, Edward (Oliver Twist)
LEWSOME (Martin Chuzzlewit)
MALLARD (Pickwick Papers)
MANETTE, Dr/Lucie (A Tale of Two Cities)
MEAGLES (Little Dorrit)
MINERVA (Pickwick Papers)
MOWCHER, Miss (David Copperfield)
NADGETT (Martin Chuzzlewit)
NECKETT, Charlotte/Emma/Tom (Bleak House)
NUBBLES, Christopher (The Old Curiosity Shop)
NUPKINS, George (Pickwick Papers)
PAWKINS, Major (Martin Chuzzlewit)
PILKINS, Dr (Dombey and Son)
PIPCHIN, Mrs (Dombey and Son)
PODSNAP, Georgiana/Mr (Our Mutual Friend)
QUINION (David Copperfield)

7 —continued

SAMPSON, George (Our Mutual Friend)
SCADDER, Zephaniah (Martin Chuzzlewit)
SCROOGE, Ebenezer (A Christmas Carol)
SIMMONS, William (Martin Chuzzlewit)
SKEWTON, Hon Mrs (Dombey and Son)
SKYLARK, Mr (David Copperfield)
SLAMMER, Dr (Pickwick Papers)
SLUMKEY, Hon Samuel (Pickwick Papers)
SNAGSBY (Bleak House)
SNAWLEY (Nicholas Nickleby)
SNUBBIN, Sergeant (Pickwick Papers)
SPARSIT, Mrs (Hard Times)
SPENLOW, Dora (David Copperfield)
SQUEERS, Fanny/Wackford (Nicholas
  Nickleby)
STARTOP (Great Expectations)
STRYVER, C J (A Tale of Two Cities)
TAMAROO, Miss (Martin Chuzzlewit)
TODGERS, Mrs (Martin Chuzzlewit)
TROTTER, Job (Pickwick Papers)
TRUNDLE (Pickwick Papers)
WACKLES, Jane/Melissa/Sophie (The Old
  Curiosity Shop)
WATKINS (Nicholas Nickleby)
WEMMICK (Great Expectations)
WICKHAM, Mrs (Dombey and Son)
WITHERS (Dombey and Son)

8

AKERSHEM, Sophronia (Our Mutual Friend)
BAGSTOCK, Major (Dombey and Son)
BARNWELL, B B (Martin Chuzzlewit)
BILLIKIN, Mrs (Edwin Drood)
BLATHERS (Oliver Twist)
BOYTHORN, Lawrence (Bleak House)
BRAVASSA, Miss (Nicholas Nickleby)
BROWNLOW, Mr (Oliver Twist)
CLAYPOLE, Noah (Oliver Twist)
CLUPPINS (Pickwick Papers)
CRADDOCK, Mrs (Pickwick Papers)
CRATCHIT, Belinda/Bob/Tiny Tim (A
  Christmas Carol)
CRIPPLES, Mr (Little Dorrit)
CRUMMLES, Ninetta/Vincent (Nicholas
  Nickleby)
CRUNCHER, Jeremiah/Jerry (A Tale of Two
  Cities)
CRUSHTON, Hon Mr (Pickwick Papers)
DATCHERY, Dick (Edwin Drood)
D'AULNAIS (A Tale of Two Cities)
FINCHING, Mrs Flora (Little Dorrit)
FLEDGEBY, Old/Young (Our Mutual Friend)
GASHFORD (Barnaby Rudge)
HAREDALE, Emma/Geoffrey/Reuben
  (Barnaby Rudge)
HAVISHAM, Miss (Great Expectations)
HORTENSE (Bleak House)
JARNDYCE, John (Bleak House)
LA CREEVY, Miss (Nicholas Nickleby)
LANDLESS, Helena/Neville (Edwin Drood)
LANGDALE (Barnaby Rudge)

8 —continued

LENVILLE (Nicholas Nickleby)
LITTIMER (David Copperfield)
LOSBERNE (Oliver Twist)
MAGWITCH, Abel (Great Expectations)
MARY ANNE (David Copperfield)
MATTHEWS (Nicholas Nickleby)
MICAWBER, Wilkins (David Copperfield)
MUTANHED, Lord (Pickwick Papers)
NICKLEBY, Godfrey/Kate/Nicholas/Ralph
  (Nicholas Nickleby)
PEGGOTTY, Clara/Daniel/Ham/Little Em'ly
  (David Copperfield)
PICKWICK, Samuel (Pickwick Papers)
PLORNISH, Thomas (Little Dorrit)
POTATOES (David Copperfield)
SCADGERS, Lady (Hard Times)
SKIFFINS, Miss (Great Expectations)
SKIMPOLE, Arethusa/Harold/Kitty/Laura
  (Bleak House)
SKITTLES, Sir Barnet (Dombey and Son)
SMIGGERS, Joseph (Pickwick Papers)
SPARKLER, Edmund (Little Dorrit)
STIGGINS (Pickwick Papers)
TRADDLES, Tom (David Copperfield)
TROTWOOD, Betsey (David Copperfield)
WESTLOCK, John (Martin Chuzzlewit)
WRAYBURN, Eugene (Our Mutual Friend)

9

BELVAWNEY, Miss (Nicholas Nickleby)
BERINTHIA (Dombey and Son)
BLACKPOOL, Stephen (Hard Times)
BOUNDERBY, Josiah (Hard Times)
CHARLOTTE (Oliver Twist)
CHEERYBLE, Charles/Frank/Ned (Nicholas
  Nickleby)
CHICKWEED, Conkey (Oliver Twist)
CHUCKSTER (The Old Curiosity Shop)
COMPEYSON (Great Expectations)
FIBBITSON, Mrs (David Copperfield)
GRADGRIND, Louisa/Thomas (Hard Times)
GREGSBURY (Nicholas Nickleby)
GREWGIOUS (Edwin Drood)
HARTHOUSE, James (Hard Times)
HEADSTONE, Bradley (Our Mutual Friend)
LIGHTWOOD, Mortimer (Our Mutual Friend)
LILLYVICK (Nicholas Nickleby)
MANTALINI, Mr (Nicholas Nickleby)
MURDSTONE, Edward/Jane (David
  Copperfield)
OLD BARLEY (Great Expectations)
PARDIGGLE, Francis/O A (Bleak House)
PECKSNIFF, Charity/Mercy/Seth (Martin
  Chuzzlewit)
PRISCILLA (Bleak House)
RIDERHOOD, Pleasant/Roger (Our Mutual
  Friend)
SMALLWEED, Bartholomew/Joshua/Judy
  (Bleak House)
SMORLTORK, Count (Pickwick Papers)
SNODGRASS, Augustus (Pickwick Papers)

9 —continued
SUMMERSON, Esther (Bleak House)
SWIVELLER, Richard (The Old Curiosity Shop)
TAPPERTIT, Simon (Barnaby Rudge)
VENEERING, Anastasia/Hamilton (Our Mutual Friend)
VERISOPHT, Lord Frederick (Nicholas Nickleby)
WICKFIELD, Agnes/Mr (David Copperfield)
WITHERDEN, Mr (The Old Curiosity Shop)
WOODCOURT, Allan (Bleak House)

10
AYRESLEIGH, Mr (Pickwick Papers)
CHUZZLEWIT, Anthony/Diggory/George/Jonas/Martin/Mrs Ned/Toby (Martin Chuzzlewit)
CRISPARKLE, Rev Septimus (Edwin Drood)
FLINTWINCH, Affery/Ephraim/Jeremiah (Little Dorrit)
MACSTINGER, Mrs (Dombey and Son)
ROUNCEWELL, Mrs (Bleak House)
SNEVELLICI, Miss (Nicholas Nickleby)
SOWERBERRY (Oliver Twist)
STARELEIGH, Justice (Pickwick Papers)
STEERFORTH, James (David Copperfield)
TATTYCORAM (Little Dorrit)

10 —continued
TURVEYDROP, Prince (Bleak House)
TWINKLETON, Miss (Edwin Drood)
WATERBROOK (David Copperfield)
WITITTERLY, Julia (Nicholas Nickleby)

11
COPPERFIELD, Clara/David (David Copperfield)
'DISMAL JIMMY' (Pickwick Papers)
'GAME CHICKEN', The (Dombey and Son)
MARCHIONESS, The (The Old Curiosity Shop)
PUMBLECHOOK (Great Expectations)
SPOTTLETOES, Mrs (Martin Chuzzlewit)
ST EVREMONDE, Marquis de/Marquise de (A Tale of Two Cities)
SWEEDLEPIPE, Paul (Martin Chuzzlewit)
TULKINGHORN (Bleak House)

12
HONEYTHUNDER, Luke (Edwin Drood)
'SHINY WILLIAM' (Pickwick Papers)
SWEET WILLIAM (The Old Curiosity Shop)
TITE-BARNACLE, Clarence/Ferdinand/Junior/Lord Decimus/Mr (Little Dorrit)

15
VON KOELDWETHOUT (Nicholas Nickleby)

SHAKESPEAREAN CHARACTERS

CHARACTER (Play)

3
HAL (1 Henry IV)
NYM (Henry V, The Merry Wives of Windsor)

4
ADAM (As You Like It)
AJAX (Troilus and Cressida)
EROS (Antony and Cleopatra)
FORD, Mistress (The Merry Wives of Windsor)
GREY (Henry V)
HERO (Much Ado About Nothing)
IAGO (Othello)
IRAS (Antony and Cleopatra)
LEAR (King Lear)
PAGE, Mistress (The Merry Wives of Windsor)
PETO (2 Henry IV)
PUCK (A Midsummer Night's Dream)
SNUG (A Midsummer Night's Dream)

5
AARON (Titus Andronicus)
ARIEL (The Tempest)
BELCH, Sir Toby (Twelfth Night)
BLUNT (2 Henry IV)
CAIUS, Doctor (The Merry Wives of Windsor)
CELIA (As You Like It)
CLEON (Pericles)

5 —continued
CORIN (As You Like It)
DIANA (All's Well that Ends Well)
EDGAR (King Lear)
ELBOW (Measure for Measure)
FESTE (Twelfth Night)
FLUTE (A Midsummer Night's Dream)
FROTH (Measure for Measure)
GOBBO, Launcelot (The Merchant of Venice)
JULIA (The Two Gentlemen of Verona)
LAFEW (All's Well That Ends Well)
MARIA (Love's Labour's Lost, Twelfth Night)
PARIS (Troilus and Cressida)
PERCY (1 Henry IV)
PHEBE (As You Like It)
PINCH (The Comedy of Errors)
POINS (1 Henry IV, 2 Henry IV)
PRIAM (Troilus and Cressida)
REGAN (King Lear)
ROMEO (Romeo and Juliet)
SNOUT (A Midsummer Night's Dream)
TIMON (Timon of Athens)
TITUS (Titus Andronicus)
VIOLA (Twelfth Night)

6

AEGEON (The Comedy of Errors)
ALONSO (The Tempest)
ANGELO (Measure for Measure)
ANTONY (Antony and Cleopatra)
ARCITE (The Two Noble Kinsmen)
ARMADO (Love's Labour's Lost)
AUDREY (As You Like It)
BANQUO (Macbeth)
BIANCA (The Taming of the Shrew, Othello)
BOTTOM (A Midsummer Night's Dream)
BRUTUS (Coriolanus, Julius Caesar)
CASSIO (Othello)
CHIRON (Titus Andronicus)
CLOTEN (Cymbeline)
DENNIS (As You Like It)
DROMIO (The Comedy of Errors)
DUMAIN (Love's Labour's Lost)
DUNCAN (Macbeth)
EDMUND (King Lear)
EMILIA (Othello, The Two Noble Kinsmen)
FABIAN (Twelfth Night)
FENTON (The Merry Wives of Windsor)
FULVIA (Antony and Cleopatra)
HAMLET (Hamlet)
HECATE (Macbeth)
HECTOR (Troilus and Cressida)
HELENA (A Midsummer Night's Dream, All's
  Well That Ends Well)
HERMIA (A Midsummer Night's Dream)
IMOGEN (Cymbeline)
JULIET (Romeo and Juliet, Measure for
  Measure)
LUCIUS (Titus Andronicus)
MARINA (Pericles)
MUTIUS (Titus Andronicus)
OBERON (A Midsummer Night's Dream)
OLIVER (As You Like It)
OLIVIA (Twelfth Night)
ORSINO (Twelfth Night)
OSWALD (King Lear)
PISTOL (2 Henry IV, Henry V, The Merry Wives
  of Windsor)
POMPEY (Measure for Measure, Antony and
  Cleopatra)
PORTIA (The Merchant of Venice)
QUINCE (A Midsummer Night's Dream)
RUMOUR (2 Henry IV)
SCROOP (2 Henry IV, 2 Henry V)
SILVIA (The Two Gentlemen of Verona)
TAMORA (Titus Andronicus)
THASIA (Pericles)
THURIO (The Two Gentlemen of Verona)
TYBALT (Romeo and Juliet)
VERGES (Much Ado About Nothing)

7

ADRIANA (The Comedy of Errors)
AEMILIA (The Comedy of Errors)
AGRIPPA (Antony and Cleopatra)
ALARBUS (Titus Andronicus)

7 —continued

ANTONIO (The Merchant of Venice, The
  Tempest)
BEROWNE (Love's Labour's Lost)
BERTRAM (All's Well That Ends Well)
CALCHAS (Troilus and Cressida)
CALIBAN (The Tempest)
CAPULET (Romeo and Juliet)
CESARIO (Twelfth Night)
CLAUDIO (Much Ado About Nothing, Measure
  for Measure)
COSTARD (Love's Labour's Lost)
DIONYZA (Pericles)
DOUGLAS (1 Henry IV)
ESCALUS (Measure for Measure)
FLAVIUS (Timon of Athens)
FLEANCE (Macbeth)
GONERIL (King Lear)
GONZALO (The Tempest)
HORATIO (Hamlet)
HOTSPUR (1 Henry IV)
IACHIMO (Cymbeline)
JACQUES (As You Like It)
JESSICA (The Merchant of Venice)
LAERTES (Hamlet)
LAVINIA (Titus Andronicus)
LEONTES (The Winter's Tale)
LORENZO (The Merchant of Venice)
LUCIANA (The Comedy of Errors)
MACBETH (Macbeth)
MACDUFF (Macbeth)
MALCOLM (Macbeth)
MARIANA (Measure for Measure, All's Well
  That Ends Well)
MARTIUS (Titus Andronicus)
MIRANDA (The Tempest)
NERISSA (The Merchant of Venice)
OCTAVIA (Antony and Cleopatra)
OPHELIA (Hamlet)
ORLANDO (As You Like It)
OTHELLO (Othello)
PALAMON (The Two Noble Kinsmen)
PAULINA (The Winter's Tale)
PERDITA (The Winter's Tale)
PISANIO (Cymbeline)
PROTEUS (The Two Gentlemen of Verona)
QUICKLY, Mistress (1 Henry IV, 2 Henry IV,
  The Merry Wives of Windsor)
QUINTUS (Titus Andronicus)
SHALLOW, Justice (2 Henry IV, The Merry
  Wives of Windsor)
SHYLOCK (The Merchant of Venice)
SILENCE (2 Henry IV)
SILVIUS (As You Like It)
SLENDER (The Merry Wives of Windsor)
SOLINUS (The Comedy of Errors)
THESEUS (A Midsummer Night's Dream,
  The Two Noble Kinsmen)
TITANIA (A Midsummer Night's Dream)
TROILUS (Troilus and Cressida)
ULYSSES (Troilus and Cressida)

7 —continued

WILLIAM (As You Like It)

8

ACHILLES (Troilus and Cressida)
AUFIDIUS (Coriolanus)
BAPTISTA (The Taming of the Shrew)
BARDOLPH (Henry IV, Henry V, The Merry
  Wives of Windsor)
BASSANIO (The Merchant of Venice)
BEATRICE (Much Ado About Nothing)
BELARIUS (Cymbeline)
BENEDICK (Much Ado About Nothing)
BENVOLIO (Romeo and Juliet)
CHARMIAN (Antony and Cleopatra)
CLAUDIUS (Hamlet)
COMINIUS (Coriolanus)
CORDELIA (King Lear)
CRESSIDA (Troilus and Cressida)
DIOMEDES (Antony and Cleopatra, Troilus
  and Cressida)
DOGBERRY (Much Ado About Nothing)
DON PEDRO (Much Ado About Nothing)
FALSTAFF (The Merry Wives of Windsor,
  Henry IV)
FLORIZEL (The Winter's Tale)
GERTRUDE (Hamlet)
GRATIANO (The Merchant of Venice)
HERMIONE (The Winter's Tale)
ISABELLA (Measure for Measure)
LUCENTIO (The Taming of the Shrew)
LYSANDER (A Midsummer Night's Dream)
MALVOLIO (Twelfth Night)
MENENIUS (Coriolanus)
MERCUTIO (Romeo and Juliet)
MONTAGUE (Romeo and Juliet)
MORTIMER (1 Henry IV)
OCTAVIUS (Antony and Cleopatra)
PANDARUS (Troilus and Cressida)
PAROLLES (All's Well That Ends Well)
PERICLES (Pericles)
PHILOTEN (Pericles)
POLONIUS (Hamlet)
PROSPERO (The Tempest)
RODERIGO (Othello)
ROSALIND (As You Like It)
ROSALINE (Love's Labour's Lost)
SICINIUS (Coriolanus)
STEPHANO (The Tempest)
TRINCULO (The Tempest)
VIOLENTA (All's Well That Ends Well)
VOLUMNIA (Coriolanus)

9

ANTIOCHUS (Pericles)

9 —continued

ARVIRAGUS (Cymbeline)
AUGECHEEK, Sir Andrew (Twelfth Night)
BASSIANUS (Titus Andronicus)
BRABANTIO (Othello)
CAMBRIDGE (Henry V)
CLEOPATRA (Antony and Cleopatra)
CYMBELINE (Cymbeline)
DEMETRIUS (A Midsummer Night's Dream,
  Antony and Cleopatra, Titus Andronicus)
DESDEMONA (Othello)
ENOBARBUS (Antony and Cleopatra)
FERDINAND (Loves Labours Lost, The
  Tempest)
FREDERICK (As You Like It)
GLENDOWER, Owen (1 Henry IV)
GUIDERIUS (Cymbeline)
HELICANUS (Pericles)
HIPPOLYTA (A Midsummer Night's Dream,
  The Two Noble Kinsmen)
HORTENSIO (The Taming of the Shrew)
KATHERINA (The Taming of the Shrew)
KATHERINE (Henry V, Love's Labour's Lost)
MAMILLIUS (The Winter's Tale)
PATROCLUS (Troilus and Cressida)
PETRUCHIO (The Taming of the Shrew)
POLIXENES (The Winter's Tale)
SEBASTIAN (The Tempest, Twelfth Night)
TEARSHEET, Doll (2 Henry IV)
VALENTINE (The Two Gentlemen of Verona)
VINCENTIO (Measure for Measure, The
  Taming of the Shrew)

10

ALCIBIADES (Timon of Athens)
ANTIPHOLUS (The Comedy of Errors)
CORIOLANUS (Coriolanus)
FORTINBRAS (Hamlet)
JAQUENETTA (Love's Labour's Lost)
LONGAVILLE (Love's Labour's Lost)
LYSIMACHUS (Pericles)
POSTHUMOUS (Cymbeline)
SATURNINUS (Titus Andronicus)
TOUCHSTONE (As You Like It)

11

ROSENCRANTZ (Hamlet)

12

GUILDENSTERN (Hamlet)

14

CHRISTOPHER SLY (The Taming of the
  Shrew)

GILBERT AND SULLIVAN

OPERAS

THESPIS (The Gods Grown Old)
TRIAL BY JURY
THE SORCERER
HMS PINAFORE (The Lass that Loved a
   Sailor)
THE PIRATES OF PENZANCE (The Slave of
   Duty)
PATIENCE (Bunthorne's Bride)
IOLANTHE (The Peer and the Peri)
PRINCESS IDA (Castle Adamant)
THE MIKADO (The Town of Titipu)
RUDDIGORE (The Witch's Curse)
THE YEOMEN OF THE GUARD (The
   Merryman and his Maid)
THE GONDOLIERS (The King of Barataria)
UTOPIA, LIMITED (The Flowers of Progress)
THE GRAND DUKE (The Statutory Duel)

CHARACTERS (*Operas*)

4
ADAM (*Ruddigore*)
ELLA (*Patience*)
GAMA (*Princess Ida*)
INEZ (*The Gondoliers*)
JANE (*Patience*)
KATE (*The Pirates of Penzance*)
KO-KO (*The Mikado*)
LUIZ (*The Gondoliers*)
RUTH (*The Pirates of Penzance*)

5
ALINE (*The Sorcerer*)
CELIA (*Iolanthe*)
CYRIL (*Princess Ida*)
EDITH (*The Pirates of Penzance*)
EDWIN (*Trial by Jury*)
FLETA (*Iolanthe*)
LEILA (*Iolanthe*)
MABEL (*The Pirates of Penzance*)
TESSA (*The Gondoliers*)

6
ALEXIS (*The Sorcerer*)
ANGELA (*Patience*)
ISABEL (*The Pirates of Penzance*)
PEEP-BO (*The Mikado*)
SAPHIR (*Patience*)
YUM-YUM (*The Mikado*)

7
CASILDA (*The Gondoliers*)
FLORIAN (*Princess Ida*)
KATISHA (*The Mikado*)
LEONARD (*The Yeomen of the Guard*)

7 —continued
MELISSA (*Princess Ida*)
PHYLLIS (*Iolanthe*)
POOH-BAH (*The Mikado*)

8
ANGELINA (*Trial by Jury*)
FREDERIC (*The Pirates of Penzance*)
GIANETTA (*The Gondoliers*)
HILARION (*Princess Ida*)
IOLANTHE (*Iolanthe*)
NANKI-POO (*The Mikado*)
PATIENCE (*Patience*)
PISH-TUSH (*The Mikado*)
SERGEANT (*The Pirates of Penzance*)
STREPHON (*Iolanthe*)

9
BUNTHORNE (*Patience*)
JACK POINT (*The Yeomen of the Guard*)
JOSEPHINE (*HMS Pinafore*)
PITTI-SING (*The Mikado*)

10
DAME HANNAH (*Ruddigore*)
HILDEBRAND (*Princess Ida*)
LADY PSYCHE (*Princess Ida*)
PIRATE KING (*The Pirates of Penzance*)
ROSE MAYBUD (*Ruddigore*)
SIR RODERIC (*Ruddigore*)

11
DICK DEADEYE (*HMS Pinafore*)
LADY BLANCHE (*Princess Ida*)
MAD MARGARET (*Ruddigore*)
MOUNTARARAT (*Iolanthe*)
PRINCESS IDA (*Princess Ida*)

12
ELSIE MAYNARD (*The Yeomen of the Guard*)
PHOEBE MERYLL (*The Yeomen of the Guard*)
SIR MARMADUKE (*The Sorcerer*)

13
LADY SANGAZURE (*The Sorcerer*)
MARCO PALMIERI (*The Gondoliers*)
ROBIN OAKAPPLE (*Ruddigore*)

14
COLONEL FAIRFAX (*The Yeomen of the
   Guard*)
DAME CARRUTHERS (*The Yeomen of the
   Guard*)
RALPH RACKSTRAW (*HMS Pinafore*)

15
CAPTAIN CORCORAN (*HMS Pinafore*)
DUKE OF DUNSTABLE (*Patience*)
DUKE OF PLAZA TORO (*The Gondoliers*)

15 —continued
EARL OF TOLLOLLER (*Iolanthe*)
LITTLE BUTTERCUP (*HMS Pinafore*)
SIR JOSEPH PORTER (*HMS Pinafore*)
WILFRED SHADBOLT (*The Yeomen of the Guard*)

16
COLONEL CALVERLEY (*Patience*)
GIUSEPPE PALMIERI (*The Gondoliers*)
RICHARD DAUNTLESS (*Ruddigore*)

18
ARCHIBALD GROSVENOR (*Patience*)

19
JOHN WELLINGTON WELLS (*The Sorcerer*)
MAJOR-GENERAL STANLEY (*The Pirates of Penzance*)

20
SIR DESPARD MURGATROYD (*Ruddigore*)
SIR RICHARD CHOLMONDELEY (*The Yeomen of the Guard*)

SCIENCE AND TECHNOLOGY

WEIGHTS AND MEASURES

2	4 —continued	5 —continued	7 —continued
CM	HAND	NEPER	DIOPTER
DR	HIDE	OUNCE	FARADAY
FT	HOUR	PERCH	FURLONG
GR	INCH	POINT	GILBERT
HL	KILO	POISE	HECTARE
IN	KNOT	POUND	KILOBAR
KG	LINE	QUART	KILOTON
KM	LINK	QUIRE	LAMBERT
LB	MILE	STADE	MAXWELL
MG	MOLE	STERE	MEGATON
ML	NAIL	STILB	OERSTED
MM	PECK	STOKE	POUNDAL
OZ	PHON	STONE	QUARTER
YD	PHOT	TESLA	QUINTAL
3	PICA	THERM	RÖNTGEN
AMP	PINT	TOISE	SCRUPLE
ARE	PIPE	TONNE	SIEMENS
BAR	POLE	WEBER	**8**
BEL	REAM	**6**	ÅNGSTROM
BIT	ROOD	AMPERE	CHALDRON
CWT	SLUG	BARREL	HOGSHEAD
DWT	SPAN	BUSHEL	KILOGRAM
ELL	TORR	CANDLE	KILOWATT
ERG	TROY	CENTAL	QUADRANT
LUX	VOLT	DEGREE	MEGAWATT
MHO	WATT	DENIER	MICROOHM
MIL	YARD	DRACHM	WATT-HOUR
MIM	**5**	FATHOM	**9**
NIT	CABLE	FIRKIN	BOARD-FOOT
OHM	CARAT	GALLON	CENTIGRAM
RAD	CHAIN	GRAMME	CUBIC FOOT
REM	CRITH	KELVIN	CUBIC INCH
ROD	CUBIT	LEAGUE	CUBIC YARD
TON	CURIE	MEGOHM	DECALITRE
TUN	CUSEC	MICRON	DECAMETRE
4	CYCLE	MINUTE	DECILITRE
ACRE	DEBYE	NEWTON	DECIMETRE
BALE	FARAD	PARSEC	FOOT-POUND
BARN	FERMI	PASCAL	HECTOGRAM
BOLT	GAUGE	RADIAN	KILOCYCLE
BYTE	GAUSS	RÉAMUR	KILOHERTZ
CASK	GRAIN	SECOND	KILOLITRE
CORD	HENRY	STOKES	KILOMETRE
CRAN	HERTZ	**7**	LIGHT-YEAR
DRAM	JOULE	CALORIE	MEGACYCLE
DYNE	LITRE	CANDELA	MEGAFARAD
FOOT	LUMEN	CENTNER	MEGAHERTZ
GILL	METRE	COULOMB	METRIC TON
GRAM	MINIM	DECIBEL	MICROGRAM

9 —continued
MICROWATT
MILLIGRAM
NANOMETRE
SCANTLING
STERADIAN
10+
BARLEYCORN
CENTILITRE

10+ —continued
CENTIMETRE
CUBIC METRE
DECAGRAMME
DECIGRAMME
FLUID OUNCE
HECTOLITRE
HORSEPOWER
HUNDREDWEIGHT

10+ —continued
KILOGRAMME
MICROFARAD
MILLILITRE
MILLIMETRE
MILLISTERES
NANOSECOND
PENNYWEIGHT

10+ —continued
RUTHERFORD
SQUARE
  CENTIMETRE
SQUARE INCH
SQUARE KILOMETRE
SQUARE MILE
SQUARE YARD

PAPER MEASURES

4
BALE
COPY
DEMY
POST
POTT
REAM
5
ATLAS
BRIEF
CROWN
DRAFT
QUIRE
ROYAL

6
BAG CAP
BUNDLE
CASING
MEDIUM
7
EMPEROR
KENT CAP
8
ELEPHANT
FOOLSCAP
HAVEN CAP

8—continued
IMPERIAL
9
CARTRIDGE
COLOMBIER
LARGE POST
MUSIC DEMY
10
DOUBLE DEMY
DOUBLE POST
GRAND EAGLE
SUPER ROYAL

11
ANTIQUARIAN
IMPERIAL CAP
PINCHED POST
14
DOUBLE ELEPHANT
15
DOUBLE LARGE
  POST

ELEMENTARY PARTICLES

2
XI
3
ETA
PHI
PSI
4
KAON
MUON
PION
5
BOSON

5—continued
GLUON
MESON
OMEGA
QUARK
SIGMA
6
BARYON
HADRON
LAMBDA
LEPTON
PHOTON

6—continued
PROTON
7
FERMION
HYPERON
NEUTRON
TACHYON
8
DEUTERON
ELECTRON
GRAVITON

8—continued
NEUTRINO
POSITRON
9
NEUTRETTO
12
ANTIPARTICLE
BETA PARTICLE
13
ALPHA PARTICLE

THE CHEMICAL ELEMENTS

NAME (SYMBOL)

ACTINIUM (AC)
ALUMINIUM (AL)
AMERICIUM (AM)
ANTIMONY (SB)

ARGON (AR)
ARSENIC (AS)
ASTATINE (AT)
BARIUM (BA)

BERKELIUM (BK)
BERYLLIUM (BE)
BISMUTH (BI)
BORON (B)

BROMINE (BR)
CADMIUM (CD)
CAESIUM (CS)
CALCIUM (CA)

CALIFORNIUM (CF)
CARBON (C)
CERIUM (CE)
CHLORINE (CL)
CHROMIUM (CR)
COBALT (CO)
COLUMBIUM (CB)
COPPER (CU)
CURIUM (CM)
DYSPROSIUM (DY)
EINSTEINIUM (ES)
ERBIUM (ER)
EUROPIUM (EU)
FERMIUM (FM)
FLUORINE (F)
FRANCIUM (FR)
GADOLINIUM (GD)
GALLIUM (GA)
GERMANIUM (GE)
GOLD (AU)
HAFNIUM (HF)
HELIUM (HE)
HOLMIUM (HO)

HYDROGEN (H)
INDIUM (IN)
IODINE (I)
IRIDIUM (IR)
IRON (FE)
KRYPTON (KR)
LANTHANUM (LA)
LAWRENCIUM (LR)
LEAD (PB)
LITHIUM (LI)
LUTETIUM (LU)
MAGNESIUM (MG)
MANGANESE (MN)
MENDELEVIUM (MD)
MERCURY (HG)
MOLYBDENUM (MO)
NEODYMIUM (ND)
NEON (NE)
NEPTUNIUM (NP)
NICKEL (NI)
NIOBIUM (NB)
NITROGEN (N)
NOBELIUM (NO)

OSMIUM (OS)
OXYGEN (O)
PALLADIUM (PD)
PHOSPHORUS (P)
PLATINUM (PT)
PLUTONIUM (PU)
POLONIUM (PO)
POTASSIUM (K)
PRASEODYMIUM
   (PR)
PROMETHIUM (PM)
PROTACTINIUM (PA)
RADIUM (RA)
RADON (RN)
RHENIUM (RE)
RHODIUM (RH)
RUBIDIUM (RB)
RUTHENIUM (RU)
SAMARIUM (SM)
SCANDIUM (SC)
SELENIUM (SE)
SILICON (SI)

SILVER (AG)
SODIUM (NA)
STRONTIUM (SR)
SULPHUR (S)
TANTALUM (TA)
TECHNETIUM (TC)
TELLURIUM (TE)
TERBIUM (TB)
THALLIUM (TL)
THORIUM (TH)
THULIUM (TM)
TIN (SN)
TITANIUM (TI)
TUNGSTEN (W)
URANIUM (U)
VANADIUM (V)
WOLFRAM (W)
XENON (XE)
YTTERBIUM (YB)
YTTRIUM (Y)
ZINC (ZN)
ZIRCONIUM (ZR)

ALLOYS

ALLOY – main components

4
ALNI – iron, nickel, aluminium, copper
BETA – titanium, aluminium, vanadium,
   chromium
5
ALPHA – titanium, aluminium, tin, copper,
   zirconium, niobium, molybdenum
BRASS – copper, zinc
INVAR – iron, nickel
MAZAC – zinc, aluminium, magnesium,
   copper
MONEL – nickel, cobalt, iron
STEEL – iron, carbon
6
ALNICO – aluminium, nickel, cobalt
BABBIT – tin, lead, antimony, copper
BRONZE – copper, tin
CUNICO – iron, cobalt, copper, nickel
CUNIFE – iron, cobalt, nickel
FEROBA – iron, barium oxide, iron oxide
PEWTER – tin, lead
SOLDER – lead, tin (soft), copper, zinc
   (brazing)
7
ALCOMAX – aluminium, cobalt, nickel,
   copper, lead, niobium
ALUMNEL – aluminium, chromium
AMALGAM – mercury, various
CHROMEL – nickel, chromium

7—continued
COLUMAN – iron, chromium, nickel,
   aluminium, nobium, copper
ELINVAR – iron, nickel, chromium, tungsten
INCONEL – nickel, chromium, iron
KANTHAL – chromium, aluminium, iron
MUMETAL – iron, nickel, copper, chromium
NIMONIC – nickel, chromium, iron, titanium,
   aluminium, manganese, silicon
8
CAST IRON – carbon, iron
DOWMETAL – magnesium, aluminium, zinc,
   manganese
GUNMETAL – copper, tin, zinc
HIPERNIK – nickel, iron
KIRKSITE – zinc, aluminium, copper
MANGANIN – copper, manganese, nickel
NICHROME – nickel, iron, chromium
VICALLOY – iron, cobalt, vanadium
ZIRCALOY – zirconium, tin, iron, nickel,
   chromium
9
DURALUMIN – aluminium, copper, silicon,
   magnesium, manganese, zinc
HASTELLOY – nickel, molybdenum, iron,
   chromium, cobalt, tungsten
PERMALLOY – nickel, iron
PERMINVAR – nickel, iron, cobalt
TYPE METAL – lead, tin, antimony

10
CONSTANTAN – copper, nickel
MISCH METAL – cerium, various
MUNTZ METAL – copper, zinc
ROSE'S METAL – bismuth, lead, tin
SUPERALLOY – type of stainless steel
WOOD'S METAL – lead, tin, bismuth, cadmium

11
CUPRONICKEL – copper, nickel
ELECTROTYPE – lead, tin, antimony
SUPERMALLOY – iron, nickel
SUPERMENDUR – iron, cobalt

12
FERROSILICON – iron, silicon
GERMAN SILVER – copper, nickel, zinc, lead, tin

12—continued
SILVER SOLDER – copper, silver, zinc

13
FERROCHROMIUM – iron, chromium
FERROTUNGSTEN – iron, tungsten
FERROVANADIUM – iron, vanadium

14
ADMIRALTY METAL – copper, zinc
BRITANNIA METAL – tin, antimony, copper
FERROMANGANESE – iron, manganese
PHOSPHOR BRONZE – copper, tin, phosphorus
STAINLESS STEEL – iron, chromium, vanadium

GEOMETRIC FIGURES AND CURVES

3
ARC

4
CONE
CUBE
KITE
LINE
LOOP
LUNE
OVAL
ROSE
ZONE

5
CHORD
CONIC
HELIX
LOCUS
NAPPE
OGIVE
PLANE
PRISM
RHOMB
SHEET
SOLID
TORUS
WEDGE
WITCH

6
CIRCLE
CONOID
FOLIUM
LAMINA
NORMAL
OCTANT
PENCIL
RADIUS

6—continued
SECTOR
SPHERE
SPIRAL
SPLINE
SQUARE

7
ANNULUS
CISSOID
CYCLOID
DECAGON
ELLIPSE
EVOLUTE
FRACTAL
HEXAGON
LIMACON
OCTAGON
PERIGON
POLYGON
PYRAMID
RHOMBUS
SEGMENT
SURFACE
TANGENT
TREFOIL
TRIDENT

8
CARDIOID
CATENARY
CATENOID
CONCHOID
CONICOID
CYLINDER
ENVELOPE
EPICYCLE
EXCIRCLE

8—continued
FRUSTRUM
GEODESIC
HEPTAGON
INCIRCLE
INVOLUTE
PARABOLA
PENTAGON
PRISMOID
QUADRANT
RHOMBOID
ROULETTE
SPHEROID
TRACTRIX
TRIANGLE
TROCHOID

9
ANTIPRISM
CRUCIFORM
DIRECTRIX
DODECAGON
ELLIPSOID
HYPERBOLA
ISOCHRONE
KOCH CURVE
LOXODROME
MULTIFOIL
PENTAGRAM
PENTANGLE
RHUMB LINE
SINE CURVE
STROPHOID
TRAPEZIUM
TRAPEZOID

10
ACUTE ANGLE

10—continued
ANCHOR RING
CYLINDROID
EPICYCLOID
HEMISPHERE
HEXAHEDRON
KAPPA CURVE
LEMNISCATE
OCTAHEDRON
PARABOLOID
PEANO CURVE
POLYHEDRON
PRISMATOID
QUADRANGLE
QUADREFOIL
RIGHT ANGLE
SEMICIRCLE
SERPENTINE
TRISECTRIX

11
CORNU SPIRAL
EPITROCHOID
HEPTAHEDRON
HYPERBOLOID
HYPOCYCLOID
ICOSAHEDRON
KLEIN BOTTLE
LATUS RECTUM
MÖBIUS STRIP
OBTUSE ANGLE
PENTAHEDRON
REFLEX ANGLE
TAUTOCHRONE
TETRAHEDRON

12
HYPOTROCHOID

12—continued
PSEUDOSPHERE
RHOMBOHEDRON
SIGMOID CURVE
13
CIRCUMFERENCE
CUBOCTAHEDRON
PARALLELOGRAM

13—continued
PARALLELOTOPE
PEDAL TRIANGLE
PERPENDICULAR
QUADRILATERAL
14
SNOWFLAKE CURVE

15
BRACHISTOCHRONE
SCALENE TRIANGLE
17
ICOSIDODECAHEDRON
ISOSCELES
 TRIANGLE

19
EQUILATERAL
 TRIANGLE

COMPUTER PROGRAMMING LANGUAGES

1
C
3
ADA
AED
APL
AWK
CPL
CSL
IAL
LEX
POL
POP
RPG

4
BCPL
FRED
LISP
LOGO
REXX
YACC
5
ALGOL
BASIC
CHILL
CLEAR

5—continued
COBOL
COMAL
CORAL
FORTH
KAPSE
MOHLL
6
EDISON
JOVIAL
MODULA
PASCAL

6—continued
PROLOG
SIMULA
SNOBOL
7
BABBAGE
FORTRAN
MACLISP
9
FRANZLISP
SMALLTALK

PLANETS AND SATELLITES

MAIN PLANETS (NAMED SATELLITES)

MERCURY
VENUS
EARTH (MOON)
MARS (PHOBOS, DEIMOS)
JUPITER (METIS, ADRASTEA, AMALTHEA,
    THEBE, IO, EUROPA, GANYMEDE,
    CALLISTO, LEDA, MILALIA, LYSITHEA,
    ELARA, ANANKE, CARME, PASIPHAE,
    SINOPE)
SATURN (MIMAS, ENCELADUS, TETHYS,
    DIONE, RHEA, TITAN, HYPERION,
    IAPETUS, PHOEBE, JANUS)
URANUS (MIRANDA, ARIEL, UMBRIEL,
    TITANIA, OBERON)
NEPTUNE (TRITON, NEREID)
PLUTO (CHARON)

MINOR PLANETS

ACHILLES
ADONIS
AMOR
APOLLO
ASTRAEA
ATEN
CERES
CHIRON
EROS
EUNOMIA
EUPHROSYNE
HEBE
HERMES
HIDALGO
HYGIEA
ICARUS
IRIS
JUNO
PALLAS
VESTA

COMETS

4
FAYE
5
BIELA
ENCKE
KOPFF
6
HALLEY
OLBERS
TUTTLE

7
BENNETT
D'ARREST
VÄISÄLÄ
WHIPPLE
8
BORRELLY
DAYLIGHT
KOHOUTEK
WESTPHAL

9
COMAS SOLÀ
CROMMELIN
10
PONS-BROOKS
SCHAUMASSE
11
AREND-ROLAND
12
PONS-WINNECKE

13
STEPHAN-OTERMA
14
BRONSEN-METCALF
15
GIACOBINI-ZINNER
GRIGG-SKIELLERUP

NAMED NEAREST AND BRIGHTEST STARS

4
ROSS
VEGA
WOLF
5
CYGNI
DENEB
RIGEL
SIRIUS
SPICA
6
ADHARA

6 —continued
ALTAIR
CASTOR
CRUCIS
KRUGER
LUYTEN
POLLUX
SHAULA
SIRIUS
7
ANTARES
CANOPUS

7 —continued
CAPELLA
LALANDE
PROCYON
REGULUS
TAU CETI
8
ACHERNAR
ARCTURUS
BARNARD'S
CENTAURI
KAPTEYN'S

9
ALDEBARAN
BELLATRIX
FOMALHAUT
10+
BETELGEUSE
EPSILON INDI
ALPHA CENTAURI
EPSILON ERIDANI
PROXIMA CENTAURI

THE CONSTELLATIONS

3
ARA
LEO
4
APUS
CRUX
GRUS
LYNX
LYRA
PAVO
VELA
5
ARIES
CETUS
DRACO
HYDRA
INDUS
LEPUS

5 —continued
LIBRA
LUPUS
MENSA
MUSCA
NORMA
ORION
PYXIS
VIRGO
6
ANTLIA
AQUILA
AURIGA
BOÖTES
CAELUM
CANCER
CARINA
CORVUS

6 —continued
CRATER
CYGNUS
DORADO
FORNAX
GEMINI
HYDRUS
OCTANS
PICTOR
PISCES
PUPPIS
SCUTUM
TAURUS
TUCANA
VOLANS
7
CEPHEUS
COLUMBA

7 —continued
LACERTA
PEGASUS
PERSEUS
PHOENIX
SAGITTA
SERPENS
SEXTANS
8
AQUARIUS
CIRCINUS
EQUULEUS
ERIDANUS
HERCULES
LEO MINOR
SCORPIUS
SCULPTOR

9
ANDROMEDA
CENTAURUS
CHAMELEON
DELPHINUS
MONOCEROS
OPHIUCHUS
RETICULUM
URSA MAJOR
URSA MINOR

9 —continued
VULPECULA
10
CANIS MAJOR
CANIS MINOR
CASSIOPEIA
HOROLOGIUM
TRIANGULUM

11
CAPRICORNUS
SAGITTARIUS
TELESCOPIUM
12+
CAMELOPARDALIS
CANES VENATICI
COMA BERENICES

12+ —continued
CORONA AUSTRALIS
CORONA BOREALIS
MICROSCOPIUM
PISCIS AUSTRINUS
TRIANGULUM
  AUSTRALE

METEOR SHOWERS

6
LYRIDS
URSIDS
7
CYGNIDS
LEONIDS

7—continued
TAURIDS
8
CEPHEIDS
GEMINIDS
ORIONIDS

8—continued
PERSEIDS
10
AUSTRALIDS
OPHIUCHIDS
PHOENICIDS

11
QUADRANTIDS
12
CAPRICORNIDS

ASTRONOMERS ROYAL

JOHN FLAMSTEED (1675–1719)
EDMUND HALLEY (1720–42)
JAMES BRADLEY (1742–62)
NATHANIEL BLISS (1762–64)
NEVIL MASKELYNE (1765–1811)
JOHN POND (1811–35)
SIR GEORGE BIDDELL AIRY (1835–81)

SIR WILLIAM H. M. CHRISTIE (1881–1910)
SIR FRANK WATSON DYSON (1910–33)
SIR HAROLD SPENCER JONES (1933–55)
SIR RICHARD WOOLLEY (1955–71)
SIR MARTIN RYLE (1972–82)
PROF. E. GRAHAM SMITH (1982–   )

GEOLOGICAL TIME SCALE

CENOZOIC	QUATERNARY	HOLOCENE
		PLEISTOCENE
	TERTIARY	PLIOCENE
		MIOCENE
		OLIGOCENE
		EOCENE
		PALAEOCENE
MESOZOIC	CRETACEOUS	
	JURASSIC	
	TRIASSIC	
PALAEOZOIC	PERMIAN	
	CARBONIFEROUS	
	DEVONIAN	
	SILURIAN	
	ORDOVICIAN	
	CAMBRIAN	
PRECAMBRIAN	PRECAMBRIAN	

CLOUDS

ALTOCUMULUS	CIRROSTRATUS	CUMULUS	STRATOCUMULUS
ALTOSTRATUS	CIRRUS	NIMBOSTRATUS	STRATUS
CIRROCUMULUS	CUMULONIMBUS		

PREHISTORIC ANIMALS

8
EOHIPPUS
RUTIODON
SMILODON
9
IGUANODON
TRACHODON
10
ALLOSAURUS
ALTISPINAX
BAROSAURUS
DIPLODOCUS
DRYOSAURUS
EUPARKERIA
MESOHIPPUS
ORTHOMERUS
PLIOHIPPUS
PTERANODON
STEGOCERAS
11
ANATOSAURUS
ANCHISAURUS
APATOSAURUS
APHANERAMMA
CETIOSAURUS
COELOPHYSIS

11—continued
DEINONYCHUS
KRITOSAURUS
MANDASUCHUS
MERYCHIPPUS
MONOCLONIUS
POLACANTHUS
PTERODACTYL
RIOJASAURUS
SAUROLOPHUS
SCOLOSAURUS
SPINOSAURUS
STEGOSAURUS
TARBOSAURUS
TRICERATOPS
12
ANKYLOSAURUS
BRONTOSAURUS
CAMPTOSAURUS
CERATOSAURUS
CHASMOSAURUS
DEINOCHEIRUS
HYLAEOSAURUS
KENTROSAURUS
LAMBEOSAURUS

12—continued
MEGALOSAURUS
ORNITHOMIMUS
OURANOSAURUS
PLATEOSAURUS
TICINOSUCHUS
13
BRACHIOSAURUS
COMPSOGNATHUS
CORYTHOSAURUS
DESMATOSUCHUS
DILOPHOSAURUS
EDMONTOSAURUS
ERYTHROSUCHUS
HYPSELOSAURUS
HYPSILOPHODON
LESOTHOSAURUS
PANOPLOSAURUS
PENTACERATOPS
PROTOCERATOPS
PTERODACTYLUS
SCELIDOSAURUS
SCLEROMOCHLUS
STYRACOSAURUS
TENONTOSAURUS

13—continued
TYRANNOSAURUS
14
BALUCHITHERIUM
CETIOSAURISCUS
CHASMATOSAURUS
EUOPLOCEPHALUS
MASSOSPONDYLUS
PSITTACOSAURUS
THESCELOSAURUS
15
PARASAUROLOPHUS
PROCHENE-
  OSAURUS
16
PACHYRHI-
  NOSAURUS
PROCOMP-
  SOGNATHUS
17
HETERO-
  DONTOSAURUS
18
PACHYCEPHALOSAURUS

ROCKS AND MINERALS

4
GOLD
MICA
OPAL
RUBY
TALC
5
AGATE
BERYL
BORAX
EMERY
FLINT
SHALE

5—continued
SHARD
SKARN
TOPAZ
TRONA
6
ACMITE
ALBITE
ARKOSE
AUGITE
BARITE
BASALT
COPPER

6—continued
DACITE
DUNITE
GABBRO
GALENA
GARNET
GNEISS
GYPSUM
HALITE
HAÜYNE
HUMITE
ILLITE
LEVYNE

6—continued
MINIUM
NORITE
NOSEAN
PELITE
PYRITE
PYROPE
QUARTZ
RUTILE
SALITE
SCHIST
SCHORL
SILICA

155

ROCKS AND MINERALS

6—continued
SILVER
SPHENE
SPINEL
URTITE
ZIRCON

7
ALNOITE
ALTAITE
ALUNITE
ANATASE
APATITE
ARSENIC
AXINITE
AZURITE
BARYTES
BAUXITE
BIOTITE
BISMUTH
BORNITE
BRECCIA
BRUCITE
CALCITE
CALOMEL
CELSIAN
CITRINE
COESITE
CUPRITE
DIAMOND
DIORITE
EMERALD
EPIDOTE
FELSITE
FOYAITE
GAHNITE
GEDRITE
GRANITE
GUMMITE
HELVITE
HESSITE
HOPEITE
HUNTITE
IJOLITE
JADEITE
KAINITE
KERNITE
KYANITE
LEUCITE
LIGNITE
MELLITE
MULLITE
OLIVINE
ORTHITE
RASPITE
REALGAR
SPARITE
SYENITE
SYLVITE
THORITE
THULITE
ZEOLITE

7—continued
ZINCITE
ZOISITE

8
AEGIRINE
ALLANITE
ALUNOGEN
ANALCIME
ANALCITE
ANDESINE
ANDORITE
ANKERITE
ANTIMONY
ARCANITE
AUGELITE
AUTUNITE
BASANITE
BIXBYITE
BLOEDITE
BLUE JOHN
BOEHMITE
BORACITE
BRAGGITE
BRAUNITE
BRAVOITE
BRONZITE
BROOKITE
CALAMINE
CHIOLITE
CHLORITE
CHROMITE
CINNABAR
CORUNDUM
CROCOITE
CRYOLITE
CUBANITE
DATOLITE
DIALLAGE
DIASPORE
DIGENITE
DIOPSIDE
DIOPTASE
DOLERITE
DOLOMITE
ECLOGITE
ENARGITE
EPSOMITE
ESSEXITE
EULYTITE
EUXENITE
FAYALITE
FELDSPAR
FLUORITE
GIBBSITE
GOETHITE
GRAPHITE
HANKSITE
HAWAIITE
HEMATITE
HYACINTH
IDOCRASE

8—continued
ILMENITE
IODYRITE
JAROSITE
LAZURITE
LIMONITE
LITHARGE
MARSHITE
MEIONITE
MELANITE
MELILITE
MESOLITE
MIERSITE
MIMETITE
MONAZITE
MONETITE
MYLONITE
NEPHRITE
ORPIMENT
PARISITE
PERIDOTE
PERTHITE
PETALITE
PLATINUM
PORPHYRY
PREHNITE
PSAMMITE
PYRIBOLE
PYROXENE
RHYOLITE
ROCKSALT
SANIDINE
SAPPHIRE
SELLAITE
SIDERITE
SMECTITE
SODALITE
STANNITE
STEATITE
STIBNITE
STILBITE
STOLSITE
STRUVITE
TITANITE
TONALITE
TRACHYTE
VARISITE
VATERITE
WEHRLITE
WURTZITE
XENOTIME

9
ACANTHITE
ALMANDINE
ALUMINITE
AMPHIBOLE
ANDRADITE
ANGLESITE
ANHYDRITE
ANORTHITE
ARAGONITE

9—continued
ARGENTITE
ATACAMITE
BENITOITE
BRIMSTONE
BROMYRITE
BUNSENITE
BYTOWNITE
CARNALITE
CARNOTITE
CELESTITE
CERUSSITE
CHABAZITE
CHINACLAY
COBALTITE
COLUMBITE
COPIAPITE
COTUNNITE
COVELLITE
DANBURITE
DERBYLITE
DIATOMITE
ENSTATITE
ERYTHRITE
EUCAIRITE
EUCLASITE
EUDIALITE
FERBERITE
FIBROLITE
FLUORSPAR
GEHLENITE
GMELINITE
GOSLARITE
GRANULITE
GREYWACKE
GROSSULAR
GRUNERITE
HARMOTOME
HERCYNITE
HERDERITE
HORNSTONE
KAOLINITE
KIESERITE
LANARKITE
LAWSONITE
LEUCITITE
LIMESTONE
LODESTONE
MAGNESITE
MAGNETITE
MALACHITE
MALIGNITE
MANGANITE
MARCASITE
MARGARITE
MARIALITE
MENDIPITE
MICROLITE
MIGMATITE
MILLERITE
MISPICKEL

9—continued	10—continued	10—continued	11—continued
MONZONITE	CACOXENITE	PYROCHLORE	GLAUBER SALT
MORDENITE	CALEDONITE	PYROLUSITE	GLAUCOPHANE
MUGEARITE	CANCRINITE	PYRRHOTITE	GREENOCKITE
MUSCOVITE	CERVANTITE	RHYODACITE	HARZBURGITE
NANTOKITE	CHALCEDONY	RICHTERITE	HASTINGSITE
NATROLITE	CHALCOCITE	RIEBECKITE	HAUSMANNITE
NEPHELINE	CHLORITOID	SAFFLORITE	HYPERSTHENE
NICCOLITE	CHRYSOLITE	SAMARSKITE	ICELAND SPAR
OLDHAMITE	CLAUDETITE	SAPPHIRINE	KATOPHORITE
OLIVENITE	CLINTONITE	SERPENTINE	LAPIS LAZULI
PECTOLITE	COLEMANITE	SHONKINITE	LEADHILLITE
PENNINITE	CONNELLITE	SPERRYLITE	LOELLINGITE
PERCYLITE	COQUIMBITE	SPHALERITE	MANGANOSITE
PERICLASE	CORDIERITE	STAUROLITE	MELANTERITE
PHENAKITE	DOUGLASITE	STERCORITE	MOLYBDENITE
PHONOLITE	DYSCRASITE	STISHOVITE	MONTROYDITE
PIGEONITE	EMPLECTITE	TESCHENITE	NEPHELINITE
PISTACITE	EMPRESSITE	THENARDITE	NORDMARKITE
POLLUCITE	EPIDIORITE	THOMSONITE	PENFIELDITE
POWELLITE	FORSTERITE	THORIANITE	PENTLANDITE
PROUSTITE	GANOMALITE	TORBERNITE	PHILLIPSITE
PULASKITE	GARNIERITE	TOURMALINE	PITCHBLENDE
QUARTZITE	GAYLUSSITE	TRAVERTINE	PLAGIOCLASE
RHODONITE	GEIKIELITE	TROEGERITE	PSILOMELANE
SANDSTONE	GLAUBERITE	ULLMANNITE	PUMPELLYITE
SCAPOLITE	GLAUCONITE	ULVÓSPINEL	PYRARGYRITE
SCHEELITE	GREENSTONE	VANADINITE	PYROCHROITE
SCOLECITE	HAMBERGITE	VITROPHYRE	RADIOLARITE
SCORODITE	HEULANDITE	WEBSTERITE	ROCK CRYSTAL
SMALLTITE	HORNBLENDE	WHEWELLITE	SILLIMANITE
SOAPSTONE	HUEBNERITE	WOLFRAMITE	SMITHSONITE
SPODUMENE	IGNIMBRITE	ZINCBLENDE	SPESSARTITE
STRENGITE	JAMESONITE		TITANAUGITE
SYLVANITE	KIMBERLITE	**11**	TRIPHYLLITE
TACHYLITE	LANTHANITE	ALLEMONTITE	VALENTINITE
TANTALITE	LAUMONTITE	AMBLYGONITE	VERMICULITE
TAPIOLITE	LAURIONITE	ANORTHOSITE	VESUVIANITE
THERALITE	LEPIDOLITE	APOPHYLLITE	VILLIAUMITE
THOLEIITE	LHERZOLITE	BADDELEYITE	ZINNWALDITE
TREMOLITE	LIMBURGITE	BERTRANDITE	
TRIDYMITE	MASCAGNITE	BERYLLONITE	**12**
TURQUOISE	MATLOCKITE	BROCHANTITE	ANORTHOCLASE
URANINITE	MEERSCHAUM	CALCARENITE	ARSENOPYRITE
VIVIANITE	MELILITITE	CALCILUTITE	BISMUTHINITE
WAGNERITE	MELTEIGITE	CALCIRUDITE	BOULANGERITE
WAVELLITE	MICROCLINE	CARBONATITE	CALCISILTITE
WILLEMITE	MIRABILITE	CARBORUNDUM	CHALCANTHITE
WITHERITE	MOISSANITE	CASSITERITE	CHALCOPYRITE
WULFENITE	NEWBERYITE	CERARGYRITE	CLAY MINERALS
ZEUNERITE	OLIGOCLASE	CHARNOCKITE	CLINOPTOLITE
10	ORTHOCLASE	CHIASTOLITE	CLINOZOISITE
ACTINOLITE	PARAGONITE	CHLOANTHITE	CRISTOBALITE
ÅKERMANITE	PEKOVSKITE	CHONDRODITE	EDDINGTONITE
ALABANDITE	PERIDOTITE	CHRYSOBERYL	FELDSPATHOID
ANDALUSITE	PERTHOSITE	CHRYSOCOLLA	FERGUSSONITE
ANKARAMITE	PHLOGOPITE	CLINOCHLORE	FLUORAPATITE
ARSENOLITE	PHOSGENITE	COBALTBLOOM	GROSSULARITE
BOROLONITE	PIEMONTITE	DAUBREELITE	HEDENBERGITE
BOURNONITE	POLYBASITE	EGLESTONITE	HEMIMORPHITE
BRONZITITE	PYRALSPITE	FERROAUGITE	LUXULLIANITE
		FRANKLINITE	METACINNABAR

12—continued	13	14	16
MONTICELLITE	ANTHOPHYLLITE	CRYOLITHIONITE	GALENABISMUTHITE
PYROMORPHITE	BREITHAUPTITE	HYDROMAGNESITE	ORTHOFERROSILITE
PYROPHYLLITE	CLINOPYROXENE	LECHATELIERITE	PHARMACOSIDERITE
RHODOCROSITE	CUMMINGTONITE	LITHIOPHYLLITE	**17**
SENARMONTITE	JACUPIRANGITE	ORTHOQUARTZITE	HYDROGROSSU-
SKUTTERUDITE	KALIOPHYLLITE	PSEUDOBROOKITE	LARITE
STRONTIANITE	LEPIDOCROCITE	RAMMELSBERGITE	TELLUROBIS-
SYENODIORITE	LITCHFIELDITE	TRACHYANDESITE	MUTHITE
TERLINGUAITE	ORTHOPYROXENE	XANTHOPHYLLITE	
TETRAHEDRITE	QUARTZARENITE	**15**	
THOMSENOLITE	RHODOCHROSITE	MONTMORILLONITE	
TRACHYBASALT	STILPNOMELANE	PSEUDOTACHYLITE	
WOLLASTONITE	THERMONATRITE	STIBIOTANTALITE	
	UNCOMPAHGRITE		

ORES

ELEMENT – ore(s)

3
TIN – cassiterite

4
IRON – haematite, magnetite
LEAD – galena
ZINC – sphalerite, smithsonite, calamine

5
BORON – kernite

6
BARIUM – barite, witherite
CERIUM – monazite, bastnaesite
COBALT – cobaltite, smaltite, erythrite
COPPER – malachite, azurite, chalcopyrite,
   bornite, cuprite
ERBIUM – monazite, bastnaesite
INDIUM – sphalerite, smithsonite, calamine
NICKEL – pentlandite, pyrrhotite
OSMIUM – iridosime
RADIUM – pitchblende, carnotite
SILVER – argentite, horn silver
SODIUM – salt

7
ARSENIC – realgar, orpiment, arsenopyrite
CADMIUM – greenockite
CAESIUM – lepidolite, pollucite
CALCIUM – limestone, gypsum, fluorite
GALLIUM
HAFNIUM – zircon
HOLMIUM – monazite
IRIDIUM
LITHIUM – lepidolite, spodumene
MERCURY – cinnabar
NIOBIUM – columbite-tantalite, pyrochlore,
   euxenite
RHENIUM – molybdenite
RHODIUM
SILICON – silica

7—continued
THORIUM – monazite
THULIUM – monazite
URANIUM – pitchblende, uraninite, carnotite
YTTRIUM – monazite

8
ANTIMONY – stibnite
CHROMIUM – chromite
LUTETIUM – monazite
PLATINUM – sperrylite
RUBIDIUM – lepidolite
SAMARIUM – monazite, bastnaesite
SCANDIUM – thortveitite, davidite
SELENIUM – pyrites
TANTALUM – columbite-tantalite
THALLIUM – pyrites
TITANIUM – rutile, ilmenite, sphere
TUNGSTEN – wolframite, scheelite
VANADIUM – carnotite, roscoelite, vanadinite

9
ALUMINIUM – bauxite
BERYLLIUM – beryl
GERMANIUM – germanite, argyrodite
LANTHANUM – monazite, bastnaesite
MAGNESIUM – magnesite, dolomite
MANGANESE – pyrolusite, rhodochrosite
NEODYMIUM – monazite, bastnaesite
PALLADIUM
POTASSIUM – sylvite, carnallite, polyhalite
RUTHENIUM – pentlandite, pyroxinite
STRONTIUM – celestite, strontianite
TELLURIUM
YTTERBIUM – monazite

10
DYSPROSIUM – monazite, bastnaesite
GADOLINIUM – monazite, bastnaesite
MOLYBDENUM – molybdenite, wulfenite
PHOSPHORUS – apatite

12
PRASEODYMIUM – monazite, bastnaesite

12—continued
PROTACTINIUM – pitchblende

GEMSTONES

STONE (colour)

4
JADE (green, mauve, brown)
ONYX (various colours, banded)
OPAL (white, milky blue, or black with rainbow-
   coloured reflections)
RUBY (red)

5
AGATE (brown, red, blue, green, yellow)
BERYL (green, blue, pink)
TOPAZ (usually yellow or colourless)

6
GARNET (red)
ZIRCON (all colours)

7
CITRINE (yellow)
DIAMOND (colourless)
EMERALD (green)

8
AMETHYST (purple)

8—continued
SAPPHIRE (blue and other colours except
   red)
SUNSTONE (whitish-red-brown flecked with
   gold)

9
MALACHITE (dark green banded)
MOONSTONE (white with bluish tinge)
SOAPSTONE (white or greenish)
TURQUOISE (greenish-blue)

10
AQUAMARINE (turquoise, greenish-blue)
BLOODSTONE (green with red spots)
CHALCEDONY (red, brown, grey, or black)
SERPENTINE (usually green or white)
TOURMALINE (all colours)

11
LAPIS LAZULI (deep blue)

MEDICAL TERMS

3	5—continued	5—continued	6—continued
GUT	FEMUR	TIBIA	PELVIS
HIP	FOVEA	UVULA	PEPSIN
JAW	HEART	VALVE	RADIUS
RIB	HYOID	VOMER	RECTUM
4	ILEUM	WRIST	REFLEX
ANUS	ILIUM	**6**	RENNET
BILE	INCUS	ARTERY	RETINA
CUSP	JOINT	ATRIUM	SACRUM
GALL	LIVER	BICEPS	SALIVA
HEEL	MALAR	CAECUM	SCLERA
IRIS	MEDIA	CARDIA	SQUAMA
LENS	NARES	CARPAL	STAPES
NOSE	NASAL	CARPUS	TARSUS
ULNA	NERVE	COCCYX	TENDON
VEIN	OPTIC	CORNEA	TONGUE
5	PUBIS	CUBOID	TUNICA
ANKLE	PULSE	DERMIS	URETER
AORTA	PUPIL	FIBULA	VASTUS
BOLUS	SENSE	GULLET	VENULE
BOWEL	SINEW	KIDNEY	VESSEL
CHYLE	SINUS	LUNATE	**7**
CHYME	SKULL	MUSCLE	AURICLE
COLON	SPINE	MYELIN	BLADDER
	TALUS		

7—continued
CAROTID
CHOROID
COCHLEA
CRANIUM
CUTICLE
DELTOID
ECCRINE
ETHMOID
FRONTAL
GEMMULE
GLOTTIS
HUMERUS
INGESTA
JEJUNUM
JUGULAR
LACTEAL
MALLEUS
MAMMARY
MEDULLA
NEPHRON
NEURONE
NOSTRIL
PATELLA
PHALANX
PHARYNX
PTYALIN
PYLORUS
SAPHENA
SCAPULA
SENSORY
STERNUM
STOMACH
SYNAPSE
SYSTOLE
THYROID
TRICEPS
URETHRA

8
ADDUCTOR
APOCRINE
APPENDIX
BACKBONE
BILE DUCT
CEREBRUM

8—continued
CLAVICLE
CORONARY
DIASTOLE
DUODENUM
EXOCRINE
GANGLION
LIGAMENT
MANDIBLE
MENINGES
PALATINE
PANCREAS
PARIETAL
PERINEUM
PISIFORM
RECEPTOR
SACCULUS
SALIVARY
SCAPHOID
SPHENOID
TEMPORAL
TUBINATE
TYMPANUM
UNCIFORM
VENA CAVA
VERTEBRA

9
ARTERIOLE
BILIRUBIN
BRAINSTEM
CAPILLARY
CUNEIFORM
DIAPHRAGM
DIGESTION
ENDOCRINE
ENDORPHIN
EPICARDIA
EPIDERMIS
GOLGI BODY
HAMSTRING
INGESTION
INTESTINE
LACHRYMAL
LYMPHATIC
LYMPH NODE

9—continued
MAXILLARY
NAVICULAR
OCCIPITAL
PACEMAKER
SPHINCTER
TASTE BUDS
TRAPEZIUM
TRAPEZIUS
TRAPEZOID
UTRICULUS
VENTRICLE

10
ADAM'S APPLE
ADRENALINE
ASTRAGALUS
BILIVERDIN
BREASTBONE
CEREBELLUM
COLLAR BONE
EPICARDIUM
EPIGLOTTIS
GREY MATTER
HEMISPHERE
HENLE'S LOOP
INNOMINATE
METACARPAL
METACARPUS
METATARSAL
METATARSUS
MYOCARDIUM
QUADRICEPS
SUPRARENAL

11
CONJUNCTIVA
ENDOCARDIUM
GALL BLADDER
PERICARDIUM
PERISTALSIS
VASA VASORUM

12
ADRENAL GLAND
HAIR FOLLICLE
MOTOR NEURONE

12—continued
PELVIC GIRDLE
RECEPTACULUM
SCHWANN CELLS
SCIATIC NERVE
SPINAL COLUMN
SUBMAXILLARY

13
AQUEOUS HUMOUR
BICUSPID VALVE
BLOOD PRESSURE
KUPFFER'S CELLS
NERVOUS SYSTEM
NODE OF RANVIER
NORADRENALINE
PEYER'S PATCHES
PURKINJE CELLS
SUBMANDIBULAR

14
ACHILLES TENDON
BOWMAN'S
  CAPSULE
BRUNNER'S GLANDS
EUSTACHIAN TUBE
PURKINJE FIBRES
VITREOUS HUMOUR

15
ALIMENTARY CANAL
MALPIGHIAN LAYER
OBTURATOR
  MUSCLE
ORGAN OF
  JACOBSON
PECTORAL
  MUSCLES

16
MEDULLA
  OBLONGATA

18
ISLETS OF
  LANGERHANS
SEMICIRCULAR
  CANALS

RELIGION AND MYTHOLOGY

BOOKS OF THE BIBLE

OLD TESTAMENT

GENESIS
EXODUS
LEVITICUS
NUMBERS
DEUTERONOMY
JOSHUA
JUDGES
RUTH
1 SAMUEL
2 SAMUEL
1 KINGS
2 KINGS
1 CHRONICLES
2 CHRONICLES
EZRA
NEHEMIAH
ESTHER
JOB
PSALMS
PROVERBS
ECCLESIASTES
SONG OF SOLOMON
ISAIAH

JEREMIAH
LAMENTATIONS
EZEKIEL
DANIEL
HOSEA
JOEL
AMOS
OBADIAH
JONAH
MICAH
NAHUM
HABAKKUK
ZEPHANIAH
HAGGAI
ZECHARIAH
MALACHI

APOCRYPHA

I ESDRAS
II ESDRAS
TOBIT
JUDITH
THE REST OF
    ESTHER

WISDOM
ECCLESIASTICUS
BARUCH, WITH
    EPISTLE OF
    JEREMIAH
SONG OF THE
    THREE CHILDREN
SUSANNA
BEL AND THE
    DRAGON
PRAYER OF
    MANASSES
I MACCABEES
II MACCABEES

NEW TESTAMENT

MATTHEW
MARK
LUKE
JOHN
THE ACTS
ROMANS
1 CORINTHIANS

2 CORINTHIANS
GALATIANS
EPHESIANS
PHILIPPIANS
COLOSSIANS
1 THESSALONIANS
2 THESSALONIANS
1 TIMOTHY
2 TIMOTHY
TITUS
PHILEMON
HEBREWS
JAMES
1 PETER
2 PETER
1 JOHN
2 JOHN
3 JOHN
JUDE
REVELATION

BIBLICAL CHARACTERS

OLD TESTAMENT

AARON – elder brother of Moses; 1st high priest of Hebrews

ABEL – second son of Adam and Eve; murdered by brother Cain

ABRAHAM – father of Hebrew nation

ABSALOM – David's spoilt third son; killed after plotting against his father

ADAM – the first man created; husband of Eve

BAAL – fertility god of Canaanites and Phoenicians

BATHSHEBA – mother of Solomon

BELSHAZZAR – last king of Babylon, son of Nebuchadnezzar; Daniel interpreted his vision of writing on the wall as foretelling the downfall of his kingdom

BENJAMIN – youngest son of Jacob and Rachel. His descendants formed one of the 12 tribes of Israel

CAIN – first son of Adam and Eve; murdered his brother Abel

DANIEL – prophet at the court of Nebuchadnezzar with a gift for interpreting dreams

DAVID – slayed the giant Goliath

DELILAH – a Philistine seducer and betrayer of Samson

ELIJAH – Hebrew prophet, taken into heaven in a fiery chariot

ELISHA – prophet and disciple of Elijah

ENOCH – father of Methuselah

EPHRAIM – son of Joseph; founded one of the 12 tribes of Israel

ESAU – elder of Isaac's twin sons; tricked out of his birthright by his younger brother Jacob

ESTHER – beautiful Israelite woman; heroically protected her people

EVE – first woman; created as companion for Adam in Garden of Eden

EZEKIEL – prophet of Israel captured by Babylonians

GIDEON – Israelite hero and judge

GOLIATH – Philistine giant killed by David

HEZEKIAH – king of Judah (c. 715–686 BC)

ISAAC – son of Abraham and Sarah, conceived in their old age; father of Jacob and Esau

ISAIAH – the greatest old testament prophet

ISHMAEL – Abraham's son by Hagar, hand-maiden to his wife, Sarah; rival of Isaac

ISRAEL – new name given to Jacob after his reconciliation with Esau

JACOB – second son of Isaac and Rebekah, younger twin of Esau whom he tricked out of his inheritance. The 12 tribes of Israel were named after his 12 descendents

JEREMIAH – one of the great prophets; foretold destruction of Jerusalem

JEZEBEL – cruel and lustful wife of Ahab, king of Israel

JOB – long-suffering and pious inhabitant of Uz

JONAH – after ignoring God's commands he was swallowed by a whale

JONATHAN – eldest son of Saul and close friend of David

JOSEPH – favourite son of Jacob and Rachel with his "coat of many colours"; sold into slavery by his jealous brothers

JOSHUA – succeeded Moses and led Israelites against Canaan. He defeated Jericho where the walls fell down

JUDAH – son of Jacob and Leah; founded tribe of Judah

LOT – nephew of Abraham; he escaped the destruction of Sodom, but his wife was turned into a pillar of salt for looking back

METHUSELAH – son of Enoch, the oldest person ever (969 years)

MIRIAM – sister of Aaron and Moses whom she looked after as a baby; prophetess and leader of Israelites

MOSES – Israel's great leader and lawgiver, he led the Israelites out of captivity in Egypt to the promised land of Canaan. Received ten commandments from Jehovah on Mt Sinai

NATHAN – Hebrew prophet at courts of David and Solomon

NEBUCHADNEZZAR – king of Babylon

NOAH – grandson of Methuselah, father of Shem, Ham, and Japheth; built ark to save his family and all animal species from the great flood

REBEKAH – wife of Isaac, mother of Jacob and Esau

RUTH – Moabite who accompanied her mother-in-law Naomi to Bethlehem. Remembered for her loyalty

SAMSON – Israelite judge of great physical strength; seduced and betrayed by Delilah

SAMUEL – prophet and judge of Israel

SARAH – wife of Abraham, mother of Isaac

SAUL – first king of Israel

SOLOMON – son of David and Bathsheba; remembered for his great wisdom and wealth

NEW TESTAMENT

ANDREW – fisherman and brother of Peter; one of 12 Apostles

BARABAS – Cypriot missionary; introduced Paul to the Church

BARABBAS – robber and murderer; in prison with Jesus and released instead of him

BARTHOLOMEW – possibly same person as Nathaniel, one of the 12 Apostles

CAIAPHAS – high priest of the Jews; Jesus brought to him after arrest

GABRIEL – angel who announced birth of Jesus to Mary; and of John the Baptist to Zechariah

HEROD – 1. the Great, ruled when Jesus was born 2. Antipas, son of Herod the Great, ruled when John the Baptist was murdered 3. Agrippa, killed James (brother of John) 4. Agrippa II, before whom Paul was tried

JAMES – 1. the Greater, one of 12 Apostles, brother of John 2. the Less, one of 12 Apostles 3. leader of the Church in Jerusalem and author of the New Testament epistle

JESUS – founder of Christianity

JOHN – youngest of 12 Apostles

JOHN THE BAPTIST – announced coming of Jesus, and baptized him

JOSEPH – 1. husband of Mary the mother of Jesus 2. of Arimathea, a secret disciple of Jesus

JUDAS ISCARIOT – the disciple who betrayed Jesus

LAZARUS – brother of Mary and Martha, raised from the dead by Jesus

LUKE – companion of Paul, author of Luke and Acts

MARK – author of the gospel; companion of Paul, Barnabas, and Peter

MARTHA – sister of Mary and Lazarus, friend of Jesus

MARY – 1. mother of Jesus 2. sister of Martha and Lazarus 3. Magdalene, cured by Jesus and the first to see him after the resurrection

MATTHEW – one of 12 Apostles, author of the gospel

MATTHIAS – chosen to replace the apostle Judas

MICHAEL – a chief archangel

NATHANIEL – *see* Bartholomew

NICODEMUS – a Pharisee who had a secret meeting with Jesus

PAUL – formerly Saul of Tarsus, persecutor of Christians; renamed after his conversion. Apostle to the Gentiles and author of epistles

PETER – Simon, one of 12 Apostles; denied Jesus before the crucifixion but later became leader of the Church

PHILIP – one of 12 Apostles

PILATE – Roman procurator of Judea; allowed Jesus to be crucified

SALOME – **1.** wife of Zebedee, mother of James and John **2.** daughter of Herodias; danced before Herod for the head of John the Baptist

SAUL – *see* Paul

SIMON – **1.** Simon Peter *see* Peter **2.** the Canaanite, one of 12 Apostles **3.** one of Jesus' four brothers **4.** the leper, in whose house Jesus was anointed **5.** of Cyrene, carried the cross of Jesus **6.** the tanner, in whose house Peter had his vision

STEPHEN – Christian martyr, stoned to death

THOMAS – one of 12 Apostles, named 'Doubting' because he doubted the resurrection

TIMOTHY – Paul's fellow missionary; two of Paul's epistles are to him

TITUS – convert and companion of Paul, who wrote him one epistle

PATRON SAINTS

NAME (Patron of)

AGATHA (bell-founders)

ALBERT THE GREAT (students of natural sciences)

ANDREW (Scotland)

BARBARA (gunners and miners)

BERNARD OF MONTJOUX (mountaineers)

CAMILLUS (nurses)

CASIMIR (Poland)

CECILIA (musicians)

CHRISTOPHER (wayfarers)

CRISPIN (shoemakers)

DAVID (Wales)

DIONYSIUS (DENIS) OF PARIS (France)

DUNSTAN (goldsmiths, jewellers, and locksmiths)

DYMPNA (insane)

ELIGIUS *or* ELOI (metalworkers)

ERASMUS (sailors)

FIACRE (gardeners)

FRANCES CABRINI (emigrants)

FRANCES OF ROME (motorists)

FRANCIS DE SALES (writers)

FRANCIS XAVIER (foreign missions)

FRIDESWIDE (Oxford)

GEORGE (England)

GILES (cripples)

HUBERT (huntsmen)

JEROME EMILIANI (orphans and abandoned children)

JOHN OF GOD (hospitals and booksellers)

JUDE (hopeless causes)

JULIAN (innkeepers, boatmen, travellers)

KATHERINE OF ALEXANDRIA (students, philosophers, and craftsmen)

LUKE (physicians and surgeons)

MARTHA (housewives)

NICHOLAS (children, sailors, unmarried girls, merchants, pawnbrokers, apothecaries, and perfumeries)

PATRICK (Ireland)

PETER NOLASCO (midwives)

SAVA (Serbian people)

VALENTINE (lovers)

VITUS (epilepsy and nervous diseases)

WENCESLAS (Czechoslovakia)

ZITA (domestic servants)

RELIGIOUS MOVEMENTS

3	3—continued	4	5
BON	ZEN	AINU	BOSCI
I AM			ISLAM

5—continued
KEGON
THAGS
THUGS
6
BABISM
PARSIS
QUAKER
SHINTO
TAOISM
VOODOO
7
AJIVIKA
BAHAISM
GIDEONS
JAINISM
JUDAISM
JUMPERS
LAMAISM
MORMONS
PARSEES
SHAKERS
SIKHISM
WAHABIS
ZIONISM

8
ABELIANS
ABELITES
ACOEMETI
ADAMITES
ADMADIYA
AHMADIYA
AMARITES
BAPTISTS
BUDDHISM
CATHOLIC
HINDUISM
HUMANISM
MAR THOMA
NICHIREN
NOSAIRIS
PURITANS
STUDITES
9
CALVINISM
CHUNTOKYO
FRANKISTS
HICKSITES
HUGUENOTS
JANSENISM
METHODIST

9—continued
PANTHEISM
10
ABSTINENTS
ADVENTISTS
AGONIZANTS
AMBROSIANS
BUCHANITES
CALIXTINES
11
ABODE OF LOVE
ABRAHAMITES
ANABAPTISTS
ANGLICANISM
ARMINIANISM
BASILIDEANS
BERNARDINES
COVENANTERS
12
ABECEDARIANS
BENEDICTINES
CHRISTIANITY
PRESBYTERIAN
SPIRITUALISM
UNITARIANISM

13
MOHAMMEDANISM
PROTESTANTISM
REDEMPTORISTS
ROMAN CATHOLIC
SALVATION ARMY
14
CONGREGATIONAL
FUNDAMENTALISM
16
ABYSSINIAN
  CHURCH
CHRISTIAN SCIENCE
MORAVIAN
  BRETHREN
PLYMOUTH
  BRETHREN
17
ANTIPAEDOBAP-
  TISTS
JEHOVAH'S
  WITNESSES

RELIGIOUS ORDERS

AUGUSTINIAN
BARNABITE
BENEDICTINE
BRIGITTINE
CAMALDOLESE
CAPUCHINS
CARMELITE

CARTHUSIAN
CISTERCIAN
DOMINICAN
FRANCISCAN
HOSPITALLERS
JERONYMITE
MINIMS

POOR CLARES
PREMONSTRATEN-
  SIAN
SALESIAN
SERVITE
SYLVESTRINE
TEMPLARS

THEATINE
TRAPPIST
TRINITARIAN
URSULINE
VISITANDINE,
  VISITATION

CLERGY

ARCHBISHOP
ARCHDEACON
BISHOP
CANON
CARDINAL

CHAPLAIN
CURATE
DEACON
DEAN

ELDER
MINISTER
PARSON
POPE

PRIEST
RECTOR
VICAR
VICAR-FORANE

POPES

POPE (DATE OF ACCESSION)

ST PETER (42)
ST LINUS (67)

ST ANACLETUS
  (Cletus) (76)

ST CLEMENT I (88)
ST EVARISTUS (97)

ST ALEXANDER I
  (105)

ST SIXTUS I (115)
ST TELESPHORUS
    (125)
ST HYGINUS (136)
ST PIUS I (140)
ST ANICETUS (155)
ST SOTERUS (166)
ST ELEUTHERIUS
    (175)
ST VICTOR I (189)
ST ZEPHYRINUS
    (199)
ST CALLISTUS I (217)
ST URBAN I (222)
ST PONTIAN (230)
ST ANTERUS (235)
ST FABIAN (236)
ST CORNELIUS (251)
ST LUCIUS I (253)
ST STEPHEN I (254)
ST SIXTUS II (257)
ST DIONYSIUS (259)
ST FELIX I (269)
ST EUTYCHIAN (275)
ST CAIUS (283)
ST MARCELLINUS
    (296)
ST MARCELLUS I
    (308)
ST EUSEBIUS (309)
ST MELCHIADES
    (311)
ST SYLVESTER I
    (314)
ST MARCUS (336)
ST JULIUS I (337)
LIBERIUS (352)
ST DAMASUS I (366)
ST SIRICIUS (384)
ST ANASTASIUS I
    (399)
ST INNOCENT I (401)
ST ZOSIMUS (417)
ST BONIFACE I (418)
ST CELESTINE I (422)
ST SIXTUS III (432)
ST LEO I (the Great)
    (440)
ST HILARY (461)
ST SIMPLICIUS (468)
ST FELIX III (483)
ST GELASIUS I (492)
ANASTASIUS II (496)
ST SYMMACHUS
    (498)
ST HORMISDAS (514)
ST JOHN I (523)
ST FELIX IV (526)
BONIFACE II (530)
JOHN II (533)
ST AGAPETUS I (535)

ST SILVERIUS (536)
VIGILIUS (537)
PELAGIUS I (556)
JOHN III (561)
BENEDICT I (575)
PELAGIUS II (579)
ST GREGORY I (the
    Great) (590)
SABINIANUS (604)
BONIFACE III (607)
ST BONIFACE IV
    (608)
ST DEUSDEDIT
    (Adeodatus I) (615)
BONIFACE V (619)
HONORIUS I (625)
SEVERINUS (640)
JOHN IV (640)
THEODORE I (642)
ST MARTIN I (649)
ST EUGENE I (654)
ST VITALIAN (657)
ADEODATUS II (672)
DONUS (676)
ST AGATHO (678)
ST LEO II (682)
ST BENEDICT II (684)
JOHN V (685)
CONON (686)
ST SERGIUS I (687)
JOHN VI (701)
JOHN VII (705)
SISINNIUS (708)
CONSTANTINE (708)
ST GREGORY II (715)
ST GREGORY III (731)
ST ZACHARY (741)
STEPHEN II (III)*
    (752)
ST PAUL I (757)
STEPHEN III (IV) (768)
ADRIAN I (772)
ST LEO III (795)
STEPHEN IV (V) (816)
ST PASCHAL I (817)
EUGENE II (824)
VALENTINE (827)
GREGORY IV (827)
SERGIUS II (844)
ST LEO IV (847)
BENEDICT III (855)
ST NICHOLAS I (858)
ADRIAN II (867)
JOHN VIII (872)
MARINUS I (882)
ST ADRIAN III (884)
STEPHEN V (VI) (885)
FORMOSUS (891)
BONIFACE VI (896)
STEPHEN VI (VII)
    (896)

ROMANUS (897)
THEODORE II (897)
JOHN IX (898)
BENEDICT IV (900)
LEO V (903)
SERGIUS III (904)
ANASTASIUS III (911)
LANDUS (913)
JOHN X (914)
LEO VI (928)
STEPHEN VII (VIII)
    (928)
JOHN XI (931)
LEO VII (936)
STEPHEN VIII (IX)
    (939)
MARINUS II (942)
AGAPETUS II (946)
JOHN XII (955)
LEO VIII (963)
BENEDICT V (964)
JOHN XIII (965)
BENEDICT VI (973)
BENEDICT VII (974)
JOHN XIV (983)
JOHN XV (985)
GREGORY V (996)
SYLVESTER II (999)
JOHN XVII (1003)
JOHN XVIII (1004)
SERGIUS IV (1009)
BENEDICT VIII (1012)
JOHN XIX (1024)
BENEDICT IX (1032)
GREGORY VI (1045)
CLEMENT II (1046)
BENEDICT IX (1047)
DAMASUS II (1048)
ST LEO IX (1049)
VICTOR II (1055)
STEPHEN IX (X)
    (1057)
NICHOLAS II (1059)
ALEXANDER II (1061)
ST GREGORY VII
    (1073)
VICTOR III (1086)
URBAN II (1088)
PASCHAL II (1099)
GELASIUS II (1118)
CALLISTUS II (1119)
HONORIUS II (1124)
INNOCENT II (1130)
CELESTINE II (1143)
LUCIUS II (1144)
EUGENE III (1145)
ANASTASIUS IV
    (1153)
ADRIAN IV (1154)
ALEXANDER III (1159)
LUCIUS III (1181)

URBAN III (1185)
GREGORY VIII (1187)
CLEMENT III (1187)
CELESTINE III (1191)
INNOCENT III (1198)
HONORIUS III (1216)
GREGORY IX (1227)
CELESTINE IV (1241)
INNOCENT IV (1243)
ALEXANDER IV
    (1254)
URBAN IV (1261)
CLEMENT IV (1265)
GREGORY X (1271)
INNOCENT V (1276)
ADRIAN V (1276)
JOHN XXI (1276)
NICHOLAS III (1277)
MARTIN IV (1281)
HONORIUS IV (1285)
NICHOLAS IV (1288)
ST CELESTINE V
    (1294)
BONIFACE VIII (1294)
BENEDICT XI (1303)
CLEMENT V (1305)
JOHN XXII (1316)
BENEDICT XII (1334)
CLEMENT VI (1342)
INNOCENT VI (1352)
URBAN V (1362)
GREGORY XI (1370)
URBAN VI (1378)
BONIFACE IX (1389)
INNOCENT VII (1404)
GREGORY XII (1406)
MARTIN V (1417)
EUGENE IV (1431)
NICHOLAS V (1447)
CALLISTUS III (1455)
PIUS II (1458)
PAUL II (1464)
SIXTUS IV (1471)
INNOCENT VIII (1484)
ALEXANDER VI
    (1492)
PIUS III (1503)
JULIUS II (1503)
LEO X (1513)
ADRIAN VI (1522)
CLEMENT VII (1523)
PAUL III (1534)
JULIUS III (1550)
MARCELLUS II (1555)
PAUL IV (1555)
PIUS IV (1559)
ST PIUS V (1566)
GREGORY XIII (1572)
SIXTUS V (1585)
URBAN VII (1590)
GREGORY XIV (1590)

INNOCENT IX (1591)
CLEMENT VIII (1592)
LEO XI (1605)
PAUL V (1605)
GREGORY XV (1621)
URBAN VIII (1623)
INNOCENT X (1644)
ALEXANDER VII
  (1655)
CLEMENT IX (1667)
CLEMENT X (1670)
INNOCENT XI (1676)

ALEXANDER VIII
  (1689)
INNOCENT XII (1691)
CLEMENT XI (1700)
INNOCENT XIII (1721)
BENEDICT XIII (1724)
CLEMENT XII (1730)
BENEDICT XIV (1740)
CLEMENT XIII (1758)
CLEMENT XIV (1769)
PIUS VI (1775)

PIUS VII (1800)
LEO XII (1823)
PIUS VIII (1829)
GREGORY XVI (1831)
PIUS IX (1846)
LEO XIII (1878)
ST PIUS X (1903)
BENEDICT XV (1914)
PIUS XI (1922)
PIUS XII (1939)
JOHN XXIII (1958)

PAUL VI (1963)
JOHN PAUL I (1978)
JOHN PAUL II (1978)

*Stephen II died
  before consecration
  and was dropped
  from the list of
  popes in 1961;
  Stephen III became
  Stephen II

ARCHBISHOPS OF CANTERBURY

ARCHBISHOP (DATE OF ACCESSION)

AUGUSTINE (597)
LAURENTIUS (604)
MELLITUS (619)
JUSTUS (624)
HONORIUS (627)
DEUSDEDIT (655)
THEODORUS (668)
BEORHTWEALD (693)
TATWINE (731)
NOTHELM (735)
CUTHBEORHT (740)
BREGUWINE (761)
JAENBEORHT (765)
ÆTHELHEARD (793)
WULFRED (805)
FEOLOGILD (832)
CEOLNOTH (833)
ÆTHELRED (870)
PLEGMUND (890)
ÆTHELHELM (914)
WULFHELM (923)
ODA (942)
ÆLFSIGE (959)
BEORHTHELM (959)
DUNSTAN (960)
ÆTHELGAR (988)
SIGERIC SERIO (990)
ÆLFRIC (995)
ÆLFHEAH (1005)
LYFING (1013)
ÆTHELNOTH (1020)
EADSIGE (1038)
ROBERT OF
  JUMIÈGES (1051)
STIGAND (1052)
LANFRANC (1070)
ANSELM (1093)
RALPH D'ESCURES
  (1114)
WILLIAM OF
  CORBEIL (1123)

THEOBALD OF BEC
  (1139)
THOMAS BECKET
  (1162)
RICHARD OF DOVER
  (1174)
BALDWIN (1184)
REGINALD
  FITZJOCELIN
  (1191)
HUBERT WALTER
  (1193)
REGINALD (1205)
JOHN DE GRAY
  (1205)
STEPHEN LANGTON
  (1213)
WALTER OF
  EVESHAM (1128)
RICHARD GRANT
  (Wethershed) (1229)
RALPH NEVILL (1231)
JOHN OF
  SITTINGBOURNE
  (1232)
JOHN BLUND (1232)
EDMUND RICH (1234)
BONIFACE OF
  SAVOY (1245)
ADAM OF
  CHILLENDEN
  (1270)
ROBERT KILWARDBY
  (1273)
ROBERT BURNELL
  (1278)
JOHN PECHAM
  (1279)
ROBERT
  WINCHELSEY
  (1295)

THOMAS COBHAM
  (1313)
WALTER REYNOLDS
  (1314)
SIMON MEPHAM
  (1328)
JOHN STRATFORD
  (1334)
JOHN OFFORD (1348)
THOMAS
  BRADWARDINE
  (1349)
SIMON ISLIP (1349)
SIMON LANGHAM
  (1366)
WILLIAM
  WHITTLESEY
  (1369)
SIMON SUDBURY
  (1375)
WILLIAM
  COURTENAY
  (1381)
THOMAS ARUNDEL
  (1397)
ROGER WALDEN
  (1398)
THOMAS ARUNDEL
  (1399)
HENRY CHICHELE
  (1414)
JOHN STAFFORD
  (1443)
JOHN KEMPE (1452)
THOMAS
  BOURGCHIER
  (1454)
JOHN MORTON
  (1486)
HENRY DEANE
  (1501)

WILLIAM WARHAM
  (1504)
THOMAS CRANMER
  (1533)
REGINALD POLE
  (1556)
MATTHEW PARKER
  (1559)
EDMUND GRINDAL
  (1576)
JOHN WHITGIFT
  (1583)
RICHARD BANCROFT
  (1604)
GEORGE ABBOT
  (1611)
WILLIAM LAUD (1633)
WILLIAM JUXON
  (1660)
GILBERT SHELDON
  (1663)
WILLIAM SANCROFT
  (1678)
JOHN TILLOTSON
  (1691)
THOMAS TENISON
  (1695)
WILLIAM WAKE
  (1716)
JOHN POTTER (1737)
THOMAS HERRING
  (1747)
MATTHEW HUTTON
  (1757)
THOMAS SECKER
  (1758)
FREDERICK
  CORNWALLIS
  (1768)
JOHN MOORE (1783)

CHARLES MANNERS SUTTON (1805)
WILLIAM HOWLEY (1828)
JOHN BIRD SUMNER (1848)
CHARLES THOMAS LONGLEY (1862)

ARCHIBALD CAMPBELL TAIT (1868)
EDWARD WHITE BENSON (1883)
FREDERICK TEMPLE (1896)
RANDALL THOMAS DAVIDSON (1903)

COSMO GORDON LANG (1928)
GEOFFREY FRANCIS FISHER (1945)
ARTHUR MICHAEL RAMSEY (1961)
FREDERICK DONALD COGGAN (1974)

ROBERT ALEXANDER KENNEDY RUNCIE (1980)

RELIGIOUS TERMS

2	5	5—continued	6—continued
BA	ABBOT	SYNOD	MANTRA
HO	ABYSS	TOTEM	MATINS
OM	AGATI	USHER	MISSAL
3	AISLE	VEDAS	NIGGUN
ALB	ALLEY	WAFER	NIMBUS
ARA	ALTAR	**6**	ORATIO
AUM	AMBRY	ABBACY	ORISON
HAJ	AMICE	ABODAH	PARVIS
PEW	ANGEL	ADVENT	PESACH
PIX	APRON	AGUNAH	PRAYER
PYX	ARMOR	AHIMSA	PULPIT
YAD	BANNS	AKASHA	ROCHET
4	BASON	AKEDAH	ROSARY
AMBO	BEADS	AL CHET	SANGHA
APSE	BIBLE	ANOINT	SERMON
AZAN	BIMAH	ANTHEM	SERVER
BEMA	BODHI	AUMBRY	SHARI'A
BUJI	BRIEF	AVODAH	SHRIVE
BULL	BUGIA	BARSOM	SPIRIT
COPE	BURSE	BAT KOL	SUTRAS
COWL	COTTA	BEADLE	TAUHID
FONT	CREED	BELFRY	TIPPET
HADJ	CROSS	CANTOR	VERGER
HAJJ	CRUET	CHOHAN	VESTRY
HALO	DIKKA	CHOVAH	**7**
HELL	EMETH	CHRISM	ACCIDIA
HOOD	EPHOD	CLERGY	ACCIDIE
HOST	FALDA	DHARMA	ACOLYTE
HYMN	GOHEI	DHYANA	AGRAPHA
JUBE	HYLIC	DITTHI	AMPULLA
KAMA	IHRAM	DOSSAL	ANGELUS
KNOP	KALPA	DUCHAN	APOSTIL
LENT	KARMA	EASTER	APOSTLE
MACE	LAVER	FLECHE	APPAREL
MASS	LIMBO	FRATER	ASHAMNU
NAOS	MOTZI	GLORIA	ATHEISM
NAVE	NICHE	HEAVEN	AUREOLE
OLAH	PASCH	HEKHAL	BADCHAN
RAMA	PESAH	HESPED	BANKERS
SOMA	PESHA	KAIROS	BAPTISM
TIEN	PSALM	KIBLAH	BATHING
VOID	ROSHI	KISMET	BELL COT
WAKE	SHIVA	KITTEL	BERAKAH
YOGA	STOUP	LITANY	BIRETTA

7—continued

CASSOCK
CHALICE
CHAMETZ
CHANCEL
CHANTRY
CHAPTER
CHAZZAN
CHRISOM
COLLECT
COMPLIN
CORNICE
CROSIER
CROZIER
DHARANI
DIOCESE
DIPTYCH
EILETON
FISTULA
GAYATRI
GELILAH
GEULLAH
GRADINE
GREMIAL
HASSOCK
HEATHEN
HEKDESH
INTROIT
KHEREBU
LECTERN
LOCULUS
MANIPLE
MINARET
MOZETTA
NARTHEX
NIRVANA
NOCTURN
PALLIUM
PENANCE
PILGRIM
PURUSHA
REQUIEM
REREDOS
SAMSARA
STHIBEL
TALLITH
TONSURE

7—continued

TRINITY
TZADDIK
VESPERS
WORSHIP

8

ABLUTION
ABSTEMII
A CAPELLA
AFFLATUS
AFFUSION
AFIKOMEN
AGNUS DEI
ANTIPHON
ARMORIUM
AUTO DA FE
AVE MARIA
BEADROLL
BELL COTE
BEMIDBAR
BENEFICE
BREVIARY
BUTSUDEN
CANCELLI
CANTICLE
CIBORIUM
CINCTURE
COMPLINE
CONCLAVE
CORPORAL
CRUCIFIX
DALMATIC
DIKERION
DISCIPLE
DOXOLOGY
EPIPHANY
EVENSONG
FRONTLET
HABDALAH
MANIPULE
NATIVITY
NER TAMID
NIVARANA
OBLATION
PAROKHET
PASSOVER
PREDELLA

8—continued

RESPONSE
SACRISTY
SURPLICE
TASHLICH
TRIPTYCH
VESTMENT

9

ADIAPHORA
ANAMNESIS
APOCRYPHA
ARBA KOSOT
ARCHANGEL
ASPERSION
CANDLEMAS
CARTOUCHE
CATACOMBS
CATECHISM
CERECLOTH
CHALITZAH
CHRISTMAS
COLLATION
COMMUNION
EPHPHETHA
EUCHARIST
FALDSTOOL
FLABELLUM
FORMULARY
MUNDATORY
OFFERTORY
PACE-AISLE
PURGATORY
SANCTUARY
YOM KIPPUR

10

ABSOLUTION
AGATHOLOGY
ALLOCUTION
AMBULATORY
ANTECHAPEL
APOCALYPSE
BALDACHINO
BAR MITZVAH
BAS MITZVAH
BAT MITZVAH
BENEDICTUS

10—continued

CATAFALQUE
CLERESTORY
CUTTY STOOL
HAGIOSCOPE
INDULGENCE
INTINCTION
INVOCATION
LADY CHAPEL
PRESBYTERY
SEXAGESIMA

11

ABBREVIATOR
ABOMINATION
AGNOSTICISM
ALITURGICAL
ANTEPENDIUM
ANTIMINSION
ASPERGILLUM
BENEDICTION
CHRISTENING
HUMERAL VEIL
INQUISITION
INVESTITURE
SCRIPTORIUM

12

ANTILEGOMENA
ARON HA-KODESH
ASH WEDNESDAY
CONFIRMATION
CONGREGATION
SEPTUAGESIMA

13

BEATIFICATION
BIRKAT HA-MAZON
EPITRACHELION

14

FOLDED CHASUBLE
MAUNDY THURSDAY

17

CONSUBSTANTIA-
TION

RELIGIOUS BUILDINGS

3

WAT

4

CELL
KIRK

5

ABBEY

5—continued

BET AM
CELLA
DUOMO
HONDO
JINGU
JINJA

6

CHAPEL
CHURCH
MOSQUE
PAGODA
PRIORY

7

CHANTRY
CONVENT
DEANERY
MINSTER

8

BASILICA

8—continued	9	12	13
CLOISTER	BADRINATH	BET HA-KNESSET	ANGELUS TEMPLE
HOUNFORT	CATHEDRAL	BET HA-MIDRASH	
LAMASERY	MONASTERY	CHAPTER HOUSE	
	SYNAGOGUE	MEETINGHOUSE	

HINDU DEITIES

BRAHMA - the Creator
SHIVA - the Destroyer
VISHNU - the Preserver
INDRA - king of the gods; god of war and storm
AGNI - god of fire
AHI or IHI - the Sistrum Player
AMRITA - water of life
YAMA - king of the dead
VARUNA - god of water
SURYA - the sun-god
VAYU - god of the wind
KUBERA - god of wealth; guardian of the north
KARTTIKEYA - war-god; god of bravery
VISVAKARMA - architect for the gods
KAMA - god of desire
SARASVATI - goddess of speech
LAKSHMI - goddess of fortune

DEVI - a mother goddess
ADITI - goddess of heaven; mother of the gods
SARANYU - goddess of the clouds
PRITHIVI - earth-goddess; goddess of fertility
DITI - mother of the demons
MANASA - sacred mountain and lake
SHITALA - goddess of smallpox
GANESHA - god of literature, wisdom, and prosperity
GARUDA - the devourer, identified with fire and the sun
HANUMAN - a monkey chief
SUGRIVA - monkey king
BALI - demon who became king of heaven and earth
AMARAVATI - city of the gods
GANDHARVAS - celestial musicians
JYESTHA - goddess of misfortune
SOMA - ambrosial offering to the gods

GREEK AND ROMAN MYTHOLOGY

Mythological Characters

ACHILLES – Greek hero; invulnerable except for his heel
ADONIS – renowned for his beauty
AGAMEMNON – king of Mycenae
AJAX – Greek warrior
ATLAS – bore heaven on his shoulders
BELLEROPHON – Corinthian hero who rode winged horse Pegasus
BOREAS – the north wind
CERBERUS – three-headed dog, guarded Hades
CHARON – boatman who rowed dead across river Styx
CHARYBDIS – violent whirlpool
CIRCE – sorceress who had the power to turn men into beasts
CYCLOPS – one of a race of one-eyed giants (cyclopes)
DAEDALUS – craftsman; designed and built the labyrinth in Crete

GORGONS – three sisters (Stheno, Euryale, and Medusa) who had snakes for hair and whose appearance turned people to stone
HADES – the Underworld
HELEN OF TROY – famed for her beauty; cause of Trojan war
HERACLES – famed for his courage and strength; performed the twelve labours
HERCULES – Roman name for HERACLES
HYDRA – many-headed snake
JASON – led the Argonauts in search of the Golden Fleece
LETHE – river in Hades whose water caused forgetfulness
MIDAS – King of Phrygia whose touch turned everything to gold
MINOTAUR – monster with the head of a bull and the body of a man. It was kept in the Cretan labyrinth and fed with human flesh
NARCISSUS – beautiful youth who fell in love with his own reflection
ODYSSEUS – Greek hero of the Trojan war

OEDIPUS – king of Thebes; married his
mother

OLYMPUS – a mountain; the home of the
gods

ORPHEUS – skilled musician

PANDORA – the first woman; opened the box
that released all varieties of evil

PERSEUS – Greek hero who killed the
Gorgon Medusa

POLYPHEMUS – leader of the Cyclopes

ROMULUS – founder of Rome

SATYRS – hoofed spirits of forests, fields,
and streams

SCYLLA – six-headed sea monster

SIBYL – a prophetess

SIRENS – creatures depicted as half women,
half birds, who lured sailors to their deaths

STYX – main river of Hades, across which
Charon ferried the souls of the dead

THESEUS – Greek hero who killed the Cretan
Minotaur

ULYSSES – Roman name for ODYSSEUS

GREEK GODS (ROMAN EQUIVALENT)

APHRODITE – goddess of beauty and love
(VENUS)

APOLLO – god of poetry, music, and
prophecy (APOLLO)

ARES – god of war (MARS)

ARTEMIS – goddess of the moon (DIANA)

ASCLEPIUS – god of medical art
(AESCULAPIUS)

ATHENE – goddess of wisdom (MINERVA)

CHARITES – 3 daughters of Zeus:
Euphrosyne, Aglaia, and Thalia; personified
grace, beauty, and charm (GRACES)

CRONOS – god of agriculture (SATURN)

DEMETER – goddess of agriculture (CERES)

DIONYSUS – god of wine and fertility
(BACCHUS)

EOS – goddess of dawn (AURORA)

EROS – god of love (CUPID)

FATES – 3 goddesses who determine man's
destiny: Clotho, Lachesis, and Atropos

HEBE – goddess of youth (JUVENTAS)

HECATE – goddess of witchcraft (HECATE)

HELIOS – god of the sun (SOL)

HEPHAESTUS – god of destructive fire
(VULCAN)

HERA – queen of heaven, goddess of women
and marriage (JUNO)

HERMES – messenger of gods (MERCURY)

HESTIA – goddess of the hearth (VESTA)

HYPNOS – god of sleep (SOMNUS)

NEMESIS – goddess of retribution

PAN – god of woods and fields (FAUNUS)

PERSEPHONE – goddess of the Underworld
(PROSERPINE)

PLUTO – god of the Underworld (PLUTO)

PLUTUS – god of wealth

POSEIDON – god of the sea (NEPTUNE)

RHEA – goddess of nature (CYBELE)

SELENE – goddess of the moon (LUNA)

THANATOS – god of death (MORS)

ZEUS – supreme god; god of sky and weather
(JUPITER)

**ROMAN GODS
(GREEK EQUIVALENT)**

AESCULAPIUS
(ASCLEPIUS)

APOLLO (APOLLO)

AURORA (EOS)

BACCHUS
(DIONYSUS)

CERES (DEMETER)

CUPID (EROS)

CYBELE (RHEA)

DIANA (ARTEMIS)

FAUNUS (PAN)

GRACES (CHARITES)

HECATE (HECATE)

JUNO (HERA)

JUPITER (ZEUS)

JUVENTAS (HEBE)

LUNA (SELENE)

MARS (ARES)

MERCURY (HERMES)

MINERVA (ATHENE)

MORS (THANATOS)

NEPTUNE
(POSEIDON)

PLUTO (PLUTO)

PROSERPINE
(PERSEPHONE)

SATURN (CRONOS)

SOL (HELIOS)

SOMNUS (HYPNOS)

VENUS (APHRODITE)

VESTA (HESTIA)

VULCAN
(HEPHAESTUS)

THE NINE MUSES

CALLIOPE (EPIC
POETRY)

CLIO (HISTORY)

ERATO (LOVE
POETRY)

EUTERPE (LYRIC
POETRY)

MELPOMENE
(TRAGEDY)

POLYHYMNIA
(SACRED SONG)

TERPSICHORE
(DANCING)

THALIA (COMEDY)

URANIA
(ASTRONOMY)

**THE TWELVE
LABOURS OF
HERCULES**

THE NEMEAN LION

THE LERNAEAN
HYDRA

THE WILD BOAR OF
ERYMANTHUS

THE STYMPHALIAN
BIRDS

THE CERYNEIAN
HIND

THE AUGEAN
STABLES

THE CRETAN BULL

THE MARES OF
DIOMEDES

THE GIRDLE OF
HIPPOLYTE

THE CATTLE OF
GERYON

THE GOLDEN
APPLES OF THE
HESPERIDES

THE CAPTURE OF
CERBERUS

NORSE MYTHOLOGY

AEGIR — god of the sea

ALFHEIM — part of Asgard inhabited by the light elves

ASGARD — the home of the gods

ASK — name of the first man created, from a fallen tree

BALDER — god of the summer sun

BRAGI — god of poetry

EIR — goddess of healing

EMBLA — name of first woman, created from a fallen tree

FORSETI — god of justice

FREY — god of fertility and crops

FREYJA — goddess of love and night

FRIGG — Odin's wife; supreme goddess

GUNGNIR — Odin's magic spear

HEIMDAL — guardian of Asgard

HEL — goddess of the dead

HÖDUR — god of night

IDUN — wife of Bragi; guardian of the golden apples of youth

LOKI — god of evil

MIDGARD — the world of men

NORNS — three goddesses of destiny: Urd (Fate), Skuld (Being), and Verdandi (Necessity)

ODIN — supreme god; god of battle, inspiration, and death

RAGNAROK — final battle between gods and giants, in which virtually all life is destroyed

SIF — wife of Thor; her golden hair was cut off by Loki

SLEIPNIR — Odin's eight-legged horse

THOR — god of thunder

TYR — god of war

VALHALLA — hall in Asgard where Odin welcomed the souls of heroes killed in battle

VALKYRIES — nine handmaidens of Odin who chose men doomed to die in battle

YGGDRASILL — the World Tree, an ash linking all the worlds

YMIR — giant from whose body the world was formed

EGYPTIAN MYTHOLOGY

AMON-RA — supreme god

ANUBIS — jackel-headed son of Osiris; god of the dead

BES — god of marriage

GEB — earth-god

HATHOR — cow-headed goddess of love

HORUS — hawk-headed god of light

ISIS — goddess of fertility

MAAT — goddess of law, truth, and justice

MONT — god of war

MUT — wife of Amon-Ra

NEHEH — god of eternity

NUN or NU — the primordial Ocean

NUT — goddess of the sky

OSIRIS — ruler of the afterlife

PTAH — god of the arts

RA — the sun god

RENPET — goddess of youth

SEKHMET — goddess of war

SET or SETH — god of evil

SHU — god of air

TEFNUT — goddess of dew and rain

THOTH — god of wisdom

UPUAUT — warrior-god; god of the dead

ARTHURIAN LEGEND

ARTHUR — legendary British leader of the Knights of the Round Table

AVALON — paradise

CAMELOT — capital of Arthur's kingdom

EXCALIBUR — Arthur's magic sword

GALAHAD — son of Lancelot; purest of the Knights of the Round Table; succeeded in the quest of the Grail

GAWAIN — nephew of Arthur, son of Morgan Le Fay; searched for the Grail

GRAIL (SANGREAL, THE HOLY GRAIL) –
said to be the vessel of the Last Supper; in
the custody of the Fisher King

GUINEVERE – wife of Arthur, lover of
Lancelot

KAY – foster brother of Arthur

LANCELOT *or* LAUNCELOT – knight and
lover of Queen Guinevere

MERLIN – magician and bard who prepared
Arthur for kingship

MODRED *or* MORDRED – nephew of Arthur,
son of Morgan Le Fay

MORGAN LE FAY – sorceress and healer;
sister of Arthur

PERCIVAL *or* PERCEVAL –knight who vowed
to seek the Grail

UTHER PENDRAGON – father of Arthur

VIVIANE – the Lady of the Lake

WORK

PROFESSIONS, TRADES, AND OCCUPATIONS

2	5—continued	5—continued	6—continued
GP	BAKER	QUILL	BUSKER
MD	BONZE	RABBI	BUTLER
MO	BOOTS	RATER	CABBIE
PA	BOSUN	REEVE	CABMAN
PM	CADDY	RUNER	CALKER
3	CHOIR	SCOUT	CANNER
DOC	CLERK	SEWER	CARTER
DON	CLOWN	SHOER	CARVER
GYP	COACH	SLAVE	CASUAL
PRO	COMIC	SMITH	CENSOR
REP	CRIER	SOWER	CLERGY
SPY	CRIMP	STAFF	CLERIC
VET	CURER	SWEEP	CODIST
4	DAILY	TAMER	COINER
AMAH	ENVOY	TAWER	COMBER
AYAH	EXTRA	TAXER	CONDER
BABU	FAKIR	TILER	COOLIE
BARD	FENCE	TUNER	COOPER
BOSS	FIFER	TUTOR	COPPER
CHAR	FILER	TYLER	CO-STAR
CHEF	FINER	USHER	COSTER
COOK	FLIER	VALET	COWBOY
CREW	GIPSY	VINER	COWMAN
DIVA	GLUER	**6**	CRITIC
DYER	GROOM	AIRMAN	CUTLER
GANG	GUARD	ARCHER	CUTTER
GRIP	GUIDE	ARTIST	DANCER
HACK	GUILD	AURIST	DEALER
HAND	HAKIM	AUTHOR	DIGGER
HEAD	HARPY	BAGMAN	DOCKER
HERD	HELOT	BAILER	DOCTOR
HIND	HIRER	BAILOR	DOWSER
MAGI	HIVER	BALKER	DRAPER
MAID	HOPPO	BANKER	DRAWER
MATE	LAMIA	BARBER	DRIVER
MIME	LEECH	BARGEE	DROVER
PAGE	LUTER	BARKER	EDITOR
PEON	MASON	BARMAN	FABLER
POET	MEDIC	BATMAN	FACTOR
SEER	MINER	BEARER	FARMER
SERF	NAVVY	BINDER	FELLER
SYCE	NURSE	BOFFIN	FICTOR
TOUT	OILER	BOOKIE	FISHER
WARD	OWLER	BOWMAN	FITTER
WHIP	PILOT	BREWER	FLAYER
5	PIPER	BROKER	FORGER
ACTOR	PLYER	BUGLER	FOWLER
AD-MAN	PUPIL	BURLER	FRAMER
AGENT	QUACK	BURSAR	FULLER

6—continued	6—continued	6—continued	6—continued
GAFFER	MUMPER	SERVER	WEEDER
GANGER	MYSTIC	SETTER	WELDER
GAOLER	NAILER	SEXTON	WHALER
GAUCHO	NOTARY	SHROFF	WORKER
GAUGER	NURSER	SINGER	WRIGHT
GIGOLO	OBOIST	SIRCAR	WRITER
GILDER	OILMAN	SKIVVY	**7**
GILLIE	ORATOR	SLATER	ABACIST
GLAZER	OSTLER	SLAVER	ABIGAIL
GLOVER	PACKER	SLAVEY	ACOLYTE
GRAVER	PARSON	SLEUTH	ACOLYTH
GROCER	PASTOR	SNARER	ACROBAT
GUIDER	PAVIER	SOCMAN	ACTRESS
GUIDON	PAVIOR	SORTER	ACTUARY
GUNMAN	PEDANT	SOUTER	ALEWIFE
GUNNER	PEDLAR	SPICER	ALMONER
HARPER	PENMAN	SQUIRE	ANALYST
HATTER	PICKER	STAGER	APPOSER
HAWKER	PIEMAN	STOKER	ARABIST
HEALER	PIRATE	STORER	ARBITER
HEAVER	PITMAN	SUTLER	ARTISAN
HODMAN	PLATER	TABLER	ARTISTE
HOOPER	PLAYER	TAILOR	ASSAYER
HORNER	PORTER	TAMPER	ASSIZER
HOSIER	POTBOY	TANNER	ASSURED
HUNTER	POTTER	TASKER	ASSURER
INTERN	PRIEST	TASTER	AUDITOR
ISSUER	PRUNER	TELLER	AVIATOR
JAILER	PURSER	TERMER	AWARDER
JAILOR	QUERRY	TESTER	BAILIFF
JOBBER	RABBIN	TILLER	BANDMAN
JOCKEY	RAGMAN	TINKER	BARMAID
JOINER	RANGER	TINMAN	BELLBOY
JOWTER	RATTER	TINNER	BELLHOP
JURIST	READER	TOLLER	BEST BOY
KEELER	REAPER	TOUTER	BIRDMAN
KEEPER	REAVER	TRACER	BLASTER
KILLER	RECTOR	TRADER	BLENDER
LACKEY	REGENT	TUBMAN	BOATMAN
LANDER	RELIEF	TURNER	BONDMAN
LASCAR	RENTER	TYCOON	BOOKMAN
LAWYER	RIGGER	TYPIST	BOTTLER
LECTOR	RINGER	USURER	BRIGAND
LENDER	ROBBER	VACHER	BUILDER
LOADER	ROOFER	VALUER	BURGLAR
LOGMAN	ROOTER	VAMPER	BUTCHER
LUMPER	SACKER	VANMAN	BUTTONS
MARKER	SAILOR	VASSAL	CALLBOY
MATRON	SALTER	VENDER	CAMBIST
MEDICO	SALVOR	VENDOR	CARRIER
MENDER	SAPPER	VERGER	CASEMAN
MENIAL	SARTOR	VERSER	CASHIER
MENTOR	SAWYER	VIEWER	CATERER
MERCER	SCRIBE	WAITER	CAULKER
MILKER	SEA-DOG	WALLER	CELLIST
MILLER	SEALER	WARDEN	CHANTER
MINTER	SEAMAN	WARDER	CHAPMAN
MONGER	SEINER	WARPER	CHEMIST
MORISK	SEIZOR	WASHER	CHORIST
MUMMER	SELLER	WEAVER	CLEANER

7—continued	**7—continued**	**7—continued**	**7—continued**
CLICKER	GRAINER	PEDDLER	TAXI-MAN
CLIPPIE	GRANGER	PIANIST	TEACHER
COALMAN	GRANTEE	PICADOR	TIPSTER
COBBLER	GRANTOR	PLANNER	TRACKER
COCKLER	GRAZIER	PLANTER	TRAINER
COLLIER	GRINDER	PLEADER	TRAPPER
CO-PILOT	GYMNAST	PLUMBER	TRAWLER
COPYIST	HACKLER	POACHER	TRIMMER
CORONER	HARPIST	POSTBOY	TRUCKER
CORSAIR	HAULIER	POSTMAN	TRUSTEE
COUNSEL	HELOTRY	PRESSER	TUMBLER
COURIER	HERBIST	PRESTOR	TURNKEY
COWHERD	HERDMAN	PRINTER	VINTNER
COWPOKE	HERITOR	PUDDLER	VIOLIST
CROFTER	HIGGLER	RANCHER	WAGONER
CROPPER	HOGHERD	REALTOR	WARRIOR
CURATOR	HOSTLER	REFINER	WEBSTER
CURRIER	INDEXER	RIVETER	WEIGHER
CUSTODE	INLAYER	ROADMAN	WHEELER
DANSEUR	IRONIST	ROASTER	WHETTER
DENTIST	JANITOR	RUSTLER	WIREMAN
DIALIST	JUGGLER	SACRIST	WOODMAN
DIETIST	JUNKMAN	SADDLER	WOOLMAN
DITCHER	JURYMAN	SAMPLER	WORKMAN
DOMINIE	KEELMAN	SAMURAI	WRAPPER
DOORMAN	KNACKER	SCOURER	**8**
DRAGMAN	KNITTER	SCRAPER	ADSCRIPT
DRAPIER	LACEMAN	SERVANT	AERONAUT
DRAWBOY	LINKBOY	SETTLER	ALGERINE
DRAYMAN	LINKMAN	SHARPER	ANALYSER
DREDGER	LOCKMAN	SHEARER	APHORIST
DRESSER	LOMBARD	SHIPPER	APIARIST
DROGMAN	MALTMAN	SHOPBOY	APRON-MAN
DRUMMER	MANAGER	SHOWMAN	ARBORIST
DUSTMAN	MANGLER	SHUNTER	ARMORIST
FARRIER	MARBLER	SILKMAN	ARMOURER
FASCIST	MARCHER	SIMPLER	ARRESTOR
FIDDLER	MARINER	SKINNER	ASSESSOR
FIREMAN	MARSHAL	SKIPPER	ATTORNEY
FLESHER	MATADOR	SLIPPER	BAGMAKER
FLORIST	MATELOT	SMELTER	BAGPIPER
FLUNKEY	MEALMAN	SNIPPER	BANDSMAN
FLUTIST	MEATMAN	SOCAGER	BARGEMAN
FOOTBOY	MIDWIFE	SOLDIER	BEARHERD
FOOTMAN	MILKMAN	SOLOIST	BEDESMAN
FOOTPAD	MODISTE	SPENCER	BEDMAKER
FOREMAN	MONEYER	SPINNER	BIT-MAKER
FOUNDER	MONITOR	SPOTTER	BLEACHER
FRISEUR	MOOTMAN	STAINER	BOATSMAN
FROGMAN	MOULDER	STAMPER	BONDMAID
FUELLER	NEWSBOY	STAPLER	BONDSMAN
FURRIER	OCULIST	STATIST	BOTANIST
GATEMAN	OFFICER	STEERER	BOWMAKER
GIRDLER	ORDERER	STEWARD	BOXMAKER
GLAZIER	ORDERLY	SURGEON	BREWSTER
GLEANER	PACKMAN	SWABBER	BROACHER
GLEEMAN	PAGEBOY	SWEEPER	CABIN BOY
GLOSSER	PAINTER	TABORER	CELLARER
GRAFFER	PALMIST	TALLIER	CERAMIST
GRAFTER	PANTLER	TAPSTER	CHANDLER

8—continued	8—continued	8—continued	8—continued
CHOIRBOY	GANGSTER	MILLHAND	RIVETTER
CIDERIST	GARDENER	MILLINER	ROMANCER
CLAQUEUR	GAVELMAN	MINISTER	RUGMAKER
CLOTHIER	GENDARME	MINSTREL	RUMOURER
COACHMAN	GLASSMAN	MODELLER	SALESMAN
CO-AUTHOR	GOATHERD	MULETEER	SATIRIST
CODIFIER	GODSMITH	MURALIST	SAWBONES
COISTRIL	GOSSIPER	MUSICIAN	SCULLION
COLLATOR	GOVERNOR	NEWSHAWK	SCULPTOR
COMEDIAN	GUARDIAN	NOVELIST	SEAMSTER
COMPILER	GUNSMITH	ONION-MAN	SEA-ROVER
COMPOSER	HAMMERER	OPERATOR	SEASONER
CONCLAVE	HANDMAID	OPTICIAN	SEEDSMAN
CONJURER	HANDYMAN	ORDAINER	SEMPSTER
CONVEYOR	HATMAKER	ORDINAND	SERVITOR
COURTIER	HAYMAKER	ORGANIST	SHEARMAN
COW-LEECH	HEAD COOK	OUTRIDER	SHEPHERD
COXSWAIN	HEADSMAN	OVERSEER	SHIPMATE
CROUPIER	HELMSMAN	PARGETER	SHIP'S BOY
CUTPURSE	HENCHMAN	PARODIST	SHOPGIRL
DAIRYMAN	HERDSMAN	PENMAKER	SHOWGIRL
DANSEUSE	HIRELING	PERFUMER	SIDESMAN
DECKHAND	HISTRION	PETERMAN	SIMPLIST
DEFENDER	HOME HELP	PEWTERER	SKETCHER
DESIGNER	HOTELIER	PICAROON	SMUGGLER
DIRECTOR	HOUSEBOY	PLOUGHER	SOLDIERY
DOG-LEECH	HUCKSTER	POLISHER	SPACEMAN
DOMESTIC	HUNTSMAN	PORTRESS	SPEARMAN
DOUGHBOY	IMPORTER	POSTILER	SPEEDCOP
DRAGOMAN	IMPROVER	POTMAKER	SPURRIER
DRUGGIST	INKMAKER	PREACHER	STARCHER
EDUCATOR	INVENTOR	PREFACER	STITCHER
EMBALMER	JAPANNER	PRELUDER	STOCKMAN
EMISSARY	JET PILOT	PRESSMAN	STOREMAN
ENGINEER	JEWELLER	PROBATOR	STRIPPER
ENGRAVER	JONGLEUR	PROCURER	STRUMMER
ENROLLER	KIPPERER	PROMOTER	STUNTMAN
EPIC POET	LABOURER	PROMPTER	SUPPLIER
ESSAYIST	LANDGIRL	PROSAIST	SURVEYOR
ESSOINER	LANDLADY	PROVIDER	SWINDLER
EXORCIST	LANDLORD	PSALMIST	TABOURER
EXPLORER	LAPIDARY	PUBLICAN	TALLYMAN
EXPORTER	LARCENER	PUGILIST	TAVERNER
FABULIST	LARDERER	PURVEYOR	TEAMSTER
FACTOTUM	LEADSMAN	QUARRIER	THATCHER
FALCONER	LECTURER	RAFTSMAN	THESPIAN
FAMULIST	LINESMAN	RANCHERO	THRESHER
FARMHAND	LUMBERER	RAPPEREE	TIN MINER
FERRYMAN	MAGICIAN	RECEIVER	TINSMITH
FIGURANT	MAGISTER	REGRATER	TORTURER
FILMSTAR	MALTSTER	RELESSEE	TOYMAKER
FINISHER	MASSEUSE	RELESSOR	TRIPEMAN
FISHWIFE	MEASURER	REPAIRER	TRUCKMAN
FLATFOOT	MECHANIC	REPORTER	TURNCOCK
FLAUTIST	MEDALIST	RESETTER	TURNSPIT
FLETCHER	MELODIST	RESTORER	TUTORESS
FODDERER	MERCATOR	RETAILER	UNIONIST
FORESTER	MERCHANT	RETAINER	VALUATOR
FORGEMAN	METAL-MAN	REVIEWER	VINTAGER
FUGLEMAN	MILKMAID	REWRITER	VIRTUOSO

8—continued

VOCALIST
VOLUMIST
WAITRESS
WALKER-ON
WARDRESS
WARRENER
WATCHMAN
WATERMAN
WET NURSE
WHALEMAN
WHITENER
WHITSTER
WIGMAKER
WINNOWER
WOOL-DYER
WRESTLER

9

ALCHEMIST
ALLUMINOR
ANATOMIST
ANNOTATOR
ANNOUNCER
ARBORATOR
ARCHERESS
ARCHITECT
ARCHIVIST
ART CRITIC
ART DEALER
ARTIFICER
ASTRONAUT
ATTENDANT
AUTHORESS
BALLADIST
BALLERINA
BANK AGENT
BARRISTER
BARROW BOY
BEEFEATER
BEEKEEPER
BIOLOGIST
BOATSWAIN
BODYGUARD
BOILERMAN
BONDSLAVE
BONDWOMAN
BOOKMAKER
BOOTBLACK
BOOTMAKER
BUCCANEER
BURNISHER
BUS DRIVER
CAB DRIVER
CAFÉ OWNER
CAMERAMAN
CAR DRIVER
CARETAKER
CARPENTER
CARVANEER
CASEMAKER
CATECHIST

9—continued

CELLARMAN
CHARWOMAN
CHAUFFEUR
CHEAPJACK
CHORISTER
CLARIFIER
CLERGYMAN
CLINICIAN
CLOGMAKER
COALMINER
COALOWNER
COLLECTOR
COLOURIST
COLUMNIST
COMPRADOR
CONCIERGE
CONDUCTOR
CONSERVER
COSMONAUT
COST CLERK
COSTUMIER
COURTESAN
COUTURIER
COWFEEDER
COWKEEPER
CRACKSMAN
CRAFTSMAN
CRAYONIST
CYMBALIST
DAILY HELP
DAIRYMAID
DECORATOR
DECRETIST
DESK CLERK
DETECTIVE
DICE-MAKER
DIE-SINKER
DIETETIST
DIETITIAN
DIRECTRIX
DISPENSER
DISSECTOR
DISTILLER
DOCTORESS
DRAFTSMAN
DRAMATIST
DRAWLATCH
DRUM-MAKER
DRYSALTER
ECOLOGIST
EMBEZZLER
ENAMELLER
ENGINEMAN
ENGROSSER
EPITOMIST
ERRAND BOY
ESTIMATOR
EXAMINANT
EXCAVATOR
EXCERPTOR

9—continued

EXCHANGER
EXCISEMAN
EXECUTIVE
EXERCITOR
EXORCISER
FABRICANT
FASHIONER
FELT-MAKER
FIGURANTE
FILM ACTOR
FILM EXTRA
FILM-MAKER
FINANCIER
FIRE-EATER
FISH-CURER
FISHERMAN
FISH-WOMAN
FLAG-MAKER
FLAX-WENCH
FLYFISHER
FREELANCE
FREIGHTER
FRIPPERER
FRUITERER
FURBISHER
FURNISHER
GALVANIST
GASFITTER
GAZETTEER
GEM-CUTTER
GEOLOGIST
GLADIATOR
GLUEMAKER
GOLDSMITH
GONDOLIER
GOSPELLER
GOVERNESS
GROUNDMAN
GUARDSMAN
GUERRILLA
GUITARIST
GUN-RUNNER
HARLEQUIN
HARMONIST
HARPOONER
HARVESTER
HELLENIST
HERBALIST
HERBARIAN
HERBORIST
HERB-WOMAN
HIRED HAND
HIRED HELP
HISTORIAN
HOG-RINGER
HOMEOPATH
HOP-PICKER
HOSTELLER
HOUSEMAID
HOUSEWIFE

9—continued

HYGIENIST
HYPNOTIST
INCUMBENT
INGRAFTER
INNHOLDER
INNKEEPER
INSCRIBER
INSPECTOR
INTENDANT
IRONSMITH
ITINERANT
JACK-SMITH
JOB-MASTER
KENNEL-MAN
LACEMAKER
LACQUERER
LADY'S MAID
LAND AGENT
LANDREEVE
LARCENIST
LAUNDERER
LAUNDRESS
LEGIONARY
LIBRARIAN
LINOTYPER
LIONTAMER
LIVERYMAN
LOAN AGENT
LOCKMAKER
LOCKSMITH
LOG-ROLLER
LUMBERMAN
MACHINIST
MAGNETIST
MAJORDOMO
MALE MODEL
MALE NURSE
MAN-AT-ARMS
MANNEQUIN
MECHANIST
MEDALLIST
MEMOIRIST
MERCENARY
MESMERIST
MESSENGER
METALLIST
METRICIAN
MILL-OWNER
MODELGIRL
MORTICIAN
MUFFIN-MAN
MUSKETEER
MUSKETOON
MYOLOGIST
NAVIGATOR
NEGOTIANT
NEOLOGIAN
NEOLOGIST
NEWSAGENT
NURSEMAID

PROFESSIONS, TRADES, AND OCCUPATIONS

9—continued	9—continued	9—continued	10—continued
ODD JOB MAN	SCARIFIER	VARNISHER	BOOKBINDER
OFFICE BOY	SCAVENGER	VERSIFIER	BOOKHOLDER
OPERATIVE	SCENARIST	VETTURINO	BOOKKEEPER
ORDINATOR	SCHOLIAST	VEXILLARY	BOOKSELLER
OSTEOPATH	SCHOOLMAN	VIOLINIST	BOOTLEGGER
OTOLOGIST	SCIENTIST	VOLCANIST	BRICKLAYER
OUTFITTER	SCRIVENER	VOLTIGEUR	BRICKMAKER
PASQUILER	SCYTHEMAN	WADSETTER	BRUSHMAKER
PAYMASTER	SEA-ROBBER	WARRANTEE	BUREAUCRAT
PEDAGOGUE	SECRETARY	WARRANTER	BUTTERWIFE
PERFORMER	SHIPOWNER	WASHERMAN	CAREER GIRL
PHYSICIAN	SHIP'S MATE	WAXWORKER	CARTOONIST
PHYSICIST	SHOEBLACK	WHITESTER	CARTWRIGHT
PINKMAKER	SHOEMAKER	WINEMAKER	CASH-KEEPER
PITSAWYER	SIGHTSMAN	WOOD-REEVE	CAT BREEDER
PLANISHER	SIGNALMAN	WORKWOMAN	CAT BURGLAR
PLASTERER	SINOLOGUE	ZOOKEEPER	CERAMICIST
PLOUGHBOY	SOAPMAKER	ZOOLOGIST	CHAIR-MAKER
PLOUGHMAN	SOLICITOR	ZOOTOMIST	CHARGEHAND
PLURALIST	SONNETEER	**10**	CHARIOTEER
POETASTER	SORCERESS	ABLE SEAMAN	CHIRURGEON
POINTSMAN	STABLEBOY	ACCOMPTANT	CHORUS GIRL
POLICEMAN	STABLEMAN	ACCOUCHEUR	CHRONICLER
POP ARTIST	STAGEHAND	ACCOUNTANT	CIRCUITEER
PORTERESS	STATIONER	ACOLOTHIST	CLAIM AGENT
PORTRAYER	STAY-MAKER	ADVERTISER	CLAPPER BOY
PORTREEVE	STEERSMAN	AEROLOGIST	CLOCKMAKER
POSTILION	STEVEDORE	AGROLOGIST	CLOG DANCER
POSTWOMAN	SUBEDITOR	AGRONOMIST	CLOTH MAKER
POULTERER	SUCCENTOR	AIR HOSTESS	COACHMAKER
PRACTISER	SUR-MASTER	AIR STEWARD	COAL-BACKER
PRECENTOR	SWAN-UPPER	ALGEBRAIST	COAL-FITTER
PRECEPTOR	SWINEHERD	AMANUENSIS	COALHEAVER
PREDICANT	SWITCHMAN	APOTHECARY	COAL-MASTER
PRELECTOR	SWORDSMAN	APPRENTICE	CO-ASSESSOR
PRIESTESS	SYNDICATE	ARBALISTER	COASTGUARD
PRIVATEER	SYNOPTIST	ARBITRATOR	COLLOCUTOR
PROFESSOR	TABLEMAID	ASTROLOGER	COLLOQUIST
PROFILIST	TACTICIAN	ASTRONOMER	COLPORTEUR
PROVEDORE	TAILORESS	ATMOLOGIST	COMEDIENNE
PUBLICIST	TEATASTER	AUCTIONEER	COMPOSITOR
PUBLISHER	TENTMAKER	AUDIT CLERK	COMPOUNDER
PULPITEER	TEST PILOT	BALLOONIST	CONCORDIST
PUPPETEER	THERAPIST	BALLPLAYER	CONTRACTOR
PYTHONESS	THEURGIST	BANDMASTER	CONTROLLER
QUALIFIER	THROWSTER	BASEBALLER	COPYHOLDER
QUARRYMAN	TIMBERMAN	BASSOONIST	COPYWRITER
RACKETEER	TIRE-WOMAN	BEADSWOMAN	CORDWAINER
RAILMAKER	TOOLSMITH	BEAUTICIAN	COUNSELLOR
RECRUITER	TOWN CLERK	BELL-HANGER	CULTIVATOR
REFORMIST	TOWNCRIER	BELL-RINGER	CUSTOMS MAN
REHEARSER	TRADESMAN	BIOCHEMIST	CYTOLOGIST
RIBBONMAN	TRAGEDIAN	BIOGRAPHER	DELINEATOR
ROADMAKER	TRAVELLER	BLACKSMITH	DIRECTRESS
ROPEMAKER	TREASURER	BLADESMITH	DISC JOCKEY
ROUNDSMAN	TREPANNER	BLOCKMAKER	DISCOUNTER
RUM-RUNNER	TRIBUTARY	BLUEJACKET	DISCOVERER
SACRISTAN	TRUMPETER	BOMBARDIER	DISHWASHER
SAFEMAKER	TYMPANIST	BONDSWOMAN	DISPATCHER
SAILMAKER	USHERETTE	BONESETTER	DISTRAINER

10—continued	10—continued	10—continued	10—continued
DISTRAINOR	HOROLOGIST	PASQUILANT	SIGNWRITER
DOCKMASTER	HORSECOPER	PASTRY-COOK	SILENTIARY
DOG BREEDER	HORSE-LEECH	PATHFINDER	SILK-MERCER
DOG-FANCIER	HOUSE AGENT	PAWNBROKER	SILK-WEAVER
DOORKEEPER	HUCKSTRESS	PEARL-DIVER	SINOLOGIST
DRAMATURGE	HUSBANDMAN	PEDIATRIST	SKIRMISHER
DRESSMAKER	INOCULATOR	PEDICURIST	SLOP SELLER
DRUMMER-BOY	INSTITUTOR	PELTMONGER	SNEAK THIEF
DRY CLEANER	INSTRUCTOR	PENOLOGIST	SOAP-BOILER
EMBLAZONER	INTERAGENT	PERRUQUIER	SPECIALIST
EMBOWELLER	IRONMONGER	PHARMACIST	STAFF NURSE
ENAMELLIST	IRONWORKER	PHILOLOGER	STEERSMATE
EPHEMERIST	JOURNALIST	PIANO TUNER	STEWARDESS
EPITAPHIST	JOURNEYMAN	PICKPOCKET	STIPULATOR
EPITOMIZER	KENNELMAID	PLATELAYER	STOCKTAKER
EVANGELIST	KEYBOARDER	PLAYWRIGHT	STONE-BORER
EXAMINATOR	LAUNDRYMAN	POLITICIAN	STONEMASON
EXPLORATOR	LAW OFFICER	PORTIONIST	STRATEGIST
EYE-SERVANT	LEGISLATOR	POSTILLION	STREET-WARD
FELL-MONGER	LIBRETTIST	POSTMASTER	SUPERCARGO
FILE-CUTTER	LIGHTERMAN	PRESCRIBER	SUPERVISER
FILIBUSTER	LIME-BURNER	PRIMA DONNA	SURCHARGER
FILM EDITOR	LINOTYPIST	PRIVATE EYE	SURFACE-MAN
FIREMASTER	LIQUIDATOR	PROCURATOR	SWAN-KEEPER
FIRE-WORKER	LOBSTERMAN	PROGRAMMER	SYMPHONIST
FISHMONGER	LOCK-KEEPER	PRONOUNCER	TALLY CLERK
FLIGHT CREW	LUMBERJACK	PROPRIETOR	TASKMASTER
FLOWERGIRL	MAGISTRATE	PROSPECTOR	TAXI-DRIVER
FLUVIALIST	MANAGERESS	PROTRACTOR	TEA-BLENDER
FOLK-DANCER	MANICURIST	PROVEDITOR	TEA PLANTER
FOLK-SINGER	MANSERVANT	PUNCTURIST	TECHNICIAN
FORECASTER	MATCHMAKER	PYROLOGIST	TECHNOCRAT
FRAME-MAKER	MEAT-HAWKER	QUIZ-MASTER	THEOGONIST
FREEBOOTER	MEDICAL MAN	RAILWAYMAN	THEOLOGIAN
FUND RAISER	MILITIAMAN	RAT-CATCHER	THEOLOGIST
GAMEKEEPER	MILLWRIGHT	RECITALIST	THRENODIST
GAME WARDEN	MINERALIST	RESEARCHER	TIMEKEEPER
GEAR-CUTTER	MINISTRESS	RINGMASTER	TRACTARIAN
GEISHA GIRL	MINTMASTER	ROADMENDER	TRADE UNION
GENETICIST	MISSIONARY	ROPEDANCER	TRAFFIC COP
GEOGRAPHER	MOONSHINER	ROUGHRIDER	TRAFFICKER
GLEE-SINGER	NATURALIST	SAFEBLOWER	TRAM-DRIVER
GLOSSARIST	NAUTCH GIRL	SALES FORCE	TRANSACTOR
GLUE-BOILER	NEGOTIATOR	SALESWOMAN	TRANSLATOR
GOLD-BEATER	NEWSCASTER	SCHOOLMARM	TRAWLERMAN
GOLD-DIGGER	NEWS EDITOR	SCRUTINEER	TREASURESS
GOLD-WASHER	NEWSVENDOR	SCULPTRESS	TROUBADOUR
GOVERNANTE	NEWSWRITER	SEA-CAPTAIN	TYPESETTER
GRAMMARIAN	NIGHT NURSE	SEAMSTRESS	UNDERTAKER
GUNSLINGER	NOSOLOGIST	SECOND MATE	VETERINARY
HACKNEY-MAN	NURSERYMAN	SEMINARIST	VICTUALLER
HALL PORTER	OBITUARIST	SERVING-MAN	VIVANDIÈRE
HANDMAIDEN	OIL PAINTER	SEXOLOGIST	VOCABULIST
HARVESTMAN	ORCHARDIST	SHIP-BROKER	WAINWRIGHT
HATCHELLER	OSTEOLOGER	SHIP-HOLDER	WARRIORESS
HEAD PORTER	OVERLOOKER	SHIPMASTER	WATCHMAKER
HEAD WAITER	PANEGYRIST	SHIPWRIGHT	WATERGUARD
HIEROPHANT	PANTRYMAID	SHOPFITTER	WHARFINGER
HIGHWAYMAN	PARK-KEEPER	SHOPKEEPER	WHITESMITH
HORN PLAYER	PARK-RANGER	SHOPWALKER	WHOLESALER

10—continued

WINEGROWER
WINE-WAITER
WIREWORKER
WOODCARVER
WOODCUTTER
WOOD-MONGER
WOODWORKER
WOOL-CARDER
WOOL-COMBER
WOOL-DRIVER
WOOL-GROWER
WOOL-SORTER
WOOL-TRADER
WOOL-WINDER
YARDMASTER
ZINC-WORKER
ZOOGRAPHER
ZYMOLOGIST

11

ACCOMPANIST
ACCOUCHEUSE
ACOUSTICIAN
ADJUDICATOR
ALLOPATHIST
ANNUNCIATOR
ANTIQUARIAN
APPLE-GROWER
ARBITRATRIX
ARMY OFFICER
ARQUEBUSIER
ARTILLERIST
AUDIO TYPIST
AUSCULTATOR
BANK CASHIER
BANK MANAGER
BARGEMASTER
BASKETMAKER
BATTI-WALLAH
BATTOLOGIST
BEACHCOMBER
BELL-FOUNDER
BILL-STICKER
BIRD-CATCHER
BIRD-FANCIER
BIRD-WATCHER
BOATBUILDER
BODY SERVANT
BOILERSMITH
BONDSERVANT
BOOT-CATCHER
BROADCASTER
BULLFIGHTER
CANDLEMAKER
CAR SALESMAN
CAT'S-MEAT-MAN
CHAIR-MENDER
CHALK-CUTTER
CHAMBERMAID
CHIFFONNIER
CHIROLOGIST

11—continued

CHIROMANCER
CHIROPODIST
CHOIRMASTER
CHRONOLOGER
CINDER-WENCH
CLOCK-SETTER
CLOTH-WORKER
COAL-WHIPPER
COFFIN-MAKER
COGNOSCENTE
COLLAR-MAKER
CONDISCIPLE
CONDOTTIERE
CONDUCTRESS
CONFEDERATE
CONGRESSMAN
CONSECRATOR
CONSERVATOR
CONSTITUENT
CONVEYANCER
COPPERSMITH
COSMOGONIST
COSMOLOGIST
CRANE DRIVER
CRIMEWRITER
CUB REPORTER
CYPHER CLERK
DELIVERY MAN
DEMOGRAPHER
DISPENSATOR
DRAUGHTSMAN
DUTY OFFICER
ELECTRICIAN
EMBLEMATIST
EMBROIDERER
ENTERTAINER
ESTATE AGENT
ETHNOLOGIST
ETYMOLOGIST
EXECUTIONER
EXTORTIONER
FACE-PAINTER
FACTORY HAND
FAITH HEALER
FANCY-MONGER
FIELD WORKER
FIGURE-MAKER
FILING CLERK
FINESTILLER
FIRE BRIGADE
FIRE INSURER
FLAX-DRESSER
FLESH-MONGER
FOURBISSEUR
FRINGE-MAKER
FRUIT PICKER
FUNAMBULIST
GALLEY-SLAVE
GENEALOGIST
GHOSTWRITER

11—continued

GLASS-BENDER
GLASS-BLOWER
GLASS-CUTTER
GLASS-WORKER
GRAVE-DIGGER
GREENGROCER
HABERDASHER
HAGIOLOGIST
HAIRDRESSER
HAIR STYLIST
HARDWAREMAN
HEDGE-PRIEST
HEDGE-WRITER
HIEROLOGIST
HISTOLOGIST
HORSE DOCTOR
HORSE TRADER
HOSPITALLER
HOTEL-KEEPER
HOUSEMASTER
HOUSEMOTHER
HYMNOLOGIST
ILLUMINATOR
ILLUSIONIST
ILLUSTRATOR
INFANTRYMAN
INSTITUTIST
INTERPRETER
INTERVIEWER
IRON-FOUNDER
IVORY-CARVER
IVORY-TURNER
IVORY-WORKER
KITCHENMAID
LAMPLIGHTER
LAND STEWARD
LAUNDRYMAID
LEADING LADY
LEDGER CLERK
LIFEBOATMAN
LIGHTKEEPER
LINEN DRAPER
LITHOLOGIST
LITHOTOMIST
LORRY DRIVER
MADRIGALIST
MAIDSERVANT
MAMMALOGIST
MASTER BAKER
MECHANICIAN
MEDICINE MAN
MEMORIALIST
MERCHANTMAN
METAL WORKER
MINIATURIST
MONEY-BROKER
MONEY-LENDER
MONOGRAPHER
MULE-SPINNER
MUSIC CRITIC

11—continued

MUSIC MASTER
MYOGRAPHIST
MYSTERIARCH
MYTHOLOGIST
NECROLOGIST
NECROMANCER
NEEDLEWOMAN
NEUROLOGIST
NEUROTOMIST
NIGHT PORTER
NIGHTWORKER
NOMENCLATOR
NUMISMATIST
OFFICE STAFF
ONION-SELLER
OPERA SINGER
OPHIOLOGIST
ORIENTALIST
ORTHOPEDIST
OSTEOLOGIST
PAMPHLETEER
PANEL-BEATER
PANTOMIMIST
PAPERHANGER
PARLOURMAID
PATHOLOGIST
PATTENMAKER
PEARLFISHER
PETROLOGIST
PETTIFOGGER
PHILATELIST
PHILOLOGIST
PHONOLOGIST
PHYTOLOGIST
POLYPHONIST
PORK BUTCHER
PORTRAITIST
PRECEPTRESS
PRINT-SELLER
PROBATIONER
PROMULGATOR
PROOFREADER
PROPERTY MAN
PROPRIETRIX
QUESTIONARY
RADIOLOGIST
RAG MERCHANT
REPRESENTER
REPUBLISHER
RHETORICIAN
ROADSWEEPER
SAFEBREAKER
SANDWICH MAN
SANSCRITIST
SAXOPHONIST
SCOUTMASTER
SCRAPDEALER
SCRIP-HOLDER
SECRET AGENT
SEDITIONARY

11—continued	12—continued	12—continued	12—continued
SERVANT GIRL	AMBULANCE MAN	FAMILY DOCTOR	MICROSCOPIST
SERVING-MAID	ANAESTHETIST	FARM LABOURER	MINERALOGIST
SHARE-BROKER	ANIMALCULIST	FILM DIRECTOR	MISCELLANIST
SHEEPFARMER	ARCHEOLOGIST	FILM PRODUCER	MONEY-CHANGER
SHEPHERDESS	ARTILLERYMAN	FIRST OFFICER	MONOGRAPHIST
SHIPBREAKER	BALLET DANCER	FLYING DOCTOR	MORRIS-DANCER
SHIPBUILDER	BALLET MASTER	FOOTPLATEMAN	MOSAIC-ARTIST
SHIP'S MASTER	BANTAMWEIGHT	GEOMETRICIAN	MOSAIC-WORKER
SHOPSTEWARD	BELLOWS-MAKER	GERIATRICIAN	MYTHOGRAPHER
SILK-THROWER	BIBLIOLOGIST	GLASS-GRINDER	NEWSPAPERMAN
SILVERSMITH	BIBLIOPEGIST	GLOSSOLOGIST	NUTRITIONIST
SLAUGHTERER	BIBLIOPOLIST	GREASEMONKEY	OBSTETRICIAN
SLAVE-DRIVER	BOOKING CLERK	GUILD BROTHER	OFFICE JUNIOR
SLAVE-HOLDER	BUS CONDUCTOR	GYMNOSOPHIST	ONEIROCRITIC
SMALLHOLDER	CABINET-MAKER	GYNECOLOGIST	ORCHESTRATOR
SOCIOLOGIST	CALLIGRAPHER	HAGIOGRAPHER	ORGAN-BUILDER
STAGE-DRIVER	CARICATURIST	HALIOGRAPHER	ORGAN-GRINDER
STEEPLEJACK	CARPET-FITTER	HARNESS-MAKER	ORTHODONTIST
STOCKBROKER	CARTOGRAPHER	HEAD GARDENER	ORTHOGRAPHER
STOCKJOBBER	CATACLYSMIST	HOMEOPATHIST	OVARIOTOMIST
STONECUTTER	CEROGRAPHIST	HORSE-BREAKER	PAPER-STAINER
STOREKEEPER	CHEESEMONGER	HORSE-COURSER	PATTERN-MAKER
SUNDRIESMAN	CHIEF CASHIER	HORSE-KNACKER	PEDIATRICIAN
SYSTEM-MAKER	CHIMNEY-SWEEP	HOTEL MANAGER	PHONOGRAPHER
TAXIDERMIST	CHIROPRACTOR	HOUSEBREAKER	PHOTOGRAPHER
TELEGRAPHER	CHRONOLOGIST	HOUSEPAINTER	PHRENOLOGIST
TELEPHONIST	CHURCHWARDEN	HOUSE STEWARD	PHYSIOLOGIST
TICKET AGENT	CIRCUIT RIDER	HOUSE SURGEON	PLANT MANAGER
TOASTMASTER	CIVIL SERVANT	HYDROGRAPHER	PLOUGHWRIGHT
TOBACCONIST	CLARINETTIST	HYDROPATHIST	PLUMBER'S MATE
TOOTH-DRAWER	CLERK OF WORKS	HYPOTHECATOR	PLYER-FOR-HIRE
TOPOGRAPHER	CLOTH-SHEARER	IMMUNOLOGIST	POSTMISTRESS
TORCH-BEARER	COACH-BUILDER	IMPROPRIATOR	PRACTITIONER
TOWN PLANNER	COLEOPTERIST	INSTRUCTRESS	PRESS OFFICER
TOXOPHILITE	COMMISSIONER	INVOICE CLERK	PRESTIGIATOR
TRAIN-BEARER	CONCHOLOGIST	JERRY-BUILDER	PRISON WARDER
TRANSCRIBER	CONFECTIONER	JOINT-TRUSTEE	PRIZE-FIGHTER
TRANSPORTER	CORN CHANDLER	JURISCONSULT	PROFESSIONAL
TRAVEL AGENT	COSMOGRAPHER	JUVENILE LEAD	PROPAGANDIST
TYPE-FOUNDER	COSTERMONGER	KING'S COUNSEL	PROPRIETRESS
TYPOGRAPHER	CRAFTS-MASTER	KNIFE-GRINDER	PSYCHIATRIST
UNDERBEARER	CRANIOLOGIST	KNIFE-THROWER	PSYCHOLOGIST
UNDERLETTER	CRYPTOGAMIST	LABOURING MAN	PUBLICITY MAN
UNDERWRITER	DANCE HOSTESS	LAND SURVEYOR	PUPIL-TEACHER
UPHOLSTERER	DEEP-SEA DIVER	LATH-SPLITTER	PUPPET-PLAYER
VERSEMONGER	DEMONOLOGIST	LEADER-WRITER	QUARRY MASTER
VINE-DRESSER	DEMONSTRATOR	LEXICOLOGIST	RACING DRIVER
WASHERWOMAN	DENDROLOGIST	LITHOGRAPHER	RADIOGRAPHER
WATCHKEEPER	DRAMATURGIST	LONGSHOREMAN	RECEPTIONIST
WAX-CHANDLER	ECCLESIASTIC	LOSS ADJUSTER	REMEMBRANCER
WHEEL-CUTTER	EGYPTOLOGIST	LUMBER-DEALER	RESTAURATEUR
WHEELWRIGHT	ELECUTIONIST	MAITRE D'HOTEL	RIDING-MASTER
WHITEWASHER	ENGASTRIMUTH	MAKE-UP ARTIST	RIGHT-HAND MAN
WITCH-DOCTOR	ENGINE-DRIVER	MALACOLOGIST	RUBBER-GRADER
WOOL-STAPLER	ENTOMOLOGIST	MANUAL WORKER	SALES MANAGER
XYLOPHONIST	ENTOMOTOMIST	MANUFACTURER	SCENE-PAINTER
ZOOGRAPHIST	ENTREPRENEUR	MASS PRODUCER	SCENE-SHIFTER
12	ESCAPOLOGIST	MEAT-SALESMAN	SCHOOLMASTER
ACCORDIONIST	ETHNOGRAPHER	METALLURGIST	SCREENWRITER
ACTOR MANAGER	EXPERIMENTER	MEZZO SOPRANO	SCRIPTWRITER

12—continued

SCULLERY-MAID
SEED-MERCHANT
SEISMOLOGIST
SHARECROPPER
SHARPSHOOTER
SHIP CHANDLER
SHIP'S HUSBAND
SHOE-REPAIRER
SILVER-BEATER
SLAUGHTERMAN
SNAKE-CHARMER
SOCIAL WORKER
SOIL MECHANIC
SPECIAL AGENT
SPEECHWRITER
SPICE-BLENDER
SPORTSCASTER
SPORTSWRITER
STAGE MANAGER
STATISTICIAN
STENOGRAPHER
STONEBREAKER
STONEDRESSER
STONESQUARER
STREET-TRADER
STREET-WALKER
SUGAR-REFINER
TAX-COLLECTOR
TECHNOLOGIST
TELEGRAPH BOY
TELEGRAPHIST
TEST ENGINEER
THERAPEUTIST
THIEF-CATCHER
TICKET-PORTER
TIMBER TRADER
TOLL-GATHERER
TOURIST AGENT
TOXICOLOGIST
TRADESPEOPLE
TRANSPLANTER
TRICHOLOGIST
UNDERMANAGER
UNDERSERVANT
VETERINARIAN
WAITING-WOMAN
WAREHOUSEMAN
WATER DIVINER
WINE MERCHANT
WOOD-ENGRAVER
WORKS MANAGER
ZINCOGRAPHER

13

ADMINISTRATOR
AGRICULTURIST
ANTIQUE DEALER
ARACHNOLOGIST
ARCHAEOLOGIST
ARITHMETICIAN
ARTICLED CLERK

13—continued

ASSYRIOLOGIST
BARBER-SURGEON
BIBLIOGRAPHER
CALICO-PRINTER
CAMPANOLOGIST
CARTOGRAPHIST
CHARTOGRAPHER
CHICKEN-FARMER
CHIROGRAPHIST
CHOREOGRAPHER
CHRONOGRAPHER
CIVIL ENGINEER
CLEARSTARCHER
COFFEE-PLANTER
COMETOGRAPHER
CONTORTIONIST
CONTRABANDIST
COTTON-SPINNER
COUNTER-CASTER
COUNTERFEITER
CRANIOSCOPIST
CRYPTOGRAPHER
DANCING MASTER
DEIPNOSOPHIST
DERMATOLOGIST
DIAGNOSTICIAN
DIAMOND-CUTTER
DRAUGHTSWOMAN
DRAWING-MASTER
DRESS DESIGNER
DRILL SERGEANT
ELECTROPLATER
ELECTROTYPIST
EMIGRATIONIST
ENCYCLOPEDIST
ENTOZOOLOGIST
EPIGRAMMATIST
ESTATE MANAGER
EXHIBITIONIST
FENCING-MASTER
FORTUNE-TELLER
FRIEGHT-BROKER
GALVANOLOGIST
GASTRILOQUIST
GLOSSOGRAPHER
GLYPHOGRAPHER
GROUND-BAILIFF
GYNAECOLOGIST
HARBOUR MASTER
HIEROGLYPHIST
HORSE-MILLINER
HOSPITAL NURSE
ICHTHYOLOGIST
INDUSTRIALIST
INTELLIGENCER
JOINT-EXECUTOR
LETTER-CARRIER
LETTER-FOUNDER
LEXICOGRAPHER
LIGHTHOUSE-MAN

13—continued

MAID-OF-ALL-WORK
MASTER-BUILDER
MASTER MARINER
MATHEMATICIAN
MELODRAMATIST
METAPHYSICIAN
METEOROLOGIST
METOPOSCOPIST
MUSIC MISTRESS
NIGHT-WATCHMAN
OLD-CLOTHES-MAN
ORNITHOLOGIST
ORTHOGRAPHIST
PARK ATTENDANT
PERIODICALIST
PHARMACEUTIST
PHYSIOGNOMIST
PHYSIOGRAPHER
POSTURE-MASTER
POULTRY FARMER
PRIVATEERSMAN
PROCESS-SERVER
PSALMOGRAPHER
PSYCHOANALYST
PTERIDOLOGIST
PUBLIC SPEAKER
QUEEN'S COUNSEL
RACING-TIPSTER
REVOLUTIONARY
REVOLUTIONIST
RUBBER-PLANTER
SAILING MASTER
SCHOOLTEACHER
SCIENCE MASTER
SHOP ASSISTANT
SILK-THROWSTER
SINGING-MASTER
STATION-MASTER
STENOGRAPHIST
STEREOSCOPIST
STETHOSCOPIST
STREET-SWEEPER
SUB-CONTRACTOR
SUPERINTENDER
SUPERNUMERARY
THAUMATURGIST
THIMBLE-RIGGER
TOLL COLLECTOR
TRADE UNIONIST
TRAMCAR-DRIVER
TRAM CONDUCTOR
VENTRILOQUIST
VIOLONCELLIST
WINDOW-CLEANER
WINDOW-DRESSER
WOOLLEN-DRAPER
WRITING-MASTER

14

ADMINISTRATRIX
ANTHROPOLOGIST

14—continued

AUTOBIOGRAPHER
BACTERIOLOGIST
BALLET MISTRESS
BILLIARD-MARKER
BILLIARD-PLAYER
CHAMBER-COUNSEL
CHIMNEY-SWEEPER
CITIZEN-SOLDIER
CLASSICS MASTER
COLOUR SERGEANT
COMMISSIONAIRE
DANCING PARTNER
DISCOUNT-BROKER
ECCLESIOLOGIST
EDUCATIONALIST
ENCYCLOPAEDIST
EXCHANGE-BROKER
GRAMMATICASTER
HANDICRAFTSMAN
HERESIOGRAPHER
HORTICULTURIST
HOUSE DECORATOR
HOUSE FURNISHER
LANGUAGE MASTER
LEATHER-DRESSER
MANUAL LABOURER
MARKET-GARDENER
MEDICAL OFFICER
MERCHANT-TAILOR
MISCELLANARIAN
MONEY-SCRIVENER
MOTHER-SUPERIOR
MUSIC PUBLISHER
NAVAL PENSIONER
OPTHALMOLOGIST
PAINTER-STAINER
PHARMACOLOGIST
PNEUMATOLOGIST
PSALMOGRAPHIST
RECEPTION CLERK
REPRESENTATIVE
SCHOOLMISTRESS
SHIP'S-CARPENTER
SIDEROGRAPHIST
SPECTACLE-MAKER
SPECTROSCOPIST
SUPERINTENDENT
SYSTEMS ANALYST
TALLOW CHANDLER
WATER-COLOURIST
WEATHER PROPHET

15

ARBORICULTURIST
ASSISTANT MASTER
BOW STREET
  RUNNER
CROSSING-
  SWEEPER
CRUSTACEOLOGIST
DANCING MISTRESS

15—continued	15—continued	15—continued	15—continued
DIAMOND MERCHANT	HEART SPECIALIST	PALAEONTOLOGIST	RAILWAY ENGINEER
DOMESTIC SERVANT	HELMINTHOLOGIST	PLATFORM-SPEAKER	RESURRECTIONIST
FORWARDING AGENT	HIEROGRAMMATIST	PORTRAIT-PAINTER	SCRIPTURE-READER
GENTLEMAN-FARMER	HISTORIOGRAPHER	PROFESSIONAL MAN	SLEEPING PARTNER
HACKNEY COACHMAN	INSTRUMENTALIST	PROGRAMME SELLER	STRETCHER-BEARER
	INSURANCE BROKER		TICKET COLLECTOR
	MUSICAL DIRECTOR	PROVISION DEALER	TIGHTROPE WALKER
	NUMISMATOLOGIST		

TOOLS

3	4—continued	5—continued	6—continued
AWL	TOOL	LEVER	DIBBLE
AXE	TRUG	MOWER	DOFFER
BIT	VICE	PARER	DREDGE
DIE	WHIM	PLANE	DRIVER
FAN	**5**	PLUMB	FANNER
GAD	ANVIL	PREEN	FAUCET
GIN	AUGER	PRISE	FERRET
HOD	BEELE	PRONG	FOLDER
HOE	BENCH	PUNCH	GIMLET
JIG	BESOM	QUERN	GRAVER
LOY	BETTY	QUOIN	HACKLE
SAW	BEVEL	RATCH	HAMMER
ZAX	BLADE	RAZOR	HARROW
4	BORER	SARSE	JAGGER
ADZE	BRACE	SCREW	JIGGER
BILL	BURIN	SPADE	JIG SAW
BORE	CHUCK	SPIKE	LADDER
BROG	CHURN	SPILE	MALLET
BURR	CLAMP	SPILL	MORTAR
CART	CLAMS	SWAGE	MULLER
CELT	CLASP	TEMSE	OLIVER
CRAB	CLEAT	TOMMY	PALLET
FILE	CRAMP	TONGS	PENCIL
FORK	CRANE	TROMP	PESTLE
FROW	CROOM	TRONE	PITSAW
GAGE	CROZE	WEDGE	PLANER
HINK	CUPEL	WINCH	PLIERS
HOOK	DOLLY	**6**	PLOUGH
JACK	DRILL	BARROW	PONTEE
LAST	FLAIL	BENDER	POOLER
LOOM	FLANG	BLOWER	RAMMER
MALL	FORGE	BODKIN	RASPER
MAUL	GAUGE	BORCER	REAPER
MULE	GAVEL	BOW-SAW	RIDDLE
NAIL	GOUGE	BRAYER	RIPSAW
PICK	HOIST	BROACH	RUBBER
PIKE	INCUS	BURTON	SANDER
PLOW	JACKS	CHASER	SAW-SET
RAKE	JEMMY	CHISEL	SCREEN
RASP	JIMMY	COLTER	SCYTHE
RULE	KNIFE	CREVET	SEGGER
SOCK	LATHE	CRUSET	SHEARS
SPUD	LEVEL	DIBBER	SHOVEL

6—continued	7—continued	8—continued	9—continued
SICKLE	POUNDER	LEAD MILL	HANDSPIKE
SIFTER	PRICKER	MITRE BOX	HOLING AXE
SKEWER	SALT-PAN	MOLEGRIP	HUMMELLER
SLEDGE	SCALPEL	MUCK RAKE	IMPLEMENT
SLICER	SCAUPER	NUT SCREW	JACKKNIFE
SQUARE	SCRAPER	OILSTONE	JACKPLANE
STIDDY	SCREWER	PAINT PAD	JACKSCREW
STITHY	SCRIBER	PANEL SAW	LACE FRAME
STRIKE	SEED LOP	PICKLOCK	LAWNMOWER
TACKLE	SPADDLE	PINCHERS	NAIL PUNCH
TENTER	SPANNER	PLUMB BOB	NUT WRENCH
TREPAN	SPITTLE	POLISHER	PITCH FORK
TROWEL	SPRAYER	POWER SAW	PLANE IRON
TUBBER	STROCAL	PRONG-HOE	PLANISHER
TURREL	TENONER	PUNCHEON	PLUMBLINE
WIMBLE	THIMBLE	REAP HOOK	PLUMBRULE
WRENCH	TRESTLE	SAW WREST	SCREWJACK
	TRIBLET	SCISSORS	SCRIBE AWL
7	T-SQUARE	SCUFFLER	SHEARLEGS
BOASTER	TWIBILL	SLATE AXE	SHEEP HOOK
BRADAWL	TWISTER	STILETTO	STEELYARD
CAPSTAN	WHIP-SAW	STRICKLE	SUGAR MILL
CATLING	WHITTLE	TENON SAW	TIN OPENER
CAUTERY	WOOLDER	THROSTLE	TRY SQUARE
CHAMFER		TOOTH KEY	TURF SPADE
CHIP-AXE	**8**	TWEEZERS	TURN BENCH
CHOPPER	BARK MILL	TWIST BIT	TURNSCREW
CLEAVER	BAR SHEAR	WATERCAN	WATERMILL
COULOIR	BEAKIRON	WATER RAM	
COULTER	BENCH PEG	WEED HOOK	**10**
CRAMPON	BILL HOOK	WINDLASS	BUSH HARROW
CRISPER	BISTOURY	WINDMILL	CLASPKNIFE
CROWBAR	BLOOMARY		CLAWHAMMER
CUVETTE	BLOWLAMP	**9**	COLD CHISEL
DERRICK	BLOWPIPE	BELT PUNCH	CRANE'S BILL
DIAMOND	BOATHOOK	BENCH HOOK	CULTIVATOR
DOG-BELT	BOWDRILL	BOLT AUGER	DRAY PLOUGH
DRUDGER	BULL NOSE	BOOT CRIMP	DRIFT BOLTS
FISTUCA	BUTTERIS	CANKER BIT	DRILLPRESS
FORCEPS	CALIPERS	CANNIPERS	DRILLSTOCK
FRETSAW	CANTHOOK	CAN OPENER	EMERY WHEEL
FRUGGIN	CHOPNESS	CENTRE BIT	FIRE ENGINE
GRADINE	CROW MILL	COMPASSES	FIRING IRON
GRAINER	CRUCIBLE	CORKSCREW	GRINDSTONE
GRAPNEL	DIE STOCK	COTTON GIN	INSTRUMENT
GRUB AXE	DOWEL BIT	CRAMP IRON	MASONRY BIT
HACKSAW	DRILL BOW	CURRY COMB	MASTICATOR
HANDSAW	EDGE TOOL	CUTTER BAR	MITRE BLOCK
HATCHET	FILATORY	DOG CLUTCH	MOTOR MOWER
HAY FORK	FIRE KILN	DRAW KNIFE	MOULD BOARD
JOINTER	FLAME GUN	DRAW-PLATE	NAIL DRAWER
MANDREL	FLAX COMB	EXCAVATOR	PAINTBRUSH
MATTOCK	GAVELOCK	EYELETEER	PERFORATOR
NIPPERS	GEE CRAMP	FILLISTER	PIPE WRENCH
NUT HOOK	HANDLOOM	FINING POT	POINTED AWL
PICKAXE	HANDMILL	FORK CHUCK	SAFETY LAMP
PIERCER	HAND VICE	GAS PLIERS	SCREW PRESS
PINCERS	HAY KNIFE	HAMMER AXE	SLEEK STONE
PLUMMET	HORSE HOE	HANDBRACE	SNOWPLOUGH
POLE AXE	LAPSTONE	HANDSCREW	SPOKESHAVE

10—continued
STEAM PRESS
STEPLADDER
TENTERHOOK
THUMBSCREW
THUMBSTALL
TILT HAMMER
TRIP HAMMER
TURF CUTTER
TURNBUCKLE
WATERCRANE
WATERGAUGE
WATERLEVEL
WHEEL BRACE

11
BRACE-AND-BIT
BREAST DRILL
CHAFF CUTTER
CHAIN BLOCKS
CHAIN WRENCH
CHEESE PRESS
COUNTERSINK
CRAZING MILL
CRISPING PIN
CROSSCUT SAW
DRILL BARROW
DRILL HARROW
DRILL PLOUGH
FANNING MILL
GRUBBING HOE
HELVEHAMMER
JAGGING IRON
MACHINE TOOL
MONKEY BLOCK
PAINT ROLLER
PLOUGHSHARE
PRUNING HOOK

11—continued
RABBET PLANE
REAPING-HOOK
SAWING STOOL
SCREWDRIVER
SINGLE-EDGED
SKIM COULTER
SNATCH BLOCK
SPIRIT LEVEL
SQUARING ROD
STEAM HAMMER
STONE HAMMER
STRAW CUTTER
STRIKE BLOCK
STUBBLE RAKE
SWARD CUTTER
SWINGPLOUGH
TAPEMEASURE
TURFING IRON
TWO-FOOT RULE
WARPING HOOK
WARPING POST
WEEDING FORK
WEEDING HOOK
WEEDING RHIM
WHEELBARROW

12
BARKING IRONS
BELT ADJUSTER
BRANDING IRON
BREASTPLOUGH
CAULKING TOOL
COUNTER GAUGE
CRADEL SCYTHE
CRAMPING IRON
CRIMPING IRON
CRISPING IRON

12—continued
CURLING TONGS
DRILL GRUBBER
DRIVING SHAFT
DRIVING WHEEL
EMERY GRINDER
FLOUR DRESSER
GLASS FURNACE
HYDRAULIC RAM
MANDREL LATHE
MARLINE SPIKE
MONKEY WRENCH
PRUNING KNIFE
PULLEY BLOCKS
RUNNING BLOCK
SCRIBING IRON
SLEDGE HAMMER
SLIDING BEVEL
SOCKET CHISEL
STONE BREAKER
STRAIGHTEDGE
SWINGLE KNIFE
TOUCH NEEDLES
TRENCH PLOUGH
TURFING SPADE
TURNING LATHE
WATER BELLOWS
WEEDING TONGS

13
BUTCHER'S BROOM
CHOPPING BLOCK
CHOPPING KNIFE
CYLINDER PRESS
ELECTRIC DRILL
GRAPPLING-IRON
HYDRAULIC JACK
PACKING NEEDLE

13—continued
SCRIBING BLOCK
SEWING MACHINE
SOLDERING BOLT
SOLDERING IRON
SOWING MACHINE
SPINNING JENNY
SPINNING WHEEL
STOCKING FRAME
SUBSOIL PLOUGH
TWO-HOLE PLIERS
WEEDING CHISEL

14
BLOWING MACHINE
CARDING MACHINE
DRAINING ENGINE
DRAINING PLOUGH
PENUMATIC DRILL
REAPING MACHINE
SMOOTHING PLANE
SWINGLING KNIFE
THRUSTING SCREW
WEEDING FORCEPS

15
CARPENTER'S
  BENCH
CRIMPING MACHINE
DREDGING MACHINE
DRILLING MACHINE
ENTRENCHING TOOL
PESTLE AND
  MORTAR
PUMP
  SCREWDRIVER
WEIGHING MACHINE

MILITARY TERMS

TITLES

ARMY RANKS

FIELD MARSHAL
GENERAL
LIEUTENANT-
  GENERAL
MAJOR-GENERAL
BRIGADIER
COLONEL
LIEUTENANT-
  COLONEL
MAJOR
CAPTAIN
LIEUTENANT
SECOND-
  LIEUTENANT
SERGEANT-MAJOR
QUARTERMASTER-
  SERGEANT
SERGEANT
CORPORAL
LANCE-CORPORAL
BOMBARDIER
PRIVATE

ROYAL NAVY RANKS

ADMIRAL OF THE
  FLEET
ADMIRAL
VICE-ADMIRAL
REAR-ADMIRAL
COMMODORE
CAPTAIN
COMMANDER
LIEUTENANT-
  COMMANDER
LIEUTENANT
SUB-LIEUTENANT
CHIEF PETTY
  OFFICER
PETTY OFFICER
LEADING SEAMAN
ABLE SEAMAN
ORDINARY SEAMAN
JUNIOR SEAMAN

**ROYAL AIR FORCE
RANKS**

MARSHAL OF THE
  ROYAL AIR FORCE
AIR CHIEF MARSHAL
AIR MARSHAL
AIR VICE-MARSHAL
AIR COMMODORE
GROUP CAPTAIN
WING COMMANDER
SQUADRON LEADER
FLIGHT LIEUTENANT
FLYING OFFICER
PILOT OFFICER
MASTER AIR
  LOADMASTER
MASTER AIR
  ELECTRONIC
  OPERATOR

MASTER ENGINEER
MASTER NAVIGATOR
MASTER SIGNALLER
MASTER PILOT
WARRANT OFFICER
CHIEF TECHNICIAN
FLIGHT SERGEANT
SERGEANT
CORPORAL
JUNIOR TECHNICIAN
SENIOR
  AIRCRAFTMAN
LEADING
  AIRCRAFTMAN
AIRCRAFTMAN 1ST
  CLASS
AIRCRAFTMAN 2ND
  CLASS

DECORATIONS AND MEDALS

AIR FORCE CROSS (AFC)
AIR FORCE MEDAL (AFM)
ALBERT MEDAL (AM)
CONSPICUOUS GALLANTRY MEDAL (CGM)
DISTINGUISHED FLYING CROSS (DFC)
DISTINGUISHED FLYING MEDAL (DFM)
DISTINGUISHED SERVICE CROSS (DSC)
DISTINGUISHED SERVICE MEDAL (DSM)
GEORGE CROSS (GC)

GEORGE MEDAL (GM)
MEDAL FOR DISTINGUISHED CONDUCT IN
  THE FIELD (DCM)
MILITARY CROSS (MC)
MILITARY MEDAL (MM)
THE DISTINGUISHED SERVICE ORDER
  (DSO)
VICTORIA CROSS (VC)

BATTLES

2
RÉ, ÎLE DE (1627, Anglo-French Wars)
3
ACS (1849, Hungarian Rising)
AIX, ÎLE D' (1758, Seven Years' War)
DEE, BRIG OF (1639, Bishops' War)

3—continued
DIU (1537, 1545, Portuguese in India)
GOA (1511, 1570, Portuguese Conquest)
HUÉ (1968, Vietnam War)
UJI (1180, Taira War)
ULM (1805, Napoleonic Wars)

3—continued

ZAB, THE (590, Bahram's Revolt)

4

ACRE (1189–1191, Third Crusade; 1291,
  Crusader-Turkish Wars; 1799, French
  Revolutionary Wars; 1840, Egyptian Revolt)
AGRA (1713, Farrukhsiyar's Rebellion; 1803,
  Second British-Maratha War; 1857, Indian
  Mutiny)
ALMA (1854, Crimean War)
AONG (1857, Indian Mutiny)
ARAS (1775, First British-Maratha War)
AVUS (198 B.C., Second Macedonian War)
BAZA (1489, Spanish-Muslim Wars)
BEDR (623, Islamic Wars)
BEGA (1696, Ottoman Wars)
CUBA (1953, Castro Revolt)
CYME (474 B.C., Etruscan-Greek Wars)
DEEG (1780, First British-Maratha War; 1804,
  Second British-Maratha War)
DYLE (896, German States' Wars)
GAZA (332 B.C., Alexander's Asiatic
  Campaigns; 312 B.C., Wars of Alexander's
  Successors; 1917, World War I)
GELT, THE (1570, Anglo-Scottish Wars)
GUAM (1944, World War II)
IRUN (1837, First Carlist War)
ISLY (1844, Abd-el-Kader's Rebellion)
IVRY (1590, French Religious Wars)
JENA (1806, Napoleonic Wars)
KARS (1855, Crimean War; 1877, Russo-
  Turkish War)
KIEV (1941, World War II)
KISO (1180, Taira War)
KULM (1813, Napoleonic Wars)
LADE (494 B.C., Ionian War; 201 B.C.,
  Macedonian Wars)
LAON (1814, Napoleonic Wars)
LECK, THE (1632, Thirty Years' War)
LENS (1648, Thirty Years' War)
LÓDŹ (1914, World War I)
LOJA (1482, Spanish-Muslim Wars)
MAIN, THE (9 B.C., Germanic War)
MAYA, COLDE (1813, Peninsular War)
METZ (1870, Franco-Prussian War)
MUTA (636, Muslim Invasion of Syria)
NEON (354 B.C., Sacred War)
NILE (1798, French Revolutionary Wars)
NIVE (1813, Peninsular War)
NOVI (1799, French Revolutionary Wars)
OFEN (1849, Hungarian Rising)
OHUD (623, Mohammed's War with the
  Koreish)
ONAO (1857, Indian Mutiny)
ORAN (1509, Spanish Invasion of Morocco;
  1940, World War II)
OREL (1943, World War II)
ORUO (1862, Bolivian Civil War)
POLA (1380, War of Chioggia)
RAAB (1809, Napoleonic Wars)
RIGA (1621, Swedish-Polish Wars)

4—continued

ROME (387 B.C., First Invasion of the Gauls;
  408, Wars of the Western Roman Empire;
  472, Ricimer's Rebellion; 537, 546, Wars of
  the Byzantine Empire; 1082, Norman
  Seizure; 1527, Wars of Charles V; 1849,
  Italian Wars of Independence)
SCIO (1769, Ottoman Wars)
SETA (1183, Yoshinaka's Rebellion)
SOHR (1745, War of the Austrian Succession)
ST LÔ (1944, World War II)
TOBA (1868, Japanese Revolution)
TORO (1476, War of the Castilian Succession)
TROY (1100 B.C.)
TRUK (1944, World War II)
TYRE (332 B.C., Alexander's Asiatic
  Campaigns)
VEII (405 B.C., Rise of Rome)
ZAMA (202 B.C., Second Punic War)
ZEIM (1877, Russo-Turkish War)
ZELA (67 B.C., Third Mithridatic War; 47 B.C.,
  Wars of the First Triumvirate)

5

ACCRA (1824, 1825, First British-Ashanti War)
ADUWA (1896, Italian Invasion of Ethiopia)
ALAMO, STORMING OF THE (1836, Texan
  Rising)
ALAND (1714, Great Northern War)
ALLIA, THE (390 B.C., The First Invasion of the
  Gauls)
ALSEN (1864, Schleswig-Holstein War)
AMBUR (1749, Carnatic War; 1767, First
  British-Mysore War)
AMIDA (359, Roman-Persian Wars)
ANZIO (1944, World War II)
ARCOT (1751, Carnatic War)
ARGOS (195 B.C., Roman Invasion of Greece)
ARIUS (214 B.C., The Wars of the Hellenistic
  Monarchies)
ARNEE (1751, Carnatic War; 1782, First
  British-Mysore War)
ARRAH (1857, Indian Mutiny)
ARRAS (1654, Wars of Louis XIV; 1917, World
  War I)
A SHAU (1966, Vietnam War)
AURAY (1364, Hundred Years' War)
BAHUR (1752, Seven Years' War)
BANDA (1858, Indian Mutiny)
BANDS, THE (961, Danish Invasion of
  Scotland)
BASRA (665, Islamic Wars)
BAVAY (57 B.C., Gallic Wars)
BEREA (1852, Kaffir Wars)
BETWA, THE (1858, Indian Mutiny)
BOSRA (632, Muslim Invasion of Syria)
BOYNE, THE (1690, War of the Grand
  Alliance)
BREST (1512, War of the Holy League)
BRILL (1572, Netherlands War of
  Independence)
BURMA (1942, 1943, World War II)

5—continued

BUXAR (1764, British Conquest of Bengal)
CADIZ (1587, Anglo-Spanish War)
CAIRO (1517, Ottoman Wars)
CANEA (1644, Candian War)
CAPUA (212 B.C., Second Punic War)
CARPI (1701, War of the Spanish Succession)
CESME (1770, Ottoman Wars)
CHIOS (357 B.C., Social War; 201 B.C., Wars of
   the Hellenistic Monarchies)
CRÉCY (1346, Hundred Years' War)
CRETE (1941, World War II)
CUZCO (1536, Conquest of Peru)
DAK TO (1967, Vietnam War)
DAMME (1213, Wars of Philip Augustus)
DELHI (1297, First Tatar Invasion of India;
   1398, Second Tatar Invasion; 1803, Second
   British-Maratha War; 1804, Second British-
   Maratha War; 1857, Indian Mutiny)
DOUAI (1710, War of the Spanish Succession)
DOURO (1809, Peninsular War)
DOVER (1652, Anglo-Dutch Wars)
DOWNS, THE (1666, Anglo-Dutch Wars)
DREUX (1562, French Religious Wars)
DUBBA (1843, Sind Campaign)
DUNES (1658, Wars of Louis XIV)
DWINA, THE (1701, Swedish-Polish War)
ELENA (1877, Russo-Turkish War)
EL TEB (1884, British-Sudan Campaigns)
EMESA (272, Wars of the Roman Empire)
ENGEN (1800, French Revolutionary Wars)
EYLAU (1807, Napoleonic Wars)
GENOA (1746, Patriotic Rising; 1795, 1800,
   French Revolutionary Wars)
GIHON, THE (1362, Wars of Tamerlane)
GINGI (1689, Mughal Invasion of the Deccan)
GOITS (1848, Italian Wars of Independence)
GUBAT (1885, British Sudan Campaigns)
HANAU (1813, Napoleonic Wars)
HERAT (1220, Tatar Invasion of Afghanistan;
   1837, Persian-Afghan Wars)
HIPPO (430, Wars of the Western Roman
   Empire)
IMMAC (218, Revolt of Elagabalus)
IMOLA (1797, French Revolutionary Wars)
INDUS, THE (1221, Tatar Invasion of Central
   Asia)
IPSUS (306 B.C., Wars of Alexander's
   Successors)
ISSUS (333 B.C., Alexander's Asiatic
   Campaigns; 1488, Ottoman Wars)
JASSY (1620, Ottoman Wars)
JIRON (1829, Peruvian-Colombian War)
JUNÍN (1824, Peruvian War of Independence)
KAGUL (1770, Ottoman Wars)
KALPI (1858, Indian Mutiny)
KAREE (1900, Second Boer War)
KAZAN (1774, Cossack Rising)
KIÖGE (1677, Northern War)
KOLIN (1757, Seven Years' War)
KOTAH (1858, Indian Mutiny)

5—continued

KUMAI (1355, Moronoshi's Rebellion)
LAGOS (1693, War of the Grand Alliance)
LA PAZ (1865, Bolivian Civil War)
LARGS (1263, Norse Invasion of Scotland)
LESNO (1708, Russo-Swedish War)
LEWES (1264, Barons' Wars)
LEYTE (1944, World War II)
LIÈGE (1914, World War I)
LIGNY (1815, Napoleonic Wars)
LILLE (1708, War of the Spanish Succession)
LIPPE (11 B.C., Germanic Wars)
LISSA (1866, Seven Weeks' War)
LUZON (1945, World War II)
LYONS (197, Civil Wars of the Roman Empire)
MAIDA (1806, Napoleonic Wars)
MALTA (1565, Ottoman Wars; 1798, French
   Revolutionary Wars; 1942, World War II)
MARNE (1914, 1918, World War I)
MAXEN (1759, Seven Years' War)
MAYPO (1818, Chilean War of Independence)
MERTA (1561, Mughal Invasion of the Deccan)
MORAT (1476, Burgundian Wars)
MOTYA (398 B.C., Carthaginian Invasion of
   Sicily)
MUDKI (1845, First British-Sikh War)
MUNDA (45 B.C., Civil War of Caesar and
   Pompey)
MURET (1213, Albigensian Crusade)
MURSA (351, Civil Wars of the Roman Empire)
MYLAE (260 B.C., First Punic War)
MYLEX (36 B.C., Wars of the Second
   Triumvirate)
NAMUR (1914, World War I)
NARVA (1700, Great Northern War)
NAXOS (376 B.C., Wars of the Greek City
   States)
NIKKO (1868, Japanese Revolution)
NISSA (1064, Scandinavian Wars)
NIZIB (1839, Mehmet Ali's Second Rebellion)
OLPAE (426 B.C., Great Peloponnesian War)
OSTIA (1500, Italian Wars)
OTRAR (1219, Tatar Invasion of Khorezm)
PARIS (1814, Napoleonic Wars; 1870, Franco-
   Prussian War)
PARMA (1734, War of the Polish Succession)
PATAY (1429, Hundred Years' War)
PAVIA (271, Invasion of the Alemanni; 568,
   Lombard Conquest of Italy; 1431, Italian
   Wars; 1525, Wars of Charles V)
PERED (1849, Hungarian Rising)
PETRA (549, Persian Wars)
PIROT (1885, Serbo-Bulgarian War)
PODOL (1866, Seven Weeks' War)
POONA (1802, Maratha Wars)
PRUTH, THE (1770, Ottoman Wars)
PYDNA (168 B.C., Third Macedonian War)
RAMLA (1177, Crusader-Turkish Wars)
REBEC (1524, Wars of Charles V)
REDAN, THE GREAT (1855, Crimean War)
REIMS (1814, Napoleonic Wars)

5—continued

REVAL (1790, Russo-Swedish Wars)
RIETI (1821, Italian Wars of Independence)
ROUEN (1418, Hundred Years' War)
SEDAN (1870, Franco-Prussian War)
SELBY (1644, English Civil War)
SEOUL (1950, Korean War)
SLUYS (1340, Hundred Years' War)
SOMME (1916, 1918, World War I)
SPIRA (1703, War of the Spanish Succession)
SPURS (1302, Flemish War; 1513, Anglo-
   French Wars)
STOKE (1487, Lambert Simnel's Rebellion)
SUERO, THE (75 B.C., Civil War of Sertorius)
TACNA (1880, Peruvian-Chilean War)
TAMAI (1884, British Sudan Campaigns)
TEGEA (473 B.C., Wars of Sparta)
TEXEL (1653, Anglo-Dutch Wars)
THALA (22, Numidian Revolt)
THORN (1702, Great Northern War)
TOURS (732, Muslim Invasion of France)
TUNIS (255 B.C., First Punic War; 1270, Eighth
   Crusade)
TURIN (312, Civil Wars of the Roman Empire;
   1706, War of the Spanish Succession)
UCLES (1109, Spanish-Muslim Wars)
UTICA (49 B.C., Civil War of Caesar and
   Pompey; 694, Muslim Conquest of Africa)
VALMY (1792, French Revolutionary Wars)
VARNA (1444, Anti-Turkish Crusade; 1828,
   Ottoman Wars)
VARUS, DEFEAT OF (A.D. 9, Wars of the
   Roman Empire)
VASAQ (1442, Ottoman Wars)
WAVRE (1815, Napoleonic Wars)
WISBY (1613, Danish-Swedish Wars)
WÖRTH (1870, Franco-Prussian War)
XERES (711, Spanish-Muslim Wars)
YPRES (1914, 1915, 1917, World War I)
ZENTA (1679, Ottoman Wars)
ZNAIM (1809, Napoleonic Wars)

6

AACHEN (1944, World War II)
ABUKIR (1799, 1801, French Revolutionary
   Wars)
ABU KRU (1885, British Sudan Campaigns)
ACTIUM (31 B.C., Wars of the Second
   Triumvirate)
ÆGINA (458 B.C., Third Messenian War)
ÆGUSA (241 B.C., First Punic War)
ALEPPO (638, Muslim Invasion of Syria; 1400,
   Tatar Invasion of Syria; 1516, Ottoman
   Wars)
ALESIA (52 B.C., Gallic Wars)
ALFORD (1645, English Civil War)
ALHAMA (1482, Spanish-Muslim Wars)
ALIWAL (1846, First British-Sikh War)
AMBATE (1532, Conquest of Peru)
AMIENS (1870, Franco-Prussian War)
ANCONA (1860, Italian Wars of Independence)
ANGORA (1402, Tatar Invasion of Asia Minor)

6—continued

ANTIUM (1378, War of Chioggia)
ARBELA (331 B.C., Alexander's Asiatic
   Campaigns)
ARCOLA (1796, French Revolutionary Wars)
ARGAON (1803, Second British-Maratha War)
ARKLOW (1798, Irish Rebellion)
ARNHEM (1944, World War II)
ARQUES (1589, French Religious Wars)
ARSOUF (1191, Third Crusade)
ARTOIS (1915, World War I)
ASHTEE (1818, Third British-Maratha War)
ASIAGO (1916, World War I)
ASPERN (1809, Napoleonic Wars)
ASSAYE (1803, Second British-Maratha War)
ATBARA (1898, British Sudan Campaigns)
AUSSIG (1426, Hussite War)
AZORES (1591, Anglo-Spanish War)
BAMIAN (1221, Tatar Invasion of Kharismia)
BARDIA (1941, World War II)
BARNET (1471, Wars of the Roses)
BASING (871, Danish Invasion of Britain)
BAYLEN (1808, Peninsular War)
BEAUGÉ (1421, Hundred Years' War)
BENDER (1768, Ottoman Wars)
BERGEN (1759, Seven Years' War)
BEYLAN (1831, Egyptian Revolt)
BILBAO (1836, First Carlist War; 1937, Spanish
   Civil War)
BINGEN (70, Gallic Revolt)
BIRUAN (1221, Tatar Invasion of Kharismia)
BOYACÁ (1819, Colombian War of
   Independence)
BUSACO (1810, Peninsular War)
CABALA (379 B.C., Second Carthaginian
   Invasion of Sicily)
CABRIA (72 B.C., Third Mithridatic War)
CALAIS (1346, Hundred Years' War; 1558,
   Anglo-French Wars)
CALLAO (1866, Peruvian War of
   Independence)
CALVEN, THE (1499, Swiss-Swabian War)
CAMDEN (1780, American Revolutionary War)
CAMPEN (1759, Seven Years' War)
CANDIA (1648, Candian War)
CANNAE (216 B.C., Second Punic War)
CEPEDA (1859, Argentine Civil War)
CHANDA (1818, Third British-Maratha War)
CHIARI (1701, War of the Spanish Succession)
CHILOE (1826, Chilean War of Independence)
CHIZAI (1372, Hundred Years' War)
CHUNAR (1538, Hindu-Mughal Wars)
CNIDUS (394 B.C., Wars of Greek City States)
CONCON (1891, Chilean Civil War)
CUNAXA (401 B.C., Expedition of Cyrus the
   Younger)
CYSSUS (191 B.C., Wars of the Hellenistic
   Monarchies)
DANZIG (1627, Thirty Years' War; 1807, 1813,
   Napoleonic Wars)

6—continued

DARGAI (1897, British Northwest Frontier Campaign)
DELIUM (424 B.C., Peloponnesian War)
DELPHI (355 B.C., Sacred War)
DENAIN (1712, War of the Spanish Succession)
DESSAU (1626, Thirty Years' War)
DIEPPE (1942, World War II)
DIPAEA (471 B.C., Arcadian War)
DJERBA (1560, Ottoman Wars)
DOLLAR (875, Danish Invasions of Scotland)
DUNBAR (1296, 1339, Wars of Scottish Independence; 1650, Cromwell's Scottish Campaign)
DUNDEE (1899, Second Boer War)
DÜPPEL (1864, Schleswig-Holstein War)
EDESSA (259, Persian Wars)
ELINGA (206 B.C., Second Punic War)
EMBATA (356 B.C., Social War)
ERBACH (1800, French Revolutionary Wars)
FAENZA (541, Wars of the Byzantine Empire)
FERKEH (1896, British Sudan Campaigns)
GAZALA (1942, World War II)
GEBORA (1811, Peninsular War)
GERONA (1809, Peninsular War)
GHAZNI (1839, First British-Afghan War)
GISORS (1197, Anglo-French Wars)
GROZKA (1739, Ottoman Wars)
HALLUE (1870, Franco-Prussian War)
HARLAW (1411, Scottish Civil Wars)
HASHIN (1885, British Sudan Campaigns)
HATVAN (1849, Hungarian Rising)
HAVANA (1748, War of the Austrian Succession; 1762, Seven Years' War)
HEXHAM (1464, Wars of the Roses)
HIMERA (480 B.C., First Carthaginian Invasion of Sicily; 409 B.C., Second Carthaginian Invasion of Sicily)
HÖCHST (1622, Thirty Years' War)
HONAIN (629, Muslim Conquest of Arabia)
HUESCA (1105, Spanish-Muslim Wars; 1837, First Carlist War)
HYSIAE (668 B.C., Sparta against Argos)
INCHON (1950, Korean War)
INGAVI (1841, Bolivian-Peruvian War)
INGOGO (1881, First Boer War)
ISMAIL (1790, Ottoman Wars)
ISONZO (1915, World War I)
JALULA (637, Muslim Invasion of Persia)
JARNAC (1569, Third French Religious War)
JERSEY (1550, Anglo-French Wars)
JHANSI (1857, Indian Mutiny)
KAPPEL (1531, Swiss Religious Wars)
KARAKU (1218, Tatar Invasion of Khwarizm)
KHELAT (1839, First British-Afghan War)
KIRKEE (1817, Third British-Maratha War)
KOKEIN (1824, First Burma War)
KOMORN (1849, Hungarian Rising)
KONIAH (1831, Mehemet Ali's First Rebellion)
KOTZIN (1622, 1673, Ottoman Wars)

6—continued

KRONIA (1738, Ottoman Wars)
LAHORE (1296, First Tatar Invasion of India)
LANDAU (1702, War of the Spanish Succession)
LANDEN (1693, War of the Grand Alliance)
LANNOY (1567, Netherlands War of Independence)
LARCAY (1829, Chilean Revolution)
LAUPEN (1339, Burgundian Wars)
LAWARI (1803, Second British-Maratha War)
LE MANS (1871, Franco-Prussian War)
LERIDA (1642, 1647, Thirty Years' War)
LEYDEN (1574, Netherlands War of Independence)
LONATO (1796, French Revolutionary Wars)
LUCENA (1483, Spanish-Muslim Wars)
LUNDEN (1676, Danish-Swedish Wars)
LUTTER (1626, Thirty Years' War)
LÜTZEN (1632, Thirty Years' War; 1813, Napoleonic Wars)
MACALO (1427, Italian Wars)
MADRAS (1746, War of the Austrian Succession; 1758, Seven Years' War)
MADRID (1936, Spanish Civil War)
MAIDAN (1842, First British-Afghan War)
MAJUBA (1881, First Boer War)
MALAGA (1487, Spanish-Muslim Wars; 1704, War of the Spanish Succession)
MALAYA (1941, World War II)
MALDON (991, Danish Invasions of Britain)
MANILA (1898, Spanish-American War)
MANTUA (1797, French Revolutionary Wars)
MARDIS (315, War of the Two Empires)
MARGUS (285, Civil Wars of the Roman Empire)
MEDINA (625, Muslim Conquest of Arabia)
MEDOLA (1796, French Revolutionary Wars)
MEERUT (1398, Second Tatar Invasion of India)
MERIDA (712, Spanish-Muslim Wars)
MERTON (871, Danish Invasions of Britain)
MEXICO (1520, Conquest of Mexico)
MINDEN (1759, Seven Years' War)
MIYAKO (1353, Moronoshi's Rebellion; 1391, Mitsuyakis' Revolt)
MOHACZ (1526, 1687, Ottoman Wars)
MORAWA (1443, Ottoman Wars)
MOSCOW (1941, World War II)
MUKDEN (1905, Russo-Japanese War; 1948, Chinese Civil War)
MULTAN (1848, Second British-Sikh War)
MUTHUL, THE (108 B.C., Jugurthine War)
MUTINA (43 B.C., Roman Civil Wars)
MYCALE (479 B.C., Persian-Greek Wars)
MYTTON (1319, Wars of Scottish Independence)
NACHOD (1866, Seven Weeks' War)
NÁJARA (1367, Hundred Years' War)
NANHAN (1904, Russo-Japanese War)
NASEBY (1645, English Civil War)

6—continued

NICAEA (1097, First Crusade)
NORWAY (1940, World War II)
NOTIUM (407 B.C., Peloponnesian War)
NOVARA (1513, Italian Wars; 1849, Italian Wars of Independence)
OCKLEY (851, Danish Invasions of Britain)
OLMEDO (1467, War of the Castilian Succession)
OLMÜTZ (1758, Seven Years' War)
OPORTO (1809, Peninsular War)
ORTHEZ (1814, Peninsular War)
OSTEND (1601, Netherlands War of Independence)
OSWEGO (1756, Seven Years' War)
OTUMBA (1520, Spanish Conquest of Mexico)
PANION (198 B.C., Wars of the Hellenistic Monarchies)
PARANA (1866, Paraguayan War)
PATILA (1394, Tatar Invasion of Persia)
PEKING (1214, Tatar Invasion of China)
PLEI ME (1965, Vietnam War)
PLEVNA (1877, Russo-Turkish War)
POLAND (1939, World War II)
PONANI (1780, First British-Mysore War)
POTOSI (1825, Bolivian War of Independence)
PRAGUE (1620, Thirty Years' War; 1757, Seven Years' War)
PUENTE (1816, Colombian War of Independence)
QUEBEC (1759, 1760, Seven Years' War)
RABAUL (1943, World War II)
RAGATZ (1446, Armagnac War)
RAPHIA (217 B.C., Wars of the Hellenistic Monarchies)
RASZYN (1809, Napoleonic Wars)
RHODES (1480, Ottoman Wars)
RIVOLI (1797, French Revolutionary Wars)
ROCROI (1643, Thirty Years' War)
ROLICA (1808, Peninsular War)
RUMANI (1915, World War I)
SACILE (1809, Napoleonic Wars)
SADOWA (1866, Seven Weeks' War)
SAIGON (1968, Vietnam War)
SAINTS, THE (1782, American Revolutionary War)
SALADO (1340, Spanish-Muslim Wars)
SANGRO (1943, World War II)
SARDIS (280 B.C., Wars of Alexander's Successors)
SEPEIA (494 B.C., Argive War)
SESKAR (1790, Russo-Swedish Wars)
SHILOH (1862, American Civil War)
SICILY (1943, World War II)
SIFFIN (657, Muslim Civil Wars)
SILPIA (206 B.C., Second Punic War)
SINOPE (1853, Crimean War)
SON-TAI (1883, Tongking War)
SORATA (1780, Inca Rising)
STE FOY (1760, Seven Years' War)
ST KITS (1667, Anglo-Dutch Wars)

6—continued

SYBOTA (433 B.C., Peloponnesian Wars)
TAURIS (47 B.C., Civil War of Caesar and Pompey)
TEGYRA (373 B.C., Boeotian War)
TERTRY (687, Rise of the Franks)
TETUÁN (1860, Spanish-Moroccan War)
THEBES (335 B.C., Macedonian Conquest)
THURII (282 B.C., Roman Civil Wars)
TIFLIS (1386, Tatar Invasion of the Caucasus)
TIGRIS (363, Persian Wars)
TOBRUK (1941, 1942, World War II)
TOFREK (1885, British-Sudan Campaigns)
TORGAU (1760, Seven Years' War)
TOULON (1707, War of the Spanish Succession; 1744, War of the Austrian Succession; 1793, French Revolutionary Wars)
TOWTON (1461, Wars of the Roses)
TSINAN (1948, Chinese Civil War)
TUDELA (1808, Peninsular War)
ULUNDI (1879, Zulu-British War)
UROSAN (1595, Japanese Invasion of Korea)
USHANT (1794, French Revolutionary Wars)
VARESE (1859, Italian Wars of Independence)
VARMAS (1813, Colombian War of Independence)
VENICE (1848, Italian Wars of Independence)
VERDUN (1916, World War I)
VERONA (312, Civil Wars of the Roman Empire)
VIENNA (1529, 1683, Ottoman Wars)
VYBORG (1918, Russo-Finnish War)
WAGRAM (1809, Napoleonic Wars)
WAIZAN (1849, Hungarian Rising)
WARSAW (1831, Second Polish Rising; 1914, World War I; 1918, Russo-Polish War; 1939, 1944, World War II)
WERBEN (1631, Thirty Years' War)
WIAZMA (1812, Napoleonic Wars)
YARMUK (636, Muslim Invasion of Syria)
YAWATA (1353, War of the Northern and Southern Empires)
ZALAKA (1086, Moorish against Castile)
ZAMORA (901, Spanish-Muslim Wars)
ZÜRICH (1799, French Revolutionary Wars)

7

ABRAHAM, PLAINS OF (1759, Seven Years' War)
ABU KLEA (1885, British Sudan Campaigns)
ACRAGAS (406 B.C., Second Carthaginian Invasion of Sicily)
AGORDAT (1893, Italian Sudan Campaigns)
ALARCOS (1195, Spanish-Muslim Wars)
ALBUERA (1811, Peninsular War)
ALCOLEA (1868, Isabel II of Spain Deposed)
ALGHERO (1353, Aragonese Conquest of Sardinia)
ALGIERS (1775, Spanish-Algerian War; 1816, Bombardment of)
ALIGARH (1803, First British-Maratha War)

7—continued

ALKMAAR (1573, Netherlands War of
Independence; 1799, French Revolutionary
Wars)
ALMANSA (1707, War of the Spanish
Succession)
ALMORAH (1815, British-Gurkha War)
ALNWICK (1093, Anglo-Scottish Wars)
AMAKUSA (1638, Revolt of the Christians in
Japan)
AMOAFUL (1874, Second British-Ashanti War)
AMORIUM (838, Muslim Invasion of Asia
Minor)
ANCYRAE (242 B.C., Hierax's Rebellion)
ANTIOCH (244 BC., Syrian Wars; 1097, First
Crusade)
ANTWERP (1576, Netherlands War of
Independence; 1832, Liberation of Belgium;
1914, World War I)
ARAUSIO (105 B.C., Fourth Gallic Invasion)
ARIKERA (1791, Second British-Mysore War)
ASCALON (1099, First Crusade)
ASCULUM (279 B.C., Pyrrhus' Invasion of Italy;
89 B.C., Social War)
ASHDOWN (871, Danish Invasion of Britain)
ATHENRY (1316, Conquest of Ireland)
AUGHRIM (1691, War of the English
Succession)
BAGHDAD (1401, Mongul Invasion of
Mesopotamia)
BALKANS (1940, 1944, World War II)
BAPAUME (1871, Franco-Prussian War)
BAROSSA (1811, Peninsular War)
BASSANO (1796, French Revolutionary Wars)
BASSEIN (1780, First British-Maratha War)
BATAVIA (1811, Napoleonic Wars)
BATOCHE (1885, Riel's Second Rebellion)
BAUTZEN (1813, Napoleonic Wars)
BELMONT (1899, Second Boer War)
BENBURB (1646, Great Irish Rebellion)
BÉTHUNE (1707, War of the Spanish
Succession)
BETIOCA (1813, Colombian War of
Independence)
BEZETHA (66, Jewish Wars of Roman Empire)
BIBERAC (1796, French Revolutionary Wars)
BITONTO (1734, War of the Polish
Succession)
BOKHARA (1220, Tatar Invasion of Kharismia)
BOURBON (1810, Napleonic Wars)
BRESCIA (1849, Italian Rising)
BRESLAU (1757, Seven Years' War)
BRIENNE (1814, Napoleonic Wars)
BULL RUN (1861, 1862, American Civil War)
CADESIA (636, Muslim Invasion of Persia)
CADSAND (1357, Hundred Years' War)
CALAFAT (1854, Crimean War)
CALICUT (1790, Second British-Mysore War)
CARACHA (1813, Colombian War of
Independence)
CARIGAT (1791, Second British-Mysore War)

7—continued

CARNOUL (1739, Persian Invasion of India)
CARRHAE (53 B.C., Parthian War)
CASSANO (1705, War of the Spanish
Succession)
CASSINO (1944, World War II)
CHÂLONS (271, Revolt of the Legions of
Aquitaine; 366, Invasion of the Alemanni;
451, Wars of the Western Roman Empire)
CHETATÉ (1854, Crimean War)
CHOCZIM (1769, Ottoman Wars)
CHONG-JU (1904, Russo-Japanese War)
CIBALIS (315, War of the Two Empires)
CLISSAU (1702, Swedish-Polish Wars)
CLUSIUM (225 B.C., Conquest of Cisalpine
Gaul)
COLENSO (1899, Second Boer War)
COLOMBO (1796, French Revolutionary Wars)
CORDOVA (1010, Spanish-Muslim Wars)
CORINTH (429 B.C., Peloponnesian War; 394
B.C., Corinthian War; 1862, American Civil
War)
CORONEA (447 B.C., First Peloponnesian War;
394 B.C., Corinthian War)
CORONEL (1914, World War I)
CORUMBA (1877, Paraguayan War)
CORUNNA (1809, Peninsular War)
COUTRAS (1587, French Religious Wars)
CRAONNE (1814, Napoleonic Wars)
CRAVANT (1423, Hundred Years' War)
CREFELD (1758, Seven Years' War)
CREMONA (198 B.C., Second Gallic Invasion;
69, Civil Wars of the Roman Empire; 1702,
War of the Spanish Succession)
CRONION (379 B.C., Second Carthaginian
Invasion of Sicily)
CROTONE (982, German Invasion of Italy)
CROTOYE (1347, Hundred Years' War)
CUASPAD (1862, Ecuador-Colombia War)
CURICTA (49 B.C., Civil War of Caesar and
Pompey)
CUSTOZA (1866, Italian Wars of
Independence)
CYZICUS (410 B.C., Peloponnesian War; 88
B.C., First Mithridatic War)
CZASLAU (1742, War of the Austrian
Succession)
DAZAIFU (1281, Chinese Invasion of Japan)
DEORHAM (577, Wessex against the Welsh)
DODOWAH (1826, First British-Ashanti War)
DONABEW (1825, First Burma War)
DRESDEN (1813, Napleonic Wars)
DRISTEN (973, Wars of the Byzantine Empire)
DUNDALK (1318, Scottish Invasion of Ireland)
DUNKELD (1689, Jacobite Rising)
DUNKIRK (1940, World War II)
DUPPLIN (1332, Baliol's Rising)
DURAZZO (1081, Norman Invasion of Italy)
ECKMÜHL (1809, Napoleonic Wars)
ECNOMUS (256 B.C., First Punic War)
EL CANEY (1898, Spanish-American War)

7—continued

ELK HORN (1862, American Civil War)
ENTHOLM (1676, Northern Wars)
EPHESUS (499 B.C., Ionian War; 262 B.C., Gallic Invasion of Asia)
ESSLING (1809, Napoleonic Wars)
ETAMPES (604, Burgundians against Neustrians)
EVESHAM (1265, Barons' War)
FALKIRK (1298, Wars of Scottish Independence; 1746, The Forty-five Rebellion)
FERRARA (1815, Napoleon's Hundred Days)
FLEURUS (1622, Thirty Years' War; 1690, War of the Grand Alliance; 1794, French Revolutionary Wars)
FLODDEN (1513, Anglo-Scottish Wars)
FOCSANI (1789, Ottoman Wars)
FORNOVO (1495, Italian Wars)
FRANLIN (1864, American Civil War)
FULFORD (1066, Norse Invasion of England)
FUSHIMI (1868, Japanese Revolution)
GALICIA (1914, World War I)
GATE PAH (1864, Maori-British War)
GHERAIN (1763, British Conquest of Bengal)
GHOAINE (1842, First British-Afghan War)
GORARIA (1857, Indian Mutiny)
GORLICE (1915, World War I)
GRANADA (1319, 1491, Spanish-Muslim Wars)
GRANGAM (1721, Great Northern War)
GRANSON (1476, Burgundian Wars)
GRASPAN (1899, Second Boer War)
GRENADA (1779, American Revolutionary War; 1983, American Invasion)
GROCHÓW (1831, Second Polish Rising)
GUJERAT (1849, Second British-Sikh War)
GWALIOR (1780, First British-Maratha War; 1858, Indian Mutiny)
HAARLEM (1572, Netherlands War of Independence)
HASLACH (1805, Napoleonic Wars)
HELORUS (492 B.C., Wars of Sicily)
HERNANI (1836, 1837, First Carlist War)
HERRERA (1837, First Carlist War)
HILL 875 (1967, Vietnam War)
HILL 881 (1967, Vietnam War)
HOGLAND (1789, Russo-Swedish Wars)
HOOGHLY, THE (1759, Anglo-Dutch Wars in India)
HUMAITA (1866, 1868, Paraguayan War)
HWAI-HAI (1948, Chinese Civil War)
ISASZCQ (1849, Hungarian Rising)
IWO-JIMA (1945, World War II)
JAMAICA (1655, Anglo-Spanish Wars)
JAVA SEA (1942, World War II)
JITGURH (1815, British Gurkha War)
JUTLAND (1916, World War I)
KAIPING (1895, Sino-Japanese War)
KALISCH (1706, Great Northern War)
KALUNGA (1814, British-Gurkha War)
KAMARUT (1824, First Burma War)

7—continued

KAMBULA (1879, Zulu War)
KAPOLNA (1849, Hungarian Rising)
KASHGAL (1883, British Sudan Campaigns)
KHARKOV (1942, 1943, World War II)
KHE SANH (1968, Vietnam War)
KILSYTH (1645, English Civil War)
KINEYRI (1848, Second British-Sikh War)
KINLOSS (1009, Danish Invasion of Scotland)
KINSALE (1601, O'Neill's Rebellion)
KIUCHAU (1904, Russo-Japanese War)
KOJENDE (1219, Tatar Invasion of Central Asia)
KOMATSU (1062, Japanese Nine Years' War)
KOSSOVA (1398, 1448, Ottoman Wars)
KRASNOI (1812, Napoleonic Wars)
KROTZKA (1739, Ottoman Wars)
KURDLAH (1795, Maratha Wars)
LA HOGUE (1692, War of the Grand Alliance)
LARISSA (171 B.C., Third Macedonian War)
L'ECLUSE (1340, Hundred Years' War)
LEGHORN (1653, Anglo-Dutch Wars)
LEGNANO (1176, Wars of the Lombard League)
LEIPZIG (1631, Thirty Years' War; 1813, Napoleonic Wars)
LEPANTO (1571, Cyprus War)
LEUCTRA (371 B.C., Wars of the Greek City States)
LEUTHEN (1757, Seven Years' War)
LINCOLN, FAIR OF (1217, First Barons' War)
LINDLEY (1900, Second Boer War)
LOCNINH (1967, Vietnam War)
LOFTCHA (1877, Russo-Turkish War)
LUCKNOW (1857, Indian Mutiny)
LUZZARA (1702, War of the Spanish Succession)
MAGENTA (1859, Italian Wars of Independence)
MAIWAND (1880, Second British-Afghan War)
MALACCA (1513, Portuguese Conquests)
MALAKOV (1855, Crimean War)
MALNATE (1859, Italian Wars of Independence)
MANSURA (1250, Seventh Crusade)
MARENGO (1800, French Revolutionary Wars)
MARGATE (1387, Hundred Years' War)
MAROSCH, THE (101, Roman Empire Wars)
MATAPAN, CAPE (1941, World War II)
MATCHIN (1791, Ottoman Wars)
MEEANEE (1843, Sind Campaign)
MEMPHIS (459 B.C., Athenian Expedition to Egypt; 638, Muslim Conquest of Egypt; 1862, American Civil War)
MENTANA (1867, Italian Wars of Independence)
MESSINA (1284, Aragonese Conquest of Sicily; 1718, War of the Quadruple Alliance)
METHVEN (1306, Wars of Scottish Independence)

7—continued

MILAZZO (1860, Italian Wars of
Independence)
MINORCA (1756, Seven Years' War; 1762,
American Revolutionary War)
MOGILEV (1812, Napoleonic Wars)
MONARDA (1501, Moorish Insurrection)
MONTIEL (1369, Castilian Civil War)
MORELLA (1840, First Carlist War)
MORTARA (1849, Italian Wars of
Independence)
MOSKOWA (1812, Napoleonic Wars)
NAEFELS (1388, Swiss-Austrian Wars)
NAISSUS (269, Gothic Invasion of the Roman
Empire)
NAM DONG (1964, Vietnam War)
NANKING (1949, Chinese Civil War)
NEUWIED (1797, French Revolutionary Wars)
NEWBURN (1640, Anglo-Scottish Wars)
NEWBURY (1643, 1644, English Civil War)
NEW ROSS (1798, Irish Rebellion)
NIAGARA (1759, Seven Years' War)
NINEVEH (627, Persian Wars)
NISIBIS (338, 346, 350, Persian Wars of the
Roman Empire)
NIVELLE (1813, Peninsular War)
OCZAKOV (1737, Ottoman Wars)
ODAWARA (1590, Hojo Rebellion)
OKINAWA (1945, World War II)
OOSCATA (1768, First British-Mysore War)
OPEQUAN (1864, American Civil War)
ORLÉANS (1428, Hundred Years' War)
PAGAHAR (1825, First Burma War)
PALERMO (1848, Italian Wars of
Independence)
PALMYRA (272, Roman Empire Wars)
PANIPAT (1526, Third Mughal Invasion of
India; 1556, Hindu Revolt; 1759, Afghan-
Maratha Wars)
PARKANY (1663, Ottoman Wars)
PLASSEY (1757, Seven Years' War)
PLATAEA (479 B.C., Third Persian Invasion;
429 B.C., Great Peloponnesian War)
PLESCOW (1615, Russo-Swedish Wars)
PLOVDIV (1878, Russo-Turkish War)
POLOTSK (1812, Napoleonic Wars)
PRESTON (1648, English Civil War; 1715, The
Fifteen Rebellion)
PULTAVA (1709, Great Northern War)
PULTUSK (1703, Great Northern War; 1806,
Napoleonic Wars)
PUNNIAR (1843, Gwalior Campaign)
RASTADT (1796, French Revolutionary Wars)
RAVENNA (729, Byzantine Empire Wars; 1512,
War of the Holy League)
READING (871, Danish Invasions of Britain)
REVOLAX (1808, Russo-Swedish Wars)
RIMNITZ (1789, Ottoman Wars)
RIO SECO (1808, Peninsular War)
ROSTOCK (1677, Danish-Swedish Wars)

7—continued

ROUCOUX (1746, War of the Austrian
Succession)
RUMANIA (1916, World War I)
RUSPINA (46 B.C., Civil War of Caesar and
Pompey)
SABUGAL (1811, Peninsular War)
SAGUNTO (1811, Peninsular War)
SALAMIS (480 B.C., Third Persian Invasion;
307 B.C., Wars of Alexander's Successors)
SALERNO (1943, World War II)
SAN JUAN (1898, Spanish-American War)
SÁRKÁNY (1848, Hungarian Rising)
SCUTARI (1474, Ottoman Wars)
SEALION, OPERATION (1940, World War II)
SECCHIA, THE (1734, War of the Polish
Succession)
SEGEWÁR (1849, Hungarian Rising)
SELINUS (409 B.C., Second Carthaginian
Invasion of Sicily)
SEMPACH (1386, Swiss War of Independence)
SENEFFE (1674, Wars of Louis XIV)
SENEKAL (1900, Second Boer War)
SHARQAT (1918, World War I)
SIMGARA (348, 360, Persian Wars of the
Roman Empire)
SINNACA (53 B.C., Parthian War)
SINUIJU (1951, Korean War)
SKALITZ (1866, Seven Weeks' War)
SOBRAON (1846, First British-Sikh War)
SOCZAWA (1676, Ottoman Wars)
SOMNATH (1024, Mahmud's Twelfth Invasion
of India)
ST DENIS (1567, French Religious Wars; 1837,
French-Canadian Rising)
ST LUCIA (1794, French Revolutionary Wars)
SURINAM (1804, Napoleonic Wars)
SURSUTI, THE (1191, 1192, Mohammed
Ghori's Invasion)
SVISTOV (1877, Russo-Turkish War)
SZIGETH (1566, Ottoman Wars)
TABRACA (398, Revolt of Gildon)
TAGINAE (552, Byzantine Empire Wars)
TALKHAN (1221, Tatar Invasion of Khorassan)
TALNEER (1818, Third British-Maratha War)
TANAGRA (457 B.C., Peloponnesian Wars)
TANJORE (1758, Seven Years' War; 1773,
First British-Mysore War)
TARANTO (1501, Italian Wars; 1940, World
War II)
TELAMON (225 B.C., Conquest of Cisalpine
Gaul)
TE-LI-SSU (1904, Russo-Japanese War)
TERGOES (1572, Netherlands War of
Independence)
THAPSUS (46 B.C., Civil War of Caesar and
Pompey)
TICINUS (218 B.C., Second Punic War)
TOLBIAC (496, Rise of the Franks)
TOLENUS (90 B.C., Social War)

7—continued

TOURNAI (1581, Netherlands War of Independence; 1709, War of the Spanish Succession)

TREBBIA (218 B.C., Second Punic War; 1799, French Revolutionary Wars)

TREVERI (55 B.C., Gallic Wars)

TRIPOLI (643, Muslim Conquest of Africa)

TUNISIA (1942, World War II)

TURBIGO (1859, Italian Wars of Independence)

UKRAINE (1943, World War II)

UPPSALA (1520, 1521, Danish-Swedish Wars)

VESERIS (339 B.C., Latin War)

VIGO BAY (1702, War of the Spanish Succession)

VILLACH (1492, Ottoman Wars)

VILLETA (1868, Paraguayan War)

VIMEIRO (1808, Peninsular War)

VINAROZ (1938, Spanish Civil War)

VITORIA (1813, Peninsular War)

VOUILLÉ (507, Rise of the Franks)

WARBURG (1760, Seven Years' War)

WARGAOM (1779, First British-Maratha War)

WEPENER (1900, Second Boer War)

WIMPFEN (1622, Thirty Years' War)

WINKOVO (1812, Napoleonic Wars)

YASHIMA (1184, Taira War)

ZLOTSOW (1676, Ottoman Wars)

ZURAKOW (1676, Ottoman Wars)

ZUTPHEN (1586, Netherlands War of Independence)

8

ABERDEEN (1644, English Civil War)

ABU HAMED (1897, British Sudan Campaigns)

ACAPULCO (1855, Mexican Liberal Rising)

ADUATUCA (52 B.C., Gallic Wars)

AIZNADIN (634, Muslim Invasion of Syria)

ALICANTE (1706, War of the Spanish Succession)

ALMENARA (1710, War of the Spanish Succession)

AMALINDE (1818, Kaffir Wars)

ANAQUITO (1546, Conquest of Peru)

ANTIETAM (1862, American Civil War)

AQUILEIA (394, Roman Civil Wars)

ARRETIUM (283 B.C., Etruscan War)

ASIRGHAR (1819, Third British-Maratha War)

ASPENDUS (191 B.C., Wars of the Hellenistic Monarchies)

ASSUNDUN (1016, Danish Invasions of Britain)

ATLANTIC (1917, World War I)

AUGSBURG (900, Germans verus Hungarians)

AULDEARN (1645, English Civil War)

AVARICUM (53 B.C., Gallic Wars)

AXARQUIA (1483, Spanish-Muslim Wars)

AYACUCHO (1824, Peruvian War of Independence)

AZIMGHUR (1858, Indian Mutiny)

8—continued

BAGRADAS (49 B.C., Wars of the First Triumvirate)

BASTOGNE (1944, World War II)

BEAUMONT (1870, Franco-Prussian War)

BEDA FOMM (1941, World War II)

BELGRADE (1456, 1717, 1789, Ottoman Wars)

BELLEVUE (1870, Franco-Prussian War)

BEREZINA (1812, Napoleonic War)

BEYMAROO (1841, First British-Afghan War)

BIBRACTE (58 B.C., Gallic Wars)

BISMARCK (1941, World War II)

BLENHEIM (1704, War of the Spanish Succession)

BLUEBERG (1806, Napoleonic Wars)

BORNHOLM (1676, Northern War)

BORODINO (1812, Napoleonic Wars)

BOULOGNE (1544, Anglo-French Wars)

BOUVINES (1214, Anglo-French Wars)

BOVIANUM (305 B.C., Second Samnite War)

BRIHUEGA (1710, War of the Spanish Succession)

BROOKLYN (1776, American Revolutionary War)

BUZENVAL (1871, Franco-Prussian War)

CALCUTTA (1756, Seven Years' War)

CALDIERO (1796, French Revolutionary Wars; 1805, Napoleonic Wars)

CAPE BONA (468, Wars of the Western Roman Empire)

CARABOBO (1821, Venezuelan War of Independence)

CARLISLE (1745, The Forty-five Rebellion)

CARRICAL (1758, Seven Years' War)

CARTHAGE (152 B.C., Third Punic War; 533, Byzantine Empire Wars)

CASTELLA (1813, Peninsular War)

CAWNPORE (1857, Indian Mutiny)

CHERITON (1644, English Civil War)

CHEVILLY (1870, Franco-Prussian War)

CHIOGGIA (1380, War of Chioggia)

CHIPPEWA (1814, War of 1812)

CLONTARF (1014, Norse Invasion of Ireland)

COCHEREL (1364, Hundred Years' War)

COLOMBEY (1870, Franco-Prussian War)

COPRATUS, THE (316 B.C., Wars of Alexander's Successors)

CORAL SEA (1942, World War II)

COURTRAI (1302, Flemish War)

CRAYFORD (456, Jutish Invasion)

CRIMISUS (341 B.C., Third Carthaginian Invasion of Sicily)

CULLODEN (1746, The Forty-five Rebellion)

CZARNOVO (1806, Napoleonic Wars)

DAMASCUS (635, Muslim Invasion of Syria; 1401, Tatar Invasion of Syria; 1918, World War I)

DAN-NO-URA (1185, Taira War)

DNIESTER (1769, Ottoman Wars)

DOMINICA (1782, American Revolutionary War)

8—continued

DREPANUM (249 B.C., First Punic Wars)

DROGHEDA (1641, Great Irish Rebellion; 1649, Cromwell's Campaign in Ireland)

DRUMCLOG (1679, Covenanters' Rising)

EDGEHILL (1642, English Civil War)

ESPINOSA (1808, Peninsular War)

ETHANDUN (878, Danish Invasions of Britain)

FAIR OAKS (1862, American Civil War)

FAVENTIA (82 B.C., Civil War of Marius and Sulla)

FLANDERS (1940, World War II)

FLORENCE (406, Wars of the Western Roman Empire)

FLUSHING (1809, Napoleonic Wars)

FONTENOY (1745, War of the Austrian Succession)

FORMIGNY (1450, Hundred Years' War)

FRASTENZ (1499, Swiss-Swabian War)

FREIBURG (1644, Thirty Years' War)

FRETEVAL (1194, Anglo-French Wars)

GADEBESK (1712, Great Northern War)

GAULAULI (1858, Indian Mutiny)

GEMBLOUX (1578, Netherlands War of Independence)

GEOK TEPE (1878, Russian Conquest of Central Asia)

GERBEROI (1080, Norman Revolt)

GERGOVIA (52 B.C., Gallic Wars)

GISLIKON (1847, War of the Sonderbund)

GITSCHIN (1866, Seven Weeks' War)

GOODWINS, THE (1666, Anglo-Dutch Wars)

GRAF SPEE (1939, World War II)

GRANICUS, THE (334 B.C., Alexander's Asiatic Campaigns)

GÜNZBURG (1805, Napoleonic Wars)

HADRANUM (344 B.C., Sicilian Wars)

HAHOZAKI (1274, Tatar Invasion of Japan)

HASTINGS (1066, Norman Conquest)

HERACLEA (280 B.C., Pyrrhus' Invasion of Italy; 313, Roman Civil Wars)

HERDONEA (210 B.C., Second Punic War)

HERRINGS, THE (1429, Hundred Years' War)

HONG KONG (1941, World War II)

HYDASPES, THE (326 B.C., Alexander's Asiatic Campaigns)

INKERMAN (1854, Crimean War)

ITABITSU (740, Hirotsuke's Rebellion)

JEMAPPES (1792, French Revolutionary Wars)

JIDBALLI (1904, Somali Expedition)

JOTAPATA (67 A.D., Jewish Wars of Roman Empire)

KANDAHAR (1221, Tatar Invasion of Afghanistan; 1545, Mughal Invasion of Afghanistan; 1648, Perso-Afghan Wars; 1834, Afghan Tribal Wars; 1880, Second British-Afghan War)

KATZBACH (1813, Napoleonic Wars)

KHARTOUM (1884, British-Sudan Campaigns)

KIRBEKAN (1885, British Sudan Campaigns)

8—continued

KLUSHINO (1610, Russo-Polish Wars)

KORYGAOM (1818, Third British-Maratha War)

KULEVCHA (1829, Ottoman Wars)

KUMAMOTO (1876, Satsuma Rebellion)

KUMANOVO (1912, 1st Balkan War)

LANGPORT (1645, English Civil War)

LANGSIDE (1568, Scottish Civil Wars)

LA PUEBLA (1862, 1863, Franco-Mexican War)

LARISSUS, THE (209 B.C., Wars of the Achaean League)

LAUFFELD (1747, War of the Austrian Succession)

LAUTULAE (316 B.C., Second Samnite War)

LE CATEAU (1914, World War I)

LEITSKAU (1813, Napoleonic Wars)

LEONTINI (211 B.C., Second Punic War)

LIAOYANG (1904, Russo-Japanese War)

LIEGNITZ (1760, Seven Years' War)

LOBOSITZ (1756, Seven Years' War)

LUNCARTY (980, Danish Invasions of Scotland)

LYS RIVER (1918, World War I)

MAFEKING (1899, Second Boer War)

MAGNESIA (190 B.C., Wars of the Hellenistic Monarchies)

MAHIDPUR (1817, Third British-Maratha War)

MANDONIA (338 B.C., Macedonian Wars)

MANTINEA (418 B.C., Peloponnesian War; 362 B.C., Wars of the Greek City States; 208 B.C., Wars of the Achaean League)

MARATHON (490 B.C., Persian-Greek Wars)

MEDELLIN (1809, Peninsular War)

MEDENINE (1943, World War II)

MELITENE (578, Persian-Byzantine Wars)

MESSINES (1917, World War I)

METAURUS (207 B.C., Second Punic War)

MOLLWITZ (1741, War of the Austrian Succession)

MONTREAL (1760, Seven Years' War)

MORTLACK (1010, Danish Invasions of Scotland)

MORTMANT (1814, Napoleonic Wars)

MÖSKIRCH (1800, French Revolutionary Wars)

MOUSCRON (1794, French Revolutionary Wars)

MÜHLBERG (1547, German Reformation Wars)

MÜHLDORF (1322, Civil War of the Holy Roman Empire)

MUSA BAGH (1858, Indian Mutiny)

MYTILENE (428 B.C., 406 B.C., Great Peloponnesian War)

NAVARINO (1827, Greek War of Independence)

NEHAVEND (A.D. 641, Muslim Invasion of Persia)

NIQUITAS (1813, Colombian War of Independence)

8—continued

NUMANTIA (142 B.C., Lusitanian War)
OBLIGADO (1845, Uruguayan Civil War)
OMDURMAN (1898, British-Sudan Campaigns)
ONESSANT (1778, American Revolutionary
War)
OSTROWNO (1812, Napoleonic Wars)
OVERLORD, OPERATION (1944, World War II)
PALESTRO (1859, Italian Wars of
Independence)
PALO ALTO (1846, American-Mexican War)
PANDOSIA (331 B.C., Macedonian Wars)
PANORMUS (251 B.C., First Punic War)
PEA RIDGE (1862, American Civil War)
PELUSIUM (525 B.C., Persian Conquest of
Egypt; 321 B.C., War of Alexander's
Successors)
PESHAWAR (1001, Afghan Invasion of India)
PHILIPPI (42 B.C., Roman Civil Wars)
PODHAJCE (1667, Polish-Turkish Wars)
POITIERS (507, Gothic Invasion of France;
1356, Hundred Years' War)
PORTLAND (1653, Anglo-Dutch Wars)
PYRAMIDS (1798, French Revolutionary Wars)
PYRENEES (1813, Peninsular War)
RATHENOW (1675, Swedish Invasion of
Brandenburg)
RICHMOND (1862, American Civil War)
ROSSBACH (1757, Seven Years' War)
ROVEREDO (1796, French Revolutionary
Wars)
SAALFELD (1806, Napoleonic Wars)
SAMAGHAR (1658, Rebellion of Aurungzebe)
SANTAREM (1834, Portuguese Civil War)
SAPIENZA (1490, Ottoman Wars)
SARATOGA (1777, American Revolutionary
War)
SAUCOURT (861, Norse Invasion of France)
SEMINARA (1495, French Wars in Italy)
SENTINUM (298 B.C., Third Samnite War)
SHANGHAI (1937, Sino-Japanese War)
SHOLAPUR (1818, Third British-Maratha War)
SIDASSIR (1799, Third British-Mysore War)
SIKAJOKI (1808, Russo-Swedish Wars)
SILISTRA (1854, Crimean War)
SINSHEIM (1674, Wars of Louis XIV)
SLIVNICA (1885, Serbo-Bulgarian War)
SMOLENSK (1708, Great Northern War; 1812,
Napoleonic Wars; 1941, World War II)
SOISSONS (486, Rise of the Franks)
SORAUREN (1813, Peninsular War)
SPION KOP (1900, Second Boer War)
SPLITTER (1679, Swedish Invasion of
Brandenburg)
ST ALBANS (1455, 1461, Wars of the Roses)
STANDARD, THE (1138, Anglo-Scottish Wars)
STE CROIX (1807, Napoleonic Wars)
ST GEORGE (1500, Ottoman Wars)
ST MIHIEL (1918, World War I)
STOCKACH (1799, French Revolutionary
Wars)

8—continued

ST PRIVAT (1870, Franco-Prussian War)
STRATTON (1643, English Civil War)
ST THOMAS (1807, Napoleonic Wars)
SYRACUSE (415 B.C., Peloponnesian Wars;
387 B.C., Second Carthaginian Invasion of
Sicily; 213 B.C., Second Punic War)
TACUBAYA (1859, Mexican Liberal Rising)
TALAVERA (1809, Peninsular War)
TARAPACÁ (1879, Peruvian-Chilean War)
TAYEIZAN (1868, Japanese Revolution)
TEMESVAR (1849, Hungarian Rising)
THETFORD (870, Danish Invasions of
England)
TIBERIAS (1187, Crusader-Saracen Wars)
TOULOUSE (1814, Napoleonic Wars)
TRINIDAD (1797, French Revolutionary Wars)
TSINGTAO (1914, World War I)
TSUSHIMA (1419, Mongol Invasion of Japan)
TURNHOUT (1597, Netherlands War of
Independence)
VALLETTA (1798, French Revolutionary Wars)
VALUTINO (1812, Napoleonic Wars)
VELENEZE (1848, Hungarian Rising)
VELLETRI (1849, Italian Wars of
Independence)
VERNEUIL (1424, Hundred Years' War)
VILLIERS (1870, Franco-Prussian War)
VOLTURNO (1860, Italian Wars of
Independence)
WATERLOO (1815, Napoleonic Wars)
WATIGAON (1825, First Burma War)
WIESLOCH (1622, Thirty Years' War)
YAMAZAKI (1582, Mitsuhide Rebellion)
YENIKALE, GULF OF (1790, Ottoman Wars)
YORKTOWN (1781, American Revolutionary
War; 1862, American Civil War)
ZENDECAN (1039, Turkish Invasion of
Afghanistan)
ZORNDORF (1758, Seven Years' War)

9

ABENSBERG (1809, Napoleonic Wars)
AGENDICUM (52 B.C., Gallic Wars)
AGINCOURT (1415, Hundred Years' War)
AGNADELLO (1509, War of the League of
Cambrai)
AHMADABAD (1780, First British-Maratha
War)
AHMED KHEL (1880, Second British-Afghan
War)
AIGUILLON (1347, Hundred Years' War)
ALCÁNTARA (1580, Spanish Conquest of
Portugal; 1706, War of the Spanish
Succession)
ALHANDEGA (939, Spanish-Muslim Wars)
ALRESFORD (1644, English Civil War)
ALTENDORF (1632, Thirty Years' War)
AMSTETTEN (1805, Napoleonic Wars)
ANGOSTURA (1847, American-Mexican War;
1868, Paraguayan War)
AQUIDABAN (1870, Paraguayan War)

9—continued

ARGINUSAE (406 B.C., Great Peloponnesian War)
ARKENHOLM (1455, Douglas Rebellion)
ASKULTSIK (1828, Ottoman Wars)
ASTRAKHAN (1569, Turkish Invasion of Russia)
ATAHUALPA (1531, Conquest of Peru)
AUERSTADT (1806, Napoleonic Wars)
AYLESFORD (456, Jutish Invasion of Britain)
BALACLAVA (1854, Crimean War)
BALLYMORE (1798, Irish Rebellion)
BANGALORE (1791, Second British-Mysore War)
BARCELONA (1705, War of the Spanish Succession; 1938, Spanish Civil War)
BEDRIACUM (69, Civil Wars of the Roman Empire)
BENEVENTO (1266, Franco-Italian Wars)
BERGFRIED (1807, Napleonic Wars)
BHURTPORE (1805, Second British-Maratha War; 1827, Second Siege of)
BLACK ROCK (1812, War of 1812)
BLUFF COVE (1982, Falkland Isles)
BOIS-LE-DUC (1794, French Revolutionary Wars)
BORGHETTO (1796, French Revolutionary Wars)
BORNHÖVED (1227, War of Scandinavia)
BRENTFORD (1642, English Civil War)
BRIG OF DEE (1639, Bishops' Wars)
BUCHAREST (1771, Ottoman Wars)
BURNS HILL (1847, Kaffir Wars)
BYZANTIUM (318 B.C., Wars of Alexander's Successors; 323, Civil Wars of the Roman Empire)
CAMERINUM (298 B.C., Third Samnite War)
CAPE HENRY (1781, American Revolutionary War)
CAPORETTO (1917, World War I)
CAPRYSEMA (743 B.C., First Messenian War)
CASILINUM (554, Byzantine Empire Wars)
CASTILLON (1453, Hundred Years' War)
CERIGNOLA (1503, Italian Wars)
CHACABUCO (1817, Chilean War of Independence)
CHAERONEA (338 B.C., Amphictyonic War; 86 B.C., First Mithridatic War)
CHALCEDON (74 B.C., Third Mithridatic War)
CHAMPAGNE (1915, World War I)
CHARASIAB (1879, Second British-Afghan War)
CHARENTON (1649, War of the Fronde)
CHE-MUL-PHO (1904, Russo-Japanese War)
CHORILLOS (1861, Peruvian-Chilean War)
CHOTUSITZ (1742, War of the Austrian Succession)
CIVITELLA (1033, Norman Invasion of Italy)
CORRICHIE (1562, Huntly's Rebellion)
COULMIERS (1870, Franco-Prussian War)
CROSSKEYS (1862, American Civil War)

9—continued

CUDDALORE (1783, American Revolutionary War)
CURUPAYTI (1866, Paraguayan War)
CYNOSSEMA (411 B.C., Peloponnesian War)
DENNEWITZ (1813, Napoleonic Wars)
DETTINGEN (1743, War of the Austrian Succession)
DEVICOTTA (1749, Carnatic War)
DORYLAEUM (1097, First Crusade)
DUNSINANE (1054, Anglo-Scottish Wars)
EBRO RIVER (1938, Spanish Civil War)
EDERSBERG (1809, Napoleonic Wars)
EDGEWORTH (1469, Wars of the Roses)
EL ALAMEIN (1942, World War II)
ELCHINGEN (1805, Napoleonic Wars)
ELLANDUNE (825, Wessex versus Mercia)
ELLEPORUS (389 B.C., Italiot Invasion of Sicily)
EMPINGHAM (1470, Wars of the Roses)
EURYMEDON, THE (466 B.C., Third Persian Invasion)
FAMAGUSTA (1570, Cyprus War)
FISH CREEK (1855, Riel's Second Rebellion)
FIVE FORKS (1865, American Civil War)
FRIEDLAND (1807, Napoleonic Wars)
FRONTIERS, BATTLE OF THE (1914, World War I)
GALLIPOLI (1915, World War I)
GERMAGHAH (1193, Tatar Conquest of Central Asia)
GIBRALTAR (1704, War of the Spanish Succession; 1779, American Revolutionary War)
GLADSMUIR (1745, The Forty-five Rebellion)
GLEN FRUIN (1604, Scottish Civil Wars)
GLENLIVET (1594, Huntly's Rebellion)
GRAMPIANS, THE (Roman Invasion of Scotland)
GRANDELLA (1266, Italian Wars)
GUAL-EL-RAS (1860, Spanish-Moroccan War)
GUINEGATE (1513, Anglo-French Wars)
GUMBINNEN (1914, World War I)
HALIARTUS (395 B.C., Wars of Greek City-States)
HEILSBERG (1807, Napoleonic Wars)
HEMUSHAGU (1595, Japanese Invasion of Korea)
HÉRICOURT (1474, Burgundian Wars)
HOCHKIRCH (1758, Seven Years' War)
HÖCHSTÄDT (1800, French Revolutionary Wars)
HYDERABAD (1843, Conquest of Sind)
JERUSALEM (70 A.D., Jewish Wars of Roman Empire; 637, Muslim Invasion of Syria; 1099, First Crusade; 1187, Crusader-Turkish Wars; 1917, World War I; 1948, Israeli-Arab Wars)
JUGDULLUK (1842, First British-Afghan War)
KAGOSHIMA (1877, Satsuma Rebellion)
KARA BURUR (1791, Ottoman Wars)
KARAGAULA (1774, Cossack Rising)

9—continued

KARAMURAN (1225, Tatar Conquest of
  Central Asia)
KASSASSIN (1882, Egyptian Revolt)
KEMENDINE (1824, First Burma War)
KERESZTES (1596, Ottoman Wars)
KHARISMIA (1220, Tatar Invasion of Central
  Asia)
KIMBERLEY (1899, Second Boer War)
KISSINGEN (1866, Seven Weeks' War)
KIZIL-TEPE (1877, Russo-Turkish War)
KRAKOVICZ (1475, Ottoman Wars)
KUNOBITZA (1443, Ottoman Wars)
LADYSMITH (1899, Second Boer War)
LANG'S NECK (1881, First Boer War)
LANSDOWNE (1643, English Civil Wars)
LE BOURGET (1870, Franco-Prussian War)
LENINGRAD (1944, World War II)
LEXINGTON (1775, American Revolutionary
  War; 1861, American Civil War)
LEYTE GULF (1944, World War II)
LILYBAEUM (250 B.C., First Punic War)
LINKÖPING (1598, Swedish-Polish Wars)
LÖWENBERG (1813, Napoleonic Wars)
MAGDEBURG (1631, Thirty Years' War)
MALAVILLY (1799, Third British-Mysore War)
MALEGNANO (1859, Italian Wars of
  Independence)
MANGALORE (1783, First British-Mysore War)
MANSFIELD (1864, American Civil War)
MARIA ZELL (1805, Napoleonic Wars)
MARIGNANO (1515, Italian Wars)
MARSAGLIA (1693, War of the Grand Alliance)
MERSEBURG (934, Germans against
  Hungarians)
MILLESIMO (1796, French Revolutionary
  Wars)
MIOHOSAKI (764, Oshikatsa's Rebellion)
MITA CABAN (1362, Tatar Wars)
MOHRUNGEN (1807, Napoleonic Wars)
MONTEREAU (1814, Napoleonic Wars)
MONTERREY (1846, Amercian-Mexican War)
MONTLHÉRY (1465, Franco-Burgundian War)
MORAZZONE (1848, Italian Wars of
  Independence)
MUKWANPUR (1816, British-Gurkha War)
MYONNESUS (190 B.C., Wars of the
  Hellenistic Monarchies)
NAGY-SARLO (1849, Hungarian Rising)
NASHVILLE (1863, American Civil War)
NAULOCHUS (36 B.C., Wars of the Second
  Triumvirate)
NAUPACTUS (429 B.C., Great Peloponnesian
  War)
NAVARRETE (1367, Hundred Years' War)
NEGAPATAM (1746, War of the Austrian
  Succession; 1781, Second British Mysore
  War; 1782, American Revolutionary War)
NEW GUINEA (1942, World War II)
NEW MARKET (1864, American Civil War)

9—continued

NICOPOLIS (66 B.C., 47 B.C., Third Mithridatic
  War; 1396, Ottoman Wars; 1877, Russo-
  Turkish War)
NUJUFGHUR (1857, Indian Mutiny)
OCEAN POND (1864, American Civil War)
OENOPHYTA (457 B.C., First Peloponnesian
  War)
OLTENITZA (1853, Crimean War)
OTTERBURN (1388, Wars of Scottish
  Independence)
OUDENARDE (1708, War of the Spanish
  Succession)
PELEKANON (1329, Ottoman Wars)
PELISCHAT (1877, Russo-Turkish War)
PERISABOR (363, Persian Wars)
PERPIGNAN (1474, Franco-Spanish War)
PHARSALUS (48 B.C., Civil War of Caesar and
  Pompey; 1897, Greco-Turkish Wars)
PLACENTIA (271, Invasion of the Alemanni)
POLLENTIA (402, Wars of the Western Roman
  Empire)
POLLICORE (1781, First British-Mysore War)
PONTEVERT (57 B.C., Gallic Wars)
PORTO NOVO (1781, First British-Mysore
  War)
PRIMOLANÓ (1796, French Revolutionary
  Wars)
PRINCETON (1777, American Revolutionary
  War)
PYONGYANG (1894, Sino-Japanese War)
QUISTELLO (1734, War of the Polish
  Succession)
RAMILLIES (1706, War of the Spanish
  Succession)
RAMNUGGUR (1849, Second British-Sikh
  War)
RATHMINES (1649, Cromwell's Campaign in
  Ireland)
RHINELAND, THE (1945, World War II)
RIACHUELA (1865, Paraguayan War)
ROSBECQUE (1382, Flemish-French Wars)
ROSEBURGH (1460, Anglo-Scottish Wars)
RYNEMANTS (1578, Netherlands War of
  Independence)
SADULAPUR (1848, Second British-Sikh War)
SALAMANCA (1812, Peninsular War; 1858,
  Mexican Liberal Rising)
SAMARKAND (1220, Tatar Invasion of
  Khorezm)
SAN LAZARO (1746, War of the Austrian
  Succession)
SANTANDER (1937, Spanish Civil War)
SARAGOSSA (1700, War of the Spanish
  Succession; 1808, Peninsular War)
SAXA RUBRA (312, Revolt of Maxentius)
SCARPHEIA (146 B.C., War of the Achaean
  League)
SCHWECHAT (1848, Hungarian Rising)
SEDGEMOOR (1685, Monmouth's Rebellion)
SERINGHAM (1753, Carnatic War)

9—continued

SEVENOAKS (1450, Cade's Rebellion)
SHAHJEHAN (1221, Tatar Invasion of Khorezm)
SHALDIRAN (1514, Ottoman Wars)
SHEERNESS (1667, Anglo-Dutch Wars)
SHERSTONE (1016, Danish Invasion of England)
SHINOWARA (1183, Yoshinaka's Rebellion)
SHIROGAWA (1876, Satsuma Rebellion)
SHOLINGUR (1781, First British-Mysore War)
SINGAPORE (1942, World War II)
SITABALDI (1817, Third British-Maratha War)
SOLFERINO (1859, Italian Wars of Independence)
SOUTHWARK (1450, Cade's Rebellion)
SPICHEREN (1870, Franco-Prussian War)
STADTLOHN (1623, Thirty Years' War)
STAFFARDA (1690, War of the Grand Alliance)
ST CHARLES (1837, French-Canadian Rising)
ST GOTHARD (1664, Ottoman Wars)
STORMBERG (1899, Second Boer War)
ST QUENTIN (1557, Franco-Spanish Wars; 1871, Franco-Prussian War)
STRALSUND (1628, Thirty Years' War; 1715, Great Northern War)
SUDDASAIN (1848, Second British-Sikh War)
TAKASHIMA (1281, Chinese Invasion of Japan)
TAKU FORTS (1859, Second China War)
TARRAGONA (1811, Peninsular War)
TCHERNAYA (1855, Crimean War)
TOLENTINO (1815, Napoleonic Wars)
TOU MORONG (1966, Vietnam War)
TOURCOING (1794, French Revolutionary Wars)
TRAFALGAR (1805, Napoleonic Wars)
TRAUTENAU (1866, Seven Weeks' War)
TREBIZOND (1461, Ottoman Wars)
TRINKITAT (1884, British-Sudan Campaigns)
VAALKRANZ (1900, Second Boer War)
VARAVILLE (1058, Rise of Normandy)
VAUCHAMPS (1814, Napoleonic Wars)
VERCELLAE (101 B.C., Cimbric War)
VICKSBURG (1862, American Civil War)
VIMY RIDGE (1917, World War I)
VIONVILLE (1870, Franco-Prussian War)
WAKAMATSU (1868, Japanese Revolution)
WAKEFIELD (1460, Wars of the Roses)
WANDIWASH (1760, Seven Years' War; 1780, First British-Mysore War)
WEI-HAI-WEI (1895, Sino-Japanese War)
WORCESTER (1651, English Civil War)
WÜRZBURG (1796, French Revolutionary Wars)
WYNANDAEL (1708, War of the Spanish Succession)
YALU RIVER (1894, Sino-Japanese War; 1904, Russo-Japanese War)
ZEUGMINUM (1168, Hungarian Wars)

9—continued

ZUYDER ZEE (1573, Netherlands War of Indpendence)

10

ACULTZINGO (1862, Franco-Mexican War)
ADRIANOPLE (1205, Fourth Crusade; 1913, First Balkan War)
AHMADNAGAR (1593, Mughal Invasion of the Deccan)
ALADJA DAGH (1877, Russo-Turkish War)
ALEXANDRIA (642, Muslim Invasion of Egypt; 1801, British Invasion of Egypt; 1881, Egyptian Revolt)
ALTO PASCIO (1325, Guelfs and Ghibellines)
AMPHIPOLIS (422 B.C., Great Peloponnesian War)
ANCRUM MOOR (1545, Anglo-Scottish Wars)
ARGENTARIA (378, Invasion of the Alemanni)
ARTOIS-LOOS (1915, World War I)
ASPROMONTE (1862, Italian Wars of Independence)
AUSTERLITZ (1805, Napoleonic Wars)
BALL'S BLUFF (1861, American Civil War)
BEACHY HEAD (1690, War of the Grand Alliance)
BEAUSÉJOUR (1755, Seven Year's War)
BENEVENTUM (275 B.C., Pyrrhus' Invasion of Italy; 214 B.C., 212 B.C., Second Punic War)
BENNINGTON (1777, American Revolutionary War)
BERESTECKO (1651, Polish-Cossack War)
BLACKHEATH (1497, Flammock's Rebellion)
BLACKWATER (1598, O'Neill's Rebellion)
BLORE HEATH (1459, Wars of the Roses)
BRANDYWINE (1777, American Revolutionary War)
BRUNANBURH (937, Danish Invasion)
BUENA VISTA (1846, American-Mexican War)
CALATAFIMI (1860, Italian Wars of Independence)
CAMPALDINO (1289, Guelfs and Ghibellines)
CAMPERDOWN (1797, French Revolutionary Wars)
CAMPO SANTO (1743, War of the Austrian Succession)
CARAGUATAY (1869, Paraguayan War)
CARTHAGENA (1741, War of the Austrian Succession)
CEDAR CREEK (1864, American Civil War)
CERISOLLES (1544, Wars of Charles V)
CHARLESTON (1863, American Civil War)
CHEVY CHASE (1388, Wars of Scottish Independence)
CHINGLEPUT (1752, Carnatic War)
CHIPPENHAM (878, Danish Invasions of Britain)
COPENHAGEN (1801, French Revolutionary Wars; 1807, Napoleonic Wars)
CORTE NUOVA (1237, Guelfs and Ghibellines)
CORUPEDION (281 B.C., Wars of the Hellenistic Monarchies)

10—continued

DALMANUTHA (1900, Second Boer War)
DOGGER BANK (1781, American
  Revolutionary War; 1915, World War I)
DONAUWÖRTH (1704, War of the Spanish
  Succession)
DUFFINDALE (1549, Kett's Rebellion)
DUNGANHILL (1647, Great Irish Rebellion)
DYRRACHIUM (48 B.C., Civil War of Caesar
  and Pompey)
ENGLEFIELD (871, Danish Invasion of Britain)
FEHRBELLIN (1675, Swedish Invasion of
  Brandenburg)
FEROZESHAH (1845, First British-Sikh War)
FETHANLEAG (584, Saxon Conquests)
FUTTEYPORE (1857, Indian Mutiny)
GAINES' MILL (1862, American Civil War)
GARIGLIANO (1503, Italian Wars; 1850, Italian
  Wars of Independence)
GERMANTOWN (1777, American
  Revolutionary War)
GETTYSBURG (1863, American Civil War)
GLEN MALONE (1580, Colonization of Ireland)
GOLDEN ROCK (1753, Carnatic War)
GORODECZNO (1812, Napoleonic Wars)
GOTHIC LINE (1944, World War II)
GRANT'S HILL (1758, Seven Years' War)
GRAVELINES (1558, Franco-Spanish Wars)
GRAVELOTTE (1870, Franco-Prussian War)
GUADELOUPE (1794, French Revolutionary
  Wars)
HABBANIYAH (1941, World War II)
HARDENBERG (1580, Netherlands War of
  Independence)
HASTENBECK (1757, Seven Years' War)
HEATHFIELD (633, Mercia against
  Northumbria)
HEKITAI-KAN (1595, Japanese Invasion of
  Korea)
HELIGOLAND (1807, Napoleonic Wars)
HELIOPOLIS (1800, French Revolutionary
  Wars)
HELLESPONT (323, War of the Two Empires)
HOLLABRUNN (1805, Napleonic Wars)
HUMBLEBECK (1700, Great Northern War)
ICHINOTANI (1189, Taira War)
INVERLOCHY (1645, English Civil War)
JELLALABAD (1842, First British-Afghan War)
KHOJAH PASS (1842, First British-Afghan
  War)
KÖNIGGRÄTZ (1866, Seven Weeks' War)
KORNSPRUIT (1900, Second Boer War)
KRINGELLEN (1612, Danish-Swedish Wars)
KUNERSDORF (1759, Seven Years' War)
KUT-EL-AMARA (1915, World War I)
LA FAVORITA (1797, French Revolutionary
  Wars)
LAKE GEORGE (1755, Seven Years' War)
LANDSKRONE (1676, Danish-Swedish Wars)
LA PLACILLA (1891, Chilean Civil War)

10—continued

LA ROCHELLE (1372, Hundred Years' War;
  1627, French Religious Wars)
LA ROTHIÈRE (1814, Napoleonic Wars)
LAS SALINAS (1538, Conquest of Peru)
LEUCOPETRA (146 B.C., Wars of the Achaean
  League)
LOUDON HILL (1307, Wars of Scottish
  Independence)
LOUISBOURG (1745, War of the Austrian
  Succession; 1758, Seven Years' War)
LÜLEBÜRGAZ (1912, Balkan Wars)
LUNDY'S LANE (1814, War of 1812)
MAASTRICHT (1579, Netherlands War of
  Independence)
MAHARAJPUR (1843, Gwalior Campaign;
  1857, Indian Mutiny)
MALPLAQUET (1709, War of the Spanish
  Succession)
MARETH LINE (1943, World War II)
MARIENDAHL (1645, Thirty Years' War)
MARS-LA-TOUR (1870, Franco-Prussian War)
MARTINESTI (1789, Ottoman Wars)
MARTINIQUE (1794, French Revolutionary
  Wars; 1809, Napoleonic Wars)
MASERFIELD (642, Northumbria against
  Mercia)
MELANTHIAS (559, Wars of the Byzantine
  Empire)
MICHELBERG (1805, Napoleonic Wars)
MIDDELBURG (1593, Netherlands War of
  Independence)
MIRAFLORES (1881, Peruvian-Chilean War)
MONTEBELLO (1800, French Revolutionary
  Wars; 1859, Italian Wars of Independence)
MONTENOTTE (1796, French Revolutionary
  Wars)
MONTEVIDEO (1807, Napoleonic Wars; 1843,
  1851, 1863, Uruguayan Civil War)
MONTFAUCON (886, Norman Invasion of
  France)
MONTMIRAIL (1814, Napoleonic Wars)
MORTGARTEN (1315, First Swiss-Austrian
  War)
MOUNT TABOR (1799, French Revolutionary
  Wars)
MÜHLHAUSEN (58 B.C., Gallic War)
NAROCH LAKE (1916, World War I)
NEERWINDEN (1693, War of the Grand
  Alliance; 1793, French Revolutionary Wars)
NEW ORLEANS (1814, War of 1812; 1862,
  American Civil War)
NIEUWPOORT (1600, Netherlands War of
  Independence)
NÖRDLINGEN (1634, 1645, Thirty Year's War)
ORCHOMENUS (85 B.C., First Mithridatic War)
OSTROLENKA (1853, Crimean War)
PAARDEBERG (1900, Second Boer War)
PALESTRINA (1849, Italian Wars of
  Independence)
PANDU NADDI (1857, Indian Mutiny)

10—continued

PEN SELWOOD (1016, Danish Invasions of Britain)

PEREMBACUM (1780, First British-Mysore War)

PERRYVILLE (1862, American Civil War)

PERSEPOLIS (316 B.C., Wars of Alexander's Successors)

PETERSBURG (1864, American Civil War)

PIAVE RIVER (1918, World War I)

PONT VALAIN (1370, Hundred Years' War)

PORT ARTHUR (1894, Sino-Japanese War; 1904, Russo-Japanese Wars)

PORT HUDSON (1863, American Civil War)

PORTO BELLO (1740, War of the Austrian Succession)

QUATRE BRAS (1815, Napoleonic Wars)

QUIPUAYPAN (1532, Conquest of Peru)

RAKERSBERG (1416, Ottoman Wars)

ROMERSWAEL (1574, Netherlands War of Independence)

RUHR POCKET (1945, World War II)

RUMERSHEIM (1709, War of the Spanish Successsion)

SALANKEMEN (1691, Ottoman Wars)

SAN ISODORO (1870, Paraguayan War)

SAN JACINTO (1836, Texan Rising; 1867, Franco-Mexican War)

SANNA'S POST (1900, Second Boer War)

SANTA LUCIA (1842, Rio Grande Rising)

SAVANDROOG (1791, Second British-Mysore War)

SEINE MOUTH (1416, Hundred Years' War)

SEKIGAHARA (1600, Rebellion of Hideyori)

SEVASTOPOL (1854, Crimean War)

SEVEN PINES (1862, American Civil War)

SHREWSBURY (1403, Percy's Rebellion)

SHROPSHIRE (A.D. 50, Roman Conquest of Britain)

SIDI REZEGH (1941, World War II)

SOLWAY MOSS (1542, Anglo-Scottish Wars)

SPHACTERIA (425 B.C., Great Peloponnesian War)

STALINGRAD (1942, World War II)

STEENKERKE (1692, War of the Grand Alliance)

ST EUSTACHE (1837, French-Canadian Rising)

STILLWATER (1777, American Revolutionary War)

STOLHOFFEN (1707, War of the Spanish Succession)

STONE RIVER (1862, American Civil War)

TAIKEN GATE (1157, Hogen Insurrection)

TALANA HILL (1899, Second Boer War)

TANNENBERG (1410, German-Polish Wars; 1914, World War I)

TASHKESSEN (1877, Russo-Turkish War)

TEL-EL-KEBIR (1882, Egyptian Revolt)

TETTENHALL (910, Danish Invasions of England)

10—continued

TEWKESBURY (1471, Wars of the Roses)

TINCHEBRAI (1106, Norman Civil War)

TIPPERMUIR (1644, English Civil War)

TRAVANCORE (1789, Second British-Mysore War)

TRICAMERON (533, Invasion of the Vandals)

UTSONOMIYA (1868, Japanese Revolution)

VAL-ÈS-DUNES (1047, Rise of Normandy)

VELESTINOS (1897, Greco-Turkish War)

WARTEMBERG (1813, Napoleonic Wars)

WATTIGNIES (1793, French Revolutionary Wars)

WILDERNESS, THE (1864, American Civil War)

WINCHESTER (1863, American Civil War)

ZIEZICKSEE (1302, Flemish War)

11

ÆGOSPOTAMI (405 B.C., Peloponnesian War)

ALAM EL HALFA (1942, World War II)

ALESSANDRIA (1799, French Revolutionary Wars)

ALJUBAROTTA (1385, Spanish-Portuguese Wars)

AN LAO VALLEY (1966, Vietnam War)

AQUAE SEXTIA (102 B.C., Cimbric War)

BANNOCKBURN (1314, Wars of Scottish Independence)

BELLEAU WOOD (1918, World War I)

BISMARCK SEA (1943, World War II)

BLADENSBURG (1814, War of 1812)

BLANQUEFORT (1450, Hundred Years' War)

BORYSTHENES, THE (1512, Russo-Polish Wars)

BRAMHAM MOOR (1408, Northumberland's Rebellion)

BREITENFELD (1642, Thirty Years' War)

BRENNEVILLE (1119, Anglo-French Wars)

BUENOS AIRES (1806, 1807, Napoleonic Wars; 1874, Mitre's Rebellion)

BUNKER'S HILL (1775, American Revolutionary War)

CALPULALPAM (1860, Mexican Liberal Rising)

CAMELODUNUM (43, Roman Invasion of Britain)

CAPE PASSERO (1718, War of the Quadruple Alliance)

CARBIESDALE (1650, English Civil War)

CARENAGE BAY (1778, American Revolutionary War)

CASTIGLIONE (1706, War of the Spanish Succession; 1796, French Revolutionary Wars)

CASTILLEJOS (1860, Spanish-Moroccan War)

CECRYPHALEA (458 B.C., Third Messenian War)

CHAMPAUBERT (1814, Napoleonic Wars)

CHAPULTEPEC (1847, American-Mexican War)

CHATEAUGUAY (1813, War of 1812)

11—continued

CHATTANOOGA (1863, American Civil War)
CHICKAMAUGA (1863, American Civil War)
CHILIANWALA (1849, Second British-Sikh War)
CHRYSOPOLIS (324, War of the Two Empires)
COLDHARBOUR (1864, American Civil War)
COLLINE GATE (82 B.C., Civil War of Marius and Sulla)
CONSTANTINE (1836, Conquest of Algeria)
DEUTSCHBROD (1422, Hussite War)
DIAMOND HILL (1900, Second Boer War)
DINGAAN'S DAY (1838, Afrikaner-Zulu War)
DOLNI-DUBNIK (1877, Russo-Turkish War)
DRIEFONTEIN (1900, Second Boer War)
DÜRRENSTEIN (1805, Napoleonic Wars)
ELANDS RIVER (1900, Second Boer War)
FARRUKHABAD (1804, Second British-Maratha War)
FERRYBRIDGE (1461, Wars of the Roses)
FISHER'S HILL (1864, American Civil War)
FORT ST DAVID (1758, Seven Years' War)
FRAUBRUNNEN (1376, Invasion of the 'Guglers')
FRAUENSTADT (1706, Great Northern War)
GIBBEL RUTTS (1798, Irish Rebellion)
GORNI-DUBNIK (1877, Russo-Turkish War)
GROSS-BEEREN (1813, Napoleonic Wars)
GUADALAJARA (1937, Spanish Civil War)
GUADALCANAL (1942, World War II)
HADRIANOPLE (323, War of the Two Empires; 378, Second Gothic Invasion of the East)
HALIDON HILL (1333, Wars of Scottish Independence)
HEAVENFIELD (634, Northumbria against the British)
HEILIGERLEE (1568, Netherlands War of Independence)
HELSINGBORG (1710, Great Northern War)
HENNERSDORF (1745, War of the Austrian Succession)
HERMANSTADT (1442, Ottoman Wars)
HOHENLINDEN (1800, French Revolutionary Wars)
HONDSCHOOTE (1793, French Revolutionary Wars)
ÎLE DE FRANCE (1810, Napoleonic Wars)
ISANDHLWANA (1879, Zulu-British War)
KLAUSENBURG (1660, Ottoman Wars)
LAKE KERGUEL (1391, Tatar Invasion of Russia)
LAKE VADIMON (283 B.C., Gallic Invasion of Italy)
LANGENSALZA (1866, Seven Weeks' War)
LONDONDERRY (1689, War of the Grand Alliance)
LOSTWITHIEL (1644, English Civil War)
MACIEJOWICE (1794, First Polish Rising)
MALVERN HILL (1862, American Civil War)
MAOGAMALCHA (363, Persian Wars)
MARSTON MOOR (1644, English Civil War)

11—continued

MASULIPATAM (1759, Seven Years' War)
MEGALOPOLIS (331 B.C., Macedonian Wars; 226 B.C., Wars of the Achaean League)
MERSA MATRÛH (1942, World War II)
MILETOPOLIS (86 B.C., First Mithridatic War)
MILL SPRINGS (1862, American Civil War)
MISSOLONGHI (1821, Greek War of Independence)
MODDER RIVER (1899, Second Boer War)
MONTCONTOUR (1569, Third French Religious War)
MONTE APERTO (1260, Guelfs and Ghibellines)
MONTE LEZINO (1796, French Revolutionary Wars)
MONTMORENCI (1759, Seven Years' War)
MOOKERHEIDE (1574, Netherlands War of Independence)
MORSHEDABAD (1763, British Conquest of Bengal)
MOUNT TAURUS (804, Muslim Invasion of Asia Minor)
MOUNT TIFATA (83 B.C., Civil War of Marius and Sulla)
NOISSEVILLE (1870, Franco-Prussian War)
NORTHAMPTON (1460, Wars of the Roses)
PEARL HARBOR (1941, World War II)
PEIWAR KOTAL (1878, Second British-Afghan War)
PENA CERRADA (1838, First Carlist War)
PHILIPHAUGH (1645, English Civil War)
PIETER'S HILL (1900, Second Boer War)
PONDICHERRY (1748, War of the Austrian Succession; 1760, Seven Years' War; 1778, 1783, American Revolutionary War)
PRESTONPANS (1745, The Forty-five Rebellion)
QUIBERON BAY (1759, Seven Years' War)
RAJAHMUNDRY (1758, Seven Years' War)
REDDERSBERG (1900, Second Boer War)
RHEINFELDEN (1638, Thirty Years' War)
RIETFONTEIN (1899, Second Boer War)
RORKE'S DRIFT (1879, Zulu-British War)
ROTTO FREDDO (1746, War of the Austrian Succession)
ROWTON HEATH (1645, English Civil War)
SACRIPONTUS (82 B.C., Civil War of Marius and Sulla)
SALDANHA BAY (1796, French Revolutionary Wars)
SAN GIOVANNI (1799, French Revolutionary Wars)
SAUCHIE BURN (1488, Rebellion of the Scottish Barons)
SCHIPKA PASS (1877, Russo-Turkish War)
SHERIFFMUIR (1715, The Fifteen Rebellion)
SHIJO NAWATE (1339, War of the Northern and Southern Empires)
SIDI BARRÂNI (1940, World War II)
STAVRICHANI (1739, Ottoman Wars)

11—continued

TAGLIACOZZO (1268, Guelfs and Ghibellines)
TAILLEBOURG (1242, Anglo-French Wars)
TANSARA SAKA (1876, Satsuma Rebellion)
TARAWA-MAKIN (1943, World War II)
TEL-EL-MAHUTA (1882, Egyptian Revolt)
TELLICHERRY (1780, First British-Mysore War)
TEUTTLINGEN (1643, Thirty Years' War)
THERMOPYLAE (480 B.C., Third Persian Invasion; 191 B.C., Wars of the Hellenistic Monarchies)
TICONDEROGA (1758, Seven Years' War; 1777, American Revolutionary War)
TRINCOMALEE (1759, Seven Years' War; 1767, First British-Mysore War; 1782, American Revolutionary War)
VINEGAR HILL (1798, Irish Rebellion)
VÖGELINSECK (1402, Appenzel Rebellion)
WALTERSDORF (1807, Napoleonic Wars)
WEDNESFIELD (911, Danish Invasions of England)
WEISSENBURG (1870, Franco-Prussian War)
WHITE RUSSIA (1943, World War II)

12

ADWALTON MOOR (1643, English Civil War)
ALGECIRAS BAY (1801, French Revolutionary Wars)
ARCIS-SUR-AUBE (1814, Napoleonic Wars)
ARGENTORATUM (357, Invasion of the Alemanni)
ARROYO GRANDE (1842, Uruguayan Civil War)
ATHERTON MOOR (1643, English Civil War)
BANDA ISLANDS (1796, French Revolutionary Wars)
BARQUISIMETO (1813, Colombian War of Independence)
BERGEN-OP-ZOOM (1747, War of the Austrian Succession; 1799, French Revolutionary Wars)
BLOEMFONTEIN (1900, Second Boer War)
BRADDOCK DOWN (1643, English Civil War)
CAUDINE FORKS (321 B.C., Second Samnite War)
CHICKAHOMINY (1864, American Civil War)
CONCHA RAYADA (1818, Chilean War of Independence)
ELANDSLAAGTE (1899, Second Boer War)
EUTAW SPRINGS (1781, American Revolutionary War)
FORT DONELSON (1862, American Civil War)
FREDRIKSHALD (1718, Great Northern War)
HAMPTON ROADS (1862, American Civil War)
HARPER'S FERRY (1862, American Civil War)
HEDGELEY MOOR (1464, Wars of the Roses)
HENGESTESDUN (837, Danish Invasions of Britain)
HOMILDON HILL (1402, Anglo-Scottish Wars)
ICLISTAVISUS (16 A.D., Germanic Wars)

12—continued

KIRCH-DENKERN (1761, Seven Years' War)
KIU-LIEN-CHENG (1904, Russo-Japanese War)
KÖNIGSWARTHA (1813, Napoleonic Wars)
KURSK SALIENT (1943, World War II)
LAKE REGILLUS (497 B.C., Roman Civil Wars)
LYNN HAVEN BAY (1781, American Revolutionary War)
MALAKAND PASS (1895, Chitral Campaign)
MIDWAY ISLAND (1942, World War II)
MONS-EN-PÉVÈLE (1304, Flemish War)
MONTE CASEROS (1852, Argentine Civil War)
MONT VALÉRIEN (1871, Franco-Prussian War)
MÜNCHENGRÄTZ (1866, Seven Weeks' War)
MURFREESBORO (1862, American Civil War)
NECHTAN'S MERE (685, Northumbrian Invasion of Scotland)
NOVA CARTHAGO (209 B.C., Second Punic War)
OONDWA NULLAH (1763, British Conquest of Bengal)
PENOBSCOT BAY (1779, American Revolutionary War)
PETERWARDEIN (1716, Ottoman Wars)
PHILIPPSBURG (1734, War of the Polish Succession)
PINKIE CLEUGH (1547, Anglo-Scottish Wars)
PORT REPUBLIC (1862, American Civil War)
PRAIRIE GROVE (1862, American Civil War)
RADCOT BRIDGE (1387, Appellants' Rebellion)
RICH MOUNTAIN (1861, American Civil War)
RONCESVALLES (778, Charlemagne's Conquests; 1813, Peninsular War)
ROUNDWAY DOWN (1643, English Civil War)
RULLION GREEN (1666, Covenanters' Rising)
SAN SEBASTIAN (1813, Peninsular War; 1836, First Carlist War)
SECUNDERBAGH (1857, Indian Mutiny)
SERINGAPATAM (1792, Second British-Mysore War; 1799, Third British-Mysore War)
SOUTHWOLD BAY (1672, Anglo-Dutch Wars)
SPOTSYLVANIA (1864, American Civil War)
ST MARY'S CLYST (1549, Arundel's Rebellion)
SUNGARI RIVER (1947, Chinese Civil War)
TET OFFENSIVE, THE (1968, Vietnam War)
TIGRANOCERTA (69 B.C., Third Mithridatic War)
VALENCIENNES (1566, Netherlands War of Independence; 1656, Franco-Spanish Wars)
VILLA VICIOSA (1710, War of the Spanish Succession)
WILLIAMSBURG (1862, American Civil War)
WILSON'S CREEK (1861, American Civil War)
WROTHAM HEATH (1554, Wyatt's Insurrection)

13

ADMAGETOBRIGA (61 B.C., Gallic Tribal Wars)

AIX-LA-CHAPELLE (1795, French Revolutionary Wars)

AMBRACIAN GULF (435 B.C., Corcyrean-Corinthian War)

BADULI-KI-SERAI (1857, Indian Mutiny)

BELLE-ÎLE-EN-MER (1759, 1761, Seven Years' War; 1795, French Revolutionary Wars)

BOROUGHBRIDGE (1322, Rebellion of the Marches)

BOSWORTH FIELD (1485, Wars of the Roses)

CAPE ST VINCENT (1797, French Revolutionary Wars)

CASTELFIDARDO (1860, Italian Wars of Independence)

CASTELNAUDARY (1632, French Civil Wars)

CEDAR MOUNTAIN (1862, American Civil War)

CHANDERNAGORE (1757, Seven Years' War)

CHRISTIANOPLE (1611, Danish-Swedish Wars)

CHRYSLER'S FARM (1813, War of 1812)

CIUDAD RODRIGO (1812, Peninsular War)

CYNOSCEPHALAE (364 B.C., Wars of Greek City States; 197 B.C., Second Macedonian War)

FALKLAND ISLES (1914, World War I; 1982, Falklands War)

FARQUHAR'S FARM (1899, Second Boer War)

FORT FRONTENAC (1758, Seven Years' War)

FRANKENHAUSEN (1525, Peasants' War)

GLENMARRESTON (683, Angles' Invasion of Britain)

HORNS OF HATTIN (1187, Crusader-Saracen Wars)

INVERKEITHING (1317, Anglo-Scottish Wars)

KASSERINE PASS (1943, World War II)

KILLIECRANKIE (1689, Jacobite Rising)

LITTLE BIG HORN (1876, Sioux Rising)

LOIGNY-POUPREY (1870, Franco-Prussian War)

MAGERSFONTEIN (1899, Second Boer War)

MARCIANOPOLIS (376, Gothic Invasion of Thrace)

MASURIAN LAKES (1914, 1915, World War I)

MEGALETAPHRUS (740 B.C., First Messenian War)

MOLINOS DEL REY (1808, Peninsular War)

MOUNT SELEUCUS (353, Civil Wars of the Roman Empire)

NEVILLE'S CROSS (1346, Anglo-Scottish Wars)

NEWTOWN BUTLER (1689, War of the Grand Alliance)

NORTHALLERTON (1138, Anglo-Scottish Wars)

NORTH FORELAND (1666, Anglo-Dutch Wars)

PAGASAEAN GULF (352 B.C., Sacred War)

PALAIS GALLIEN (1649, War of the Fronde)

13—continued

PASSCHENDAELE (1917, World War I)

PELELIU-ANGAUR (1944, World War II)

PHILIPPINE SEA (1944, World War II)

PHILIPPOPOLIS (251, First Gothic Invasion of the Roman Empire; 1878, Russo-Turkish War)

PORTO PRAIA BAY (1781, American Revolutionary War)

ROANOKE ISLAND (1862, American Civil War)

SANTA VITTORIA (1702, War of the Spanish Succession)

SIEVERSHAUSEN (1553, German Reformation Wars)

SOUTH MOUNTAIN (1862, American Civil War)

SPANISH ARMADA (1588, Anglo-Spanish War)

SUDLEY SPRINGS (1862, American Civil War)

SUGAR-LOAF ROCK (1753, Carnatic War)

WHITE OAK SWAMP (1862, American Civil War)

YOUGHIOGHENNY (1754, Seven Years' War)

ZUSMARSHAUSEN (1647, Thirty Years' War)

14

BERWICK-ON-TWEED (1296, Wars of Scottish Independence)

BOTHWELL BRIDGE (1679, Covenanters' Rising)

BRISTOE STATION (1863, American Civil War)

CAMPUS CASTORUM (69, Revolt of Vitellius)

CAPE FINISTERRE (1747, War of the Austrian Succession; 1805, Napoleonic Wars)

CHALGROVE FIELD (1643, English Civil War)

CHÂTEAU-THIERRY (1814, Napoleonic Wars)

CONSTANTINOPLE (668, Muslim Invasion of Europe; 1203–04, Fourth Crusade; 1261, Reconquest by Byzantines; 1422, Ottoman Invasion of Europe; 1453, Turkish Conquest)

CROPREDY BRIDGE (1644, English Civil War)

DRUMMOSSIE MOOR (1746, The Forty-five Rebellion)

FREDERICKSBURG (1862, American Civil War)

FUENTES DE OÑORO (1811, Peninsular War)

HOHENFRIEDBERG (1745, War of the Austrian Succession)

KOVEL-STANISLAV (1916, World War I)

LA BELLE FAMILLE (1759, Seven Years' War)

LOOSECOAT FIELD (1470, Wars of the Roses)

MARIANA ISLANDS (1944, World War II)

MORTIMER'S CROSS (1461, Wars of the Roses)

MOUNT LACTARIUS (553, Wars of the Byzantine Empire)

NICHOLSON'S NECK (1899, Second Boer War)

PASO DE LA PATRIA (1866, Paraguayan War)

PEACH TREE CREEK (1864, American Civil War)

14—continued

PORTE ST ANTOINE (1652, War of the Fronde)

PUSAN PERIMETER (1950, Korean War)

ROUVRAY-ST-DENIS (1429, Hundred Years' War)

SANTIAGO DE CUBA (1898, Spanish-American War)

SAVAGE'S STATION (1862, American Civil War)

SECESSIONVILLE (1862, American Civil War)

SINAI PENINSULA (1956, Israeli-Arab War)

SOLOMON ISLANDS (1942, World War II)

STAMFORD BRIDGE (1066, Norse Invasion of Britain; 1453, Wars of the Roses)

STIRLING BRIDGE (1297, Wars of Scottish Independence)

TEARLESS BATTLE (368 B.C., Wars of Sparta)

TONDEMAN'S WOODS (1754, Carnatic War)

TSUSHIMA STRAIT (1905, Russo-Japanese War)

VITTORIO VENETO (1918, World War I)

15

ALEUTIAN ISLANDS (1943, World War II)

AMATOLA MOUNTAIN (1846, Kaffir Wars)

APPOMATTOX RIVER (1865, American Civil War)

BATTLE OF BRITAIN (1940, World War II)

BEAUNE-LA-ROLANDE (1870, Franco-Prussian War)

BEAVER'S DAM CREEK (1862, American Civil War)

FORUM TEREBRONII (251, First Gothic Invasion of the Roman Empire)

FRANKFURT-ON-ODER (1631, Thirty Years' War)

GROSS-JÄGERSDORF (1757, Seven Years' War)

HELIGOLAND BIGHT (1914, World War I)

KHOORD KABUL PASS (1842, First British-Afghan War)

MALOYAROSLAVETS (1812, Napoleonic Wars)

MISSIONARY RIDGE (1863, American Civil War)

PLAINS OF ABRAHAM (1759, Seven Years' War)

PUENTE DE LA REYNA (1872, Second Carlist War)

SEVEN DAYS' BATTLE (1862, American Civil War)

SPANISH GALLEONS (1702, War of the Spanish Succession)

16

BATAAN-CORREGIDOR (1941, World War II)

BRONKHORST SPRUIT (1880, First Boer War)

CAMBRAI-ST QUENTIN (1918, World War I)

CHANCELLORSVILLE (1863, American Civil War)

16—continued

FARRINGTON BRIDGE (1549, Arundel's Rebellion)

FORT WILLIAM HENRY (1757, Seven Years' War)

KINNESAW MOUNTAIN (1864, American Civil War)

LAS NAVAS DE TOLOSA (1212, Spanish-Muslim Wars)

LIPARAEAN ISLANDS (257 B.C., First Punic War)

MADONNA DELL'OLENO (1744, War of the Austrian Succession)

MONONGAHELA RIVER (1755, Seven Years' War)

QUEENSTON HEIGHTS (1812, War of 1812)

SALUM-HALFAYA PASS (1941, World War II)

SAMPFORD COURTNEY (1549, Arundel's Rebellion)

ST JAKOB AN DER BIRS (1444, Armagnac War)

17

BURLINGTON HEIGHTS (1813, War of 1812)

DODECANESE ISLANDS (1943, World War II)

GUSTAV-CASSINO LINE (1943, World War II)

INHLOBANE MOUNTAIN (1879, Zulu War)

KWAJALEIN-ENIWETOK (1944, World War II)

LA FÈRE CHAMPENOISE (1814, Napoleonic Wars)

PITTSBURGH LANDING (1862, American Civil War)

POLAND-EAST PRUSSIA (1944, World War II)

VAN TUONG PENINSULA (1965, Vietnam War)

18

FORNHAM ST GENEVIÈVE (1173, Rebellion of the Princes)

GUILFORD COURTHOUSE (1781, American Revolutionary War)

MEUSE-ARGONNE FOREST (1918, World War I)

PYLOS AND SPHACTERIA (425 B.C., Great Peloponnesian War)

19

CHU PONG-IA DRANG RIVER (1965, Vietnam War)

'GLORIOUS FIRST OF JUNE' (1794, French Revolutionary Wars)

20+

BARBOSTHENIAN MOUNTAINS (192 B.C., Wars of the Achaean League)

PARAETAKENE MOUNTAINS (316 B.C., Wars of Alexander's Successors)

RHINE AND THE RUHR POCKET, THE (1945, World War II)

SHANNON AND CHESAPEAKE (1813, War of 1812)

THIRTY-EIGHTH PARALLEL (1951, Korean War)

ARMOUR

4	6 —continued	8	9 —continued
JACK	MASCLE	ALLECRET	CHAIN MAIL
MAIL	MESAIL	BARDINGS	CHAMPFRON
5	MORIAN	BASCINET	CHAUSSONS
ARMET	MORION	BAUDRICK	EPAULETTE
BACYN	SALADE	BRASSARD	HAUSSE-COL
BUFFE	SHIELD	BRAYETTE	JACK BOOTS
CREST	TABARD	BUFF COAT	POURPOINT
CULET	UMBRIL	BURGINOT	REREBRACE
GIPON	**7**	BURGONET	SABATYNES
IMBER	AILETES	CABASSET	**10**
JUPEL	BACINET	CHAMPONS	AVENTAILLE
JUPON	BALDRIC	CHANFRON	BANDED MAIL
LAMES	BARBUTE	CHAUCHES	BARREL HELM
SALET	BASINET	CHAUSSES	BRICHETTES
VISOR	BUCKLER	COD PIECE	BRIGANDINE
6	CHAUCES	COLLERET	CROISSANTS
ALETES	CORSLET	COLLETIN	ECREVISSES
BASNET	CRUPPER	CORSELET	EMBOITMENT
BHANJU	CUIRASS	CRINIERE	FLANCHARDS
BRACER	CUISSES	GAUNTLET	LAMBREQUIN
BRIDLE	CULESET	HALECRET	**11**
BRUGNE	FENDACE	JAMBEAUX	BREASTPLATE
CALOTE	FRONTAL	JAZERANT	BREASTSTRAP
CAMAIL	GAUCHET	PAULDRON	BRIGANDYRON
CASQUE	GOUCHET	PECTORAL	BRIGANTAYLE
CASSIS	GREAVES	PLASTRON	CHAPEL DE FER
CELATE	HAUBERK	SABATONS	ESPALLIERES
CHEEKS	HOGUINE	SOLARETS	PLATE ARMOUR
CRENEL	LANIERS	SOLERETS	**13**
CRINET	MURSAIL	TESTIERE	ARMING DOUBLET
CUELLO	PANACHE	**9**	**15**
GORGET	PLACARD	BAINBERGS	IMBRICATE ARMOUR
GUSSET	POITRAL	BEINBERGS	
HEAUME	SURCOAT		
HELMET	VISIERE		

WEAPONS

2	3 —continued	4 —continued	4 —continued
NU	TNT	FANG	TUCK
V1	**4**	FOIL	**5**
V2	ADZE	KORA	A-BOMB
3	BARB	KRIS	ANCUS
AXE	BILL	MACE	ANKUS
BOW	BOLO	MINE	ANLAS
DAG	BOLT	PIKE	ARROW
DAS	BOMB	SHOT	ASWAR
GUN	CLUB	TANK	BATON
GYN	DIRK	TOCK	BIDAG

5 —continued

BILBO
BOLAS
BOSON
BRAND
ESTOC
FLAIL
FUSEE
FUSIL
GUPTI
H-BOMB
KERIS
KHORA
KILIG
KILIJ
KNIFE
KUKRI
KYLIE
LANCE
LATCH
PILUM
PRODD
RIFLE
SABRE
SHELL
SLING
SPEAR
STAKE
STAVE
SWORD
TACHI
WADDY

6

AMUKTA
ARMLET
BARKAL
BARONG
BASTON
BODKIN
BULLET
CANNON
CARCAS
CEMTEX
CUDGEL
DAGGER
DAISHO
DRAGON
DUM-DUM
DUSACK
EXOCET
KATANA
KERRIE
KHANDA
KIKUKI
KODOGU
MASSUE
MAZULE
MORTAR
MUSKET
NAPALM
PARANG

6 —continued

PETARD
PISTOL
POP GUN
QILLIJ
QUIVER
RAMROD
RAPIER
ROCKET
SCYTHE
SEMTEX
SUMPIT
TALWAR
VGO GUN

7

ASSEGAI
AWL-PIKE
BALASAN
BALISTA
BAYONET
BELFREY
BILIONG
BOMBARD
BOURDON
BREN GUN
CALIVER
CALTRAP
CARABEN
CARBINE
CARREAU
CHAKRAM
CHALCOS
CHOPPER
CURRIER
CUTLASS
DUDGEON
DUSSACK
FAUCHON
FIRE-POT
GRENADE
HALBARD
HALBART
HALBERD
HAND GUN
HARPOON
KASTANE
KINDJAL
LONG BOW
MISSILE
MUSQUET
PONIARD
PUNT GUN
QUARREL
SHASHQA
SHINKEN
STEN GUN
TORPEDO
TRIDENT

8

AMUSETTE

8 —continued

ARBALEST
ARBALETE
ARQUEBUS
ATOM BOMB
AXE-KNIFE
BASELARD
BASILARD
BLOWPIPE
CALTHORP
CANISTER
CARABINE
CATAPULT
CHACHEKA
CLADIBAS
CLAYMORE
CROSSBOW
DERINGER
DESTRIER
FALCHION
FALCONET
FAUCHARD
FIRELOCK
HACKBUTT
HAIL SHOT
HAQUEBUT
HASSEGAI
HOWITZER
PETRONEL
POIGNARD
QUERQUER
REPEATER
REVOLVER
SCIMITAR
SHAMSHIR
SHRAPNEL
SPONTOON
SUMPITAN
TOMAHAWK
TOMMY GUN

9

ACK-ACK GUN
ARTILLERY
BADELAIRE
BANDELEER
BANDOLIER
BANNEROLE
BATTLE-AXE
BIG BERTHA
BOOMERANG
CARRONADE
CARTOUCHE
CARTRIDGE
CHAIN SHOT
DETONATOR
DOODLE-BUG
FALCASTRA
FLAGELLUM
FLAMBERGE
FLINTLOCK
GELIGNITE

9 —continued

GRAPESHOT
GUNPOWDER
HARQUEBUS
KNOBSTICK
MATCHLOCK
MAZZUELLE
MILLS BOMB
MUSKETOON
POM-POM GUN
SLUNG SHOT
TRUNCHEON

10

ARTILLATOR
BANDEROLLE
BRANDESTOC
BROAD ARROW
BROADSWORD
CANNON BALL
FIRE-STICKS
FLICK KNIFE
GATLING GUN
KNOBKERRIE
LETTER BOMB
LIMPET MINE
MACHINE GUN
PEA-SHOOTER
POWDERHORN
SIDEWINDER
SMALL SWORD
SWORD STICK

11

ANTI-TANK GUN
ARMOURED CAR
BLUNDERBUSS
HAND GRENADE
KHYBER KNIFE
MISERICORDE
NEUTRON BOMB

12

BATTERING RAM
BREECH LOADER
BRIDLE CUTTER
FIRE CARRIAGE
FLAME-THROWER
HYDROGEN BOMB

13

BRASS KNUCKLES
DUELLING SWORD
GUIDED MISSILE
KNUCKLE DUSTER
THROWING KNIFE

14

DUELLING PISTOL
INCENDIARY BOMB
NUCLEAR WEAPONS
ROCKET LAUNCHER
SAWN-OFF
  SHOTGUN

14 —continued
TWO-HANDED
  SWORD

15
ANTI-AIRCRAFT GUN

16
BALLISTIC MISSILE

18
HEAT-SEEKING
  MISSILE

20+
DOUBLE-
  BARRELLED
  SHOTGUN

TRANSPORT

VEHICLES

3
BMX
BUS
CAB
CAR
FLY
GIG
VAN

4
AUTO
BIKE
CART
DRAG
DRAY
EKKA
HACK
JEEP
LUGE
SHAY
SLED
TAXI
TRAM
TRAP
TUBE
WAIN

5
ARABA
BRAKE
BUGGY
COACH
COUPÉ
CRATE
CYCLE
DANDY
DOOLY
LORRY
METRO
MOPED
MOTOR
PALKI
SEDAN
SULKY
TONGA
TRAIN
TRUCK
WAGON

6
BERLIN
CALASH
CHAISE
DIESEL

6—continued
FIACRE
GO-CART
HANSOM
HEARSE
HOTROD
HURDLE
JALOPY
JITNEY
LANDAU
LIMBER
LITTER
MAGLEV
MODEL-T
ROCKET
SALOON
SLEDGE
SLEIGH
SNOCAT
SURREY
TANDEM
TANKER
TOURER
TRICAR
WEASEL

7
AUTOBUS
AUTOCAR
BICYCLE
BOB-SLED
BRITZKA
BROWSER
CALÈCHE
CARAVAN
CAROCHE
CHARIOT
COASTER
DOG-CART
DROSHKY
FLIVVER
GROWLER
HACKERY
HARD-TOP
OMNIBUS
OPEN-CAR
PHÆTON
PULLMAN
SCOOTER
SHUNTER
SIDE-CAR
TALLY-HO

7—continued
TAXI-CAB
TILBURY
TRACTOR
TRAILER
TROLLEY
TUMBRIL
TWO-DOOR
UNICORN
VIS-À-VIS
WHISKEY

8
BAROUCHE
BRANCARD
BROUGHAM
CABLE-CAR
CAPE-CART
CARRIAGE
CARRIOLE
CLARENCE
CURRICLE
DEAD-CART
DORMEUSE
FOUR-DOOR
HORSE-BUS
HORSE-CAB
HORSE-VAN
ICE-YACHT
KIBITZKA
MONORAIL
MOTOR-CAR
MOTOR-VAN
OLD CROCK
PONY-CART
PUSH-BIKE
QUADRIGA
RICKSHAW
ROADSTER
RUNABOUT
SOCIABLE
STAFF CAR
STEAM-CAR
TOBOGGAN
TRICYCLE
UNICYCLE
VICTORIA

9
AMBULANCE
BOAT-TRAIN
BOB-SLEIGH
BUBBLECAR

9—continued
BUCKBOARD
CABRIOLET
CHAR-À-BANC
DILIGENCE
ESTATE-CAR
FUNICULAR
HORSE-CART
LIMOUSINE
MAIL-COACH
MILKFLOAT
MILK TRAIN
MONOCYCLE
MOTOR-BIKE
PALANKEEN
PALANQUIN
RACING CAR
SPORTS CAR
STREET-CAR
STRETCHER
TARANTASS
TIN LIZZIE
TWO-SEATER
WAGONETTE

10
AUTOMOBILE
BAIL GHARRY
BEACHWAGON
BLACK MARIA
FIRE-ENGINE
FOUR-IN-HAND
GOODS TRAIN
JINRICKSHA
LOCAL TRAIN
LOCOMOTIVE
MOTOR-COACH
MOTOR-CYCLE
NIGHT TRAIN
OUTSIDE CAR
PADDYWAGON
PEDAL-CYCLE
PONY-ENGINE
POST-CHAISE
RATTLETRAP
SEDAN-CHAIR
SHANDRYDAN
SINCLAIR C5
SNOWPLOUGH
STAGE-COACH
STAGE-WAGON

10—continued
STATE COACH
TROLLEY-BUS
TROLLEY-CAR
TWO-WHEELER
VELOCIPEDE
11
BONE-BREAKER
BULLOCK-CART
CONVERTIBLE
DIESEL TRAIN
FOUR-WHEELER
GUN-CARRIAGE
JAUNTING-CAR
JINRICKSHAW
LANDAULETTE
MAIL-PHÆTON
QUADRICYCLE

11—continued
SIT-UP-AND-BEG
SOUPED-UP CAR
STEAM-ENGINE
STEAM-ROLLER
THIKA-GHARRY
WHITECHAPEL
12
COACH AND FOUR
DÉSOBLIGEANT
DOUBLE-DECKER
EXPRESS TRAIN
FREIGHT TRAIN
HORSE-AND-CART
LUGGAGE TRAIN
PANTECHNICON
PUFFING BILLY
RAILWAY TRAIN

12—continued
SINGLE-DECKER
STATION-WAGON
STEAM-OMNIBUS
THROUGH TRAIN
13
CYCLE-RICKSHAW
ELECTRIC TRAIN
GOVERNESS-CART
HORSE-CARRIAGE
PENNYFARTHING
RACING CHARIOT
SHOOTING-BRAKE
14
PASSENGER TRAIN
RIDING-CARRIAGE
TRACTION ENGINE

15
HACKNEY-CARRIAGE
PRAIRIE-SCHOONER
16
MOTORIZED
  BICYCLE
UNDERGROUND
  TRAIN
17
HORSELESS
  CARRIAGE
18
TRAVELLING
  CARRIAGE

SHIPS AND BOATS

3
ARK
COG
HOY
TUG
4
ARGO
BARK
BOAT
BRIG
BUSS
DHOW
DORY
GRAB
JUNK
PROA
PUNT
RAFT
SAIC
SNOW
TROW
YAWL
5
BARGE
CANOE
COBLE
DANDY
FERRY
FUNNY
KAYAK
KETCH
LINER
NOBBY
PRAHU
SHELL
SKIFF

5—continued
SLOOP
SMACK
TRAMP
U-BOAT
UMIAK
XEBEC
YACHT
6
BARQUE
BAWLEY
BIREME
CAIQUE
CARVEL
CUTTER
DINGHY
DOGGER
DUG-OUT
GALLEY
HOOKER
HOPPER
LAUNCH
LORCHA
LUGGER
PACKET
RANDAN
SAMPAN
SEALER
SLAVER
TANKER
TENDER
WHALER
7
BUMBOAT
CARAVEL
CARRACK

7—continued
CLIPPER
COASTER
COLLIER
CORACLE
CORSAIR
CURRACH
DREDGER
DRIFTER
DROMOND
FELUCCA
FLY-BOAT
FRIGATE
GABBARD
GALLEON
GONDOLA
JANGADA
PINNACE
PIRAGUA
POLACCA
POLACRE
ROWBOAT
SCULLER
STEAMER
TARTANE
TOWBOAT
TRAWLER
TRIREME
WAR SHIP
8
BILANDER
BUDGEROW
COCKBOAT
CORVETTE
CRUMSTER
DAHABIYA

8—continued
FIRESHIP
FOLDBOAT
GALLIVAT
LIFEBOAT
LONG-BOAT
MAIL-SHIP
NOAH'S ARK
OUTBOARD
SAILBOAT
SCHOONER
SHOWBOAT
9
BUCENTAUR
CARGO-BOAT
CATAMARAN
CRIS-CRAFT
FREIGHTER
HOUSE BOAT
JOLLY-BOAT
LIGHTSHIP
MOTORBOAT
MOTORSHIP
MUD-HOPPER
OUTRIGGER
RIVER-BOAT
ROTOR SHIP
SHIP'S BOAT
SLAVE-SHIP
SPEEDBOAT
STEAMBOAT
STEAMSHIP
STORESHIP
SUBMARINE
10
BANANA-BOAT

10—continued
BRIGANTINE
PADDLE-BOAT
PICKET BOAT
PIRATE-SHIP
PRISON-SHIP
QUADRIREME
ROWING BOAT
TEA-CLIPPER
TRAIN-FERRY
VIKING-SHIP
WIND-JAMMER

11
BARQUENTINE
CHASSE-MARÉE
COCKLE-SHELL
DOUBLE-CANOE
FISHING-BOAT
HOPPER-BARGE
MAIL-STEAMER
PENTECONTER
PILOT VESSEL
QUINQUEREME
SAILING-SHIP

11—continued
THREE-MASTER
12
CABIN-CRUISER
ESCORT VESSEL
FISHING SMACK
HOSPITAL SHIP
MERCHANT SHIP
PLEASURE BOAT
SAILING BARGE
STERN-WHEELER

13
HERRING-FISHER
PASSENGER SHIP
TRANSPORT SHIP
14
CHANNEL STEAMER
COASTING VESSEL
FLOATING PALACE
OCEAN GREYHOUND

AIRCRAFT

3
JET
4
KITE
5
PLANE
6
AIR CAR
BOMBER
GLIDER
7
AIRSHIP
BALLOON
BIPLANE
CLIPPER

7—continued
FIGHTER
JUMP-JET
SHUTTLE
8
AEROSTAT
AIRPLANE
AUTOGIRO
CONCORDE
JUMBO-JET
ROTODYNE
SEA-PLANE
TRIPLANE
TURBO-JET
WARPLANE
ZEPPELIN

9
AEROPLANE
DIRIGIBLE
MAIL-PLANE
MONOPLANE
SAILPLANE
TURBO-PROP
10
FLYING-BOAT
GAS-BALLOON
HELICOPTER
HOVERCRAFT
HYDROPLANE
11
FIRE-BALLOON

12
FREIGHT-PLANE
13
STRATOCRUISER
14
FLYING BEDSTEAD
PASSENGER PLANE
18
MONTGOLFIER
 BALLOON

MOTORING TERMS

2
C.C.
3
BHP
CAM
FAN
HUB
JET
REV
ROD
4
AXLE
BOOT
BUSH
COIL
GEAR
HORN
LOCK
SUMP

4—continued
TYRE
5
BRAKE
CHOKE
SERVO
SHAFT
VALVE
WHEEL
6
BIG END
BONNET
CAMBER
CLUTCH
DAMPER
DECOKE
DYNAMO
ENGINE
FILTER

6—continued
GASKET
HEATER
HUB CAP
IDLING
PISTON
REBORE
STROKE
TAPPET
TORQUE
TUNING
7
BATTERY
BEARING
BRACKET
CHASSIS
DYNAMIC
EXHAUST
FAN BELT

7—continued
GEARBOX
OIL SEAL
8
ADHESION
BRAKE PAD
BULKHEAD
CALLIPER
CAMSHAFT
CROSS-PLY
CYLINDER
DIPSTICK
FLYWHEEL
FUEL PUMP
IGNITION
KICK-DOWN
KNOCKING
LIVE AXLE
MANIFOLD

8—continued
MOUNTING
RADIATOR
ROTOR ARM
SELECTOR
SILENCER
SMALL END
STEERING
THROTTLE
TRACK ROD

9
BRAKESHOE
CONDENSER
DISC BRAKE
DRUM BRAKE
GEAR STICK
GENERATOR
HALF-SHAFT
HANDBRAKE
INDUCTION
MISFIRING
OVERDRIVE
OVERSTEER
PROP SHAFT
RADIAL-PLY
SIDE VALVE
SPARK PLUG

9—continued
TWO-STROKE
UNDERSEAL
WHEELBASE

10
AIR CLEANER
ALTERNATOR
BRAKE FLUID
CRANKSHAFT
DETONATION
DRIVE SHAFT
FOUR-STROKE
GUDGEON PIN
HORSEPOWER
PISTON RING
REV COUNTER
SUSPENSION
TACHOMETER
THERMOSTAT
UNDERSTEER
WINDSCREEN

11
ANTI-ROLL BAR
CARBURETTER
CARBURETTOR
COMPRESSION

11—continued
CROSSMEMBER
DISTRIBUTOR
SERVO SYSTEM
SYNCHROMESH

12
ACCELERATION
CYLINDER HEAD
DIESEL ENGINE
DIFFERENTIAL
SPARKING PLUG
SUPERCHARGER
TRANSMISSION
TURBOCHARGER
VISCOUS DRIVE

13
COOLING SYSTEM
DECARBONIZING
FUEL INJECTION
OVERHEAD VALVE
POWER STEERING
RACK-AND-PINION
SHOCK ABSORBER
SLAVE CYLINDER
SPARK IGNITION

14
FOUR-WHEEL DRIVE
PROPELLER SHAFT
UNIVERSAL JOINT

15
FRONT-WHEEL
   DRIVE
HYDRAULIC SYSTEM
PETROL INJECTION

17
INDUCTION
   MANIFOLD
REVOLUTION
   COUNTER

19
CROWN WHEEL AND
   PINION

20+
AUTOMATIC
   TRANSMISSION
INDEPENDENT
   SUSPENSION
POWER ASSISTED
   STEERING

NAUTICAL TERMS

3
AFT
BOW
FID
LEE

4
ALEE
BEAM
BITT
BOOM
FORE
HOLD
HULL
KEEL
KNOT
LIST
MATE
POOP
PORT
PROW
STAY
STEM
WAKE
WARP

5
ABAFT
ABEAM

5—continued
ABOUT
ALOFT
AVAST
BELAY
BELLS
BILGE
BOSUN
CABLE
CAULK
CLEAT
DAVIT
HATCH
HAWSE
STERN
TRICK
TRUCK
WAIST
WEIGH
WINCH

6
BRIDGE
BUNKER
FATHOM
FENDER
FLUKES
FO'C'SLE

6—continued
GALLEY
HAWSER
JETSAM
LEAGUE
LEEWAY
OFFING
PURSER
SHROUD
YAWING

7
ADMIRAL
BALLAST
BOLLARD
BULWARK
CAPSTAN
CATWALK
COAMING
DRAUGHT
FLOTSAM
GANGWAY
GRAPNEL
GUNWALE
INBOARD
LANYARD
MOORING
QUARTER

7—continued
RIGGING
SEA MILE
TONNAGE
TOPSIDE
WATCHES

8
BINNACLE
BOWSPRIT
BULKHEAD
COXSWAIN
DOG WATCH
HALYARDS
HATCHWAY
LARBOARD
PITCHING
RATLINES
SCUPPERS
SPLICING
TAFFRAIL
WINDLASS
WINDWARD

9
AMIDSHIPS
COMPANION
CROW'S NEST
FREEBOARD

9—continued
SHIP'S BELL
STARBOARD
WATER-LINE
10
BATTEN DOWN
DEADLIGHTS
DEADWEIGHT
FIRST WATCH

10—continued
FORE-AND-AFT
FORECASTLE
NIGHT WATCH
11
MIDDLE WATCH
QUARTER-DECK
WEATHER SIDE

12
DISPLACEMENT
JACOB'S LADDER
MARLINE SPIKE
NAUTICAL MILE
PLIMSOLL LINE
13
QUARTERMASTER

14
SUPERSTRUCTURE
15
COMPANION-
  LADDER
DAVY JONES'
  LOCKER

CLOTHES AND MATERIALS

CLOTHES

3
ABA
ALB
BAL
BAS
BAT
BIB
BRA
COP
FEZ
HAT
LEI
OBI
TAM

4
ABBA
AGAL
ALBA
APEX
BAJU
BARB
BECK
BELT
BENN
BOTA
BUSK
CACK
CAPE
CLOG
COAT
COPE
COTE
COWL
DAPS
DIDO
DISK
GARB
GETA
GOWN
HAIK
HOOD
HOSE
IZAR
JAMA
KEPI
KILT
MASK
MAXI
MIDI
MINI

4 —continued
MITT
MUFF
MULE
PUMP
ROBE
RUFF
SARI
SASH
SAYA
SHOE
SLIP
SLOP
SOCK
SPAT
SUIT
TABI
TOGA
TOGS
TOPI
TUTU
VAMP
VEIL
VEST
WRAP

5
ABNET
ACTON
AEGIS
AMICE
AMPYX
APRON
ARCAN
ARMET
ARMOR
ASCOT
BARBE
BARRY
BENJY
BERET
BLAKE
BLUEY
BOINA
BOOTS
BURKA
BUSBY
CABAS
CADET
CAPPA
CHALE

5 —continued
CHAPS
CHOGA
CHOLI
CLOAK
CORDY
COTTA
COTTE
CREST
CROWN
CURCH
CYLAS
CYMAR
DERBY
DHOTI
EPHOD
FICHU
FROCK
GANSY
GILET
GIPPO
GLOVE
HABIT
HULLS
IHRAM
JABOT
JAMAH
JEANS
JELAB
JUPON
LAMMY
LODEN
LUNGI
MIDDY
MUFTI
NUBIA
PAGNE
PAGRI
PALLA
PANTS
PARKA
PILCH
PIRNY
PUMPS
SABOT
SAREE
SCARF
SHAKO
SHAWL
SHIFT

5 —continued
SHIRT
SKIRT
SMOCK
SNOOD
STOCK
STOLA
STOLE
TAILS
TEDDY
TIARA
TONGS
TOPEE
TOQUE
TREWS
TUNIC
VISOR
VIZOR
WEEDS

6
ABOLLA
ALMUCE
ANADEM
ANALAV
ANKLET
ANORAK
ARCTIC
ARTOIS
BALKAN
BANYAN
BARRET
BARVEL
BASQUE
BAUTTA
BEANIE
BEAVER
BÈQUIN
BERTHA
BICORN
BIETLE
BIGGIN
BIKINI
BIRRUS
BISHOP
BLAZER
BLIAUD
BLOUSE
BOATER
BODICE
BOLERO

6 —continued	6 —continued	6 —continued	7 —continued
BONNET	GAUCHO	TWEEDS	CHRISOM
BOOTEE	GILLIE	ULSTER	CHUDDAR
BOWLER	GUIMPE	UNDIES	CHUDDER
BOXERS	HALTER	UPLIFT	COMMODE
BRACAE	HENNIN	VAMPAY	CORONEL
BRACES	HUIPIL	VESTEE	CORONET
BRAGAS	JACKET	WIMPLE	COSSACK
BRAIES	JERKIN	WOOLLY	COXCOMB
BRETON	JERSEY	ZOUAVE	CREPIDA
BRIEFS	JUBBAH	**7**	CRISPIN
BROGAN	JUMPER	AMICTUS	CUCULLA
BROGUE	KABAYA	APPAREL	CUIRASS
BUSKIN	KIMONO	ARISARD	CULOTTE
BYRNIE	KIRTLE	ARM BAND	CURCHEF
BYRRUS	KITTEL	BABOOSH	CUTAWAY
CABAAN	LAMMIE	BALDRIC	DOPATTA
CADDIE	LOAFER	BALTEUS	DOUBLET
CAFTAN	LUNGEE	BANDEAU	DRAWERS
CALASH	MAGYAR	BANDORE	DULBAND
CALCEI	MANTEE	BARBUTE	DUL HOSE
CALIGA	MANTLE	BAROQUE	EARMUFF
CALPAC	MANTUA	BASHLYK	ETON CAP
CAMAIL	MITTEN	BASINET	EVERETT
CAMISA	MOBCAP	BAVETTE	FANCHON
CAMISE	MOGGAN	BAVOLET	FASHION
CAPOTE	OUTFIT	BEDIZEN	FILIBEG
CAPUCE	PEG-TOP	BELCHER	FLATCAP
CAPUTI	PEPLOS	BERDASH	GARMENT
CARACO	PEPLUM	BERETTA	GHILLIE
CASQUE	PILEUS	BETSIES	G STRING
CASTOR	PINNER	BIRETTA	GUM BOOT
CAUSIA	PIRNIE	BOTTINE	GUM SHOE
CESTUS	PONCHO	BOX CAPE	GYM SHOE
CHADAR	PUGREE	BOX COAT	HANDBAG
CHITON	PUTTEE	BRIMMER	HIGH-LOW
CHOKER	RAGLAN	BROIGNE	HOMBURG
CILICE	REEFER	BURNOUS	HOSIERY
CIMIER	RUFFLE	BUSSKIN	JODHPUR
CLAQUE	SANDAL	CALEÇON	KLOMPEN
CLOCHE	SARONG	CALOTTE	LAYETTE
COBCAB	SERAPE	CAMOURO	LEOTARD
COCKET	SHIMMY	CANEZOU	MAILLOT
CORNET	SHORTS	CAPE HAT	MANTEAU
CORONA	SHROUD	CAPUCHE	MONTERA
CORSET	SLACKS	CAPULET	MONTERO
COTHUM	SONTAG	CASAQUE	MUFFLER
COVERT	STEP-IN	CASSOCK	OLIVERS
CRAVAT	SUN HAT	CATSKIN	OVERALL
DIADEM	TABARD	CAUBEEN	OXFORDS
DICKEY	TAMISE	CEREVIS	PANTIES
DIRNDL	TIGHTS	CHAINSE	PARASOL
DOLMAN	TIPPET	CHALWAR	PATTERN
DOMINO	TOP HAT	CHAPLET	PELISSE
DUSTER	TOPPER	CHEMISE	PETASOS
EARCAP	TRILBY	CHEVRON	PIERROT
FEDORA	TRUNKS	CHIMERE	PILLBOX
FILLET	T-SHIRT	CHIP HAT	PLUVIAL
GAITER	TUCKER	CHLAMYS	PUGGREE
GANSEY	TURBAN	CHOPINE	PYJAMAS
GARTER	TUXEDO	CHOU HAT	RAIMENT

7 —continued	8 —continued	8 —continued	9 —continued
REGALIA	BOTTEKIN	LINGERIE	BILLYCOCK
ROMPERS	BREECHES	LIRIPIPE	BLOUSETTE
RUBBERS	BURGONET	MANTELET	BODY LINEN
SARAFAN	BURNOOSE	MANTILLA	BOURRELET
SCOGGER	BYCOCKET	MOCCASIN	BRASSIÈRE
SHALWAR	CABASSET	NECKLACE	BROADBRIM
SILK HAT	CAMISOLE	NIGHTCAP	BRODEQUIN
SINGLET	CANOTIER	OPERA HAT	BRUNSWICK
SKI BOOT	CAPE COAT	OVERALLS	BYZANTINE
SLIPPER	CAPELINE	OVERCOAT	CABRIOLET
SLYDERS	CAPRIOLE	OVERSHOE	CAPE DRESS
SMICKET	CAPUCINE	PARAMENT	CAPE STOLE
SNEAKER	CAPUTIUM	PEASECOD	CARTWHEEL
SOUTANE	CARCANET	PEIGNOIR	CASENTINO
SPENCER	CARDIGAN	PHILIBEG	CASQUETTE
SPORRAN	CARDINAL	PILEOLUS	CASSIMERE
SULTANE	CAROLINE	PINAFORE	CHEMILOON
SUN SUIT	CASAQUIN	PLASTRON	CHIN-CLOTH
SURCOAT	CATERCAP	PLATINUM	CHIVARRAS
SURTOUT	CHANDAIL	PLIMSOLL	CHOLO COAT
SWEATER	CHAPERON	PULLOVER	COAT DRESS
TANK TOP	CHAQUETA	SABOTINE	COAT SHIRT
TEA GOWN	CHASUBLE	SKULL-CAP	COCKED HAT
TOP BOOT	CHAUSSES	SLIP-OVER	COOLIE HAT
TOP COAT	CHONGSAM	SNOWSHOE	COPINTANK
TRAHEEN	COLOBIUM	SOMBRERO	CORNERCAP
TRICORN	COPATAIN	STOCKING	COVERSLUT
TUNICLE	CORSELET	SURPLICE	COWBOY HAT
TWIN SET	COUCH HAT	SWIM SUIT	CREEDMORE
UNIFORM	COVERALL	TAIL COAT	CRINOLINE
VEILING	CRUSH HAT	TAILLEUR	DOG COLLAR
WATTEAU	CUCULLUS	TARBOOSH	DOMINICAL
WEDGIES	DANCE SET	TOQUETTE	DRESS COAT
WING TIE	DANDY HAT	TRAINERS	DRESS SHOE
WOOLLEN	DJELLABA	TRENCHER	DRESS SUIT
WRAPPER	DOM PEDRO	TRICORNE	DUNGAREES
YASHMAK	DORMEUSE	TROUSERS	DUNSTABLE
Y-FRONTS	DUCK-BILL	TWO-PIECE	ESCOFFIAN
ZIMARRA	DUNCE CAP	WOOLLENS	FORAGE CAP
8	DUST COAT	WOOLLIES	FROCK COAT
ABBÉ CAPE	DUTCH CAP	ZOOT SUIT	FULL DRESS
ALL-IN-ONE	FALDETTA	**9**	GABARDINE
ANALABOS	FLANNELS	AFTERWELT	GABERDINE
ANTELOPE	FLIMSIES	ALPARGATA	GARIBALDI
BABUSHKA	FOOTWEAR	ALPINE HAT	GLENGARRY
BALADRAN	GAMASHES	ANKLE BOOT	GREATCOAT
BALMORAL	GAUNTLET	APON DRESS	HEADDRESS
BANDANNA	GUERNSEY	ARMILAUSA	HEADPIECE
BARBETTE	HALF-HOSE	BABY SKIRT	HELMET CAP
BASQUINE	HALF SLIP	BALAYEUSE	HOURI-COAT
BATH ROBE	HEADGEAR	BALL DRESS	HOUSE-COAT
BEARSKIN	JACK BOOT	BALMACAAN	HULA SKIRT
BED SOCKS	JUDO COAT	BAMBIN HAT	INVERNESS
BENJAMIN	JUMP SUIT	BANDOLEER	JOCKEY CAP
BIGGONET	KERCHIEF	BARCELONA	JULIET CAP
BINNOGUE	KNICKERS	BEAVERTOP	LOINCLOTH
BLOOMERS	KNITWEAR	BED JACKET	MILLINERY
BODY COAT	LARRIGAN	BEEGUM HAT	NECKCLOTH
BOMBARDS	LAVA-LAVA	BELL SKIRT	NIGHTGOWN
BOOT-HOSE	LEGGINGS	BILLICOCK	OUTERWEAR

9 —continued	10 —continued	10 —continued	11 —continued
OVERDRESS	BUSH JACKET	POKE BONNET	RUNNING SHOE
OVERSHIRT	BUSK JACKET	PORK PIE HAT	RUSSIAN BOOT
OVERSKIRT	CALZONERAS	RIDING-HOOD	SEWING APRON
PANAMA HAT	CANVAS SHOE	SERVICE CAP	SNAP-BRIM HAT
PANTALETS	CAPE COLLAR	SHIRTWAIST	SOUP-AND-FISH
PANTOFFLE	CAPPA MAGNA	SPORTS COAT	SOUTHWESTER
PANTY HOSE	CARMAGNOLE	SPORT SHIRT	SPATTERDASH
PEA JACKET	CERVELIÈRE	SPORTSWEAR	STOCKING CAP
PETTICOAT	CHARTREUSE	STICHARION	STRING GLOVE
PILOT COAT	CHATELAINE	STRING VEST	SWAGGER COAT
PLUS FOURS	CHEMISETTE	SUNDAY BEST	TAM-O'SHANTER
POLONAISE	CHIGNON CAP	SUSPENDERS	TYROLEAN HAT
QUAKER HAT	CHOUQUETTE	SWEAT SHIRT	UNDERGIRDLE
REDINGOTE	CLOCK-MUTCH	THREE-PIECE	UNDERTHINGS
SANBENITO	COOLIE COAT	TRENCH COAT	WALKING SHOE
SHAKSHEER	COQUELUCHE	UNDERDRESS	WEDDING GOWN
SHINTIYAN	CORPS PIQUÉ	UNDERLINEN	WEDDING VEIL
SHOVEL HAT	COSSACK CAP	UNDERPANTS	WELLINGTONS
SLOPPY JOE	COTE-HARDIE	UNDERSHIRT	WINDBREAKER
SLOUCH HAT	COUVRE-CHEF	UNDERSKIRT	WINDCHEATER
SNEAKERS	COVERCHIEF	VELDSCHOEN	
SOU'WESTER	COVERT COAT	WINDSOR TIE	**12**
STOMACHER	CROSSCLOTH	WING COLLAR	AMISH COSTUME
STRING TIE	CUMMERBUND		BALKAN BLOUSE
SUNBONNET	DANCE DRESS	**11**	BALLOON SKIRT
SURCINGLE	DESHABILLE	ALSATIAN BOW	BASEBALL BOOT
TENT DRESS	DINNER SUIT	BATHING SUIT	BATTLE JACKET
THIGH BOOT	DIPLOIDIAN	BIB-AND-BRACE	BELLY DOUBLET
TROUSSEAU	DOUILLETTE	BOILED SHIRT	BLOOMER DRESS
TRUNK-HOSE	DRESS PLAID	BOXER SHORTS	BUSINESS SUIT
UNDERCOAT	DRESS SHIRT	BRACONNIÈRE	CAMICIA ROSSA
UNDERGOWN	DUFFEL COAT	BREECHCLOTH	CAVALIER BOOT
UNDERVEST	ECLIPSE TIE	BRITISH WARM	CHEMISE DRESS
UNDERWEAR	ESPADRILLE	CANCAN DRESS	CHEMISE FROCK
VESTMENTS	ETON JACKET	CAVALIER HAT	CHESTERFIELD
VICTORINE	EUGÉNIE HAT	CHAPEAU BRAS	CHUKKER SHIRT
WAISTCOAT	FANCY DRESS	CHAPEL DE FER	CIGARETTE MIT
WATCH COAT	FASCINATOR	CIRCASSIENE	CORSET BODICE
WIDE-AWAKE	FLYING SUIT	COMBINATION	COTTAGE CLOAK
WITCH'S HAT	FORE-AND-AFT	CORSET COVER	CRUSADER HOOD
WYLIECOAT	FUSTANELLA	COWBOY BOOTS	DINNER JACKET
10	GARMENTURE	DANCING CLOG	DIVIDED SKIRT
ANGELUS CAP	GRASS SKIRT	DEERSTALKER	DORIC CHILTON
APRON TUNIC	HAREM SKIRT	DINNER DRESS	DRESS CLOTHES
BABY BONNET	HUG-ME-TIGHT	EMPIRE SKIRT	DRESSING GOWN
BASIC DRESS	JIGGER COAT	ESPADRILLES	EASTER BONNET
BATHING CAP	LIRIPIPIUM	EVENING GOWN	ENGLISH DRAPE
BEER JACKET	LOUNGE SUIT	EVENING SLIP	EVENING DRESS
BELLBOY CAP	LUMBERJACK	FORMAL DRESS	EVENING SHOES
BERRETTINO	MESS JACKET	FORTUNY GOWN	EVENING SKIRT
BIBI BONNET	NIGHTDRESS	GALLIGASKIN	HANDKERCHIEF
BICYCLE BAL	NIGHTSHIRT	HOBBLE SKIRT	HEADKERCHIEF
BLOUSE COAT	OPERA CLOAK	HOSTESS GOWN	HELMET BONNET
BOBBY SOCKS	OVERBLOUSE	HOUPPELANDE	KNEE BREECHES
BOSOM SHIRT	OVERGAITER	HUNTING BOOT	LOUNGING ROBE
BOUDOIR CAP	OXFORD BAGS	MIDDY BLOUSE	MANDARIN COAT
BRIGANDINE	OXFORD GOWN	NECKERCHIEF	MONKEY JACKET
BRUNCH COAT	PANTALOONS	OVERGARMENT	MORNING DRESS
BUCKET TOPS	PICTURE HAT	PANTY GIRDLE	MOTORING VEIL
BUMPER BRIM	PITH HELMET	RIDING HABIT	PEDAL PUSHERS
		RUBBER APRON	PENITENTIALS

12 —continued
QUAKER BONNET
ROLL-ON GIRDLE
SCOTCH BONNET
SHIRTWAISTER
SLEEPING COAT
SLEEPING SUIT
SMALLCLOTHES
STOVEPIPE HAT
SUGAR-LOAF HAT
TAILORED SUIT
TEN-GALLON HAT
TROUSERETTES
UNDERCLOTHES
UNDERGARMENT
WIDE-AWAKE HAT
ZOUAVE JACKET

13
ACROBATIC SHOE
AFTER-SKI SOCKS
BACK-STRAP SHOE
BEEFEATER'S HAT
BELLBOY JACKET
BUNGALOW APRON
COACHMAN'S COAT
COMBING JACKET
COTTAGE BONNET
DRESSING SAQUE
ELEVATOR SHOES

13 —continued
HAWAIIAN SKIRT
MOTHER HUBBARD
MOURNING DRESS
NORFOLK JACKET
PEEK-A-BOO WAIST
PRINCESS DRESS
SAM BROWNE BELT
SMOKING JACKET
SPORTS CLOTHES
SUSPENDER-BELT
TEDDYBEAR COAT
TRUNK-BREECHES
UNDERCLOTHING

14
AFTERNOON DRESS
BAREFOOT SANDAL
BATHING COSTUME
BICYCLE CLIP HAT
CABBAGE-TREE HAT
CACHE-POUSSIÈRE
CAMOUFLAGE SUIT
CARDIGAN BODICE
CONGRESS GAITOR
CONTINENTAL HAT
DRESSING JACKET
DRESSMAKER SUIT
EGYPTIAN SANDAL
EVENING SWEATER

14 —continued
KNICKERBOCKERS
SHOOTING JACKET

15
BOUDOIR SLIPPERS
CARDIGAN
 SWEATER
CHAPEAU FRANCAIS
CHEMISE À LA REINE
CHEVALIER BONNET
DOUBLE-DUTY
 DRESS
ENVELOPE CHEMISE
FAIR ISLE SWEATER
MONTGOMERY
 BERET

16
BALLERINA
 COSTUME
BUTCHER BOY
 BLOUSE
CALMEL'S HAIR
 SHAWL
CHICKEN SKIN
 GLOVE
EISENHOWER
 JACKET

16 —continued
ELBERT HUBBARD
 TIE
GOING-AWAY
 COSTUME
SWADDLING
 CLOTHES

17
CHEMISE À
 L'ANGLAISE
COAL SCUTTLE
 BONNET
CONFIRMATION
 DRESS
FOUNDATION
 GARMENT
SWALLOW-TAILED
 COAT

18
BETHLEHEM
 HEADDRESS
CHARLOTTE
 CORDAY CAP

19
SALVATION ARMY
 BONNET

MATERIALS

3
ABB
BAN
FUR
NET
REP

4
ACCA
ALMA
BAKU
BRIN
BURE
CALF
CORD
CREA
FELT
FUJI
GROS
HEMP
HIDE
JEAN
LACE
LAMÉ
LAWN
LYNX

4 —continued
MULL
PELT
ROAN
SILK
SKIN
VAIR
WOOL

5
ABACA
ACELE
ACETA
ARDIL
BAIZE
BASCO
BASIN
CADIS
CAFFA
CASHA
CLOTH
CRAPE
CRASH
CRISP
CROWN
DENIM

5 —continued
DORIA
FITCH
GAUZE
GENET
GUNNY
HONAN
JUPON
KAPOK
LAINE
LAPIN
LINEN
LINON
LISLE
LLAMA
LUREX
MOIRE
NINON
NYLON
ORLON
OTTER
PEKIN
PIQUÉ
PLUSH
PRINT

5 —continued
RAYON
SATIN
SCRIM
SERGE
SISAL
SISOL
SKUNK
STRAW
STUFF
SUEDE
SURAH
TAMMY
TISSU
TOILE
TULLE
TWEED
TWILL
UNION
VOILE

6
ALACHA
ALASKA
ALPACA
AMAZON

6 —continued	6 —continued	7 —continued	7 —continued
ANGORA	MANTUA	CARACAL	PIGSKIN
ARALAC	MARMOT	CARACUL	RACCOON
ARIDEX	MARTEN	CATALIN	RAWHIDE
ARMURE	MELTON	CHALLIS	RAW SILK
BALINE	MERINO	CHAMOIS	ROMAINE
BARÉGE	MILIUM	CHARVET	SACKING
BEAVER	MOHAIR	CHEKMAK	SAFFIAN
BENGAL	MOUTON	CHEVIOT	SATINET
BERBER	MULMUL	CHEYNEY	SUITING
BIRETZ	MUSLIN	CHIFFON	TAFFETA
BLATTA	NAPERY	COOTHAY	TEXTILE
BOTANY	NUTRIA	COWHIDE	TICKING
BUREAU	OCELOT	DAMMASÉ	TIE SILK
BURLAP	OSPREY	DELAINE	TIFFANY
BURNET	OXFORD	DOESKIN	TUSSORE
BURRAH	PAILLE	DORNICK	VALENCE
BYSSUS	PONGEE	DRABBET	VELOURS
CAFFOY	POPLIN	DRUGGET	VISCOSE
CALICO	PYTHON	DUCHESS	VIYELLA
CAMACA	RABBIT	DURANCE	WEBBING
CAMLET	RED FOX	DUVETYN	WOOLLEN
CANGAN	RIBBON	EARL GLO	WORSTED
CANVAS	RUBBER	ÉPINGLÉ	**8**
CASTOR	SAMITE	ESPARTO	AGA BANEE
CATGUT	SATEEN	ETAMINE	ALOE LACE
CHILLO	SAXONY	FAKE FUR	ANTELOPE
CHINTZ	SENNIT	FISHNET	ARMOZEEN
CHROME	SHODDY	FITCHEW	ARMOZINE
CHUNAN	SISSOL	FLANNEL	ART LINEN
COBURG	SKIVER	FOULARD	ASBESTOS
CONTRO	SOUPLE	FUR FELT	BAGHEERA
COSSAS	TARTAN	FUSTIAN	BARATHEA
CÔTELÉ	TINSEL	GALATEA	BARRACAN
CREPON	TISSUE	GINGHAM	BATSWING
CROISE	TRICOT	GOBELIN	BAUDEKIN
CUBICA	TUSSAH	GROGRAM	BEUTANOL
DAMASK	TUSSEH	GUANACO	BLANCARD
DIAPER	VELURE	GUIPURE	BOBBINET
DIMITY	VELVET	HESSIAN	BOMBAZET
DJERSA	VICUNA	HOLLAND	BOX CLOTH
DOMETT	WINCEY	JACONET	BUCKSKIN
DOWLAS	WITNEY	JAP SILK	BUFFSKIN
DUCAPE	**7**	KASHMIR	CALFSKIN
ÉPONGE	ACRILON	KIDSKIN	CAPESKIN
ERMINE	ACRYLIC	LEATHER	CASHMERE
FABRIC	ALAMODE	LEGHORN	CELANESE
FAILLE	ART SILK	LEOPARD	CELENESE
FISHER	BAGGING	LIBERTY	CHAMBRAY
FORFAR	BATISTE	MINIVER	CHARMEEN
FRIEZE	BATTING	MOROCCO	CHENILLE
GALYAC	BEMBERG	NANKEEN	CHIRIMEN
GALYAK	BLUE FOX	NETTING	CHIVERET
GRENAI	BRABANT	OILSKIN	CIVET CAT
GURRAH	BRUNETE	ORGANDY	CORDUROY
KERSEY	BUNTING	ORGANZA	COTELINE
LAMPAS	BUSTIAN	OTTOMAN	CRETONNE
LASTEX	CAMBAYE	PAISLEY	CROSS FOX
LINENE	CAMBRIC	PARAGON	DIAPHANE
LIZARD	CANTOON	PECCARY	DRAP D'ÉTÉ
MADRAS	CAPENET	PERCALE	DUCHESSE

8 —continued

ÉCRU SILK
EOLIENNE
ESTAMENE
EVERFAST
FARADINE
FLORENCE
GOATSKIN
GOSSAMER
HOMESPUN
INDIENNE
KOLINSKY
LAMBSKIN
LUSTRINE
LUSTRING
MARABOUT
MARCELLA
MAROCAIN
MATERIAL
MILANESE
MOGADORE
MOLESKIN
MOQUETTE
MUSLINET
MUSQUASH
NAINSOOK
OILCLOTH
ORGANDIE
PURE SILK
SARCENET
SARSENET
SEALSKIN
SHAGREEN
SHANTUNG
SHIRTING
SHOT SILK
SQUIRREL
TAPESTRY
TARLATAN
TARLETAN
TOILINET
VALENCIA
WAX CLOTH
WHIPCORD
WHITE FOX
WILD MINK
WILD SILK
ZIBELINE

9

ADA CANVAS
AGRA GAUZE
ALBATROSS
ALLIGATOR
ASBESTALL
ASTRAKHAN
ASTRAKHAN
BARK CLOTH
BARK CREPE
BENGALINE
BOMBAZINE
BOMBYCINE

9 —continued

BOOK CLOTH
BOOK LINEN
BROCATELL
BYRD CLOTH
CALAMANCO
CANNEQUIN
CATALOWNE
CHARMEUSE
CHINA SILK
COTTONADE
COTTON REP
CREPELINE
CRINOLINE
CUT VELVET
DACCA SILK
ÉCRU CLOTH
ÉLASTIQUE
FLANNELET
FUR FABRIC
GABARDINE
GEORGETTE
GRENADINE
GROSGRAIN
HAIRCLOTH
HORSEHAIR
HUCKABACK
LONGCLOTH
MARCELINE
MESSALINE
MOSS CREPE
ORGANZINE
PATCHWORK
PETERSHAM
RANCH MINK
SACKCLOTH
SAIL CLOTH
SATINETTE
SHARKSKIN
SHEEPSKIN
SILVER FOX
SNAKESKIN
STOCKINET
SWANSDOWN
TARPAULIN
TOWELLING
TRICOTINE
VELVETEEN
WOLVERINE
WORCESTER

10

ABBOT CLOTH
AIDA CANVAS
ANGOLA YARN
AUSTINIZED
BALBRIGGAN
BARLEYCORN
BAUM MARTEN
BEAVERETTE
BEAVERTEEN
BOOK MUSLIN

10 —continued

BOUCLÉ YARN
BROADCLOTH
BROAD GOODS
CADET CLOTH
CAMBRESINE
CHINCHILLA
CHINO CLOTH
CIRCASSIAN
CONGO CLOTH
CREPE LISSE
DRESS LINEN
GRASS CLOTH
HOP SACKING
HORSECLOTH
INDIAN LAMB
IRISH LINEN
MARSEILLES
MOUSSELINE
PEAU DE SOIE
PIECE GOODS
PILOT CLOTH
SEERSUCKER
SUEDE CLOTH
TERRY CLOTH
TOILINETTE
WINCEYETTE

11

ABRADED YARN
AERATED YARN
ALBERT CREPE
ARABIAN LACE
ARMURE-LAINE
BABY FLANNEL
BAG SHEETING
BANDLE LINEN
BASKET CLOTH
BATH COATING
BEDFORD CORD
BOMBER CLOTH
BRUSHED WOOL
CANTON CREPE
CANTON LINEN
CHAMOISETTE
CHEESECLOTH
CHESS CANVAS
CHINA COTTON
CLAY WORSTED
COTTON CREPE
DACCA MUSLIN
DIAPER CLOTH
DOTTED SWISS
DRAP DE BERRY
DREADNOUGHT
DRUID'S CLOTH
DU PONT RAYON
ESKIMO CLOTH
EVERLASTING
FLANNELETTE
HARRIS TWEED
IRISH POPLIN

11 —continued

LEATHERETTE
MARQUISETTE
NAPA LEATHER
NUN'S VEILING
OVERCOATING
PANNE VELVET
PERSIAN LAMB
POODLE CLOTH
POULT-DE-SOIE
SCOTCH PLAID
SPONGE CLOTH
STONE MARTEN
TOILE DE JOUY
WAFFLE CLOTH

12

ACETATE RAYON
BALLOON CLOTH
BERLIN CANVAS
BOLIVIA CLOTH
BOLTING CLOTH
BRILLIANTINE
BROWN HOLLAND
BRUSHED RAYON
BUTCHER LINEN
CARACUL CLOTH
CAVALRY TWILL
CONVENT CLOTH
COTTON VELVET
CRINKLE CLOTH
CROISÉ VELVET
DENMARK SATIN
DOUBLE DAMASK
DRESS FLANNEL
ELEMENT CLOTH
EMPRESS CLOTH
GLAZED CHINTZ
MUTATION MINK
SHETLAND WOOL
SLIPPER SATIN
SUMMER ERMINE
VISCOSE RAYON
WELSH FLANNEL

13

AIRPLANE CLOTH
AMERICAN CLOTH
ARMURE-SATINÉE
BRITTANY CLOTH
CANTON FLANNEL
CARDINAL CLOTH
CASEMENT CLOTH
CLOISTER CLOTH
COSTUME VELVET
COTTON FLANNEL
COTTON SUITING
COTTON WORSTED
CRUSHED VELVET
DIAGONAL CLOTH
DIAPER FLANNEL
EGYPTIAN CLOTH

13 —continued
END-TO-END CLOTH
LINSEY-WOOLSEY
PATENT LEATHER
RUSSIA LEATHER
14
ALGERIAN STRIPE
AMERICAN COTTON
ARGENTINE CLOTH
BANDOLIER CLOTH
BARONETTE SATIN
BROADTAIL CLOTH
CORKSCREW TWILL
EGYPTIAN COTTON

14 —continued
ELECTORAL CLOTH
FRUIT OF THE LOOM
HONEYCOMB CLOTH
JACQUARD FABRIC
SHEPHERD'S PLAID
15
ABSORBENT
   COTTON
ADMIRALITY CLOTH
CACHEMIRE DE SOIE
CAMEL'S HAIR
   CLOTH

15 —continued
EMBROIDERY LINEN
OSTRICH FEATHERS
PARACHUTE FABRIC
SEA-ISLAND
   COTTON
SHIRTING FLANNEL
TATTERSALL CHECK
TATTERSALL PLAID
TROPICAL SUITING
16
CANDLEWICK
   FABRIC

16 —continued
CONSTITUTION
   CORD
MERCERIZED
   COTTON
TURKISH
   TOWELLING
17
CROSS-STITCH
   CANVAS
CUPRAMMONIUM
   RAYON

FOOD AND DRINK

COOKERY TERMS

4
BARD
BEAT
BLEU (AU)
BOIL
BONE
CHOP
COAT
HANG
HASH
LARD
PIPE
RARE
TOSS

5
BASTE
BERNY
BLANC (À)
BLANC (AU)
BROIL
BROWN
BRULÉ
CARVE
CHILL
CROWN
DAUBE
DRAIN
DRESS
GLAZE
GRILL
KNEAD
MELBA
PLUCK
POACH
POINT (À)
PROVE
PURÉE
REINE (À LA)

5—continued
ROAST
RUB IN
SAUTÉ
SCALD
STEAM
SWEAT
TRUSS

6
AURORE
BRAISE
CONFIT
CRÉOLE (À LA)
DECANT
DESALT
DIABLE (À LA)
FILLET
FONDUE
GRATIN
GREASE
MAISON
MIGNON
NATURE
REDUCE
SIMMER
ZEPHYR

7
AL DENTE
ARRÊTER
BLANCHE
BLONDIR
CHEMISE (EN)
COLBERT
CROUTON
DEGLAZE
EMINCER
FLAMBER
GRECQUE (À LA)

7—continued
MARENGO
MÉDICIS
NICOISE (À LA)
REFRESH
SUPRÊME
TARTARE (À LA)

8
ALLONGER
ANGLAISE (À L')
APPAREIL
ASSATION
BARBECUE
BELLEVUE (EN)
BRETONNE (À LA)
CATALANE (À LA)
CHAMBORD
CHASSEUR
CHEMISER
CRUDITÉS
DAUPHINE (À LA)
DEVILLED
DUCHESSE (À LA)
EMULSION
ESCALOPE
FERMIÈRE (À LA)
FLAMANDE (ÀLA)
INFUSION
JULIENNE
MACERATE
MARINATE
MEUNIÈRE (À LA)
PISTACHE
POT-ROAST
SURPRISE (EN)

9
ACIDULATE
BAKE BLIND

9—continued
CANELLING
DETAILLER
DIEPPOISE (À LA)
ESPAGNOLE (À L')
FRICASSÉE
KNOCK BACK
LIÉGEOISE (À LA)
LYONNAISE (À LA)
MARINIÈRE (À LA)
MEDALLION
MILANAISE (À LA)

10
ANTILLAISE (À L')
BALLOTTINE
BLANQUETTE
BONNE FEMME
BORDELAISE (À LA)
BOULANGÈRE (À LA)
CHAUD-FROID
DIJONNAISE (À LA)
FLORENTINE (À LA)
PROVENCALE (À LA)

11
BELLE-HÉLÈNE
BOURGUIGNON
CHARCUTERIE
DAUPHINOISE (À LA)
HOLLANDAISE (À LA)

13
BOURGUIGNONNE (À LA)
CLARIFICATION
DEEP-FAT FRYING

KITCHEN UTENSILS AND TABLEWARE

3
CUP
HOB
JAR
JUG

3—continued
LID
MUG
PAN
POT

3—continued
TIN
WOK

4
BOWL

4—continued
DISH
EWER
FORK
MILL

4—continued	6—continued	8—continued	10—continued
RACK	SHAKER	SCISSORS	SLOW COOKER
SPIT	SHEARS	STOCKPOT	STERILIZER
TIAN	SIPHON	STRAINER	WAFFLE IRON
TRAY	SKEWER	TART RING	**11**
5	STRING	TASTE-VIN	BAKING SHEET
BAHUT	TAJINE	TRENCHER	BRAISING PAN
BASIN	TOUPIN	**9**	CANDISSOIRE
BOARD	TUREEN	ALCARRAZA	CHAFING DISH
CHOPE	**7**	AUTOCLAVE	CHEESECLOTH
CHURN	ALEMBIC	BAIN-MARIE	COFFEE MAKER
FLUTE	ATTELET	BAKING TIN	DOUGH TROUGH
GRILL	BLENDER	CAFETIÈRE	DRIPPING PAN
KNIFE	BROILER	CASSEROLE	FRUIT STONER
LADLE	CAISSES	COMPOTIER	GARGOULETTE
MIXER	CHINOIS	CORKSCREW	JAMBONNIÈRE
MOULD	CHIP PAN	CRUMB TRAY	NUTCRACKERS
PELLE	CHOPPER	DÉCOUPOIR	PASTRY BRUSH
PLATE	COCOTTE	FISH SLICE	PASTRY WHEEL
PRESS	DRAINER	FRYING-PAN	SERVING DISH
RUSSE	DREDGER	KILNER JAR	THERMOMETER
SIEVE	ÉCUELLE	MANDOLINE	YOGURT-MAKER
SPOON	GRINDER	MIJOTEUSE	**12**
STEEL	MARMITE	PASTRY BAG	CARVING KNIFE
STRAW	PITCHER	PIPING BAG	DEEP-FAT FRYER
TONGS	RAMEKIN	RING MOULD	MEASURING JUG
WHISK	RONDEAU	SALAD BOWL	PALETTE KNIFE
6	SALT BOX	SAUCEBOAT	PASTRY CUTTER
BASKET	SAMOVAR	SHARPENER	TURBOT KETTLE
BUCKET	SKILLET	STEAK BATT	**13**
CARAFE	SKIMMER	TISANIÈRE	BUTCHER'S BLOCK
CLOCHE	SPATULA	TOURTIÈRE	FOOD PROCESSOR
COOLER	SYRINGE	**10**	ICE-CREAM MAKER
CRIBLE	TÂTE-VIN	APPLE-CORER	KITCHEN SCALES
DIABLE	TOASTER	CAISSETTES	LARDING NEEDLE
EGG CUP	**8**	CASSOLETTE	PRESERVING JAR
FUNNEL	CAQUELON	CHOPSTICKS	SACCHAROMETER
GOBLET	CAULDRON	CRUET STAND	VEGETABLE DISH
GRADIN	COLANDER	DIPPING PIN	**14**
GRATER	CRÊPE PAN	FISH KETTLE	JUICE EXTRACTOR
KETTLE	CROCKERY	LIQUIDISER	KNEADING TROUGH
MINCER	DAUBIÈRE	MUSTARD POT	KNIFE SHARPENER
MORTAR	EGG TIMER	PERCOLATOR	PRESSURE COOKER
MUSLIN	FLAN RING	ROLLING PIN	TRUSSING NEEDLE
PESTLE	HOTPLATE	ROTISSERIE	**16**
PICHET	MAZAGRAN	SALAMANDER	MEAT-CARVING
PITTER	MOUVETTE	SALT CELLAR	TONGS
POÊLON	SAUCEPAN	SALTING TUB	
SAUCER	SAUTÉ PAN		

BAKING

3	3—continued	4—continued	5
BAP	PIE	FLAN	BAGEL
BUN	**4**	PAVÉ	BÂTON
COB	BABA	RUSK	BREAD
FAR	CHOU	TART	CRÊPE

CEREALS (continued list)

5—continued
FLÛTE
ICING
PLAIT
SABLÉ
SCONE
STICK
TOAST

6
COOKIE
CORNET
ÉCLAIR
LEAVEN
MUFFIN
OUBLIE
ROCHER
TOURTE
WAFFLE

7
BAKLAVA
BANNOCK
BISCUIT
BLOOMER
BRIOCHE

7—continued
CHAPATI
COTTAGE
CRACKER
CRUMPET
FICELLE
FRITTER
GALETTE
PALMIER
PANCAKE
PRALINE
PRETZEL
STOLLEN
STRUDEL
TARTINE
TARTLET

8
AMANDINE
BAGUETTE
BARM CAKE
BÂTONNET
BISCOTTE
DOUGHNUT
DUCHESSE

8—continued
DUMPLING
EMPANADA
FROSTING
GRISSINI
SANDWICH
SPLIT TIN
TORTILLA
TURNOVER

9
ALLUMETTE
BARQUETTE
CROISSANT
FEUILLETÉ
FRIANDISE
KUGELHOPF
PETIT FOUR
VOL-AU-VENT

10
CRISPBREAD
FRANGIPANE
PÂTISSERIE

10—continued
PUFF PASTRY
RELIGIEUSE
SHORTBREAD
SPONGE CAKE

11
CHOUX PASTRY
LINZERTORTE
PETIT-BEURRE
PROFITEROLE

12
LANGUE-DE-CHAT
PUMPERNICKEL
SPONGE FINGER

13
GENOESE SPONGE

14
PAIN AU CHOCOLAT

15
SAVOY SPONGE
  CAKE

CEREALS

3
RYE

4
BRAN
CORN
OATS
RICE

5
MAIZE
SPELT
WHEAT

6
BARLEY
BULGUR

6—continued
MÉTEIL
MILLET

7
BURGHUL
FROMENT
SORGHUM

9
BUCKWHEAT

12
CRACKED WHEAT

CHEESES

4
BRIE (France)
CURD (CHEESE)
EDAM (Netherlands)
FETA (Greece)
TOME (France)

5
BANON (France)
BRICK (US)
CABOC (Scotland)
COMTÉ (France)
DANBO (Denmark)
DERBY (England)
FETTA (Greece)
GOUDA (Netherlands)
HERVE (Belgium)

5—continued
LEIGH (England)
MOLBO (Denmark)
MUROL (France)
NIOLO (Corsica)
TAMIÉ (France)

6
ASIAGO (Italy)
BAGNES (Switzerland)
BRESSE (France)
CACHAT (France)
CANTAL (France)
CENDRÉ (France)
DUNLOP (Scotland)
FOURME (France)
GAPRON (France)

6—continued
GÉROMÉ (France)
HALUMI (Greece)
HRAMSA (Scotland)
LEIDEN (Netherlands)
MORVEN (Scotland)
OLIVET (France)
POURLY (France)
ROLLOT (France)
SALERS (France)
SAMSOË (Denmark)
SBRINZ (Switzerland)
SURATI (India)
TILSIT (Switzerland; Germany; Austria)
VENACO (Corsica)

7
BONDARD (France)
BRINZEN (Hungary)
BROCCIO (Corsica)
BROCCIU (Corsica)
BROUSSE (France)
BRUCCIU (Corsica)
BRYNDZA (Hungary)
CABÉCOU (France)
CHEDDAR (England)
CROWDIE (Scotland)
DAUPHIN (France)
DEMI-SEL (France)
FONTINA (Italy)
GAPERON (France)
GJETÖST (Norway)
GRUYÈRE (France; Switzerland)
JONCHÉE (France)
LANGRES (France)
LEVROUX (France)
LIMBURG (Belgium)
LIVAROT (France)
MACQUÉE (France)
MONT-D'OR (France)
MORBIER (France)
MÜNSTER (France)
NANTAIS (France)
PICODON (France)
QUARGEL (Austria)
RICOTTA (Italy)
SAPSAGO (Switzerland)
STILTON (England)
VENDÔME (France)

8
AUVERGNE (France)
AYRSHIRE (Scotland)
BEAUFORT (France)
BEL PAESE (Italy)
BERGKÄSE (Austria)
BOULETTE (France)
CHAOURCE (France)
CHESHIRE (England)
EDELPILZ (Germany)
EMMENTAL (Switzerland)
EPOISSES (France)

8—continued
MANCHEGO (Spain)
PARMESAN (Italy)
PECORINO (Italy)
PÉLARDON (France)
REMOUDOU (Belgium)
SCAMORZE (Italy)
TALEGGIO (Italy)
VACHERIN (Switzerland)
VALENÇAY (France)

9
APPENZELL (Switzerland)
BROODKAAS (Netherlands)
CAITHNESS (Scotland)
CAMBOZOLA (Italy; Germany)
CAMEMBERT (France)
CHABICHOU (France)
CHEVRETON (France)
EMMENTHAL (Switzerland)
EXCELSIOR (France)
GAMMELÖST (Norway)
LA BOUILLE (France)
LEICESTER (England)
LIMBURGER (Belgium)
MAROILLES (France)
MIMOLETTE (France)
PAVÉ D'AUGE (France)
PORT-SALUT (France)
PROVOLONE (Italy)
REBLOCHON (France)
ROQUEFORT (France)
SOVIETSKI (USSR)

10
CAERPHILLY (Wales)
DANISH BLUE (Denmark)
DOLCELATTE (Italy)
GLOUCESTER (England)
GORGONZOLA (Italy)
LANCASHIRE (England)
MOZZARELLA (Italy)
NEUFCHÂTEL (Switzerland)
PITHIVIERS (France)
RED WINDSOR (England)
SAINGORLON (France)
STRACCHINO (Italy)

11
CARRÉ DE L'EST (France)
COEUR DE BRAY (France)
COULOMMIERS (France)
KATSHKAWALJ (Bulgaria)
PETIT-SUISSE (France)
PONT-L'ÉVÊQUE (France)
SAINTE-MAURE (France)
SAINT-PAULIN (France)
SCHABZIEGER (Switzerland)
SCHLOSSKÄSE (Austria)
TÊTE-DE-MOINE (Switzerland)
WEISSLACKER (Germany)
WENSLEYDALE (England)

12
CACIOCAVALLO (Italy)
RED LEICESTER (England)
SOUMAINTRAIN (France)

13
SAINT-NECTAIRE (France)
SELLES-SUR-CHER (France)

14
BRILLAT-SAVARIN (France)
FEUILLE DE DREUX (France)
LAGUIOLE-AUBRAC (France)
SAINT-FLORENTIN (France)
SAINT-MARCELLIN (France)
TRAPPISTENKÄSE (Germany)

15
BOUTON-DE-CULOTTE (France)

16
DOUBLE GLOUCESTER (England)

17
RIGOTTE DE PELUSSIN (France)

18
CHEVROTIN DES ARAVIS (France)
CROTTIN DE CHAVIGNOL (France)

19
POULIGNY-SAINT-PIERRE (France)

HERBS AND SPICES

3
BAY
RUE

4
BALM
DILL
MINT
SAGE

5
ANISE
BASIL
CHIVE
CLOVE
CUMIN
TANSY
THYME

6
BETONY
BORAGE
BURNET

6 —continued
CICELY
FENNEL
GARLIC
GINGER
LOVAGE
PEPPER
SAVORY
SESAME
SORREL

7
BONESET
CARAWAY
CHERVIL
COMFREY
DITTANY
MUSTARD
OREGANO
PAPRIKA

7 —continued
PARSLEY
PERILLA
PIMENTO
SAFFRON
SALSIFY
TABASCO
VANILLA

8
ALLSPICE
ANGELICA
CAMOMILE
CARDAMOM
CARDAMON
CINNAMON
DROPWORT
FEVERFEW
MARJORAM
ROSEMARY

8 —continued
TARRAGON
TURMERIC

9
CHAMOMILE
CORIANDER
FENUGREEK
SPEARMINT

10+
ASAFOETIDA
BLACK-EYED SUSAN
HERB OF GRACE
HORSERADISH
HOTTENTOT FIG
OYSTER PLANT
PEPPERMINT
POT MARIGOLD
VEGETABLE OYSTER

DRINKS

WINES AND APERITIFS

4
FINO
HOCK
PORT

5
BYRRH
CRÉPY
FITOU
MÉDOC
MOSEL
RIOJA

5—continued
TAVEL
TOKAY

6
ALSACE
BANDOL
BAROLO
BARSAC
BEAUNE
CAHORS
CASSIS

6—continued
CHINON
CLARET
FRANGY
GRAVES
MÁLAGA
SAUMUR
SHERRY
VOLNAY

7
ALIGOTÉ

7—continued
CAMPARI
CHABLIS
CHIANTI
CLAIRET
CRÉMANT
FALERNO
GAILLAC
MADEIRA
MARGAUX
MARSALA

7—continued
MARTINI
MOSELLE
ORVIETO
POMMARD
RETSINA
VOUVRAY

8
BORDEAUX
BROUILLY
DUBONNET
GIGONDAS
MERCUREY
MONTAGNY
MONTILLA
MUSCADET
PAUILLAC
RIESLING
ROSÉ WINE
SANCERRE
SANTENAY
VALENCAY
VERMOUTH
VIN JAUNE

9
BOURGUEIL
CHAMPAGNE

9—continued
CLAIRETTE
CÔTE-RÔTIE
HERMITAGE
LAMBRUSCO
MEURSAULT
MONTLOUIS
SAUTERNES

10
BARBARESCO
BEAUJOLAIS
BULL'S BLOOD
MANZANILLA
MONTRACHET
RICHEBOURG
RIVESALTES
VINHO VERDE

11
ALOXE-CORTON
AMONTILLADO
MONBAZILLAC
POUILLY-FUMÉ
SAINT JULIEN
VIN DE PAILLE

12
CÔTES-DU-RHÔNE
ROMANÉE-CONTI

12—continued
SAINT-EMILION
SAINT ESTEPHE
VALPOLICELLA
VOSNE-ROMANÉE

13
CHÂTEAU D'YQUEM
CHÂTEAU LAFITE
CHÂTEAU LATOUR
ENTRE-DEUX-MERS
POUILLY-FUISSÉ

14
CHÂTEAU MARGAUX
CÔTES-DU-VENTOUX
GEWÜRZTRAMINER
LACRIMA CHRISTI

15
CÔTES-DE-
  PROVENCE
CÔTES-DU-VIVARAIS
CROZES-HERMITAGE
HAUT POITOU WINES
MOREY-SAINT-DENIS

16
CHAMBOLLE-
  MUSIGNY

16—continued
CHÂTEAU HAUT-
  BRION
GEVREY-
  CHAMBERTIN
SAVIGNY-LÈS-
  BEAUNE

17
CORTON-
  CHARLEMAGNE
CÔTES-DU-
  ROUSSILLON
NUITS-SAINT-
  GEORGES

18
BLANQUETTE DE
  LIMOUX

19
CHASSAGNE-
  MONTRACHET

20
CHÂTEAU MOUTON-
  ROTHSCHILD

COCKTAILS AND MIXED DRINKS

3
FIX
KIR
NOG

4
FIZZ
FLIP
GROG
RAKI
SOUR

5
JULEP
NEGUS
PUNCH
TODDY

6
BEADLE
BISHOP
GIMLET
POSSET

7
BACARDI

7—continued
MARTINI
SANGRIA
SIDECAR
WALDORF

8
APPLE CAR
DAIQUIRI
GIN AND IT
GIN SLING
HIGHBALL
NIGHTCAP
PINK LADY
WHIZ BANG

9
ALEXANDER
APPLEJACK
BEE'S KNEES
BUCK JONES
BUCKS FIZZ
COMMODORE
MANHATTAN

9—continued
MINT JULEP
MOONLIGHT
MOONSHINE
MULLED ALE
WHITE LADY

10
ANGEL'S KISS
ARCHBISHOP
BLACK MARIA
BLOODY MARY
HORSE'S NECK
MERRY WIDOW
MULLED WINE
PINA COLADA
RUM COLLINS
TOM COLLINS

11
BEACHCOMBER
BLACK VELVET
FALLEN ANGEL
JOHN COLLINS

11—continued
WASSAIL BOWL

12
CHURCHWARDEN
ELEPHANT'S EAR
FINE AND DANDY
OLD-FASHIONED
WHITE GIN SOUR

13
CHAMPAGNE BUCK
CORPSE REVIVER
KNICKERBOCKER
MAIDEN'S PRAYER
PLANTER'S PUNCH
PRAIRIE OYSTER

16
BETWEEN THE
  SHEETS
HARVEY
  WALLBANGER

BEERS AND BEVERAGES

3
ALE

4
MEAD

4—continued
MILD

5
CIDER

5—continued
KVASS
LAGER
PERRY
STOUT

6
BITTER
LAMBIC
SHANDY

8
GUINNESS
HYDROMEL

10
BARLEY BEER
BARLEY WINE

SPIRITS

3
GIN
RUM
4
ARAK
MARC
OUZO
5
CHOUM
VODKA
6
BOUKHA
BRANDY

6—continued
CHICHA
COGNAC
GRAPPA
KIRSCH
MESCAL
METAXA
PASTIS
PERNOD
PULQUE
WHISKY
7
AKVAVIT

7—continued
AQUAVIT
BACARDI
BOUKHRA
BOURBON
SCHNAPS
TEQUILA
WHISKEY
8
ARMAGNAC
CALVADOS

8—continued
FALERNUM
SCHNAPPS
9
FRAMBOISE
SLIVOVITZ
10
RYE WHISKEY
11
AGUARDIENTE

LIQUEURS

4
SAKÉ
SAKI
5
ANISE
ANRAM
6
CASSIS
KÜMMEL
MÊLISS
QETSCH
SCUBAC
STREGA
7
ALCAMAS

7—continued
ALLASCH
BAILEYS
CURACAO
ESCUBAC
RATAFIA
SAMBUCA
8
ABSINTHE
ADVOCAAT
ANISETTE
DRAMBUIE
PERSICOT
PRUNELLE

9
ARQUEBUSE
COINTREAU
FRAMBOISE
GUIGNOLET
MIRABELLE
TRIPLE SEC
10
BROU DE NOIX
CHARTREUSE
MARASCHINO
11
BENEDICTINE
TRAPPISTINE

12
CHERRY BRANDY
CRÈME DE CACAO
GRAND MARNIER
13
CRÈME DE MENTHE
15
SOUTHERN
   COMFORT
17
AMARETTO DI
   SARANNO

NON-ALCOHOLIC DRINKS

3
CHA (TEA)
TEA
4
CHAR (TEA)
COLA
MATÉ
SODA
5
LASSI

5—continued
WATER
6
COFFEE
ORGEAT
TISANE
7
BEEF TEA

7—continued
DIABOLO
SELTZER
8
LEMONADE
9
GRENADINE

9—continued
MILKSHAKE
ORANGEADE
10
GINGER BEER
TONIC WATER

SPORT AND RECREATION

SPORTS

4
GOLF
JUDO
PATO
POLO

5
BOWLS
FIVES
KENDO
RALLY
RODEO

6
AIKIDO
BOULES
BOXING
HOCKEY
KARATE
KUNG FU
PELOTA
ROWING
SHINTY
SKIING
TENNIS

7
ANGLING
ARCHERY
BOWLING
CRICKET
CROQUET
CURLING
FENCING
HURLING
JUJITSU
KABADDI
KARTING

7—continued
NETBALL
RACKETS
SHOT PUT

8
BASEBALL
BIATHLON
CANOEING
COURSING
DRESSAGE
FALCONRY
GYMKHANA
HANDBALL
HURDLING
LACROSSE
LONG JUMP
MARATHON
PETANQUE
PING-PONG
ROUNDERS
SHOOTING
SPEEDWAY
SWIMMING
TUG OF WAR

9
ATHLETICS
BADMINTON
DECATHLON
ICE HOCKEY
MOTO-CROSS
POLE VAULT
SKYDIVING
TAE KWON-DO
WATER POLO
WRESTLING

10
BASKETBALL
DRAG RACING
FLAT RACING
FOXHUNTING
GYMNASTICS
ICE SKATING
REAL TENNIS
RUGBY UNION
TRIPLE JUMP
VOLLEYBALL

11
BEARBAITING
BLOOD SPORTS
BOBSLEDDING
BULLBAITING
DISCUS THROW
HAMMER THROW
HAND-GLIDING
HORSE RACING
HORSE TRAILS
MARTIAL ARTS
MOTOR RACING
PARACHUTING
PENTHATHLON
RUGBY LEAGUE
SEPAK TAKRAW
TABLE TENNIS
TOBOGGANING
WATER SKIING

12
BULLFIGHTING
CABER TOSSING
COCKFIGHTING

12—continued
ETON WALL GAME
JAVELIN THROW
ORIENTEERING
PIGEON RACING
POINT-TO-POINT
STEEPLECHASE

13
EQUESTRIANISM
HARNESS RACING
SKATEBOARDING
SQUASH RACKETS
WEIGHT LIFTING

14
FOOTBALL LEAGUE
MOUNTAINEERING
STOCK-CAR RACING

15
GREYHOUND
  RACING

16
AMERICAN
  FOOTBALL
MOTORCYCLE
  RACING

18
CLAY-PIGEON
  SHOOTING
FREESTYLE
  WRESTLING

19
ASSOCIATION
  FOOTBALL

GAMES

2
GO

4
BRAG
POOL
SNAP

5
BINGO
CAVES
CHESS

5—continued
CRAPS
DARTS
FIVES
POKER
RUMMY
SHOGI
SPOOF
WHIST

6
CLUEDO
PAC-MAN
QUOITS
TIPCAT

7
BEZIQUE
CANASTA

7—continued
DOBBERS
MAHJONG
MARBLES
MATADOR
OLD MAID
PACHISI
PONTOON

7—continued	8—continued	10—continued	13—continued
SNOOKER	SCRABBLE	CASABLANCA	SPACE INVADERS
YAHTZEE	SKITTLES	RUNNING OUT	**14**
8	**9**	**11**	CONTRACT BRIDGE
BACCARAT	AUNT SALLY	CHEMIN DE FER	TRIVIAL PURSUIT
BIRD CAGE	BILLIARDS	TIDDLYWINKS	**16**
CRIBBAGE	BLACKJACK	**12**	SNAKES AND
DADDLUMS	POKER DICE	BAR BILLIARDS	LADDERS
DOMINOES	SNAKE-EYES	KNUR AND SPELL	**20**
DRAUGHTS	VINGT-ET-UN	SHOVE HA'PENNY	DEVIL AMONG THE
LIAR DICE	**10**	**13**	TAILORS
MONOPOLY	BACKGAMMON	HAPPY FAMILIES	
PATIENCE	BAT AND TRAP		
ROULETTE			

DANCES

3	5—continued	6—continued	7—continued
DOG	RUMBA	SHIMMY	MADISON
GIG	SAMBA	TIRANA	MAYPOLE
JIG	SARBA	VALETA	MAZURKA
OLE	SHAKE	VELETA	MEASURE
	SIBEL	YUMARI	MILONGA
4	SIBYL	**7**	MUNEIRA
AHIR	STOMP	ABRASAX	PASILLO
BUMP	TANGO	ABRAXAS	PERICON
CANA	TRATA	AHIDOUS	PLANXTY
HAKA	TWIST	APARIMA	PURPURI
HORA	VELAL	ARNAOUT	SARDANA
JIVE	WALTZ	BABORÁK	SATACEK
JOTA	**6**	BALL PLA	SIKINIK
POGO	ABUANG	BAMBUCO	TANDAVA
SHAG	AMENER	BANJARA	TANTARA
VIRA	ATINGA	BATUQUE	TRAIPSE
	BATUTA	BHARANG	WAKAMBA
5	BOLERO	BOURRÉE	**8**
BARIS	BOOGIE	CANARIE	ALEGRIAS
BULBA	CALATA	CANARIO	À MOLESON
CAROL	CANARY	CINQ PAS	AURRESKU
CONGA	CAN-CAN	CSARDAS	BALZTANZ
CUECA	CAROLE	FORLANA	BULL-FOOT
DANSA	CEBELL	FOX-TROT	CACHUCHA
DEBKA	CHA CHA	FURIANT	CAKEWALK
GAVOT	DJOGED	FURLANA	CANACUAS
GIGUE	EIXIDA	GAVOTTE	CANDIOTE
GOPAK	GANGAR	GERANOS	CHARRADA
HALOA	GIENYS	GLOCSEN	COURANTE
HOPAK	HUSTLE	GOMBEYS	FANDANGO
KUMMI	JACARA	GONDHAL	GALLIARD
L'AG-YA	JARABE	GOSHIKI	GYMNASKA
LIMBO	JARANA	HIMINAU	HABANERA
LOURE	KAGURA	JABADAO	HAND JIVE
MAMBO	KALELA	JON-NUK.E	HORNPIPE
NAZUN	MINUET	LAMENTO	HUAPANGO
NUMBA	PAVANE	LANCERS	MAILEHEN
OKINA	PESSAH	LANDLER	MOHOBELO
POLKA	POLSKA	LLORONA	MOONWALK
RUEDA			

8—continued
MUTCHICO
OXDANSEN
PERICOTE
RIGAUDON
RUTUBURI
TSAMIKOS

9
BAGUETTES
BAILECITO
BARN DANCE
BOULANGER
CARDADORA
CLOG DANCE
COTILLION
ECOSSAISE
FARANDOLE
GALLEGADA
HAJDUTÂNC
HORN DANCE
JITTERBUG
KOLOMEJKA
MISTLETOE
MOKOROTLO
PASSEPIED
POLONAISE
QUADRILLE

9—continued
QUICKSTEP
RENNINGEN
ROCK 'N' ROLL
SARABANDE
SATECKOVA
TAMBORITO
TROYANATS

10
ATNUMOKITA
BANDLTANTZ
BATON DANCE
BERGERETTA
CHANIOTIKO
CHARLESTON
ESPRINGALE
FACKELTANZ
FARANDOULO
FURRY DANCE
GAY GORDONS
HOKEY-COKEY
KYNDELDANS
LAUTERBACH
LOCOMOTION
RUNNING SET
STRATHSPEY
STRIP TEASE

10—continued
SURUVAKARY
TARANTELLA
TRENCHMORE
TURKEY TROT

11
BABORASCHKA
BLACKBOTTOM
DANSURINGUR
DITHYRAMBOS
FLORAL DANCE
GHARBA DANCE
LAMBETH WALK
MORRIS DANCE
PALAIS GLIDE
PAMPERRUQUE
ROCK AND ROLL
SCHOTTISCHE
SQUARE DANCE
TEWRDANNCKH

12
BREAKDANCING
CREUX DE VERVI
DAMHSA NAM BOC
DANSE MACABRE

12—continued
FUNKY CHICKEN
GREEN GARTERS
REEL O'TULLOCH

13
EIGHTSOME REEL
GHILLIE CALLUM
HIGHLAND FLING

14
BABBITY BOWSTER
MILKMAIDS' DANCE
STRIP THE WILLOW

15
COUNTRY BUMPKIIN
MILITARY TWO-STEP
SELLINGER'S
  ROUND

17
HASTE TO THE
  WEDDING

18
SIR ROGER DE
  COVERLEY

HOBBIES AND CRAFTS

3
DIY

5
BATIK
BINGO

6
BONSAI
SEWING

7
COLLAGE
COOKERY
CROCHET
KEEP FIT
MACRAMÉ
MOSAICS
ORIGAMI
POTTERY
READING
TATTING
TOPIARY
WEAVING

8
AEROBICS
APPLIQUÉ
BASKETRY
CANEWORK

8—continued
FRETWORK
KNITTING
LAPIDARY
PAINTING
QUILTING
SPINNING
TAPESTRY
WOODWORK

9
ASTROLOGY
ASTRONOMY
DÉCOUPAGE
GARDENING
GENEALOGY
MARQUETRY
PALMISTRY
PATCHWORK
PHILATELY
RUG MAKING

10
BEE-KEEPING
BEER MAKING
CROSSWORDS
EMBROIDERY
ENAMELLING
KITE FLYING

10—continued
LACE MAKING
UPHOLSTERY
WINE MAKING

11
ARCHAEOLOGY
BARK RUBBING
BOOK BINDING
CALLIGRAPHY
DRESS MAKING
HANG GLIDING
LEPIDOPTERY
MODEL MAKING
PHOTOGRAPHY
STENCILLING
VINTAGE CARS

12
BEACH COMBING
BIRD WATCHING
BRASS RUBBING
CANDLE-MAKING
FLOWER DRYING
TROPICAL FISH

13
FOSSIL HUNTING
JIG-SAW PUZZLES

13—continued
MODEL RAILWAYS
TRAIN SPOTTING

14
BADGER WATCHING
CAKE DECORATING
COIN COLLECTING
FLOWER PRESSING
GLASS ENGRAVING
PIGEON FANCYING

15
FLOWER
  ARRANGING
LAMPSHADE MAKING
SHELL COLLECTING
STAMP COLLECTING

16
AMATEUR
  DRAMATICS
AUTOGRAPH
  HUNTING

19
BUTTERFLY
  COLLECTING

STADIUMS AND VENUES

AINTREE (horse racing)
ANAHEIM STADIUM, CALIFORNIA (baseball)
ASCOT (horse racing)
AZTECA STADIUM, MEXICO CITY (olympics, football)
BELFRY, THE (golf)
BELMONT PARK, LONG ISLAND (horse racing)
BERNABAU STADIUM, MADRID (football)
BIG FOUR CURLING RINK (curling)
BRANDS HATCH (motor racing)
BROOKLANDS (motor racing)
CAESAR'S PALACE, LAS VEGAS (boxing)
CARDIFF ARMS PARK (rugby union)
CENTRAL STADIUM, KIEV (football)
CLEVELAND MUNICIPAL STADIUM (baseball)
CORPORATION STADIUM, CALICUR (cricket)
CROKE PARK, DUBLIN (Gaelic football, hurling)
CRUCIBAL, SHEFFIELD (snooker)
CRYSTAL PALACE (athletics)
DAYTONA INTERNATIONAL SPEEDWAY (motor racing, motor cycling)
EDEN GARDENS, CALCUTTA (cricket)
EDGBASTON (cricket)
EPSOM DOWNS (horse racing)
FORUM, THE (gymnastics)
FRANCORCHAMPS, BELGIUM (motor racing)
HAMPDEN PARK, GLASGOW (football)
HEADINGLEY (cricket)
HEYSEL STADIUM, BRUSSELS (football)
LAHORE (cricket)

LANDSDOWNE ROAD, BELFAST (rugby union)
LENIN STADIUM, MOSCOW (football)
LORDS CRICKET GROUND (cricket)
LOUISIANA SUPERDOME (most sports)
MARACANA STADIUM, BRAZIL (football)
MEADOWBANK (athletics)
MEMORIAL COLISEUM, LOS ANGELES (most sports)
MOOR PARK, RICKMANSWORTH (golf)
MUNICH OLYMPIC STADIUM (athletics, football)
MURRAYFIELD (rugby union)
NEWMARKET (horse racing)
NOU CAMP, BARCELONA (football)
ODSAL STADIUM, BRADFORD (rugby league)
OLD TRAFFORD (cricket)
OVAL, THE (cricket)
ROYAL AND ANCIENT GOLF CLUB OF ST ANDREWS (golf)
SENAYAN MAIN STADIUM, JAKARTA (cricket)
SHANGHAI STADIUM (gymnastics)
SILVERSTONE (motor racing)
STAHOV STADIUM, PRAGUE (gymnastics)
TEXAS STADIUM (most sports)
TWICKENHAM (rugby union)
WEMBLEY CONFERENCE CENTRE (darts)
WEMBLEY STADIUM (football, rugby)
WHITE CITY (greyhound racing)
WIMBLEDON (tennis)
WINDSOR PARK, BELFAST (football)

TROPHIES, EVENTS, AND AWARDS

ADMIRAL'S CUP (sailing)
AFRICAN NATIONS CUP (football)
AIR CANADA SILVER BROOM (curling)
ALL-IRELAND CHAMPIONSHIP (Gaelic football)
ALL-IRELAND CHAMPIONSHIPS (hurling)
ALPINE CHAMPIONSHIPS (skiing)
AMERICA'S CUP (sailing)
ASHES (cricket)
BADMINTON THREE DAY EVENT (equestrian)
BBC SPORTS PERSONALITY OF THE YEAR (all-round)
BENSON HEDGES CUP (cricket)
BOAT RACE (rowing)
BRITISH OPEN CHAMPIONSHIP (golf)
BRONZE MEDAL (most sports)

CAMANACHD ASSOCIATION CHALLENGE CUP (shinty)
CHELTENHAM GOLD CUP (horse racing)
CLASSICS (horse racing)
COMMONWEALTH GAMES (athletics)
CORNHILL TEST (cricket)
DAVIS CUP (tennis)
DAYTONA 500 (motor racing)
DECATHLON (athletics)
DERBY (horse racing)
EMBASSY WORLD INDOOR BOWLS CROWN (bowls)
EMBASSY WORLD PROFESSIONAL SNOOKER CHAMPIONSHIP (snooker)
ENGLISH GREYHOUND DERBY (greyhound racing)

EUROPEAN CHAMPION CLUBS CUP
(football)
EUROPEAN CHAMPIONS CUP (basketball)
EUROPEAN CHAMPIONSHIPS (football)
EUROPEAN CUP WINNERS' CUP (football)
EUROPEAN FOOTBALLER OF THE YEAR
(football)
EUROPEAN SUPER CUP (football)
FEDERATION CUP (tennis)
FOOTBALL ASSOCIATION CHALLENGE CUP
(football)
FOOTBALL ASSOCIATION CHARITY SHIELD
(football)
FOOTBALL LEAGUE CHAMPIONSHIP
(football)
FOOTBALL LEAGUE CUP (football)
FULL CAP (football, rugby)
FWA FOOTBALLER OF THE YEAR (football)
GILLETTE CUP (cricket)
GOLDEN BOOT AWARD (football)
GOLD MEDAL (most sports)
GORDEN INTERNATIONAL MEDAL (curling)
GRAND NATIONAL (greyhound racing)
GRAND NATIONAL STEEPLECHASE (horse
racing)
GRAND PRIX (motor racing)
GUINNESS TROPHY (tiddlywinks)
HARMSWORTH TROPHY (power boat racing)
HENLEY REGATTA (rowing)
HENRI DELANEY TROPHY (football)
HIGHLAND GAMES
ICY SMITH CUP (ice hockey)
INDIANAPOLIS 500 (motor racing)
INTERNATIONAL CHAMPIONSHIP (bowls)
INTERNATIONAL CROSS-COUNTRY
CHAMPIONSHIP (athletics)
INTERNATIONAL INTER-CITY INDUSTRIAL
FAIRS CUP (football)
IROQUOIS CUP (lacrosse)
ISLE OF MAN TT (motorcycle racing)
JOHN PLAYER CUP (rugby league)
JOHN PLAYER LEAGUE (cricket)
JULES RIMET TROPHY (football)
KING GEORGE V GOLD CUP (equestrian)
KINNAIRD CUP (fives)
LE MANS 24 HOUR (motor racing)
LITTLEWOODS CHALLENGE CUP (football)
LOMBARD RALLY (motor racing)
LONSDALE BELT (boxing)
MACROBERTSON INTERNATIONAL SHIELD
(croquet)
MAN OF THE MATCH (football)
MARATHON (athletics)
MIDDLESEX SEVENS (rugby union)
MILK CUP (football)
MILK RACE (cycling)
MONTE CARLO RALLY (motor racing)
MOST VALUABLE PLAYER (American
football)

NATIONAL ANGLING CHAMPIONSHIP (horse
racing)
NATIONAL HUNT JOCKEY CHAMPIONSHIP
(horse racing)
NATIONAL WESTMINSTER BANK TROPHY
(cricket)
NORDIC CHAMPIONSHIPS (skiing)
OAKS (horse racing)
OLYMPIC GAMES (most sports)
ONE THOUSAND GUINEAS (horse racing)
OPEN CROQUET CHAMPIONSHIP (croquet)
OXFORD BLUE (most sports)
PALIO
PENTATHLON
PFA FOOTBALLER OF THE YEAR (football)
PRUDENTIAL WORLD CUP (cricket)
PYONGYANG
QUEEN ELIZABETH II CUP (equestrian)
RAC TOURIST TROPHY (motor racing)
ROSE BOWL (American football)
ROYAL HUNT CUP (horse racing)
RUGBY LEAGUE CHALLENGE CUP (rugby
league)
RUNNERS-UP MEDAL (most sports)
RYDER CUP (golf)
SCOTTISH FOOTBALL ASSOCIATION CUP
(football)
SILVER MEDAL (most sports)
SIMOD CUP (football)
SKOL CUP (football)
SOUTH AMERICAN CHAMPIONSHIP (football)
STANLEY CUP (ice hockey)
ST LEGER (horse racing)
STRATHCONA CUP (curling)
SUPER BOWL (American football)
SUPER CUP (handball)
SWAYTHLING CUP (table tennis)
THOMAS CUP (badminton)
TOUR DE FRANCE (cycling)
TRIPLE CROWN (rugby union)
TWO THOUSAND GUINEAS (horse racing)
UBER CUP (badminton)
U.E.F.A. CUP (Union of European Football
Associations) (football)
UNIROYAL WORLD JUNIOR
CHAMPIONSHIPS (curling)
WALKER CUP (golf)
WIGHTMAN CUP (sailing)
WIMBLEDON (tennis)
WINGFIELD SKULLS (rowing)
WINNERS MEDAL (most sports)
WOODEN SPOON! (most sports)
WORLD CLUB CHAMPIONSHIP (football)
WORLD MASTERS CHAMPIONSHIPS (darts)
WORLD SERIES (baseball)
YELLOW JERSEY (cycling)

FOOTBALL TEAMS

TEAM	GROUND	NICKNAME
ABERDEEN	PITTODRIE STADIUM	DONS
AIRDRIEONIANS	BROOMFIELD PARK	DIAMONDS; WAYSIDERS
ALBION ROVERS	CLIFTON HALL	WEE ROVERS
ALDERSHOT	RECREATION GROUND	SHOTS
ALLOA	RECREATION PARK	WASPS
ARBROATH	GAYFIELD PARK	RED LICHTIES
ARSENAL	HIGHBURY	GUNNERS
ASTON VILLA	VILLA PARK	VILLANS
AYR UNITED	SOMERSET PARK	HONEST MEN
BARNSLEY	OAKWELL GROUND	TYKES; REDS; COLLIERS
BERWICK RANGERS	SHIELFIELD PARK	BORDERERS
BIRMINGHAM CITY	ST ANDREWS	BLUES
BLACKBURN ROVERS	EWOOD PARK	BLUE WHITES; ROVERS
BLACKPOOL	BLOMMFIELD ROAD	SEASIDERS
BOLTON WANDERERS	BURNDEN PARK	TROTTERS
BOURNEMOUTH	DEAN COURT	CHERRIES
BRADFORD CITY	VALLEY PARADE	BANTAMS
BRECHIN CITY	GLEBE PARK	CITY
BRENTFORD	GRIFFIN PARK	BEES
BRIGHTON HOVE ALBION	GOLDSTONE GROUND	SEAGULLS
BRISTOL CITY	ASHTON GATE	ROBINS
BRISTOL ROVERS	TWERTON PARK	PIRATES
BURNLEY	TURF MOOR	CLARETS
BURY	GIGG LANE	SHAKERS
CAMBRIDGE UNITED	ABBEY STADIUM	UNITED
CARDIFF CITY	NINIAN PARK	BLUEBIRDS
CARLISLE UNITED	BRUNTON PARK	CUMBRIANS; BLUES
CELTIC	CELTIC PARK	BHOYS
CHARLTON ATHLETIC	SELHURST PARK	HADDICKS; ROBINS; VALIANTS
CHELSEA	STAMFORD BRIDGE	BLUES
CHESTER CITY	SEALAND ROAD	BLUES
CHESTERFIELD	RECREATION GROUND	BLUES; SPIREITES
CLYDEBANK	KILBOWIE PARK	BANKIES
CLYDE	FIRHILL PARK	BULLY WEE
COLCHESTER UNITED	LAYER ROAD	U'S
COVENTRY CITY	HIGHFIELD ROAD	SKY BLUES
COWDENBEATH	CENTRAL PARK	COWDEN
CREWE ALEXANDRA	GRESTY ROAD	RAILWAYMEN
CRYSTAL PALACE	SELHURST PARK	EAGLES
DARLINGTON	FEETHAMS GROUND	QUAKERS
DERBY COUNTY	BASEBALL GROUND	RAMS
DONCASTER ROVERS	BELLE VUE GROUND	ROVERS
DUMBARTON	BOGHEAD PARK	SONS
DUNDEE	DENS PARK	DARK BLUES; DEE
DUNDEE UNITED	TANNADICE PARK	TERRORS
DUNFERMLINE ATHLETIC	EAST END PARK	PARS
EAST FIFE	BAYVIEW PARK	FIFERS
EAST STIRLINGSHIRE	FIRS PARK	SHIRE
EVERTON	GOODISON PARK	TOFFEES
EXETER CITY	ST JAMES PARK	GRECIANS
FALKIRK	BROCKVILLE PARK	BAIRNS
FORFAR ATHELTIC	STATION PARK	SKY BLUES

FULHAM	CRAVEN COTTAGE	COTTAGERS
GILLINGHAM	PRIESTFIELD STADIUM	GILLS
GRIMSBY TOWN	BLUNDELL PARK	MARINERS
HALIFAX TOWN	SHAY GROUND	SHAYMEN
HAMILTON ACADEMICAL	DOUGLAS PARK	ACCES
HARTLEPOOL UNITED	VICTORIA GROUND	POOL
HEART OF MIDLOTHIAN	TYNECASTLE PARK	HEARTS
HEREFORD UNITED	EDGAR STREET	UNITED
HIBERNIAN	EASTER ROAD	HIBEES
HUDDERSFIELD TOWN	LEEDS ROAD	TERRIERS
HULL CITY	BOOTHFERRY PARK	TIGERS
IPSWICH TOWN	PORTMAN ROAD	BLUES; TOWN
KILMARNOCK	RUGBY PARK	KILLIE
LEEDS UNITED	ELLAND ROAD	UNITED
LEICESTER CITY	FILBERT STREET	FILBERTS; FOXES
LEYTON ORIENT	BRISBANE ROAD	O'S
LINCOLN CITY	SINCIL BANK	RED IMPS
LIVERPOOL	ANFIELD	REDS; POOL
LUTON TOWN	KENILWORTH ROAD	HATTERS
MANCHESTER CITY	MAINE ROAD	BLUES
MANCHESTER UNITED	OLD TRAFFORD	RED DEVILS
MANSFIELD TOWN	FIELD MILL GROUND	STAGS
MEADOWBANK THISTLE	MEADOWBANK STADIUM	THISTLE; WEE JAGS
MIDDLESBROUGH	AYRESOME PARK	BORO
MILLWALL	THE DEN	LIONS
MONTROSE	LINKS PARK	GABLE ENDERS
MORTON	CAPPIELOW PARK	TON
MOTHERWELL	FIR PARK	WELL
NEWCASTLE UNITED	ST JAMES PARK	MAGPIES
NORTHAMPTON TOWN	COUNTY GROUND	COBBLERS
NORWICH CITY	CARROW ROAD	CANARIES
NOTTINGHAM FOREST	CITY GROUND	REDS; FOREST
NOTTS COUNTY	MEADOW LANE	MAGPIES
OLDHAM ATHLETIC	BOUNDARY PARK	LATICS
OXFORD UNITED	MANOR GROUND	U'S
PARTICK THISTLE	FIRHILL PARK	JAGS
PETERBOROUGH UNITED	LONDON ROAD	POSH
PLYMOUTH ARGYLE	HOME PARK	PILGRIMS
PORTSMOUTH	FRATTON PARK	POMPEY
PORT VALE	VALE PARK	VALIANTS
PRESTON NORTH END	DEEPDALE	LILYWHITES; NORTH END
QUEEN OF THE SOUTH	PALMERSTON PARK	DOONHAMERS
QUEEN'S PARK	HAMPDEN PARK	SPIDERS
QUEEN'S PARK RANGERS	LOFTUS ROAD	RANGERS; R'S
RAITH ROVERS	STARK'S PARK	ROVERS
RANGERS	IBROX STADIUM	GERS
READING	ELM PARK	ROYALS
ROCHDALE	SPOTLAND	DALE
ROTHERHAM UNITED	MILLMOOR GROUND	MERRY MILLERS
SCARBOROUGH	SEAMER ROAD	BORO
SCUNTHORPE UNITED	GLANFORD PARK	IRON
SHEFFIELD UNITED	BRAMALL LANE	BLADES
SHEFFIELD WEDNESDAY	HILLSBOROUGH	OWLS
SHREWSBURY TOWN	GAY MEADOW	SHREWS; TOWN
SOUTHAMPTON	DELL	SAINTS
SOUTHEND UNITED	ROOTS HALL	SHRIMPERS
STENHOUSEMUIR	OCHILVIEW PARK	WARRIORS
STIRLING ALBION	ANNFIELD PARK	ALBION
ST JOHNSTONE	MUIRTON PARK	SAINTS
ST MIRREN	LOVE STREET	BUDDIES; PAISLEY SAINTS
STOCKPORT COUNTY	EDGELEY PARK	COUNTY; HATTERS

STOKE CITY	VICTORIA GROUND	POTTERS
STRANRAER	STAIR PARK	BLUES
SUNDERLAND	ROKER PARK	ROKERITES
SWANSEA CITY	VETCH FIELD	SWANS
SWINDON TOWN	COUNTY GROUND	ROBINS
TORQUAY UNITED	PLAINMOOR GROUND	GULLS
TOTTENHAM HOTSPUR	WHITE HART LANE	SPURS
TRANMERE ROVERS	PRENTON PARK	ROVERS
WALSALL	FELLOWS PARK	SADDLERS
WATFORD	VICARAGE ROAD	HORNETS
WEST BROMWICH ALBION	HAWTHORNS	THROSTLES; BAGGIES; ALBION
WEST HAM UNITED	UPTON PARK	HAMMERS
WIGAN ATHLETIC	SPRINGFIED PARK	LATICS
WIMBLEDON	PLOUGH LANE	DONS
WOLVERHAMPTON WANDERERS	MOLINEUX	WOLVES
WREXHAM	RACECOURSE GROUND	ROBINS
YORK CITY	BOOTHAM CRESCENT	MINSTERMEN

MISCELLANEOUS

COLOURS

3	5 —continued	6 —continued	7 —continued
AAL	GREEN	MADDER	OLD ROSE
ABA	GRÈGE	MAROON	PEARLED
DUN	HAZEL	MATARA	PLATINA
JET	HENNA	MOTLEY	SAFFRON
RED	IVORY	ORANGE	SCARLET
TAN	JASPÉ	ORCHID	SEA BLUE
4	JAUNE	OYSTER	SKY BLUE
BLEU	JEWEL	PASTEL	TEA ROSE
BLUE	KHAKI	PEARLY	THISTLE
BOIS	LODEN	PIRNED	TILE RED
BURE	MAIZE	PURPLE	TILLEUL
CUIR	MAUVE	RACHEL	TUSSORE
DRAB	OCHRE	RAISIN	VIOLINE
EBON	OLIVE	RESEDA	**8**
ÉCRU	OMBRÉ	RUSSET	ABSINTHE
GOLD	PEACH	SALMON	ALIZARIN
GREY	PEARL	SHRIMP	AMARANTH
GRIS	PÊCHE	SILVER	AURULENT
HOPI	PRUNE	TITIAN	BABY BLUE
IRIS	ROUGE	VIOLET	BABY PINK
JADE	SEPIA	YELLOW	BORDEAUX
LAKE	SHADE	ZIRCON	BURGUNDY
LARK	TAUPE	**7**	CAPUCINE
NAVY	TOPAZ	ANAMITE	CHALDERA
NOIR	UMBER	APRICOT	CHÂTAINE
ONYX	WHITE	ARDOISE	CHESTNUT
OPAL	**6**	AUREATE	CIEL BLUE
PIED	ACAJOU	BISCUIT	CINNAMON
PINK	ALESAN	CALDRON	CREVETTE
PLUM	ARGENT	CARAMEL	CYCLAMEN
PUCE	AUBURN	CARMINE	EAU DE NIL
ROSE	BASANÉ	CHAMOIS	ÉCARLATE
RUBY	BISTRE	CORBEAU	EGGPLANT
SAND	BLONDE	CRIMSON	EGGSHELL
SHOT	BRONZE	EMERALD	GRIZZLED
VERT	BURNET	FILBERT	GUN METAL
5	CASTOR	FUCHSIA	HAZEL NUT
AMBER	CENDRÉ	GRIZZLE	HYACINTH
BEIGE	CERISE	HEATHER	LARKSPUR
BLACK	CHERRY	INGÉNUE	LAVENDER
BROWN	CHROMA	JACINTH	MAHOGANY
CAMEL	CITRON	JONQUIL	MOLE GREY
CAPRI	CLARET	LACQUER	MULBERRY
CHAIR	COPPER	LAVANDE	NAVY BLUE
COCOA	DORADO	MAGENTA	PEA GREEN
CORAL	FLAXEN	MOTTLED	PISTACHE
CREAM	GARNET	MUSTARD	POPPY RED
CYMAR	GOLDEN	NACARAT	PRIMROSE
DELFT	INDIGO	NATURAL	SAPPHIRE
FLESH	JASPER	NEUTRAL	SEA GREEN

8 —continued
SHAGREEN
SPECTRUM
VIRIDIAN

9
ALICE BLUE
AUBERGINE
AZURE BLUE
BLUE-GREEN
CADET BLUE
CADET GREY
CARNATION
CARNELIAN
CHAMPAGNE
CHOCOLATE
COCHINEAL
DELPH BLUE
DUTCH BLUE
FLESH PINK
GREEN-BLUE
HARLEQUIN
LEAF GREEN
LIME GREEN
MOONSTONE
MOSS GREEN
NILE GREEN
OLIVE DRAB
PARCHMENT
PEARL GREY
RASPBERRY
ROYAL BLUE

9 —continued
TANGERINE
TOMATO RED
TURKEY RED
VERDIGRIS
VERMILION
WALLY BLUE

10
AQUAMARINE
AURICOMOUS
BOIS DE ROSE
CAFÉ AU LAIT
CASTOR GREY
COBALT BLUE
CONGO BROWN
ENSIGN BLUE
LIVER BROWN
MARINA BLUE
MARINE BLUE
OXFORD BLUE
PETROL BLUE
POLYCHROME
POWDER BLUE
TERRACOTTA
ZENITH BLUE

11
BOTTLE GREEN
BURNT ALMOND
CARDINAL RED
CLAIR DE LUNE

11 —continued
FOREST GREEN
GOBELIN BLUE
HORIZON BLUE
HUNTER'S PINK
LAPIS LAZULI
LEMON YELLOW
LIPSTICK RED
PARROT GREEN
PEACOCK BLUE
POMEGRANATE
SMOKED PEARL
SOLID COLOUR
ULTRAMARINE
VERSICOLOUR
WALNUT BROWN
YELLOW OCHRE

12
BALL PARK BLUE
CANARY YELLOW
CARROT COLOUR
CASTILIAN RED
CELADON GREEN
HUNTER'S GREEN
HYACINTH BLUE
LOGWOOD BROWN
MIDNIGHT BLUE
OVERSEAS BLUE
SAPPHIRE BLUE
SOLFERINO RED

12 —continued
TYRIAN PURPLE
VERDANT GREEN

13
BISHOP'S PURPLE
BISHOP'S VIOLET
CAMBRIDGE BLUE
MOTHER-OF-PEARL
MULTICOLOURED
PARTI-COLOURED
PEPPER-AND-SALT
PRIMARY COLOUR
TORTOISE SHELL
TURQUOISE BLUE

14
HEATHER MIXTURE
PERIWINKLE BLUE
PISTACHIO GREEN
TURQUOISE GREEN

15
CALEDONIAN
  BROWN
CHARTREUSE
  GREEN
SECONDARY
  COLOUR

16
CHARTREUSE
  YELLOW

CALENDARS

GREGORIAN
JANUARY
FEBRUARY
MARCH
APRIL
MAY
JUNE
JULY
AUGUST
SEPTEMBER
OCTOBER
NOVEMBER
DECEMBER

HEBREW
SHEVAT (Jan/Feb)
ADAR (Feb/Mar)
NISAN (Mar/Apr)
IYAR (Apr/May)
SIVAN (May/June)
TAMMUZ (June/July)
AV (July/Aug)
ELUL (Aug/Sept)
TISHRI (Sept/Oct)
HESHVAN (Oct/Nov)
KISLEV (Nov/Dec)
TEVET (Dec/Jan)

ISLAMIC
MUHARRAN (Jan)
SAFAR (Feb)
RAB I (Mar)
RAB II (Apr)
JUMĀDĀ I (May)
JUMĀDĀ II (June)
RAJAB (July)
SHA'BAN (Aug)
RAMADĀN (Sept)
SHAWWĀL (Oct)
DHŪAL-QA'DAH (Nov)
DHŪAL-HIJJAH (Dec)

CHINESE
XIAO HAN (Jan)
DA HAN (Jan/Feb)
LI CHUN (Feb)
YU SHUI (Feb/Mar)
JING ZHE (Mar)
CHUN FEN (Mar/Apr)
QING MING (Apr)
GU YU (Apr/May)
LI XIA (May)
XIAO MAN (May/
  June)
MANG ZHONG (June)
XIA ZHI (June/July)
XIAO SHU (July)
DA SHU (July/Aug)
LI QUI (Aug)
CHU SHU (Aug/Sept)
BAI LU (Sept)
QUI FEN (Sept/Oct)
HAN LU (Oct)
SHUANG JIANG (Oct/
  Nov)
LI DONG (Nov)
XIAO XUE (Nov/Dec)
DA XUE (Dec)
DONG ZHI (Dec/Jan)

FRENCH REVOLUTIONARY
VENDÉMIAIRE –
  Vintage (Sept)
BRUMAIRE – Fog
  (Oct)
FRIMAIRE – Sleet
  (Nov)
NIVÔSE – Snow
  (Dec)
PLUVIÔSE – Rain
  (Jan)
VENTÔSE – Wind
  (Feb)
GERMINAL – Seed
  (Mar)
FLOREAL – Blossom
  (Apr)
PRAIRIAL – Pasture
  (May)
MESSIDOR – Harvest
  (June)
THERMIDOR – Heat
  (July)
FRUCTIDOR – Fruit
  (Aug)

THE SIGNS OF THE ZODIAC

SIGN (Symbol; Dates)

ARIES (Ram; 21 Mar–19 Apr)
TAURUS (Bull; 20 Apr–20 May)
GEMINI (Twins; 21 May–21 June)
CANCER (Crab; 22 June–22 July)
LEO (Lion; 23 July–22 Aug)
VIRGO (Virgin; 23 Aug–22 Sept)

LIBRA (Scales; 23 Sept–23 Oct)
SCORPIO (Scorpion; 24 Oct–21 Nov)
SAGITTARIUS (Archer; 22 Nov–21 Dec)
CAPRICORN (Goat; 22 Dec–19 Jan)
AQUARIUS (Water-carrier; 20 Jan–18 Feb)
PISCES (Fish; 19 Feb–20 Mar)

THE TWELVE SIGNS OF THE CHINESE ZODIAC

RAT	RABBIT	HORSE	ROOSTER
OX	DRAGON	SHEEP	DOG
TIGER	SNAKE	MONKEY	BOAR

BIRTHSTONES

Month – STONE

January – GARNET
February – AMETHYST
March – BLOODSTONE/AQUAMARINE
April – DIAMOND
May – EMERALD
June – PEARL

July – RUBY
August – SARDONYX/PERIDOT
September – SAPPHIRE
October – OPAL
November – TOPAZ
December – TURQUOISE

WEDDING ANNIVERSARIES

1st – PAPER
2nd – COTTON
3rd – LEATHER
4th – FRUIT/FLOWERS
5th – WOOD
6th – IRON
7th – WOOL/COPPER
8th – BRONZE/POTTERY
9th – POTTERY/WILLOW
10th – TIN/ALUMINIUM
11th – STEEL
12th – SILK/LINEN

13th – LACE
14th – IVORY
15th – CRYSTAL
20th – CHINA
25th – SILVER
30th – PEARL
35th – CORAL
40th – RUBY
45th – SAPPHIRE
50th – GOLD
55th – EMERALD
60th – DIAMOND

PEERAGE

DUKE	DUCHESS	MARQUIS	MARCHIONESS
EARL	BARONESS	MARQUESS	VISCOUNTESS
BARON	COUNTESS	VISCOUNT	

HERALDIC TERMS

TINCTURES
OR (gold)
ARGENT (silver)
ERMINE
VAIR
POTENT
AZURE (blue)
GULES (red)
SABLE (black)
VERT (green)
PURPURE (purple)

DIVISIONS OF FIELDS
PER PALE
PER FESS
PER CROSS
PER BEND
PER SALTIRE
PER CHEVRON

DESCRIPTIONS OF FIELDS

PARTY
BARRY
BURELY
BENDY
QUARTERLY
ENTY
FRETTY
GIRONNY
BEZANTY

PARTS OF THE ESCUTCHEON
DEXTER (right)
SINISTER (left)
MIDDLE
CHIEF (top)
FLANK (side)
BASE
NOMBRIL
FESS POINT
HONOUR POINT

TRESSURE (border)

LINES
ENGRAILED
EMBATTLED
INDENTED
INVECTED
WAVY, UNDY
NEBULY
DANCETTY
RAGULY
POTENTÉ
DOVETAILED
URDY

CROSSES
FORMY
PATY
FLORY
MOLINE
BOTONNY

CROSLETTED
FITCHY
SALTIRE

OTHER OBJECTS AND DECORATIONS

LOZENGES
ROUNDELS (circles)
ANNELETS (rings)
FOUNTAINS (wavey lines on a circle)
BILLETS (upright objects)
MOLET (star)
RAMPANT (rearing up)
COUCHANT (sleeping or sitting)
PASSANT (standing)
BAR

SEVEN DEADLY SINS

PRIDE	LUST	GLUTTONY	SLOTH
COVETOUSNESS	ENVY	ANGER	

SEVEN WONDERS OF THE WORLD

THE PYRAMIDS OF EGYPT
THE COLOSSUS OF RHODES
THE HANGING GARDENS OF BABYLON
THE MAUSOLEUM OF HALICARNASSUS

THE STATUE OF ZEUS AT OLYMPIA
THE TEMPLE OF ARTEMIS AT EPHESUS
THE PHAROS OF ALEXANDRIA

SEVEN VIRTUES

FAITH	HOPE	LOVE (CHARITY)	TEMPERANCE
FORTITUDE	JUSTICE	PRUDENCE	

MONEY

1 & 2	4 —continued	6	7 —continued
AS	UNIK	AMANIA	UNICORN
D	**5**	AUREUS	**8**
L	ANGEL	BAUBEE	AMBROSIN
P	ASPER	BAWBEE	DENARIUS
S	BELGA	BEZART	DIDRACHM
3	BETSO	CONDOR	DOUBLOON
BIT	BROAD	COPANG	DUCATOON
BOB	CONTO	COPPER	FARTHING
COB	COPEC	DÉCIME	FLORENCE
DAM	CROWN	DOBLON	JOHANNES
ECU	DARIC	FLORIN	KREUTZER
FAR	DUCAT	FUORTE	LOUIS D'OR
KIP	EAGLE	GUINEA	MARAVEDI
LAT	GROAT	GULDEN	NAPOLEON
MIL	LIARD	KOPECK	PICAYUNE
MNA	LIBRA	MONKEY	QUETZALE
PIE	LITAS	NICKEL	SESTERCE
REE	LIVRE	PAGODE	SHILLING
REI	LOCHO	SCEATT	SIXPENCE
SHO	LOUIS	SEQUIN	**9**
SOL	MEDIO	STATER	BOLIVIANO
SOU	MOHAR	STIVER	CUARTILLO
4	MOHUR	TALARI	DIDRACHMA
ANNA	NOBLE	TALENT	DUPONDIUS
BEKA	OBANG	TANNER	GOLD BROAD
BIGA	PAOLO	TESTER	GOLD NOBLE
BUCK	PENCE	TESTON	GOLD PENNY
CASH	PENGO	THALER	HALFPENNY
DAUM	PENNY	TOMAUN	PISTAREEN
DIME	PLACK	ZECHIN	RIXDOLLAR
DOIT	QURSH	**7**	ROSE-NOBLE
JOEY	SCEAT	ANGELOT	SESTERTII
KRAN	SCUDI	CAROLUS	SOVEREIGN
MAIL	SCUDO	CENTAVA	SPUR ROYAL
MERK	SEMIS	DENARII	YELLOW BOY
MITE	SOLDO	GUILDER	**10**
OBOL	STICA	JACOBUS	EASTERLING
PEAG	STYCA	MILREIS	FIRST BRASS
PICE	SYCEE	MOIDORE	GOLD STATER
PONY	TICAL	NGUSANG	QUADRUSSIS
QUID	TICCY	PISTOLE	SESTERTIUM
REAL	TOMAN	QUARTER	SILVERLING
RYAL	UNCIA	SEXTANS	STOUR-ROYAL
TAEL	UNITE	STOOTER	THREEPENCE
		TESTOON	

COLLECTIVE NAMES

ACROBATS – troupe
APES – shrewdness
ASSES – pace
BABOONS – troop
BAKERS – tabernacle
BARBERS – babble
BARMEN – promise
BAYONETS – grove
BEES – erst, swarm
BELLS – change
BISHOPS – bench, psalter
BISON – herd
BREWERS – feast
BUFFALOES – obstinacy
BULLFINCHES – bellowing
BULLOCKS – drove
BUTCHERS – goring
BUTLERS – sneer
CANONS – chapter, dignity
CATERPILLARS – army
CATTLE – herd
CHOUGHS – chattering
COBBLERS – cutting
CROCODILES – bask
CROWS – murder
DEANS – decanter, decorum
DONS – obscuration
DUCKS – paddling, safe
ELEPHANTS – herd, parade
FERRETS – busyness
FLIES – swarm
GAMBLERS – talent
GEESE – gaggle
GOLDFINCHES – charm
GOVERNESSES – galaxy
GRAMMARIANS – conjunction
HARES – down
HARPISTS – melody
HERONS – serge
HIPPOPOTOMI – bloat
HUNTERS – blast
JELLYFISH – fluther, smack
JUGGLERS – neverthriving

KITTENS – litter
LAPWING – desert
LARKS – exaltation
LEOPARDS – leap, lepe
LIONS – pride, sawt, sowse
LOCUSTS – swarm
MAGPIES – tittering
MERCHANTS – faith
MESSENGERS – diligence
MOLES – labour
MULES – span
NIGHTINGALES – watch
ORCHIDS – coterie
OWLS – parliament, stare
PAINTERS – curse, illusion
PARROTS – pandemonium
PEKINGESE – pomp
PENGUINS – parcel
PIGS – litter
PIPERS – skirl
PORPOISES – turmoil
PREACHERS – converting
RABBITS – bury
RHINOCEROS – crash
ROBBERS – band
SHEEP – flock
SHERIFFS – posse
SHIPS – fleet, armada
SHOEMAKERS – blackening
STARLINGS – murmuration
SWALLOWS – gulp
SWINE – doylt
TAILORS – disguising
TAVERNERS – closing
TROUT – hover
TURKEY – rafter
TURTLES – turn
UNDERTAKERS – unction
WIDOWS – ambush
WILDCATS – destruction, dout
WOODPECKERS – descent
WRITERS – worship
ZEBRAS – zeal

TYPEFACES

3	6—continued	7—continued	8—continued
DOW	FUTURA	MADISON	SOUVENIR
4	GLYPHA	MEMPHIS	**9**
BELL	GOTHIC	NEUZEIT	AMERICANA
GILL	HORLEY	PLANTIN	ATHENAEUM
ZAPF	ITALIA	RALEIGH	BARCELONA
5	JANSON	SPARTAN	BRITANNIC
ASTER	LUCIAN	STEMPEL	CALEDONIA
BEMBO	MELIOR	TIFFANY	CLARENDON
BLOCK	MODERN	UNIVERS	CLEARFACE
DORIC	OLIVER	WEXFORD	CRITERION
ERBAR	ONDINE	WINDSOR	DOMINANTE
FOLIO	OPTIMA	**8**	EUROSTILE
GOUDY	ROMANA	BENGUIAT	EXCELSIOR
IONIC	**7**	BERKELEY	FAIRFIELD
KABEL	ANTIQUE	BREUGHEL	GROTESQUE
LOTUS	BASILIA	CLOISTER	HELVETICA
MITRA	BAUHAUS	CONCORDE	WORCESTER
SABON	BERNARD	EGYPTIAN	**10**
TIMES	BOOKMAN	EHRHARDT	AVANT GARDE
6	BRAMLEY	FOURNIER	CHELTENHAM
AACHEN	CANDIDA	FRANKLIN	CHURCHWARD
ADROIT	CENTURY	FRUTIGER	DEVANAGARI
AURIGA	CORONET	GALLIARD	EGYPTIENNE
BECKET	CUSHING	GARAMOND	LEAMINGTON
BODONI	ELECTRA	KENNERLY	**11**
BULMER	FLOREAL	NOVARESE	BASKERVILLE
CASLON	IMPRINT	OLYMPIAN	COPPERPLATE
COCHIN	IRIDIUM	PALATINO	**14**
COOPER	KORINNA	PERPETUA	TRUMP MEDIAEVAL
CORONA	LUBALIN	ROCKWELL	
FENICE			

AMERICAN INDIANS

3	5—continued	6—continued	6—continued
FOX	CREEK	APACHE	PAIUTE
OTO	HAIDA	ATSINA	PAWNEE
UTE	HURON	CAYUGA	QUAPAW
4	KASKA	DAKOTA	SALISH
CREE	KIOWA	DOGRIB	SANTEE
CROW	OMAHA	MANDAN	SENECA
HOPI	OSAGE	MICMAC	TANANA
HUPA	SIOUX	MIXTEC	TOLTEC
IOWA	SLAVE	MOHAWK	YAKIMA
SAUK	TETON	NAVAJO	**7**
TUPI	WAPPO	NOOTKA	ARIKARA
5	YUROK	OJIBWA	BEOTHUK
AZTEC	**6**	ONEIDA	CATAWBA
CADDO	ABNAKI	OTTAWA	CHINOOK

7 —continued
CHOKTAW
HIDATSA
INGALIK
KUTCHIN
NATCHEZ
SHAWNEE
SHUSWAP
TLINGIT
WICHITA
WYANDOT

8
CHEROKEE
CHEYENNE
COMANCHE
DELAWARE
ILLINOIS
IROQUOIS
KICKAPOO
NEZ PERCÉ
OKANOGAN
ONONDAGA
SHOSHONI

8 —continued
TUTCHONE

9
ALGONQUIN
BLACKFOOT
CHICKASAW
CHIPEWYAN
CHIPPEWAY
MENOMINEE
PENOBSCOT
TAHAGMIUT
TILLAMOOK

9 —continued
TSIMSHIAN
TUSCARORA
WINNEBAGO

10+
KAVIAGMIUT
PASAMAQUODDY
POTAWATOMI

LANGUAGE

LANGUAGES OF THE WORLD

2
WU
3
MIN
4
URDU
5
DUTCH
GREEK
HINDI
IRISH
MALAY
ORIYA
TAMIL
WELSH
6
ARABIC
BIHARI

6 —continued
BRETON
DANISH
FRENCH
GAELIC
GERMAN
KOREAN
PAHARI
POLISH
ROMANY
SINDHI
SLOVAK
TELUGU
7
BENGALI
CATALAN
ENGLISH
FRISIAN

7 —continued
ITALIAN
LATVIAN
MARATHI
PUNJABI
RUSSIAN
SLOVENE
SORBIAN
SPANISH
SWEDISH
TURKISH
8
ASSAMESE
GUJARATI
JAPANESE
JAVANESE
KASHMIRI
MANDARIN

8 —continued
ROMANSCH
RUMANIAN
UKRANIAN
9
AFRIKAANS
BULGARIAN
CANTONESE
ICELANDIC
NORWEGIAN
SINHALESE
10
LITHUANIAN
PORTUGUESE
RAJASTHANI
SERBO-CROAT

THE GREEK ALPHABET

ALPHA
BETA
GAMMA
DELTA
EPSILON
ZETA
ETA
THETA
IOTA
KAPPA
LAMBDA
MU

NU
XI
OMICRON
PI
RHO
SIGMA
TAU
UPSILON
PHI
CHI
PSI
OMEGA

THE HEBREW ALPHABET

ALEPH
BETH
GIMEL
DALETH
HE
VAV
ZAYIN

CHETH
TETH
YOD
KAPH
LAMED
MEM
NUN

SAMEKH		RESH
AYIN		SHIN
PE		SIN
SADI		TAV
KOPH		

FOREIGN WORDS

ENGLISH	FRENCH	GERMAN	ITALIAN	SPANISH	LATIN
AND	ET	UND	E, ED	E	ET
BUT	MAIS	ABER	MA	PERO	SED
FOR	POUR	FÜR	PER	PARA, POR	PER
TO	À	AUF, NACH	A	A	AD
WITH	AVEC	MIT	CON	CON	CUM
MISTER, MR.	MONSIEUR, M.	HERR, HR., HRN.	SIGNOR, SIG.	SEÑOR, SR.	DOMINUS
MADAME, MRS.	MADAME, MME.	FRAU, FR.	SIGNORA, SIG.A., SIG.RA.	SEÑORA, SRA.	DOMINA
MISS, MS.	MADEMOI-SELLE, MLLE.	FRÄULEIN, FRL.	SIGNORINA, SIG.NA.	SEÑORITA, SRTA.	
FROM	DE	AUS, VON	DA	DE	AB
OF	DE	VON	DI	DE	DE
GIRL	FILLE	MÄDCHEN	RAGAZZA	CHICA, NIÑA	PUELLA
BOY	GARÇON	JUNGE	RAGAZZO	CHICO, NIÑO	PUER
BIG	GRAND	GROSS	GRANDE	GRANDE	MAGNUS
LITTLE	PETIT	KLEIN	PICCOLO	PEQUENO, CHICO, POCO	PAUCUS
VERY	TRÈS	SEHR	MOLTO	MUCHO	
FASHIONABLE	À LA MODE	MODISCH	DI MODA	DE MODA	
GENTLEMAN	MONSIEUR	HERR	SIGNORE	CABALLERO	DOMINUS
LADY	DAME	DAME	SIGNORA	SEÑORA	DOMINA
MAN	HOMME	MANN	UOMO	HOMBRE	HOMO
WOMAN	FEMME	FRAU	DONNA	DOÑA	MULIER
WHO	QUI	WER	CHI	QUIÉN, QUE	QUIS
I	JE	ICH	IO	YO	EGO
YOU	TU, VOUS	DU, SIE, IHR	TU, VOI, LEI	TU, VOSOTROS/AS	TU, VOS
WHAT	QUOI, QUEL	WAS	CHE COSA	QUE	QUOD
HE	IL	ER	EGLI	EL	IS
SHE	ELLE	SIE	ELLA	ELLA	EA
WE	NOUS	WIR	NOI	NOSOTROS/AS	NOS
THEY	ILS, ELLES	SIE	ESSI/E, LORO	ELLOS, ELLAS	EI, EAE
AT HOME	CHEZ MOI/NOUS *OR* À LA MAISON	ZU HAUSE	A CASA	EN CASA	DOMO
HOUSE	MAISON	HAUS	CASA	CASA	VILLA, DOMUS
STREET	RUE	STRASSE	STRADA	CALLE	VIA
ROAD	ROUTE	WEG	VIA	CAMINO	VIA
BY	PAR	BEI	PER	POR	PER
BEFORE	AVANT	VOR	PRIMA	(DEL) ANTE	ANTE
AFTER	APRÈS	NACH	DOPO	DESPUES	POST

ENGLISH	FRENCH	GERMAN	ITALIAN	SPANISH	LATIN
UNDER	SOUS	UNTER	SOTTO	(DE)BAJO	SUB
OVER	SUR	OBER	SOPRA, SU	SOBRE	SUPER
NEAR	PRÈS DE	NAHE, BEI	VICINO	CERCA	PROPE
OUT	DEHORS	AUS	VIA, FUORI	FUERA	EX
IN	DANS	IN	IN	EN	IN
HOW	COMMENT	WIE	COME	COMO	QUO MODO
WHY	POURQUOI	WARUM	PERCHE	POR QUÉ	CUR
THE	LE, LA, LES	DER, DIE, DAS	IL, LO, LA, I, GLI, LE	EL, LA, LO, LOS, LAS	
A	UN, UNE	EIN, EINE	UN, UNO, UNA	UN, UNA	
RED	ROUGE	ROT	ROSSO	ROJO	RUBER
BLUE	BLEU	BLAU	AZZURRO	AZUL	CAERULEUS
YELLOW	JAUNE	GELB	GIALLO	AMARILLO	FULVUS
GREEN	VERT	GRÜN	VERDE	VERDE	VIRIDIS
BLACK	NOIR	SCHWARZ	NERO	NEGRO	NIGER
WHITE	BLANC *OR* BLANCHE	WEISS	BIANCO	BLANCO	ALBUS
SHORT	COURT	KURZ	CORTO, BREVE	CORTO	BREVIS
LONG	LONG	LANG	LUNGO	LARGO	LONGUS

NUMBERS

ENGLISH	ROMAN NUMERALS	FRENCH	GERMAN	ITALIAN	SPANISH
ONE	I	UN	EIN	UNO	UNO
TWO	II	DEUX	ZWEI	DUE	DOS
THREE	III	TROIS	DREI	TRE	TRES
FOUR	IV	QUATRE	VIER	QUATTRO	CUATRO
FIVE	V	CINQ	FÜNF	CINQUE	CINCO
SIX	VI	SIX	SECHS	SEI	SEIS
SEVEN	VII	SEPT	SIEBEN	SETTE	SIETE
EIGHT	VIII	HUIT	ACHT	OTTO	OCHO
NINE	IX	NEUF	NEUN	NOVE	NUEVE
TEN	X	DIX	ZEHN	DIECI	DIEZ
TWENTY	XX	VINGT	ZWANZIG	VENTI	VEINTE
TWENTY-FIVE	XV	VINGT-CINQ	FÜNF UND ZWANZIG	VENTICINQUE	VEINTICINCO
THIRTY	XXX	TRENTE	DREISSIG	TRENTA	TREINTA
FORTY	XL	QUARANTE	VIERZIG	QUARANTA	CUARENTA
FIFTY	L	CINQUANTE	FÜNFZIG	CINQUANTA	CINCUENTA
SIXTY	LX	SOIXANTE	SECHZIG	SESSANTA	SESENTA
SEVENTY	LXX	SOIXANTE-DIX	SIEBZIG	SETTANTA	SETENTA
EIGHTY	LXXX	QUATRE-VINGT	ACHTZIG	OTTANTA	OCHENTA
NINETY	XC	QUANTRE-VINGT-DIX	NEUNZIG	NOVANTA	NOVENTA
ONE HUNDRED	C	CENT	HUNDERT	CENTO	CIEN (CIENTO)
FIVE HUNDRED	D	CINQ CENTS	FÜNFHUNDERT	CINQUECENTO	QUINIENTOS
ONE THOUSAND	M	MILLE	TAUSEND	MILLE	MIL

FRENCH PHRASES

5
MÊLÉE – brawl
ON DIT – piece of gossip, rumour
6
DE TROP – unwelcome
7
À LA MODE – fashionable
À PROPOS – to the point
CAP-À-PIE – from head to foot
DE RÈGLE – customary
EN MASSE – all together
EN ROUTE – on the way
8
BÊTE NOIR – person or thing particularly
 disliked
IDÉE FIXE – obsession
MAL DE MER – seasickness
MOT JUSTE – the appropriate word
9
DE RIGUEUR – required by custom
EN PASSANT – by the way
EN RAPPORT – in harmony
ENTRE NOUS – between you and me
10
À BON MARCHÉ – cheap
BILLET DOUX – love letter
DERNIER CRI – latest fashion, the last word
NOM DE PLUME – writer's assumed name
PENSE À BIEN – think for the best
11
AMOUR PROPRE – self-esteem
GARDEZ LA FOI – keep the faith

11 —continued
LÈSE MAJESTÉ – treason
NOM DE GUERRE – assumed name
RAISON D'ÊTRE – justification for existence
SAVOIR FAIRE – address, tact
TOUR DE FORCE – feat or accomplishment
 of great strength
12
FORCE MAJEURE – irresistible force or
 compulsion
HORS DE COMBAT – out of the fight,
 disabled
SANS DIEU RIEN – nothing without God
VENTRE À TERRE – at great speed
14
DOUBLE ENTENDRE – double meaning
ENFANT TERRIBLE – child who causes
 embarrassment
NOBLESSE OBLIGE – privilege entails
 responsibility
PREUX CHEVALIER – gallant knight
VÉRITÉ SANS PEUR – truth without fear
15
AMENDE HONORABLE – reparation
CHERCHEZ LA FEMME – look for the woman
17
PIÈCE DE RÉSISTANCE – most outstanding
 item; main dish at a meal
20+
AUTRE TEMPS, AUTRES MOEURS – other
 times, other manners

LATIN PHRASES

4
FIAT – let it be done or made
IN RE – concerning
STET – let it stand
5
AD HOC – for this special purpose
AD LIB – to speak off the cuff, without notes
AD REM – to the point
CIRCA – about
FECIT – he did it
6
AD USUM – as customary
IN SITU – in its original situation
IN TOTO – entirely

6 —continued
IN VIVO – in life, describing biological
 occurrences within living bodies
PRO TEM – temporary, for the time being
7
AD FINEM – to the end
A PRIORI – by deduction
CUI BONO? – whom does it benefit?
DE FACTO – in fact
FIAT LUX – let there be light
IN VITRO – in glass, describing biological
 experiments outside a body
PECCAVI – a confession of guilt (I have
 sinned)

7 —continued
PER DIEM – by the day
SINE DIE – without a day being appointed
SUB ROSA – confidential
UNA VOCE – with one voice, unanimously

8
ALTER EGO – another self
BONA FIDE – in good faith
EMERITUS – one retired from active official duties
MEA CULPA – an acknowledgement of guilt (I am to blame)
NOTA BENE – observe or note well
PRO FORMA – for the sake of form
UT PROSIM – that I may be of use

9
AD INTERIM – meanwhile
AD LITERAM – to the letter
AD NAUSEAM – to a disgusting, sickening degree
DEI GRATIA – by the grace of God
ET TU, BRUTE – and you, Brutus
EXCELSIOR – still higher
EX OFFICIO – by right of position or office
HIC ET NUNC – here and now
INTER ALIA – among other things
PRO PATRIA – for our country
STATUS QUO – the existing situation or state of affairs
SUB JUDICE – under consideration
VICE VERSA – the terms being exchanged, the other way round
VOX POPULI – popular opinion

10
ANNO DOMINI – in the year of our Lord
DEO GRATIAS – thanks be to God
EX CATHEDRA – with authority
IN EXTREMIS – in dire straits, at the the point of death
IN MEMORIAM – to the memory of
LOCO CITATO – in the place quoted
POST MORTEM – after death
PRIMA FACIE – at first sight
SINE QUA NON – something indispensable
TERRA FIRMA – solid ground

11
AD INFINITUM – endlessly, to infinity
ANIMO ET FIDE – by courage and faith
DE DIE IN DIEM – from day to day
DE PROFUNDIS – from the depths of misery
EX POST FACTO – after the event
GLORIA PATRI – glory to the Father
LOCUS STANDI – the right to be heard (in a law case)
NON SEQUITUR – an unwarranted conclusion
PAX VOBISCUM – peace be with you
TEMPUS FUGIT – time flies

12
ANTE MERIDIEM – before noon

12 —continued
CAVEAT EMPTOR – let the buyer beware
COMPOS MENTIS – of sane mind
FESTINA LENTE – hasten slowly, be quick without impetuosity
JACTA EST ALEA – the die is cast
PERSEVERANDO – by perseverance
POST MERIDIEM – after noon
SERVABO FIDEM – I will keep faith
VENI, VIDI, VICI – I came, I saw, I conquered
VOLO NON VALEO – I am willing but unable

13
CORPUS DELICTI – body of facts that constitute an offence
DUM SPIRO, SPERO – while I breathe, I hope
IN VINO VERITAS – there is truth in wine, that is, the truth comes out
MODUS OPERANDI – a method of operating
NE FRONTI CREDE – trust not to appearances
VINCIT VERITAS – truth conquers
VIRTUTIS AMORE – By love of virtue

14
CETERIS PARIBUS – other things being equal
EDITIO PRINCEPS – the original edition
IN LOCO PARENTIS – in place of a parent
NIL DESPERANDUM – never despair
PRO BONO PUBLICO – for the public good

15
ANIMO NON ASTUTIA – by courage not by craft
FORTITER ET RECTE – courageously and honourably
FORTUNA SEQUATUR – let fortune follow
INFRA DIGNITATEM – beneath one's dignity
NON COMPOS MENTIS – mentally unsound
OMNIA VINCIT AMOR – love conquers all things
PERSONA NON GRATA – an unacceptable person

16
GLORIA IN EXCELSIS – glory to God in the highest

17
LABOR IPSE VOLUPTAS – labour itself is pleasure
NUNQUAM NON PARATUS – always ready
PROBUM NON PAENITET – honesty repents not
VER NON SEMPER VIRET – Spring does not always flourish

18
NEC TEMERE NEC TIMIDE – neither rashly nor timidly
PRO REGE, LEGE, ET GREGE – for the king, the law, and the people
REDUCTIO AD ABSURDAM – reducing to absurdity

19

CANDIDE ET CONSTANTER – fairly and firmly

SOLA NOBILITAS VIRTUS – virtue alone is true nobility

VIRTUTI NON ARMIS FIDO – I trust to virtue and not to arms

20+

DE MORTUIS NIL NISI BONUM – speak only good of the dead

DULCE ET DECORUM EST PRO PATRIA MORI – it is sweet and seemly to die for one's country

20+ —continued

FORTUNA FAVET FORTIBUS – fortune favours the brave

PATRIA CARA CARIOR LIBERTAS – my country is dear, but liberty is dearer

QUOD ERAT DEMONSTRANDUM – which was to be demonstrated

SIC TRANSIT GLORIA MUNDI – thus passes the glory from the world

TIMEO DANAOS ET DONA FERENTES – I fear the Greeks, even when bearing gifts

VIVIT POST FUNERA VIRTUS – virtue survives the grave

AMERICANISMS

BRITISH	AMERICAN	BRITISH	AMERICAN
ACTION REPLAY	INSTANT REPLAY	DEMISEMIQUAVER	THIRTY-SECOND NOTE
ADRENALINE	EPINEPHRINE		
AERODROME	AIRDROME	DICKY	RUMBLE SEAT
AEROFOIL	AIRFOIL	DINNER JACKET	TUXEDO
AEROPLANE	AIRPLANE	DOSSHOUSE	FLOPHOUSE
ANAESTHETIST	ANESTHESIOLOGIST	DOWNPIPE	DOWNSPOUT
ANAESTHETICS	ANESTHESIOLOGY	DRAUGHTS	CHECKERS
ARMISTICE DAY	VETERANS DAY	DRAWING PIN	THUMBTACK
AUBERGINE	EGGPLANT	DUAL CARRIAGEWAY	DIVIDED HIGHWAY
AUTOCUE	TELEPROMPTER	DUMBWAITER	LAZY SUSAN
BACK BOILER	WATER BACK	DUSTBIN	GARBAGE CAN; TRASH CAN
BARYTES	BARITE		
BEETROOT	RED BEET	DUSTCART	GARBAGE TRUCK
BILL	CHECK	DUSTER	DUST CLOTH
BISCUIT	COOKIE	ÉTRIER	STIRRUP
BLACK PUDDING	BLOOD SAUSAGE	FANLIGHT	TRANSOM
BLOWLAMP	BLOWTORCH	FLAT	APARTMENT
BLUE-EYED BOY	FAIR-HAIRED BOY	FLEX	CORD
BONNET	HOOD	FLY-PAST	FLYOVER
BOOT	TRUNK	FOUR-STROKE	FOUR-CYCLE
BOWLER	DERBY	FRENCH WINDOWS	FRENCH DOORS
BRACES	SUSPENDER	FRIESIAN	HOLSTEIN
BREATHALYZER	DRUNKOMETER	FUNERAL PARLOUR	FUNERAL HOME
BREEZE BLOCK	CINDER BLOCK	FUNNY BONE	CRAZY BONE
CAMBERWELL BEAUTY	MOURNING CLOAK	GRAMOPHONE	PHONOGRAPH
		GREY MULLET	MULLET
CANDYFLOSS	COTTON CANDY	GUDGEON PIN	WRIST PIN
CARAVAN	TRAILER	HAIRSLIDE	BARRETTE
CATAPULT	SLINGSHOT	HEMIDEMISEMI-QUAVER	SIXTY-FOURTH NOTE
CATCH PIT	CATCH BASIN		
CENTRAL RESERVE	MEDIAN STRIP	HEMLOCK	POISON HEMLOCK
CORNFLOUR	CORNSTARCH	HEN HARRIER	MARSH HAWK; MARSH HARRIER
COS	ROMAINE		
COURGETTE	ZUCCHINI	HOLDALL	CARRYALL
CREEPING THISTLE	CANADA THISTLE	INSULATING TAPE	FRICTION TAPE
CROTCHET	QUARTER NOTE	JELLY	JELLO
CURRENT ACCOUNT	CHECKING ACCOUNT	JUMP LEADS	JUMPER CABLES
CUTTHROAT	STRAIGHT RAZOR	KENNEL	DOGHOUSE
DELIVERY VAN		LADYBIRD	
	PANEL TRUCK		LADYBUG

BRITISH	AMERICAN	BRITISH	AMERICAN
LEFT-LUGGAGE OFFICE	CHECKROOM	RING ROAD	BELTWAY
		ROOF RACK	CARRIER
LEVEL CROSSING	GRADE CROSSING	ROUNDABOUT	TRAFFIC CIRCLE
LIFT	ELEVATOR	RUBBER	ERASER
LIGNOCAINE	LIDOCAINE	RUCKSACK	BACKPACK
LOOSE COVER	SLIPCOVER	SEASON TICKET	COMMUTATION TICKET
LORRY	TRUCK		
LOUD-HAILER	BULLHORN	SEMIBREVE	WHOLE NOTE
LOUDSPEAKER VAN	SOUND TRUCK	SEMIQUAVER	SIXTEENTH NOTE
LUGGAGE VAN	BAGGAGE CAR	SHOPWALKER	FLOORWALKER
MAIZE	CORN	SHORTHAND TYPIST	STENOGRAPHER
MERRY-GO-ROUND	CAROUSEL	SILENCER	MUFFLER
MILEOMETER	ODOMETER	SKIRTING BOARD	BASEBOARD; MOPBOARD
MILLEFEUILLE	NAPOLEON		
MINIM	HALF-NOTE	SLEEVE	JACKET
MUDGUARD	FENDER	SOCKET	OUTLET
MUSIC HALL	VAUDEVILLE	STEAM ORGAN	CALLIOPE
NAPPY	DIAPER	STOCKBROKER BELT	EXURBIA
NORADRENALINE	NOREPINEPHRINE	SUSPENDER BELT	GARTER BELT
NOSEBAG	FEEDBAG	SWALLOW DIVE	SWAN DIVE
NOTICE BOARD	BULLETIN BOARD	SWEDE	RUTABAGA
OPEN DAY	OPEN HOUSE	TAP	FAUCET
ORDINARY SHARES	COMMON STOCK	TEA TOWEL	DISHTOWEL
OVERHEAD-VALVE ENGINE	VALVE-IN-HEAD ENGINE	TERYLENE	DACRON
		THORN APPLE	JIMSON WEED
PATIENCE	SOLITAIRE	TIE	NECKTIE
PAVEMENT	SIDEWALK	TIEPIN	STICK PIN
PEDESTRIAN CROSSING	CROSSWALK	TORSK	CUSK
		TRAM	STREETCAR; TROLLEY CAR
PENNY-FARTHING	ORDINARY		
PEPPERWORT	PEPPERGRASS	TRAPEZIUM	TRAPEZOID
PETROL	GASOLINE	TREACLE	MOLASSES
PLOUGH	BIG DIPPER	TRUNCHEON	NIGHT STICK
PRAM	BABY CARRIAGE	TURN UP	CUFF
PREFERENCE SHARES	PREFERRED STOCK	UNDERGROUND	SUBWAY
		UNDERSEAL	UNDERCOAT
PROTEOSE	ALBUMOSE	URSA MINOR	LITTLE DIPPER
QUAVER	EIGHTH NOTE	VALVE	VACUUM TUBE
RAGWORM	CLAMWORM	VIRGINIA CREEPER	BOSTON IVY
REAR LIGHT	TAILLIGHT; TAIL LAMP	WAISTCOAT	VEST
		WINDMILL	PINWHEEL
RED MULLET	GOATFISH	WINDSCREEN	WINDSHIELD
REPERTORY COMPANY	STOCK COMPANY	WINDSCREEN WIPER	WINDSHIELD WIPER
		WING	FENDER
REVERSING LIGHT	BACK-UP LIGHT	WINTERGREEN	SHINLEAF
RIGHT-ANGLED TRIANGLE	RIGHT TRIANGLE		

COMMON SAYINGS

PROVERBS

A bad penny always turns up.
A bad workman always blames his tools.
A bird in the hand is worth two in the bush.
Absence makes the heart grow fonder.
A cat has nine lives.
A cat may look at a king.
Accidents will happen in the best regulated
families.
A chain is no stronger than its weakest link.
Actions speak louder than words.
A drowning man will clutch at a straw.
A fool and his money are soon parted.
A fool at forty is a fool indeed.
A friend in need is a friend indeed.
All cats are grey in the dark.
All good things must come to an end.
All is fair in love and war.
All roads lead to Rome.
All's grist that comes to the mill.
All's well that ends well.
All that glitters is not gold.
All the world loves a lover.
All work and no play makes Jack a dull boy.
A miss is as good as a mile.
An apple a day keeps the doctor away.
An Englishman's home is his castle.
An Englishman's word is his bond.
A nod is as good as a wink to a blind horse.
Any port in a storm.
Any publicity is good publicity.
A trouble shared is a trouble halved.
Attack is the best form of defence.
A watched pot never boils.
A woman's work is never done.
A young physician fattens the churchyard.
Bad news travels fast.
Beauty is in the eye of the beholder.
Beauty is only skin-deep.
Beggars can't be choosers.
Better be an old man's darling than a young
man's slave.
Better be safe than sorry.
Better late than never.
Birds of a feather flock together.
Blood is thicker than water.
Books and friends should be few but good.
Caesar's wife must be above suspicion.
Charity begins at home.
Christmas comes but once a year.
Civility costs nothing.

Cold hands, warm heart.
Constant dripping wears away the stone.
Curiosity killed the cat.
Cut your coat according to your cloth.
Dead men tell no tales.
Death is the great leveller.
Divide and rule.
Do as I say, not as I do.
Do as you would be done by.
Dog does not eat dog.
Don't count your chickens before they are
hatched.
Don't cross the bridge till you get to it.
Don't cut off your nose to spite your face.
Don't meet troubles half-way.
Don't put all your eggs in one basket.
Don't spoil the ship for a ha'porth of tar.
Don't teach your grandmother to suck eggs.
Don't throw the baby out with the bathwater.
Don't wash your dirty linen in public.
Early to bed and early to rise, makes a man
healthy, wealthy and wise.
Easier said than done.
East, west, home's best.
Easy come, easy go.
Empty vessels make the greatest sound.
Even a worm will turn.
Every cloud has a silver lining.
Every dog has his day.
Every dog is allowed one bite.
Every man for himself, and the devil take the
hindmost.
Everything comes to him who waits.
Experience is the best teacher.
Faith will move mountains.
Familiarity breeds contempt.
Fight fire with fire.
Fine feathers make fine birds.
Fine words butter no parsnips.
Fish and guests smell in three days.
Forewarned is forearmed.
Forgive and forget.
For want of a nail the shoe was lost; for want
of a shoe the horse was lost; for want of a
horse the rider was lost.
From clogs to clogs in only three generations.
Give a dog a bad name and hang him.
Give him an inch and he'll take a yard.
Great minds think alike.
Great oaks from little acorns grow.

Handsome is as handsome does.

He that fights and runs away, may live to fight another day.

He travels fastest who travels alone.

He who hesitates is lost.

He who lives by the sword dies by the sword.

He who pays the piper calls the tune.

He who sups with the devil should have a long spoon.

History repeats itself.

Honesty is the best policy.

If a job's worth doing, it's worth doing well.

If at first you don't succeed, try, try, try again.

If the mountain will not come to Mahomet, Mahomet must go to the mountain.

If you don't like the heat, get out of the kitchen.

Imitation is the sincerest form of flattery.

In for a penny, in for a pound.

In the country of the blind, the one-eyed man is king.

It is no use crying over spilt milk.

It never rains but it pours.

It's an ill wind that blows nobody any good.

It's too late to shut the stable door after the horse has bolted.

It will all come right in the wash.

It will be all the same in a hundred years.

Jack of all trades, master of none.

Keep something for a rainy day.

Kill not the goose that lays the golden egg.

Least said soonest mended.

Let bygones be bygones.

Let sleeping dogs lie.

Let the cobbler stick to his last.

Life begins at forty.

Life is just a bowl of cherries.

Life is not all beer and skittles.

Look before you leap.

Love is blind.

Love laughs at locksmiths.

Lucky at cards, unlucky in love.

Many a true word is spoken in jest.

Many hands make light work.

March comes in like a lion and goes out like a lamb.

March winds and April showers bring forth May flowers.

Marry in haste, and repent at leisure.

More haste, less speed.

Necessity is the mother of invention.

Needs must when the devil drives.

Ne'er cast a clout till May be out.

Never look a gift horse in the mouth.

No time like the present.

Old habits die hard.

Old sins cast long shadows.

One for sorrow, two for joy; three for a girl, four for a boy; five for silver, six for gold; seven for a secret, not to be told; eight for heaven, nine for hell; and ten for the devil's own sel.

One good turn deserves another.

One man's meat is another man's poison.

One swallow does not make a summer.

Out of sight, out of mind.

Patience is a virtue.

Penny wise, pound foolish.

Prevention is better than cure.

Red sky at night, shepherd's delight; red sky in the morning, shepherd's warning.

Revenge is a dish that tastes better cold.

Revenge is sweet.

See a pin and pick it up, all the day you'll have good luck; see a pin and let it lie, you'll want a pin before you die.

Seeing is believing.

See Naples and die.

Silence is golden.

Spare the rod and spoil the child.

Sticks and stones may break my bones, but words will never hurt me.

Still waters run deep.

St. Swithin's Day, if thou dost rain, for forty days it will remain; St. Swithin's Day, if thou be fair, for forty days 'twill rain no more.

Take a hair of the dog that bit you.

The darkest hour is just before the dawn.

The devil finds work for idle hands to do.

The devil looks after his own.

The early bird catches the worm.

The end justifies the means.

The exception proves the rule.

The hand that rocks the cradle rules the world.

Time is a great healer.

There is honour among thieves.

There is more than one way to skin a cat.

There is no accounting for tastes.

There is safety in numbers.

There's many a good tune played on an old fiddle.

There's many a slip' twixt the cup and the lip.

There's no place like home.

There's no smoke without fire.

The road to hell is paved with good intentions.

Time and tide wait for no man.

Time is a great healer.

Too many cooks spoil the broth.

Truth is stranger than fiction.

Two heads are better than one.

Two wrongs do not make a right.

United we stand, divided we fall.

Waste not, want not.

We must learn to walk before we can run.

What you lose on the swings you gain on the roundabouts.

When poverty comes in at the door, love flies out of the window.

When the cat's away, the mice will play.

When the wine is in, the wit is out.

Where there's a will there's a way.
Why keep a dog and bark yourself?
You can lead a horse to the water, but you can't make him drink.
You cannot run with the hare and hunt with the hounds.

You can't make an omelette without breaking eggs.
You can't teach an old dog new tricks.
You can't tell a book by its cover.

SIMILES

as bald as a coot
as black as pitch
as black as the ace of spades
as blind as a bat
as blind as a mole
as bold as brass
as bright as a button
as busy as a bee
as calm as a millpond
as cheap as dirt
as chirpy as a cricket
as clean as a whistle
as clear as a bell
as clear as crystal
as clear as mud
as cold as charity
as common as muck
as cool as a cucumber
as cross as two sticks
as daft as a brush
as dead as a dodo
as dead as a doornail
as dead as mutton
as deaf as a post
as different as chalk and cheese
as drunk as a lord
as dry as a bone
as dry as dust
as dull as dishwater
as easy as falling off a log
as easy as pie
as fit as a flea
as flat as a pancake
as free as a bird
as free as air
as free as the wind
as fresh as a daisy
as good as gold
as green as grass
as happy as a lark
as happy as a sandboy
as happy as Larry
as happy as the day is long
as hard as nails
as keen as mustard
as large as life
as light as a feather
as like as two peas in a pod

as lively as a cricket
as mad as a hatter
as mad as a March hare
as meek as a lamb
as merry as a cricket
as neat as a new pin
as nutty as a fruitcake
as obstinate as a mule
as old as the hills
as pale as death
as plain as a pikestaff
as plain as the nose on your face
as pleased as Punch
as poor as a church mouse
as poor as Lazarus
as pretty as a picture
as proud as a peacock
as pure as the driven snow
as quick as a flash
as quick as lightning
as quick as thought
as quiet as a mouse
as quiet as the grave
as red as a beetroot
as regular as clockwork
as rich as Croesus
as right as rain
as safe as houses
as sharp as a needle
as sick as a dog
as simple as falling off a log
as slippery as an eel
as snug as a bug in a rug
as sound as a bell
as steady as a rock
as stiff as a board
as stiff as a poker
as stiff as a ramrod
as straight as a die
as straight as an arrow
as stubborn as a mule
as sure as eggs is eggs
as sure as hell
as thick as thieves
as thick as two short planks
as thin as a lath
as thin as a rake
as thin as a stick

as tough as nails
as tough as old boots
as ugly as sin
as warm as toast

as weak as a kitten
as weak as dishwater
as welcome as the flowers in May
as white as a sheet

NURSERY RHYMES

A frog he would a-wooing go,
Heigh ho! says Rowley,
A frog he would a-wooing go,
Whether his mother would let him or no.
With a rowley, powley, gammon and spinach,
Heigh ho! says Anthony Rowley.

As I was going to St Ives,
I met a man with seven wives.
Each wife had seven sacks
Each sack had seven cats,
Each cat had seven kits,
How many were going to St Ives?

Baa, baa, black sheep,
Have you any wool?
Yes, sir, yes, sir,
Three bags full;
One for the master,
And one for the dame,
And one for the little boy
Who lives down the lane.

Bobby Shafto's gone to sea,
Silver buckles on his knee;
He'll come back and marry me,
Bonny Bobby Shafto!

Come, let's to bed
Says Sleepy-head;
Tarry a while, says Slow;
Put on the pan;
Says Greedy Nan,
Let's sup before we go.

Ding dong, bell,
Pussy's in the well.
Who put her in?
Little Johnny Green.
Who pulled her out?
Little Tommy Stout.

Doctor Foster went to Gloucester
In a shower of rain:
He stepped in a puddle,
Right up to his middle,
And never went there again.

Georgie Porgie, pudding and pie,
Kissed the girls and made them cry;
When the boys came out to play,
Georgie Porgie ran away.

Goosey, goosey gander,
Whither shall I wander?

Upstairs and downstairs
And in my lady's chamber.

Hey diddle diddle,
The cat and the fiddle,
The cow jumped over the moon;
The little dog laughed
To see such sport,
And the dish ran away with the spoon.

Hickory, dickory, dock,
The mouse ran up the clock.
The clock struck one,
The mouse ran down,
Hickory, dickory, dock.

Jack and Jill went up the hill
To fetch a pail of water;
Jack fell down and broke his crown,
And Jill came tumbling after.

Little Bo-peep has lost her sheep,
And can't tell where to find them;
Leave them alone, and they'll come home,
Bringing their tails behind them.

Little Boy Blue,
Come blow your horn,
The sheep's in the meadow,
The cow's in the corn.

Little Jack Horner
Sat in the corner,
Eating a Christmas pie;
He put in his thumb,
And pulled out a plum,
And said, What a good boy am I!

Little Miss Muffet
Sat on a tuffet,
Eating her curds and whey;
There came a big spider,
Who sat down beside her
And frightened Miss Muffet away.

Little Tommy Tucker,
Sings for his supper:
What shall we give him?
White bread and butter
How shall he cut it
Without a knife?
How will he be married
Without a wife?

Mary, Mary, quite contrary,

How does your garden grow?
With silver bells and cockle shells,
And pretty maids all in a row.

Monday's child is fair of face,
Tuesday's child is full of grace,
Wednesday's child is full of woe,
Thursday's child has far to go,
Friday's child is loving and giving,
Saturday's child works hard for his living,
And the child that is born on the Sabbath day
Is bonny and blithe, and good and gay.

Oh! the grand old Duke of York
He had ten thousand men;
He marched them up to the top of the hill,
And he marched them down again.
And when they were up they were up,
And when they were down they were down,
And when they were only half way up,
They were neither up nor down.

Old King Cole
Was a merry old soul,
And a merry old soul was he;
He called for his pipe,
And he called for his bowl,
And he called for his fiddlers three.

Old Mother Hubbard
Went to the cupboard,
To fetch her poor dog a bone;
But when she got there
The cupboard was bare
And so the poor dog had none.

One, two,
Buckle my shoe;
Three, four,
Knock at the door.
Five, six,
Pick up sticks;
Seven, eight,
Close the gate.
Nine, ten,
Big fat hen;
Eleven, twelve,
Dig and delve.
Thirteen, fourteen,
Maid's a'courting;
Fifteen, sixteen,
Maids in the kitchen.
Seventeen, eighteen,
Maids a'waiting;
Nineteen, twenty,
My plate's empty.

Oranges and lemons,
Say the bells of St Clement's.
You owe me five farthings,
Say the bells of St Martin's.
When will you pay me?
Say the bells of Old Bailey.
When I grow rich,

Say the bells of Shoreditch.
When will that be?
Say the bells of Stepney.
I'm sure I don't know,
Says the great bell at Bow.
Here comes a candle to light you to bed,
Here comes a chopper to chop off your head.

Peter Piper picked a peck of pickled pepper;
A peck of pickled pepper Peter Piper picked;
If Peter Piper picked a peck of pickled pepper,
Where's the peck of pickled pepper Peter
    Piper picked?

Polly put the kettle on,
Polly put the kettle on,
Polly put the kettle on,
We'll all have tea.
Sukey take it off again,
Sukey take it off again,
Sukey take it off again,
They've all gone away.

Pussy cat, pussy cat, where have you been?
I've been to London to look at the queen.
Pussy cat, pussy cat, what did you there?
I frightened a little mouse under her chair.

Ride a cock-horse to Banbury Cross,
To see a fine lady upon a white horse;
Rings on her fingers and bells on her toes,
And she shall have music wherever she goes.

Ring-a-ring o'roses,
A pocket full of posies,
A-tishoo! A-tishoo!
We all fall down.

Rub-a-dub-dub,
Three men in a tub,
And who do you think they be?
The butcher, the baker,
The candlestick-maker,
And they all sailed out to sea.

See-saw, Margery Daw,
Jacky shall have a new master;
Jacky shall have but a penny a day,
Because he can't work any faster.

Simple Simon met a pieman,
Going to the fair;
Says Simple Simon to the pieman,
Let me taste your ware.
Says the pieman to Simple Simon,
Show me first your penny;
Says Simple Simon to the pieman,
Indeed I have not any.

Sing a song of sixpence,
A pocket full of rye;
Four and twenty blackbirds,
Baked in a pie.
When the pie was opened,
The birds began to sing;
Was not that a dainty dish,

To set before the king?
The king was in his counting-house,
Counting out his money;
The queen was in the parlour,
Eating bread and honey.
The maid was in the garden,
Hanging out the clothes,
When down came a blackbird,
And pecked off her nose.

Solomon Grundy,
Born on a Monday,
Christened on Tuesday,
Married on Wednesday,
Took ill on Thursday,
Worse on Friday,
Died on Saturday,
Buried on Sunday.
This is the end
Of Solomon Grundy.

The lion and the unicorn
Were fighting for the crown;
The lion beat the unicorn
All round about the town.

There was a crooked man, and he walked a
    crooked mile,
He found a crooked sixpence against a
    crooked stile:
He bought a crooked cat, which caught a
    crooked mouse,
And they all lived together in a little crooked
    house.

There was an old woman who lived in a shoe,
She had so many children she didn't know
    what to do;
She gave them some broth without any bread;
She whipped them all soundly and put them to
    bed.

The twelfth day of Christmas,
My true love sent to me
Twelve lords a-leaping,
Eleven ladies dancing,
Ten pipers piping,
Nine drummers drumming,
Eight maids a-milking,
Seven swans a-swimming,
Six geese a-laying,
Five gold rings,
Four colly birds,
Three French hens,
Two turtle doves, and
A partridge in a pear tree.

Thirty days hath September,
April, June, and November;
All the rest have thirty-one,
Excepting February alone
And that has twenty-eight days clear
And twenty-nine in each leap year.

This little piggy went to market,

This little piggy stayed at home,
This little piggy had roast beef,
This little piggy had none,
And this little piggy cried, Wee-wee-wee-wee-
    wee,
I can't find my way home.

Three blind mice, see how they run!
They all run after the farmer's wife,
Who cut off their tails with a carving knife,
Did you ever see such a thing in your life,
As three blind mice?

Tinker,
Tailor,
Soldier,
Sailor,
Rich man,
Poor man,
Beggarman,
Thief.

Tom, Tom, the piper's son,
Stole a pig and away he run;
The pig was eat
And Tom was beat,
And Tom went howling down the street.

Two little dicky birds,
Sitting on a wall;
One named Peter,
The other named Paul,
Fly away, Peter!
Fly away, Paul!
Come back, Peter!
Come back, Paul!

Wee Willie Winkie runs through the town
Upstairs and downstairs and in his nightgown,
Rapping at the window, crying through the
    lock,
Are the children all in bed? It's past eight
    o'clock.

What are little boys made of?
Frogs and snails
And puppy-dogs' tails,
That's what little boys are made of.
What are little girls made of?
Sugar and spice
And all that's nice,
That's what little girls are made of.

Who killed Cock Robin?
I, said the Sparrow,
With my bow and arrow,
I killed Cock Robin.
Who saw him die?
I, said the Fly,
With my little eye,
I saw him die.

Jack Sprat could eat no fat,
His wife could eat no lean,
And so between them both you see,

They licked the platter clean.

How many miles to Babylon?
Three score miles and ten.
Can I get there by candle-light?
Yes, and back again.
If your heels are nimble and light,

You may get there by candle-light.

Humpty Dumpty sat on a wall,
Humpty Dumpty had a great fall.
All the king's horses and
All the king's men,
Couldn't put Humpty together again.

MOTTOES

A DEO ET REGE − By God and the King (Earl of Chesterfield)

AD MAJOREM DEI GLORIAM − to the greater glory of God (The Jesuits)

A MARI USQUE AD MARE − from sea to sea (Canada)

APRES NOUS LE DELUGE − after us the deluge (617 Squadron, 'The Dam Busters', RAF)

ARS LONGA, VITA BREVIS − art is long, life is short (Millais)

AUDI, VIDE, TACE − hear, see, keep silence (United Grand Lodge of Freemasons)

AUSPICIUM MELIORIS AEVI − the sign of a better age (Duke of St Albans, Order of St Michael and St George)

BE PREPARED − Scout Association, 1908

CAVENDO TUTUS − safe by being cautious (Duke of Devonshire)

CHE SERA SERA − what will be will be (Duke of Bedford)

DARE QUAM ACCIPERE − to give rather than to receive (Guy's Hospital)

DE PRAESCIENTIA DEI − from the foreknowledge of God (Barbers' Company, 1461)

DICTUM MEUM PACTUM − my word is my bond (Stock Exchange)

DIEU ET MON DROIT − God and my right (British Sovereigns)

DILIGENT AND SECRET (College of Arms, 1484)

DOMINE DIRIGE NOS − Lord, guide us (City of London)

DOMINUS ILLUMINATIO MEA − the Lord is my light (Oxford University)

DONORUM DEI DISPENSATIO FIDELIS − faithful dispensation of the gifts of God (Harrow School)

ENTALENTÉ À PARLER D'ARMES − equipped to speak of arms (The Heraldry Society, 1957)

ESPÉRANCE EN DIEU − hope in God (Duke of Northumberland)

FIDES ATQUE INTEGRITAS − faith and integrity (Society of Incorporated Accountants and Auditors)

FLOREAT ETONA − may Eton flourish (Eton College)

FOR COUNTRY NOT FOR SELF (226 Squadron, RAF)

GARDEZ BIEN − watch well (Montgomery)

HEAVEN'S LIGHT OUR GUIDE (Order of the Star of India)

HELP (Foundling Hospital, London)

HINC LUCEM ET POCULA SACRA − hence light and sacred cups (Cambridge University)

HONI SOIT QUI MAL Y PENSE − evil be to him who evil thinks (Order of the Garter)

HONNEUR ET PATRIE − honour and country (Order of the Legion of Honour)

ICH DIEN − I serve (Prince of Wales)

IMPERATRICUS AUSPICIIS − imperial in its auspices (Order of the Indian Empire)

IN ACTION FAITHFUL AND IN HONOUR CLEAR (Order of the Companions of Honour, 1917)

IN FIDE SALUS − safety in faith (Star of Rumania)

IN SOMNO SECURITAS − security in sleep (Association of Anaesthetists of Great Britain and Ireland)

JUSTITA VIRTUTUM REGINA − justice is queen of the virtues (Goldsmiths' Company)

LABORARE EST ORARE − to labour is to pray (Benedictine Order)

LABOR VIRIS CONVENIT − labour becomes men (Richard I)

LIFE IN OUR HANDS (Institute of Hospital Engineers)

MIHI ET MEA − to me and mine (Anne Boleyn)

NATION SHALL SPEAK PEACE UNTO NATION (British Broadcasting Corporation)

NEC ASPERA TERRENT − difficulties do not daunt (3rd Foot, 'The Buffs', East Kent Regiment)

NEC CUPIAS NEC METUAS − neither desire nor fear (Earl of Hardwicke)

NEMO ME IMPUNE LACESSIT − no one injures me with impunity (Order of the Thistle)

NOLI ME TANGERE − touch me not (Graeme of Garvock, 103 Squadron, RAF)

NON EST VIVERE SED VALERE VITA – life is not living, but health is life (Royal Society of Medicine)

NON SIBI, SED PATRIAE – not for himself, but for his country (Earl of Romney)

NULLIUS IN VERBA – in no man's words (Royal Society)

PAX IN BELLO – peace in war (Godolphin, Duke of Leeds)

PEACE THROUGH UNDERSTANDING (President Eisenhower)

PER ARDUA AD ASTRA – through endeavour to the stars (RAF motto)

PER CAELUM VIA NOSTRA – our way through heaven (Guild of Air Pilots and Navigators)

PISCATORES HOMINUM – fishers of men (National Society)

POWER IN TRUST (Central Electricity Generating Board)

QUIS SEPARABIT? – who shall separate? (Order of St Patrick)

QUOD PETIS HIC EST – here is what you seek (Institute of British Engineers)

RATIONE ET CONCILIO – by reason and counsel (Magistrates Association)

RERUM COGNOSCERE CAUSAS – to know the causes of things (Institute of Brewing)

SEMPER FIDELIS – always faithful (Devonshire regiment, East Devon Militia)

SEMPER PARATUS – always prepared (207 Squadron, RAF)

SOLA VIRTUS INVICTA – virtue alone is invincible (Duke of Norfolk)

TOUCH NOT THE CAT BOT A GLOVE (Macpherson Clan)

TRIA JUNCTA IN UNO – three joined in one (Order of the Bath)

UNITATE FORTIOR – stronger by union (Building Societies Association; Army and Navy Club)

VER NON SEMPER VIRET – the spring does not always flourish

VERNON SEMPER VIRET – *Vernon* always flourishes (Lord Lyveden)

WHO DARES WINS (Special Air Service)

WORDS

PALINDROMES

3	3—continued	4—continued	5—continued
AHA	NUN	DEED	SAGAS
BIB	OHO	KOOK	SEXES
BOB	PAP	MA'AM	SHAHS
DAD	PEP	NOON	SOLOS
DID	PIP	PEEP	TENET
DUD	POP	POOP	**6**
ERE	PUP	SEES	DENNED
EVE	SIS	TOOT	HALLAH
EWE	SOS	**5**	HANNAH
EYE	TAT	CIVIC	REDDER
GAG	TIT	KAYAK	TERRET
GIG	TNT	LEVEL	TUT-TUT
HAH	TOT	MADAM	**9**
HEH	TUT	MINIM	MALAYALAM
HUH	WOW	RADAR	ROTAVATOR
MAM	**4**	REFER	
MOM	BOOB	ROTOR	
MUM			

BACK WORDS

2	3—continued	3—continued	3—continued
AH – HA	BOY – YOB	GUT – TUG	PAR – RAP
AM – MA	BUD – DUB	HOD – DOH	PAT – TAP
AT – TA	BUN – NUB	JAR – RAJ	PAY – YAP
EH – HE	BUS – SUB	LAG – GAL	PER – REP
HA – AH	BUT – TUB	LAP – PAL	PIN – NIP
HE – EH	DAB – BAD	LEE – EEL	PIT – TIP
HO – OH	DAM – MAD	LEG – GEL	POT – TOP
IT – TI	DEW – WED	MAD – DAM	PUS – SUP
MA – AM	DIM – MID	MAR – RAM	RAJ – JAR
MP – PM	DNA – AND	MAY – YAM	RAM – MAR
NO – ON	DOG – GOD	MID – DIM	RAP – PAR
OH – HO	DOH – HOD	MUG – GUM	RAT – TAR
ON – NO	DON – NOD	NAB – BAN	RAW – WAR
PM – MP	DOT – TOD	NAP – PAN	REP – PER
TA – AT	DUB – BUD	NET – TEN	ROT – TOR
TI – IT	EEL – LEE	NIB – BIN	SAG – GAS
3	GAB – BAG	NIP – PIN	SUB – BUS
AND – DNA	GAL – LAG	NIT – TIN	SUP – PUS
BAD – DAB	GAS – SAG	NOD – DON	TAB – BAT
BAG – GAB	GEL – LEG	NOT – TON	TAP – PAT
BAN – NAB	GOB – BOG	NOW – WON	TAR – RAT
BAT – TAB	GOD – DOG	NUB – BUN	TEN – NET
BIN – NIB	GOT – TOG	PAL – LAP	TIN – NIT
BOG – GOB	GUM – MUG	PAN – NAP	TIP – PIT

3—continued	4—continued	4—continued	5—continued
TOD – DOT	LEEK – KEEL	STAR – RATS	RECAP – PACER
TOG – GOT	LEER – REEL	STEP – PETS	REGAL – LAGER
TON – NOT	LIAR – RAIL	STEW – WETS	REMIT – TIMER
TOP – POT	LIVE – EVIL	STOP – POTS	REPEL – LEPER
TOR – ROT	LOOP – POOL	STUB – BUTS	REVEL – LEVER
TUB – BUT	LOOT – TOOL	STUN – NUTS	SALTA – ATLAS
TUG – GUT	MACS – SCAM	SWAM – MAWS	SERAC – CARES
WAR – RAW	MADE – EDAM	SWAP – PAWS	SERIF – FIRES
WAY – YAW	MAPS – SPAM	SWAY – YAWS	SLEEK – KEELS
WED – DEW	MAWS – SWAM	SWOT – TOWS	SLOOP – POOLS
WON – NOW	MEET – TEEM	TANG – GNAT	SMART – TRAMS
YAM – MAY	MOOD – DOOM	TAPS – SPAT	SNIPS – SPINS
YAP – PAY	MOOR – ROOM	TEEM – MEET	SPINS – SNIPS
YAW – WAY	NAPS – SPAN	TIDE – EDIT	SPOOL – LOOPS
YOB – BOY	NIPS – SPIN	TIME – EMIT	SPOTS – STOPS
4	NUTS – STUN	TIPS – SPIT	STOPS – SPOTS
ABLE – ELBA	OGRE – ERGO	TONS – SNOT	STRAP – PARTS
ABUT – TUBA	PALS – SLAP	TOOL – LOOT	STRAW – WARTS
BARD – DRAB	PANS – SNAP	TOPS – SPOT	STROP – PORTS
BATS – STAB	PART – TRAP	TORT – TROT	TIMER – REMIT
BRAG – GARB	PAWS – SWAP	TOWS – SWOT	TRAMS – SMART
BUNS – SNUB	PEEK – KEEP	TRAP – PART	TUBER – REBUT
BUTS – STUB	PETS – STEP	TROT – TORT	WARTS – STRAW
DEER – REED	PINS – SNIP	TUBA – ABUT	**6**
DIAL – LAID	PLUG – GULP	WARD – DRAW	ANIMAL – LAMINA
DOOM – MOOD	POOH – HOOP	WETS – STEW	DELIAN – NAILED
DOOR – ROOD	POOL – LOOP	WOLF – FLOW	DENIER – REINED
DRAB – BARD	POTS – STOP	YAPS – SPAY	DIAPER – REPAID
DRAW – WARD	RAIL – LIAR	YARD – DRAY	DRAWER – REWARD
DRAY – YARD	RAPS – SPAR	YAWS – SWAY	HARRIS – SIRRAH
DUAL – LAUD	RATS – STAR	**5**	LAMINA – ANIMAL
EDAM – MADE	REED – DEER	ANNAM – MANNA	LOOTER – RETOOL
EDIT – TIDE	REEL – LEER	ATLAS – SALTA	NAILED – DELIAN
ELBA – ABLE	RIAL – LAIR	CARES – SERAC	PUPILS – SLIP-UP
EMIR – RIME	RIME – EMIR	DARAF – FARAD	RECAPS – SPACER
EMIT – TIME	ROOD – DOOR	DECAL – LACED	REINED – DENIER
ERGO – OGRE	ROOM – MOOR	DENIM – MINED	RENNET – TENNER
ET AL – LATE	SCAM – MACS	DEVIL – LIVED	REPAID – DIAPER
EVIL – LIVE	SLAG – GALS	FARAD – DARAF	RETOOL – LOOTER
FLOG – GOLF	SLAP – PALS	FIRES – SERIF	REWARD – DRAWER
FLOW – WOLF	SMUG – GUMS	KEELS – SLEEK	SERVES – SEVRES
GALS – SLAG	SNAP – PANS	LACED – DECAL	SEVRES – SERVES
GARB – BRAG	SNIP – PINS	LAGER – REGAL	SIRRAH – HARRIS
GNAT – TANG	SNOT – TONS	LEPER – REPEL	SLIP-UP – PUPILS
GOLF – FLOG	SNUB – BUNS	LEVER – REVEL	SNOOPS – SPOONS
GULP – PLUG	SNUG – GUNS	LIVED – DEVIL	SPACER – RECAPS
GUMS – SMUG	SPAM – MAPS	LOOPS – SPOOL	SPOONS – SNOOPS
GUNS – SNUG	SPAN – NAPS	MANNA – ANNAM	TENNER – RENNET
HOOP – POOH	SPAR – RAPS	MINED – DENIM	**8**
KEEL – LEEK	SPAT – TAPS	PACER – RECAP	DESSERTS –
KEEP – PEEK	SPAY – YAPS	PARTS – STRAP	STRESSED
LAID – DIAL	SPIN – NIPS	POOLS – SLOOP	STRESSED –
LAIR – RIAL	SPIT – TIPS	PORTS – STROP	DESSERTS
LATE – ET AL	SPOT – TOPS	REBUT – TUBER	
LAUD – DUAL	STAB – BATS		

HOMOPHONES

ACCESSARY – ACCESSORY
ACCESSORY – ACCESSARY
AERIAL – ARIEL
AERIE – AIRY
AIL – ALE
AIR – AIRE, E'ER, ERE, EYRE, HEIR
AIRE – AIR, E'ER, ERE, EYRE, HEIR
AIRSHIP – HEIRSHIP
AIRY – AERIE
AISLE – I'LL, ISLE
AIT – EIGHT, ATE
ALE – AIL
ALL – AWL, ORLE
ALMS – ARMS
ALTAR – ALTER
ALTER – ALTAR
AMAH – ARMOUR
ANTE – ANTI
ANTI – ANTE
ARC – ARK
AREN'T – AUNT
ARES – ARIES
ARIEL – AERIAL
ARIES – ARES
ARK – ARC
ARMOUR – AMAH
ARMS – ALMS
ASCENT – ASSENT
ASSENT – ASCENT
ATE – AIT, EIGHT
AUK – ORC
AUNT – AREN'T
AURAL – ORAL
AUSTERE – OSTIA
AWAY – AWEIGH
AWE – OAR, O'ER, ORE
AWEIGH – AWAY
AWL – ALL, ORLE
AXEL – AXLE
AXLE – AXEL
AY – AYE, EYE, I
AYAH – IRE
AYE – AY, EYE, I
AYES – EYES
BAA – BAH, BAR
BAAL – BASLE
BAH – BAA, BAR
BAIL – BALE
BALE – BAIL
BALL – BAWL
BALM – BARM
BALMY – BARMY
BAR – BAA, BAH
BARE – BEAR

BARM – BALM
BARMY – BALMY
BARON – BARREN
BARREN – BARON
BASE – BASS
BASLE – BAAL
BASS – BASE
BAUD – BAWD, BOARD
BAWD – BAUD, BOARD
BAWL – BALL
BAY – BEY
BEACH – BEECH
BEAN – BEEN
BEAR – BARE
BEAT – BEET
BEATER – BETA
BEAU – BOH, BOW
BEECH – BEACH
BEEN – BEAN
BEER – BIER
BEET – BEAT
BEL – BELL, BELLE
BELL – BEL, BELLE
BELLE – BEL, BELL
BERRY – BURY
BERTH – BIRTH
BETA – BEATER
BEY – BAY
BHAI – BI, BUY, BY, BYE
BI – BHAI, BUY, BY, BYE
BIER – BEER
BIGHT – BITE, BYTE
BIRTH – BERTH
BITE – BIGHT, BYTE
BLEW – BLUE
BLUE – BLEW
BOAR – BOER, BOOR, BORE
BOARD – BAUD, BAWD
BOARDER – BORDER
BOART – BOUGHT
BOER – BOAR, BOOR, BORE
BOH – BEAU, BOW
BOLE – BOWL
BOLT – BOULT
BOOR – BOAR, BOER, BORE
BOOTIE – BOOTY
BOOTY – BOOTIE
BORDER – BOARDER
BORE – BOAR, BOER, BOOR
BORN – BORNE
BORNE – BORN
BOUGH – BOW
BOUGHT – BOART
BOULT – BOLT

BOW – BEAU, BOH
BOW – BOUGH
BOWL – BOLE
BOY – BUOY
BRAKE – BREAK
BREAD – BRED
BREAK – BRAKE
BRED – BREAD
BREDE – BREED, BREID
BREED – BREDE, BREID
BREID – BREDE, BREED
BRIDAL – BRIDLE
BRIDLE – BRIDAL
BROACH – BROOCH
BROOCH – BROACH
BUNION – BUNYAN
BUNYAN – BUNION
BUOY – BOY
BURGER – BURGHER
BURGHER – BURGER
BURY – BERRY
BUS – BUSS
BUSS – BUS
BUY – BHAI, BI, BY, BYE
BUYER – BYRE
BY – BHAI, BI, BUY, BYE
BYE – BHAI, BI, BUY, BY
BYRE – BUYER
BYTE – BIGHT, BITE
CACHE – CASH
CACHOU – CASHEW
CAIN – CANE, KAIN
CALL – CAUL
CALLAS – CALLOUS, CALLUS
CALLOUS – CALLAS, CALLUS
CALLUS – CALLAS, CALLOUS
CANAPÉ – CANOPY
CANE – CAIN, KAIN
CANOPY – CANAPÉ
CARAT – CARROT, KARAT
CARROT – CARAT, KARAT
CART – CARTE, KART
CARTE – CART, KART
CASH – CACHE
CASHEW – CACHOU
CASHMERE – KASHMIR
CAST – CASTE, KARST
CASTE – CAST, KARST
CAUGHT – COURT
CAUL – CALL
CAW – COR, CORE, CORPS
CEDAR – SEEDER
CEDE – SEED
CEIL – SEEL, SEAL
CELL – SELL, SZELL
CELLAR – SELLER
CENSER – CENSOR, SENSOR
CENSOR – CENSER, SENSOR
CENT – SCENT, SENT
CERE – SEAR, SEER
CEREAL – SERIAL

CESSION – SESSION
CHAW – CHORE
CHEAP – CHEEP
CHECK – CZECH
CHEEP – CHEAP
CHOIR – QUIRE
CHOLER – COLLAR
CHORD – CORD
CHORE – CHAW
CHOTT – SHOT, SHOTT
CHOU – SHOE, SHOO
CHOUGH – CHUFF
CHUFF – CHOUGH
CHUTE – SHOOT, SHUTE
CITE – SIGHT, SITE
CLACK – CLAQUE
CLAQUE – CLACK
CLIMB – CLIME
CLIME – CLIMB
COAL – COLE, KOHL
COARSE – CORSE, COURSE
COLE – COAL, KOHL
COLLAR – CHOLER
COLONEL – KERNEL
COLOUR – CULLER
COME – CUM
COMPLEMENTARY – COMPLIMENTARY
COMPLIMENTARY – COMPLEMENTARY
COO – COUP
COOP – COUPE
COR – CAW, CORE, CORPS
CORD – CHORD
CORE – CAW, COR, CORPS
CORNFLOUR – CORNFLOWER
CORNFLOWER – CORNFLOUR
CORPS – CAW, COR, CORE
CORSE – COARSE, COURSE
COUNCIL – COUNSEL
COUNSEL – COUNCIL
COUP – COO
COUPE – COOP
COURSE – COARSE, CORSE
COURT – CAUGHT
CREAK – CREEK
CREEK – CREAK
CULLER – COLOUR
CUM – COME
CURB – KERB
CURRANT – CURRENT
CURRENT – CURRANT
CYGNET – SIGNET
CYMBAL – SYMBOL
CZECH – CHECK
DAM – DAMN
DAMN – DAM
DAW – DOOR, DOR
DAYS – DAZE
DAZE – DAYS
DEAR – DEER
DEER – DEAR
DESCENT – DISSENT

DESERT – DESSERT
DESSERT – DESERT
DEW – DUE
DINAH – DINER
DINE – DYNE
DINER – DINAH
DISSENT – DESCENT
DOE – DOH, DOUGH
DOH – DOE, DOUGH
DONE – DONNE, DUN
DONNE – DONE, DUN
DOOR – DAW, DOR
DOR – DAW, DOOR
DOST – DUST
DOUGH – DOE, DOH
DRAFT – DRAUGHT
DRAUGHT – DRAFT
DROOP – DRUPE
DRUPE – DROOP
DUAL – DUEL
DUCKS – DUX
DUE – DEW
DUEL – DUAL
DUN – DONE, DONNE
DUST – DOST
DUX – DUCKS
DYEING – DYING
DYING – DYEING
DYNE – DINE
EARN – URN
EATEN – ETON
E'ER – AIR, AIRE, ERE, EYRE, HEIR
EERIE – EYRIE
EIDER – IDA
EIGHT – AIT, ATE
EIRE – EYRA
ELATION – ILLATION
ELICIT – ILLICIT
ELUDE – ILLUDE
ELUSORY – ILLUSORY
EMERGE – IMMERGE
EMERSED – IMMERSED
EMERSION – IMMERSION
ERE – AIR, AIRE, E'ER, EYRE, HEIR
ERK – IRK
ERR – UR
ESTER – ESTHER
ESTHER – ESTER
ETON – EATEN
EWE – YEW, YOU
EYE – AY, AYE, I
EYED – I'D, IDE
EYELET – ISLET
EYES – AYES
EYRA – EIRE
EYRE – AIR, AIRE, E'ER, ERE, HEIR
EYRIE – EERIE
FA – FAR
FAIN – FANE, FEIGN
FAINT – FEIGNT
FAIR – FARE

FANE – FAIN, FEIGN
FAR – FA
FARE – FAIR
FARO – PHARAOH
FARTHER – FATHER
FATE – FÊTE
FATHER – FARTHER
FAUGH – FOR, FOUR, FORE
FAUN – FAWN
FAWN – FAUN
FAZE – PHASE
FEAT – FEET
FEET – FEAT
FEIGN – FAIN, FANE
FEIGNT – FAINT
FELLOE – FELLOW
FELLOW – FELLOE
FELT – VELD, VELDT
FETA – FETTER
FÊTE – FATE
FETTER – FETA
FEU – FEW, PHEW
FEW – FEU, PHEW
FIR – FUR
FISHER – FISSURE
FISSURE – FISHER
FIZZ – PHIZ
FLAIR – FLARE
FLARE – FLAIR
FLAW – FLOOR
FLEA – FLEE
FLEE – FLEA
FLEW – FLU, FLUE
FLOE – FLOW
FLOOR – FLAW
FLOUR – FLOWER
FLOW – FLOE
FLOWER – FLOUR
FLU – FLEW, FLUE
FLUE – FLEW, FLU
FOR – FAUGH, FOUR, FORE
FORE – FAUGH, FOR, FOUR
FORT – FOUGHT
FORTE – FORTY
FORTH – FOURTH
FORTY – FORTE
FOUGHT – FORT
FOUL – FOWL
FOUR – FAUGH, FOR, FORE
FOURTH – FORTH
FOWL – FOUL
FRIAR – FRIER
FRIER – FRIAR
FUR – FIR
GAIL – GALE
GAIT – GATE
GALE – GAIL
GALLOP – GALLUP
GALLUP – GALLOP
GAMBLE – GAMBOL
GAMBOL – GAMBLE

GATE – GAIT
GAWKY – GORKY
GENE – JEAN
GIN – JINN
GLADDEN – GLADDON
GLADDON – GLADDEN
GNASH – NASH
GNAT – NAT
GNAW – NOR
GORKY – GAWKY
GRATER – GREATER
GREATER – GRATER
GROAN – GROWN
GROWN – GROAN
HAE – HAY, HEH, HEY
HAIL – HALE
HAIR – HARE
HALE – HAIL
HALL – HAUL
HANDEL – HANDLE
HANDLE – HANDEL
HANGAR – HANGER
HANGER – HANGAR
HARE – HAIR
HART – HEART
HAUD – HOARD, HORDE
HAUL – HALL
HAW – HOARE, WHORE
HAY – HAE, HEH, HEY
HEAR – HERE
HEART – HART
HEH – HAE, HAY, HEY
HEIR – AIR, AIRE, E'ER, ERE, EYRE
HEIRSHIP – AIRSHIP
HERE – HEAR
HEROIN – HEROINE
HEROINE – HEROIN
HEW – HUE
HEY – HAE, HAY, HEH
HIE – HIGH
HIGH – HIE
HIGHER – HIRE
HIM – HYMN
HIRE – HIGHER
HO – HOE
HOAR – HAW, WHORE
HOARD – HAUD, HORDE
HOARSE – HORSE
HOE – HO
HOLE – WHOLE
HOO – WHO
HORDE – HAUD, HOARD
HORSE – HOARSE
HOUR – OUR
HOURS – OURS
HUE – HEW
HYMN – HIM
I – AY, AYE, EYE
I'D – EYED, IDE
IDA – EIDER
IDE – EYED, I'D

IDLE – IDOL
IDOL – IDLE
I'LL – AISLE, ISLE
ILLATION – ELATION
ILLICIT – ELICIT
ILLUDE – ELUDE
ILLUSORY – ELUSORY
IMMERGE – EMERGE
IMMERSED – EMERSED
IMMERSION – EMERSION
IN – INN
INCITE – INSIGHT
INDICT – INDITE
INDITE – INDICT
INN – IN
INSIGHT – INCITE
INSOLE – INSOUL
INSOUL – INSOLE
ION – IRON
IRE – AYAH
IRK – ERK
IRON – ION
ISLE – AISLE, I'LL
ISLET – EYELET
JAM – JAMB, JAMBE
JAMB – JAM, JAMBE
JAMBE – JAM, JAMB
JEAN – GENE
JINKS – JINX
JINN – GIN
JINX – JINKS
KAIN – CAIN, CANE
KARAT – CARAT, CARROT
KARST – CAST, CASTE
KART – CART, CARTE
KASHMIR – CASHMERE
KERB – CURB
KERNEL – COLONEL
KEW – KYU, QUEUE
KEY – QUAY
KNAVE – NAVE
KNEAD – NEED
KNEW – NEW, NU
KNIGHT – NIGHT
KNIGHTLY – NIGHTLY
KNIT – NIT
KNOW – NOH, NO
KNOWS – NOES, NOSE
KOHL – COAL, COLE
KYU – KEW, QUEUE
LACKER – LACQUER
LACQUER – LACKER
LAIN – LANE
LANCE – LAUNCE
LANE – LAIN
LAUD – LORD
LAUNCE – LANCE
LAW – LORE
LAY – LEI, LEY
LAYS – LAZE

LAZE – LAYS
LEAD – LED
LEAF – LIEF
LEAH – LEAR, LEER, LEHR
LEAK – LEEK
LEANT – LENT
LEAR – LEAH, LEER, LEHR
LED – LEAD
LEEK – LEAK
LEER – LEAH, LEAR, LEHR
LEHR – LEAH, LEAR, LEER
LEI – LAY, LEY
LEMAN – LEMON
LEMON – LEMAN
LENT – LEANT
LESSEN – LESSON
LESSON – LESSEN
LEY – LAY, LEI
LIAR – LYRE
LIEF – LEAF
LINCS – LINKS, LYNX
LINKS – LINCS, LYNX
LOAD – LODE
LOAN – LONE
LODE – LOAD
LONE – LOAN
LORD – LAUD
LORE – LAW
LUMBAR – LUMBER
LUMBER – LUMBAR
LYNX – LINCS, LINKS
LYRE – LIAR
MA – MAAR, MAR
MAAR -- MA, MAR
MADE – MAID
MAID – MADE
MAIL – MALE
MAIN – MAINE, MANE
MAINE – MAIN, MANE
MAIZE – MAZE
MALE – MAIL
MALL – MAUL
MANE – MAIN, MAINE
MANNA – MANNER, MANOR
MANNER – MANNA, MANOR
MANOR – MANNA, MANNER
MAQUIS – MARQUEE
MAR – MA, MAAR
MARC – MARK, MARQUE
MARE – MAYOR
MARK – MARC, MARQUE
MARQUE – MARC, MARK
MARQUEE – MAQUIS
MAUL – MALL
MAW – MOR, MORE, MOOR
MAYOR – MARE
MAZE – MAIZE
MEAN – MESNE, MIEN
MEAT – MEET, METE
MEDAL – MEDDLE
MEDDLE – MEDAL

MEET – MEAT, METE
MESNE – MIEN, MEAN
METAL – METTLE
METE – MEAT, MEET
METTLE – METAL
MEWS – MUSE
MIEN – MESNE, MEAN
MIGHT – MITE
MINER – MINOR
MINOR – MINER
MITE – MIGHT
MOAN – MOWN
MOAT – MOTE
MOCHA – MOCKER
MOCKER – MOCHA
MOOR – MAW, MOR, MORE
MOOSE – MOUSSE
MOR – MAW, MORE, MOOR
MORE – MAW, MOR, MOOR
MORN – MOURN
MORNING – MOURNING
MOTE – MOAT
MOURN – MORN
MOURNING – MORNING
MOUSSE – MOOSE
MOWN – MOAN
MUSCLE – MUSSEL
MUSE – MEWS
MUSSEL – MUSCLE
NAE – NAY, NEAGH, NEIGH, NEY
NASH – GNASH
NAT – GNAT
NAUGHT – NOUGHT
NAVAL – NAVEL
NAVE – KNAVE
NAVEL – NAVAL
NAY – NAE, NEAGH, NEIGH, NEY
NEAGH – NAE, NAY, NEIGH, NEY
NEED – KNEAD
NEIGH – NAE, NAY, NEAGH, NEY
NEUK – NUKE
NEW – KNEW, NU
NEY – NAE, NAY, NEAGH, NEIGH
NIGH – NYE
NIGHT – KNIGHT
NIGHTLY – KNIGHTLY
NIT – KNIT
NO – KNOW, NOH
NOES – KNOWS, NOSE
NOH – KNOW, NO
NONE – NUN
NOR – GNAW
NOSE – KNOWS, NOES
NOUGHT – NAUGHT
NU – KNEW, NEW
NUKE – NEUK
NUN – NONE
NYE – NIGH
OAR – AWE, O'ER, ORE
O'ER – AWE, OAR, ORE
OFFA – OFFER

OFFER – OFFA
OH – OWE
ORAL – AURAL
ORC – AUK
ORE – AWE, OAR, O'ER
ORLE – ALL, AWL
OSTIA – AUSTERE
OUR – HOUR
OURS – HOURS
OUT – OWT
OVA – OVER
OVER – OVA
OWE – OH
OWT – OUT
PA – PAH, PAR, PARR, PAS
PACKED – PACT
PACT – PACKED
PAH – PA, PAR, PARR, PAS
PAIL – PALE
PAIR – PARE, PEAR
PALATE – PALETTE, PALLET
PALE – PAIL
PALETTE – PALATE, PALLET
PALLET – PALATE, PALETTE
PANDA – PANDER
PANDER – PANDA
PAR – PA, PAH, PARR, PAS
PARE – PEAR, PAIR
PARR – PA, PAH, PAR, PAS
PAS – PA, PAH, PAR, PARR
PAW – POOR, PORE, POUR
PAWKY – PORKY
PAWN – PORN
PEA – PEE
PEACE – PIECE
PEAK – PIQUE
PEAKE – PEEK, PEKE
PEAL – PEEL
PEAR – PARE, PAIR
PEARL – PURL
PEARLER – PURLER
PEDAL – PEDDLE
PEDDLE – PEDAL
PEE – PEA
PEEK – PEAKE, PEKE
PEEL – PEAL
PEKE – PEAKE, PEEK
PER – PURR
PETREL – PETROL
PETROL – PETREL
PHARAOH – FARO
PHASE – FAZE
PHEW – FEU, FEW
PHIZ – FIZZ
PI – PIE, PYE
PIE – PI, PYE
PIECE – PEACE
PILATE – PILOT
PILOT – PILATE
PIQUE – PEAK
PLACE – PLAICE

PLAICE – PLACE
PLAIN – PLANE
PLANE – PLAIN
POLE – POLL
POLL – POLE
POMACE – PUMICE
POMMEL – PUMMEL
POOR – PAW, PORE, POUR
POPULACE – POPULOUS
POPULOUS – POPULACE
PORE – PAW, POOR, POUR
PORKY – PAWKY
PORN – PAWN
POUR – PAW, POOR, PORE
PRAY – PREY
PREY – PRAY
PRINCIPAL – PRINCIPLE
PRINCIPLE – PRINCIPAL
PROFIT – PROPHET
PROPHET – PROFIT
PSALTER – SALTER
PUCKA – PUCKER
PUCKER – PUCKA
PUMICE – POMACE
PUMMEL – POMMEL
PURL – PEARL
PURLER – PEARLER
PURR – PER
PYE – PI, PIE
QUAY – KEY
QUEUE – KEW, KYU
QUIRE – CHOIR
RACK – WRACK
RACKET – RACQUET
RACQUET – RACKET
RAIN – REIGN, REIN
RAINS – REINS
RAISE – RASE
RAP – WRAP
RAPT – WRAPPED
RASE – RAISE
RAW – ROAR
READ – REDE, REED
RECK – WRECK
REDE – READ, REED
REED – READ, REDE
REEK – WREAK
REIGN – RAIN, REIN
REIN – RAIN, REIGN
REINS – RAINS
RENNES – WREN
RETCH – WRETCH
REVERE – REVERS
REVERS – REVERE
RHEUM – ROOM
RHEUMY – ROOMY
RHO – ROW, ROE
RHÔNE – ROAN, RONE
RIGHT – RITE, WRIGHT, WRITE
RING – WRING
RINGER – WRINGER

RITE – RIGHT, WRIGHT, WRITE
ROAM – ROME
ROAN – RHÔNE, RONE
ROAR – RAW
ROE – RHO, ROW
ROLE – ROLL
ROLL – ROLE
ROME – ROAM
RONE – RHÔNE, ROAN
ROOD – RUDE
ROOM – RHEUM
ROOMY – RHEUMY
ROOSE – RUSE
ROOT – ROUTE
RORT – WROUGHT
ROTE – WROTE
ROUGH – RUFF
ROUTE – ROOT
ROW – RHO, ROE
RUDE – ROOD
RUFF – ROUGH
RUNG – WRUNG
RUSE – ROOSE
RYE – WRY
SAIL – SALE
SAIN – SANE, SEINE
SALE – SAIL
SALTER – PSALTER
SANE – SAIN, SEINE
SAUCE – SOURCE
SAUT – SORT, SOUGHT
SAW – SOAR, SORE
SAWN – SORN
SCENE – SEEN
SCENT – CENT, SENT
SCULL – SKULL
SEAL – CEIL, SEEL
SEAM – SEEM
SEAR – CERE, SEER
SEED – CEDE
SEEDER – CEDAR
SEEK – SEIK, SIKH
SEEL – CEIL, SEAL
SEEM – SEAM
SEEN – SCENE
SEER – CERE, SEAR
SEIK – SEEK, SIKH
SEINE – SAIN, SANE
SELL – CELL, SZELL
SELLER – CELLAR
SENSOR – CENSER, CENSOR
SENT – CENT, SCENT
SERF – SURF
SERGE – SURGE
SERIAL – CEREAL
SESSION – CESSION
SEW – SO, SOH, SOW
SEWN – SONE, SOWN
SHAKE – SHEIK
SHEIK – SHAKE
SHIER – SHYER, SHIRE

SHIRE – SHIER, SHYER
SHOE – CHOU, SHOO
SHOO – CHOU, SHOE
SHOOT – SHUTE, CHUTE
SHOT – SHOTT, CHOTT
SHOTT – SHOT, CHOTT
SHUTE – SHOOT, CHUTE
SHYER – SHIER, SHIRE
SIGHT – CITE, SITE
SIGN – SYN
SIGNET – CYGNET
SIKH – SEEK, SEIK
SIOUX – SOU
SITE – CITE, SIGHT
SKULL – SCULL
SKY – SKYE
SKYE – SKY
SLAY – SLEIGH
SLEAVE – SLEEVE
SLEEVE – SLEAVE
SLEIGH – SLAY
SLOE – SLOW
SLOW – SLOE
SO – SEW, SOH, SOW
SOAR – SAW, SORE
SOH – SEW, SO, SOW
SOLE – SOUL
SOME – SUM
SON – SUN, SUNN
SONE – SEWN, SOWN
SONNY – SUNNI, SUNNY
SORE – SAW, SOAR
SORN – SAWN
SORT – SAUT, SOUGHT
SOU – SIOUX
SOUGHT – SAUT, SORT
SOUL – SOLE
SOURCE – SAUCE
SOW – SEW, SO, SOH
SOWN – SEWN, SONE
STAIR – STARE
STAKE – STEAK
STALK – STORK
STARE – STAIR
STEAK – STAKE
STEAL – STEEL
STEEL – STEAL
STOREY – STORY
STORK – STALK
STORY – STOREY
SUITE – SWEET
SUM – SOME
SUN – SON, SUNN
SUNDAE – SUNDAY
SUNDAY – SUNDAE
SUNN – SON, SUN
SUNNI – SONNY, SUNNY
SUNNY – SONNY, SUNNI
SURF – SERF
SURGE – SERGE
SWAT – SWOT

SWEET – SUITE
SWOT – SWAT
SYMBOL – CYMBAL
SYN – SIGN
SZELL – CELL, SELL
TACIT – TASSET
TAI – TAILLE, THAI, TIE
TAIL – TALE
TAILLE – TAI, THAI, TIE
TALE – TAIL
TALK – TORC, TORQUE
TARE – TEAR
TASSET – TACIT
TAUGHT – TAUT, TORT, TORTE
TAUT – TAUGHT, TORT, TORTE
TEA – TEE, TI
TEAM – TEEM
TEAR – TARE
TEE – TEA, TI
TEEM – TEAM
TENNER – TENOR
TENOR – TENNER
TERNE – TURN
THAI – TAI, TAILLE, TIE
THAW – THOR
THEIR – THERE, THEY'RE
THERE – THEIR, THEY'RE
THEY'RE – THEIR, THERE
THOR – THAW
THREW – THROUGH, THRU
THROE – THROW
THRONE – THROWN
THROUGH – THREW, THRU
THROW – THROE
THROWN – THRONE
THRU – THREW, THROUGH
THYME – TIME
TI – TEA, TEE
TIC – TICK
TICK – TIC
TIDE – TIED
TIE – TAI, TAILLE, THAI
TIED – TIDE
TIER – TIRE, TYRE
TIGHTEN – TITAN
TIMBER – TIMBRE
TIMBRE – TIMBER
TIME – THYME
TIRE – TIER, TYRE
TITAN – TIGHTEN
TO – TOO, TWO
TOAD – TOED, TOWED
TOE – TOW
TOED – TOAD, TOWED
TOO – TO, TWO
TOR – TORE
TORC – TALK, TORQUE
TORE – TOR
TORQUE – TALK, TORC
TORT – TAUGHT, TAUT, TORTE
TORTE – TAUGHT, TAUT, TORT

TOW – TOE
TOWED – TOAD, TOED
TROOP – TROUPE
TROUPE – TROOP
TUNA – TUNER
TUNER – TUNA
TURN – TERNE
TWO – TO, TOO
TYRE – TIER, TIRE
UR – ERR
URN – EARN
VAIL – VALE, VEIL
VAIN – VANE, VEIN
VALE – VAIL, VEIL
VANE – VAIN, VEIN
VEIL – VAIL, VALE
VEIN – VAIN, VANE
VELD – FELT, VELDT
VELDT – FELT, VELD
WAE – WAY, WHEY
WAIL – WHALE
WAIN – WANE, WAYNE
WAIST – WASTE
WAIT – WEIGHT
WAIVE – WAVE
WANE – WAIN, WAYNE
WAR – WAUGH, WAW, WORE
WARE – WEAR, WHERE
WARN – WORN
WASTE – WAIST
WATT – WHAT, WOT
WAUGH – WAR, WAW, WORE
WAVE – WAIVE
WAW – WAR, WAUGH, WORE
WAY – WAE, WHEY
WAYNE – WAIN, WANE
WEAK – WEEK
WEAKLY – WEEKLY
WEAR – WARE, WHERE
WEAVE – WE'VE
WE'D – WEED
WEED – WE'D
WEEK – WEAK
WEEKLY – WEAKLY
WEEL – WE'LL, WHEAL, WHEEL
WEIGHT – WAIT
WE'LL – WEEL, WHEAL, WHEEL
WEN – WHEN
WERE – WHIRR
WE'VE – WEAVE
WHALE – WAIL
WHAT – WATT, WOT
WHEAL – WEEL, WE'LL, WHEEL
WHEEL – WEEL, WE'LL, WHEAL
WHEN – WEN
WHERE – WARE, WEAR
WHEY – WAE, WAY
WHICH – WITCH
WHINE – WINE
WHIRR – WERE
WHITE – WIGHT, WITE

WHITHER – WITHER
WHO – HOO
WHOA – WO, WOE
WHOLE – HOLE
WHORE – HAW, HOAR
WIGHT – WHITE, WITE
WINE – WHINE
WITCH – WHICH
WITE – WHITE, WIGHT
WITHER – WHITHER
WO – WHOA, WOE
WOE – WHOA, WO
WORE – WAR, WAUGH, WAW
WORN – WARN
WOT – WATT, WHAT
WRACK – RACK
WRAP – RAP
WRAPPED – RAPT
WREAK – REEK
WRECK – RECK
WREN – RENNES

WRETCH – RETCH
WRIGHT – RIGHT, RITE, WRITE
WRING – RING
WRINGER – RINGER
WRITE – RIGHT, RITE, WRIGHT
WROTE – ROTE
WROUGHT – RORT
WRUNG – RUNG
WRY – RYE
YAW – YORE, YOUR
YAWS – YOURS
YEW – EWE, YOU
YOKE – YOLK
YOLK – YOKE
YORE – YAW, YOUR
YOU – EWE, YEW
YOU'LL – YULE
YOUR – YAW, YORE
YOURS – YAWS
YULE – YOU'LL

TWO-WORD PHRASES

FIRST WORD

ABERDEEN – ANGUS, TERRIER
ABLE – BODIED, RATING, SEAMAN
ABSOLUTE – ALCOHOL, HUMIDITY, JUDGMENT, MAGNITUDE, MAJORITY, MONARCHY, MUSIC, PITCH, TEMPERATURE, THRESHOLD, UNIT, VALUE, ZERO
ABSTRACT – EXPRESSIONISM, NOUN
ACCESS – ROAD, TIME
ACCOMMODATION – ADDRESS, BILL, LADDER, PLATFORM
ACHILLES – HEEL, TENDON
ACID – DROP, RAIN, ROCK, SOIL, TEST, VALUE
ACT – AS, FOR, ON, OUT, UP
ACTION – COMMITTEE, GROUP, PAINTING, POTENTIAL, REPLAY, STATIONS
ACTIVE – CENTRE, LIST, SERVICE, TRANSPORT, VOCABULARY, VOLCANO
ADMIRALTY – BOARD, HOUSE, ISLANDS, MILE, RANGE
ADVANCE – BOOKING, COPY, GUARD, MAN, NOTICE, POLL, RATIO
AEOLIAN – DEPOSITS, HARP, ISLANDS, MODE
AFRICAN – LILY, MAHOGANY, TIME, VIOLET
AGONY – AUNT, COLUMN
AIR – ALERT, BAG, BED, BLADDER, BRAKE, BRIDGE, COMMODORE, CONDITIONING, CORRIDOR, COVER, CURTAIN, CUSHION, CYLINDER, DAM, EMBOLISM, FORCE, GAS, GUN, HARDENING, HOLE, HOSTESS, JACKET, LETTER, MAIL, MARSHAL, MASS, MILE, OFFICER, PLANT, POCKET, POWER, PUMP, RAID, RIFLE, SAC, SCOOP, SCOUT, SHAFT, SHOT, SOCK, SPRAY, SPRING, STATION, TERMINAL, TRAFFIC, TURBINE, VALVE, VICE-MARSHAL

ALL – BLACK, CLEAR, FOURS, HAIL, IN, ONE, OUT, RIGHT, SQUARE, THERE, TOLD
ALPHA – CENTAURI, HELIX, IRON, PARTICLE, PRIVATIVE, RAY, RHYTHM
ALTAR – BOY, CLOTH, -PIECE
AMERICAN – ALOE, CHAMELEON, CHEESE, CLOTH, EAGLE, FOOTBALL, INDIAN, PLAN, REVOLUTION, SAMOA, WAKE
ANCHOR – MAN, PLATE, RING
ANCIENT – GREEK, HISTORY, LIGHTS, MONUMENT
ANGEL – CAKE, DUST, FALLS, FOOD, SHARK
ANGLE – BRACKET, DOZER, IRON, PLATE
ANIMAL – HUSBANDRY, KINGDOM, MAGNETISM, RIGHTS, SPIRITS, STARCH
ANT – BEAR, BIRD, COW, EATER, HEAP, HILL
APPLE – BLIGHT, BOX, BRANDY, BUTTER, GREEN, ISLE, JACK, MAGGOT, POLISHER, SAUCE
ARCTIC – CHAR, CIRCLE, FOX, HARE, OCEAN, TERN, WILLOW
ART – DECO, FORM, NOUVEAU, PAPER
ARTIFICIAL – INSEMINATION, INTELLIGENCE, RESPIRATION
ASH – BLOND, CAN, WEDNESDAY
ATOMIC – AGE, CLOCK, COCKTAIL, ENERGY, HEAT, MASS, NUMBER, PILE, POWER, STRUCTURE, THEORY, VOLUME, WEIGHT
AUTOMATIC – CAMERA, PILOT, REPEAT, TRANSMISSION, TYPESETTING
BABY – BOOM, BUGGY, CARRIAGE, GRAND, SNATCHER, TALK, TOOTH

BACK — BOILER, BURNER, COUNTRY, DOOR, DOWN, END, LIGHT, LIST, MARKER, MATTER, OUT, PASSAGE, PAY, REST, ROOM, SEAT, STRAIGHT, UP, YARD

BAD — BLOOD, FAITH, LANDS, NEWS

BALL — BEARING, BOY, COCK, GAME, VALVE

BANANA — OIL, REPUBLIC, SKIN, SPLIT

BANK — ACCEPTANCE, ACCOUNT, ANNUITIES, BILL, CARD, CLERK, DISCOUNT, HOLIDAY, MANAGER, ON, RATE, STATEMENT

BAR — BILLIARDS, CHART, CODE, DIAGRAM, FLY, GIRL, GRAPH, LINE, MITZVAH, SINISTER

BARLEY — SUGAR, WATER, WINE

BARN — DANCE, DOOR, OWL, SWALLOW

BASE — LOAD, METAL, RATE

BASKET — CASE, CHAIR, HILT, MAKER, WEAVE

BATH — BUN, CHAIR, CHAP, CUBE, OLIVER, SALTS, STONE

BATTLE — CRUISER, CRY, FATIGUE, ROYAL

BAY — LEAF, LYNX, RUM, STREET, TREE, WINDOW

BEACH — BALL, BOYS, BUGGY, FLEA, PLUM

BEAR — DOWN, GARDEN, HUG, OFF, OUT, UP, WITH

BEAUTY — QUEEN, SALON, SLEEP, SPOT

BED — JACKET, LINEN

BELL — BRONZE, BUOY, GLASS, HEATHER, JAR, MAGPIE, METAL, MOTH, PULL, PUNCH, PUSH, SHEEP, TENT

BELLY — DANCE, FLOP, LANDING, LAUGH

BERMUDA — GRASS, RIG, SHORTS, TRIANGLE

BEST — BOY, END, GIRL, MAN, SELLER

BICYCLE — CHAIN, CLIP, PUMP

BIG — APPLE, BAND, BANG, BEN, BERTHA, BROTHER, BUSINESS, CHEESE, CHIEF, DEAL, DIPPER, END, SCREEN, SHOT, STICK, TIME, TOP, WHEEL

BINARY — CODE, DIGIT, FISSION, FORM, NOTATION, NUMBER, STAR, WEAPON

BIRD — CALL, CHERRY, DOG, PEPPER, SPIDER, STRIKE, TABLE

BIRTH — CERTIFICATE, CONTROL, RATE

BIRTHDAY — HONOURS, SUIT

BIT — PART, RATE, SLICE

BITTER — APPLE, END, LAKES, ORANGE, PRINCIPLE

BLACK — ART, BEAN, BEAR, BEETLE, BELT, BILE, BODY, BOOK, BOTTOM, BOX, COUNTRY, DEATH, DIAMOND, ECONOMY, EYE, FLY, FOREST, FRIAR, FROST, HILLS, HOLE, ICE, MAGIC, MARIA, MARK, MARKET, MASS, MONK, MOUNTAINS, PANTHER, PEPPER, PRINCE, PUDDING, ROD, ROT, SEA, SHEEP, SPOT, SWAN, TIE, TREACLE, VELVET, WATCH, WIDOW

BLANK — CARTRIDGE, CHEQUE, ENDORSEMENT, VERSE

BLANKET — BATH, FINISH, STITCH

BLIND — ALLEY, DATE, FREDDIE, GUT, SNAKE, SPOT, STAGGERS, STAMPING

BLISTER — BEETLE, COPPER, PACK, RUST

BLOCK — DIAGRAM, IN, LETTER, OUT, PRINTING, RELEASE, SAMPLING, TIN, VOTE

BLOOD — BANK, BATH, BROTHER, CELL, COUNT, DONOR, FEUD, FLUKE, GROUP, HEAT, MONEY, ORANGE, POISONING, PRESSURE, PUDDING, RED, RELATION, SPORT, TEST, TYPE, VESSEL

BLUE — BABY, BAG, BILLY, BLOOD, CHEESE, CHIP, DEVILS, ENSIGN, FUNK, GUM, JAY, MOON, MOUNTAINS, MURDER, NILE, PENCIL, PETER, RIBAND, RIBBON, VEIN

BOARDING — HOUSE, OUT, SCHOOL

BOAT — DECK, DRILL, NECK, PEOPLE, RACE, TRAIN

BOBBY — CALF, PIN, SOCKS

BODY — BLOW, BUILDING, CAVITY, CORPORATE, IMAGE, LANGUAGE, POPPING, SHOP, SNATCHER, STOCKING, WARMER

BOG — ASPHODEL, COTTON, DEAL, DOWN, IN, MOSS, MYRTLE, OAK, ORCHID, RUSH, STANDARD

BON — MOT, TON, VIVANT, VOYAGE

BONE — ASH, CHINA, IDLE, MEAL, OIL, UP

BOOBY — HATCH, PRIZE, TRAP

BOOK — CLUB, END, IN, INTO, OUT, SCORPION, TOKEN, UP

BOTTLE — GOURD, GREEN, OUT, PARTY, TREE, UP

BOTTOM — DRAWER, END, HOUSE, LINE, OUT

BOW — LEGS, OUT, TIE, WINDOW

BOWLING — ALLEY, CREASE, GREEN

BOX — CAMERA, COAT, ELDER, GIRDER, JELLYFISH, NUMBER, OFFICE, PLEAT, SEAT, SPANNER, SPRING

BRAIN — CORAL, DEATH, DRAIN, FEVER, STEM, WAVE

BRAKE — BAND, DRUM, FLUID, HORSEPOWER, LIGHT, LINING, PARACHUTE, SHOE, VAN

BRAND — IMAGE, LEADER, NAME

BRANDY — BOTTLE, BUTTER, SNAP

BRASS — BAND, FARTHING, HAT, NECK, RUBBING, TACKS

BREAK — DANCE, DOWN, EVEN, IN, INTO, OFF, OUT, THROUGH, UP, WITH

BRING — ABOUT, DOWN, FORWARD, IN, OFF, ON, OUT, OVER, ROUND, TO, UP

BRISTOL — BOARD, CHANNEL, FASHION

BROAD — ARROW, BEAN, CHURCH, GAUGE, JUMP, SEAL

BROWN — BEAR, BOMBER, FAT, OWL, PAPER, RICE, SHIRT, SNAKE, STUDY, SUGAR

BRUSSELS — CARPET, LACE, SPROUT

BUBBLE — BATH, CAR, CHAMBER, FLOAT, GUM, MEMORY, PACK

BUCK — FEVER, RABBIT, UP

BUILDING — BLOCK, LINE, PAPER, SOCIETY

BULL — MASTIFF, NOSE, RUN, SESSION, SNAKE, TERRIER, TONGUE, TROUT

BURNT — ALMOND, OFFERING, SHALE, SIENNA, UMBER

BUS — BOY, LANE, SHELTER, STOP

BUTTER — BEAN, MUSLIN, UP

BUZZ — BOMB, OFF, SAW, WORD

CABBAGE — BUG, LETTUCE, MOTH, PALM, PALMETTO, ROSE, TREE, WHITE

CABIN — BOY, CLASS, CRUISER, FEVER

CABLE — CAR, RAILWAY, RELEASE, STITCH, TELEVISION

CALL — ALARM, BOX, DOWN, FORTH, GIRL, IN, LOAN, MONEY, NUMBER, OFF, OUT, RATE, SIGN, SLIP, UP

CAMP — DAVID, FOLLOWER, MEETING, OVEN, SITE

CANARY — CREEPER, GRASS, ISLANDS, SEED, YELLOW

CANTERBURY — BELL, LAMB, PILGRIMS

CAPE – BUFFALO, CART, COD, COLONY, COLOURED, DOCTOR, DUTCH, FLATS, GOOSEBERRY, HORN, JASMINE, PENINSULA, PIGEON, PRIMROSE, PROVINCE, SPARROW, TOWN, VERDE, YORK

CAPITAL – ACCOUNT, ALLOWANCE, ASSETS, EXPENDITURE, GAIN, GOODS, LEVY, MARKET, PUNISHMENT, SHIP, STOCK, SURPLUS

CARD – FILE, INDEX, PUNCH, READER, VOTE

CARDINAL – BEETLE, FLOWER, NUMBER, POINTS, SPIDER, VIRTUES

CARPET – BEETLE, KNIGHT, MOTH, PLOT, SHARK, SLIPPER, SNAKE, TILES

CARRIAGE – BOLT, CLOCK, DOG, LINE, TRADE

CARRIER – BAG, PIGEON, WAVE

CARRY – AWAY, BACK, FORWARD, OFF, ON, OUT, OVER, THROUGH

CARTRIDGE – BELT, CLIP, PAPER, PEN

CASH – CROP, DESK, DISCOUNT, DISPENSER, FLOW, IN, LIMIT, RATIO, REGISTER, UP

CAST – ABOUT, BACK, DOWN, IRON, ON, OUT, STEEL, UP

CAT – BURGLAR, DOOR, HOLE, LITTER, RIG, SCANNER

CATCH – BASIN, CROP, ON, OUT, PHRASE, PIT, POINTS, UP

CAULIFLOWER – CHEESE, EAR

CENTRE – BIT, FORWARD, HALF, PUNCH, SPREAD, THREE-QUARTER

CHAIN – DRIVE, GANG, GRATE, LETTER, LIGHTNING, MAIL, PRINTER, REACTION, RULE, SAW, SHOT, STITCH, STORE

CHAMBER – COUNSEL, MUSIC, ORCHESTRA, ORGAN, POT

CHARGE – ACCOUNT, DENSITY, HAND, NURSE, SHEET

CHEESE – CUTTER, MITE, SKIPPER, STRAW

CHICKEN – BREAST, FEED, LOUSE, OUT, WIRE

CHILD – ABUSE, BENEFIT, CARE, GUIDANCE, LABOUR, MINDER

CHIMNEY – BREAST, CORNER, STACK, SWALLOW, SWEEP, SWIFT

CHINA – ASTER, BARK, CLAY, INK, ROSE, SEA, TREE

CHINESE – BLOCK, CABBAGE, CHEQUERS, CHIPPENDALE, EMPIRE, GOOSEBERRY, INK, LANTERN, LEAVES, PUZZLE, WALL, WAX, WHITE, WINDLASS

CHIP – BASKET, HEATER, IN, LOG, PAN, SHOT

CHRISTMAS – BEETLE, BOX, CACTUS, CARD, DISEASE, EVE, ISLAND, PUDDING, ROSE, STOCKING, TREE

CIGARETTE – CARD, END, HOLDER, LIGHTER, PAPER

CIRCUIT – BINDING, BOARD, BREAKER, JUDGE, RIDER, TRAINING

CITY – BLUES, COMPANY, DESK, EDITOR, FATHER, HALL, MANAGER, PLANNING, SLICKER

CIVIL – DEFENCE, DISOBEDIENCE, ENGINEER, LAW, LIBERTY, LIST, MARRIAGE, RIGHTS, SERVANT, SERVICE, WAR

CLAW – BACK, HAMMER, HATCHET, OFF, SETTING

CLOCK – GOLF, OFF, ON, UP

CLOSE – CALL, COMPANY, DOWN, HARMONY, IN, OUT, PUNCTUATION, QUARTERS, SEASON, SHAVE, WITH

CLOSED – BOOK, CHAIN, CIRCUIT, CORPORATION, GAME, PRIMARY, SCHOLARSHIP, SENTENCE, SET, SHOP

CLOTHES – MOTH, PEG, POLE, PROP

CLUB – FOOT, HAND, MOSS, ROOT, SANDWICH

COAL – GAS, HEAVER, HOLE, MEASURES, OIL, POT, SACK, SCUTTLE, TAR, TIT

COCONUT – BUTTER, ICE, MATTING, OIL, PALM, SHY

COFFEE – BAG, BAR, CUP, HOUSE, MILL, MORNING, NUT, SHOP, TABLE, TREE

COLD – CALL, CHISEL, CREAM, CUTS, DUCK, FEET, FRAME, FRONT, SHOULDER, SNAP, SORE, STORAGE, SWEAT, TURKEY, WAR, WARRIOR, WAVE, WORK

COLLECTIVE – AGREEMENT, BARGAINING, FARM, FRUIT, NOUN, OWNERSHIP, SECURITY, UNCONSCIOUS

COLORADO – BEETLE, DESERT, SPRINGS

COLOUR – BAR, CODE, CONTRAST, FILTER, GUARD, INDEX, LINE, PHASE, SCHEME, SERGEANT, SUPPLEMENT, TEMPERATURE

COME – ABOUT, ACROSS, ALONG, AT, AWAY, BETWEEN, BY, FORWARD, IN, INTO, OF, OFF, OUT, OVER, ROUND, THROUGH, TO, UP, UPON

COMIC – OPERA, STRIP

COMMAND – GUIDANCE, MODULE, PAPER, PERFORMANCE, POST

COMMERCIAL – ART, BANK, COLLEGE, PAPER, TRAVELLER, VEHICLE

COMMON – COLD, DENOMINATOR, ENTRANCE, ERA, FACTOR, FEE, FRACTION, GOOD, GROUND, KNOWLEDGE, LAW, MARKET, NOUN, ROOM, SENSE, STOCK, TIME

COMMUNITY – CARE, CENTRE, CHEST, SERVICE, SINGING

COMPOUND – EYE, FLOWER, FRACTION, FRACTURE, INTEREST, LEAF, NUMBER, SENTENCE, TIME

CON – AMORE, BRIO, DOLORE, ESPRESSIONE, FUOCO, MAN, MOTO, ROD, SORDINO, SPIRITO, TRICK

CONTINENTAL – BREAKFAST, CLIMATE, DIVIDE, DRIFT, QUILT, SHELF, SYSTEM

CORAL – FERN, REEF, SEA, SNAKE, TREE

CORN – BORER, BREAD, BUNTING, DOLLY, EXCHANGE, FACTOR, LAWS, LILY, MARIGOLD, MEAL, OIL, PONE, POPPY, ROSE, ROW, SALAD, SHOCK, SHUCK, SILK, WHISKY

CORONA – AUSTRALIS, BOREALIS, DISCHARGE

COTTAGE – CHEESE, FLAT, HOSPITAL, INDUSTRY, LOAF, PIANO, PIE

COTTON – BELT, BUSH, CAKE, CANDY, FLANNEL, GRASS, ON, PICKER, SEDGE, STAINER, TO, WASTE, WOOL

COUGH – DROP, MIXTURE, UP

COUNTRY – CLUB, CODE, COUSIN, DANCE, HOUSE, MUSIC, SEAT

COURT – CARD, CIRCULAR, DRESS, MARTIAL, ROLL, SHOE

COVER – CROP, GIRL, NOTE, POINT, VERSION

CRASH – BARRIER, DIVE, HELMET, OUT, PAD

CREAM – CHEESE, CRACKER, PUFF, SAUCE, SODA, TEA

CREDIT – ACCOUNT, CARD, LINE, RATING, SQUEEZE, STANDING

CROCODILE — BIRD, CLIP, RIVER, TEARS

CRYSTAL — BALL, GAZING, MICROPHONE, PALACE, PICK-UP, SET, VIOLET

CUCKOO — BEE, CLOCK, SHRIKE, SPIT

CURTAIN — CALL, LECTURE, SPEECH, WALL

CUSTARD — APPLE, PIE, POWDER

CUT — ACROSS, ALONG, DOWN, GLASS, IN, OFF, OUT, STRING, UP

CUTTY — GRASS, SARK, STOOL

DANISH — BLUE, LOAF, PASTRY

DARK — AGES, CONTINENT, GLASSES, HORSE, LANTERN, REACTION, STAR

DAVY — JONES, LAMP

DAY — BED, LILY, NAME, NURSERY, RELEASE, RETURN, ROOM, SCHOOL, SHIFT, TRIP

DE — FACTO, FIDE, LUXE, PROFUNDIS, RIGUEUR, TROP

DEAD — BEAT, CENTRE, DUCK, END, FINISH, HAND, HEART, HEAT, LETTER, LOSS, MARCH, SEA, SET, WEIGHT

DEATH — ADDER, CAP, CELL, CERTIFICATE, DUTY, GRANT, KNELL, MASK, PENALTY, RATE, RATTLE, RAY, ROW, SEAT, VALLEY, WARRANT, WISH

DECIMAL — CLASSIFICATION, CURRENCY, FRACTION, PLACE, POINT, SYSTEM

DECK — CHAIR, HAND, OVER, TENNIS

DENTAL — CLINIC, FLOSS, HYGIENE, HYGIENIST, NURSE, PLAQUE, SURGEON

DESERT — BOOTS, COOLER, ISLAND, LYNX, OAK, PEA, RAT, SOIL

DIAMOND — ANNIVERSARY, BIRD, JUBILEE, POINT, SNAKE, WEDDING, WILLOW

DINNER — JACKET, LADY, SERVICE

DIPLOMATIC — BAG, CORPS, IMMUNITY, SERVICE

DIRECT — ACCESS, ACTION, EVIDENCE, LABOUR, METHOD, OBJECT, QUESTION, SPEECH

DISC — BRAKE, FLOWER, HARROW, JOCKEY, PLOUGH, WHEEL

DISPATCH — BOX, CASE, RIDER

DOG — BISCUIT, BOX, COLLAR, DAYS, FENNEL, HANDLER, LATIN, PADDLE, ROSE, STAR, TAG, VIOLET

DONKEY — DERBY, ENGINE, JACKET, VOTE

DOUBLE — AGENT, BACK, BAR, BASS, BASSOON, BILL, BOND, CHIN, CREAM, CROSS, DUTCH, ENTENDRE, ENTRY, EXPOSURE, FAULT, FIRST, GLAZING, GLOUCESTER, KNIT, KNITTING, NEGATION, NEGATIVE, PNEUMONIA, STANDARD, TAKE, TALK, TIME, UP

DOWN — PAYMENT, TIME, UNDER

DRAWING — BOARD, CARD, PIN, ROOM

DRESS — CIRCLE, COAT, DOWN, PARADE, REHEARSAL, SHIELD, SHIRT, SUIT, UNIFORM, UP

DRESSING — CASE, GOWN, ROOM, STATION, TABLE

DROP — AWAY, CANNON, CURTAIN, FORGE, GOAL, HAMMER, KICK, LEAF, OFF, SCONE, SHOT, TANK

DRUM — BRAKE, MAJOR, MAJORETTE, OUT, UP

DRY — BATTERY, CELL, DISTILLATION, DOCK, ICE, MARTINI, MEASURE, NURSE, OUT, ROT, RUN, UP

DUST — BOWL, COAT, COVER, DEVIL, DOWN, JACKET, SHOT, STORM

DUTCH — AUCTION, BARN, CAP, CHEESE, COURAGE, DOLL, DOOR, ELM, MEDICINE, OVEN, TREAT, UNCLE

EAR — LOBE, PIERCING, SHELL, TRUMPET

EARLY — BIRD, CLOSING, WARNING

EARTH — CLOSET, MOTHER, PILLAR, RETURN, SCIENCE, UP, WAX

EASTER — CACTUS, EGG, ISLAND, LILY

EASY — CHAIR, GAME, MEAT, MONEY, STREET

EGG — CUP, ROLL, SLICE, SPOON, TIMER, TOOTH, WHITE

ELECTRIC — BLANKET, BLUE, CHAIR, CHARGE, CONSTANT, CURRENT, EEL, EYE, FIELD, FIRE, FURNACE, GUITAR, HARE, NEEDLE, ORGAN, POTENTIAL, RAY, SHOCK, STORM

ELEPHANT — BIRD, GRASS, SEAL, SHREW

EVENING — CLASS, DRESS, PRIMROSE, STAR

EX — CATHEDRA, DIVIDEND, GRATIA, LIBRIS, OFFICIO

EYE — CONTACT, DOG, RHYME, SHADOW, SOCKET, SPLICE

FACE — CLOTH, OUT, PACK, POWDER, VALUE

FAIR — COPY, GAME, ISLE, PLAY, RENT, SEX

FAIRY — CYCLE, GODMOTHER, LIGHTS, PENGUIN, RING, SHRIMP, SWALLOW, TALE

FALL — ABOUT, AMONG, AWAY, BACK, BEHIND, DOWN, FOR, GUY, IN, OFF, ON, OVER, THROUGH, TO

FALSE — ALARM, COLOURS, DAWN, IMPRISONMENT, PRETENCES, STEP, TEETH

FAMILY — ALLOWANCE, BENEFIT, BIBLE, CIRCLE, DOCTOR, MAN, NAME, PLANNING, SKELETON, TREE

FAN — BELT, DANCE, HEATER, MAIL, VAULTING

FANCY — DRESS, GOODS, MAN, WOMAN

FAST — FOOD, LANE, MOTION, TALK

FATHER — CHRISTMAS, CONFESSOR, TIME

FIELD — ARMY, ARTILLERY, BATTERY, CENTRE, DAY, EMISSION, EVENT, GLASSES, HOSPITAL, MARSHAL, OFFICER, SPORTS, STUDY, TRIP, WORK

FIGURE — ON, OUT, SKATING

FILM — LIBRARY, PACK, SET, STAR, STRIP

FILTER — BED, OUT, PAPER, PRESS, PUMP, TIP

FINGER — BOWL, PAINTING, POST, WAVE

FIRE — ALARM, ANT, AWAY, BRIGADE, CLAY, CONTROL, DEPARTMENT, DOOR, DRILL, ENGINE, ESCAPE, HYDRANT, INSURANCE, IRONS, RAISER, SCREEN, SHIP, STATION, WALKING, WALL, WATCHER

FIRING — LINE, ORDER, PARTY, PIN, SQUAD

FIRST — AID, BASE, CLASS, FLOOR, FRUITS, LADY, LANGUAGE, LIEUTENANT, LIGHT, MATE, NAME, NIGHT, OFFENDER, OFFICER, PERSON, POST, PRINCIPLE, READING, REFUSAL, SCHOOL, WATER

FIVE — HUNDRED, KS, NATIONS, STONES, TOWNS

FLAKE — OUT, WHITE

FLASH — BURN, CARD, ELIMINATOR, FLOOD, GUN, PHOTOGRAPHY, PHOTOLYSIS, POINT, SET, SMELTING

FLAT — CAP, KNOT, RACING, SPIN, TUNING

FLIGHT — ARROW, DECK, ENGINEER, FEATHER, FORMATION, LIEUTENANT, LINE, PATH, PLAN, RECORDER, SERGEANT, SIMULATOR, STRIP, SURGEON

FLYING — BOAT, BOMB, BRIDGE, BUTTRESS, CIRCUS, COLOURS, DOCTOR, DUTCHMAN, FISH, FOX, FROG, JIB, LEMUR, LIZARD, MARE, OFFICER, PICKET, SAUCER, SQUAD, SQUIRREL, START, WING

FOLK — DANCE, MEDICINE, MEMORY, MUSIC, SINGER, SONG, TALE, WEAVE

FOOD — ADDITIVE, CHAIN, POISONING, PROCESSOR

FOOT — BRAKE, FAULT, ROT, RULE, SOLDIER

FOREIGN — AFFAIRS, AID, BILL, CORRESPONDENT, EXCHANGE, LEGION, MINISTER, MISSION, OFFICE, SERVICE

FOUL — PLAY, SHOT, UP

FOURTH — DIMENSION, ESTATE, INTERNATIONAL, REPUBLIC, WORLD

FREE — AGENT, ASSOCIATION, CHURCH, ELECTRON, ENERGY, ENTERPRISE, FALL, FLIGHT, FORM, GIFT, HAND, HOUSE, KICK, LOVE, SPACE, SPEECH, STATE, THOUGHT, THROW, TRADE, VERSE, WILL, ZONE

FRENCH — ACADEMY, BEAN, BREAD, CHALK, CRICKET, CUFF, CURVE, DOORS, DRESSING, HORN, KISS, KNICKERS, KNOT, LEAVE, LETTER, MUSTARD, PLEAT, POLISH, SEAM, STICK, TOAST, WINDOWS

FRONT — BENCH, DOOR, LINE, MAN, MATTER

FRUIT — BAT, BODY, COCKTAIL, CUP, FLY, KNIFE, MACHINE, SALAD, SUGAR, TREE

FULL — BLOOD, BOARD, DRESS, HOUSE, MOON, NELSON, PITCH, STOP, TIME, TOSS

GALLEY — PROOF, SLAVE

GALLOWS — BIRD, HUMOUR, TREE

GAME — BIRD, CHIPS, FISH, FOWL, LAWS, PARK, POINT, THEORY, WARDEN

GARDEN — CENTRE, CITY, CRESS, FLAT, FRAME, PARTY, SNAIL, SUBURB, WARBLER

GAS — BURNER, CHAMBER, CONSTANT, ENGINE, EQUATION, FIXTURE, GANGRENE, LAWS, LIGHTER, MAIN, MANTLE, MASK, METER, OIL, OVEN, POKER, RING, STATION, TURBINE

GENERAL — ANAESTHETIC, ASSEMBLY, DELIVERY, ELECTION, HOSPITAL, PRACTITIONER, STAFF, STRIKE, SYNOD, WILL

GIN — PALACE, RUMMY, SLING

GINGER — ALE, BEER, GROUP, SNAP, UP, WINE

GIRL — FRIDAY, GUIDE, SCOUT

GIVE — AWAY, IN, OFF, ONTO, OUT, OVER, UP

GLAD — EYE, HAND, RAGS

GLOVE — BOX, COMPARTMENT, PUPPET

GOLD — BASIS, BEETLE, BRICK, CERTIFICATE, COAST, DUST, FOIL, LEAF, MEDAL, MINE, NOTE, PLATE, POINT, RECORD, RESERVE, RUSH, STANDARD, STICK

GOLDEN — AGE, ASTER, CALF, CHAIN, DELICIOUS, EAGLE, FLEECE, GATE, GOOSE, HANDSHAKE, NUMBER, OLDIE, RETRIEVER, RULE, SECTION, SYRUP

GOLF — BALL, CLUB, COURSE, LINKS

GOOD — AFTERNOON, DAY, EVENING, FRIDAY, MORNING, NIGHT, SAMARITAN, SORT, TURN

GOOSE — BARNACLE, FLESH, STEP

GRAND — CANARY, CANYON, DUCHESS, DUCHY, DUKE, FINAL, GUIGNOL, JURY, LARCENY, MAL, MARNIER, MASTER, NATIONAL, OPERA, PIANO, PRIX, SEIGNEUR, SIÈCLE, SLAM, TOUR

GRANNY — BOND, FLAT, KNOT, SMITH

GRASS — BOX, CLOTH, COURT, HOCKEY, MOTH, ROOTS, SNAKE, TREE, WIDOW

GRAVY — BOAT, TRAIN

GREASE — CUP, GUN, MONKEY

GREAT — AUK, BEAR, BRITAIN, DANE, DIVIDE, LAKES, OUSE, PLAINS, SEAL, TIT, TREK, WAR,

GREEN — BEAN, BELT, BERET, CARD, DRAGON, FINGERS, LIGHT, MONKEY, MOULD, PAPER, PEPPER, PLOVER, THUMB, TURTLE, WOODPECKER

GREGORIAN — CALENDAR, CHANT, TELESCOPE, TONE

GREY — AREA, EMINENCE, FOX, FRIAR, MARKET, MATTER, SQUIRREL, WARBLER, WHALE, WOLF

GROUND — CONTROL, COVER, ENGINEER, FLOOR, GLASS, ICE, IVY, PLAN, PLATE, PROVISIONS, RENT, RULE, SWELL

GROW — BAG, INTO, ON, UP

GUIDE — DOG, ROPE

HAIR — DRYER, FOLLICLE, GEL, LACQUER, RESTORER, SHIRT, SLIDE, SPRAY, TRIGGER

HAPPY — EVENT, HOUR, MEDIUM, RELEASE

HARD — CASH, CHEESE, COPY, CORE, COURT, DISK, FEELING, HAT, HITTER, LABOUR, LINES, ROCK, SELL, SHOULDER, STANDING

HARVEST — HOME, MITE, MOON, MOUSE

HAT — STAND, TRICK

HATCHET — JOB, MAN

HEALTH — CENTRE, FOOD, SALTS, VISITOR

HEN — HARRIER, PARTY, RUN

HIGH — ALTAR, CHURCH, COMEDY, COMMAND, COMMISSIONER, COUNTRY, COURT, DAY, EXPLOSIVE, FASHION, FIDELITY, GERMAN, HAT, HOLIDAYS, JINKS, JUMP, POINT, PRIEST, SCHOOL, SEAS, SEASON, SOCIETY, SPOT, STREET, TABLE, TEA, TECH, TECHNOLOGY, TIDE, TIME, TREASON, WATER, WIRE, WYCOMBE

HIGHLAND — CATTLE, DRESS, FLING, REGION

HIP — BATH, FLASK, JOINT, POCKET

HIT — LIST, MAN, OFF, ON, OUT, PARADE

HOLD — BACK, DOWN, FORTH, IN, OFF, ON, OUT, OVER, TOGETHER, WITH

HOLY — BIBLE, CITY, COMMUNION, DAY, FATHER, GHOST, GRAIL, ISLAND, JOE, LAND, MARY, OFFICE, ORDERS, PLACE, ROLLER, ROOD, SCRIPTURE, SEE, SEPULCHRE, SPIRIT, WAR, WATER, WEEK, WRIT

HOME — AID, COUNTIES, ECONOMICS, FARM, GROUND, GUARD, HELP, LOAN, OFFICE, PLATE, RANGE, RULE, RUN, SECRETARY, STRAIGHT, TEACHER, TRUTH, UNIT

HORSE — AROUND, BEAN, BRASS, CHESTNUT, GUARDS, LAUGH, MACKEREL, MARINE, MUSHROOM, NETTLE, OPERA, PISTOL, SENSE, TRADING

HOT — AIR, DOG, LINE, METAL, MONEY, PEPPER, POTATO, ROD, SEAT, SPOT, SPRING, STUFF, UP, ZONE

HOUSE — ARREST, GUEST, LIGHTS, MARTIN, MOTH, ORGAN, PARTY, PHYSICIAN, PLANT, SPARROW, SPIDER

HUMAN — BEING, CAPITAL, INTEREST, NATURE, RESOURCES, RIGHTS

HURRICANE — DECK, LAMP

ICE — AGE, AXE, BAG, BLOCK, CREAM, FISH, HOCKEY, HOUSE, LOLLY, MACHINE, MAN, PACK, PICK, PLANT, POINT, SHEET, SHELF, SHOW, SKATE, STATION, WATER, YACHT

ILL — FEELING, HUMOUR, TEMPER, WILL

IN — ABSENTIA, AETERNUM, CAMERA, ESSE, EXTENSO, EXTREMIS, MEMORIAM, NOMINE, PERPETUUM, PERSONAM, RE, REM, SITU, TOTO, UTERO, VACUO, VITRO, VIVO

INDIA — PAPER, PRINT, RUBBER

INDIAN — CLUB, EMPIRE, FILE, HEMP, INK, MALLOW, MILLET, MUTINY, OCEAN, RED, RESERVE, ROPE-TRICK, SUMMER

INNER — CITY, EAR, HEBRIDES, LIGHT, MAN, MONGOLIA, TUBE

INSIDE — FORWARD, JOB, LANE, TRACK

IRISH — COFFEE, MOSS, POTATO, REPUBLIC, SEA, SETTER, STEW, TERRIER, WHISKEY, WOLFHOUND

IRON — AGE, CHANCELLOR, CROSS, CURTAIN, FILINGS, GUARD, HAND, HORSE, LUNG, MAIDEN, MAN, OUT, PYRITES, RATIONS

JACK — FROST, IN, PLANE, RABBIT, ROBINSON, RUSSELL, TAR, UP

KICK — ABOUT, IN, OFF, OUT, PLEAT, TURN, UP, UPSTAIRS

KIDNEY — BEAN, MACHINE, STONE, VETCH

KNIFE — EDGE, GRINDER, PLEAT, SWITCH

LADY — BOUNTIFUL, CHAPEL, DAY, FERN, MAYORESS, MUCK, ORCHID

LAND — AGENT, BANK, BRIDGE, CRAB, FORCES, GIRL, GRANT, LINE, MINE, OFFICE, RAIL, REFORM, TAX, UP, WITH

LAST — JUDGMENT, NAME, OUT, POST, QUARTER, RITES, STRAW, SUPPER, THING

LATIN — AMERICA, CROSS, QUARTER, SQUARE

LAY — ASIDE, AWAY, BROTHER, DAYS, DOWN, FIGURE, IN, INTO, OFF, ON, OUT, OVER, READER, TO, UP

LEADING — AIRCRAFTMAN, ARTICLE, DOG, EDGE, LIGHT, MAN, NOTE, QUESTION, REINS

LEAVE — BEHIND, OFF, OUT

LEFT — BANK, WING

LEMON — BALM, CHEESE, DROP, FISH, GERANIUM, GRASS, SOLE, SQUASH, SQUEEZER, VERBENA

LETTER — BOMB, BOX, CARD

LIBERTY — BODICE, CAP, HALL, HORSE, ISLAND, SHIP

LIE — DETECTOR, DOWN, IN, TO

LIFE — ASSURANCE, BELT, BUOY, CYCLE, EXPECTANCY, FORM, GUARDS, HISTORY, INSURANCE, INTEREST, JACKET, PEER, PRESERVER, RAFT, SCIENCE, SPAN, STYLE

LIGHT — BULB, FACE, FLYWEIGHT, HEAVYWEIGHT, HORSE, INTO, METER, MIDDLEWEIGHT, MUSIC, OPERA, OUT, SHOW, UP, WELTERWEIGHT, YEAR

LIVER — FLUKE, SALTS, SAUSAGE

LIVING — DEATH, FOSSIL, PICTURE, ROOM, WAGE

LOBSTER — MOTH, NEWBURG, POT, THERMIDOR

LOCAL — ANAESTHETIC, AUTHORITY, COLOUR, GOVERNMENT, TIME

LONE — HAND, WOLF

LONG — ARM, BEACH, FACE, HAUL, HOP, ISLAND, JENNY, JOHNS, JUMP, PARLIAMENT, SHOT, SUIT, TOM, VACATION, WEEKEND

LOOK — AFTER, BACK, DOWN, ON, OVER, THROUGH, UP

LOOSE — CHANGE, COVER, END

LORD — ADVOCATE, CHAMBERLAIN, CHANCELLOR, LIEUTENANT, MAYOR, MUCK, PROTECTOR, PROVOST

LOUNGE — LIZARD, SUIT

LOVE — AFFAIR, APPLE, CHILD, FEAST, GAME, KNOT, LETTER, LIFE, MATCH, NEST, POTION, SEAT, SET

LOW — CHURCH, COMEDY, COUNTRIES, FREQUENCY, PROFILE, TECH, TECHNOLOGY, TIDE

LUNAR — CAUSTIC, ECLIPSE, MODULE, MONTH, YEAR

LUNCHEON — CLUB, MEAT, VOUCHER

MACHINE — BOLT, GUN, HEAD, SHOP, TOOL

MACKEREL — BREEZE, SHARK, SKY

MAGIC — CARPET, EYE, LANTERN, MUSHROOM, NUMBER, SQUARE

MAGNETIC — CIRCUIT, COMPASS, CONSTANT, DISK, EQUATOR, FIELD, FLUX, INDUCTION, INK, LENS, MOMENT, NEEDLE, NORTH, PICK-UP, POLE, STORM, TAPE

MAIDEN — NAME, OVER, VOYAGE

MAIL — DROP, ORDER

MAKE — AFTER, AWAY, BELIEVE, FOR, OF, OFF, OUT, OVER, WITH

MALT — EXTRACT, LIQUOR, WHISKY

MANDARIN — CHINESE, COLLAR, DUCK

MARCH — BROWN, HARE, PAST

MARKET — GARDEN, GARDENING, ORDER, PRICE, RENT, RESEARCH, SHARE, TOWN, VALUE

MARRIAGE — BUREAU, GUIDANCE

MARSH — ELDER, FERN, FEVER, GAS, HARRIER, HAWK, HEN, MALLOW, MARIGOLD, ORCHID, TIT

MASTER — BUILDER, CYLINDER, KEY, RACE, SERGEANT

MATINÉE — COAT, IDOL

MAUNDY — MONEY, THURSDAY

MAY — APPLE, BEETLE, BLOBS, BLOSSOM, DAY, QUEEN, TREE

MECHANICAL — ADVANTAGE, DRAWING, ENGINEERING, INSTRUMENT

MEDICAL — CERTIFICATE, EXAMINATION, EXAMINER, JURISPRUDENCE

MEDICINE — BALL, CHEST, LODGE, MAN

MELBA — SAUCE, TOAST

MEMORY — BANK, MAPPING, SPAN, TRACE

MENTAL — AGE, BLOCK, CRUELTY, DISORDER, HANDICAP

MERCHANT — BANK, NAVY, PRINCE

MERCY — FLIGHT, KILLING, SEAT

MESS — ABOUT, HALL, JACKET, KIT

MICHAELMAS — DAISY, TERM

MICKEY — FINN, MOUSE

MIDDLE — AGE, AGES, C, CLASS, EAR, EAST, MANAGEMENT, NAME, SCHOOL, TEMPLE

MIDNIGHT — BLUE, SUN

MIDSUMMER — DAY, MADNESS

MILITARY — ACADEMY, HONOURS, LAW, ORCHID, PACE, POLICE

MILK — BAR, CHOCOLATE, FEVER, FLOAT, LEG, PUDDING, PUNCH, ROUND, RUN, SHAKE, STOUT, TOOTH

MINT — BUSH, JULEP, SAUCE

MINUTE — GUN, HAND, MARK, STEAK

MIRROR — CANON, CARP, FINISH, IMAGE, LENS, SYMMETRY, WRITING

MITRE — BLOCK, BOX, GEAR, JOINT, SQUARE

MIXED — BAG, BLESSING, DOUBLES, ECONOMY, FARMING, GRILL, MARRIAGE, METAPHOR

MONEY — MARKET, ORDER, SPIDER, SUPPLY

MONKEY — BREAD, BUSINESS, CLIMB, FLOWER, JACKET, NUT, ORCHID, PUZZLE, SUIT, TRICKS, WRENCH

MORNING — COAT, DRESS, SICKNESS, STAR, TEA, WATCH

MOSQUITO — BOAT, HAWK, NET

MOSS — AGATE, LAYER, PINK, ROSE, STITCH

MOTHER — COUNTRY, GOOSE, HUBBARD, LODE, SHIP, SHIPTON, SUPERIOR, TONGUE, WIT

MOTOR — CARAVAN, DRIVE, GENERATOR, SCOOTER, VEHICLE, VESSEL

MOUNTAIN — ASH, CAT, CHAIN, DEVIL, GOAT, LAUREL, LION, RANGE, SHEEP, SICKNESS

MUD — BATH, DAUBER, FLAT, HEN, MAP, PIE, PUPPY, TURTLE

MUSTARD — GAS, OIL, PLASTER

MYSTERY — PLAY, TOUR

NANSEN — BOTTLE, PASSPORT

NARROW — BOAT, GAUGE, SEAS

NATIONAL — ACCOUNTING, AGREEMENT, ANTHEM, ASSEMBLY, ASSISTANCE, DEBT, FRONT, GALLERY, GRID, SERVICE, TRUST

NERVE — CELL, CENTRE, FIBRE, GAS, IMPULSE

NEW — BROOM, FOREST, GUINEA, LOOK, MATHS, MOON, PENNY, TESTAMENT, TOWN, WAVE, WORLD, YEAR, YORK, ZEALAND

NEWS — AGENCY, CONFERENCE, VENDOR

NIGHT — BLINDNESS, DANCER, FIGHTER, NURSE, OWL, ROBE, SAFE, SCHOOL, SHIFT, WATCH, WATCHMAN

NINETEENTH — HOLE, MAN

NOBLE — ART, GAS, SAVAGE

NORFOLK — ISLAND, JACKET, TERRIER

NOSE — CONE, DIVE, OUT, RAG, RING

NUCLEAR — BOMB, ENERGY, FAMILY, FISSION, FUEL, FUSION, ISOMER, PHYSICS, POWER, REACTION, REACTOR, THRESHOLD, WINTER

NURSERY — RHYME, SCHOOL, SLOPES, STAKES

OFF — CHANCE, COLOUR, KEY, LIMITS, LINE, SEASON

OIL — BEETLE, CAKE, DRUM, HARDENING, PAINT, PAINTING, PALM, RIG, RIVERS, SHALE, SLICK, VARNISH, WELL

OLD — BAILEY, BILL, BIRD, BOY, CONTEMPTIBLES, COUNTRY, GIRL, GOLD, GUARD, HAND, HAT, LADY, MAID, MAN, MOON, NICK, PRETENDER, SCHOOL, STYLE, TESTAMENT, WORLD

OLIVE — BRANCH, BROWN, CROWN, DRAB, GREEN, OIL

ON — DIT, KEY, LINE

OPEN — AIR, BOOK, CHAIN, CIRCUIT, COURT, DAY, DOOR, HOUSE, LETTER, MARKET, PRISON, PUNCTUATION, SANDWICH, SESAME, UNIVERSITY, UP, VERDICT

OPERA — BUFFA, CLOAK, GLASSES, HAT, HOUSE, SERIA

OPIUM — DEN, POPPY, WARS

ORANGE — BLOSSOM, PEEL, PEKOE, STICK

ORDINARY — LEVEL, RATING, RAY, SEAMAN, SHARES

OXFORD — ACCENT, BAGS, BLUE, ENGLISH, FRAME, GROUP, MOVEMENT

OYSTER — BED, CRAB, PINK, PLANT, WHITE

PACK — ANIMAL, DRILL, ICE, IN, RAT, UP

PALM — BEACH, CIVET, OFF, OIL, SUGAR, SUNDAY, VAULTING, WINE

PANAMA — CANAL, CITY, HAT

PANIC — BOLT, BUTTON, BUYING, GRASS, STATIONS

PAPER — CHASE, FILIGREE, MONEY, MULBERRY, NAUTILUS, OVER, TAPE, TIGER

PAR — AVION, EXCELLENCE, VALUE

PARISH — CLERK, COUNCIL, PUMP, REGISTER

PARTY — LINE, MAN, POLITICS, WALL

PASSING — BELL, NOTE, SHOT

PASSION — FRUIT, PLAY, SUNDAY, WEEK

PATCH — BOARD, POCKET, QUILT, TEST

PAY — BACK, BED, DIRT, DOWN, FOR, IN, OFF, OUT, TELEVISION, UP

PEACE — CORPS, OFFERING, PIPE, RIVER, SIGN

PEG — CLIMBING, DOWN, LEG, OUT, TOP

PEN — FRIEND, NAME, PAL

PENNY — ARCADE, BLACK, WHISTLE

PER — ANNUM, CAPITA, CENT, CONTRA, DIEM, MENSEM, MILL, PRO, SE

PERSIAN — BLINDS, CARPET, CAT, EMPIRE, GREYHOUND, GULF, LAMB, MELON

PETIT — BOURGEOIS, FOUR, JURY, LARCENY, MAL, POINT

PETROL — BOMB, PUMP, STATION

PETTY — CASH, JURY, LARCENY, OFFICER, SESSIONS

PICTURE — CARD, HAT, HOUSE, MOULDING, PALACE, WINDOW, WRITING

PIECE — GOODS, OUT, RATE

PILLOW — BLOCK, FIGHT, LACE, LAVA, SHAM, TALK

PILOT — BALLOON, BIRD, BISCUIT, CLOTH, ENGINE, FILM, FISH, HOUSE, LAMP, LIGHT, OFFICER, PLANT, STUDY, WHALE

PIN — CURL, DOWN, JOINT, MONEY, RAIL, TUCK, WRENCH

PINE — CONE, END, MARTEN, NEEDLE, TAR

PINK — ELEPHANTS, GIN, NOISE, SALMON, SLIP

PIPE — CLEANER, DOWN, DREAM, MAJOR, ORGAN, ROLL, UP

PLACE — CARD, KICK, NAME, SETTING

PLAIN — CHOCOLATE, CLOTHES, FLOUR, SAILING, TEXT

PLAY — ALONG, DOWN, OFF, ON, OUT, UP, WITH

PLYMOUTH — BRETHREN, COLONY, ROCK

POCKET — BATTLESHIP, BILLIARDS, BOROUGH, GOPHER, MONEY, MOUSE

POETIC — JUSTICE, LICENCE

PONY — EXPRESS, TREKKING

POOR — BOX, LAW, MOUTH, RELATION, WHITE

POP — ART, OFF, SHOP

POST — CHAISE, HOC, HORN, HOUSE, MERIDIEM, OFFICE, ROAD, TOWN

POT — CHEESE, LIQUOR, MARIGOLD, ON, PLANT, ROAST, SHOT, STILL

POTATO — BEETLE, BLIGHT, CHIP, CRISP

POWDER — BLUE, BURN, COMPACT, FLASK, HORN, KEG, MONKEY, PUFF, ROOM

POWER — CUT, DIVE, DRILL, FACTOR, LINE, PACK, PLANT, POINT, POLITICS, STATION, STEERING, STRUCTURE

PRAIRIE — DOG, OYSTER, PROVINCES, SCHOONER, SOIL, TURNIP, WOLF

PRAYER — BEADS, BOOK, MEETING, RUG, SHAWL, WHEEL

PRESS — AGENCY, AGENT, BOX, CONFERENCE, GALLERY, GANG, RELEASE, STUD

PRESSURE — CABIN, COOKER, DRAG, GAUGE, GRADIENT, GROUP, HEAD, POINT, SUIT

PRICE — COMMISSION, CONTROL, DISCRIMINATION, RING, SUPPORT, TAG, WAR

PRICKLY — ASH, HEAT, PEAR, POPPY

PRIME — COST, MERIDIAN, MINISTER, MOVER, NUMBER, RATE, TIME, VERTICAL

PRIVATE — BAR, BILL, COMPANY, DETECTIVE, ENTERPRISE, EYE, HOTEL, INCOME, LANGUAGE, LIFE, MEMBER, PARTS, PATIENT, PRACTICE, PRESS, PROPERTY, SCHOOL, SECRETARY, SECTOR

PRIVY — CHAMBER, COUNCIL, PURSE, SEAL

PRIZE — COURT, MONEY, RING

PRO — FORMA, PATRIA, RATA, TEMPORE

PUBLIC — BAR, BILL, COMPANY, CONVENIENCE, CORPORATION, DEBT, DEFENDER, ENEMY, ENTERPRISE, EXPENDITURE, FOOTPATH, GALLERY, HOLIDAY, HOUSE, LAW, NUISANCE, OPINION, OWNERSHIP, PROSECUTOR, RELATIONS, SCHOOL, SECTOR, SERVANT, SERVICE, SPEAKING, SPENDING, TRANSPORT

PUFF — ADDER, PASTRY

PULL — ABOUT, BACK, DOWN, IN, OFF, ON, OUT, THROUGH, TOGETHER, UP

PURPLE — EMPEROR, GALLINULE, HEART, MEDIC, PATCH

PUSH — ABOUT, ALONG, BUTTON, IN, OFF, ON, THROUGH

PUT — ABOUT, ACROSS, ASIDE, AWAY, BACK, BY, DOWN, FORTH, FORWARD, IN, OFF, ON, OUT, OVER, THROUGH, UP, UPON

QUANTUM — LEAP, MECHANICS, NUMBER, STATE, STATISTICS, THEORY

QUARTER — CRACK, DAY, GRAIN, HORSE, NOTE, PLATE, ROUND, SECTION, SESSIONS, TONE

QUEEN — BEE, CONSORT, DOWAGER, MAB, MOTHER, OLIVE, POST, REGENT, REGNANT, SUBSTANCE

QUEER — FISH, STREET

QUESTION — MARK, MASTER, TIME

RAIN — CHECK, GAUGE, SHADOW, TREE

REAL — ALE, ESTATE, LIFE, NUMBER, PART, PRESENCE, PROPERTY, TENNIS, WAGES

RED — ADMIRAL, ALGAE, BAG, BARK, BEDS, BIDDY, CARPET, CEDAR, CROSS, DUSTER, DWARF, ENSIGN, FLAG, HAT, HEAT, HERRING, INDIAN, MEAT, MULLET, PEPPER, RAG, RIVER, ROSE, SALMON, SEA, SETTER, SHANK, SHIFT, SNAPPER, SPIDER, SQUIRREL, TAPE

RES — ADJUDICATA, GESTAE, JUDICATA, PUBLICA

RIGHT — ABOUT, ANGLE, ASCENSION, AWAY, HONOURABLE, OFF, ON, REVEREND, WING

ROCK — BOTTOM, CAKE, CLIMBING, GARDEN, PLANT, SALT, STEADY

ROLLER — BEARING, CAPTION, COASTER, DERBY, SKATE, TOWEL

ROMAN — ARCH, CALENDAR, CANDLE, CATHOLIC, CATHOLICISM, COLLAR, EMPIRE, HOLIDAY, LAW, MILE, NOSE, NUMERALS

ROOF — GARDEN, RACK

ROOM — SERVICE, TEMPERATURE

ROOT — BEER, CANAL, CROP, NODULE, OUT, POSITION, UP

ROTARY — CLOTHESLINE, CLUB, ENGINE, PLOUGH, PRESS, PUMP

ROUGH — COLLIE, DIAMOND, OUT, PASSAGE, SPIN, STUFF, UP

ROUND — ANGLE, CLAM, DANCE, DOWN, HAND, OFF, ON, OUT, ROBIN, TABLE, TOP, TRIP, UP

ROYAL — ACADEMY, ASSENT, BLUE, BURGH, COMMISSION, DUKE, ENGINEERS, FLUSH, HIGHNESS, ICING, JELLY, MARINES, NAVY, PURPLE, ROAD, STANDARD, TENNIS, WARRANT, WORCESTER

RUBBER — BAND, BRIDGE, CEMENT, CHEQUE, GOODS, PLANT, STAMP, TREE

RUN — ACROSS, AFTER, ALONG, AROUND, AWAY, DOWN, IN, INTO, OFF, ON, OUT, OVER, THROUGH, TO, UP

RUNNING — BOARD, COMMENTARY, HEAD, LIGHT, MATE, REPAIRS, RIGGING, STITCH

RUSSIAN — DRESSING, EMPIRE, REVOLUTION, ROULETTE, SALAD, WOLFHOUND

SAFETY — BELT, CATCH, CHAIN, CURTAIN, FACTOR, FILM, FUSE, GLASS, LAMP, MATCH, NET, PIN, RAZOR, VALVE

SALAD — DAYS, DRESSING

SALLY — ARMY, LUNN

SALT — AWAY, BATH, CAKE, DOME, FLAT, LAKE, LICK, MARSH, OUT, PORK

SAND — BAR, CASTLE, EEL, FLEA, HOPPER, LANCE, LEEK, LIZARD, MARTIN, PAINTING, SHRIMP, TABLE, TRAP, VIPER, WASP, WEDGE, YACHT

SANDWICH — BOARD, CAKE, COURSE, ISLANDS, MAN

SAUSAGE — DOG, ROLL

SCARLET — FEVER, HAT, LETTER, PIMPERNEL, RUNNER, WOMAN

SCATTER — DIAGRAM, PIN, RUG

SCOTCH — BROTH, EGG, MIST, PANCAKE, SNAP, TAPE, TERRIER

SCRAPE — IN, THROUGH, TOGETHER

SCRATCH — PAD, SHEET, TEST, TOGETHER, VIDEO

SECOND — CHILDHOOD, CLASS, COMING, COUSIN, FIDDLE, FLOOR, GENERATION, GROWTH, HAND, LANGUAGE, LIEUTENANT, MATE, NAME, NATURE, READING, SIGHT, STRING, THOUGHT, WIND

SECONDARY — COLOUR, EMISSION, PICKET, PROCESSES, QUALITIES, SCHOOL, STRESS

SECRET — AGENT, POLICE, SERVICE, SOCIETY

SEE — ABOUT, INTO, OF, OFF, OUT, OVER, THROUGH

SENIOR — AIRCRAFTMAN, CITIZEN, MANAGEMENT, SERVICE

SERVICE — AREA, CHARGE, INDUSTRY, MODULE, ROAD, STATION

SET — ABOUT, AGAINST, ASIDE, BACK, DOWN, FORTH, IN, OFF, ON, OUT, PIECE, POINT, SQUARE, THEORY, TO, UP, UPON

SETTLE — DOWN, FOR, IN, WITH

SHAKE — DOWN, OFF, UP
SHEET — ANCHOR, BEND, DOWN, LIGHTNING, METAL, MUSIC
SHOP — AROUND, ASSISTANT, FLOOR, STEWARD
SHORE — BIRD, LEAVE, PATROL
SHORT — CIRCUIT, CUT, FUSE, HEAD, LIST, ODDS, SHRIFT, STORY, STRAW, TIME, WAVE
SHOW — BILL, BUSINESS, CARD, COPY, OFF, STOPPER, TRIAL, UP
SIAMESE — CAT, TWINS
SICK — LEAVE, LIST, NOTE, PAY
SIGN — AWAY, IN, LANGUAGE, MANUAL, OFF, ON, OUT, UP
SINGLE — BOND, CREAM, DENSITY, ENTRY, FILE, TAX, THREAD, TICKET
SIT — BACK, DOWN, ON, OUT, OVER, UNDER, UP
SITTING — BULL, ROOM, TARGET, TENANT
SKI — JUMP, LIFT, PANTS, RUN, STICK, TOW
SKIN — DIVING, EFFECT, FLICK, FOOD, FRICTION, GAME, GRAFT, TEST
SLAVE — ANT, COAST, CYLINDER, DRIVER, SHIP, STATE, TRADE
SLIDE — FASTENER, GUITAR, OVER, REST, RULE, TROMBONE, VALVE
SLIP — GAUGE, RAIL, RING, ROAD, STEP, STITCH, UP
SLOW — BURN, HANDCLAP, MARCH, MOTION, TIME
SMALL — ARMS, BEER, CHANGE, FRY, HOURS, INTESTINE, SLAM, TALK
SMART — ALECK, CARD, MONEY, SET
SMOKE — BOMB, OUT, SCREEN, TREE
SNEAK — PREVIEW, THIEF
SOB — SISTER, STORY, STUFF
SOCIAL — CLIMBER, SCIENCE, SECRETARY, SECURITY, SERVICES, STUDIES, WELFARE, WORK
SODA — ASH, BISCUIT, BREAD, FOUNTAIN, JERK, LIME, NITRE, POP, SIPHON, WATER
SOFT — DRINK, FRUIT, FURNISHINGS, GOODS, LANDING, LINE, OPTION, PORN, SELL, SOAP, SPOT, TOP, TOUCH
SOLAR — ECLIPSE, FLARE, FURNACE, HEATING, MONTH, MYTH, PANEL, PLEXUS, POWER, SYSTEM, WIND, YEAR
SOUND — BARRIER, BOW, CHECK, EFFECT, HEAD, HOLE, MIXER, OFF, OUT, WAVE
SOUR — CHERRY, CREAM, GOURD, GRAPES, GUM, MASH
SPACE — AGE, BLANKET, CADET, CAPSULE, CHARACTER, HEATER, INVADERS, OPERA, PLATFORM, PROBE, SHUTTLE, STATION
SPAGHETTI — JUNCTION, WESTERN
SPARK — CHAMBER, COIL, EROSION, GAP, OFF, PLUG, TRANSMITTER
SPEAK — FOR, OUT, TO, UP
SPECIAL — ASSESSMENT, BRANCH, CASE, CONSTABLE, DELIVERY, EFFECTS, JURY, LICENCE, PLEADING, PRIVILEGE, SCHOOL, SORT
SPEED — LIMIT, TRAP, UP
SPINNING — JENNY, MULE, TOP, WHEEL
SPIRIT — GUM, LAMP, LEVEL, VARNISH
SPLIT — CANE, DECISION, INFINITIVE, PEA, PERSONALITY, SECOND, SHIFT, TIN, UP

SPONGE — BAG, BATH, CAKE, CLOTH, DOWN
SPORTS — CAR, COAT, JACKET, SHIRT
SPRING — BALANCE, CHICKEN, FEVER, LOCK, MATTRESS, ONION, ROLL, TIDE
SPUN — SILK, SUGAR, YARN
SQUARE — AWAY, BRACKET, DANCE, LEG, MEAL, NUMBER, OFF, ROOT, UP
STABLE — DOOR, FLY, LAD
STAFF — ASSOCIATION, COLLEGE, CORPORAL, NURSE, OFFICER, SERGEANT
STAG — BEETLE, PARTY
STAGE — DIRECTION, DOOR, EFFECT, FRIGHT, LEFT, MANAGER, RIGHT, WHISPER
STAMP — ACT, COLLECTING, DUTY, MILL, OUT
STAND — BY, DOWN, FOR, IN, OIL, ON, OUT, OVER, PAT, TO, UP
STAR — CHAMBER, CONNECTION, GRASS, SAPPHIRE, SHELL, STREAM, SYSTEM, THISTLE, WARS
STATUS — QUO, SYMBOL
STEEL — BAND, BLUE, GREY, GUITAR, WOOL
STICK — AROUND, AT, BY, DOWN, INSECT, OUT, TO, TOGETHER, WITH
STICKY — END, WICKET
STIRRUP — BONE, CUP, PUMP
STOCK — CAR, CERTIFICATE, COMPANY, EXCHANGE, FARM, MARKET
STOCKING — CAP, FILLER, FRAME, MASK, STITCH
STORAGE — BATTERY, CAPACITY, DEVICE, HEATER
STORM — BELT, CENTRE, CLOUD, COLLAR, CONE, DOOR, GLASS, LANTERN, PETREL, WARNING, WINDOW
STRAIGHT — BAT, FACE, FIGHT, FLUSH, MAN, OFF, UP
STRAWBERRY — BLONDE, BUSH, MARK, TOMATO, TREE
STREET — ARAB, CREDIBILITY, CRY, DOOR, PIANO, THEATRE, VALUE
STRIKE — DOWN, FAULT, NOTE, OFF, OUT, PAY, THROUGH, UP
STRING — ALONG, BAND, BASS, BEAN, COURSE, LINE, ORCHESTRA, QUARTET, TIE, VARIABLE
STRIP — CARTOON, CLUB, CROPPING, LIGHTING, MILL, MINING, OUT, POKER
SUGAR — BEET, CANDY, CANE, CORN, DADDY, DIABETES, LOAF, MAPLE
SUMMER — HOLIDAY, PUDDING, SCHOOL, SOLSTICE, TIME
SUN — BATH, BEAR, BITTERN, BLIND, BLOCK, DANCE, DECK, DISC, KING, LAMP, LOUNGE
SUPREME — BEING, COMMANDER, COURT, SACRIFICE
SURFACE — MAIL, NOISE, PLATE, STRUCTURE, TENSION
SWAN — DIVE, MAIDEN, NECK, SONG
SWEAT — GLAND, OFF, OUT, SHIRT, SUIT
SWEET — BASIL, BAY, CHERRY, CHESTNUT, CICELY, CIDER, CLOVER, CORN, FERN, FLAG, GALE, GUM, MARJORAM, MARTEN, OIL, PEA, PEPPER, POTATO, SHOP, TOOTH, WILLIAM, WOODRUFF
SWISS — CHARD, CHEESE, GUARD, MUSLIN, ROLL, TOURNAMENT
TABLE — BAY, D'HOTE, LICENCE, MONEY, MOUNTAIN, NAPKIN, SALT, TALK, TENNIS, WINE
TAIL — COAT, COVERT, END, FAN, GATE, OFF, OUT

TAKE — ABACK, AFTER, APART, AWAY, BACK, DOWN, FOR, IN, OFF, ON, OUT, OVER, TO, UP

TALK — ABOUT, AT, BACK, DOWN, INTO, OUT, ROUND, SHOW

TANK — ENGINE, FARMING, TOP, TRAP, UP, WAGON

TAX — AVOIDANCE, DISC, EVASION, EXILE, HAVEN, RATE, RETURN, SHELTER

TEA — BAG, BISCUIT, CLOTH, COSY, GARDEN, GOWN, LEAF, PARTY, ROSE, SERVICE, TOWEL, TROLLEY

TEAR — AWAY, DOWN, DUCT, GAS, INTO, OFF, SHEET

TELEPHONE — BOX, DIRECTORY, NUMBER

TERRA — ALBA, COTTA, FIRMA, INCOGNITA, SIGILLATA

TEST — ACT, BAN, CASE, MARKETING, MATCH, PAPER, PILOT, TUBE

THIRD — CLASS, DEGREE, DIMENSION, ESTATE, EYELID, MAN, PARTY, PERSON, READING, REICH, WORLD

THROW — ABOUT, IN, OFF, OUT, OVER, TOGETHER, UP, WEIGHT

TIME — BOMB, CAPSULE, CLOCK, IMMEMORIAL, MACHINE, SERIES, SHARING, SHEET, SIGNATURE, SWITCH, TRIAL, ZONE

TIN — CAN, GOD, HAT, LIZZIE, PLATE, SOLDIER, WHISTLE

TITLE — DEED, PAGE, ROLE

TOILET — PAPER, SET, SOAP, TRAINING, WATER

TONE — CLUSTER, COLOUR, CONTROL, DOWN, LANGUAGE, POEM, ROW, UP

TOP — BOOT, BRASS, DOG, DRAWER, END, GEAR, HAT, MANAGEMENT, OFF, OUT, UP

TORQUE — CONVERTER, METER, SPANNER, WRENCH

TOUCH — FOOTBALL, JUDGE, OFF, UP

TOWN — CLERK, CRIER, GAS, HALL, HOUSE, MEETING, PLANNING

TRACK — DOWN, EVENT, MEET, RECORD, ROD, SHOE

TRADE — ACCEPTANCE, CYCLE, DISCOUNT, GAP, JOURNAL, NAME, ON, PLATE, SCHOOL, SECRET, UNION, WIND

TRAFFIC — COP, COURT, ISLAND, JAM, LIGHT, OFFICER, PATTERN, WARDEN

TREASURY — BENCH, BILL, BOND, CERTIFICATE, NOTE, TAG

TRENCH — COAT, FEVER, FOOT, KNIFE, MORTAR, MOUTH, WARFARE

TRIPLE — ALLIANCE, BOND, ENTENTE, JUMP, POINT, TIME

TURKISH — BATH, COFFEE, DELIGHT, EMPIRE, TOBACCO, TOWEL

TURN — AGAINST, AWAY, BRIDGE, DOWN, IN, OFF, ON, OUT, OVER, TO, UP

TWELFTH — DAY, MAN, NIGHT

TWIN — BED, BILL, TOWN

UMBRELLA — BIRD, PINE, PLANT, STAND, TREE

UNION — CARD, JACK

UNIT — COST, FACTOR, PRICE, TRUST

UNITED — KINGDOM, NATIONS, PARTY, PROVINCES

VACUUM — CLEANER, FLASK

VALUE — ADDED, DATE, JUDGMENT

VENETIAN — BLIND, GLASS, RED

VENTURE — CAPITAL, SCOUT

VICAR — APOSTOLIC, FORANE, GENERAL

VICE — ADMIRAL, CHANCELLOR, PRESIDENT, SQUAD, VERSA

VIDEO — CASSETTE, GAME, NASTY, TAPE

VIRGIN — BIRTH, ISLANDS, MARY, WOOL

VIRGINIA — BEACH, CREEPER, DEER, REEL, STOCK

VOX — ANGELICA, HUMANA, POP, POPULI

VULGAR — FRACTION, LATIN

WALK — AWAY, INTO, OFF, OUT

WAR — BABY, BONNET, BRIDE, CHEST, CORRESPONDENT, CRIME, CRY, DANCE, GAME, MEMORIAL, OFFICE, PAINT, WHOOP

WASHING — MACHINE, POWDER, SODA

WATCH — CAP, CHAIN, COMMITTEE, FIRE, NIGHT, OUT

WEATHER — EYE, HOUSE, MAP, STATION, STRIP, VANE, WINDOW

WEDDING — BREAKFAST, CAKE, RING

WEIGH — DOWN, IN, UP

WELSH — CORGI, DRESSER, HARP, MOUNTAIN, POPPY, RABBIT, TERRIER

WET — BLANKET, CELL, DREAM, FISH, FLY, LOOK, NURSE, PACK, ROT, STEAM, SUIT

WHITE — ADMIRAL, AREA, BEAR, BIRCH, ELEPHANT, ENSIGN, FEATHER, FISH, FLAG, GOLD, HEAT, HORSE, HOUSE, KNIGHT, LADY, LEAD, LIE, LIGHT, MEAT, OUT, PAPER, PEPPER, SLAVE, SPIRIT, STICK, TIE, WHALE

WINDOW — BOX, ENVELOPE, SASH, SEAT, TAX

WINE — BAR, BOX, CELLAR, COOLER, TASTING

WING — CHAIR, COLLAR, COMMANDER, COVERT, LOADING, NUT, SHOT, TIP

WITCH — DOCTOR, HAZEL

WOLF — CUB, SPIDER, WHISTLE

WORD — ASSOCIATION, BLINDNESS, ORDER, PICTURE, PROCESSING, PROCESSOR, SQUARE

WORK — BACK, CAMP, ETHIC, FUNCTION, IN, OFF, ON, OUT, OVER, SHEET, STATION, THROUGH, UP

WORKING — BEE, CAPITAL, CLASS, DAY, DOG, DRAWING, PAPERS, PARTY, SUBSTANCE, WEEK

WRITE — DOWN, IN, OFF, OUT, UP

YELLOW — BELLY, CARD, FEVER, JACKET, PAGES, PERIL, RIVER, STREAK

YORKSHIRE — DALES, FOG, PUDDING, TERRIER

YOUNG — BLOOD, FOGEY, LADY, MAN, PRETENDER, TURK

YOUTH — CLUB, CUSTODY, HOSTEL

SECOND WORD

ABOUT — BRING, CAST, COME, FALL, HANG, KICK, KNOCK, MESS, MUCK, PUSH, PUT, RIGHT, SET, TALK, THROW

ABSOLUTE — ABLATIVE, DECREE

ACADEMY — FRENCH, MILITARY, ROYAL

ACCESS — DIRECT, RANDOM, SEQUENTIAL

ACCOUNT — BANK, BUDGET, CAPITAL, CHARGE, CONTROL, CREDIT, CURRENT, DEPOSIT, DRAWING, EXPENSE, JOINT, SAVINGS, SHORT, SUSPENSE, TRUST

ACCOUNTANT — CHARTERED, TURF

ACROSS — COME, CUT, GET, PUT, RUN

ACT — ENABLING, HOMESTEAD, JURISTIC, LOCUTIONARY, RIOT, SPEECH, STAMP, TEST

ADMIRAL — FLEET, REAR, RED, VICE, WHITE

ADVOCATE — DEVIL'S, JUDGE, LORD

AGAINST — COUNT, GO, SET, STACK, TURN

AGENCY — ADVERTISING, EMPLOYMENT, MERCANTILE, NEWS, PRESS, TRAVEL

AGENT — CROWN, DISCLOSING, DOUBLE, ESTATE, FORWARDING, FREE, HOUSE, LAND, LAW, OXIDIZING, PRESS, REDUCING, SECRET, SHIPPING, WETTING

AGREEMENT — COLLECTIVE, GENTLEMEN'S, NATIONAL, PROCEDURAL, STANDSTILL, TECHNOLOGY

AID — ARTIFICIAL, FIRST, FOREIGN, HEARING, HOME, LEGAL, TEACHING

ALARM — CALL, FALSE, FIRE

ALCOHOL — ABSOLUTE, ALLYL, AMYL, BUTYL, ETHYL, GRAIN, LAURYL, METHYL, RUBBING, WOOD

ALE — GINGER, REAL

ALLEY — BLIND, BOWLING

ALLIANCE — DUAL, HOLY, TRIPLE

ALONG — COME, CUT, GET, GO, MUDDLE, PLAY, PUSH, RUB, RUN, SING, STRING

ANGEL — DESTROYING, HELL'S, RECORDING

ANGLE — CENTRAL, COMPLEMENTARY, CRITICAL, EXTERIOR, FACIAL, HOUR, INTERIOR, OBLIQUE, PLANE, RIGHT, STRAIGHT

ANT — AMAZON, ARMY, BULLDOG, DRIVER, FIRE, LEAFCUTTER, LEGIONARY, PHARAOH, SLAVE, VELVET, WHITE, WOOD

APPLE — ADAM'S, BALSAM, BIG, BITTER, CRAB, CUSTARD, LOVE, MAY, OAK, ROSE, SUGAR, THORN

ARCADE — AMUSEMENT, PENNY

ARCH — ACUTE, FALLEN, GOTHIC, HORSESHOE, KEEL, LANCET, NORMAN, OGEE, POINTED, ROMAN, SKEW, TRIUMPHAL, ZYGOMATIC

AREA — CATCHMENT, DEVELOPMENT, GOAL, GREY, MUSH, NO-GO, PENALTY, SERVICE

ARMS — CANTING, ORDER, SIDE, SMALL

ARMY — CHURCH, FIELD, SALLY, SALVATION, STANDING, TERRITORIAL

AROUND — BAT, GET, GO, HORSE, RUN, SHOP, SLEEP, SLOP, STICK

ART — BLACK, COMMERCIAL, FINE, NOBLE, OP, PERFORMANCE, POP

ARTS — GRAPHIC, LIBERAL, PERFORMING, VISUAL

ASH — BONE, FLY, MOUNTAIN, PEARL, PRICKLY, SODA

ASIDE — BRUSH, LAY, PUT, SET

ASSEMBLY — GENERAL, LEGISLATIVE, NATIONAL, UNLAWFUL

ATTORNEY — CROWN, DISTRICT, PROSECUTING

AWAY — BLOW, BOIL, CARRY, CLEAR, COME, EXPLAIN, FALL, FIRE, GET, GIVE, GO, KEEP, LAUGH, LAY, MAKE, PUT, RIGHT, RUN, SALT, SIGN, SOCK, SQUARE, TAKE, TEAR, TRAIL, TUCK, TURN, WALK, WHILE

BABY — BLUE, JELLY, PLUNKET, RHESUS, TEST-TUBE, WAR

BACK — ANSWER, BITE, BOUNCE, CARRY, CAST, CHOKE, CLAW, DOUBLE, FALL, FIGHT, GET, GO, HANG, HARK, HOLD, KEEP, KNOCK, LADDER, LOOK, PAY, PLOUGH, PULL, PUT, RING, SET, SIT, TAKE, TALK

BAG — AIR, BLUE, BODY, CARRIER, COFFEE, COOL, DIPLOMATIC, DOGGY, DUFFEL, GLADSTONE, GROW, ICE, JELLY, JIFFY, LAVENDER, MIXED, SAG, SLEEPING, SPONGE, TEA, TOTE

BALLOON — BARRAGE, HOT-AIR, PILOT, TRIAL

BAND — BIG, BRAKE, BRASS, CITIZENS', CONDUCTION, ELASTIC, ENERGY, FREQUENCY, RUBBER, STEEL

BANK — BLOOD, CENTRAL, CLEARING, COMMERCIAL, COOPERATIVE, DATA, DOGGER, FOG, JODRELL, LAND, LEFT, MEMORY, MERCHANT, NATIONAL, PIGGY, RESERVE, SAVINGS, SOIL, SPERM

BAR — CAPSTAN, COFFEE, COLOUR, DOUBLE, HEEL, HORIZONTAL, INNER, MILK, OUTER, PINCH, PRIVATE, PUBLIC, SAND, SINGLES, SNACK, TORSION, WINE

BARRIER — CRASH, CRUSH, HEAT, SONIC, SOUND, THERMAL, TRANSONIC

BASE — AIR, DATA, FIRST, LEWIS, PRISONER'S, PYRIMIDINE

BASKET — CHIP, MOSES, POLLEN, WASTEPAPER

BASS — BLACK, DOUBLE, FIGURED, GROUND, LARGEMOUTH, ROCK, SEA, SMALLMOUTH, STONE, STRING, THOROUGH, WALKING

BAT — FRUIT, HORSESHOE, INSECTIVOROUS, STRAIGHT, VAMPIRE

BATH — BLANKET, BLOOD, BUBBLE, HIP, MUD, SALT, SPONGE, STEAM, SUN, SWIMMING, TURKISH

BEACON — BELISHA, LANDING, RADAR, RADIO

BEAN — ADSUKI, ADZUKI, BLACK, BROAD, BUTTER, CALABAR, CASTOR, COCOA, DWARF, FRENCH, GREEN, HORSE, JACK, JUMPING, KIDNEY, LIMA, MUNG, PINTO, RUNNER, SHELL, SNAP, SOYA, STRING, TONKA, WAX

BEAR — ANT, BLACK, BROWN, CINNAMON, GREAT, GRIZZLY, HONEY, KOALA, KODIAK, LITTLE, NATIVE, POLAR, SLOTH, SUN, TEDDY, WATER, WHITE, WOOLLY

BEAT — DEAD, MERSEY, WING

BEAUTY — BATHING, CAMBERWELL, SPRING

BED — AIR, APPLE-PIE, BUNK, FEATHER, OYSTER, PAY, SOFA, TRUCKLE, TRUNDLE, TWIN, WATER

BEE — CARPENTER, CUCKOO, HIVE, LEAFCUTTER, MASON, MINING, QUEEN, SPELLING, WORKING

BEER — BOCK, GINGER, KAFFIR, ROOT, SMALL, SPRUCE

BELL — CANTERBURY, DIVING, LUTINE, PASSING, SACRING, SANCTUS, SHARK, SILVER

BELT — BIBLE, BLACK, CARTRIDGE, CHASTITY, CONVEYOR, COPPER, COTTON, FAN, GREEN, LIFE, LONSDALE, SAFETY, SEAT, SHELTER, STOCKBROKER, STORM, SUSPENDER, SWORD

BENCH — FRONT, KING'S, OPTICAL, TREASURY

BENEFIT — CHILD, DISABLEMENT, FAMILY, FRINGE, HOUSING, INJURY, INVALIDITY, MATERNITY, SICKNESS, SUPPLEMENTARY, UNEMPLOYMENT, WIDOW'S

BILL — ACCOMMODATION, BUFFALO, DEMAND, DOUBLE, FINANCE, FOREIGN, OLD, PRIVATE, PUBLIC, REFORM, TREASURY, TRUE, TWIN

BIRD — ADJUTANT, ANT, BRAIN-FEVER, CROCODILE, DIAMOND, EARLY, ELEPHANT, GALLOWS, GAME, _PARSON, WATER

BISCUIT — BOURBON, CAPTAIN'S, DIGESTIVE, DOG, PILOT, SEA, SHIP'S, SODA, TARARUA, TEA, WATER

BLACK — ALL, CARBON, GAS, IVORY, JET, LARGE, PENNY, PLATINUM

BLOCK — BREEZE, BUILDING, CAVITY, CYLINDER, HEART, ICE, MENTAL, OFFICE, PSYCHOLOGICAL, SADDLE, STARTING, STUMBLING, SUN, WOOD

BLOOD — BAD, BLUE, BULL'S, DRAGON'S, FULL, WHOLE, YOUNG

BOARD — ABOVE, ADMIRALTY, BULLETIN, CATCHMENT, CIRCUIT, CRIBBAGE, DIVING, DRAFT, DRAINING, DRAWING, EMERY, FULL, HALF, IDIOT, IRONING, NOTICE, PATCH, RUNNING, SANDWICH, SCHOOL, SKIRTING, SOUNDING, WOBBLE

BOAT — CANAL, FLYING, GRAVY, JOLLY, MOSQUITO, NARROW, ROWING, SAILING, SAUCE, SWAMP, TORPEDO

BOMB — ATOM, BORER, BUZZ, CLUSTER, COBALT, FISSION, FLYING, FUSION, HYDROGEN, LETTER, MILLS, NEUTRON, NUCLEAR, PETROL, SMOKE, STINK, TIME, VOLCANIC

BOND — BAIL, CHEMICAL, COORDINATE, COVALENT, DATIVE, DOUBLE, ELECTROVALENT, ENGLISH, FLEMISH, GRANNY, HERRINGBONE, HYDROGEN, INCOME, IONIC, METALLIC, PAIR, PEPTIDE, SINGLE, TREASURY, TRIPLE

BONE — CANNON, CARTILAGE, COFFIN, CRAZY, FETTER, FRONTAL, FUNNY, HAUNCH, HEEL, INNOMINATE, MEMBRANE, OCCIPITAL, PARIETAL, SPHENOID, SPLINT, STIRRUP, TEMPORAL, TYMPANIC, ZYGOMATIC

BOOK — BLACK, CLOSED, COMMONPLACE, COOKERY, DOMESDAY, DOOMSDAY, HYMN, OPEN, PHRASE, PRAYER, REFERENCE, STATUTE, TALKING

BOTTLE — BRANDY, FEEDING, HOT-WATER, KLEIN, NANSEN, WATER

BOWL — BEGGING, DUST, FINGER, GOLDFISH, RICE

BOX — APPLE, BALLOT, BLACK, CHRISTMAS, COIN, DEED, DISPATCH, FUSE, FUZZ, GLOVE, JUNCTION, JURY, LETTER, MUSIC, PENALTY, PILLAR, POOR, PRESS, SENTRY, SHOOTING, SIGNAL, TELEPHONE, VOICE, WINDOW, WINE, WITNESS

BOY — ALTAR, BALL, BARROW, BEST, BEVIN, BLUE-EYED, CABIN, ERRAND, OFFICE, OLD, PRINCIPAL, RENT, TAR, TEDDY, WHIPPING

BRAKE — AIR, CENTRIFUGAL, DISC, DRUM, FOOT, HYDRAULIC, SHOOTING

BRETHREN — BOHEMIAN, ELDER, EXCLUSIVE, OPEN, PLYMOUTH, TRINITY

BRIDGE — AIR, AUCTION, BAILEY, BALANCE, BOARD, CABLE-STAYED, CANTILEVER, CLAPPER, CONTRACT, COUNTERPOISE, DUPLICATE, FLYING, FOUR-DEAL, LAND, PIVOT, RAINBOW, RUBBER, SNOW, SUSPENSION, SWING, TRANSPORTER, TRUSS, TURN, WHEATSTONE

BRIGADE — BOYS', FIRE, FUR, INTERNATIONAL

BROTHER — BIG, BLOOD, LAY

BUG — ASSASSIN, CABBAGE, CHINCH, CROTON, DAMSEL, DEBRIS, FLOWER, GROUND, HARLEQUIN, JUNE, KISSING, LACE, LIGHTNING, MAORI, MEALY, PILL, RHODODENDRON, SHIELD, SOW, SQUASH, WATER, WHEEL

BUGGY — BABY, BEACH, SWAMP

BUOY — BELL, BREECHES, CAN, LIFE, NUN, SPAR

BURNER — BACK, BUNSEN, GAS, LIME, WELSBACH

BUSH — BURNING, BUTTERFLY, CALICO, COTTON, CRANBERRY, CREOSOTE, DAISY, EMU, GOOSEBERRY, MINT, NATIVE, NEEDLE, ORCHARD, STRAWBERRY, SUGAR

BUSINESS — BIG, MONKEY, SHOW

BY — COME, DO, GET, GO, PASS, PUT, STAND, STICK

CAKE — ANGEL, BANBURY, BARM, COTTON, DUNDEE, ECCLES, FISH, GENOA, JOHNNY, LARDY, LAYER, MADEIRA, MARBLE, OIL, PONTEFRACT, POUND, ROCK, SALT, SANDWICH, SIMNEL, SPONGE, TIPSY, UPSIDE-DOWN, WEDDING

CALL — BIRD, CLOSE, COLD, CURTAIN, LINE, PHOTO, ROLL, TOLL, TRUNK

CAMERA — AUTOMATIC, BOX, CANDID, CINE, COMPACT, GAMMA, IN, MINIATURE, MOVIE, PINHOLE, REFLEX

CAMP — CONCENTRATION, HEALTH, HIGH, HOLIDAY, LABOUR, LOW, MOTOR, TRANSIT, WORK

CANAL — ALIMENTARY, ANAL, CALEDONIAN, ERIE, GRAND, HAVERSIAN, MITTELLAND, PANAMA, ROOT, SEMICIRCULAR, SPINAL, SUEZ, WELLAND

CAP — BATHING, CLOTH, CROWN, DEATH, DUNCE, DUTCH, FILLER, FLAT, FOOL'S, FUNNEL, JOCKEY, JULIET, LEGAL, LIBERTY, MILK, PERCUSSION, ROOT, SHAGGY, STOCKING, WATCH, WAX

CAPITAL — BLOCK, HUMAN, RISK, SMALL, VENTURE, WORKING

CAPSULE — SEED, SPACE, TIME

CARD — BANK, BANKER'S, CALLING, CHEQUE, CHRISTMAS, CIGARETTE, COURT, CREDIT, DONOR, DRAWING, FLASH, GREEN, ID, LASER, LETTER, PICTURE, PLACE, PLAYING, POSTAL, PUNCHED, SHOW, SMART, UNION, VISITING, YELLOW

CASE — ATTACHÉ, BASKET, COT, DISPATCH, DRESSING, LOWER, SPECIAL, SPORE, STATED, TEST, UPPER, WARDIAN, WORST, WRITING

CELL — BLOOD, CADMIUM, CLARK, COLLAR, CONDEMNED, DANIELL, DEATH, DRY, ELECTROLYTIC, FLAME, FUEL, GERM, GRAVITY, GUARD, LYMPH, MAST, NERVE, PADDED, PARIETAL, PHOTOELECTRIC, PRIMARY, SECONDARY, SELENIUM, SOLAR, SOMATIC, STANDARD, STEM, SWARM, UNIT, VOLTAIC, WET

CENTRE — ACTIVE, ATTENDANCE, CIVIC, COMMUNITY, COST, DAYCARE, DEAD, DETENTION, GARDEN, HEALTH, MUSIC, NERVE, REMAND, SHOPPING, STORM

CHAIN — BICYCLE, BRANCHED, CLOSED, DAISY, FOOD, GOLDEN, GRAND, GUNTER'S, LEARNER'S, MARKOV, MOUNTAIN, OPEN, SAFETY, SIDE, SNIGGING, STRAIGHT, SURVEYOR'S, WATCH

CHAIR — BATH, BOATSWAIN'S, DECK, EASY, ELECTRIC, ROCKING, SEDAN, STRAIGHT, SWIVEL, WINDSOR, WING

CHAMBER — BUBBLE, CLOUD, COMBUSTION, DECOMPRESSION, ECHO, FLOAT, GAS, INSPECTION, IONIZATION, LOWER, MAGMA, PRESENCE, PRIVY, SECOND, SPARK, STAR, UPPER

CHART — BAR, BREAKEVEN, CONTROL, FLOW, ORGANIZATION, PIE, PLANE

CHASE — PAPER, WILD-GOOSE

CHEST — COMMUNITY, HOPE, MEDICINE, SEA, SLOP, WAR, WIND

CHILD — FOSTER, LATCHKEY, LOVE, MOON

CHINA — BONE, COCHIN, COMMUNIST, DRESDEN, NATIONALIST, RED, WORCESTER

CHIP — BLUE, LOG, POTATO, SILICON

CIRCLE — ANTARCTIC, ARCTIC, DIP, DRESS, EQUINOCTIAL, FAMILY, GREAT, HOUR, HUT, MERIDIAN, PARQUET, PITCH, POLAR, TURNING, VERTICAL, VICIOUS

CLASS — CABIN, CRYSTAL, EVENING, FIRST, LOWER, MIDDLE, SECOND, THIRD, UNIVERSAL, UPPER, WORKING

CLAY — BOULDER, CHINA, FIRE, PORCELAIN

CLEF — ALTO, BASS, C, F, G, SOPRANO, TENOR, TREBLE, VIOLA

CLERK — ARTICLED, BANK, DESK, FILING, PARISH, SHIPPING, TALLY, TOWN

CLIP — BICYCLE, BULLDOG, CARTRIDGE, CROCODILE, WOOL

CLOCK — ALARM, ANALOGUE, ATOMIC, BIOLOGICAL, CAESIUM, CARRIAGE, CUCKOO, DIGITAL, GRANDFATHER, GRANDMOTHER, LONGCASE, QUARTZ, SETTLER'S, SPEAKING, TIME, TOWNHALL, WATER

CLOTH — AEROPLANE, AIRCRAFT, ALTAR, BARK, COVERT, FACE, GRASS, MONK'S, NUN'S, SPONGE, TEA, WIRE

CLUB — BOOK, CHARTERED, COUNTRY, GLEE, GOLF, INDIAN, JOCKEY, LIONS, LUNCHEON, MONDAY, PROVIDENT, PUDDING, ROTARY, STRIP, SUPPER, TRAMPING, YOUTH

COAL — BITUMINOUS, BROWN, CANNEL, GAS, HARD, SOFT, STEAM, WHITE, WOOD

COCKTAIL — ATOMIC, FRUIT, MOLOTOV

CODE — AREA, BAR, BINARY, CHARACTER, CLARENDON, COLOUR, COUNTRY, DIALLING, GENETIC, GRAY, HIGHWAY, JUSTINIAN, MORSE, NAPOLEONIC, NATIONAL, PENAL, STD, TIME, ZIP

COLLAR — CLERICAL, DOG, ETON, HEAD, MANDARIN, ROMAN, SHAWL, STORM, VANDYKE, WING

COLOUR — ACHROMATIC, CHROMATIC, COMPLEMENTARY, CROSS, LOCAL, OFF, PRIMARY, SECONDARY, TONE

COLUMN — AGONY, CORRESPONDENCE, FIFTH, PERSONAL, SPINAL, STEERING, VERTEBRAL

COMPANY — CLOSE, FINANCE, FIRE, FREE, HOLDING, JOINT-STOCK, LIMITED, PARENT, PRIVATE, PUBLIC, REPERTORY, STOCK

COMPLEX — ELECTRA, INFERIORITY, LAUNCH, OEDIPUS, PERSECUTION, SUPERIORITY

CONE — ICE-CREAM, NOSE, PINE, STORM, WIND

CORD — COMMUNICATION, SASH, SPERMATIC, SPINAL, UMBILICAL

COUNTER — CRYSTAL, GEIGER, PROPORTIONAL, REV, SCINTILLATION

COURSE — ASSAULT, BARGE, GOLF, MAGNETIC, MAIN, REFRESHER, SANDWICH

COURT — CLAY, COUNTY, CROWN, DISTRICT, DOMESTIC, GRASS, HARD, HIGH, INFERIOR, JUSTICE, JUVENILE, KANGAROO, MAGISTRATES', MOOT, OPEN, POLICE, PRIZE, PROVOST, SHERIFF, SUPERIOR, SUPREME, TERRITORIAL, TOUT, TRAFFIC, TRIAL, WORLD

COVER — AIR, DUST, EXTRA, FIRST-DAY, GROUND, LOOSE

CREAM — BARRIER, BAVARIAN, CLOTTED, COLD, DEVONSHIRE, DOUBLE, GLACIER, ICE, PASTRY, SINGLE, SOUR, VANISHING, WHIPPING

CROP — CASH, CATCH, COVER, ETON, RIDING, ROOT

CROSS — CALVARY, CELTIC, CHARING, DOUBLE, FIERY, GEORGE, GREEK, IRON, JERUSALEM, LATIN, LORRAINE, MALTESE, NORTHERN, PAPAL, PATRIARCHAL, RED, SOUTHERN, TAU, VICTORIA

CROSSING — LEVEL, PEDESTRIAN, PELICAN, ZEBRA

CROW — CARRION, HOODED, JIM

CUP — AMERICA'S, CLARET, COFFEE, DAVIS, EGG, FA, FRUIT, GRACE, GREASE, LOVING, MOUSTACHE, STIRRUP, WORLD

CURRENCY — DECIMAL, FRACTIONAL, MANAGED, RESERVE

CURRENT — ALTERNATING, CROMWELL, DARK, DIRECT, EDDY, ELECTRIC, FOUCAULT, HUMBOLDT, JAPAN, LABRADOR, PERU, THERMIONIC, TURBIDITY

CURTAIN — AIR, BAMBOO, DROP, IRON, SAFETY

CUT — BASTARD, CREW, CULEBRA, GAILLARD, NAVY, OPEN, POWER, SHORT

DASH — EM, EN, PEBBLE, SWUNG

DAYS — DOG, EMBER, HUNDRED, JURIDICAL, LAY, ROGATION, SALAD

DEATH — BLACK, BRAIN, CIVIL, COT, CRIB, HEAT, LIVING, SUDDEN

DECK — 'TWEEN, BOAT, FLIGHT, HURRICANE, LOWER, MAIN, POOP, PROMENADE, SUN, TAPE

DELIVERY — BREECH, FORWARD, GENERAL, JAIL, RECORDED, RURAL, SPECIAL

DERBY — CROWN, DONKEY, KENTUCKY, ROLLER, SAGE

DESK — CASH, CITY, COPY, ROLL-TOP, WRITING

DEVIL — DUST, MOUNTAIN, PRINTER'S, SNOW, TASMANIAN

DIAGRAM — BAR, BLOCK, INDICATOR, RUSSELL, SCATTER, VENN

DIVE — CRASH, NOSE, POWER, SWALLOW, SWAN

DOCTOR — ANGELIC, BAREFOOT, CAPE, FAMILY, FLYING, SAW, WITCH

DOG — BACKING, BIRD, CARRIAGE, COACH, ESKIMO, EYE, GREAT, GUIDE, GUN, HEADING, HOT, KANGAROO, LEADING, LITTLE, NATIVE, PARIAH, PIG, POLICE, PRAIRIE, RACCOON, SAUSAGE, SEA, SHEPHERD, SLED, SNIFFER, SPOTTED, TOP, TRACKER, WORKING

DOOR — BACK, BARN, CAT, DUTCH, FIRE, FOLDING, FRONT, NEXT, OPEN, OVERHEAD, REVOLVING, STABLE, STAGE, STORM, STREET, SWING, TRAP

DOWN — BACK, BEAR, BEAT, BOG, BOIL, BREAK, BRING, BUCKET, BUCKLE, CALL, CAST, CHANGE, CLAMP, CLIMB, CLOSE, CRACK, CRY, CUT, DIE, DO, DRAG, DRESS, DUST, FALL, GET, GO, HAND, HOLD, HUNT, KEEP, KNOCK, LAY, LET, LIE, LIVE, LOOK, MOW, NAIL, PAY, PEG, PIN, PIPE, PLAY, PULL, PUT, RIDE, ROUND, RUB, RUN, SEND, SET, SETTLE, SHAKE, SHOOT, SHOUT, SIMMER, SIT, SLAP, SPONGE, STAND, STEP, STICK, STOP, STRIKE, TAKE, TALK, TEAR, TONE, TRACK, TURN, UPSIDE, VOTE, WASH, WEAR, WEIGH, WIND, WRITE

DRESS — ACADEMIC, COAT, COURT, EVENING, FANCY, FULL, HIGHLAND, MORNING, PINAFORE, TENT

DRESSING — FRENCH, ORE, RUSSIAN, SALAD, TOP, WELL

DRILL — BOAT, FIRE, HAMMER, KERB, PACK, POWER, TWIST

DRIVE — BEETLE, CHAIN, DISK, FLUID, FOUR-WHEEL, MOTOR, WHIST

DROP — ACID, COUGH, DELAYED, DOLLY, KNEE, LEMON, MAIL

DUCK — BLUE, BOMBAY, COLD, DEAD, HARLEQUIN, LAME, MANDARIN, MUSCOVY, MUSK, PARADISE, RUDDY, SEA, TUFTED, WOOD

DUST — ANGEL, BULL, COSMIC, GOLD

DUTY — DEATH, ESTATE, POINT, STAMP

EDGE — DECKLE, KNIFE, LEADING, TRAILING

EGG — CURATE'S, DARNING, EASTER, NEST, SCOTCH

END — BACK, BEST, BIG, BITTER, BOOK, BOTTOM, BUSINESS, CIGARETTE, COD, DEAD, EAST, FAG, GABLE, LAND'S, LOOSE, ROPE'S, STICKY, TAG, TAIL, TOP, WEST

ENGINE — AERO, BEAM, BYPASS, COMPOUND, DIESEL, DONKEY, EXTERNAL-COMBUSTION, FIRE, GAS, HEAT, INTERNAL-COMBUSTION, ION, JET, LIGHT, OVERHEAD-VALVE, PILOT, PLASMA, RADIAL, REACTION, RECIPROCATING, ROCKET, ROTARY, SIDE-VALVE, STATIONARY, STIRLING, TANK, TRACTION, TURBOJET, V-TYPE, VALVE-IN-HEAD, WANKEL

ENSIGN — BLUE, RED, WHITE

EVENT — FIELD, HAPPY, MEDIA, THREE-DAY, TRACK

EVIDENCE — CIRCUMSTANTIAL, CUMULATIVE, DIRECT, HEARSAY, KING'S, PRIMA-FACIE, QUEEN'S, STATE'S

EXCHANGE — CORN, EMPLOYMENT, FOREIGN, ION, LABOUR, PART, POST, STOCK

EYE — BEADY, BLACK, COMPOUND, ELECTRIC, EVIL, GLAD, MAGIC, MIND'S, PHEASANT'S, PINEAL, POPE'S, PRIVATE, RED, SCREW, WEATHER

FACE — BOLD, EN, LIGHT, LONG, OLD, POKER, STRAIGHT

FACTOR — COMMON, CORN, GROWTH, HOUSE, LOAD, POWER, QUALITY, RH, RHESUS, SAFETY, UNIT

FEATHER — COCK, CONTOUR, FLIGHT, SHAFT, SICKLE, WHITE

FILE — CARD, CROSSCUT, INDIAN, SINGLE

FINGER — INDEX, LADY'S, RING

FINISH — BLANKET, DEAD, MIRROR, PHOTO

FIRE — BRUSH, ELECTRIC, GREEK, LIQUID, QUICK, RAPID, RED, WATCH

FLAT — ADOBE, ALKALI, COTTAGE, DOUBLE, GARDEN, GRANNY, MUD, SALT, STUDIO

FOOD — CONVENIENCE, FAST, HEALTH, JUNK, SKIN, SOUL

FORTH — CALL, GO, HOLD, PUT, SET

FORWARD — BRING, CARRY, CENTRE, COME, INSIDE, PUT

FRACTION — COMMON, COMPLEX, COMPOUND, CONTINUED, DECIMAL, IMPROPER, PACKING, PARTIAL, PROPER, SIMPLE, VULGAR

FRACTURE — COLLES', COMMINUTED, COMPOUND, GREENSTICK, POTT'S, SIMPLE

FRAME — CLIMBING, COLD, GARDEN, HALF, OXFORD, PORTAL, SAMPLING, STILL, STOCKING

FRIDAY — GIRL, GOOD, MAN

FRONT — COLD, EYES, NATIONAL, OCCLUDED, PEOPLE'S, POLAR, POPULAR, RHODESIAN, WARM, WAVE

FROST — BLACK, JACK, SILVER, WHITE

FRUIT — ACCESSORY, COLLECTIVE, FALSE, FORBIDDEN, KEY, KIWI, MULTIPLE, PASSION, SIMPLE, SOFT, STONE, WALL

GALLERY — LADIES', NATIONAL, PRESS, PUBLIC, ROGUES', SHOOTING, STRANGER'S, TATE, WHISPERING, WINNING

GAP — CREDIBILITY, DEFLATIONARY, ENERGY, GENERATION, INFLATIONARY, SPARK, TRADE, WATER, WIND

GARDEN — BEAR, BOTANICAL, COVENT, KITCHEN, KNOT, MARKET, PEBBLE, ROCK, ROOF, TEA, WINTER, ZOOLOGICAL

GAS — AIR, BOTTLED, CALOR, COAL, CS, ELECTROLYTIC, IDEAL, INERT, LAUGHING, MARSH, MUSTARD, NATURAL, NERVE, NOBLE, NORTH-SEA, PERFECT, POISON, PRODUCER, RARE, SEWAGE, TEAR, TOWN, WATER

GATE — GOLDEN, HEAD, IRON, KISSING, LICH, LYCH, MORAVIAN, STARTING, TAIL, TARANAKI, WATER

GIRL — BACHELOR, BAR, BEST, CALL, CAREER, CHORUS, CONTINUITY, COVER, DANCING, FLOWER, GIBSON, LAND, MARCHING, OLD, SWEATER

GLASS — BELL, BURNING, CHEVAL, CROWN, CUPPING, CUT, FAVRILE, FIELD, FLINT, FLOAT, GREEN, GROUND, HAND, LEAD, LIQUID, LOOKING, MAGNIFYING, MILK, MURRHINE, OBJECT, OPTICAL, PIER, PLATE, QUARTZ, REDUCING, RUBY, SAFETY, SILICA, SOLUBLE, STAINED, STORM, TIFFANY, VENETIAN, VOLCANIC, WATER, WIRE

GLASSES — DARK, FIELD, OPERA

GOAT — ANGORA, BILLY, KASHMIR, MOUNTAIN, NANNY

GOLD — FILLED, FOOL'S, FREE, MOSAIC, OLD, ROLLED, WHITE

GREEN — APPLE, BACK, BOTTLE, BOWLING, CHROME, CROWN, GRETNA, JADE, KENDAL, LIME, LINCOLN, NILE, OLIVE, PARIS, PEA, PUTTING, RIFLE, SEA

GROUND — BURIAL, CAMPING, COMMON, HOME, HUNTING, MIDDLE, PROVING, RECREATION, STAMPING, VANTAGE

GUARD — ADVANCE, COLOUR, HOME, IRON, NATIONAL, OLD, PRAETORIAN, PROVOST, RED, SECURITY, SWISS

GUIDE — BROWNIE, GIRL, HONEY, QUEEN'S

GUM — ACAROID, BLUE, BUBBLE, CHEWING, COW, FLOODED, GHOST, KAURI, RED, SNOW, SOUR, SPIRIT, SUGAR, SWEET, WATER, WHITE

HALF — BETTER, CENTRE, FLY, SCRUM

HALL — CARNEGIE, CITY, FESTIVAL, LIBERTY, MESS, MUSIC, TAMMANY, TOWN

HAND — CHARGE, CLUB, COURT, DAB, DEAD, DECK, FARM, FREE, GLAD, HELPING, HOUR, IRON, LONE, MINUTE, OLD, ROUND, SECOND, SHED, SWEEP, UPPER, WHIP

HAT — BRASS, COCKED, COSSACK, HARD, HIGH, OLD, OPERA, PANAMA, PICTURE, PORKPIE, RED, SAILOR, SCARLET, SHOVEL, SILK, SLOUCH, TEN-GALLON, TIN, TOP

HEART – BLEEDING, BULLOCK'S, DEAD, FLOATING, PURPLE, SACRED

HEAT – ATOMIC, BLACK, BLOOD, DEAD, LATENT, PRICKLY, RADIANT, RED, TOTAL, WHITE

HISTORY – ANCIENT, CASE, LIFE, NATURAL, ORAL

HITCH – BLACKWALL, CLOVE, HARNESS, MAGNUS, ROLLING, TIMBER, WEAVER'S

HOLE – AIR, BEAM, BLACK, BOLT, COAL, FUNK, GLORY, KETTLE, LUBBER'S, NINETEENTH, SOUND, SPIDER, SWALLOW, WATER, WATERING

HOLIDAY – BANK, BUSMAN'S, HALF, LEGAL, PUBLIC, ROMAN

HOME – EVENTIDE, HARVEST, MOBILE, NURSING, REMAND, STATELY, VILLA

HORSE – CHARLEY, DARK, IRON, LIBERTY, LIGHT, NIGHT, POLE, POST, QUARTER, RIVER, ROCKING, SADDLE, SEA, SHIRE, TROJAN, WHEEL, WHITE, WILLING, WOODEN

HOUR – ELEVENTH, HAPPY, LUNCH, RUSH, SIDEREAL, WITCHING, ZERO

HOUSE – ACCEPTING, ADMIRALTY, BOARDING, BROILER, BUSH, CHARNEL, CHATTEL, CLEARING, COACH, COFFEE, COUNTING, COUNTRY, CUSTOM, DISCOUNT, DISORDERLY, DOWER, FASHION, FORCING, FREE, FULL, HALFWAY, ICE, ISSUING, LODGING, MANOR, MANSION, MEETING, OPEN, OPERA, PICTURE, POST, PUBLIC, ROOMING, SAFE, SOFTWARE, SPORTING, STATE, STATION, STOREY, TERRACED, THIRD, TOWN, TRINITY, UPPER, WASH, WENDY, WHITE

HUMOUR – AQUEOUS, GALLOWS, ILL, VITREOUS

HUNT – DRAG, FOX, SCAVENGER, STILL, TREASURE

ICE – BLACK, CAMPHOR, COCONUT, DRIFT, DRY, GLAZE, GROUND, PACK, PANCAKE, SHELF, SLOB, WATER

IN – ALL, BLOCK, BLOW, BOOK, BREAK, BRING, BUILD, BURN, BUY, CALL, CASH, CAVE, CHECK, CHIP, CLOSE, COME, DIG, DO, DRAG, DRAW, FALL, FILL, FIT, GET, GIVE, GO, HAND, HANG, HOLD, HORN, INK, JACK, KEEP, KEY, KICK, LAY, LET, LIE, LISTEN, LIVE, LOG, MOVE, MUCK, PACK, PAY, PHASE, PITCH, PLUG, PULL, PUSH, PUT, RAKE, REIN, RING, ROLL, ROPE, RUB, RUN, SCRAPE, SET, SETTLE, SIGN, SINK, SLEEP, STAND, START, STEP, SUCK, SWEAR, TAKE, THROW, TIE, TUCK, TUNE, TURN, WEIGH, WELL, WHIP, WORK, WRITE, ZERO, ZOOM

INTEREST – COMPOUND, CONTROLLING, HUMAN, LIFE, SIMPLE, VESTED

IRON – ALPHA, ANGLE, BETA, CAST, CHANNEL, CORRUGATED, DELTA, GAMMA, GEM, GRAPPLING, GROZING, INGOT, LILY, MALLEABLE, PIG, PUMP, SHOOTING, SMOOTHING, SOLDERING, STEAM, TOGGLE, WROUGHT

IVY – BOSTON, GRAPE, GROUND, JAPANESE, POISON, WEEPING

JACK – JUMPING, MAN, SCREW, UNION, YELLOW

JACKET – AIR, BED, BOMBER, BUSH, DINNER, DONKEY, DUST, ETON, FLAK, HACKING, LIFE, MESS, MONKEY, NORFOLK, PEA, REEFING, SAFARI, SHELL, SMOKING, SPORTS, STEAM, WATER, YELLOW

JELLY – CALF'S-FOOT, COMB, MINERAL, PETROLEUM, ROYAL

JOE – GI, HOLY, SLOPPY

JUDGMENT – ABSOLUTE, COMPARATIVE, LAST, VALUE

JUMP – BROAD, HIGH, LONG, SKI, TRIPLE, WATER

KEY – ALLEN, CHROMA, CHURCH, CONTROL, DEAD, FUNCTION, IGNITION, MASTER, MINOR, NUT, OFF, ON, PRONG, SHIFT, SKELETON, TUNING

KICK – DROP, FLUTTER, FREE, FROG, GOAL, PENALTY, PLACE, SCISSORS, STAB

KNIFE – BOWIE, CARVING, CASE, CLASP, FLICK, FRUIT, HUNTING, PALLET, SHEATH, TRENCH

KNOT – BLACK, FISHERMAN'S, FLAT, FRENCH, GORDIAN, GRANNY, LOOP, LOVE, OVERHAND, REEF, SQUARE, STEVEDORE'S, SURGEON'S, SWORD, THUMB, TRUELOVE, WALL, WINDSOR

LACE – ALENCON, BOBBIN, BRUSSELS, CHANTILLY, CLUNY, MECHLIN, PILLOW, POINT, SEA, TORCHON

LADY – BAG, DINNER, FIRST, NAKED, OLD, OUR, PAINTED, WHITE, YOUNG

LAMP – ALDIS, DAVY, FLUORESCENT, GLOW, HURRICANE, INCANDESCENT, NEON, PILOT, SAFETY, SPIRIT, SUN, TUNGSTEN

LANGUAGE – BODY, COMPUTER, FIRST, FORMAL, MACHINE, NATURAL, PROGRAMMING, SECOND, SIGN

LANTERN – CHINESE, DARK, FRIAR'S, JAPANESE, MAGIC, STORM

LEAVE – FRENCH, MASS, MATERNITY, SHORE, SICK

LETTER – AIR, BEGGING, BLACK, CHAIN, COVERING, DEAD, DOMINICAL, FORM, FRENCH, LOVE, OPEN, POISON-PEN, SCARLET

LIBRARY – CIRCULATING, FILM, LENDING, MOBILE, SUBSCRIPTION

LICENCE – DRIVING, OCCASIONAL, POETIC, SPECIAL, TABLE

LIFE – FUTURE, LOVE, MEAN, PRIVATE, REAL, SHELF, STILL

LIGHT – ARC, BACK, BACK-UP, BENGAL, BRAKE, COURTESY, FIRST, GREEN, INNER, KLIEG, LEADING, PILOT, REAR, RED, REVERSING, RUSH, TRAFFIC, WHITE

LIGHTING – INDIRECT, STRIP, STROBE

LIGHTNING – CHAIN, FORKED, HEAT, SHEET

LIGHTS – ANCIENT, BRIGHT, FAIRY, HOUSE, NORTHERN, POLAR, SOUTHERN

LINE – ASSEMBLY, BAR, BOTTOM, BRANCH, CLEW, CONTOUR, DATE, FALL, FIRING, FLIGHT, FRONT, GOAL, HARD, HINDENBURG, HOT, LAND, LEAD, LEDGER, MAGINOT, MAIN, MASON-DIXON, NUMBER, ODER-NEISSE, OFF, ON, PARTY, PICKET, PLIMSOLL, PLUMB, POWER, PRODUCTION, PUNCH, SIEGFRIED, SNOW, STORY, TIMBER, WATER

LINK – CUFF, DRAG, MISSING

LION – MOUNTAIN, NEMEAN, SEA

LIST – BACK, CHECK, CIVIL, CLASS, HIT, HONOURS, MAILING, RESERVED, SHORT, SICK, TRANSFER, WAITING

LOCK – COMBINATION, FERMENTATION, MAN, MORTISE, PERCUSSION, SCALP, SPRING, STOCK, VAPOUR, WHEEL, YALE

LOVE – CALF, COURTLY, CUPBOARD, FREE, PUPPY

MACHINE – ADDING, ANSWERING, BATHING, FRUIT, KIDNEY, SEWING, SLOT, TIME, VENDING, WASHING

MAIL — AIR, CHAIN, ELECTRONIC, FAN, SURFACE

MAIN — RING, SPANISH, WATER

MAN — ADVANCE, ANCHOR, BEST, COMPANY, CON, CONFIDENCE, ENLISTED, FAMILY, FANCY, FRONT, HATCHET, HIT, ICE, INNER, IRON, LADIES', LEADING, MEDICINE, MUFFIN, NEANDERTHAL, PALAEOLITHIC, PARTY, PILTDOWN, RAG-AND-BONE, SANDWICH, STRAIGHT, TWELFTH, YES

MARCH — DEAD, FORCED, HUNGER, LONG, QUICK, SLOW

MARIA — AVE, BLACK, HENRIETTA, SANTA, TIA

MARK — BENCH, BLACK, EXCLAMATION, KITE, PUNCTUATION, QUESTION, QUOTATION

MARKET — BLACK, BUYERS', CAPITAL, CAPTIVE, COMMON, FLEA, KERB, MONEY, OPEN, SELLERS', SPOT, STOCK

MARRIAGE — CIVIL, COMMON-LAW, GROUP, MIXED

MASK — DEATH, GAS, LIFE, LOO, OXYGEN, SHADOW, STOCKING

MASTER — CAREERS, GRAND, HARBOUR, INTERNATIONAL, OLD, PAST, QUESTION

MATCH — FRICTION, LOVE, SAFETY, SHIELD, SLANGING, SLOW, TEST

MATE — FIRST, FOOL'S, RUNNING, SCHOLAR'S, SECOND, SOUL

MATTER — BACK, END, FRONT, GREY, SUBJECT, WHITE

MEDICINE — ALTERNATIVE, COMPLEMENTARY, DUTCH, FOLK, FORENSIC, PATENT

MILE — ADMIRALTY, AIR, GEOGRAPHICAL, NAUTICAL, ROMAN, SEA, STATUTE, SWEDISH

MILL — COFFEE, PEPPER, ROLLING, SMOCK, STAMP, STRIP, WATER

MITE — BULB, CHEESE, FLOUR, FOWL, GALL, HARVEST, ITCH, SPIDER, WIDOW'S

MONEY — BIG, BLOOD, CALL, CAUTION, COB, CONSCIENCE, DANGER, EASY, FOLDING, GATE, HEAD, HOT, HUSH, KEY, MAUNDY, NEAR, PAPER, PIN, PLASTIC, POCKET, PRIZE, READY, SEED, SHIP

MOON — BLUE, FULL, HARVEST, HUNTER'S, MOCK, NEW, OLD

MOTHER — EARTH, FOSTER, NURSING, QUEEN, REVEREND, SOLO

MOTION — FAST, HARMONIC, LINK, PERPETUAL, PROPER, SLOW

NAME — BRAND, CHRISTIAN, DAY, FAMILY, FIRST, GIVEN, HOUSEHOLD, LAST, MAIDEN, MIDDLE, PEN, PLACE, PROPRIETARY, SECOND, TRADE

NECK — BOAT, BRASS, CREW, SCOOP, SWAN, V

NEEDLE — CLEOPATRA'S, DARNING, DIP, ELECTRIC, ICE, MAGNETIC, PINE, SHEPHERD'S

NET — DRIFT, GILL, LANDING, MOSQUITO, POUND, SAFETY, SHARK

NIGHT — FIRST, GOOD, TWELFTH, WALPURGIS, WATCH

NOTE — ADVICE, AUXILIARY, BLUE, COVER, CURRENCY, DEMAND, EIGHTH, GOLD, GRACE, LEADING, PASSING, POSTAL, PROMISSORY, QUARTER, SICK, TREASURY, WHOLE

NUMBER — ACCESSION, ALGEBRAIC, ATOMIC, BACK, BINARY, BOX, CALL, CARDINAL, COMPLEX, COMPOSITE, COMPOUND, CONCRETE, E, GOLDEN, INDEX, MACH,

MAGIC, OPPOSITE, ORDINAL, PERFECT, PRIME, REAL, REGISTRATION, SERIAL, SQUARE, TELEPHONE, WHOLE, WRONG

OFFERING — BURNT, PEACE

OFFICE — BOX, CROWN, DIVINE, ELECTRONIC, EMPLOYMENT, FOREIGN, HOLY, HOME, LAND, LEFT-LUGGAGE, PATENT, POST, REGISTER, WAR

OIL — CAMPHORATED, CASTOR, COCONUT, COD-LIVER, CORN, CRUDE, DIESEL, ESSENTIAL, FATTY, GAS, LINSEED, MACASSAR, MINERAL, MUSTARD, NUT, OLIVE, PALM, PEANUT, RAPE, SASSAFRAS, SHALE, SPERM, VEGETABLE, WHALE

OPERA — BALLAD, COMIC, GRAND, HORSE, LIGHT, SOAP, SPACE

ORANGE — AGENT, BITTER, BLOOD, MOCK, NAVEL, OSAGE, SEVILLE

ORDER — AFFILIATION, APPLE-PIE, ATTIC, BANKER'S, COMMUNITY-SERVICE, COMPENSATION, ENCLOSED, FIRING, LOOSE, MAIL, MARKET, MONEY, PECKING, POSSESSION, POSTAL, RECEIVING, SHORT, STANDING, SUPERVISION, TEUTONIC, THIRD, WORD

ORDERS — HOLY, MAJOR, MARCHING, MINOR, SEALED

ORGAN — BARREL, ELECTRIC, ELECTRONIC, END, GREAT, HAMMOND, HAND, HOUSE, MOUTH, PIPE, PORTATIVE, REED, SENSE, STEAM

OVER — BIND, BLOW, BOIL, BOWL, BRING, CARRY, CHEW, DO, FALL, GET, GIVE, GLOSS, GO, HAND, HOLD, KEEL, LAY, LOOK, MAIDEN, MAKE, PAPER, PASS, PUT, ROLL, RUN, SEE, SKATE, SLIDE, SMOOTH, SPILL, STAND, TAKE, THINK, THROW, TICK, TIDE, TURN, WARM, WORK

OYSTER — BUSH, PEARL, PRAIRIE, SEED, VEGETABLE

PACK — BLISTER, BUBBLE, COLD, FACE, FILM, ICE, POWER, WET

PAD — CRASH, HARD, LAUNCHING, LILY, SCRATCH, SHOULDER

PAINT — GLOSS, OIL, POSTER, WAR

PALACE — BUCKINGHAM, CRYSTAL, GIN, PICTURE

PAPER — ART, BALLOT, BLOTTING, BOND, BROMIDE, BROWN, BUILDING, CARBON, CARTRIDGE, CIGARETTE, COMMERCIAL, CREPE, FILTER, FLOCK, GRAPH, GREEN, INDIA, LAVATORY, LINEN, MANILA, MERCANTILE, MUSIC, ORDER, RICE, TISSUE, TOILET, TRACING, WAX, WRITING

PARK — AMUSEMENT, CAR, COUNTRY, FOREST, GAME, HYDE, NATIONAL, SAFARI, SCIENCE, THEME

PARTY — BOTTLE, COMMUNIST, CONSERVATIVE, FIRING, GARDEN, HEN, HOUSE, LABOUR, LIBERAL, NATIONAL, NATIONALIST, PEOPLE'S, REPUBLICAN, SEARCH, STAG, TEA, THIRD, WORKING

PASSAGE — BACK, BRIDGE, DRAKE, MIDDLE, MONA, NORTHEAST, NORTHWEST, ROUGH, WINDWARD

PATH — BRIDLE, FLARE, FLIGHT, GLIDE, PRIMROSE, TOWING

PAY — BACK, EQUAL, SEVERANCE, SICK, STRIKE, TAKE-HOME

PEA — BLACK-EYED, DESERT, PIGEON, SPLIT, SUGAR, SWEET

PEAR — ALLIGATOR, ANCHOVY, CONFERENCE, PRICKLY, WILLIAMS

PEN — CARTRIDGE, CATCHING, DATA, FELT-TIP, FOUNTAIN, QUILL, SEA

PENSION — EN, OCCUPATIONAL, RETIREMENT

PIANO — COTTAGE, GRAND, PLAYER, PREPARED, SQUARE, STREET, UPRIGHT

PIE — COTTAGE, CUSTARD, HUMBLE, MINCE, MUD, PORK, SHEPHERD'S

PIN — BOBBY, COTTER, DRAWING, END, FIRING, GUDGEON, PANEL, ROLLING, SAFETY, SCATTER, SHEAR, STICK, SWIVEL, TAPER, WREST, WRIST

PIPE — CORNCOB, ESCAPE, FLUE, INDIAN, JET, PEACE, PITCH, RAINWATER, REED, SOIL, WASTE

PITCH — ABSOLUTE, CONCERT, FEVER, PERFECT, WOOD

PLACE — DECIMAL, HIGH, HOLY, RESTING, WATERING

PLASTER — COURT, MUSTARD, STICKING

PLATE — ANGLE, ARMOUR, BATTEN, BUTT, ECHO, FASHION, FUTTOCK, GLACIS, GOLD, GROUND, HOME, LICENSE, NICKEL, QUARTER, REGISTRATION, SCREW, SILVER, SOUP, SURFACE, SWASH, TIN, TRADE, WALL, WOBBLE

PLAY — CHILD'S, DOUBLE, FAIR, FOUL, MATCH, MIRACLE, MORALITY, MYSTERY, PASSION, SHADOW, STROKE

PLEAT — BOX, FRENCH, INVERTED, KICK, KNIFE

POCKET — AIR, HIP, PATCH, SLASH, SLIT

POINT — BOILING, BREAKING, BROWNIE, CHANGE, CLOVIS, COVER, CRITICAL, CURIE, DEAD, DECIMAL, DEW, DIAMOND, DRY, END, EQUINOCTIAL, FESSE, FIXED, FLASH, FOCAL, FREEZING, GALLINAS, GAME, GOLD, HIGH, ICE, LIMIT, MATCH, MELTING, OBJECTIVE, PETIT, POWER, PRESSURE, SAMPLE, SATURATION, SET, SPECIE, STEAM, STRONG, SUSPENSION, TRANSITION, TRIG, TRIPLE, TURNING, VANISHING, VANTAGE, WEST, YIELD

POLE — BARBER'S, CELESTIAL, MAGNETIC, NORTH, SOUTH, TOTEM

POLL — ADVANCE, DEED, GALLUP, OPINION, RED, STRAW

POST — COMMAND, FINGER, FIRST, GOAL, GRADED, GRADIENT, HITCHING, LAST, LISTENING, NEWEL, OBSERVATION, REGISTERED, STAGING, TOOL, TRADING, WINNING

POT — CHAMBER, COAL, LOBSTER, MELTING, PEPPER, WATERING

POTATO — HOT, IRISH, SEED, SWEET, WHITE

POWDER — BAKING, BLACK, BLEACHING, CHILLI, CURRY, CUSTARD, FACE, GIANT, TALCUM, TOOTH, WASHING

PRESS — DRILL, FILTER, FLY, FOLDING, GUTTER, HYDRAULIC, PRINTING, PRIVATE, RACKET, STOP

PRESSURE — ATMOSPHERIC, BAROMETRIC, BLOOD, CRITICAL, FLUID, OSMOTIC, PARTIAL, VAPOUR

PRICE — ASKING, BID, BRIDE, INTERVENTION, LIST, MARKET, OFFER, RESERVE, STARTING, UNIT

PROFESSOR — ASSISTANT, ASSOCIATE, FULL, REGIUS, VISITING

PUDDING — BLACK, BLOOD, CABINET, CHRISTMAS, COLLEGE, EVE'S, HASTY, MILK, PEASE, PLUM, SUET, SUMMER, WHITE, YORKSHIRE

PUMP — AIR, BICYCLE, CENTRIFUGAL, ELECTROMAGNETIC, FILTER, FORCE, HEAT, LIFT, PARISH, PETROL, ROTARY, STIRRUP, STOMACH, SUCTION, VACUUM

PUNCH — BELL, CARD, CENTRE, KEY, MILK, PLANTER'S, RABBIT, SUFFOLK, SUNDAY

PURSE — LONG, MERMAID'S, PRIVY, SEA

PUZZLE — CHINESE, CROSSWORD, JIGSAW, MONKEY

QUARTER — EMPTY, FIRST, LAST, LATIN

QUESTION — DIRECT, INDIRECT, LEADING, RHETORICAL

RABBIT — ANGORA, BUCK, JACK, ROCK, WELSH

RACE — ARMS, BOAT, BUMPING, CLAIMING, DRAG, EGG-AND-SPOON, MASTER, OBSTACLE, RAT, RELAY, SACK, THREE-LEGGED

RACK — CLOUD, ROOF, TOAST

RATE — BANK, BASE, BASIC, BIRTH, BIT, DEATH, EXCHANGE, LAPSE, MORTALITY, MORTGAGE, PIECE, POOR, PRIME, TAX

RECORDER — FLIGHT, INCREMENTAL, TAPE, WIRE

RED — BLOOD, BRICK, CHINESE, CHROME, CONGO, INDIAN, TURKEY, VENETIAN

RELATIONS — COMMUNITY, INDUSTRIAL, LABOUR, PUBLIC, RACE

RELIEF — HIGH, LOW, OUTDOOR, PHOTO

RENT — COST, ECONOMIC, FAIR, GROUND, MARKET, PEPPERCORN

RESERVE — CENTRAL, GOLD, INDIAN, NATURE, SCENIC

REVOLUTION — AMERICAN, BLOODLESS, CHINESE, CULTURAL, FEBRUARY, FRENCH, GLORIOUS, GREEN, INDUSTRIAL, OCTOBER, PALACE, RUSSIAN

RING — ANCHOR, ANNUAL, BENZENE, ENGAGEMENT, ETERNITY, EXTENSION, FAIRY, GAS, GROWTH, GUARD, KEEPER, NOSE, PISTON, PRICE, PRIZE, RETAINING, SEAL, SIGNET, SLIP, SNAP, TEETHING, TREE, VORTEX, WEDDING

ROAD — ACCESS, CLAY, CONCESSION, DIRT, ESCAPE, POST, RING, SERVICE, SLIP, TRUNK

ROD — AARON'S, BLACK, BLUE, CON, CONNECTING, CONTROL, DIVINING, DOWSING, DRAIN, FISHING, FLY, HOT, PISTON, STAIR, TIE, TRACK, WELDING

ROLL — BARREL, BRIDGE, COURT, DANDY, EGG, FORWARD, MUSIC, MUSTER, PIANO, PIPE, SAUSAGE, SNAP, SPRING, SWISS, VICTORY, WESTERN

ROOM — BACK, COMBINATION, COMMON, COMPOSING, CONSULTING, DAY, DINING, DRAWING, DRESSING, ENGINE, GUN, LIVING, MEN'S, OPERATIONS, ORDERLY, POWDER, PUMP, RECEPTION, RECREATION, REST, ROBING, RUMPUS, SITTING, SMOKING, STILL, TIRING, UTILITY, WAITING, WITHDRAWING

ROOT — BUTTRESS, CLUB, CUBE, CULVER'S, MALLEE, PLEURISY, PROP, SQUARE

ROT — BLACK, BROWN, DRY, FOOT, SOFT, WET

ROUND — BRING, CHANGE, COME, MILK, RALLY, SCRUB, TALK

ROW — CORN, DEATH, NOTE, SKID, TONE

ROYAL — ANNAPOLIS, BATTLE, PAIR, PORT, PRINCE, PRINCESS, RHYME

RUBBER — COLD, CREPE, HARD, INDIA, PARÁ, SMOKED, SORBO, SYNTHETIC, WILD

RULE — CHAIN, FOOT, GLOBAL, GOLDEN, GROUND, HOME, PARALLELOGRAM, PHASE, PLUMB, SETTING, SLIDE

RUN — BOMBING, BULL, DRY, DUMMY, GROUND, HEN, HOME, MILK, MOLE, SKI, TRIAL

SALAD — CORN, FRUIT, RUSSIAN, WALDORF

SALE — BOOT, BRING-AND-BUY, CAR-BOOT, JUMBLE, RUMMAGE, WHITE

SALTS — BATH, EPSOM, HEALTH, LIVER, SMELLING

SAUCE — APPLE, BÉCHAMEL, BREAD, CHILLI, CREAM, HARD, HOLLANDAISE, MELBA, MINT, MOUSSELINE, SOY, TARTAR, WHITE, WORCESTER

SAW — BACK, BAND, BUZZ, CHAIN, CIRCULAR, COMPASS, COPING, CROSSCUT, CROWN, FLOORING, FRET, GANG, PANEL, SCROLL, STONE, TENON

SCHOOL — APPROVED, BOARD, BOARDING, CHOIR, COMPREHENSIVE, CORRESPONDENCE, DAME, DAY, DIRECT-GRANT, ELEMENTARY, FINISHING, FIRST, GRAMMAR, HIGH, INDEPENDENT, INFANT, JUNIOR, LOWER, MIDDLE, NIGHT, NURSERY, PREP, PREPARATORY, PRIMARY, PRIVATE, PUBLIC, RESIDENTIAL, SECONDARY, SPECIAL, STATE, SUMMER, SUNDAY, UPPER

SCIENCE — BEHAVIOURAL, CHRISTIAN, COGNITIVE, DOMESTIC, EARTH, HARD, INFORMATION, LIFE, NATURAL, PHYSICAL, POLICY, POLITICAL, RURAL, SOCIAL, VETERINARY

SCOUT — AIR, BOY, CUB, GIRL, KING'S, QUEEN'S, SEA, TALENT, VENTURE

SCREEN — BIG, FIRE, ORGAN, ROOD, SILVER, SMALL, SMOKE

SCREW — ARCHIMEDES', CAP, COACH, GRUB, ICE, INTERRUPTED, LAG, LEAD, LEVELLING, LUG, MACHINE, MICROMETER, PHILLIPS

SEASON — CLOSE, HIGH, OFF, SILLY

SEAT — BACK, BOX, BUCKET, COUNTRY, COUNTY, DEATH, EJECTION, HOT, JUMP, LOVE, MERCY, RUMBLE, SAFE, SLIDING, WINDOW

SECRETARY — COMPANY, HOME, PARLIAMENTARY, PRIVATE, SOCIAL

SERVICE — ACTIVE, CIVIL, COMMUNITY, DINNER, DIPLOMATIC, DIVINE, FOREIGN, LIP, NATIONAL, PUBLIC, ROOM, SECRET, SENIOR, SILVER, TEA

SET — CLOSED, COMPANION, CRYSTAL, DATA, DEAD, FILM, FLASH, JET, LOVE, NAIL, OPEN, ORDERED, PERMANENT, POWER, SAW, SMART, SOLUTION, TOILET, TRUTH

SHAFT — AIR, BUTT, DRIVE, ESCAPE, PROPELLER

SHEET — BALANCE, CHARGE, CRIME, DOPE, FLOW, FLY, ICE, SCRATCH, SWINDLE, TEAR, THUNDER, TIME, WINDING, WORK

SHIFT — BACK, BLUE, DAY, EINSTEIN, FUNCTION, NIGHT, RED, SOUND, SPLIT, SWING

SHIRT — BOILED, BROWN, DRESS, HAIR, SPORTS, STUFFED, SWEAT, TEE

SHOE — BLOCKED, BRAKE, COURT, GYM, HOT, LAUNCHING, PILE, TENNIS, TRACK

SHOP — BETTING, BODY, BUCKET, CLOSED, COFFEE, DUTY-FREE, FISH-AND-CHIP, JUNK, MACHINE, OPEN, PRINT, SEX, SWAP, SWEET, TALKING, TUCK, UNION

SHOT — APPROACH, BIG, BOOSTER, DIRECT-MAIL, DROP, FCUL, JUMP, LONG, PARTHIAN, PASSING, POT

SHOW — CHAT, DUMB, FLOOR, ICE, LIGHT, MINSTREL, RAREE, ROAD, TALK

SICKNESS — ALTITUDE, BUSH, DECOMPRESSION, FALLING, MILK, MORNING, MOTION, MOUNTAIN, RADIATION, SERUM, SLEEPING, SWEATING

SIDE — DISTAFF, FLIP, PROMPT, SPEAR, SUNNY

SLEEVE — BALLOON, BATWING, BISHOP, DOLMAN

SOAP — CASTILE, GREEN, JOE, METALLIC, SADDLE, SOFT, SUGAR, TOILET

SODA — CAUSTIC, CREAM, ICE-CREAM, WASHING

SOLDIER — FOOT, GALLANT, OLD, RETURNED, TIN, UNKNOWN, WAGON, WATER

SONG — FOLK, PART, PATTER, PRICK, SWAN, THEME, TORCH

SPEECH — CURTAIN, DIRECT, FREE, INDIRECT, KING'S, QUEEN'S, REPORTED

SPIRIT — HOLY, PROOF, SURGICAL, TEAM, WHITE, WOOD

SPOT — BEAUTY, BLACK, BLIND, HIGH, HOT, LEAF, SOFT, TROUBLE

SQUAD — FIRING, FLYING, FRAUD, SNATCH, VICE

SQUARE — ALL, BEVEL, LATIN, MAGIC, MITRE, SET, TIMES, WORD

STAMP — DATE, POSTAGE, RUBBER, TRADING

STAND — HALL, HAT, MUSIC, ONE-NIGHT, UMBRELLA

STANDARD — DOUBLE, GOLD, LAMP, ROYAL, SILVER

STAR — BINARY, BLAZING, DARK, DOG, DOUBLE, DWARF, EVENING, EXPLODING, FALLING, FEATHER, FILM, FIXED, FLARE, GIANT, MORNING, MULTIPLE, NEUTRON, NORTH, POLE, PULSATING, RADIO, SHOOTING

START — BUMP, FLYING, HEAD

STEAK — MINUTE, T-BONE, TARTAR

STICK — BIG, CANCER, COCKTAIL, CONTROL, FRENCH, JOSS, POGO, SHOOTING, SKI, SWAGGER, SWIZZLE, WALKING, WHITE

STITCH — BLANKET, BUTTONHOLE, CABLE, CHAIN, GARTER, LOCK, MOSS, RUNNING, SATIN, SLIP, STOCKING, TENT

STOCK — CAPITAL, COMMON, DEAD, JOINT, LAUGHING, PREFERRED, ROLLING, VIRGINIA

STONE — BATH, BLARNEY, CINNAMON, COPING, FOUNDATION, IMPOSING, KIDNEY, MOCHA, OAMARU, PAVING, PHILOSOPHER'S, PRECIOUS, ROSETTA, STEPPING

STOOL — CUCKING, CUTTY, DUCKING, MILKING, PIANO

STRAW — CHEESE, LAST, SHORT

STRIKE — BIRD, GENERAL, HUNGER, OFFICIAL, SIT-DOWN, SYMPATHY, TOKEN, WILDCAT

STUDY — BROWN, CASE, FEASIBILITY, FIELD, MOTION, NATURE, PILOT, TIME

STUFF — HOT, KIDS', ROUGH, SMALL, SOB

SUGAR — BARLEY, BEET, BROWN, CANE, CASTER, CONFECTIONERS', FRUIT, GRANULATED, GRAPE, ICING, INVERT, LOAF, MAPLE, MILK, PALM, SPUN, WOOD

SUIT — BATHING, BIRTHDAY, BOILER, DIVING, DRESS, JUMP, LONG, LOUNGE, MAJOR, MAO, MINOR, MONKEY, PATERNITY, PRESSURE, SAFARI, SAILOR, SLACK, TROUSER, WET, ZOOT

ABBREVIATIONS

TABLE – BIRD, COFFEE, DRESSING, GATE-LEG, GLACIER, HIGH, LEAGUE, LIFE, MULTIPLICATION, OCCASIONAL, OPERATING, PEMBROKE, PERIODIC, POOL, REFECTORY, ROUND, SAND, TIDE, WATER, WOOL, WRITING

TALK – BABY, DOUBLE, PEP, PILLOW, SALES, SMALL

TAPE – CHROME, FRICTION, GAFFER, GRIP, IDIOT, INSULATING, MAGNETIC, MASKING, PAPER, PERFORATED, PUNCHED, RED, SCOTCH, TICKER, VIDEO

TAR – COAL, JACK, MINERAL, PINE, WOOD

TENNIS – COURT, DECK, LAWN, REAL, ROYAL, TABLE

TERM – HALF, HILARY, INKHORN, LAW, LENT, MICHAELMAS, TRINITY

THROUGH – BREAK, CARRY, COME, FOLLOW, MUDDLE, PULL, PUSH, PUT, ROMP, RUN, SCRAPE, SEE, WALK, WORK

TICKET – MEAL, ONE-WAY, PARKING, PAWN, PLATFORM, RETURN, ROUND-TRIP, SEASON, SINGLE

TIDE – HIGH, LOW, NEAP, RED, SPRING

TIE – BLACK, BOW, CUP, ENGLISHMAN'S, STRING, WHITE, WINDSOR

TIME – BIG, BORROWED, CLOSING, COMMON, COMPOUND, CORE, DAYLIGHT-SAVING, DOUBLE, DOWN, DRINKING-UP, EXTRA, FATHER, FOUR-FOUR, FULL, HIGH, IDLE, INJURY, LIGHTING-UP, LOCAL, MEAN, OPENING, PRIME, QUADRUPLE, QUESTION, QUICK, RESPONSE, SHORT, SIX-EIGHT, SLOW, STANDARD, SUMMER, THREE-FOUR, TRIPLE, TWO-FOUR, UNIVERSAL

TO – BRING, COME, FALL, GO, HEAVE, KEEP, RISE, RUN, SET, SPEAK, STAND, STICK, TAKE, TUMBLE, TURN

TOGETHER – GO, HANG, HOLD, LIVE, PULL, SCRAPE, SCRATCH, STICK, THROW

TOM – LONG, PEEPING, UNCLE

TOOTH – BABY, EGG, MILK, SWEET, WISDOM

TOP – BIG, DOUBLE, FIGHTING, HUMMING, PEG, ROUND, SCREW, SOFT, SPINNING, TANK

TOWN – BOOM, CAPE, COUNTY, GEORGE, GHOST, MARKET, NEW, POST, TWIN

TRADE – CARRIAGE, FREE, RAG, SLAVE

TRAIN – BOAT, DOG, GRAVY, WAGON, WAVE

TRAP – BOOBY, LIVE, POVERTY, RADAR, SAND, SPEED, STEAM, STENCH, STINK, TANK

TRIANGLE – BERMUDA, CIRCULAR, ETERNAL, PASCAL'S, RIGHT, RIGHT-ANGLED, SPHERICAL

TRICK – CON, CONFIDENCE, DIRTY, HAT, THREE-CARD

TRIP – DAY, EGO, FIELD, ROUND

TROT – JOG, RISING, SITTING, TURKEY

TUBE – CAPILLARY, CATHODE-RAY, DRIFT, ELECTRON, EUSTACHIAN, FALLOPIAN, GEISSLER, INNER, NIXIE, PICTURE, PITOT, POLLEN, SHOCK, SIEVE, SPEAKING, STATIC, TELEVISION, TEST, VACUUM

TURN – ABOUT, GOOD, KICK, LODGING, PARALLEL, STEM, THREE-POINT

UNDER – DOWN, GO, KEEP, KNUCKLE, SIT

WALL – ANTONINE, CAVITY, CELL, CHINESE, CLIMBING, CURTAIN, FIRE, HADRIAN'S, HANGING, PARTY, RETAINING, SEA, WAILING, WESTERN

WATCH – BLACK, MIDDLE, MORNING, NIGHT

WAVE – BRAIN, ELECTROMAGNETIC, FINGER, GROUND, HEAT, LONG, LONGITUDINAL, MEDIUM, NEW, PERMANENT, RADIO, SEISMIC, SHOCK, SHORT, SKY, SOUND, STANDING, STATIONARY, TIDAL

WAX – CHINESE, COBBLER'S, EARTH, JAPAN, MINERAL, MONTAN, PARAFFIN, SEALING, VEGETABLE

WAY – APPIAN, EACH, FLAMINIAN, FLY, FOSSE, MILKY, PENNINE, PERMANENT, UNDER

WHEEL – BALANCE, BIG, BUFFING, CATHERINE, CROWN, DISC, DRIVING, EMERY, ESCAPE, FERRIS, GRINDING, PADDLE, POTTER'S, PRAYER, SPINNING, STEERING, STITCH, TAIL, WATER, WIRE

WHISKEY – IRISH, CORN, MALT

WHISTLE – PENNY, STEAM, TIN, WOLF

WINDOW – BAY, BOW, COMPASS, GABLE, JESSE, LANCET, LAUNCH, PICTURE, RADIO, ROSE, SASH, STORM, WEATHER, WHEEL

WIRE – BARBED, CHICKEN, FENCING, HIGH, LIVE, RAZOR

WITH – BEAR, BREAK, CLOSE, DEAL, GO, LIVE, PLAY, SETTLE, SLEEP, STICK

WOMAN – FANCY, LITTLE, OLD, PAINTED, SCARLET, WIDOW

WORK – FIELD, NUMBER, OUTSIDE, SOCIAL

YARD – BACK, MAIN, SCOTLAND

YEAR – ASTRONOMICAL, CALENDAR, CIVIL, EQUINOCTIAL, FINANCIAL, FISCAL, GREAT, HOLY, LEAP, LIGHT, LUNAR, NEW, SABBATICAL, SCHOOL, SIDEREAL, SOLAR, TROPICAL

ZONE – ECONOMIC, ENTERPRISE, FREE, FRIGID, HOT, NUCLEAR-FREE, SKIP, SMOKELESS, TEMPERATE, TIME, TORRID, TWILIGHT

ABBREVIATIONS

AA (Alcoholics Anonymous; Automobile Association)
AAA (Amateur Athletic Association)
AB (able seaman)
ABA (Amateur Boxing Association)
ABP (archbishop)
ABTA (Association of British Travel Agents)
AC (alternating current; account)

ACA (Associate of the Institute of Chartered Accountants)
ACAS (Advisory Conciliation and Arbitration Service)
ACIS (Associate of the Chartered Institute of Secretaries)
AD (anno domini)
ADC (aide-de-camp; amateur dramatic club)

ADJ (adjective)
ADM (Admiral)
ADV (adverb)
AD VAL (ad valorem)
AFA (Amateur Football Association)
AFC (Air Force Cross)
AFM (Air Force Medal)
AGM (annual general meeting)
AI (artificial insemination; artificial intelligence)
AIB (Associate of the Institute of Bankers)
AIDS (Acquired Immune Deficiency Syndrome)
ALA (Alabama)
AM (ante meridiem)
AMU (atomic mass unit)
ANON (anonymous)
AOB (any other business)
AOC (Air Officer Commanding)
APEX (Association of Professional, Executive, Clerical, and Computer Staff)
APOCR (Apocrypha)
APPROX (approximate)
APT (Advanced Passenger Train)
ARA (Associate of the Royal Academy)
ARAM (Associate of the Royal Academy of Music)
ARCM (Associate of the Royal College of Music)
ARCS (Associate of the Royal College of Science)
ARIBA (Associate of the Royal Institute of British Architects)
ARIZ (Arizona)
ARK (Arkansas)
ASA (Advertising Standards Authority)
ASAP (as soon as possible)
ASH (Action on Smoking and Health)
ASLEF (Associated Society of Locomotive Engineers and Firemen)
AT (atomic)
ATC (air traffic control; Air Training Corps)
ATS (Auxiliary Territorial Service)
ATTN (for the attention of)
ATTRIB (attributive)
AT WT (atomic weight)
AU (Ångstrom unit; astronomical unit)
AUEW (Amalgamated Union of Engineering Workers)
AUG (August)
AV (ad valorem; Authorized Version)
AVDP (avoirdupois)
AVE (avenue)
AWOL (absent without leave)
BA (Bachelor of Arts; British Academy; British Airways; British Association)
BAA (British Airports Authority)
BAFTA (British Academy of Film and Television Arts)
B ARCH (Bachelor of Architecture)
BART (baronet)
BBC (British Broadcasting Corporation)
BC (before Christ)

BCH (Bachelor of Surgery)
BCL (Bachelor of Civil Law)
BCOM (Bachelor of Commerce)
BD (Bachelor of Divinity)
BDA (British Dental Association)
BDS (Bachelor of Dental Surgery)
BE (bill of exchange)
B ED (Bachelor of Education)
B ENG (Bachelor of Engineering)
BHP (brake horsepower)
BIM (British Institute of Management)
B LITT (Bachelor of Letters)
BMA (British Medical Association)
BMC (British Medical Council)
BMJ (British Medical Journal)
BMUS (Bachelor of Music)
BN (billion)
BOC (British Oxygen Company)
BP (bishop)
BPAS (British Pregnancy Advisory Service)
BPHARM (Bachelor of Pharmacy)
BPHIL (Bachelor of Philosophy)
BR (British Rail)
BRCS (British Red Cross Society)
BROS (brothers)
BSC (Bachelor of Science)
BSI (British Standards Institution)
BST (British Standard Time; British Summer Time)
BT (Baronet)
BTA (British Tourist Authority)
BVA (British Veterinary Association)
C (centigrade; circa)
CA (chartered accountant)
CAA (Civil Aviation Authority)
CAD (computer-aided design)
CADCAM (computer-aided design and manufacture)
CAL (California; calorie)
CAM (computer-aided manufacture)
CAMRA (Campaign for Real Ale)
C AND G (City and Guilds)
C AND W (country and western)
CANT (canticles)
CANTAB (of Cambridge — used with academic awards)
CAP (capital)
CAPT (captain)
CARD (Cardinal)
CB (Citizens' Band; Companion of the Bath)
CBE (Commander of the British Empire)
CBI (Confederation of British Industry)
CC (County Council; Cricket Club; cubic centimetre)
CDR (Commander)
CDRE (Commodore)
CE (Church of England; civil engineer)
CEGB (Central Electricity Generating Board)
C ENG (Chartered Engineer)
CENTO (Central Treaty Organization)
CERT (certificate; certified; certify)

CET (Central European Time)
CF (compare)
CFE (College of Further Education)
CFI (cost, freight, and insurance)
CGM (Conspicuous Gallantry Medal)
CH (chapter; church; Companion of Honour)
CHAS (Charles)
CI (curie; Order of the Crown of India)
CIA (Central Intelligence Agency)
CID (Criminal Investigation Department)
CIE (Companion of the Indian Empire)
CIF (cost, insurance, and freight)
CII (Chartered Insurance Institute)
C IN C (Commander in Chief)
CIS (Chartered Institute of Secretaries)
CL (centilitre)
CLLR (councillor)
CM (centimetre)
CMG (Companion of St Michael and St George)
CNAA (Council for National Academic Awards)
CND (Campaign for Nuclear Disarmament)
CO (commanding officer; company; county)
COD (cash on delivery)
C OF E (Church of England)
C OF S (Church of Scotland)
COHSE (Confederation of Health Service Employees)
COL (colonel; Colorado; Colossians)
CONN (Connecticut)
CONT (continued)
COR (Corinthians)
COS (cosine)
CR (credit)
CRO (cathode ray oscilloscope; Criminal Records Office)
CSE (Certificate of Secondary Education)
CSI (Companion of the Star of India)
CSM (Company Sergeant Major)
CU (cubic)
CV (curriculum vitae)
CVO (Commander of the Victorian Order)
CWT (hundredweight)
D (daughter; died; penny)
DA (District Attorney)
DAK (Dakota)
DAN (Daniel)
DBE (Dame Commander of the British Empire)
DC (Detective Constable; direct current; from the beginning)
DCB (Dame Commander of the Bath)
DCL (Doctor of Civil Law)
DCM (Distinguished Conduct Medal)
DCMG (Dame Commander of St Michael and St George)
DCVO (Dame Commander of the Victorian Order)
DD (direct debit; Doctor of Divinity)
DDS (Doctor of Dental Surgery)
DEL (Delaware)
DEPT (department)

DES (Department of Education and Science)
DEUT (Deuteronomy)
DF (Defender of the Faith)
DFC (Distinguished Flying Cross)
DFM (Distinguished Flying Medal)
DG (by the grace of God)
DHSS (Department of Health and Social Security)
DI (Detective Inspector)
DIAL (dialect)
DIP (Diploma)
DIP ED (Diploma in Education)
DIY (do-it-yourself)
D LITT (Doctor of Literature)
DM (Doctor of Medicine)
D MUS (Doctor of Music)
DNB (Dictionary of National Biography)
DO (ditto)
DOA (dead on arrival)
DOB (date of birth)
DOE (Department of the Environment)
DOM (to God, the best and greatest)
DOZ (dozen)
DPHIL (Doctor of Philosophy)
DPP (Director of Public Prosecutions)
DR (debtor; doctor; drive)
DSC (Distinguished Service Cross; Doctor of Science)
DSM (Distinguished Service Medal)
DSO (Distinguished Service Order)
DT (delirium tremens)
DV (God willing)
DVLC (Driver and Vehicle Licensing Centre)
E (East; Easterly; Eastern)
EA (each)
EC (East Central – London postal district)
ECCLES (Ecclesiastes)
ECCLUS (Ecclesiasticus)
ECG (electrocardiogram)
ECS (European Communication Satellite)
EE (Early English)
EEC (European Economic Community)
EEG (electroencephalogram)
EFTA (European Free Trade Association)
EG (for example)
EMA (European Monetary Agreement)
EMF (electromotive force)
ENC (enclosed; enclosure)
ENE (east-northeast)
ENSA (Entertainments National Service Association)
ENT (ear, nose and throat)
EOC (Equal Opportunities Commission)
EOF (end of file)
EP (electroplate; epistle)
EPH (Ephesians)
EPNS (electroplated nickel silver)
EPROM (erasable programmable read only memory)
ER (Edward Rex; Elizabeth Regina)
ESE (east-southeast)

ESN (educationally subnormal)
ESQ (esquire)
ESTH (Esther)
ETA (estimated time of arrival)
ETC (etcetera)
ETD (estimated time of departure)
ET SEQ (and the following one)
EX DIV (without dividend)
EX LIB (from the books)
EXOD (Exodus)
EZEK (Ezekiel)
F (Fahrenheit; franc)
FA (Football Association)
FANY (First Aid Nursing Yeomanry)
FAS (free alongside ship)
FBA (Fellow of the British Academy)
FBI (Federal Bureau of Investigation)
FC (Football Club)
FCA (Fellow of the Institute of Chartered
   Accountants)
FCII (Fellow of the Chartered Insurance
   Institute)
FCIS (Fellow of the Chartered Institute of
   Secretaries)
FCO (Foreign and Commonwealth Office)
FIFA (International Football Federation)
FL (flourished)
FLA (Florida)
FO (Field Officer; Flying Officer; Foreign
   Office)
FOB (free on board)
FOC (Father of the Chapel; free of charge)
FPA (Family Planning Association)
FRAM (Fellow of the Royal Academy of Music)
FRAS (Fellow of the Royal Astronomical
   Society)
FRCM (Fellow of the Royal College of Music)
FRCO (Fellow of the Royal College of
   Organists)
FRCOG (Fellow of the Royal College of
   Obstetricians and Gynaecologists)
FRCP (Fellow of the Royal College of
   Physicians)
FRCS (Fellow of the Royal College of
   Surgeons)
FRCVS (Fellow of the Royal College of
   Veterinary Surgeons)
FRGS (Fellow of the Royal Geographical
   Society)
FRIBA (Fellow of the Royal Institute of British
   Architects)
FRIC (Fellow of the Royal Institute of
   Chemistry)
FRICS (Fellow of the Royal Institution of
   Chartered Surveyors)
FRPS (Fellow of the Royal Photographic
   Society)
FRS (Fellow of the Royal Society)
FRSA (Fellow of the Royal Society of Arts)
FSA (Fellow of the Society of Antiquaries)
FZS (Fellow of the Zoological Society)

G (gram)
GA (Georgia)
GAL (Galatians)
GATT (General Agreement on Tariffs and
   Trade)
GB (Great Britain)
GBE (Knight/Dame Grand Cross of the British
   Empire)
GBH (grievous bodily harm)
GC (George Cross)
GCB (Knight/Dame Grand Cross of the Bath)
GCE (General Certificate of Education)
GCHQ (Government Communications
   Headquarters)
GCIE (Grand Commander of the Indian
   Empire)
GCMG (Knight/Dame Grand Cross of St
   Michael and St George)
GCSE (General Certificate of Secondary
   Education)
GCVO (Knight/Dame Grand Cross of the
   Victorian Order)
GDP (gross domestic product)
GDR (German Democratic Republic)
GEO (George)
GER (German)
GHQ (general headquarters)
GIB (Gibraltar)
GLC (Greater London Council)
GM (George Medal; gram)
GMT (Greenwich Mean Time)
GNP (gross national product)
GOM (grand old man)
GP (general practitioner)
GPO (general post office)
H (hour)
HCF (highest common factor)
HEB (Hebrews)
HF (high frequency)
HGV (heavy goods vehicle)
HIH (His/Her Imperial Highness)
HIM (His/Her Imperial Majesty)
HM (headmaster; headmistress; His/Her
   Majesty)
HMI (His/Her Majesty's Inspector)
HMS (His/Her Majesty's Ship)
HMSO (His/Her Majesty's Stationery Office)
HNC (Higher National Certificate)
HND (Higher National Diploma)
HO (Home Office; house)
HON (honorary; honour; honourable)
HONS (honours)
HON SEC (Honorary Secretary)
HOS (Hosea)
HP (hire purchase; horsepower)
HQ (headquarters)
HR (holiday route; hour)
HRH (His/Her Royal Highness)
HSH (His/Her Serene Highness)
HT (height)
HV (high velocity; high-voltage)

IA (Institute of Actuaries; Iowa)
IAAF (International Amateur Athletic
  Federation)
IABA (International Amateur Boxing
  Association)
IATA (International Air Transport Association)
IB (ibidem; Institute of Bankers)
IBA (Independent Broadcasting Authority)
IBID (ibidem)
IC (in charge; integrated circuit)
ICE (Institution of Civil Engineers)
ICHEME (Institute of Chemical Engineers)
ID (idem; identification)
IE (that is)
IEE (Institution of Electrical Engineers)
IHS (Jesus)
ILL (Illinois)
I MECH E (Institution of Mechanical
  Engineers)
IMF (International Monetary Fund)
INC (incorporated)
INCL (included; including; inclusive)
IND (Indiana)
INST (instant)
IOM (Isle of Man)
IOW (Isle of Wight)
IPA (International Phonetic Alphabet)
IQ (intelligence quotient)
IR (Inland Revenue)
IRA (Irish Republican Army)
IS (Isaiah)
ISO (Imperial Service Order)
ITA (initial teaching alphabet)
ITAL (italic; italicized)
ITV (Independent Television)
JAM (James)
JC (Jesus Christ; Julius Caesar)
JER (Jeremiah)
JP (Justice of the Peace)
JR (junior)
KAN (Kansas)
KB (King's Bench)
KBE (Knight Commander of the British
  Empire)
KC (King's Counsel)
KCB (Knight Commander of the Bath)
KCIE (Knight Commander of the Indian
  Empire)
KCMG (Knight Commander of St Michael and
  St George)
KCSI (Knight Commander of the Star of India)
KCVO (Knight Commander of the Victorian
  Order)
KG (kilogram; Knight of the Garter)
KGB (Soviet State Security Committee)
KKK (Ku Klux Klan)
KM (kilometre)
KO (knock-out)
KP (Knight of St Patrick)
KSTJ (Knight of St John)
KT (Knight of the Thistle)

KY (Kentucky)
L (Latin; learner; pound)
LA (Louisiana)
LAT (latitude)
LB (pound)
LBW (leg before wicket)
LCD (liquid crystal display; lowest common
  denominator)
LCJ (Lord Chief Justice)
LEA (Local Education Authority)
LEV (Leviticus)
LF (low frequency)
LIEUT (Lieutenant)
LITT D (Doctor of Letters; Doctor of Literature)
LJ (Lord Justice)
LJJ (Lords Justices)
LLB (Bachelor of Laws)
LLD (Doctor of Laws)
LLM (Master of Laws)
LOC CIT (in the place cited)
LOQ (he/she speaks)
LPG (liquefied petroleum gas)
LPO (London Philharmonic Orchestra)
LPS (Lord Privy Seal)
LRAM (Licentiate of the Royal Academy of
  Music)
LS (locus sigilli)
LSD (pounds, shillings, and pence)
LSE (London School of Economics)
LSO (London Symphony Orchestra)
LTD (limited)
LW (long wave)
M (male; married; motorway; thousand)
MA (Master of Arts)
MACC (Maccabees)
MAJ (Major)
MAL (Malachi)
MASH (mobile army surgical hospital)
MASS (Massachusetts)
MATT (Matthew)
MB (Bachelor of Medicine)
MBE (Member of the British Empire)
MC (Master of Ceremonies)
MCC (Marylebone Cricket Club)
MCP (male chauvinist pig)
MD (Doctor of Medicine; Managing Director;
  Maryland)
ME (Maine)
MEP (Member of the European Parliament)
MET (meteorological; meteorology;
  metropolitan)
MF (medium frequency)
MG (milligram)
MIC (Micah)
MICH (Michigan)
MINN (Minnesota)
MISS (Mississippi)
ML (millilitre)
M LITT (Master of Letters)
MLR (minimum lending rate)
MM (millimetre)

MO (Medical Officer; Missouri)
MOC (Mother of the Chapel)
MOD (Ministry of Defence)
MOH (Medical Officer of Health)
MONT (Montana)
MP (Member of Parliament; Metropolitan
   Police; Military Police)
MPG (miles per gallon)
MPH (miles per hour)
MPHIL (Master of Philosophy)
MR (Master of the Rolls)
MRCOG (Member of the Royal College of
   Obstetricians and Gynaecologists)
MRCP (Member of the Royal College of
   Physicians)
MRCS (Member of the Royal College of
   Surgeons)
MRCVS (Member of the Royal College of
   Veterinary Surgeons)
MS (manuscript; multiple sclerosis)
MSC (Master of Science)
MSM (Meritorious Service Medal)
MSS (manuscripts)
MT (Mount)
MVO (Member of the Victorian Order)
N (North)
NA (North America; not applicable)
NAAFI (Navy, Army, and Air Force Institutes)
NALGO (National and Local Government
   Officers Association)
NASA (National Aeronautics and Space
   Administration)
NAT (Nathaniel)
NATO (North Atlantic Treaty Organization)
NATSOPA (National Society of Operative
   Printers, Graphical and Media Personnel)
NB (note well)
NCB (National Coal Board)
NCO (non-commissioned officer)
NCP (National Car Parks)
NCT (National Childbirth Trust)
NCV (no commercial value)
NDAK (North Dakota)
NE (Northeast)
NEB (Nebraska)
NEC (National Executive Committee)
NEH (Nehemiah)
NEV (Nevada)
NFU (National Farmers' Union)
NGA (National Graphical Association)
NHS (National Health Service)
NI (National Insurance; Northern Ireland)
NNE (north-northeast)
NNW (north-northwest)
NO (not out; number)
NORM (normal)
NOS (numbers)
NP (new paragraph)
NR (near; Northern Region)
NSB (National Savings Bank)

NSPCC (National Society for the Prevention of
   Cruelty to Children)
NT (National Trust; New Testament)
NUBE (National Union of Bank Employees)
NUGMW (National Union of General and
   Municipal Workers)
NUJ (National Union of Journalists)
NUM (National Union of Mineworkers)
NUPE (National Union of Public Employees)
NUR (National Union of Railwaymen)
NUS (National Union of Seamen; National
   Union of Students)
NUT (National Union of Teachers)
NW (Northwest)
NY (New York)
O (Ohio)
OAP (old-age pensioner)
OB (outside broadcast)
OBAD (Obadiah)
OBE (Officer of the British Empire)
OCTU (Officer Cadets Training Unit)
OFM (Order of Friars Minor)
OHMS (On His/Her Majesty's Service)
OKLA (Oklahoma)
OM (Order of Merit)
ONC (Ordinary National Certificate)
OND (Ordinary National Diploma)
ONO (or near offer)
OP (opus)
OP CIT (in the work cited)
OPEC (Organization of Petroleum Exporting
   Countries)
OPS (operations)
OREG (Oregon)
OS (ordinary seaman; Ordnance Survey)
OSA (Order of St Augustine)
OSB (Order of St Benedict)
OSF (Order of St Francis)
OT (occupational therapy; Old Testament)
OTC (Officers' Training Corps)
OU (Open University)
OUDS (Oxford University Dramatic Society)
OXFAM (Oxford Committee for Famine Relief)
OZ (ounce)
P (page; penny; purl)
PA (Pennsylvania; per annum; personal
   assistant; public address system)
PAYE (pay as you earn)
PC (per cent; personal computer; police
   constable)
PD (paid)
PDSA (People's Dispensary for Sick Animals)
PE (physical education)
PEI (Prince Edward Island)
PER PRO (by the agency of)
PG (paying guest; postgraduate)
PHD (Doctor of Philosophy)
PHIL (Philippians)
PL (place; plural)
PLC (public limited company)
PLO (Palestine Liberation Organization)

PM (post meridiem; Prime Minister)
PO (Petty Officer; Pilot Officer; postal order; Post Office)
POW (prisoner of war)
PP (pages; per pro)
PPS (further postscript; Parliamentary Private Secretary)
PR (public relations)
PRAM (programmable random access memory)
PRO (Public Records Office; public relations officer)
PROM (programmable read-only memory)
PROV (Proverbs)
PS (postscript; Private Secretary)
PT (physical training)
PTA (Parent-Teacher Association)
PTO (please turn over)
PVA (polyvinyl acetate)
PVC (polyvinyl chloride)
QB (Queen's Bench)
QC (Queen's Counsel)
QED (which was to be demonstrated)
QM (quartermaster)
QR (quarter; quire)
QT (quart)
QV (which see)
R (king; queen; right; river)
RA (Royal Academy; Royal Artillery)
RAC (Royal Automobile Club)
RADA (Royal Academy of Dramatic Art)
RAF (Royal Air Force)
RAM (random access memory; Royal Academy of Music)
RAMC (Royal Army Medical Corps)
R AND D (research and development)
RBA (Royal Society of British Artists)
RBS (Royal Society of British Sculptors)
RC (Roman Catholic)
RCA (Royal College of Art)
RCM (Royal College of Music)
RCN (Royal College of Nursing)
RCP (Royal College of Physicians)
RCS (Royal College of Surgeons)
RCVS (Royal College of Veterinary Surgeons)
RD (road)
RE (religious education; Royal Engineers)
REME (Royal Electrical and Mechanical Engineers)
REV (Reverend)
RFC (Royal Flying Corps)
RH (Royal Highness; right hand)
RHA (Royal Horse Artillery)
RI (religous instruction)
RIBA (Royal Institute of British Architects)
RIC (Royal Institute of Chemistry)
RICS (Royal Institution of Chartered Surveyors)
RIP (may he rest in peace)
RK (religious knowledge)

RM (Resident Magistrate; Royal Mail; Royal Marines)
RMA (Royal Military Academy)
RN (Royal Navy)
RNIB (Royal National Institute for the Blind)
RNLI (Royal National Lifeboat Institution)
ROM (read only memory)
ROSPA (Royal Society for the Prevention of Accidents)
RPM (revolutions per minute)
RS (Royal Society)
RSA (Royal Society of Arts)
RSC (Royal Shakespeare Company)
RSM (Regimental Sergeant Major; Royal Society of Medicine)
RSPB (Royal Society for the Protection of Birds)
RSPCA (Royal Society for the Prevention of Cruelty to Animals)
RSVP (please answer)
RT HON (Right Honourable)
RT REV (Right Reverend)
RU (Rugby Union)
RUC (Royal Ulster Constabulary)
S (second; shilling; South)
SA (Salvation Army; sex appeal)
SAE (stamped addressed envelope)
SALT (Strategic Arms Limitation Talks)
SAS (Special Air Service)
SATB (soprano, alto, tenor, bass)
SAYE (save-as-you-earn)
SCD (Doctor of Science)
SE (southeast)
SEC (second; secretary)
SEN (senior; State Enrolled Nurse)
SEQ (the following)
SF (science fiction)
SGT (Sergeant)
SHAPE (Supreme Headquarters Allied Powers Europe)
SI (International System of Units)
SIN (sine)
SLADE (Society of Lithographic Artists, Designers, and Etchers)
SLR (single lens reflex)
SNCF (French National Railways)
SNP (Scottish National Party)
SNR (senior)
SOGAT (Society of Graphical and Allied Trades)
SOP (soprano)
SQ (square)
SRN (State Registered Nurse)
SSE (south-southeast)
SSW (south-southwest)
ST (saint; street)
STD (subscriber trunk dialling)
SW (southwest)
TA (Territorial Army)
TAN (tangent)

TASS (official news agency of the Soviet
  Union)
TB (tubercle bacillus)
TCCB (Test and County Cricket Board)
TEFL (teaching English as a foreign language)
TENN (Tennessee)
TEX (Texas)
TGWU (Transport and General Workers'
  Union)
THESS (Thessalonians)
THOS (Thomas)
TM (trademark; transcendental meditation)
TOPS (Training Opportunities Scheme)
TSB (Trustee Savings Bank)
TT (teetotal; teetotaller)
TU (trade union)
TUC (Trades Union Congress)
TV (television)
UC (upper case)
UCATT (Union of Construction, Allied Trades,
  and Technicians)
UCCA (Universities Central Council on
  Admissions)
UCL (University College, London)
UDI (unilateral declaration of independence)
UEFA (Union of European Football
  Associations)
UHF (ultrahigh frequency)
UHT (ultrahigh temperature)
UK (United Kingdom)
ULT (ultimo)
UN (United Nations)
UNCTAD (United Nations Commission for
  Trade and Development)
UNESCO (United Nations Educational,
  Scientific, and Cultural Organization)
UNO (United Nations Organization)
UPOW (Union of Post Office Workers)
US (United States)
USA (United States of America)
USDAW (Union of Shop, Distributive, and
  Allied Workers)
USSR (Union of Soviet Socialist Republics)
V (verse; versus; volt)
VA (Order of Victoria and Albert; Virginia)

VAT (value-added tax)
VB (verb)
VC (Vice Chancellor; Victoria Cross)
VD (venereal disease)
VDU (visual display unit)
VE (Victory in Europe)
VG (very good)
VHF (very high frequency)
VIP (very important person)
VIZ (namely)
VLF (very low frequency)
VR (Victoria Regina; Volunteer Reserve)
VS (verse)
VSO (Voluntary Service Overseas)
VT (Vermont)
W (west)
WAAC (Women's Army Auxiliary Corps)
WAAF (Women's Auxiliary Air Force)
WC (water closet; West Central)
WI (West Indies; Women's Institute)
WIS (Wisconsin)
WK (week)
WM (William)
WNW (west-northwest)
WO (Warrant Officer)
WP (word processor)
WPC (Woman Police Constable)
WPM (words per minute)
WRAC (Women's Royal Army Corps)
WRAF (Women's Royal Air Force)
WRNS (Women's Royal Naval Service)
WRVS (Women's Royal Voluntary Service)
WSW (west-southwest)
WT (weight)
WW (Word War)
WWF (World Wildlife Fund)
WYO (Wyoming)
XL (extra large)
YHA (Youth Hostels Association)
YMCA (Young Men's Christian Association)
YR (year)
YWCA (Young Women's Christian
  Association)
ZECH (Zechariah)
ZEPH (Zephania)

FIRST NAMES

GIRLS' NAMES

2	3—continued	4—continued	4—continued
DI	MEL	CARY	HOPE
EM	MIA	CASS	ILMA
JO	NAN	CATH	ILSE
VI	NAT	CERI	IMMY
3	ONA	CISS	INEZ
ADA	PAM	CLEM	IOLA
AMY	PAT	CLEO	IONA
ANN	PEG	CORA	IRIS
AUD	PEN	DAFF	IRMA
AVA	PIA	DALE	ISLA
BAB	PRU	DANA	IVAH
BEA	RAE	DAPH	JADE
BEE	RIA	DAWN	JAEL
BEL	ROS	DOLL	JANE
CIS	SAL	DORA	JEAN
DEB	SAM	EDEN	JESS
DEE	SIB	EDIE	JILL
DOT	SUE	EDNA	JOAN
EDA	UNA	EILY	JODI
ENA	VAL	EIRA	JODY
ETH	VIV	ELLA	JOSS
EVA	WIN	ELMA	JUDI
EVE	ZOË	ELSA	JUDY
FAN		EMMA	JUNE
FAY	**4**	ENID	KARA
FLO	ABBY	ERIN	KATE
GAY	ADAH	ERYL	KATH
GUS	ADDY	ESME	KATY
IDA	AINE	ETTA	KERI
INA	ALDA	ETTY	KYLE
ISA	ALEX	EVIE	LANA
ITA	ALIX	FAYE	LELA
IVY	ALLY	FERN	LENA
JAN	ALMA	FIFI	LETA
JAY	ALVA	FLOY	LILA
JEN	ALYS	FRAN	LILI
JOY	ANIS	GABI	LILY
KAY	ANNA	GABY	LINA
KIM	ANNE	GAIL	LISA
KIT	ANYA	GALE	LISE
LEE	AVIS	GAYE	LITA
LES	BABS	GERT	LIZA
LIL	BEAT	GILL	LOIS
LIZ	BELL	GINA	LOLA
LOU	BESS	GLAD	LORA
LYN	BETA	GWEN	LORI
MAE	BETH	GWYN	LORN
MAY	BINA	HEBE	LUCE
MEG	CARA	HEDY	LUCY

4—continued	4—continued	5—continued	5—continued
LULU	TRIX	BETSY	ERICA
LYNN	TYRA	BETTE	ERIKA
LYRA	VERA	BETTY	ESMEE
MAIR	VIDA	BIDDY	ESSIE
MARA	VINA	BONNY	ETHEL
MARY	VITA	BRIDE	ETHNE
MAUD	VIVA	BRITA	ETTIE
META	VIVA	BRITT	EVITA
MIMA	WYNN	CANDY	FAITH
MIMI	ZANA	CAREY	FANNY
MINA	ZARA	CARLA	FARON
MIRA	ZENA	CARLY	FIONA
MOLL	ZITA	CAROL	FLEUR
MONA	ZOLA	CARYL	FLORA
MYRA	ZORA	CARYS	FLOSS
NADA	**5**	CASEY	FREDA
NELL	ABBEY	CATHY	FREYA
NEST	ABBIE	CELIA	GABBY
NEVA	ADDIE	CERYS	GAYLE
NINA	ADELA	CHLOE	GEMMA
NITA	ADELE	CHRIS	GERDA
NOLA	ADLAI	CILLA	GERRY
NONA	AGGIE	CINDY	GILDA
NORA	AGNES	CISSY	GINNY
NOVA	AILIE	CLARA	GRACE
OLGA	AILIS	CLARE	GRETA
OONA	AILSA	CORAL	GUSTA
OPAL	AIMEE	DAISY	HAGAR
OZZY	ALANA	DARCY	HATTY
PETA	ALEXA	DEBRA	HAZEL
PHIL	ALICE	DELIA	HEDDA
POLL	ALINA	DELLA	HEIDI
PRUE	ALINE	DELMA	HELEN
RENA	ALLIE	DERYN	HELGA
RENE	ALVIE	DIANA	HENNY
RHEA	AMATA	DIANE	HEPSY
RICA	AMBER	DILYS	HETTY
RIKA	AMICE	DINAH	HILDA
RINA	ANGEL	DIONE	HOLLY
RITA	ANGIE	DODIE	HORRY
ROMA	ANITA	DOLLY	HULDA
RONA	ANNIE	DONNA	HYLDA
ROSA	ANNIS	DORIA	ILONA
ROSE	ANONA	DORIS	IRENE
ROXY	ANWEN	DREDA	ISMAY
RUBY	APHRA	DULCE	JACKY
RUTH	APRIL	EDITH	JANET
SARA	ASTRA	EFFIE	JANEY
SIAN	AUDRA	ELAIN	JANIE
SÍLE	AUREA	ELENA	JANIS
SÌNE	AVICE	ELISE	JAYNE
SUZY	AVRIL	ELIZA	JEMMA
TACY	BEATA	ELLEN	JENNA
TARA	BECKY	ELLIE	JENNY
TESS	BELLA	ELROY	JEWEL
THEA	BELLE	ELSIE	JINNY
TINA	BERNY	ELVIE	JODIE
TONI	BERRY	EMILY	JOSIE
TRIS	BERTA	EMMIE	JOYCE
	BERYL	EPPIE	JUDOC
	BESSY		

5—continued	5—continued	5—continued	5—continued
JULIA	MARTI	PEGGY	TILDA
JULIE	MARTY	PENNY	TILLY
KAREN	MATTY	PETRA	TISHA
KARIN	MAUDE	PHEBE	TONIA
KATHY	MAURA	PIPPA	TONYA
KATIE	MAVIS	POLLY	TOPSY
KELDA	MEAVE	POPPY	TOTTY
KELLY	MEGAN	RAINA	TRACY
KEREN	MEGGY	RAINE	TRINA
KERRI	MELBA	REINE	TRUDI
KERRY	MELVA	RENÉE	TRUDY
KEZIA	MERCY	RENIE	UNITY
KIRBY	MERLE	RHIAN	VALDA
KITTY	MERRY	RHODA	VANDA
KYLIE	MERYL	RHONA	VELDA
LAURA	MILLY	ROBYN	VELMA
LAURI	MINNA	RONNA	VENUS
LEIGH	MINTY	ROSIE	VERNA
LEILA	MITZI	ROWAN	VICKI
LENNY	MOIRA	SADIE	VICKY
LEONA	MOLLY	SALLY	VIKKI
LETTY	MORAG	SAMMY	VILMA
LIANA	MORNA	SANDY	VINNY
LIBBY	MOYNA	SARAH	VIOLA
LIDDY	MOYRA	SARAI	VIVIA
LIESL	MYRNA	SARRA	WANDA
LILAC	MYSIE	SELMA	WENDA
LILLA	NADIA	SENGA	WENDY
LINDA	NAHUM	SHANI	WILLA
LINDY	NANCE	SHARI	WILMA
LIZZY	NANCY	SHEBA	WYNNE
LOLLY	NANNY	SHENA	XENIA
LOREN	NAOMI	SHIRL	ZELDA
LORNA	NELLY	SHONA	ZELMA
LORNE	NERYS	SIBBY	ZORAH
LOTTY	NESSA	SIBYL	**6**
LUCIA	NESTA	SISSY	AGACIA
LUCIE	NETTA	SONIA	AGATHA
LUCKY	NICKY	SONJA	AGNETA
LYDIA	NIKKI	SONYA	AILEEN
LYNDA	NOELE	SOPHY	AILITH
LYNNE	NORAH	STACY	AITHNE
MABEL	NORMA	SUKEY	ALANNA
MABLE	NUAŁA	SUSAN	ALBINA
MADDY	NYREE	SUSIE	ALDITH
MADGE	ODILE	SYBIL	ALEXIA
MAEVE	OLIFF	TACEY	ALEXIS
MAGDA	OLIVE	TAMAR	ALICIA
MAIRE	OLLIE	TAMMY	ALISON
MAMIE	OLWEN	TANIA	ALTHEA
MANDY	OLWYN	TANSY	ALVINA
MARAH	ORIEL	TANYA	AMABEL
MARCY	OWENA	TEGAN	AMALIA
MARGE	PANSY	TERRI	AMALIE
MARGO	PATSY	TERRY	AMANDA
MARIA	PATTI	TESSA	AMELIA
MARIE	PATTY	TETTY	AMICIA
MARLA	PAULA	THORA	AMINTA
MARNI	PEACE	THYRA	ANDREA
MARTA	PEARL	TIBBY	ANDRÉE

6—continued	6—continued	6—continued	6—continued
ANEIRA	CECILY	EVELYN	ISOLDE
ANGELA	CELINA	EVONNE	JACKIE
ANNICE	CELINE	FARRAN	JACOBA
ANNIKA	CHARIS	FARREN	JACQUI
ANNORA	CHERIE	FEDORA	JANICE
ANSTEY	CHERRY	FELICE	JANINE
ANTHEA	CHERYL	FINOLA	JANSIS
ARIANE	CICELY	FLAVIA	JEANIE
ARLEEN	CISSIE	FLOWER	JEANNE
ARLENE	CLAIRE	FOSTER	JEHANE
ARLINE	COLINA	FRANCA	JEMIMA
ARMINA	CONNIE	FRANNY	JENNIE
ARMINE	DAGMAR	FRIEDA	JESSIE
ASHLEY	DANITA	GABBIE	JOANNA
ASTRID	DANUTA	GAENOR	JOANNE
ATHENE	DAPHNE	GARNET	JOLEEN
AUDREY	DAVIDA	GAYNOR	JOLENE
AURIEL	DAVINA	GERTIE	JUDITH
AURIOL	DEANNA	GINGER	JULIET
AURORA	DEANNE	GISELA	KARINA
AURORE	DEBBIE	GLADYS	KEELEY
AVERIL	DECIMA	GLENDA	KELLIE
BARBIE	DELWEN	GLENIS	KENDRA
BARBRA	DELWYN	GLENNA	KERRIE
BAUBIE	DELYTH	GLENYS	KEZIAH
BEATTY	DENISE	GLINYS	KIRSTY
BENITA	DENNIE	GLORIA	LALAGE
BERNIE	DIANNE	GLYNIS	LAUREL
BERTHA	DIONNE	GOLDIE	LAUREN
BESSIE	DORCAS	GRACIE	LAURIE
BETHAN	DOREEN	GRANIA	LAVENA
BETHIA	DORICE	GRETEL	LAVINA
BEULAH	DORITA	GRIZEL	LEANNE
BIANCA	DORRIE	GUSSIE	LEILAH
BILLIE	DOTTIE	GWENDA	LENNIE
BIRDIE	DULCIE	HAIDEE	LENORE
BIRGIT	DYMPNA	HANNAH	LEONIE
BLANCH	EARTHA	HATTIE	LESLEY
BLODYN	EASTER	HAYLEY	LESLIE
BLYTHE	EDWINA	HEDWIG	LETTIE
BOBBIE	EILEEN	HELENA	LIANNE
BONITA	EILWEN	HELENE	LIESEL
BONNIE	EIRIAN	HENNIE	LILIAN
BRENDA	EITHNE	HEPSEY	LILIAS
BRIDIE	ELAINE	HEPSIE	LILITH
BRIGID	ELINED	HERMIA	LILLAH
BRIGIT	ELINOR	HESTER	LILLIE
BRIONY	ELISHA	HILARY	LINNET
BRYONY	ELISSA	HONORA	LIZZIE
CANICE	ELOISA	HOWARD	LLINOS
CARINA	ELOISE	HULDAH	LOLITA
CARITA	ELSPIE	IANTHE	LOREEN
CARMEL	ELUNED	IDONEA	LOTTIE
CARMEN	ELVINA	IMOGEN	LOUISA
CAROLA	ELVIRA	INGRID	LOUISE
CAROLE	EMELYN	ISABEL	LUCINA
CARRIE	EMILIA	ISEULT	LUELLA
CASSIE	ESTHER	ISHBEL	MADDIE
CATRIN	EUNICE	ISOBEL	MAGGIE
CECILE	EVADNE	ISOLDA	MAHALA

6—continued	**6—continued**	**6—continued**	**7—continued**
MAIDIE	QUEENA	THELMA	ARIANNA
MAIRIN	QUEENY	THIRSA	ARLETTA
MAISIE	RACHEL	THIRZA	ARLETTE
MARCIA	RAMONA	TIRZAH	ASPASIA
MARCIE	REGINA	TRACEY	AUGUSTA
MARGIE	RENATA	TRICIA	AURELIA
MARGOT	RHONDA	TRISHA	AUREOLA
MARIAM	ROBINA	TRIXIE	AUREOLE
MARIAN	ROISIN	TRUDIE	AVELINE
MARIEL	ROSINA	ULRICA	BABETTE
MARINA	ROSITA	URSULA	BARBARA
MARION	ROSLYN	VASHTI	BARBARY
MARISA	ROWENA	VERENA	BASILIA
MARITA	ROXANA	VERITY	BASILIE
MARLIN	ROXANE	VERONA	BASILLA
MARLYN	RUBINA	VICKIE	BEATRIX
MARNIE	RUTHIE	VINNIE	BEATTIE
MARSHA	SABINA	VIOLET	BEDELIA
MARTHA	SALENA	VIVIAN	BELINDA
MARTIE	SALINA	VIVIEN	BERNICE
MATTIE	SALOME	VYVYAN	BETHANY
MAUDIE	SANDIE	WALLIS	BETTINA
MAXINE	SANDRA	WINNIE	BETTRYS
MEGGIE	SARINA	XANTHE	BEVERLY
MEGHAN	SARITA	YASMIN	BLANCHE
MEHALA	SELENA	YVETTE	BLODWEN
MELODY	SELINA	YVONNE	BLOSSOM
MERCIA	SERENA	ZANDRA	BRANWEN
MERIEL	SHARON	ZILLAH	BRIDGET
MIGNON	SHAUNA	ZINNIA	BRIGHID
MILLIE	SHEENA	**7**	BRONWEN
MINNIE	SHEILA	ABIGAIL	BRONWYN
MIRIAM	SHELLY	ADAMINA	CAITLIN
MONICA	SHERRI	ADELINA	CAMILLA
MURIEL	SHERRY	ADELINE	CAMILLE
MYRTLE	SHERYL	ADRIANA	CANDACE
NADINE	SIBBIE	AINSLEY	CANDICE
NELLIE	SIDONY	AINSLIE	CANDIDA
NERINA	SILVIA	AISLING	CARLEEN
NESSIE	SIMONA	AISLINN	CARLENE
NETTIE	SIMONE	ALBERTA	CARMELA
NICOLA	SINEAD	ALBINIA	CAROLYN
NICOLE	SISLEY	ALBREDA	CECILIA
NOELLE	SISSIE	ALDREDA	CECILIE
NOREEN	SOPHIA	ALEDWEN	CEINWEN
ODETTE	SOPHIE	ALETHEA	CELESTE
ODILIA	SORCHA	ALFREDA	CHARITY
OLIVET	STACEY	ALLEGRA	CHARLEY
OLIVIA	STELLA	ALLISON	CHARLIE
OONAGH	STEVIE	ALOISIA	CHATTIE
ORIANA	SYLVIA	ALOYSIA	CHRISSY
PAMELA	SYLVIE	ANNABEL	CHRISTY
PATTIE	TAMARA	ANNAPLE	CLARICE
PEPITA	TAMSIN	ANNETTE	CLARRIE
PETULA	TANITH	ANOUSKA	CLAUDIA
PHEMIE	TEGWEN	ANSELMA	CLODAGH
PHOEBE	TERESA	ANSTICE	COLETTE
PORTIA	TESSIE	ANTOINE	COLLEEN
PRISCA	THECLA	ANTONIA	CORALIE
PRISSY	THEKLA	ARIADNE	

7—continued	7—continued	7—continued	7—continued
CORINNA	GWYNETH	LORINDA	PANDORA
CORINNE	HALCYON	LOUELLA	PASCALE
CRYSTAL	HARRIET	LOVEDAY	PAULINE
CYNTHIA	HEATHER	LUCASTA	PEARLIE
DAMARIS	HÉLOÏSE	LUCETTA	PERDITA
DANETTE	HEULWEN	LUCETTE	PERONEL
DARLENE	HILLARY	LUCIANA	PETRINA
DAVINIA	HONORIA	LUCILLA	PHILLIS
DEBORAH	HORATIA	LUCILLE	PHYLLIS
DEIRDRE	HYPATIA	LUCINDA	QUEENIE
DELILAH	ISADORA	LUCRECE	RACHAEL
DEMELZA	ISIDORA	LYNETTE	RAELENE
DESIREE	JACINTA	MABELLA	RAFAELA
DIAMOND	JACINTH	MABELLE	REBECCA
DOLORES	JANETTA	MAHALAH	REBEKAH
DONALDA	JANETTE	MAHALIA	RHONWEN
DORETTE	JASMINE	MALVINA	RICARDA
DORINDA	JEANNIE	MANUELA	RICHMAL
DOROTHY	JENIFER	MARILYN	ROBERTA
DYMPHNA	JESSICA	MARISSA	ROMAINE
EILUNED	JILLIAN	MARLENE	RONALDA
ELDREDA	JOCASTA	MARTINA	ROSABEL
ELEANOR	JOCELYN	MARTINE	ROSALIA
ELFREDA	JOHANNA	MATILDA	ROSALIE
ELFRIDA	JONQUIL	MAUREEN	ROSALYN
ELSPETH	JOSEPHA	MEHALAH	ROSANNA
EMELINE	JOSETTE	MEHALIA	ROSANNE
EMERALD	JUANITA	MEIRION	ROSEANN
ESTELLA	JULIANA	MELANIA	ROSELYN
ESTELLE	JULITTA	MELANIE	ROSETTA
EUGENIA	JUSTINA	MELINDA	ROSSLYN
EUGENIE	JUSTINE	MELIORA	ROXANNA
EULALIA	KATHRYN	MELISSA	ROXANNE
EULALIE	KATRINA	MELODIE	RUPERTA
EVELEEN	KATRINE	MELVINA	SABRINA
EVELINA	KETURAH	MERILYN	SAFFRON
EVELINE	KIRSTEN	MERRION	SANCHIA
FABIANA	KRISTEN	MICHELE	SARANNA
FELICIA	KRISTIN	MILDRED	SCARLET
FENELLA	LARAINE	MINERVA	SEPTIMA
FEODORA	LARISSA	MIRABEL	SHANNON
FIDELIA	LAUREEN	MIRANDA	SHARRON
FLORRIE	LAURINA	MODESTY	SHEILAH
FLOSSIE	LAVERNE	MONIQUE	SHELAGH˙
FORTUNE	LAVINIA	MYFANWY	SHELLEY
FRANCES	LEONORA	NANETTE	SHIRLEY
FRANCIE	LETITIA	NATALIA	SIBELLA
FRANKIE	LETTICE	NATALIE	SIBILLA
FRANNIE	LILLIAN	NATASHA	SIBYLLA
GENEVRA	LILLIAS	NERISSA	SIDONIA
GEORGIA	LINDSAY	NICHOLA	SIDONIE
GEORGIE	LINDSEY	NINETTE	SILVANA
GILLIAN	LINETTE	NOELEEN	SIOBHAN
GINETTE	LISBETH	NOELINE	SUSANNA
GINEVRA	LISETTE	OCTAVIA	SUSANNE
GISELLE	LIZANNE	OLYMPIA	SUZANNA
GRAINNE	LIZBETH	OPHELIA	SUZANNE
GRIZZEL	LORAINE	OTTILIA	SUZETTE
GWLADYS	LORETTA	OTTILIE	SYBELLA
GWYNEDD	LORETTE	PAMELIA	

7—continued	8—continued	8—continued	8—continued
SYBILLA	CORDELIA	LAETITIA	ROSEMARY
TABITHA	CORNELIA	LARRAINE	SAMANTHA
TALITHA	COURTNEY	LAURAINE	SAPPHIRA
TATIANA	CRESSIDA	LAURETTA	SAPPHIRE
THERESA	CYTHEREA	LAURETTE	SCARLETT
THÉRÈSE	DANIELLA	LAURINDA	SHEELAGH
TIFFANY	DANIELLE	LORRAINE	SHUSHANA
TRISSIE	DELPHINE	LUCIENNE	STEFANIE
VALERIA	DIONYSIA	LUCRETIA	SUSANNAH
VALERIE	DOMINICA	LUCREZIA	TALLULAH
VANESSA	DOROTHEA	LYNNETTE	TAMASINE
VENETIA	DOWSABEL	MADELINA	THEODORA
VIVIANA	DRUSILLA	MADELINE	THERESIA
YOLANDA	ELEANORA	MAGDALEN	THOMASIN
YOLANDE	ELEONORA	MAGNOLIA	TIMOTHEA
ZENOBIA	EMANUELA	MARCELLA	TRYPHENA
ZULEIKA	EMMELINE	MARCELLE	VERONICA
8	EUPHEMIA	MARGARET	VICTORIA
ADELAIDE	EUSTACIA	MARIAMNE	VIOLETTA
ADELHEID	FAUSTINA	MARIANNE	VIOLETTE
ADRIANNE	FELICITY	MARIETTA	VIRGINIA
ADRIENNE	FLORENCE	MARIETTE	VIVIENNE
ANGELICA	FLORETTA	MARIGOLD	WALBURGA
ANGELINA	FLORETTE	MARJORIE	WILFREDA
ANGELINE	FLORINDA	MELICENT	WILFRIDA
ANGHARAD	FRANCINE	MELISENT	WINEFRED
ANNALISA	FREDRICA	MELLONEY	WINIFRED
ANTONINA	FREDRIKA	MERCEDES	**9**
ANTONNIA	GEORGINA	MEREDITH	ALBERTINA
APPOLINA	GERMAINE	MERRILYN	ALBERTINE
APPOLINE	GERTRUDE	MICHAELA	ALEXANDRA
ARABELLA	GILBERTA	MICHELLE	AMARYLLIS
ARAMINTA	GRETCHEN	MORWENNA	AMBROSINA
BEATRICE	GRISELDA	MYRTILLA	AMBROSINE
BERENICE	GULIELMA	PATIENCE	ANASTASIA
BEVERLEY	GWYNNETH	PATRICIA	ANGELIQUE
BIRGITTA	HADASSAH	PAULETTE	ANNABELLA
BRIGITTA	HELEWISE	PENELOPE	ANNABELLE
BRIGITTE	HEPZIBAH	PERPETUA	ANNELIESE
BRUNETTA	HERMIONE	PHILIPPA	APOLLONIA
CARLOTTA	HORTENSE	PHILLIDA	ARTEMISIA
CAROLINA	HYACINTH	PHILLIPA	ARTHURINA
CAROLINE	INGEBORG	PHYLLIDA	ARTHURINE
CATHLEEN	IOLANTHE	PRIMROSE	AUGUSTINA
CATRIONA	ISABELLA	PRUDENCE	BATHSHEBA
CERIDWEN	ISABELLE	PRUNELLA	BENEDICTA
CHARISSA	JACOBINA	RAPHAELA	BERNADINA
CHARLENE	JAMESINA	RAYMONDE	BERNADINE
CHARMIAN	JEANETTE	RHIANNON	BRITANNIA
CHRISSIE	JEANNINE	RICHENDA	CARMELITA
CHRISTIE	JENNIFER	ROCHELLE	CASSANDRA
CLARIBEL	JESSAMYN	RONNETTE	CATHARINE
CLARINDA	JOSCELIN	ROSALEEN	CATHERINE
CLARISSA	JULIANNE	ROSALIND	CELESTINA
CLAUDINE	JULIENNE	ROSALINE	CELESTINE
CLEMENCE	JULIETTE	ROSAMOND	CHARLOTTE
CLEMENCY	KATHLEEN	ROSAMUND	CHARMAINE
CLOTILDA	KIMBERLY	ROSEANNA	CHRISTIAN
CONCEPTA	KRISTINA	ROSEANNE	CHRISTINA
CONCETTA	KRISTINE	ROSELINE	CHRISTINE

9—continued	9—continued	9—continued	10—continued
CHRISTMAS	GWENLLIAN	PHILOMENA	CLEMENTINA
CLAUDETTE	HARRIETTE	PLEASANCE	CLEMENTINE
CLEMENTIA	HENRIETTA	POLLYANNA	CONSTANTIA
CLEOPATRA	HENRIETTE	PRISCILLA	DULCIBELLA
COLUMBINA	HEPHZIBAH	ROSABELLA	ERMINTRUDE
COLUMBINE	HILDEGARD	ROSABELLE	ERMYNTRUDE
CONSTANCE	HIPPOLYTA	ROSALINDA	ETHELDREDA
CONSTANCY	HORTENSIA	ROSEMARIE	EVANGELINA
COURTENAY	HYACINTHA	SERAPHINA	EVANGELINE
DESDEMONA	JACQUELYN	SHUSHANNA	GILBERTINE
DOMINIQUE	JACQUETTA	SOPHRONIA	GWENDOLINE
DONALDINA	JEANNETTE	STEPHANIE	HILDEGARDE
ELISABETH	JESSAMINE	THEODOSIA	JACQUELINE
ELIZABETH	JOSEPHINE	THEOPHILA	KINBOROUGH
EMMANUELA	KATHARINE	THOMASINA	MARGARETTA
ERNESTINE	KATHERINE	THOMASINE	MARGUERITA
ESMERALDA	KIMBERLEY	VALENTINA	MARGUERITE
ETHELINDA	LAURENCIA	VALENTINE	MARIABELLA
FIONNUALA	LAURENTIA	VÉRONIQUE	MILBOROUGH
FRANCESCA	MADELEINE	VICTORINE	PETRONELLA
FRANCISCA	MAGDALENA	VINCENTIA	PETRONILLA
FREDERICA	MAGDALENE	WINNIFRED	TEMPERANCE
FREDERIKA	MARGARETA	**10**	THEOPHANIA
GABRIELLA	MARGARITA	ALEXANDRIA	WILHELMINA
GABRIELLE	MEHETABEL	ALPHONSINE	WILLIAMINA
GENEVIEVE	MEHITABEL	ANTOINETTE	**11**
GEORGETTE	MÉLISANDE	ARTHURETTA	ALEXANDRINA
GEORGIANA	MILLICENT	BERENGARIA	CHRISTIANIA
GERALDINE	MIRABELLA	BERNADETTE	FIONNGHUALA
GHISLAINE	MIRABELLE	BERNARDINA	**12**
GUENDOLEN	NICOLETTE	BERNARDINE	KERENHAPPUCH
GUINEVERE	PARTHENIA	CHRISTABEL	PHILADELPHIA
GWENDOLEN	PHILLIPPA	CHRISTIANA	
GWENDOLYN		CINDERELLA	

BOYS' NAMES

2	3—continued	3—continued	3—continued
AL	DEE	IRA	LEW
CY	DEL	IVO	LEX
ED	DES	JAN	LOU
TY	DON	JAY	LYN
3	DUD	JED	MAT
ABE	ELI	JEM	MAX
ALF	ERN	JIM	MEL
ART	GIB	JOB	NAT
ASA	GIL	JOE	NED
BAS	GUS	JON	NYE
BAT	GUY	KAY	ODO
BAZ	HAL	KEN	PAT
BEN	HAM	KIM	PIP
BOB	HEW	KIT	RAB
BUD	HOB	LEE	RAY
CAI	HUW	LEN	REG
DAI	IAN	LEO	REX
DAN	IKE	LES	ROB

3—continued	4—continued	4—continued	4—continued
ROD	DAVE	JUDE	SEAN
RON	DAVY	KANE	SETH
ROY	DEAN	KARL	SHAW
SAM	DEWI	KEIR	SHEM
SEB	DICK	KENT	STAN
SID	DION	KING	STEW
SIM	DIRK	KIRK	THEO
STU	DOUG	KRIS	THOM
SYD	DREW	KURT	TOBY
TAM	DUKE	KYLE	TODD
TED	EARL	LARS	TONY
TEL	EBEN	LEON	TREV
TEX	EDDY	LEVI	TROY
TIM	EDEN	LIAM	VERE
TOM	EDOM	LORI	VICK
VIC	EMIL	LORN	WADE
VIN	ENOS	LUDO	WALT
WAL	ERIC	LUKE	WARD
WAT	ERIK	LYLE	WILF
WIN	ERLE	MARC	WILL
ZAK	ESAU	MARK	WYNN
4	ESME	MATT	YVES
ABEL	EVAN	MERV	ZACK
ADAM	EWAN	MICK	ZANE
ALAN	EWEN	MIKE	ZEKE
ALDO	EZRA	MILO	**5**
ALEC	FRED	MORT	AARON
ALED	GARY	MOSS	ABNER
ALEX	GENE	MUIR	ABRAM
ALGY	GLEN	NEAL	ADAIR
ALUN	GLYN	NEIL	ADOLF
ALVA	GREG	NICK	AIDAN
AMOS	GWYN	NOAH	ALAIN
ANDY	HAMO	NOEL	ALBAN
ARTY	HANK	NORM	ALBIN
AXEL	HANS	OLAF	ALDEN
BART	HERB	OLAV	ALDIS
BEAU	HUEY	OMAR	ALDUS
BERT	HUGH	OSSY	ALFIE
BILL	HUGO	OTHO	ALGAR
BING	IAGO	OTIS	ALGER
BOAZ	IAIN	OTTO	ALGIE
BOYD	IFOR	OWEN	ALICK
BRAD	IGOR	PAUL	ALLAN
BRAM	IOLO	PETE	ALLEN
BRET	IVAN	PHIL	ALVAH
BRYN	IVES	RAFE	ALVAR
BURT	IVOR	RENÉ	ALVIE
CARL	JACK	RHYS	ALVIN
CARY	JAGO	RICH	ALVIS
CERI	JAKE	RICK	ALWYN
CHAD	JEFF	ROLF	AMIAS
CHAS	JOCK	ROLY	AMYAS
CHAY	JOEL	RORY	ANCEL
CLEM	JOEY	ROSS	ANDRÉ
COLM	JOHN	RUDI	ANGEL
CONN	JOSÉ	RUDY	ANGUS
CURT	JOSH	RUSS	ANSEL
DALE	JUAN	RYAN	ANTON
DANA	JUDD	SAUL	ARCHY

5—continued	5—continued	5—continued	5—continued
ARMIN	CYRIL	GLENN	LLOYD
ARTIE	CYRUS	GRANT	LOREN
ASHER	DAMON	GREGG	LORIN
ATHOL	DANNY	GUIDO	LORNE
AULAY	DANTE	GYLES	LOUIE
AVERY	DARBY	HAMON	LOUIS
BARON	DARCY	HARDY	LUCAS
BARRY	DARYL	HARRY	LYULF
BASIE	DAVID	HAYDN	MADOC
BASIL	DENIS	HEATH	MANNY
BENET	DENNY	HEBER	MANUS
BENJY	DENYS	HENRI	MARCO
BENNY	DERBY	HENRY	MARIO
BERNY	DEREK	HERVÉ	MARTY
BERRY	DERRY	HIRAM	MICAH
BEVIS	DERYK	HOMER	MICKY
BILLY	DICKY	HONOR	MILES
BJORN	DIGBY	HORRY	MITCH
BLAIR	DONAL	HOWEL	MONTE
BLAKE	DONNY	HUMPH	MONTY
BLANE	DORAN	HYMAN	MORAY
BLASE	DROGO	HYMIE	MORTY
BOBBY	DUANE	HYWEL	MOSES
BONAR	DYLAN	IDRIS	MOSHE
BORIS	EAMON	INIGO	MUNGO
BOYCE	EDDIE	IRVIN	MYLES
BRENT	EDGAR	IRWIN	MYRON
BRETT	EDWIN	ISAAC	NEDDY
BRIAN	EDWYN	ITHEL	NEILL
BRICE	ELDON	IZAAK	NEVIL
BROCK	ELIAS	JABEZ	NIALL
BRUCE	ELIHU	JACKY	NICKY
BRUNO	ELIOT	JACOB	NICOL
BRYAN	ELLIS	JAMES	NIGEL
BRYCE	ELMER	JAMIE	NIKKI
BYRON	ELTON	JARED	NOLAN
CADEL	ELVIN	JASON	OGDEN
CAIUS	ELVIS	JEMMY	OLAVE
CALEB	ELWYN	JERRY	OLLIE
CALUM	EMERY	JESSE	ORSON
CAREY	EMILE	JESUS	ORVAL
CARLO	EMLYN	JIMMY	OSCAR
CAROL	EMRYS	JONAH	OSSIE
CASEY	ENOCH	JONAS	OSWIN
CECIL	EPPIE	JUDAH	OWAIN
CHRIS	ERNIE	JUDAS	OZZIE
CHUCK	ERROL	JULES	PABLO
CLARK	ETHAN	KAROL	PADDY
CLAUD	FARON	KEITH	PAOLO
CLIFF	FELIX	KENNY	PARRY
CLINT	FIDEL	KEVIN	PEDRO
CLIVE	FLOYD	KIRBY	PERCE
CLYDE	FRANK	LABAN	PERCY
COLIN	GAIUS	LANCE	PERRY
COLUM	GARRY	LANTY	PETER
CONAN	GARTH	LARRY	PIERS
CONOR	GAVIN	LAURI	PIRAN
COSMO	GEOFF	LEIGH	QUINN
CRAIG	GERRY	LEROY	RALPH
CUDDY	GILES	LEWIS	RAMON

5—continued	6—continued	6—continued	6—continued
RANDY	ALDWYN	CORNEY	GARRET
RAOUL	ALEXIS	COSIMO	GASPAR
RICKI	ALFRED	CUDDIE	GAWAIN
RICKY	ALONSO	CURTIS	GEORGE
RIKKI	ALONZO	DAFYDD	GERALD
ROALD	ALURED	DAMIAN	GERARD
ROBIN	ANDREW	DAMIEN	GERWYN
RODDY	ANGELO	DANIEL	GETHIN
RODGE	ANSELL	DARREL	GIDEON
ROGER	ANSELM	DARREN	GILROY
ROLLO	ANTONY	DARRYL	GODWIN
ROLLY	AQUILA	DECLAN	GORDON
ROLPH	ARCHER	DENNIS	GRAEME
ROWAN	ARCHIE	DENZIL	GRAHAM
ROYAL	ARMAND	DERMOT	GREGOR
RUFUS	ARNAUD	DERYCK	GROVER
SACHA	ARNOLD	DEXTER	GUNTER
SAMMY	ARTHUR	DICKIE	GUSSIE
SAXON	ASHLEY	DICKON	GUSTAF
SCOTT	AUBERT	DILLON	GUSTAV
SELBY	AUBREY	DONALD	GWILYM
SERGE	AUGUST	DORIAN	GWYLIM
SHANE	AUSTEN	DOUGAL	HAMISH
SHAUN	AUSTIN	DOUGIE	HAMLET
SHAWN	AYLMER	DUDLEY	HAMLYN
SILAS	AYLWIN	DUGALD	HAMNET
SIMON	BALDIE	DUGGIE	HARLEY
SOLLY	BARNET	DUNCAN	HAROLD
STEVE	BARNEY	DURAND	HARVEY
TAFFY	BARRIE	DUSTIN	HAYDEN
TEDDY	BARRON	DWAYNE	HAYDON
TERRI	BARTLE	DWIGHT	HECTOR
TERRY	BENITO	EAMONN	HEDLEY
TIMMY	BENNET	EASTER	HERBIE
TITUS	BERNIE	EDMOND	HERMAN
TOLLY	BERTIE	EDMUND	HERVEY
TOMMY	BETHEL	EDWARD	HILARY
TUDOR	BILLIE	EGBERT	HOBART
ULRIC	BLAINE	ELDRED	HOLDEN
UPTON	BLAISE	ELIJAH	HONOUR
URBAN	BOBBIE	ELLERY	HORACE
URIAH	BONAMY	ELLIOT	HOWARD
VINCE	BOTOLF	EOGHAN	HOWELL
VITUS	BOTULF	ERNEST	HUBERT
WALDO	BUSTER	ESMOND	HUGHIE
WALLY	CADELL	EUGENE	INGRAM
WAYNE	CAESAR	EVELYN	IRVINE
WILLY	CALLUM	FABIAN	IRVING
WYATT	CALVIN	FARRAN	ISAIAH
WYNNE	CARLOS	FARREN	ISRAEL
6	CAROLE	FERGIE	JACKIE
ADOLPH	CARTER	FERGUS	JACQUI
ADRIAN	CASPAR	FINLAY	JARRED.
AENEAS	CEDRIC	FLURRY	JARROD
ALARIC	CERDIC	FRANCO	JARVIS
ALBANY	CLAUDE	FRASER	JASPER
ALBERT	COLLEY	FRAZER	JEREMY
ALDOUS	CONNOR	FREDDY	JEROME
ALDRED	CONRAD	GARETH	JETHRO
ALDWIN	CORMAC	GARNET	JOHNNY

6—continued	6—continued	6—continued	7—continued
JOLYON	MURRAY	SHAMUS	BALDWIN
JORDAN	NATHAN	SHELLY	BARCLAY
JOSEPH	NEDDIE	SHOLTO	BARNABY
JOSHUA	NELSON	SIDNEY	BARNARD
JOSIAH	NEWTON	SIMEON	BARRETT
JOSIAS	NINIAN	STEVEN	BARTLET
JOTHAM	NORMAN	STEVIE	BASTIAN
JULIAN	NORRIS	ST JOHN	BEDFORD
JULIUS	NORTON	STUART	BENNETT
JUNIOR	NOWELL	SYDNEY	BENTLEY
JUSTIN	OBERON	TALBOT	BERNARD
KELVIN	OLIVER	TAYLOR	BERTRAM
KENDAL	ORRELL	TEDDIE	BETHELL
KENELM	OSBERT	THOMAS	BOTOLPH
KENTON	OSBORN	TOBIAS	BRADLEY
KESTER	OSMOND	TRAVIS	BRANDAN
KIERAN	OSMUND	TREFOR	BRANDON
LAUNCE	OSWALD	TREVOR	BRENDAN
LAUREN	PALMER	TYBALT	CAMERON
LAURIE	PARKER	TYRONE	CARADOC
LAWRIE	PASCAL	VAUGHN	CARADOG
LAYTON	PASCOE	VERNON	CARLTON
LEMUEL	PELHAM	VICTOR	CAROLUS
LENNOX	PHILIP	VIRGIL	CEDRYCH
LESLIE	PIERRE	WALLIS	CHARLES
LESTER	POLDIE	WALTER	CHARLEY
LIONEL	PRINCE	WARNER	CHARLIE
LONNIE	QUINCY	WARREN	CHAUNCY
LOVELL	RABBIE	WESLEY	CHESTER
LOWELL	RAFAEL	WILBUR	CHRISTY
LUCIAN	RAINER	WILLIE	CLAYTON
LUCIEN	RAMSAY	WILLIS	CLEDWYN
LUCIUS	RAMSEY	WILMER	CLEMENT
LUTHER	RANALD	WILMOT	CLIFTON
LYNDON	RANDAL	WINNIE	CLINTON
LYULPH	RAYNER	WYBERT	COLUMBA
MAGNUS	RAYNOR	WYSTAN	CRISPIN
MALISE	REGGIE	XAVIER	CRYSTAL
MALORY	REUBEN	YEHUDI	CYPRIAN
MALVIN	RICHIE	**7**	DARRELL
MANLEY	ROBBIE	ABRAHAM	DECIMUS
MANSEL	ROBERT	ABSALOM	DENHOLM
MANUEL	RODGER	ABSOLON	DERRICK
MARCEL	RODNEY	ADAMNAN	DESMOND
MARCUS	ROLAND	ADOLPHE	DIGGORY
MARIUS	RONALD	AINSLEY	DOMINIC
MARTIN	RONNIE	AINSLIE	DONOVAN
MARTYN	RUDOLF	ALBERIC	DOUGLAS
MARVIN	RUPERT	ALDHELM	DUNSTAN
MARVYN	RUSSEL	ALFONSO	EARNEST
MELVIN	SAMSON	AMBROSE	ELEAZAR
MELVYN	SAMUEL	ANDREAS	ELKANAH
MERLIN	SEAMUS	ANEIRIN	ELLIOTT
MERTON	SEFTON	ANEURIN	EMANUEL
MERVIN	SELWYN	ANTHONY	EPHRAIM
MERVYN	SERGEI	ANTONIO	ERASMUS
MICKEY	SERGIO	ARTEMAS	EUSTACE
MILTON	SEUMAS	ARTEMUS	EVERARD
MORGAN	SEWARD	AUBERON	EZEKIEL
MORRIS	SEXTUS	AZARIAH	FEARGUS

7—continued	7—continued	7—continued	8—continued
FITZROY	LINDSAY	STANLEY	CHARLTON
FLORIAN	LORENZO	STEPHEN	CHAUNCEY
FRANCIS	LUDOVIC	STEWART	CHRISTIE
FRANKIE	MALACHI	SWITHIN	CHRYSTAL
FREDDIE	MALACHY	TANCRED	CLARENCE
FREDRIC	MALCOLM	TERENCE	CLAUDIUS
FULBERT	MALLORY	TERTIUS	CLIFFORD
GABRIEL	MANFRED	THORLEY	CONSTANT
GARRETT	MANSELL	TIMOTHY	COURTNEY
GARRICK	MATTHEW	TORQUIL	CRISPIAN
GAYLORD	MAURICE	TRAVERS	CUTHBERT
GEORDIE	MAXWELL	TRISTAN	DIARMAIT
GEORGIE	MAYNARD	ULYSSES	DIARMUID
GERAINT	MEIRION	VAUGHAN	DOMINICK
GERRARD	MERRION	VINCENT	EBENEZER
GERSHOM	MICHAEL	WALLACE	EMMANUEL
GERVAIS	MILBURN	WARWICK	ETHELRED
GERVASE	MONTAGU	WENDELL	FARQUHAR
GILBERT	MURDOCH	WILBERT	FERNANDO
GILLEAN	MURTAGH	WILFRED	FLETCHER
GILLIAN	NEVILLE	WILFRID	FLORENCE
GODFREY	NICOLAS	WILLARD	FLUELLEN
GOLDWIN	NORBERT	WILLIAM	FRANKLIN
GOLDWYN	OBADIAH	WINDSOR	FREDERIC
GRAHAME	OLIVIER	WINFRED	FREDRICK
GREGORY	ORLANDO	WINFRID	GAMALIEL
GUNTHER	ORVILLE	WINSTON	GARFIELD
GUSTAVE	OSBORNE	WOODROW	GEOFFREY
GWYNFOR	PADRAIG	WYNDHAM	GRAYBURN
HADRIAN	PATRICK	WYNFORD	GRIFFITH
HAMMOND	PHILLIP	ZACHARY	GUSTAVUS
HARTLEY	PHINEAS	**8**	HAMILTON
HERBERT	PRESTON	ADOLPHUS	HANNIBAL
HERMANN	QUENTIN	ALASDAIR	HARRISON
HILLARY	QUINTIN	ALASTAIR	HERCULES
HORATIO	RANDALL	ALGERNON	HEREWARD
HUMBERT	RAPHAEL	ALISTAIR	HEZEKIAH
ICHABOD	RAYMOND	ALOYSIUS	HUMPHREY
ISIDORE	RAYMUND	ALPHONSE	IGNATIUS
JACQUES	REDVERS	ALPHONSO	IORWERTH
JAPHETH	REYNARD	AUGUSTIN	JEDIDIAH
JEFFERY	REYNOLD	AUGUSTUS	JEPHTHAH
JEFFREY	RICARDO	AURELIAN	JEREMIAH
JILLIAN	RICHARD	BARDOLPH	JEREMIAS
JOACHIM	RODOLPH	BARNABAS	JERMAINE
JOCELYN	RODRIGO	BARTLETT	JOHANNES
JOHNNIE	ROWLAND	BENEDICK	JONATHAN
KENDALL	ROYSTON	BENEDICT	JOSCELIN
KENNETH	RUDOLPH	BENJAMIN	KIMBERLY
KENRICK	RUSSELL	BERENGER	KINGSLEY
KIMBALL	SALAMON	BERKELEY	LANCELOT
LACHLAN	SAMPSON	BERNHARD	LAURENCE
LAMBERT	SERGIUS	BERTHOLD	LAWRENCE
LAZARUS	SEYMOUR	BERTRAND	LEIGHTON
LEANDER	SHANNON	BEVERLEY	LLEWELYN
LEOFRIC	SHELDON	BONIFACE	MANASSEH
LEOLINE	SHELLEY	CAMILLUS	MANASSES
LEONARD	SIGMUND	CAMPBELL	MARSHALL
LEOPOLD	SOLOMON	CARLETON	MATTHIAS
LINCOLN	SPENCER	CARTHACH	MELVILLE

8—continued
MEREDITH
MITCHELL
MONTAGUE
MORDECAI
MORTIMER
NAPOLEON
NEHEMIAH
NICHOLAS
OCTAVIAN
OCTAVIUS
PERCEVAL
PERCIVAL
PHILEMON
PHINEHAS
RADCLIFF
RANDOLPH
REGINALD
RODERICK
SALVADOR
SEPTIMUS
SHERIDAN
SILVANUS
SINCLAIR
STAFFORD
STANFORD
STIRLING
SYLVANUS
TALIESIN
TERRENCE

8—continued
THADDEUS
THEOBALD
THEODORE
THORNTON
THURSTAN
THURSTON
TRISTRAM
TURLOUGH
WINTHROP
ZEDEKIAH

9
ALEXANDER
ALPHONSUS
AMBROSIUS
ARCHELAUS
ARCHIBALD
ATHELSTAN
AUGUSTINE
BALTHASAR
BALTHAZAR
BRODERICK
CADWALADR
CHRISTIAN
CHRISTMAS
CORNELIUS
COURTENAY
DIONYSIUS
ETHELBERT

9—continued
FERDINAND
FRANCESCO
FRANCISCO
FREDERICK
GERONTIUS
GRANVILLE
GRENVILLE
JEFFERSON
KENTIGERN
KIMBERLEY
LAUNCELOT
LLEWELLYN
MARCELLUS
MARMADUKE
NATHANAEL
NATHANIEL
NICODEMUS
ONUPHRIUS
PEREGRINE
PHILIBERT
RADCLIFFE
SALVATORE
SEBASTIAN
SIEGFRIED
SIGISMUND
SILVESTER
STANISLAS
SYLVESTER

9—continued
THEODORIC
VALENTINE
ZACCHAEUS
ZACHARIAH
ZACHARIAS
ZECHARIAH
ZEPHANIAH

10
BARRINGTON
CARACTACUS
FORTUNATUS
HIERONYMUS
HILDEBRAND
HIPPOLYTUS
MAXIMILIAN
MONTGOMERY
STANISLAUS
THEOPHILUS
WASHINGTON
WILLOUGHBY

11
BARTHOLOMEW
CADWALLADER
CHRISTOPHER
CONSTANTINE
SACHEVERELL

INDEX

Entries in bold face type (e.g. **COUNTRIES OF THE WORLD** 1) refer to tables or lists in the text, with their page numbers. Other index entries suggest tables that might be useful (e.g., SHELLS *see* SEASHELLS, or CHARACTER *try* DICKENSIAN CHARACTERS; GILBERT AND SULLIVAN; FICTIONAL CHARACTERS). We have also included a selection of cue words for cryptic clues (e.g., the word ZERO often indicates the letter O).

NOTES

NOTES

NOTES

NOTES

NOTES

NOTES

NOTES